Fo
Southeast
Asia

Fodor's Travel Publications, Inc.
New York and London

Fodor's Southeast Asia

Editor: Candice Gianetti
Contributors: Reynaldo Alejandro, Shann Davies, John English, Nigel Fisher, Luis Francia, Robert Halliday, En Hooi Knaw, Steven Levingston, John Major, Linda Miller, Jack Moore, Bruce Shu, Joan Warner
Art Director: Fabrizio La Rocca
Cartographer: David Lindroth
Illustrator: Karl Tanner
Cover Photograph: Owen Franken

Design: Vignelli Associates

Special Sales

Fodor's Travel Publications are available at special discounts for bulk purchases (100 copies or more) for sales promotions or premiums. Special editions, including personalized covers, excerpts of existing guides, and corporate imprints, can be created in large quantities for special needs. For more information write to Special Marketing, Fodor's Travel Publications, 201 East 50th St., New York, NY 10022. Inquiries from the United Kingdom should be sent to Fodor's Travel Publications, 30-32 Bedford Square, London WC1B 3SG.

Contents

Vocabulary *491*

Index *498*

Maps

Foreword

In compiling this guide to the vast area of Southeast Asia, we have had to make some difficult choices. Rather than provide skeletal coverage of all areas of the countries included, we have selected the most popular areas and covered them in depth, although we have tried to provide at least a hint of character of some of the lesser-known, but fascinating areas.

This is an exciting time for Fodor's, as we continue our ambitious program to rewrite, reformat, and redesign all 140 of our guides. Here are just a few of the new features:

★ Brand-new computer-generated maps locating all the top attractions, hotels, restaurants, and shops

★ A unique system of numbers and legends to help readers move effortlessly between text and maps

★ A new star rating system for hotels and restaurants

★ Restaurant reviews by major food critics around the world

★ Stamped, self-addressed postcards, bound into every guide, give readers a chance to help evaluate hotels and restaurants

★ Complete page redesign for instant retrieval of information

★ ITINERARIES—The experts help you decide where to go

★ FODOR'S CHOICE—Our favorite museums, beaches, cafés, romantic hideaways, festivals, and more

★ HIGHLIGHTS—An insider's look at the most important developments in tourism during the past year

★ TIME OUT—The best and most convenient lunch stops along exploring routes

★ Exclusive background essays create a powerful portrait of each destination

★ A mini-journal for travelers to keep track of their own itineraries and addresses

For the invaluable assistance they have provided us in putting together this guide, we would like to extend our sincere appreciation to the following: Philippine Air Lines, Philippine Department of Tourism (New York and Manila), and Philippine Convention and Visitors' Corporation (Manila); China Airlines and Taiwan Visitors Association (New York and Taipei); Thai International Airways; United Airlines; Didien Junaedy of Pt. Natourin, Indonesia; Garuda Indonesian Airways; Indonesian Tourist Promotion Board; Singapore Tourist Promotion Board.

While every care has been taken to ensure the accuracy of the information in this guide, the passage of time will always bring change, and consequently, the publisher cannot accept responsibility for errors that may occur.

All prices and opening times quoted here are based on information available to us at press time. Hours and admission fees may change, however, and the prudent traveler will avoid inconvenience by calling ahead.

Fodor's wants to hear about your travel experiences, both pleasant and unpleasant. When a hotel or restaurant fails to live up to its billing, let us know and we will investigate the complaint and revise our entries where the facts warrant it.

Send your letters to the editors of Fodor's Travel Publications, 201 E. 50th Street, New York, NY 10022.

Highlights '90 and Fodor's Choice

Highlights '90

Hong Kong

With the opening of the spectacular **Convention & Exhibition Centre** at the end of 1988, Hong Kong moved into the big league for large international meetings. Fortunately, there are now enough hotel rooms to meet their needs, thanks to the opening in 1989 of several four- and five-star hotels, including the **Hyatt Regency**'s superb new flagship (built atop the Convention Centre along with a **New World Hotels** property).

The newest landmark on the Kowloon waterfront is the **Hong Kong Cultural Centre,** where local and international artists perform in plays and concerts. Hong Kong's latest engineering marvel is a second **cross-harbor tunnel,** completed in late 1989, which connects eastern Hong Kong Island with eastern Kowloon.

In Macau there has also been something of a hotel building boom, with the opening of the **Beverly Plaza, Ritz,** and **Guia.** Another welcome event last year was the inauguration of a greatly enlarged and renovated **race track,** where flat racing has replaced trotting.

Indonesia

Indonesia, with its diverse cultures, astounding architecture, and thousands of islands, is becoming the newly discovered vacation destination with tourism increasing at a rate of 20% yearly. To accommodate this climb, some 87 hotels are either expanding or being newly constructed, creating 14,000 more guest rooms. Bali, for example, is an area of major growth, with a new **Hyatt** and **Sheraton** opening in 1990.

Malaysia

For years Malaysia has quietly gone about its business of national development, and now it's one of the emerging nations of Southeast Asia. Facilities have dramatically improved in recent times, and now many hotels are world-class—especially the **Penang Mutiara,** the **Kuching Hilton,** the **Tanjung Aru Beach Hotel** in Kota Kinabalu, and the **Shangri-La** in Kuala Lumpur. In Kuala Lumpur, large mansions of Chinese tycoons have been turned into restaurants like **Yazmin** and the **Terrace Garden.**

In 1989 Malacca was granted **special historical status** and began a program of restoration and renovation of its historic buildings. A new outdoor **sound-and-light show** highlights the city's colonial past with narration and lighting of monuments and ruins.

Philippines

The decline in tourism of the last years of the Marcos regime has shifted, yet visitors are advised that travel should be confined to urban areas and major tourist destinations. Due to unsettled conditions, tourists should check with the consular section of the embassy in Manila prior to arrival in the Philippines.

The exchange rate has stood still for the past two years, though that may change as the economy improves. The country has just one international airport (in Manila), but there are plans to open the **airports** in Cebu and Laoag to more international flights (Cebu already receives some flights from Tokyo).

An expensive new resort has been added to the growing number in the country: **Dayak Beach Resort** in northern Mindanao. Surfers from Australia, Japan, and the United States are beginning to discover the island of Catanduanes, off the Pacific coast of southern Luzon. Finally, the Department of Tourism is planning a Homestay Program for the provinces, that will let foreign visitors board with local families, providing an opportunity for a closer look at the Philippine culture.

The current trend in Philippine cuisine is the emergence of contemporary interpretations of traditional and regional specialties. For instance, **Gene's Bistro** in Manila prepares vichyssoise using native yams.

Singapore

Singapore has undertaken a **S$1 billion program** to enhance its attractiveness as a destination. Some projects have been completed; others continue through 1990 and 1991. A large part of the plan involves resurrecting and revitalizing some historic buildings and areas that were destroyed in Singapore's rush to modernity.

Empress Place, which housed innumerable government offices over the past century, reopened in 1989 after a S$25 million renovation and will be used as a cultural museum. **Bugis Street,** once a popular spot with bars and clubs offering transvestite and other bawdy floor shows, was torn down to make way for a subway station but is being rebuilt, with the completion date set for late 1990.

The eccentric **Haw Par Villa (Tiger Balm Gardens),** with elaborate, brightly painted statues and murals of Chinese mythological figures, has been closed since July 1988 for major renovations and expansion, and is scheduled for completion in April 1990. The original exhibits are being carefully restored and a new high-tech "adventureland" of Chinese folklore added.

Charming storefront **restaurants** in terraced houses, such as **Aziza's,** are proliferating, as are restaurants offering seafood fresh from the tank. Combination buffet/à la carte lunches are newly popular. Try **Latour** and **Chateaubriand.**

Exciting developments in transportation are in various stages of completion. The **MV** *Orient Express,* owned by a subsidiary of the luxury train company, will begin using Singapore as a base for winter-season cruises to Bali and other Southeast Asian ports in late 1990. A **second airline terminal** will be finished in late 1990, doubling Changi's present capacity, while a second line of Singapore's excellent **Mass Rapid Transit Railway (MRT)** subway system is set to open in 1990.

Taiwan

In recent years, the Taiwanese government has turned its attention to the development of tourism to complement the massive growth of the island's commerce and industry. The progress of tourist hotels continues apace with the recent completion of two new hotels as well as renovations of several others. The **International Convention Center,** completed in 1989, rounded out development of the Taipei World Trade Center. Taiwan also has begun opening up its scenic areas. The results are evident in the magnificent facilities at the **Caesar Park Hotel** on the southern coast at Kenting.

The Chinese preoccupation with food, spurred on by new wealth, has made Taiwan's lively dining scene even livelier. Traditional street-level eateries like those in Hsimenting attract as many diners as ever, and in fine dining, a new, more imaginative cuisine is being created.

Thailand

Since the much-publicized "Visit Thailand Year," 1987, Bangkok's dining scene has become one of the world's most vital. One development is the appearance of first-class restaurants featuring non-Thai Asian cuisines, like the new **Mandalay,** with excellent Burmese food.

Thailand's own cuisine is available in restaurants in a much greater variety. Obscure regional recipes have been brought to town, where they are pleasing crowds at a new generation of elegantly decorated, quiet, air-conditioned places. Also new and worth exploring are enormous outdoor seafood restaurants, such as **Tumnak Thai,** with riverside settings and good, cheap food.

Thailand's spectacular beaches have become a magnet for tourists, and to keep up with the influx, new resort areas are developing rapidly. For instance, Phi Phi Island has recently opened a new luxury hotel, the **P.P. International Resort.** Also, Chiang Mai, which was once a quiet provincial town studded with temples, is presently experiencing a tremendous development boom, with new hotels, like the **Mae Ping Hotel,** going up all the time.

Thailand's industry is booming too. Most of this new wealth and economic growth is centered in or close to Bangkok, and until recently has outstripped expansions of the city's infrastructure. But improvements are being made slowly.

Fodor's Choice

Special Moments

Hong Kong The dazzling view of Hong Kong from the Peak

Finding familiar names in the Old Protestant Cemetery in Macau

Indonesia Morning at Jakarta's fish market, Pasar Ikan

Sunrise at Prambanan temple, Jogjakarta

Ramayana Ballet at Prambanan, Jogjakarta

Singapore Cricket on the Padang

Sunday breakfast at a bird-singing café

Sunsets from Mt. Faber

Taiwan Ocean view from the bluffs at Opuanpi

Train through the forest on Alishan mountain

Thailand Scuba diving off Phi Phi Island

Sunset at Nai Harn Bay, Phuket

Dining

Hong Kong Gaddi's (*Very Expensive*)

Hugo's (*Very Expensive*)

Jimmy's Kitchen (*Moderate*)

A Galera, Macau (*Moderate*)

Chili Club (*Moderate*)

Yung Kee (*Moderate*)

Indonesia The Spice Garden, Jakarta (*Expensive*)

Spice Islander, Bali (*Expensive*)

Sari Kuring, Jakarta (*Moderate*)

Ny Suharti, Jogjakarta (*Inexpensive*)

Malaysia Brasserie, Penang (*Expensive*)

La Farfalla, Penang (*Expensive*)

Eden, Penang (*Moderate*)

Yazmin, Kuala Lumpur (*Moderate*)

Minah, Penang (*Inexpensive*)

Philippines Copper Grill, Baguio City (*Very Expensive*)

Lantaw Seafoods Restaurant, Cebu City (*Expensive*)

Kamayan Restaurant, Manila (*Moderate*)

Sunset Terrace, Iloilo City (*Moderate*)

Alavar's, Zamboanga City (*Inexpensive*)

Cafe by the Ruins, Baguio City (*Inexpensive*)

Gene's Bistro, Manila (*Inexpensive*)

Singapore Latour (*Very Expensive*)

Li Bai (*Very Expensive–Expensive*)

Nadaman (*Expensive*)

Tandoor (*Expensive*)

Banana Leaf Apollo (*Inexpensive*)

Taiwan Trader's Grill, Taipei (*Very Expensive*)

The Chinese Restaurant, Taipei (*Expensive*)

Hizen-ya, Taipei (*Inexpensive*)

Thailand Le Normandie, Bangkok (*Very Expensive*)

Amanpuri, Phuket (*Expensive*)

Royal Kitchen, Bangkok (*Expensive*)

Sala Rim Naam, Bangkok (*Moderate*)

Baen Suan, Chiang Mai (*Moderate*)

Lodging

Hong Kong Mandarin Oriental, Hong Kong Island (*Very Expensive*)

Peninsula, Kowloon (*Very Expensive*)

The Regent, Kowloon (*Very Expensive*)

Hyatt Regency, Macau (*Expensive*)

Pousada de Sao Tiago, Macau (*Expensive*)

Taipa Island Resort, Macau (*Expensive*)

Ritz, Kowloon (*Inexpensive*)

Indonesia Kupu Kupu Barong, Ubud, Bali (*Very Expensive*)

Mandarin Oriental, Jakarta (*Very Expensive*)

Oberoi, Legian, Bali (*Very Expensive*)

Ambarrukmo Palace, Jogjakarta (*Expensive*)

Tanjung Sari, Sanur, Bali (*Expensive*)

Hotel Garuda, Jogjakarta (*Moderate*)

Hotel Misiliana, Rantepao, Sulawesi (*Moderate*)

Kusuma Sahid Prince Hotel, Solo (*Moderate*)

Malaysia Kuching Hilton, Kuching (*Very Expensive*)

Penang Mutiara, Penang *(Very Expensive)*

Shangri-La, Kuala Lumpur (*Very Expensive*)

Tanjung Aru Beach Hotel, Kota Kinabalu
(*Very Expensive*)

Eastern & Oriental Hotel, Penang (*Moderate*)

Merlin, Kuala Lumpur (*Moderate*)

Philippines Cebu Plaza, Lanug (*Very Expensive*)

Manila Peninsula, Manila (*Very Expensive*)

Philippine Plaza, Manilla (*Very Expensive*)

Hyatt Terraces, Baguio City (*Moderate*)

Hotel Del Rio, Iloilo City (*Moderate*)

Casa Amapola, Baguio City (*Inexpensive*)

Singapore Goodwood Park (*Very Expensive*)

The Dynasty (*Expensive*)

Ladyhill Hotel (*Moderate*)

RELC International House (*Inexpensive*)

Taiwan Howard Plaza, Taipei (*Very Expensive*)

Grand Hotel, Taipei (*Expensive*)

YMCA International Guest House (*Inexpensive*)

Thailand Amanpuri, Phuket (*Very Expensive*)

Oriental, Bangkok (*Expensive*)

Shangri-La, Bangkok (*Expensive*)

River View Lodge, Chiang Mai (*Inexpensive*)

Museums

Hong Kong Railway Museum, Tai Po

Maritime Museum in Macau, one of Asia's finest

Indonesia National Museum, Jakarta

Singapore Peranakan Place

Pioneers of Singapore/Surrender Chambers

Taiwan Taiwan Folk Art Museum, Peitou

National Palace Museum, Taipei

Thailand National Museum, Bangkok

Temples, Shrines, and Buildings

Hong Kong Temple of 10,000 Buddhas, Shatin

A-Ma Temple, Macau

Indonesia	Borobudur, Jogjakarta
	Prambanan, Jogjakarta
	Ceremonial Houses of the Toraja, Sulawesi
	Hall of Justice, Bali
Philippines	Miagao and Molo churches, Iloilo City
	Manila Cathedral, Quiapo, and San Agustin churches, Manila
Singapore	Fuk Tak Chi Temple
	Sri Mariamman Temple
Thailand	Suan Pakkard Palace, Bangkok
	Wat Benjamabopit-Marble Temple, Bangkok
	Wat Chaimongkol, Chiang Mai
	Wat Phanan Choeng, Ayutthaya
	Wat Phra Keo-Temple of the Emerald Buddha, Bangkok
	Wat Traimitr-Temple of the Golden Buddha, Bangkok

Sights

Hong Kong	The view of the coastline from the Ocean Park cable car
	Crossing the harbor on the Star Ferry—second class, at water level
	Tram ride from Kennedy Town to North Point
	The double-decker bus ride over the bridge to Taipa Island
	A pedicab ride for leisurely sightseeing in Macau
Malaysia	Masjid Jamek Bandaraya, Kuala Lumpur
	Baba Nonya Heritage, Malacca
	Khoo Kongsi, Penang
	Mt. Kinabalu from anywhere in Sabah
	Sunset from the patio of E&O Hotel in Penang
	Night skyline of Kuala Lumpur from Ming Court balcony
Philippines	Basilica Minore del Sto. Nino, Cebu City
	Intramuros, Manila
	Villa Escudero, Metro Manila
	Banaue Rice Terraces, northern Luzon
	Sagada Burial Caves, northern Luzon
	Magellan's Cross, Visayas
	Taluksangay, Visayas
	Palawan island

Taiwan	Taroko Gorge
Thailand	Erawan Waterfall, Kanchanaburi
	Floating Market, Damnoen Saduak
	Golden Triangle, northern Thailand
	Phang Nga Bay, off Phuket
	Thai classical dancing

Parks and Walks

Hong Kong	Tai Lam Country Park, near Kowloon
	Lantau Island, Shek Pik to Tai O
	Victoria Park, Causeway Bay, to watch morning t'ai chi
	Camoes Gardens, Macau
Singapore	Singapore Zoological Gardens

Beaches

Indonesia	Legian Beach, Bali
	Lombok Island
Malaysia	Batu Ferringhi, Penang
	Pangkor Island
	Damai Beach, Sarawak
Philippines	Panglao, Bohol
	El Nido, Palawan
	Boracay and Sicogon, Panay
	Santa Cruz Island, Zamboanga
Taiwan	Fulung
Thailand	Pansea Beach, Phuket
	Nai Harn, Phuket
	Ao Phrang Bay, Krabi
	Ko Samui
	Ko Samet

Shopping

Hong Kong	Jade Market, Kansu Street, Kowloon
	Night Market at Temple Street, Kowloon
Indonesia	Antique wayang-kulit in Bali or Jogjakarta
	Batiks and leather in Jogjakarta
	Gold and Silver in Bali

Malaysia	Karyaneka Handicrafts Center, Kuala Lumpur
	Batik Malaysia Berhad, Kuala Lumpur and Penang
	Selangor Pewter, throughout Malaysia
	Antiques shops of Jonker Street, Malacca
Singapore	Singapore Handicraft Centre
	P. Govindasamy Pillai for Indian silks
	China Silk House for Chinese silks
Taiwan	Lin Tien Cooperage, Taipei
Thailand	Sapphires and rubies in Bangkok
	Thai silk in Chiang Mai and Bangkok

Taipei

TAIWAN

P A C I F I C

O C E A N

Laoag

LUZON

Baguio

Manila

PHILIPPINES

MINDORO

PALAU

V I S A Y A S

Iloilo City

PANAY

SAMAR

Cebu City

NEGROS

MINDANAO

Sulu Sea

Davao

Celebes Sea

HALMAHERA

Makassar Strait

M O L U C C A S

SULUWESI
(The Celebes)

SERAM

BURU

IRIAN JAYA

**PAPUA-
NEW GUINEA**

*KEPULAUAN
ARU*

A N D S

Ujung
Pandang

Banda Sea

Flores Sea

I S L A N D S

*KEPULAUAN
TANIMBAR*

S E R   S U N D A

FLORES

TIMOR

Timor Sea

SUMBA

xxii

World Time Zones

Numbers below vertical bands relate each zone to Greenwich Mean Time (0 hrs.).
Local times may differ, as indicated by lightface numbers on the map.

Algiers, **29**
Anchorage, **3**
Athens, **41**
Auckland, **1**
Baghdad, **46**
Bangkok, **50**
Beijing, **54**

Berlin, **34**
Bogotá, **19**
Budapest, **37**
Buenos Aires, **24**
Caracas, **22**
Chicago, **9**
Copenhagen, **33**
Dallas, **10**

Delhi, **48**
Denver, **8**
Djakarta, **53**
Dublin, **26**
Edmonton, **7**
Hong Kong, **56**
Honolulu, **2**

Istanbul, **40**
Jerusalem, **42**
Johannesburg, **44**
Lima, **20**
Lisbon, **28**
London (Greenwich), **27**
Los Angeles, **6**
Madrid, **38**
Manila, **57**

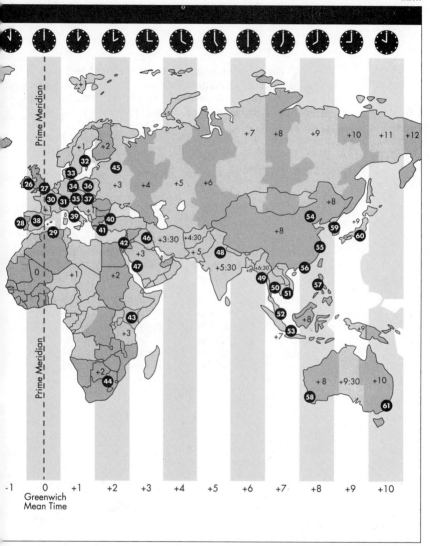

Introduction

Any attempt to generalize about Southeast Asia is doomed to failure. This vast, varied region encompasses every level of civilization, from booming, bustling Hong Kong and Singapore—with their ultra-luxury hotels, sophisticated restaurants, and world-class shopping—to the tribal villages of Sulawesi and of Borneo, where headhunting was a way of life, discarded only within recent memory.

A large part of Southeast Asia's fascination lies in the quiet beauty found in such rice-paddy landscapes as that captured in the photograph on the cover of this book—the glimpse into a simpler time that we in the West have left behind. But no matter where you go, do not expect to leave modern life entirely behind. As tourism among these simpler societies grows, it subtly or grossly succeeds in changing them irrevocably.

Because of political and social instability, Burma (now officially renamed the Union of Myanmar) and Indochina—including Vietnam, Cambodia (known also as Kampuchea), and Laos—are not included in this book. Once these nations welcome and are able to accommodate foreign guests, we will again give them the coverage they deserve. The following capsule portraits should help point you in the direction of the countries most likely to offer the kinds of excursions you are after in your journey to this exciting and richly complex land.

Brunei, primarily a stopover between Sabah and Sarawak in East Malaysia, covers less than 3,584 sq km (2,226 sq mi). The tiny Malay sultanate is rich in oil revenues but still limited as to tourist facilities. Its population of 200,000 is found mostly in the sleepy tropical capital, Bandar Seri Begawan, and in longhouses on stilts along the water nearby. A traveler can visit the country's attractions in a couple of days.

Hong Kong is compact, well organized, well equipped, and convenient. The British Crown—encompassing about 652 sq km (405 sq mi) on 235 islands and with a population of around 5.6 million—is one of the most exciting places in the world. Your first impression will be of the magnificent natural setting; your second, of the vibrantly colorful life of the Chinese who make up 98% of the population. Then you can enjoy the food, nightlife, shopping, and cosmopolitan atmosphere of the colony. You can see Hong Kong in about a week. One benefit of its amazing economic achievement is that the colony is brilliantly organized for tourism of all kinds, especially for people who want lots of good eating

and shopping, plus recreation and sightseeing in exotic surroundings.

Indonesia is made up of five large and 13,600 small islands
totaling more than 936,464 sq km (581,655 sq mi), with a
population of 175 million. Its principal tourist destinations
are Bali and Java. Java, the smallest of the main islands,
has the capital city of Jakarta (population 7 million), which
clearly reflects the successive influences of Indonesian culture: Local markets cater to its native people, the National
Museum displays the heritage of former kingdoms, the cuisine is a fabulous mixture of Chinese and Dutch, and the
architecture includes the pompous projects that remain
from the Sukarno era. Central Java is home to Borobudur,
the world's greatest Buddhist monument, and the palaces
of the sultans in Jogjakarta and Solo.

Bali is only about 145 km (90 mi) long but has more than 3
million people and probably more than 10,000 temples.
Since the destruction of Tibet, this is the only remaining example in the world today of a completely traditional society
in which all facets of life—agriculture, economics, politics,
technology, social customs, the arts—are welded by the
Hindu religion. The beaches of Bali's southern coast are
highly developed to accommodate tourists, but it is in the
interior that you catch the Balinese passionate and beautiful way of life.

Sumatra to the north, with exciting ethnic minorities and a
charming hill station at Lake Toba, has lately become a regular tourist stop, as have the Toraja highlands on the island
of Sulawesi. Allow a minimum of two weeks to see Indonesia, more if you plan to go beyond Jakarta and Bali.
Although conditions in Indonesia are improving, tourists
do best by working through a travel agency.

Macau, still Portuguese-administered, was once a quiet
European rather than Oriental town. Recent construction
is increasingly disrupting the antique atmosphere of this
island—spanning only 9.6 sq km (6 sq mi), with a population of 400,000. Three-quarters of an hour or so by jetfoil
from Hong Kong, Macau can easily be seen on foot in one
day, but since the nightlife includes legal gambling, you
may want to stay over.

Malaysia's more than 204,978 sq km (127,316 sq mi) are divided into two parts, peninsular and eastern Malaysia. Its
population of 16 million is made up of about 56% Malays,
34% Chinese, and 10% Indians. Peninsular Malaysia, with
83% of the population, contains the chief cities, sights, and
resorts. English is common everywhere, and the country is
prosperous, with modern facilities that are bargains by
Western standards. The scenery is spectacular, with jungles and rugged hills in the interior, plantations and superb
beaches in the coastal areas.

The capital, Kuala Lumpur (population 1.6 million), is clean and comfortable, with striking Victorian-Moorish architecture. The city is within easy reach of Penang (the other main tourist center) and is near the Genting and Cameron highlands.

The states of Sarawak and Sabah in northern Borneo constitute eastern Malaysia. For tourists, this is frontier country. It has limited facilities (other than a few new luxury resorts) but offers wild jungle and mountain scenery and fascinating close-up glimpses of tribal life. Malaysia's major highlights can be seen in 7 to 10 days. (Be aware that a United States travel advisory for Malaysia warns that convicted drug traffickers will receive the death penalty.)

The Philippines has a population of 62 million and an area of nearly 186,488 sq km (115,831 sq mi), including seven major and 7,100 minor islands. The economic, political, and cultural center is still Manila (population 8 million), though the country's capital is Quezon City. Tourism is concentrated in the Metro Manila area, where there are modern hotels, restaurants, and shops. Elsewhere on the main island of Luzon, hill resorts, beaches, subtropical scenery, and friendly people also draw visitors.

The Philippines contains about 55 ethnic groups, each with distinctive languages, customs, and traditions. The five major cultures are the Ilocanos, Tagalogs, Visayans, Bicolanos, and Muslims.

At press time, unsettled conditions in Manila have calmed and the Department of State has withdrawn advice that Americans should avoid travel to the Philippines. Tourists should be aware, however, that problems still persist, especially in the south, where Muslim factions continue to oppose central government. At press time, there is a U.S. State Department Advisory against travel to the island of Mindanao and the provinces of Lanao del Sur, Lanao del Norte, Zamboanga del Sur, Zamboanga del Norte, and all of the Sulu Archipelago. Anyone traveling outside the regular tourist areas should contact the embassy in Manila or the consulate in Cebu for the latest information. A couple of days will suffice to visit Manila, but if you want to see the upcountry areas and the exotic southern islands such as Cebu, plan on spending two weeks or more.

Singapore is something of an anomaly: an independent city-state, an efficient economy, a tightly run welfare system, and a remarkable multiracial social environment. With a population of 2.6 million and about 362 sq km (225 sq mi), Singapore has lost the mystery and romance of the "exotic Orient." What you will find instead is a bright, clean, modern tropical city that has neither the excitement and glamour of Hong Kong nor, mercifully, its brutal contrasts of wealth and squalor. Although the population is predominantly Chinese, Singapore's national culture is truly multiracial. A major port and shopping center, Singapore boasts excellent tourist facilities. Sightseeing takes only two or three days, but shopping often keeps visitors busy much longer.

Taiwan, once sparsely settled and undeveloped, now has a population just over 19.6 million. The nearly 22,368-sq-km (13,893-sq-mi) island was taken over in 1949 by the millions of refugees who fled Communism in mainland China. These industrious people have created an economic miracle, a modern state that preserves an antique cultural heritage. Tourism in Taiwan is often limited to a stopover in the capital city of Taipei (population 3 million), which is a pity, as the island has many other attractions. The city itself is colorless at first glance; you have to look closely to find the bazaars, temples, shrines, restaurants, theaters, shops, and side streets where you can get the feel of Chinese life. Beyond Taipei are resorts, including Taroko Gorge, Mount Ali, and the beaches at Oluanpi. Transportation is good; conditions in general are clean, modern, and efficient; and Taipei has many new hotels. Four to six days are adequate for a visit.

Thailand, with a population of 54 million and an area of almost 319,513 sq km (198,455 sq mi), has become one of the world's top tourist destinations. Most of the traffic is centered on the capital city of Bangkok (population 6 million), which has wonderful hotels, restaurants, nightclubs, luxury shops, banks, offices, and other big-city facilities. The level of development makes the city very convenient, but this air-conditioned little world is misleading. Much of Bangkok is chaotic and hideous—like Tokyo, a monument to the horrors of sudden, unplanned growth and commercialization.

Outside the capital, chief excursions are to important temples and ruins, mostly in smaller towns in the Bangkok basin—a hot, flat, wet, rice-growing plain that epitomizes subtropical Asia. The eastern and northeastern parts of the country are arid and poor, with little to interest the traveler. In the north, Chiang Mai, the rapidly developing second city, is a pleasant provincial town on a cool mountain plateau, with several good hotels, and a tranquil atmosphere. A number of beach resorts are gradually opening up for tourism. Pattaya is the leader: almost 137 km (85 mi) south of Bangkok, it is Asia's largest resort. Toward the Malaysian border are miles of sand beaches—such as the resort area of Phuket—fishing villages, and jungle regions, including that of the famous River Kwai. At least a week is needed to see even the superficial sights.

1 Essential Information

Before You Go

Government Tourist Offices

Call or write the following organizations for free brochures; listings of hotels, restaurants, sights, and shops; and up-to-date calendars of events. The **Pacific Asia Travel Association** (1 Montgomery St., San Francisco, CA 94104, tel. 415/986–4646) can answer some general questions about the area. It also sells a Pacific Asia Information Offices brochure (with tourist board locations for 34 countries) for $3. (For tourist offices in the United Kingdom, *see* Tips for British Travelers, below.)

In the United States
Brunei Brunei has no tourist office in the United States. For information, contact the Embassy of Brunei (Consular Section, Watergate, Suite 300, 2600 Virginia Ave. NW, Washington, DC 20037, tel. 202/342–0159) or the **Brunei Permanent Mission to the United Nations** (866 United Nations Plaza, Room 248, New York, NY 10016, tel. 212/838–1600).

Hong Kong **Hong Kong Tourist Association** (590 Fifth Ave., New York, NY 10036, tel. 212/869–5008; 333 N. Michigan Ave., Chicago, IL 60601, tel. 312/782–3872; 360 Post St., San Francisco, CA 94108, tel. 415/781–4582; 10940 Wilshire Blvd., Suite 1220, Los Angeles, CA 90024, tel. 213/208–4582).

Indonesia **Indonesia Tourist Promotion Board** (3457 Wilshire Blvd., Los Angeles, CA 90010, tel. 213/387–2078).

Macau **Macau Tourist Information Bureau** (608 Fifth Ave., Suite 309, New York, NY 10020, tel. 212/581–7465; Box 1860, Los Angeles, CA 90078, tel. 213/851–3402; Box 22188, Honolulu, HI 96822, tel. 808/538–7613).

Malaysia **Malaysia Tourist Information Center** (818 W. 7th St., Los Angeles, CA 90017, tel. 213/689–9702).

Philippines **Philippine Ministry of Tourism** (556 Fifth Ave., New York, NY 10036, tel. 212/575–7915; 30 N. Michigan Ave., Suite 1111, Chicago, IL 60602, tel. 312/782–1707; 3460 Wilshire Blvd., Los Angeles, CA 90010, tel. 213/487–4525).

Singapore **Singapore Tourist Promotion Board** (590 Fifth Ave., 12th floor, New York, NY 10036, tel. 212/302–4861; 333 N. Michigan Ave., Suite 818, Chicago, IL 60601, tel. 312/704–4200; 8484 Wilshire Blvd., Suite 510, Beverly Hills, CA 90211, tel. 213/852–1901).

Taiwan **Taiwan Visitors Association** (1 World Trade Center, Suite 7953, New York, NY 10048, tel. 212/466–0691; 333 N. Michigan Ave., Suite 2329, Chicago, IL 60601, tel. 312/346–1037; 166 Geary St., Suite 1605, San Francisco, CA 94108, tel. 415/989–8677).

Thailand **Tourism Authority of Thailand** (5 World Trade Center, Suite 2449, New York, NY 10048, tel. 212/432–0433; 3440 Wilshire Blvd., Los Angeles, CA 90010, tel. 213/382–2353).

In Canada Indonesia, the Philippines, Taiwan, and Thailand have no tourist offices in Canada. For information, write to any U.S. office.

Brunei Brunei has no tourist office in Canada. For information, write to the **Embassy of Brunei** in Washington, DC, or the Permanent Mission to the United Nations in New York.

Hong Kong **Hong Kong Tourist Association** (347 Bay St., Suite 909, Toronto, Ont. M5H 2R7, tel. 416/366–2389).

Macau **Macau Tourist Information Bureau** (475 Main St., Vancouver, B.C. V6A 2T7, tel. 604/687–3316).

Malaysia **Malaysia Tourist Information Center** (830 Burrard St., Vancouver, B.C. V6C 2K4, tel. 604/689–8899).

Singapore **Singapore Tourist Promotion Board** (175 Bloor St. E, Suite 1112, North Tower, Toronto, Ont. M4W 3R8, tel. 416/323–9139).

Tour Groups

Package tours are a good idea if you are willing to trade independence for a guide who knows the language, a fairly solid guarantee that you will see the highlights, and some savings on airfare, hotels, and ground transportation. Listed below is a select sampling of tour operators serving the region, and of the tours they offer. Operators mix and match Southeast Asian countries in seemingly infinite varieties, so chances are that one has just the tour you had in mind. Often you can customize existing tours to suit your preferences. If you'd like to keep group travel to a minimum, look for tours with plenty of free or optional days.

When considering a tour, be sure to find out (1) exactly what expenses are included in the price, particularly tips, taxes, side trips, meals, and entertainment; (2) ratings of all hotels on the itinerary and the facilities they offer; (3) cancellation policies for both you and the tour operator; (4) the number of travelers in your group; and (5), if you are traveling alone, the cost of the single supplement. Most tour operators request that bookings be made through a travel agent, and in most cases there is no additional charge for doing so.

General-Interest Deluxe-tour packager **Abercrombie & Kent International** (1420 Tours Kensington Rd., Oak Brook, IL 60521, tel. 312/954–2944 or *Multicountry* 800/323–7308) offers a "Silks and Sails" tour of Hong Kong and Thailand, plus the exotic "Borneo and Beyond" trip to Bangkok, Kuala Lumpur, Borneo, and Hong Kong. **Globus-Gateway** (150 S. Los Robles Ave., Pasadena, CA 91101, tel. 818/449–2019 or 800/556–5454 from western U.S., 800/221–0090 from eastern U.S.) teams Manila, Bangkok, and Hong Kong in a 13-day package or Tokyo, Hong Kong, Chiang Mai, Bangkok, Kuala Lumpur, Singapore, and Bali in its 21-day "Exotic Orient" tour. "Orient Highlights" from **Maupintour** (1515 St. Andrew's Dr., Lawrence, KS 66046, tel. 913/843–1211 or 800/255–4266) includes Hong Kong, Bangkok, and Singapore.

TBI Tours (787 7th Ave., Suite 1101, New York, NY 10019, tel. 212/489–1919 or 800/223–0266) serves up Bali, Hong Kong, Singapore, China, and Japan in its grand samplers. **InterPacific Tours International** (111 E. 15th St., New York, NY 10003, tel. 212/953–6010 or 800/221–3594) has a base of operations in Hong Kong and a wide range of Orient packages (and prices) as a result. **American Express Vacations** (100 Church St., New York, NY 10007, tel. 800/241–1700) is another supermarket of Orient packages. **Pacific Delight Tours** (132 Madison Ave., New York, NY 10016, tel. 212/684–7707 or 800/221–7179) offers single-country packages to Singapore, Thailand, or Hong Kong as well as mixed Orient tours. **Travel Plans International** (1200 Harger Rd., Oak Brook, IL 60521, tel. 312/573–1400) travels out-of-the-ordinary routes in Southeast Asia. Its deluxe 18-day

"Route of the Spice Traders" visits the boat-shaped houses and mountain tribes of Sulawesi in Indonesia, as well as Singapore, Jogjakarta, Bali, and Hong Kong. **Cultural Tours** (9920 La Cienega Blvd., Suite 715, Englewood, CA 90301, tel. 213/216–1332, 800/282–8898, or in CA, 800/282–8899) offers a 15-day "Orient Shangri-La" tour to Hong Kong, Bangkok, Singapore, and Bali, as well as a 12-day tour of Manila, Cebu, and Hong Kong.

Single-Country Several of the operators listed above also offer single-country tours. **Globus-Gateway** has all-Hong Kong tours. **Cultural Tours** has Hong Kong, Indonesia, and Philippines tours. **Abercrombie & Kent** runs Indonesia and Philippines tours. **Odyssey Tours** (1821 Wilshire Blvd., Santa Monica, CA 90403, tel. 213/453–1042 or 800/654–7975) offers single-country trips to Hong Kong, Singapore, Taiwan, and Thailand.

Special-Interest **Sobek Expeditions** (Box 1089, Angels Camp, CA 95222, tel. 209/
Tours 736–4524 or 800/777–7939) offers several adventure outings,
Adventure including sailing and hiking in Thailand and exploring the caves, jungles, and beaches of Malaysia by canoe and on foot. In Indonesia's remote outpost Irian Jaya, a Sobek tour visits Melanesian tribes with roots in the Stone Age. The eight-day "Sumatran Alas River Adventure" is a rafting trip through the jungle. **Mountain Travel** (6420 Fairmount Ave., El Cerrito, CA 94530, tel. 800/227–2384), a specialist in adventure travel, has a 16-day "Thai Elephant Safari" tour, in which you visit remote hill tribes and stay in simple village houses.

Art **InnerAsia Expeditions** (2627 Lombard St., San Francisco, CA 94123, tel. 415/922–0448 or 800/551–1769) offers an in-depth look at the art of Singapore, Bangkok, Hong Kong, and China. **Select Tours International** (901A N. Pacific Coast Hwy., Suite 212B, Redondo Beach, CA 90278, tel. 213/379–8999 or 800/356–6680) offers art and photography tours, including its 25-day "Art Expedition to the Indonesian Archipelago," focusing on textile arts.

Bicycling **Backroads Bicycle Touring** (1516 Fifth St., Berkeley, CA 94710–1713, tel. 415/527–1555 or 800/533–2573) offers a 12-day "Cycle Bali" tour in spring.

Business **Asian Corporate Travel Service** (Odyssey Tours, 1821 Wilshire Blvd., Santa Monica, CA 90403, tel. 213/453–1042 or 800/654–7975), in addition to air and first-class accommodations, provides such services as bilingual business cards, letter of introduction in the language of your destination, list of business contacts, and pretrip counseling on local business practices.

Culinary For the serious chef, **InnerAsia** (*see* Art, above) opens the doors to cooking schools in Singapore and Bangkok. Led by a noted authority on Oriental cooking, the group goes behind the scenes at restaurants and into the markets. Offered in conjunction with the California Culinary Academy.

Natural History "Thailand and Malaysia" is a 23-day nature and culture tour from **Questers Worldwide Nature Tours** (257 Park Ave. S, New York, NY 10010, tel. 212/673–3120). The group will follow wild elephant tracks, looking for gibbons and tropical birds; boat down the Kok River; and take in a wealth of temples and shrines. **Sobek Expeditions** (*see* Adventure, above) offers a 10-

day natural-history tour of Bali and Java, called "Islands of Fire."

Scuba **Tropical Adventures Travel** (170 Denny Way, Seattle, WA 98109, tel. 206/441–3483 or 800/247–3483), a specialist in scuba cruises, visits some of the best dive spots in Indonesia and Thailand. Other water-sports equipment is available on the 36-passenger ship.

Cruises **Society Expeditions Cruises** (3131 Elliott Ave., Suite 700, Seattle, WA 98121, tel. 206/285–9400 or 800/426–7794) offers cruises around Indonesia, Sumatra, and Borneo. The line is noted for its high-caliber onboard lectures and programs by experts in the history, natural history, culture, and other facets of its destinations. Reserve six months to a year in advance.

Pearl Cruises (1510 S.E. 17th St., Fort Lauderdale, FL 33316, tel. 800/338–1700 or 800/426–3588) offers a 20-day "Great Cities of Asia" land-sea "CruiseTour" to Bangkok, Singapore, Malaysia, Brunei, Manila, Canton, and Hong Kong. The 19-day "Spice Islands" tour calls at Singapore, Penang, Phuket, and several Indonesian islands.

Cunard Cruise Lines (555 Fifth Ave., New York, NY 10017, tel. 800/458–9000) offers the ultimate in luxury cruises aboard the *Sea Goddess II*. Seven- to 14-day cruises visit major and less-traveled Southeast Asian ports. The 11-day "Malaysia/China" cruise calls at Singapore, Kuching, Brunei, Kota Kinabalu, Manila, Canton, and Hong Kong.

The luxury cruise ship **MV** *Orient-Express* (Venice Simplon-Orient-Express, 1 World Trade Center, Suite 2565, New York, NY 10048, tel. 212/938–6830 or 800/524–2420) has departures from Singapore during the winter season. A five-day cruise visits Thailand and the Malay Peninsula; a nine-day cruise visits Indonesia. These can be combined as a 14-day tour.

Package Deals for Independent Travelers

Most packages include air transportation, accommodations, and transfers to and from your hotel. Some add on meals and sightseeing and make local representatives available to answer questions and offer advice. The travel section of a local newspaper and a good travel agent are your best sources for shopping around. The airlines also provide individualized service for the independent traveler. For example, **Singapore Airlines** offers a flexible "Driveaway Holiday" fly/drive/hotel package. **Thai Airways International's** "Royal Orchid Holiday Discover Tours" are fly/hotel packages.

Japan & Orient Tours (250 E. 1st St., Los Angeles, CA 90012, tel. 800/877–8777 or in CA, 800/327–6471) offers flexible packages that let you design your own itinerary with options for hotels, air and ground transportation, and sightseeing. **InterPacific Tours International** (*see* Tour Groups, above) has three-day "Pacific à la Carte" packages. **Tourcrafters** (30 S. Michigan Ave., Chicago, IL 60603, tel. 312/726–3886 or 800/621–2259) has two-day (or longer) "Short Stay" packages offering hotels in all ranges. Other good sources of independent packages are **American Express** (*see* Tour Groups) and **United Airlines Vacations** (Box 3633, Culver City, CA 90231, tel. 800/592–2244 or 213/410–0246).

Tips for British Travelers

Government Tourist Offices Contact the following offices for brochures and tourist information: The **Brunei High Commission** (49 Cromwell Rd., London SW7 2ED, tel. 01/581–0521); **Hong Kong Tourist Association** (125 Pall Mall, London SW1Y 5EA, tel. 01/930–4775); **Macau Tourist Information Bureau** (22 Devonshire St., Suite 01-01, London W1N 1RL, tel. 01/224–3390); **Malaysian Tourist Development Corporation** (17 Curzon St., London W1Y 7FE, tel. 01/499–7388); **Philippines Department of Tourism** (199 Piccadilly, London W1V 9LE, tel. 01/439–3481); **Singapore Tourist Promotion Board** (1 Carrington House, 126–130 Regent St., London W1R 5FE, tel. 01/437–0033); **Thailand Tourist Office** (49 Albemarle St., London W1X 3FE, tel. 01/499–7679). *Note:* There is no tourist office or government agency in Britain for Taiwan.

Passports/Visas *See* general Passports and Visas section, below.

Customs Returning to the United Kingdom, those 17 or older may take home: (1) 200 cigarettes or 100 cigarillos or 50 cigars or 250 grams of tobacco; (2) two liters of table wine and (a) one liter of alcohol over 22% by volume (most spirits), (b) two liters of alcohol under 22% by volume (fortified or sparkling wine), or (c) two more liters of table wine; (3) 50 grams of perfume and 0.25 liter of toilet water; and (4) other goods up to a value of £32. For Customs policies of the Southeast Asian countries, *see* general Customs section, below.

Insurance We recommend that you insure yourself against health or motoring mishaps with **Europ Assistance** (252 High St., Croydon, Surrey CR0 1NF, tel. 01/680–1234). It is also wise to take out insurance to cover the loss of luggage (although check that such loss isn't covered in a homeowner's policy you may already have) and trip cancellation. **The Association of British Insurers** (Aldermary House, Queen St., London EC4, tel. 01/248–4477) gives comprehensive advice on all aspects of holiday insurance.

Tour Operators **Bales Tours Ltd** (Bales House, Barrington Rd., Dorking, Surrey RH4 3EJ, tel. 0306/76881) specializes in escorted tours, such as a 13-day tour of Burma and Thailand, a 12-day tour of Indonesia, 10 days in northern or southern Thailand, 17 days in Bangkok and Singapore, or 14 days in Malaysia.

Kuoni Travel Ltd (Kuoni House, Dorking, Surrey RH5 4AZ, tel. 0306/740500) covers all the main Southeast Asian centers. Offerings include 13 days in Thailand; 13 days in Singapore, Hong Kong, and Bangkok; a 20-day cruise taking in Thailand, Singapore, Malaysia, Brunei, the Philippines, and Hong Kong; and a 7-day "Beaches of Malaysia" package.

Sovereign Worldwide (Groundstar House, London Rd., Crawley RH10 2TB, tel. 0293/560777) offers 7 to 14 nights in Bangkok and 7-night stays in Phuket or Malaysia.

Tradewinds Faraway Holidays (Station House, 81–83 Fulham High St., London SW6 3JP, tel. 01/731–8000) offers 7-night Singapore tours and 14-day "Around Thailand" tours.

Airlines and Airfares **British Airways** and **Singapore Airlines** fly to Singapore; the APEX economy fare is £650 return in the low season (Oct.–June), £850 in the high season. **British Airways** and **Malaysian Airlines** serve Kuala Lumpur; the APEX low-season return fare is £650. **British Airways** and **Thai International Airlines**

travel to Bangkok; the APEX low-season return fare is £598.
Cathay Pacific and **British Airways** fly to Hong Kong; APEX
fare is £542, rising to £742 in high season. Check *Time Out* and
the Sunday papers for charters. **Thomas Cook Ltd** can often
book you on inexpensive flights. Call the branch nearest you
and ask to be put through to the "Airfare Warehouse."

When to Go

Hong Kong and Macau
Hong Kong's high tourist season, October–late December, is
popular for a reason: The weather is pleasant, with sunny days
and comfortable, cool nights. January, February, and sometimes early March are not only cold but also dank, with long
periods of overcast skies and rain. March and April can be either cold and miserable or beautiful and sunny. By May, the
cold, damp spell has broken and the temperature is warm and
comfortable. The months of June through September are the
typhoon season, when the weather is hot and sticky, with lots
of rain.

Macau's summers are slightly cooler and wetter than Hong
Kong's. In the 19th century, many Hong Kong residents sum-
mered in Macau to escape the heat.

Climate The following are average daily maximum and minimum temperatures for Hong Kong.

Jan.	64F	18C	**May**	82F	28C	**Sept.**	85F	29C
	56	13		74	23		77	25
Feb.	63F	17C	**June**	85F	29C	**Oct.**	81F	27C
	55	13		78	26		73	23
Mar.	67F	19C	**July**	87F	31C	**Nov.**	74F	23C
	60	16		78	26		65	18
Apr.	75F	24C	**Aug.**	87F	31C	**Dec.**	68F	20C
	67	19		78	26		59	15

Indonesia
Indonesia's low-lying regions are uniformly hot and humid
year-round. Temperatures can reach 90°F (32°C) soon after
midday, and they drop no lower than 70°F (21°C) at night. The
weather at higher altitudes is up to 20°F (11°C) cooler.

The best months for traveling are April–May and September–
October, when you are most likely to miss the rains and the
crowds. The west monsoon, from November through March,
brings heavy rains: It can drizzle for several days in a row or
pour half the day, with only occasional dry spells. Since most of
Indonesia's attractions are under the open sky—temples and
other architecture, beaches, and outdoor festivals—the monsoon can very literally dampen your enjoyment.

In the peak tourist months, June and July, popular areas (especially Torajaland) are crammed with visitors. Bali hotels also
tend to be fully booked around Christmas and New Year.

Climate The following are average daily maximum and minimum temperatures for Jakarta.

Jan.	84F	29C	May	87F	31C	Sept.	88F	31C
	74	23		74	23		74	23
Feb.	84F	29C	June	87F	31C	Oct.	87F	31C
	74	23		74	23		74	23
Mar.	85F	30C	July	87F	31C	Nov.	85F	30C
	74	23		74	23		74	23
Apr.	86F	30C	Aug.	88F	31C	Dec.	85F	30C
	74	23		74	23		74	23

Malaysia and Brunei Malaysia's equatorial climate is fairly uniform throughout the year: Temperatures range from the low 90s during the day to low 70s at night. The mountains may be 10° cooler than the lowlands. Relative humidity is usually about 90%. Rain is common all year, but showers don't last long and shouldn't slow you down much. A rainy season brought on by monsoons lasts from November through February on the east coast of peninsular Malaysia, from October through April in Sarawak, and from October through February in Sabah. The heavy rains can cause delays.

During school holidays, locals tend to fill hotels, so book in advance if you plan to visit in early April, early August, or from mid-November to early January.

Climate The following are average daily maximum and minimum temperatures for Kuala Lumpur.

Jan.	89F	32C	May	91F	33C	Sept.	89F	32C
	72	22		74	23		74	23
Feb.	91F	33C	June	91F	33C	Oct.	89F	32C
	72	22		74	23		74	23
Mar.	91F	33C	July	89F	32C	Nov.	89F	32C
	74	23		72	22		74	23
Apr.	91F	33C	Aug.	89F	32C	Dec.	89F	32C
	74	23		74	23		72	22

Brunei, which lies between 4° and 6° north of the equator, is also hot and humid. (The annual mean temperature is 80°F.) Except for a narrow coastal plain, much of the country is rugged and heavily forested. Though sudden and short-lived rainstorms are prevalent throughout the year (particularly November through May), the wettest months are December and January.

Philippines The Philippines has two seasons: dry and wet. The dry season generally runs from late October through May, with temperatures ranging from cool and breezy—even chilly—in the northern highlands to scorching hot in the lowland cities. Within this seven-month span, the coolest stretch is from November through February and, since it coincides with winter months in the West, is also the peak tourist season. During this period popular spots are crowded, major hotels have high occupancy rates, and airfares are higher. Still, there are plenty of beaches and unspoiled places where crowds are either sparse or nonexistent.

If you enjoy crackling summer heat, then March through May are the best months to visit. The Catholic penitential rites of Lent are observed in late March or early April, climaxing in nationwide rituals during Holy Week, when business and government offices shut down. In contrast, May is harvest time, when fiestas are held all over the islands in a final burst of abandon before the onset of the monsoon rains.

For travelers who find themselves in the Philippines during the rainy season—June through September—it's helpful to know that most of Mindanao lies outside the typhoon belt, which cuts across Luzon and most of the Visayas. Mindanao does get rain, but not much more than during the rest of the year. Manila, on the other hand, is subject to frequent floods, while the highlands of northern Luzon become waterlogged, and mud and rock slides frequently make the roads impassable. Be sure to pack a good raincoat.

Climate   The following are average daily maximum and minimum temperatures for Manila.

Jan.	86F	30C	May	93F	34C	Sept.	88F	31C
	70	21		75	24		75	24
Feb.	88F	31C	June	92F	33C	Oct.	88F	31C
	70	21		75	24		74	23
Mar.	91F	33C	July	88F	31C	Nov.	88F	31C
	72	22		75	24		72	22
Apr.	93F	34C	Aug.	88F	31C	Dec.	86F	30C
	74	23		75	24		70	21

Singapore   Singapore has neither peak nor off-peak tourist seasons. Hotel prices remain the same throughout the year, though during quiet spells many properties will discount room rates upon request (either in person or by mail). The busiest tourist months are December and July.

With the equator only 129 km (80 mi) to the south, Singapore is usually either hot or very hot. The average daily temperature is 80°F (26.6°C); it usually reaches 87°F (30.7°C) in the afternoon and drops to a cool 75°F (23.8°C) just before dawn. The months from November through January, during the northeast monsoon, are generally the coolest. The average daily relative humidity is 84.5%, though it drops to 65%–70% on dry afternoons.

Rain falls year-round, but the wettest months are November through January. February is usually the sunniest month; December, the most inclement. Though Singapore has been known to have as much as 512.2 mm (20 in) of rainfall in one 24-hour period, brief, frequent rainstorms are the norm, and the washed streets soon dry in the sun that follows.

Climate   The following are average daily maximum and minimum temperatures for Singapore.

Jan.	86F	30C	May	89F	32C	Sept.	88F	31C
	74	23		75	24		75	24
Feb.	88F	31C	June	88F	31C	Oct.	88F	31C
	74	23		75	24		74	23
Mar.	88F	31C	July	88F	31C	Nov.	88F	31C
	75	24		75	24		74	23
Apr.	88F	31C	Aug.	88F	31C	Dec.	88F	31C
	75	24		75	24		74	23

Taiwan   Taiwan is a moist, subtropical island. The heaviest rainfall occurs in May and June, with occasional typhoons between June and October. Humidity hovers around 80% all year. Summers are hot and sticky, with temperatures reaching 90°F (32°C). Winters are chilly and damp. The best time to visit is between either March and May or September and November. The weather is warmest in the south. If you're traveling in the central mountain range to such places as Alishan, be prepared for colder temperatures. Snow often caps the peaks.

Climate   The following are average daily maximum and minimum temperatures for Taipei.

Jan.	66F	19C	May	82F	28C	Sept.	88F	31C
	53	12		70	21		74	23
Feb.	65F	18C	June	89F	32C	Oct.	80F	27C
	53	12		74	23		60	19
Mar.	70F	21C	July	91F	33C	Nov.	75F	24C
	57	14		75	24		62	17
Apr.	77F	25C	Aug.	91F	33C	Dec.	70F	21C
	62	17		75	24		57	14

Thailand   Thailand has two climates: tropical savannah in the northern regions and tropical rainforest in the south. Three seasons run from hot (March to May) to rainy (June to September) and cool (October to February). Humidity is high all year, especially during the hot season. The cool season is pleasantly warm in the south, but in the north, especially in the hills around Chiang Mai, it can become quite chilly. The cool season is the peak season. Prices are often twice as high then as in the low seasons, yet hotels are often fully booked.

Climate   The following are average daily maximum and minimum temperatures for Bangkok. The north will generally be a degree or two cooler.

Jan.	89F	32C	May	93F	34C	Sept.	89F	32C
	68	20		77	25		75	24
Feb.	91F	33C	June	91F	33C	Oct.	88F	31C
	72	22		75	24		75	24
Mar.	93F	34C	July	89F	32C	Nov.	88F	31C
	75	24		75	24		72	22
Apr.	95F	35C	Aug.	89F	32C	Dec.	88F	31C
	77	25		75	24		68	20

WeatherTrak   Current weather information on more than 500 cities around the world may be obtained by calling the WeatherTrak information service at 900/370–8728 or in Texas, 900/575–8728. A taped message will tell you to dial a three-digit access code for the destination you're interested in. The code is either the area code (in the United States) or the first three letters of the foreign city. For a list of all access codes, send a stamped, addressed envelope to Cities, Box 7000, Dallas, TX 75209. For further information, phone 800/247–3282.

What to Pack

Pack light, because porters can be hard to find and baggage restrictions are tight on international flights—be sure to check on your airline's policies before you pack. And either leave room in your suitcase or bring expandable totes for all your bargains.

Clothing If you'll be traveling through several different types of climate, your wardrobe will have to reflect this. (For weather information on your particular destinations, *see* When to Go, above.) Light cotton or other natural-fiber clothing is appropriate for any Southeast Asian destination; drip-dry is an especially good idea, because the tropical sun and high humidity encourage frequent changes of clothing. Avoid exotic fabrics, because you may have difficulty getting them laundered.

Southeast Asia is generally informal: A sweater, shawl, or lightweight linen jacket will be sufficient for dining and evening wear, except for top international restaurants, where men will still be most comfortable in (and may in fact be required to wear) a jacket and tie. A sweater is also a good idea for cool evenings or overly air-conditioned restaurants.

Toiletries It might be wise to bring your favorite toilet articles (in plastic containers, to avoid breakage and reduce the weight of luggage)—make sure that bottles containing liquids are tightly capped to prevent leakage.

Footwear The paths leading to temples can be rough; in any case, a pair of sturdy and comfortable walking shoes is always appropriate when traveling. Slip-ons are preferable to lace-up shoes, as they must be removed before you enter most shrines and temples.

Miscellaneous Allow for the tropical sun by bringing along a hat and sunscreen. Mosquito repellent is a good idea, and toilet paper is not always supplied in public places.

Electricity Many Southeast Asian countries operate on either 110-volt or 220-volt electrical current, so if you plan to use a hair dryer, razor, travel iron, or other compact electric appliance, be sure and bring a convertor along. (The United States operates on 120-volt electric current.)

Taking Money Abroad

Traveler's checks and major U.S. credit cards—particularly Visa—are accepted in larger cities and resorts. In smaller towns and rural areas, you'll need cash. Small restaurants and shops in the cities also tend to operate on a cash basis. You won't get as good an exchange rate at home as abroad, but it's wise to change a small amount of money into the currency of your first destination before you go to avoid long lines at airport currency-exchange booths. If your local bank can't provide this service, you can exchange money through Deak International. To find the office nearest you, contact them at 630 Fifth Avenue, New York, NY 10011 (tel. 212/635–0515).

For safety and convenience, it's always best to take traveler's checks. The most recognized are American Express, Barclay's, Thomas Cook, and those issued through major commercial banks, such as Citibank and Bank of America. Some banks will issue the checks free to established customers, but most charge a 1% commission fee. Buy some of the checks in small denominations to cash toward the end of your trip. This will save you having to cash a large check and ending up with more foreign money than you need. You can also buy traveler's checks in the currencies of some Southeast Asian countries, a good idea if the dollar is falling and you want to lock in the current rate. Remember to take the addresses of offices where you can get refunds for lost or stolen traveler's checks. Banks and government-approved exchange houses give the best rates; hotels will also change currency, but generally at lower rates.

Getting Money from Home

There are at least three ways to get money from home:

(1) Have it sent through a large commercial bank with a branch in the city or town where you're staying. The drawback is that you must have an account with the bank; if not, you'll have to go through your own bank, and the process will be slower and more expensive.

(2) Have it sent through American Express. If you are a cardholder, you can cash a personal check or a counter check at an American Express office for up to $1,000; $200 will be in cash and $800 in traveler's checks. There is a 1% commission. Through the American Express MoneyGram service, you can receive up to $5,000 cash. It works this way: You call home and ask someone to go to an American Express office or a MoneyGram agent located in a retail outlet and fill out a MoneyGram. It can be paid for with cash or any major credit card. The person making the payment is given a reference number and telephones you with that number. The MoneyGram agent calls an 800 number and authorizes the transfer of funds to an American Express office or participating agency in the town where you're staying. In most cases, the money is available immediately on a 24-hour basis. You pick it up by showing identification and giving the reference number. Fees vary according to the amount of money sent. For sending $300, the fee is $22; for $5,000, $150. For the American Express MoneyGram location nearest your home, and to find out where the service is available overseas, call 800/543-4080. You do not have to be a cardholder to use this service.

(3) Have it sent through Western Union (tel. 800/325-6000). If you have a MasterCard or Visa, you can have money sent for any amount up to your credit limit. If not, have someone take cash or a certified cashier's check to a Western Union office. The money will be delivered in two business days to a bank near where you're staying. Fees vary with the amount of money sent and where it's being sent. For $1,000 the fee is $67; for $500, $57.

Cash Machines Virtually all U.S. banks now belong to a network of Automatic Teller Machines (ATMs) that dispense cash 24 hours a day. The largest of the major networks—Cirrus, owned by MasterCard, and Plus, affiliated with Visa—have now begun providing access to ATMs abroad, mostly in cities that attract large numbers of tourists and business travelers. At press time, both services were planning to open outlets in Asia (Japan, Hong Kong, Malaysia, the Philippines, Singapore) by early 1990. Each network has a toll-free number you can call to find out whether it provides service in a given city and to locate its machines in that city. (Cirrus: 800/424-7787. Plus: 800/843-7587.) Note that these "cash cards" are not issued automatically; they must be requested at your specific branch.

Cards issued by Visa, American Express, and MasterCard can also be used in the ATMs, but the fees are usually higher than the fees on bank cards (and there is a daily interest charge on the "loan"). All three companies issue directories listing the national and international outlets that accept their cards. You can pick up a Visa or MasterCard directory at your local bank. For an American Express directory, call 800/CASH–NOW (this number can also be used for general inquiries). Contact your bank for information on fees and the amount of cash you can withdraw on any given day. Although each bank individually charges for taking money with the card, using your American Express, Visa, or MasterCard at an ATM can be cheaper than exchanging money in a bank because of variations in exchange rates.

Passports and Visas

All Americans, Canadians, and Britons must have a valid passport to enter any of the countries covered in this book. In addition, each country has its own visa requirements, listed below. *(Note:* Do check with your travel agent or the consulates of the countries you are planning to visit, as regulations change.)

Also, if you have visited areas infected with yellow fever, cholera, or smallpox within six to 14 days (depending on the country) of arrival in any of the countries in the book, you will need a certificate of vaccination in order to be allowed in.

Americans. Applications for a new passport must be made in person; renewals can be obtained in person or by mail *(see* below). First-time applicants should apply well in advance of their departure date to one of the 13 U.S. Passport Agency offices. In addition, local county courthouses, many state and probate courts, and some post offices accept passport applications. Necessary documents include: (1) a completed passport application (Form DSP-11); (2) proof of citizenship (birth certificate with raised seal or naturalization papers); (3) proof of identity (driver's license, employee ID card, or any other document with your photograph and signature); (4) two recent, identical, two-inch-square photographs (black-and-white or color); (5) $42 application fee for a 10-year passport (those under 18 pay $27 for a five-year passport). Passports are mailed to you within about 10 working days.

To renew your passport by mail, you'll need a completed Form DSP-82, two recent, identical passport photographs, and a check or money order for $35.

Canadians. Send a completed application (available at any post office or passport office) to the Bureau of Passports, Complexe Guy Favreau, 200 Dorchester W, Montreal, Quebec H2Z 1X4. Include $25, two photographs, a guarantor, and proof of Canadian citizenship. Applications can be made in person at the regional passport offices in Edmonton, Halifax, Montreal, Toronto, Vancouver, or Winnipeg. Passports are valid for five years and are nonrenewable.

Britons. Applications are available from travel agencies or a main post office. Send the completed form to a regional Passport Office. The application must be countersigned by your bank manager, or by a solicitor, barrister, doctor, clergyman, or Justice of the Peace who knows you personally. In addition, you'll need two photographs and the £15 fee. The occasional tourist might opt for a British Visitor's Passport. It is valid for one year, costs £7.50, and is nonrenewable. You'll need two passport photographs and identification. Apply at your local post office.

Brunei

Americans Visas, good for stays up to 14 days, are required to enter Brunei. To apply, contact the Embassy of Brunei, Consular Section, Watergate, Suite 300, 2600 Virginia Ave. NW, Washington, DC 20037, tel. 202/342–0159, or the Brunei Permanent Mission to the United Nations, 866 United Nations Plaza, Room 248, New York, NY 10016, tel. 212/838–1600. Allow at least seven working days for applications to be processed.

Canadians Visas are not required for stays up to 14 days. Canadians planning longer stays in Brunei can apply for a visa at the UN Mission in New York or the Embassy in Washington, DC.

Britons Visas are not required for stays up to 30 days. For extensions, contact the Embassy of Brunei, 49 Cromwell Rd., London SW7 2ED, tel. 01/581–0521. Allow at least seven working days for processing.

Hong Kong Visas are not required for stays of up to one month for Americans, up to three months for Canadians, and up to six months for Britons.

Extended-stay visas may be obtained through the nearest British embassy, consulate, or high commission, or through the Immigration Department in Hong Kong (3/F, Mirror Tower, 61 Mody Rd., East Tsimshatsui, Kowloon; tel. 3/733–3111). Allow six weeks for processing.

Indonesia Passports must be valid for at least six months from arrival date, and all travelers must have proof of onward or return passage. Visas are not required for stays of up to 60 days for Americans, Canadians, and Britons.

Macau Visas are not required for stays of up to 90 days for Americans, Canadians, and Britons.

Malaysia Visas are not required for stays of up to 90 days for Americans, Canadians, and Britons.

Philippines Visas are not required for stays of up to 21 days for Americans, Canadians, and Britons, providing travelers have a ticket for a return or onward journey.

Singapore Visas are not required for stays of up to 14 days for Americans, Canadians, and Britons.

Taiwan Visas, required for Americans, Canadians, and Britons, are good for stays of up to 60 days but can be extended to a maximum of 180 days. Americans and Canadians may contact the nearest Taiwan Coordination Council for North American Affairs office in the United States—in Atlanta, Boston, Chicago, Honolulu, Houston, Kansas City (MO), Los Angeles, Miami, New York, San Francisco, Seattle, or Washington, DC.

Britons may contact the Free Chinese Center, Dorland House, 4th floor, 14–16 Regent St., London SW1Y 4PH, tel. 01/930–5767.

Thailand Visas are not required for stays of up to 15 days for Americans, Canadians, and Britons, providing visitors can show proof of onward travel arrangements.

Extended-stay visas can be obtained by contacting the nearest Thai diplomatic mission or writing the Immigration Division, Soi Suan Phlu, Sathon Tai Rd., Bangkok 10120, Thailand.

Customs and Duties

On Arrival If you are bringing any foreign-made equipment from home, such as cameras, it is wise to carry the original receipt with you or register it with U.S. Customs before you leave (Form 4457). Otherwise you may end up paying duty on your return.

Brunei Personal effects, eight ounces of tobacco, two ounces of perfume, up to 10 ounces of toilet water, and 20 ounces of liquor may be brought into Brunei duty-free.

Hong Kong Visitors may bring 200 cigarettes, 50 cigars, or 250 grams of tobacco; 1 liter of liquor; 60 milliliters of perfume; and 250 milliliters of toilet water into Hong Kong duty-free. Firearms must be declared and handed into custody until departure.

Indonesia Two bottles of liquor and 200 cigarettes may be brought into Indonesia duty-free. Restrictions apply on the import of radios and television sets.

Macau There are no Customs restrictions for travelers entering Macau.

Malaysia Such items as cameras, watches, pens, lighters, cosmetics, perfume, portable radio cassette players, cigarettes (up to 200), and liquor (one liter) may be brought into Malaysia duty-free. Visitors bringing in dutiable goods, such as video equipment, may have to pay a deposit (up to 50% of the item's value) for temporary importation, which is refundable when they leave. If you have to pay a tax or deposit, be sure to get an official receipt. The importation of illegal drugs into Malaysia carries the death penalty.

Philippines Personal effects (a reasonable amount of clothing and a small quantity of perfume), 400 cigarettes or two tins of smoking tobacco, and two liters of liquor may be brought into the Philippines duty-free.

Singapore Duty-free allowances include one liter each of spirits, wine, and beer; 200 cigarettes, 50 cigars, or 250 grams of tobacco; all personal effects; and less than S$50 in foods such as chocolates, biscuits, and cakes. The import of drugs, obscene articles and publications, seditious and treasonable materials, toy coins and currency notes, cigarette lighters of pistol/revolver shapes, or reproductions of copyrighted publications, videotapes, records, or cassettes are prohibited.

Taiwan Clothing and personal items may be brought in without charge or restriction. Travelers may also bring in one bottle of liquor, plus 25 cigars, 200 cigarettes, or one pound of tobacco.

Thailand One quart of wine or liquor, 200 cigarettes or 250 grams of smoking tobacco, and all personal effects may be brought into Thailand duty-free. Visitors may bring in any amount of foreign currency; amounts taken out may not exceed those declared upon entry. Narcotic drugs, pornographic materials, and firearms are strictly prohibited.

On Departure U.S. residents may bring home duty-free up to $400 worth of foreign goods, so long as they have been out of the country for at least 48 hours. Each member of the family is entitled to the same exemption, regardless of age, and exemptions can be pooled. For the next $1,000 worth of goods, a flat 10% rate is assessed; above $1,400, duties vary with the merchandise. Included for travelers 21 or older are one liter of alcohol, 100 cigars (non-Cuban), and 200 cigarettes. Only one bottle of perfume trademarked in the United States may be brought in. However, there is no duty on antiques or art more than 100 years old. Anything exceeding these limits will be taxed at the port of entry and may be taxed additionally in the traveler's home state. Gifts valued at less than $50 may be mailed to friends or relatives at home duty-free, but must not exceed one package per day to any one addressee and must not include perfumes costing more than $5, tobacco, or liquor.

Canadian residents have a $300 exemption and may also bring in duty-free: (1) up to 50 cigars, 200 cigarettes, and 2 pounds of tobacco; and (2) 40 ounces of liquor, provided these are declared in writing to customs on arrival and accompany the traveler in hand or checked-through baggage. Personal gifts should be mailed as "Unsolicited Gift—Value under $40." Request the Canadian Customs brochure, *I Declare*, for further details.

Brunei   The export of certain goods, such as antiques and articles of a historical nature, are restricted. Severe penalties (including death) apply to anyone caught smuggling narcotics.

Hong Kong   Hong Kong is a free port with no duty restrictions.

Indonesia   Visitors may not export more than 50,000 rupiah per person.

Macau   Travelers may bring only 200 cigarettes, 50 cigars, or 250 grams of tobacco, plus one liter of spirits, duty-free into Hong Kong from Macau. Otherwise, Macau has no export duties.

Malaysia   Restrictions exist on the export of antiquities. If in doubt about any purchase, check with the director of the Museum Negara in Kuala Lumpur.

Philippines   Restrictions exist on the export of antiques and religious and historical artifacts.

Singapore   Export permits are required for arms, ammunition, explosives, animals, gold, platinum, precious stones and jewelry, poisons, and medicinal drugs. The export of narcotic drugs is punishable by death under Singapore law.

Taiwan   Travelers are prohibited to leave Taiwan with more than 62.5 grams of gold (or 625 grams of silver) ornaments or coins; genuine Chinese antiques, coins, or paintings; arms, ammunition, explosives, and other weapons of war; publications, pictures, documents, and other articles propagating communism or in violation of anti-communist principles; and more than US$5,000 in notes or the equivalent in other foreign currency (unless a greater amount was brought in within the preceding six months and declared at the time of entry).

Thailand   Visitors may not export more than 500 baht per person or 1,000 baht per family passport.

Traveling with Film

If your camera is new, shoot and develop a few rolls before leaving home. Pack some lens tissue and an extra battery for your built-in light meter. Invest about $10 in a skylight filter and screw it onto the front of your lens. It will protect the lens and also reduce haze.

Film doesn't like hot weather. If you're driving in the heat, don't store film in the glove compartment or on the shelf under the rear window. Put it behind the front seat on the floor, on the side opposite the exhaust pipe.

On a plane trip, never pack unprocessed film in check-in luggage; if your bags are X-rayed, say good-bye to your pictures. Always carry undeveloped film with you through security, and ask to have it inspected by hand. (It helps to isolate your film in a plastic bag, ready for quick inspection.) Inspectors at American airports are required by law to honor requests for hand inspection; abroad, you'll have to depend on the kindness of strangers.

The old airport scanning machines—still in use in some countries—use heavy doses of radiation that can turn a family portrait into an early morning fog. The newer models—used in all U.S. airports—are safe for anything from five to 500 scans, depending on the speed of your film. The effects are cumulative; you can put the same roll of film through several scans without worry. After five scans, though, you're asking for trouble.

If your film gets fogged and you want an explanation, send it to the National Association of Photographic Manufacturers (600 Mamaroneck Ave., Harrison, NY 10528). They will try to determine what went wrong. The service is free.

Staying Healthy

Shots and Medications Although the countries in Southeast Asia do not require or suggest vaccinations before traveling, the United States Centers for Disease Control offer the following recommendations:

Tetanus and polio vaccinations should be up-to-date, and you should be immunized against (or immune to) measles, mumps, and rubella. If you plan to visit rural areas, where there's questionable sanitation, you'll need a gamma globulin vaccination as protection against Hepatitis A. If you are staying for longer than three weeks, and traveling into rural areas, antimalaria pills and typhoid vaccination are recommended. If staying for six months or more, you should be vaccinated against Hepatitis B, rabies, and Japanese encephalitis. For news on current outbreaks of infectious diseases, ask your physician and check with your state or local department of health.

Precautions To minimize the risk of digestive-tract infections, drink bottled water instead of tap (boiled tea is fine) and avoid raw fruits and vegetables. Use insect repellent to minimize the risk of mosquito-borne illnesses.

Doctors Many Southeast Asian hotels have physicians on call 24 hours a day. Also, the **International Association for Medical Assistance to Travelers (IAMAT;** 736 Center St., Lewiston, NY 14092, tel. 716/754–4883; 40 Regal Rd., Guelph, Ont. N1K 1B7, Canada; Gotthardstrasse 17, 6300 Zug, Switzerland) offers a list of approved English-speaking doctors abroad whose training meets British and American standards. Membership is free.

Insurance

Travelers may seek insurance coverage in three areas: health and accident, lost luggage, and trip cancellation. Your first step is to review your existing health and home-owner policies. Some health insurance plans cover health expenses incurred while traveling, some home-owner policies cover luggage theft, and some major medical plans cover emergency transportation.

Companies offering comprehensive travel insurance packages that cover personal accident, trip cancellation, lost luggage, and sometimes default and bankruptcy include **Access America, Inc.,** a subsidiary of Blue Cross/Blue Shield (600 Third Ave., Box 807, New York, NY 10163, tel. 212/490–5345 or 800/284–8300); **Near Services** (1900 N. MacArthur Blvd., Suite 210, Oklahoma City, OK 73127, tel. 405/949–2500 or 800/654–6700); **Carefree Travel Insurance** (Box 310, 120 Mineola Blvd., Mineola, NY 11501, tel. 516/294–0220 or 800/645–2424); and **Travel Guard International,** underwritten by Cygna (1100 Centerpoint Dr., Stevens Point, WI 54481, tel. 715/345–0505 or 800/782–5151).

Health and Accident Several companies offer coverage designed to supplement existing health insurance for travelers:

Carefree Travel Insurance *(see* above) provides coverage for medical evacuation. It also offers 24-hour medical advice by phone, will help find English-speaking medical and legal assistance anywhere in the world, and offers direct payment to hospitals for emergency medical care.

Wallach and Company, Inc. (243 Church St. NW, Suite 100D, Vienna, VA 22180, tel. 703/281–9500 or 800/237–6615) offers comprehensive medical coverage, including emergency evacuation for international trips of 10–90 days.

International SOS Insurance (Box 11568, Philadelphia, PA 19116, tel. 215/244–1500 or 800/523–8930) does not offer medical insurance but provides medical evacuation and repatriation services.

Travel Guard International *(see* above) offers medical insurance, with coverage for emergency evacuation when Travel Guard's representatives in the United States agree that it is necessary.

Luggage Airlines are responsible for lost or damaged property only up to $1,250 per passenger on domestic flights, and $9.07 per pound ($20 per kilo) for checked baggage on international flights, and up to $400 per passenger for unchecked baggage on international flights. If you're carrying valuables, either take them with you on the airplane or purchase additional insurance for lost luggage. Some airlines will issue additional insurance when you check in, but many do not. Rates are $1 for every $100 valuation, with a maximum of $400 valuation per passenger. Hand luggage is not included.

Insurance for lost, damaged, or stolen luggage is available through travel agents or directly through various insurance companies. Two companies that issue luggage insurance are **Tele-Trip** (3201 Farnam St., Omaha, NE 68131, tel. 800/228–9792), a subsidiary of Mutual of Omaha, and **The Travelers Insurance Co.** (Ticket and Travel Plans Dept., 1 Tower Sq.,

Hartford, CT 06183–5040, tel. 201/277–2318 or 800/243–3174). Tele-Trip, which operates sales booths at airports and also issues policies through travel agents, insures checked luggage for up to 180 days and for $500–$3,000 valuation. For one to three days, the rate for a $500 valuation is $8.25; for 180 days, $100. The Travelers insures checked or hand luggage for $500–$2,000 valuation per person, also for a maximum of 180 days. Rates for up to five days for $500 valuation are $10; for 180 days, $85. Both companies offer the same rates on domestic and international flights. Check the travel pages of your local newspaper for the names of other companies that insure luggage.

Before you go, itemize the contents of each bag in case you need to file an insurance claim. Be certain to put your home address on each piece of luggage, including carry-on bags. If your luggage is stolen and later recovered, the airline must deliver the luggage to your home free of charge.

Trip Cancellation Flight insurance is often included in the price of a ticket when paid for with an American Express, Visa, or other major credit or charge card. It is usually included in combination travel insurance packages available from most tour operators, travel agents, and insurance agents.

Student and Youth Travel

The **International Student Identity Card (ISIC)** entitles students to special fares on local transportation and discounts at museums, theaters, sports events, and many other attractions, though few, in fact, in Southeast Asia. If purchased in the United States, the $10 ISIC also includes $2,000 in emergency medical insurance, plus $100 a day for up to 60 days of hospital coverage. Apply to the Council on International Educational Exchange (CIEE; 205 E. 42nd St., New York, NY 10017, tel. 212/661–1450). In Canada, the ISIC is available for C$7.50 from the Federation of Students-Services (171 College St., Toronto, Ont. M5T 1P7).

Council Travel, a CIEE subsidiary, is the foremost U.S. student travel agency, specializing in low-cost charters and serving as the exclusive U.S. agent for many student airfare bargains and student tours. (CIEE's 80-page *Student Travel Catalog* and "Council Charter" brochure are available free from any Council Travel office in the United States; enclose $1 postage if ordering by mail.) In addition to the CIEE headquarters at 205 East 42nd Street and a branch office at 35 West 8th Street in New York City (tel. 212/254–2525), there are Council Travel offices in Amherst (MA), Austin, Berkeley, Boston, Cambridge, Chicago, Dallas, La Jolla, Long Beach, Los Angeles, Portland (OR), Providence, San Diego, San Francisco, and Seattle.

The **Educational Travel Center** (438 N. Frances St., Madison, WI 55703, tel. 608/256–5551) is another student-travel specialist with information on tours, bargain fares, and bookings.

Students who would like to work abroad should contact CIEE's **Work Abroad Department** (205 E. 42nd St., New York, NY 10017). The council arranges various types of paid and voluntary work experiences overseas for up to six months. CIEE also sponsors study programs in Latin America and Asia and publishes many books of interest to the student traveler, including

Work, Study, Travel Abroad; The Whole World Handbook ($8.95 plus $1 postage) and *Volunteer! The Comprehensive Guide to Voluntary Service in the U.S. and Abroad* ($4.95 plus $1 postage).

The Information Center at the **Institute of International Education** (IIE, 809 UN Plaza, New York, NY 10017, tel. 212/984–5413) has reference books, foreign university catalogues, study-abroad brochures, and other materials that may be consulted by students and nonstudents alike, free of charge. Open weekdays 10–4.

IIE administers a variety of grant and study programs offered by U.S. and foreign organizations and publishes a well-known annual series of study-abroad guides, including *Academic Year Abroad, Vacation Study Abroad*, and *Management Study Abroad*. The institute also publishes *Teaching Abroad*, listing employment and study opportunities overseas for U.S. teachers. For a current list of IIE publications, prices, and ordering information, write to Institute of International Education Books (809 UN Plaza, New York, NY 10017). Books must be purchased by mail or in person; telephone orders are not accepted. General information on IIE programs and services is available from the institute's regional offices in Atlanta, Chicago, Denver, Houston, San Francisco, and Washington, DC.

An **International Youth Hostel Federation** (IYHF) membership card can be used in inexpensive, dormitory-style hostels in Hong Kong, Taiwan, and Thailand. Hostels provide separate sleeping quarters for men and women at rates ranging from $7 to $15 a night per person, and are situated in a variety of buildings, including converted farmhouses, villas, restored castles, and specially constructed modern buildings. IYHF membership costs $25 a year and is available in the United States through **American Youth Hostels** (Box 37613, Washington, DC 20013, tel. 202/783–6161). AYH also publishes an extensive directory of youth hostels around the world.

Economical bicycle tours for small groups of adventurous, energetic students are another popular AYH student travel service. For information on these and other AYH services and publications, contact the AYH at the address above.

The **Hong Kong Youth Hostel Association** (Rm. 1408, Block A, Watson's Estate, Northpoint, Hong Kong, tel. 570–6222) provides information on inexpensive accommodations. For a list of hostels, write to the tourist authorities *(see* Tourist Information, above) of Singapore (ask for the booklet *Surprising Singapore)*, Taiwan (ask for the *Official Guidebook)*, and Thailand.

YMCAs are located throughout Southeast Asia. For a listing of Y's worldwide, send a stamped, addressed envelope to "Y's Way," 356 W. 34th St., New York, NY 10001, tel. 212/760–5856. They can also make reservations.

Traveling with Children

The **American Institute for Foreign Study** (AIFS; 102 Greenwich Ave., Greenwich, CT 06830, tel. 203/869–9090) offers a family-vacation program.

Rascals in Paradise (Adventure Express Travel, 185 Berry St. #5503, San Francisco, CA 94107, tel. 415/442–0799) specializes in organizing family tours to exotic destinations. Escorted tours provide children's activities, a babysitter for each family, and teacher programs.

Publications *Family Travel Times* is an eight- to 12-page newsletter published 10 times a year by TWYCH (Travel with Your Children, 80 8th Ave., New York, NY 10011, tel. 212/206–0688). The $35 subscription includes access to back issues and twice-weekly opportunities to call in for specific information. Send $1 for a sample issue.

Great Vacations with Your Kids, by Dorothy Jordan (founder of TWYCH) and Marjorie Cohen, offers complete advice on planning a trip with children (toddlers to teens) ($9.95 paperback, E.P. Dutton, 2 Park Ave., New York, NY 10016, tel. 212/725–1818; a new edition, due out January 1990, will be $11.95).

Kids and Teens in Flight is a brochure developed by the U.S. Department of Transportation on children traveling alone. To order a free copy, call 202/366–2220.

Family Travel Guides (Carousel Press, Box 6061, Albany, CA 94706, tel. 415/527–5849) is a catalog of guidebooks, games, and magazine articles geared to traveling with children. Send $1 for postage and handling.

Getting There All children, including infants, must have a passport for foreign travel; family passports are no longer issued.

On international flights, children under age two not occupying a seat pay 10% of adult fare. Various discounts apply to children 2–12. Reserve a seat behind the bulkhead of the plane, which offers more legroom and can usually fit a bassinet (supplied by the airline). At the same time, inquire about special children's meals or snacks, offered by most airlines. (See "TWYCH's Airline Guide" in the February 1990 issue of *Family Travel Times* for a rundown on children's services furnished by 46 airlines.) Ask your airline in advance if you can bring aboard your child's car seat. (For the pamphlet "Child/Infant Safety Seats Acceptable for Use in Aircraft," write the Community and Consumer Liaison Division, APA-200, Federal Aviation Administration, Washington, DC 20591, tel. 202/267–3479.)

Hotels Babysitting services are available at almost all of the better hotels, including Hilton, Inter-Continental, Marriott, and Ramada Inn, and at most YMCAs in major Southeast Asian cities. At many hotels, children can stay free in their parents' room. **Club Med** (40 W. 57th St., New York, NY 10019, tel. 800/CLUB–MED) has "Mini Clubs" for ages 4–9 and "Kids Clubs" for ages 10–11 in their Malaysian and Bali resort villages.

Hints for Disabled Travelers

Organizations The **Information Center for Individuals with Disabilities** (Fort Point Place, 1st fl., 27–43 Wormwood St., Boston, MA 02217, tel. 617/727–5540) offers useful problem-solving assistance, including lists of travel agents who specialize in tours for the disabled.

Mobility International (Box 3551, Eugene, OR 97403, tel. 503/343–1284) has information on accommodations, organized study, and accessibility problems around the world.

The **Society for the Advancement of Travel for the Handicapped** (26 Court St., Penthouse Suite, Brooklyn, NY 11242, tel. 718/858–5483) offers access information. Annual membership costs $40, $25 for senior travelers and students. Send $1 and a stamped, addressed envelope for information on a specific country.

Travel Industry and Disabled Exchange (TIDE, 5435 Donna Ave., Tarzana, CA 91356, tel. 818/343–6339) is an industry-based organization with a $15-per-person annual membership fee. Members receive a quarterly newsletter and information on travel agencies and tours.

Evergreen Travel Service (19505L 44th Avenue W, Lynnwood, WA 98036, tel. 206/776–1184 or 800/435–2288) has been specializing in unique tours for the disabled for 33 years. Its 1990 Southeast Asia itinerary will include visits to Bangkok, Singapore, and Bali.

Publications *The Itinerary* (Box 2012, Bayonne, NJ 07002, tel. 201/858–3400) is a bimonthly travel magazine for the disabled. Call for a subscription ($10 for one year, $18 for two); it's not available in stores.

Access to the World: A Travel Guide for the Handicapped, by Louise Weiss, is useful though out of date. Available from Henry Holt & Co. for $12.95 plus $2 shipping (tel. 800/247–3912; the order number is 0805 001417).

Twin Peaks Press (Box 129, Vancouver, WA 98666, tel. 206/694–2462 or 800/637–2256 for orders only) specializes in books for the disabled. *Travel for the Disabled* offers helpful hints as well as a comprehensive list of guidebooks and facilities geared to the disabled. *Directory of Travel Agencies for the Disabled* lists more than 350 agencies throughout the world. They also offer a "Traveling Nurse's Network," which provides registered nurses trained in all medical areas to accompany and assist disabled travelers.

The **Hong Kong Tourist Association**'s *A Guide for Physically Handicapped Visitors to Hong Kong* offers information about hotels, transportation, restaurants, services, and tourist attractions. For a free copy, contact the HKTA (*see* Tourist Information, above).

Hints for Older Travelers

Organizations The **American Association of Retired Persons** (AARP; 1909 K St. NW, Washington, DC 20049, tel. 202/662–4850) has a program for independent travelers called the Purchase Privilege Program, which offers discounts on hotels, airfare, car rentals, and sightseeing. The **AARP Travel Service** (4801 W. 110th St., Overland Park, KS 66211, tel. 800/365–5358) arranges group tours and cruises. AARP members must be at least 50 years old. Annual dues are $5 per person or per couple.

If you're planning to use an AARP or other senior-citizen identification card to obtain a reduced hotel rate, mention it at the time you make your reservation rather than when you check out. At restaurants, show your card to the maître d' before you're seated; discounts may be limited to certain set menus, days, or hours. Your AARP card will identify you as a retired person but will not ensure a discount in all hotels and restaurants. For a free list of hotels and restaurants that offer discounts, call or write the AARP and ask for the "Purchase Privilege" brochure or call the AARP Travel Service. When renting a car, remember that economy cars, priced at promotional rates, may cost less than the cars that are available with your ID card.

National Council of Senior Citizens (925 15th St. NW, Washington, DC 20005, tel. 202/347–8800) is a nonprofit advocacy group with some 4,000 local clubs across the country. Annual membership is $10 per person or $14 per couple. Members receive a monthly newspaper with travel information and an ID for reduced rates on hotels and car rentals.

Mature Outlook (6001 N. Clarke St., Chicago, IL 60660, tel. 800/336–6330), a subsidiary of Sears, Roebuck & Co., is a travel club for U.S. residents over 50 years of age, offering Holiday Inn discounts and a bimonthly newsletter. Annual membership is $9.95 per person or couple.

Vantage Travel Service (111 Cypress St., Brookline, MA 02146, tel. 800/322–6677) offers land/cruise tours geared toward senior citizens. The itinerary includes visits to Bangkok, Bali, Hong Kong, and Singapore. Nonsenior, adult companions are welcome.

Publications *Travel Tips for Senior Citizens* (U.S. Dept. of State Publication 8970, revised Sept. 1987) is available for $1 from the Superintendent of Documents (U.S. Government Printing Office, Washington, DC 20402–9325, tel. 202/783–3238).

The International Health Guide for Senior Citizen Travelers, by W. Robert Lang, M.D., is available for $4.95 plus $1 for shipping from Pilot Books (103 Cooper St., Babylon, NY 11702, tel. 516/422–2225).

The Discount Guide for Travelers over 55, by Caroline and Walter Weintz, lists helpful addresses, package tours, reduced-rate car rentals, etc., in the United States and abroad. To order, send $7.95 plus $3 shipping and handling to NAL/Cash Sales (Bergenfield Order Dept., 120 Woodbine St., Bergenfield, NJ 07021, tel. 800/526–0275).

Further Reading

Sources *Good Books for the Curious Traveler: Asia and the South Pacific* provides synopses of 35 texts on Southeast Asian countries in the categories of fiction, archaeology, history, nature, the performing arts, and folktales. Phileas Fogg (tel. 800/233–FOGG) offers *Asia and Southeast Asia,* a mail-order catelogue listing guidebooks, photo essays, background reading, and maps on the region, as well as language tapes.

Southeast Asia *The Travelers' Guide to Asian Customs and Manners,* by Kevin Chambers, advises on how to dine, tip, dress, make friends, do business, bargain, and do just about everything else in Asia, Australia, and New Zealand. *Shopping in Exotic Places,* by Ronald L. Krannich, Jo Reimer, and Carl Rae Krannich, discusses all major shopping districts and tells how to pick a tailor, how to bargain, how to pack. For full reservation information with detailed descriptions of lodgings in 16 countries, read Jerome E. Klein's *Best Places to Stay in Asia.* Also, *Video Night in Kathmandu,* by Pico Iyer, is a delightful collection of essays on the *Time* correspondent's recent travels through Southeast Asia.

History Three highly recommended works on Southeast Asian history are *Southeast Asia*, 3rd edition, by M. Osborne; *Southeast Asia: A History* by Lea E. Williams; and *In Search of Southeast Asia: A Modern History*, edited by David J. Steinberg.

Religion Taufik Abdullah and Sharon Siddique's *Islam and Society in Southeast Asia*.

Fiction Southeast Asia has been an inspiration for much of Joseph Conrad's work, including the novels *An Outcast of the Islands*, *Lord Jim*, *The Shadow-Line*, *Victory*, *Almayer's Folly*, and *The Rescue* and the short stories "Karain," "The Lagoon," "Youth," "The End of the Tether," "Typhoon," "Flak," "The Secret Sharer," and "Freya of the Seven Isles."

Hong Kong *History of Hong Kong*, by G. B. Endicott, traces Hong Kong from its beginnings to the 1960s. Richard Hughes's *Borrowed Time, Borrowed Place* studies the colony immediately before the signing of the 1984 Sino-British agreement, and David Bonavia's *Hong Kong 1997: The Final Settlement* provides history and analysis of the agreement.

James Clavell has written several novels with Hong Kong as a backdrop, including *Noble House; Taipan*, set in the 1840s during the Opium War; and *Hong Kong*, with a more contemporary setting. *The Honourable Schoolboy* by John LeCarré is a suspenseful spy thriller set in Hong Kong. Richard Mason's classic novel *The World of Suzy Wong* chronicles an American's adventures with a young woman in the Wanchai bar area. Also read Jan Morris's *Hong Kong*.

Indonesia *Anthology of Modern Indonesian Poetry*, edited by B. Raffle, provides insight into Indonesian society. Christopher Koch's *The Year of Living Dangerously* is a historical novel of the chaotic state of Indonesia in 1965. *The Religion of Java*, by Clifford Geertz, is a modern classic that describes the religious and social life of the Javanese.

Malaysia Denis Walls and Stella Martin's *In Malaysia* is a dramatic novel set in Malaysia. Somerset Maugham's *Ah King and Other Stories* and *The Casuarina Tree* are two volumes of short stories that capture the essence of what colonial life in Malaya was like.

Philippines *In Our Image*, by S. Karnow, is a good standard text on the history of the Philippines. The best book dealing with the revolution is *Worth Dying For*, by L. Simons. *Waltzing with a Dictator*, by R. Bonner is an in-depth study about the relationshp between the United States and the Philippines. Also try Bryan Johnson's *The Four Days of Courage: The Untold Story of the People Who Brought Marcos Down*. D. Schirmer's *Philippine Reader* is a good collection of Left-wing essays.

Singapore Maurice Collis's *Raffles* is a rich biographical account of the founder of Singapore. *Singapore Malay Society*, by T. Li, is a solid historical reference. *Saint Jack* is a novel set in Singapore, by Paul Theroux.

Taiwan *Taiwan in China's Foreign Relations, 1836–1874*, by Sophia S. Yen, and Martin Lasater's *Taiwan Issue in Sino-American Strategic Relations* are focused texts on Taiwanese politics.

Teito Hirasawa's *Taiwanese Folkliterature* explores Taiwan's folk tradition.

Thailand *Thailand: A Short History*, by D. Wyatt, is an informative study. Anna Leonowens's collected memoirs, *English Governess at the Siamese Court*, is a personalized account of the country from the early 20th-century Westerner's perspective, and was the basis for Margaret Landon's historical novel, *Anna and the King of Siam*. Also see *The Arts of Thailand*, by S. Vanbeek. *Thai Style*, by William Warren, is a glossy picture book presenting an architectural-historical digest of Thailand.

Arriving and Departing

Destinations in Southeast Asia are becoming more popular and therefore more accessible through a number of airlines.

From North America by Plane

Be certain to distinguish between (1) nonstop flights—no plane changes, no stops; (2) direct flights—no changes, but one or more stops; and (3) connecting flights—two or more planes, two or more stops.

The Airlines The following is a list of all major airlines that fly from the U.S. to Southeast Asia, and their primary trans-Pacific hub cities and routes. To break up the lengthy flight, especially from east-coast United States, you may want to plan a stopover in one of these hub cities.

From the Southeast Asian hub city listed below, the airlines branch out to myriad regional destinations. If they do not fly to your chosen destination, they often will work with other airlines that do. Generally, your trans-Pacific carrier can reserve and ticket all your flights when you make your initial reservation.

Canadian Airlines International, call 800/555–1212 for your local toll-free number (Vancouver–Hong Kong).

Cathay Pacific Airways, tel. 800/233–2742 (San Francisco–Vancouver–Hong Kong).

China Airlines, tel. 800/227–5118 (Los Angeles or San Francisco–Hong Kong).

Delta Air Lines, tel. 800/241–4141 (Portland–Tokyo–Hong Kong).

Garuda Indonesian Airways, tel. 800/342–7832 (Los Angeles–Honolulu–Biak–Bali).

Japan Air Lines, tel. 800/525–3663 (nonstops from Los Angeles, San Francisco, Seattle, New York, Atlanta, or Chicago–Tokyo–Hong Kong, Bangkok, Singapore, or Manila).

Malaysia Airlines, tel. 800/421–8641 (Los Angeles–Tokyo–Kuala Lumpur).

Northwest Airlines, tel. 800/447–4747 (Los Angeles or San Francisco–Tokyo–Hong Kong; New York–Tokyo–Hong Kong).

Philippine Airlines, tel. 800/435–9725 (San Francisco–Honolulu–Manila).

Singapore Airlines, tel. 800/742–3333 (Los Angeles or San Francisco–Honolulu, Tokyo, or Taipei–Hong Kong–Singapore).

Thai Airways International, tel. 800/426–5204 (Seattle–Tokyo–Bangkok).

United Airlines, tel. 800/538–2929 (San Francisco or Seattle–Hong Kong).

Flying Times Minimum flying time from west-coast United States can range from 13.5 hours nonstop from San Francisco to Hong Kong to 16 hours airtime only from Seattle to Bangkok. From Chicago, it is 18 hours airtime only to Hong Kong, 20 hours to Bangkok. From New York, it is 20 hours airtime only to Hong Kong, 22 hours to Bangkok. Add more time for stopovers and connections, especially if you are using more than one carrier.

Country by Country Nonstop and direct flights generally operate on certain days of the week and differ according to time of year. If your transpacific flight is on a Southeast Asian carrier, you generally will need to fly to their west coast hub city on a U.S. domestic airline. However, this can be arranged through your Southeast Asian carrier. *All flying times reflect in-air time only.*

Hong Kong Hong Kong is served by many airlines and acts as connecting point for most Southeast Asian destinations. **United Airlines** has nonstop flights from San Francisco and Seattle; direct, one-stop flights from Los Angeles and Chicago, and a direct, two-stop flight from New York. **Cathay Pacific** offers a direct, one-stop flight from San Francisco to Hong Kong. **Flying time** is 15 hours nonstop from San Francisco, 18 hours from Chicago, and 20 hours from New York.

Indonesia **Garuda Indonesian Airways,** the national carrier, offers a direct, two-stop flight from Los Angeles to Jakarta or Bali. Flying time to Bali is 19 hours from Los Angeles, 23 hours from Chicago, 25 hours from New York.

Malaysia **Malaysia Airlines,** the national carrier, offers a direct flight, with one stop in Tokyo, from Los Angeles to Kuala Lumpur. Flying time is 17 hours from Los Angeles, 21 hours from Chicago, 23 hours from New York.

Philippines **Philippine Airlines,** the national carrier, offers a direct flight, with one stop in Honolulu, from San Francisco to Manila. Flying time is 16 hours from San Francisco, 20 hours from Chicago, 22 hours from New York.

Singapore **Singapore Airlines,** the national carrier, known for superior service, and **United Airlines** offer direct, one-stop flights from Los Angeles to Singapore. Flying time is 18 hours from Los Angeles, 20 hours from San Francisco, 20 hours from Chicago, 22 hours from New York.

Taiwan **China Airlines** offers nonstop flights from Los Angeles and San Francisco to Taipei and a direct flight, with one stop in Anchorage, from New York to Taipei. **United Airlines** offers a nonstop from San Francisco and a direct, one-stop from Los Angeles. **Delta** offers a direct, one-stop flight from Portland. Flying time is 13 hours nonstop from San Francisco, 17 hours from Chicago, 19 hours from New York including the stopover time.

Thailand **Thai Airways International,** the national carrier, known for its exceptional service, offers direct, one-stop flights from Seattle to Bangkok. **United Airlines** offers a direct, one-stop flight from San Francisco to Bangkok. **Northwest Airlines** offers direct, one-stop flights from San Francisco and Seattle to Bangkok. Flying time is 16 hours from Seattle, 20 hours from Chicago, 22 hours from New York.

Stopovers For independent travelers, most airlines, including **United, Northwest,** and **Malaysia Airlines,** offer special "Circle Pacific" fares. These allow four stopovers at no extra charge, but must be purchased 14–30 days in advance and carry cancellation penalties. You usually can add on extra stopovers, including Australian and South Pacific destinations, for a nominal charge (about $50). In addition to its six-stopover "Circle Pacific" fare, **Cathay Pacific** offers a "Super Discovery" fare. This is the lowest possible fare for any Cathay Pacific itinerary but is restricted to a very limited number of seats and should be booked well in advance.

Several airlines work together to offer "Around the World" fares. Sometimes these are not much more expensive than the "Circle Pacific" fares, but you must follow a specific routing itinerary and you cannot backtrack. "Around the World" itineraries usually include several Southeast Asian destinations before continuing through Asia and Europe.

Discount Flights Because of the great number of air miles covered, fares are expensive, but it is possible to save some money off regular coach tickets. The key is to start with a flexible schedule and to make your reservations as far in advance as possible. Discounted, advance-purchase seats are limited and tend to sell out quickly. Generally, the airfare will be more economical if you travel with a tour operator.

If you are not already participating in the airline's frequent-flyer program, join. Membership is free, and all it takes is a simple application. Traveling halfway around the world will add about 22,586 km (14,000 mi) to your account. Many programs will give you additional bonus miles if you travel within a certain time period following your application submission. Some airlines are partners in American Airlines' frequent-flyer programs. For example, if you fly on Cathay Pacific, your miles are added to your American Airlines frequent-flyer account and can be used toward future American Airlines flights.

Flights Most of the major airlines offer a range of tickets that can increase the price of any given seat by more than 300%, depending on the day of purchase. As a rule, the further in advance you buy the ticket, the less expensive it is but the greater the penalty (up to 100%) for canceling. Check with airlines for details.

The best buy is not necessarily an APEX (advance purchase) ticket on one of the major airlines. APEX tickets carry certain restrictions: They must be bought in advance (usually 21 days); they restrict your travel, usually with a minimum stay of seven days and a maximum of 90; and they penalize you for changes—voluntary or not—in your travel plans. But if you can work around these drawbacks (and most can), they are among the best-value fares available.

Charter flights offer the lowest fares but often depart only on certain days, and seldom on time. Though you may be able to arrive at one city and return from another, you may lose all or most of your money if you cancel your trip. Travel agents can make bookings, though they won't encourage you, since commissions are lower than on scheduled flights. Checks should, as a rule, be made out to the bank and specific escrow account for your flight. To make sure your payment stays in this account until your departure, don't use credit cards as a method of payment. Don't sign up for a charter flight unless you've checked with a travel agency about the reputation of the packager. It's particularly important to know the packager's policy concerning refunds should a flight be canceled. One of the most popular charter operators is **Council Charter** (tel. 800/223–7402), a division of CIEE (Council on International Educational Exchange). Other companies advertise in Sunday travel sections of newspapers.

Somewhat more expensive—but up to 50% below the cost of APEX fares—are tickets purchased through companies known as consolidators, who buy blocks of tickets on scheduled airlines and sell them at wholesale prices. Here again, you may lose all or most of your money if you change plans, but at least you will be on a regularly scheduled flight with less risk of cancellation than a charter. Once you've made your reservation, call the airline to make sure you're confirmed. Among the best known consolidators are **UniTravel** (tel. 800/325–2222) and **Access International** (250 W. 57th St., Suite 511, New York, NY 10107, tel. 212/333–7280). Others advertise in the Sunday travel sections of newspapers as well.

A third option is to join a travel club that offers special discounts to its members. Three such organizations are **Moments Notice** (40 E. 49th St., New York, NY 10017, tel. 212/486–0503), **Discount Travel International** (114 Forrest Ave., Narberth, PA 19072, tel. 215/668–2182), and **Worldwide Discount Travel Club** (1674 Meridian Ave., Miami Beach, FL 33139, tel. 305/534–2082). These cut-rate tickets should be compared with APEX tickets on the major airlines.

Enjoying the Flight Flights to destinations in Southeast Asia are long and trying. Because of time difference, jet lag and fatigue are nearly inevitable. The air on a plane is dry, so it helps, while flying, to drink a lot of nonalcoholic liquids; drinking alcohol contributes to jet lag. Feet swell at high altitudes, so it's a good idea to remove your shoes while in flight. Sleepers usually prefer window seats to curl up against; those who like to move about the cabin should ask for aisle seats. Bulkhead seats (adjacent to Exit signs) have more legroom, but seat trays are attached to the arms of your seat rather than to the back of the seat in front.

Smoking If cigarette smoke bothers you, request a seat far away from the smoking section. Remember, FAA regulations require U.S. airlines to find seats for all nonsmokers.

Luggage
Labeling Luggage Put your home address on each piece of luggage, including hand baggage. If your luggage is lost and then found, the airline must deliver it to your home, at no charge to you.

Insurance *See* Insurance in Before You Go, above.

Luggage Regulations Luggage allowances vary slightly from airline to airline. Many carriers allow three checked pieces; some allow only two. Check before you go. In all cases, check-in luggage cannot weigh more than 70 pounds per piece or be larger than 62 inches (length + width + height).

Passengers on U.S. airlines are limited to two carry-on bags. For a bag you wish to store under the seat, the maximum dimensions are 9″ × 14″ × 22″; for bags to be hung in a closet or on a luggage rack, 4″ × 23″ × 45″; for bags to store in an overhead bin, 10″ × 14″ × 36″. Any item that exceeds the specified dimensions may be rejected as a carryon and taken as checked baggage. Keep in mind that an airline can adapt the rules to circumstances, so on an especially crowded flight don't be surprised if you are allowed only one carryon.

In addition to the two carryons, you may bring aboard a handbag (pocketbook or purse), an overcoat or wrap, an umbrella, a camera, a reasonable amount of reading material, an infant bag, crutches, a cane, braces, or other prosthetic device, and an infant/child safety seat.

Foreign airlines have slightly different policies. They generally allow only one piece of carry-on luggage in tourist class, in addition to handbags and bags filled with duty-free goods. Passengers in first and business class are also allowed to carry on one garment bag. It is best to call your airline to find out its current policy.

From North America by Ship

Some cruise lines, including **Cunard** (tel. 800/221–4770) and **Royal Viking** (tel. 800/426–0821), call at major Southeast Asian ports as part of their around-the-world itineraries. Plan on spending at least four weeks cruising from west coast United States to Southeast Asia, as these ships usually visit ports in the Pacific and Australia along the way. Or you can take a slow boat to China by booking passage on a freighter from Long Beach, California, to Hong Kong and Taiwan. The round-trip takes approximately 70 days. The freighters hold only 12 passengers and often are sold out a year in advance. For more information, contact **Freighter World Cruises** (180 South Lake, #335, Pasadena, CA 91101, tel. 818/449–3106).

Staying in Southeast Asia

Getting Around

By Plane Most of your international travel within the region is likely to be by air. Distances are long and fares are commensurately pricey. For example, the distance between Hong Kong and Singapore is more than 1,500 air miles, and the one-way fare can reach several hundred dollars. You can save money with excursion fares, which require a round trip but usually allow some stopovers. Some excursion fares require minimum and maximum stays.

Another option is to purchase open-connection tickets through airlines such as **Northwest,** which works with **Malaysia Airlines.** For traveling within Southeast Asia, these tickets allow flexible departure times as long as you retain the order of the cities visited. These work well if you know you want to visit Singapore, Penang, and Bangkok, for example, but are not sure how long you want to stay in each city. Tentative reservations are highly recommended, however, as these flights are often booked well in advance.

You can purchase tickets to fly within the region from travel agents in your Southeast Asian city. Bangkok is generally reckoned to be the best source of low-cost tickets within Asia. This allows even more flexibility in your schedule, but be aware that this will take time away from seeing the sights you came halfway around the globe to see. Pay close attention to make sure the tickets you receive are the ones promised. Note any expiration dates that may invalidate the ticket.

By Car Driving within the city limits of major Southeast Asian destinations probably is best left to the cabbies and chauffeurs who rule the roads here. For the adventuresome who like to explore the countryside on their own, local and international car rental agencies, including **Avis** (tel. 800/331–1084) and **Hertz** (tel. 800/654–3001), are located in the major cities. If you are planning on renting a car for most of your stay, you may get a better price if you reserve in advance through your airline's fly/drive program.

Generally, except in Malaysia, self-drive car rental is not recommended. The roads, to be sure, are good in some places, such as those from Singapore up through the scenic Malay Peninsula to Thailand. Hiring a car with driver is usually reasonably inexpensive in Asia, and can be arranged through your hotel on arrival. Even less expensive and perhaps preferable are organized tours or day trips with car and guide, which will give you a chance to see the countryside and still enjoy the convenience of city facilities (including air conditioning) on your return at night.

By Train Some countries have excellent rail systems; others are not as well equipped. International rail travel is at present limited to the Singapore–Thailand express—a delightful two-day trip, especially if you like to watch passing scenery as well as your fellow passengers. There is always at least one air-conditioned coach. Be sure to take along enough reading matter, and don't expect gourmet food.

By Public Transport Most Asians don't own cars, so public transport is actually far more developed in Asia than in America, but it is, of course, crowded. In Singapore it is excellent everywhere. The main problem is language; in many countries signs are not in Roman letters. City buses can be very confusing, so if you have a precise destination, get written instructions from your hotel clerk to show the driver. In your free time, buses can give you very cheap and realistic sightseeing tours.

Dining

One of the most exciting experiences a traveler has in visiting Southeast Asia is discovering and reveling in a host of wonderful Asian cuisines. Following are descriptions of the most prevalent and interesting; *also see* individual country chapters.

Hotels usually have several restaurants, ranging from coffee shops serving both Western and Oriental cuisine to posh places staffed by famous European chefs where the service, ambience, and food are superior. At the other end of the scale are the outdoor stalls and markets where you can eat happily for a song. (Be sure to check our recommendations in the individual chapters regarding the safety of eating in particular places—they are not all especially concerned with hygiene.)

Note: Wine in Southeast Asia is expensive, does not travel well to the tropics, and is often available only in a very limited selection. We therefore recommend that you order one of the many respectable Australian wines or stick to beers, such as Singapore's Tiger and Thailand's Singha.

Chinese   The best-known regional Chinese cuisine is **Cantonese,** with its fresh, delicate flavors. Characteristic dishes are stir-fried beef in oyster sauce; steamed fish with slivers of ginger, and deep-fried duckling with mashed taro.

Though the cooking of the **Teochew** (or Chao Zhou), mainly fisherfolk from Swatow in the eastern part of Guangdong Province, has been greatly influenced by the Cantonese, it is quite distinctive. Teochew chefs cook with clarity and freshness, often steaming or braising, with an emphasis on fish and vegetables. Oyster sauce and sesame oil—staples of Cantonese cooking—do not feature much in Teochew cooking; Teochew chefs pride themselves on enhancing the natural flavors of the foods they use.

Characteristic Teochew dishes are *lo arp* and *lo goh* (braised duck and goose), served with a vinegary chili-and-garlic sauce; crispy liver or prawn rolls; stewed, preserved vegetables; black mushrooms with fish roe; and a unique porridge called *congee*, which is eaten with small dishes of salted vegetables, fried whitebait, black olives, and preserved-carrot omelets.

The **Szechuan** style of cooking is distinguished by the use of bean paste, chilies, and garlic, as well as a wide, complex use of nuts and poultry. The result is dishes with pungent flavors of all sorts, harmoniously blended and spicy hot. Simmering and smoking are common forms of preparation, and noodles and steamed bread are preferred accompaniments. Characteristic dishes are hot-and-sour soup, sautéed chicken or prawns with dried chilies, camphor- and tea-smoked duck, and spicy fried string beans.

Pekingese cooking originated in the Imperial courts. It makes liberal use of strong-flavored roots and vegetables, such as peppers, garlic, ginger, leeks, and coriander. Dishes are usually served with noodles or dumplings and baked, steamed, or fried bread. The most famous Pekingese dish is Peking duck: The skin is lacquered with aromatic honey and baked until it looks like dark mahogany and is crackly crisp. Other choices are clear winter-melon soup, emperor's purses (stir-fried shredded beef with shredded red chili, served with crispy sesame bread), deep-fried minced shrimp on toast, and baked fish on a hot plate.

The greatest contribution made by the many arrivals from China's **Hainan** island, off the north coast of North Vietnam, is "chicken rice": Whole chickens are lightly poached with ginger and spring onions; then rice is boiled in the liquid to fluffy perfection and eaten with chopped-up pieces of chicken, which are dipped into a sour and hot chili sauce and dark soy sauce.

Fukien cuisine emphasizes soups and stews with rich, meaty stocks. Wine-sediment paste and dark soy sauce are often used, and seafood is prominently featured. Dishes to order are braised pork belly served with buns, fried oysters, and turtle soup.

Hunanese cooking is dominated by sugar and spices and tends to be more rustic. One of the most famous dishes is beggar's chicken: A whole bird is wrapped in lotus leaves and baked in a sealed covering of clay; when it's done, a mallet is used to break away the hardened clay, revealing a chicken so tender and aromatic that it is more than worthy of an emperor. Other favorites are pigeon soup in bamboo cups, fried layers of bean-curd skin, and honey ham served with bread.

Hakka food is very provincial in character and uses ingredients not normally found in other Chinese cuisines. Red-wine lees are used to great effect in dishes of fried prawns or steamed chicken, producing gravies that are delicious eaten with rice. Stuffed bean curds and beef balls are other Hakka delicacies.

Indian **Southern Indian** cuisine is generally chili-hot, relies on strong spices like mustard seed, and uses coconut milk liberally. Meals are very cheap, and eating is informal: Just survey the cooked food displayed, point to whatever you fancy, then take a seat at a table. A piece of banana leaf will be placed before you, plain rice will be spooned out, and the rest of your food will be arranged around the rice and covered generously with curry sauce.

Tempting southern Indian dishes include fish *pudichi* (fish in coconut, spices, and yogurt), fried prawns and crabs, mutton or chicken *biryani* (a meat-and-rice dish), *brinjal curry keema* (spicy minced meat), *vindaloo* (hot spiced meat), *dosai* (savory pancakes), *appam* (rice-flour pancakes), sour lime pickle, and *papadam* (flat bread). The really adventurous should sample fish-head curry, with its hot, rich, sour gravy. Try a glass of *rasam* (pepper water) to aid digestion or a glass of beer to cool things down.

Generally found in the more posh restaurants, **northern Indian** food blends the aromatic spices of Kashmiri food with a subtle Persian influence. The main differences between northern and southern Indian cuisine are that northern food is less hot and more subtly spiced than southern and that cow's milk is used as a base instead of coconut milk. Northern Indian cuisine also uses yogurt extensively to tame the pungency of the spices and depends more on puréed tomatoes and nuts to thicken gravies.

The signature northern Indian dish is Tandoori chicken (marinated in yogurt and spices and cooked in a clay urn) and fresh mint chutney, eaten with *naan chapati* and *paratha* (Indian breads). Another typical dish is *rogan josh*, lamb braised gently with yogurt until the spices blend into a delicate mix of aromas and flavors. *Ghee*, a nutty clarified butter, is used—often in lavish quantities—to cook and season rice or rice-and-meat dishes (*pulaos* and biryanis).

The **Indian Muslim** tradition yields such dishes as *roti prata* (a sort of crispy, many-layered pancake eaten with curries), *murtabak* (prata filled with a spiced, minced mutton and diced onions), *nasi biryani* (saffron-colored rice with chicken or mutton), and various curries.

Japanese The Japanese eat with studied grace, making dining a dramatic event. Dishes look like still-life paintings; flavors and textures both stimulate and soothe. Waitresses quietly appear and then vanish; the cooks welcome and chat with you.

The high art of *kaiseki* (the formal Japanese banquet) was developed by the Samurai class for tea ceremonies and is influenced by Zen philosophy. The food is served on a multitude of tiny dishes. Regulations govern the types of foods that can be served: The seasoning is light, the color schemes must be harmonious, and the foods, whenever possible, must be in their natural shapes. Everything presented is intended for conscious admiration. This stylized approach to food and service is the perfect way to mark a special occasion.

More fun for some are the forms of Japanese dining in which guests can watch the chef exercise his skills right at the table. At a *sushi* bar, for example, the setting and the performance of the chef as he skillfully wields the knife to create the elegant, colorful pieces of sushi (vinegared rice tinged with *wasabi*, or green horseradish, topped with a slice of raw fish) make the meal special. Savor the rich, incredible flavor and you will be hooked forever. Also watch the chef perform stylized movements, including knife twirling, at places serving *teppanyaki:* On a large griddle around which diners are seated, fish, meat, vegetables, and rice are lightly seared, flavored with butter and sake. *Sukiyaki* too is grilled at the table, but the meat is strictly beef and the soup is sweeter; noodles and bean curd are served at the end of the meal as fillers.

Yakitori is meat and vegetables grilled to perfection and glazed with a sweet sauce. *Yakiniku* is a grill-it-yourself meal of thin slices of beef, chicken, or Japanese fish. *Shabu-shabu* is a kind of fondue: Seafoods and meats are lightly swished in boiling stock, then dipped in a variety of sauces. *Tempura* is a sort of fritter of remarkable lightness and delicacy; the most popular kinds are made of prawns and vegetables. The dipping sauce is a mix of soy sauce and *mirin* (sweet rice wine), flavored with grated turnip and ginger.

Malay and Indonesian Malay cuisine is hot and rich. Turmeric root, lemon grass, coriander, *blachan* (prawn paste), chilies, and shallots are the ingredients used most often; coconut milk is used to create fragrant, spicy gravies. A basic method of cooking is to gently fry the *rempah* (spices, herbs, roots, chilies, and shallots ground to a paste) in oil and then, when the rempah is fragrant, add meat and either a tamarind liquid, to make a tart spicy-hot sauce, or coconut milk, to make a rich spicy-hot curry sauce. Dishes to look for are *gulai ikan* (a smooth, sweetish fish curry), *telor sambal* (eggs in hot sauce), *empalan* (beef boiled in coconut milk and then deep-fried), *tahu goreng* (fried bean curd in peanut sauce), and *ikan bilis* (fried, crispy anchovies). The best-known Malay dish is *satay*—slivers of marinated beef, chicken, or mutton threaded onto thin coconut sticks, barbecued, and served with a spicy peanut sauce.

Indonesian food is very close to Malay; both are based on rice, and both are Muslim and thus do not use pork. A meal called *nasi padang*—consisting of a number of mostly hot dishes, such as curried meat and vegetables with rice, that offer a range of tastes from sweet to salty to sour to spicy—originally comes from Indonesia.

Nonya When Hokkien immigrants settled on the Malay Peninsula, they acquired the taste for Malay spices and soon adapted Malay foods. Nonya food is one manifestation of the marriage of the two cultures, which is also seen in language, music, literature, and clothing.

Nonya cooking combines the finesse and blandness of Chinese cuisine with the spiciness of Malay cooking. Many Chinese ingredients are used—especially dried ingredients like Chinese mushrooms, fungus, anchovies, lily flowers, soybean sticks, and salted fish—along with the spices and aromatics used in Malay cooking.

The Nonya cook uses preserved soybeans, garlic, and shallots to form the rempah needed to make *chap chay* (a mixed-vegetable stew with soy sauce). Other typical dishes are *husit goreng* (an omelet fried with shark's fin and crabmeat) and *otak otak* (a sort of fish quenelle with fried spices and coconut milk). Nonya cooking also features sourish-hot dishes like *garam assam*, a fish or prawn soup made with pounded turmeric, shallots, *galangal* (a hard ginger), lemon grass, shrimp paste, and preserved tamarind, a very sour fruit.

Thai Thai cuisine, while linked with Chinese and Malay, is distinctly different in taste. On first tasting a dish, you may find it stingingly hot (tiny chilies make the cuisine so fiery), but the taste of the fresh herbs will soon surface. Thai food's characteristic flavor comes from fresh mint, basil, coriander, and citrus leaves; extensive use of lemon grass, lime, vinegar, and tamarind keeps the sour-hot taste prevalent.

Thai curries—such as chicken curry with cashews, salted egg, and mango—use coconut milk and are often served with dozens of garnishes and side dishes. Various sauces are used for dipping; *nam pla*, one favorite, is a salty, fragrant amber liquid made from salted and fermented shrimp.

Popular Thai dishes include *mee krob*, crispy fried noodles with shrimp; *tom yam kung*, hot and spicy shrimp soup (few meals start without it); *gai hor bai toey*, fried chicken wrapped in pandanus leaves; and *pu cha*, steamed crab with fresh coriander root and a little coconut milk. For drinks, try Singha beer, brewed in Thailand, or *o-liang*, the national drink, which is very strong, black iced coffee sweetened with palm-sugar syrup.

Lodging

Accommodations in Southeast Asia range from shoebox rooms with community or seatless toilets to five-star luxury. Every major city (except Rangoon) and important resort has at least one and probably several luxurious, new, international-style hotels (many part of such international chains as Sheraton, Regent, Hyatt, Hilton, Holiday Inn, and Inter-Continental) that are famous for their service and amenities. If you can afford to splurge, this is the place to do it, for the prices of even the very top hotels are still far lower than comparable digs in Europe.

If you are traveling on a tight budget, leave more time. Most bottom-end accommodations are clustered in a particular area of the city, but you will probably want to see your room before committing to stay there, and comparison-shop for the best deal. Also, plan on spending more time getting from the cheaper hotels to the major sights. They are usually not on the beaten tourist path.

In Hong Kong, the budget and moderate-range accommodations can be found in Kowloon; the mass transit railway provides a fast journey beneath the harbor from Kowloon to Hong Kong Island. In Bangkok, try the Chinese-run hotels near the train and bus stations or along the main street. In Taipei, smaller hotels are found throughout the city, particularly in the older part, near the Yuan Huan Circle. In Kuala Lumpur, try the Jalan Tuanku Abdul Rahman. In Manila, look in the Ermita and Quiapo sections. In Singapore, try Bencoolen Street and Beach Road.

You can find budget dormitory and hotel accommodations at the YMCAs in Bangkok, Hong Kong, Kuala Lumpur, Manila, Singapore, and Taipei or at hostels in Hong Kong, Thailand, the Philippines, Indonesia, Malaysia, and Taiwan. They vary greatly in quality but are generally inexpensive and clean. For more on hostels and Y's, *see* Student and Youth Travel in Before You Go, above.

You will also find some interesting Asian alternative lodging opportunities. In Sarawak, Malaysia, for example, you can stay in tribal longhouses and observe the native lifestyle, joining in meal preparation and evening entertainments. In northern Thailand, stays in village huts are part of many overnight treks to the hill tribes. For more, *see* the individual chapters.

Reservations A good rule is to reserve your hotel rooms at least two months prior to arrival. This is especially true in December and January, in autumn, at Chinese New year, and over Easter, the busiest times. The international chains have U.S. reservations offices. If you do arrive in an Asian capital without a hotel reservation, you will generally find a reservations desk at the airport, for an immediate booking. This service is usually efficient and free, and often special discounts are available.

Ratings Taiwan is the only Southeast Asian country with a system of hotel ratings. In its "Plum Blossoms" system, five plum blossoms is the equivalent of a top U. S. rating.

Shopping

Some people travel to Southeast Asia exclusively to shop. Finely tailored clothing and unique handcrafts, such as graceful ceramics, colorful textiles, and intricately engraved silver, can be found at rock-bottom prices here.

Although prices in department stores are generally fixed, be prepared to bargain with the smaller shopkeeper. It is the accepted practice in this land of few set prices. If you have time, comparison-shop for similar items in several shops to get a feel for the cost of the items. The final price will depend on your bargaining skill and the shopkeeper's mood, but generally will range from 10% to 40% off the original price.

If you can, carry the items with you instead of trusting the shopkeepers and postal services to ship them safely home. If you're shopping for larger items, such as ceramic vases or furniture, the upscale shops are generally reliable. Some credit card companies, such as American Express, guarantee that items purchased with their card will arrive home safely.

With any purchase, make sure you get a receipt for the amount paid, both for potential returns and for Customs. Also, check on Customs and shipping fees to make sure your bargain doesn't turn into a costly white elephant.

The following is a quick rundown of some of the most popular purchases in individual Southeast Asian countries.

Hong Kong: custom-tailored clothing, designer clothing, electronics, jewelry

Indonesia: batik, rod shadow puppets, handcrafts such as wooden masks and statues from Bali

Macau: jewelry, electronics

Malaysia: batik, pewterware, gold jewelry, silver, woven fabrics

Philippines: traditional clothing such as the barong Tagalog, wood furniture, and carving

Taiwan: custom-tailored clothing, jewelry, electronics, ceramics, porcelain

Thailand: silk, jewelry, ready-to-wear clothing, handcrafts such as lacquerware, pottery, and silverwork

Sports

Western-style participant sports and unique Southeast Asian spectator sports are becoming more popular with travelers to the region. The following will give you an idea of which countries provide facilities for your chosen sport.

Biking: Singapore

Deep-sea fishing: Pattaya (Thai Gulf), Ranong and Phuket (Indian Ocean in Thailand); Taiwan

Golf: Thailand, Singapore, Taiwan, Philippines

Kite-fighting: Thailand (in March and April)

River rafting: Indonesia, Taiwan

Scuba/Snorkeling: Thailand (Phuket and several marine national parks), Taiwan, Philippines (Cebu and Bohol), Malaysia (Langkawi)

Tennis: Singapore, Taiwan, Philippines

Windsurfing: Thailand, Taiwan

Beaches

Southeast Asia has some of the world's most exotic beaches, ranging from remote volcanic stretches in the Philippines to resort-strewn sites on Bali. The following is a brief rundown of the best beaches in each country. (*See* individual chapters for more information.)

Indonesia: The island of Lombok (a 20-minute flight from Bali) has a warm, dry climate, and lovely unspoiled beaches. Surfers frequent the waves at Kuta Beach in Bali, where an annual festival is held with local and Australian participation.

Malaysia: The Batu Ferringhi strip on Penang Island has fine, golden-sand beaches, often shaded by willowy casuarina and coconut trees. Pangkor and Langkawi islands, off Malaysia's northwest coast, offer more remote stretches of sand, while

Tioman Island (where the movie *Bali Hai* was filmed) provides idyllic scenery and water-sports facilities.

Philippines: This tropical archipelago of more than 7,000 islands has an abundance of beaches, from pebble-strewn coastlines and black volcanic stretches to shady white expanses. Some of the most picturesque spots are on the smaller islands, particularly on Boracay, Sicogon, Iloilo, Bohol, and Cebu. Matabungkay, a two-hour ride from Manila, is a brown-sand beach frequented by city dwellers out for a day's excursion.

Taiwan: Kenting National park, in south Taiwan, sports warm temperatures year-round and long stretches of white sand in enclosed bays. Fulung, a white-sand resort area 40 minutes north of Taipei, offers a scenic retreat for urban day-trippers.

Thailand: With its long coastlines and warm waters, Thailand offers many opportunities for beach lovers. Ko Samet, a popular Thai vacation spot, has many fine-sand beaches dotted with bungalows and cottages. (There are no big luxury resorts on the island.) Phuket, though much more commercial, boasts long, sandy beaches, cliff-sheltered coves, waterfalls, mountains, and waters that are excellent for scuba diving.

Key to Our Listings

Throughout this book, the following credit-card abbreviations are used in hotel and restaurant reviews: AE, American Express; CB, Carte Blanche; DC, Diner's Club; MC, MasterCard; V, Visa.

Price ranges in the Dining sections are based on one appetizer, one main course, and dessert, but not taxes, tips, or drinks.

In the Lodging sections, prices are based on a double room in high season.

Highly recommended establishments are indicated by a star.

Great Itineraries

The itineraries that follow suggest ways in which destinations can be combined and give an idea of reasonable (minimum) amounts of time needed in various destinations.

Elements from different itineraries can be combined to create an itinerary that suits your interests.

Note: Throughout, where flights cross the International Date Line, remember that you lose or gain a day, depending on your direction.

The Capitals Tour

Southeast Asia is more diverse than Europe, yet there is a temptation on a first visit to cover the entire area on one European-style Grand Tour. Such a trip is physically and mentally taxing and cannot begin to do justice to the complexities of Asian cultures. However, as time is often limited, this whirlwind tour encompasses the capitals and a few of the highlights of Southeast Asia in three weeks.

Begin the tour in Hong Kong, or, if you are arriving from Europe, in Singapore. Both are easy places to begin adjusting to the Orient, with a leisurely round of sightseeing interspersed with shopping. We begin in Hong Kong, visit Macau, then fly to Thailand for a look at Bangkok and the ancient capitals. We then stop in Singapore before heading on to Bali and Manila, and end in Taipei.

Length of Trip 3 weeks

Transportation Be aware that stopping in all the major regions of Southeast Asia requires the use of different airlines. Coming from the United States, you may want to consider using Thai International, a first-rate airline, or United Airlines, a U.S. airline that covers all the capital cities in Southeast Asia, as your major carriers. Coming from Great Britain, British Airways covers many of Asia's capital cities.

Itinerary
Hong Kong **Four nights.** Be sure to take the tram up to the Peak on Hong Kong Island to get your bearings. Explore Kowloon, the New Territories, Hong Kong Island and its marvelous southern coastline, including Aberdeen Harbour and Repulse Bay. Spend a day visiting Macau, using the hovercraft to cross there and back from Hong Kong, and another day shopping in Hong Kong.

Bangkok **Four nights.** Take an early morning flight to Bangkok. Explore Thailand's capital city with a look at some of its 300 temples. Go on a morning tour to Damnoen Saduak's floating market and a full-day tour to explore Ayutthaya, Thailand's ancient capital.

Chiang Mai **Two nights.** Fly to Chiang Mai. (Alternatively, take the night train the evening before from Ayutthaya.) Visit the major temples in and around town, including Doi Suthep. Spend a morning at the elephant training camp at Mae Sa and an afternoon browsing the craft showrooms and workshops along San Kamphaeng Road.

Singapore **Three nights.** Fly, by way of Bangkok, to Singapore. You may want to give yourself the morning in Chiang Mai for a little extra shopping time. Once in Singapore, explore the various ethnic neighborhoods—Chinatown, Little India, the Arab district—take an evening stroll along the Padang, the heart of colonial Singapore, check out the myriad shops on Orchard Road, and dine sumptuously on Singapore's multiethnic cuisines. Make a day excursion to Malaysia to visit the historic city of Malacca.

Bali **Three nights.** Fly to Bali. You'll want more than two days to explore the temples, the craft shops, and the town of Ubud, and more than one day on the beaches, so make plans to return next year.

Manila **Two nights.** Fly to Manila. Explore the Philippine capital, especially Intramuros, the walled city. Take an afternoon to visit the World War II battle sites, or the natural beauty of Lake Taal, or the gardens of the Hidden Valley.

Taipei **Two nights.** Fly to Taiwan. These are your last two days in the Orient, so mix sightseeing with shopping but be sure to visit the National Museum for its superb collection of Chinese art.

The Chinese Syndrome with an Iberian Flavor

These three destinations may be linked together as a three-week excursion or may be divided into separate vacation itineraries for each country.

Start in Hong Kong with a leisurely round of sightseeing interspersed with shopping and dining. Explore Hong Kong Island, Kowloon, and the New Territories. Include an overnight trip to Macau, unique for its Portuguese-influenced architecture and just steps away from the People's Republic of China. Visit Hong Kong's outlying islands.

Then take a trip over to the Philippines. In Manila, you'll feel the presence of the Spanish colonial past, and outside the capital, you'll experience the beauties of its nature. Next, make excursions first to the north, then to the south.

Then it is back to Manila by plane, connecting for a flight to Taiwan.

Hong Kong Length of Stay: 1 Week

Transportation Cathay Pacific is the Hong Kong–based carrier. United Airlines flies into Hong Kong from the United States, British Airways from Great Britain.

Itinerary **Hong Kong: four nights.** Begin your stay with a tram ride to the Peak to get your bearings, and then explore Hong Kong Island, starting at Central and working your way around the island to include Aberdeen Harbour, Stanley, and Repulse Bay. Use one morning to explore Kowloon-side (Nathan Road, Typhoon Harbour) on foot, and be sure to spend an afternoon out on Lamma or Lantau islands. Take another day to tour the New Territories.

Macau: one night. Take the Hovercraft to this Portuguese colony with its casinos and colonial architecture.

Hong Kong: one night. Return to Hong Kong for last-minute shopping.

Fly to Manila, Philippines.

Philippines Length of Trip: 1 week–10 days

Transportation Philippines Airlines is the national carrier, United Airlines is the leading U.S. carrier, and British Airways flies in from London.

Itinerary **Manila: three nights.** Tour the Philippine capital and visit Malacanang Palace, the Manila Cathedral, and, especially, the Intramuros, the walled city built in the 16th century. Exploring out of Manila, you'll want to visit the 16th-century Quiapo Church, famed for its black Nazareine stature of Jesus, and nearby Quiapo market with its colorful and exotic produce. You will surely pass the Coconut Palace, a white elephant and pet project of Imelda Marcos. Farther afield are the Pagsanjan Falls, whose cascading drama was used in the film *Apocalyse Now*. You'll also want to visit the caldera Lake Taal with its baby volcano pushing up from the crater's languid waters. The beauty of the tropical gardens at the Hidden Valley will also draw you.

Baguio: three nights. Leave Manila and make the five-hour overland trip (by train or bus) to north Luzon and the highlands. Use the vacation and provincial capital city of Baguio as your base. If you desperately need a beach, there is the new resort of Bauang with fine sandy beaches, and the hour's drive there is panoramic and thrilling. If you have an extra couple of days, make the eight-hour drive to the Banaue Rice Terraces, which look like giant steps to the sky. Nearby are the Ifugao villages with pyramid-shape huts perched on rocky crags. On the way back, pass through the tribal villages of the Bontoc, who still wear their traditional tasseled G-strings and little else.

Cebu City: two nights. Via Manila, fly to Cebu City, the capital of the Visayas and base for visiting the southern province, which can include a trip to explore Zamboanga City and time to relax on the beach on Santa Cruz Island. If you can take a few extra days, head to Boracay Island, which has the Philippines' most beautiful beaches; otherwise, travel on to Taiwan via Manila.

Taiwan Length of Trip: 1 week–10 days.

Transportation United Airlines from the U.S. and British Airways from Great Britain service Taipei. Once on Taiwan, use taxis and public transport in Taipei. For the excursions out of Taipei, a rental car gives you the most freedom. However, the itinerary can also be accomplished by train and some bus or by flying between the major destinations and using taxis or buses for local transport.

Taipei: two nights. Explore the capital city, leaving at least an afternoon for the National Palace Museum.

Taroko Gorge: one night. By plane (use Hualien airport) or train along the coast, or by road, head south to Taroko Gorge. Road travel is slow, but there is a 100-km (60-mi) stretch of exciting cliffs with wild mountain scenery. Driving will take the best part of a day.

Kenting: two nights. After visiting the Taroko Gorge and local sights, continue south and along the coast to Kenting on the southeastern tip of the island. The trip will take a full day. Relax on the beaches the following day. These beaches are Taiwan's best.

Tainan: two nights. Drive along the southern coast through Kaohsiung to Tainan, Taiwan's oldest city, with more than 200 temples.

Return to Taipei and fly home.

Hitting the Beaches

Increasingly Southeast Asia is becoming a sun and beach center. Each destination could be the entire vacation. However, you could cover several beaches in one three-week trip.

The Andaman Sea is known for its crystal-clear turquoise waters. From south Thailand to northern Malysia, beaches beckon on the shoreline and hundreds of islands offshore offer Robinson Crusoe–style exploring.

Length of Trip 3 weeks

Transportation Thailand is served by Thai International and United Airlines from the United States, Thai International and British Airways from Great Britain. With the exception of a visit to Langkawi, all travel is by plane. To reach Langkawi from the Phuket area you will take a bus, via Hattyai, into Malaysia. (However, there are flights from Phuket to Hattyai and Penang.) You may also travel the whole distance from Bangkok to Singapore by combinations of rail, bus, and ferry.

Itinerary
Bangkok **Two nights.** Arrive in Thailand and spend at least one day exploring the capital city.

Phuket **Five nights.** Fly to Phuket. Enjoy the island's 12 beaches, but do take a cruise out to Phang Nga Bay and "James Bond" island.

Phi Phi **Three nights.** Take the morning boat to Phi Phi island and the cruise around the islands where you can snorkel and scuba dive.

Hattyai **One night.** Cross by ferry to Krabi and take the bus to Hattyai and into Malaysia. Cross over to Langkawi. You may want to overnight in Hattyai.

Langkawi **Three nights.** Spend a couple of days beachcombing, soaking up the sun, and cooling off in the warm waters of this tropical island retreat.

Penang **Four nights.** Return to the mainland and travel south to cross to the island of Penang, where you can mix sightseeing with relaxing on the beach.

Singapore **One night.** Fly to this island republic and take advantage of the shopping, delicious foods, and creature comforts.

Return home.

2 Portraits of Southeast Asia

Southeast Asia
at a Glance: A Chronology

Southeast Asia

20,000 BC	First evidence of human settlement in the Philippines.
6000	Rice cultivation begins in Southeast Asia.
3000	Use of bronze begins in Thailand.

c AD 150	Coastal Indonesians establish direct trade with South India. Early Malayan rulers adopt Indian Sanskrit.
c 400	Chinese inscriptions from Province Wellesley (along the coast of Malay Peninsula) indicate presence of Mahayana Buddhism.

638–700s	Empire of Srivijaya emerges on Sumatra and power extends to Malay Peninsula and small archipelagoes to the south; West Java and southwest Borneo are influenced. Eighth-century inscriptions attest to "Old Malay," earliest-known use of national language in Southeast Asia.
c 775–856	Under Sailendra dynasty the Central Java region prospers; great monuments are built in devotion to Mahayana Buddhism.
1000–1100	Suryavarman I of Angkor conquers area that is now Thailand and Laos. Old Javanese literature flourishes.

1100–1200	Singapore Island becomes prosperous trading center, while Kediri is chief political center in East Java. Khmer Temples are built at Lopburi (the region now occupied by Thailand and Laos).
1230	Theravada Buddhist becomes ruler of Ligor (now Malaysia).
1291	Marco Polo arrives in Pasai, in northern Sumatra.
1292–93	Mongols attack Java. Northern Sumatran states adopt Islam.
1293	Majapahit, near present-day town of Modjokerto, is founded as capital of eastern Javanese kingdom.
1350–78	Siamese kingdom of Ayutthaya is founded and shortly thereafter conquers state of Sukothai.
1364	Nagarajertagama (Old Javanese survey of Indonesian culture) is completed.
1402–1500	Malacca, located along southwestern coast of Malay Peninsula, becomes greatest international trading center in eastern world, and is greatest diffusion center of Islam; Islam spreads throughout Sumatra and eastward. Buddhist reforms begin in Burma region.

The World

221 BC Ch'in dynasty under Shih Huang-ti unites China.

AD 30 Jesus is crucified in Jerusalem.

50 First human images of Buddha appear in central India.

271 First use of the magnetic compass (China).

449 Anglos, Saxons, and Jutes begin colonization of Britain.

500 Teotihuacán in central Mexico is now sixth largest city in the world, with a population of 299,000.

632 Death of Mohammed; Islam begins.

732 Printing invented in China. Arabs advance through Spain and France to Poitiers.

800 Charlemagne crowned Holy Roman Emperor in Rome.

c 1000 Vikings arrive in America (via Greenland).

1050 The Chinese learn to print from moveable type.

1096 First European Crusade to the Holy Land.

1161 Chinese use gunpowder in warfare.

1206 Mongols under Genghis Khan begin the conquest of Asia.

1275 Marco Polo reaches China.

1348 Europe is ravaged by the Black Death (Bubonic Plague) originating in Asia—75 million die in four years.

1368 Ming dynasty is established in China.

Southeast Asia

1431   Brahman political advisors are brought to Ayutthaya (capital of Siam), and king becomes divine monarch; Siamese sack Angkor.

1511   The Portuguese conquer Malacca.

1525–36   Spanish expeditions, under Charles V, claim Philippines.

1596   The Dutch arrive in Indonesia.

1600–1700   Ayutthaya becomes principal port of Far East. The French, under Louis XIV, exchange embassies with Siam; European influence on Southeast Asia increases.

1624   The Dutch establish themselves on Taiwan's west coast, which is taken over by China at the close of the century.

1633   The Dutch blockade Malacca, but do not gain control until 1641 when the Portuguese surrender the city.

1688   Siam undergoes a period of comparative isolation with France, not to be broken until the 19th century.

1767   The Burmese destroy Ayutthaya, and Sino-Siamese Phy Tak Sin, becomes monarch; Siam's capital moves to Thonburi.

1781   The Philippines enter time of prosperity as the state holds monopoly on cultivation, manufacture, and tobacco sales.

1782   The Chakri Dynasty is established in Siam.

1795   Great Britain takes over Malacca.

1807   Organized by Herman Willem Daendels (governor general), Indonesian highway that spans the length of northern coast of Java is constructed.

1811   British troops occupy Java.

1819   Under East India Company, Singapore becomes new British port south of Malacca.

1824   Britain returns Indonesia to the Dutch.

1826–32   Singapore joins with Penang and Malacca (both in present-day Malaysia) to form Straits Settlements; the territory then becomes seat of government.

The World

1445 Gutenberg prints the first book in Europe.

1492 Columbus sails to the Caribbean and "discovers" the New World. The Moors are finally expelled from Spain.

1493 Treaty of Tordesillas divides the New World between Spain and Portugal.

1521 Martin Luther is denounced—the Protestant Reformation begins.

1532 Inca Empire is destroyed by Pizarro.

1571 The Spanish conquer the Philippines.

1607 First permanent English settlement in America, at Jamestown, Virginia.

1608 Quebec founded by the French.

1620 The *Mayflower* arrives off New England.

1625 New Amsterdam is founded by Dutch colonists.

1632 The Taj Mahal is built at Agra in India.

1645 Tasman, a Dutch mariner, circumnavigates Australia and discovers New Zealand.

1656 St. Peter's in Rome is finished.

1703 The foundation of St. Petersburg, the capital of the Russian Empire.

1759–60 The British win New France—Quebec in 1759, Montreal in 1760.

1775–76 The American Revolution and the Declaration of Independence.

1798–1812 The Napoleonic Wars spread French domination across Europe and into Russia.

1803 The United States is nearly doubled in size by the Louisiana Purchase.

1807 The Slave Trade is abolished in the British Empire.

1819 The United States buys Florida from Spain.

1823 Promulgation of the Monroe Doctrine.

Southeast Asia

1834   After years of clandestinely trading sugar, abaca, and other tropical produce with Europe, Manila enters the world trade market.

1839   At outbreak of Opium War, British merchants withdraw from Canton to Hong Kong.

1842   Hong Kong's cession to Britain is confirmed by signing of Treaty of Nanking.

1851   Siam's King Rama IV begins to reestablish previously severed diplomatic relations with Western powers.

1858   China opens two ports in Taiwan to foreign trade.

1895   Following Sino-Japanese War (1894–95), Taiwan is ceded to Japan.

1896–1901   The Philippines experience a country-wide revolt led by Katipunan Society; General Alguinaldo declares the Philippines independent of Spain; instead of independence, sovereignty changes hands and United States takes control. Though Alguinaldo's troops refuse to recognize transfer, United States forces collapse of Filipino resistance.

1907–1909   Siam cedes Laos and Cambodia to France, and recognizes British control over Kedan, Kelantan, Perlis, and Trengganu.

1916   The Philippines adopt bicameral legislature.

1922   Singapore chosen as principal base for defense of British interests in Far East.

1932   Western-educated minority stages revolution in Siam, sparking what will be years of change in political power but little change in policy.

1935   Primary education is made compulsory throughout Thailand.

1941–42   Japan occupies most of Southeast Asia (Malaya, the Philippines, Hong Kong, Singapore, Taiwan, Burma, Indochina).

1945–49   Indonesia stages resistance against Dutch and declares independence. Singapore liberated from Japanese by Great Britain. China takes Taiwan. Great Britain regains possession of Hong Kong.

1946   Straits Settlements are disbanded and Singapore becomes separate colony; Malacca and Penang are incorporated into Malaya. Republic of the Philippines becomes independent. U.S. economic assistance to Thailand begins. (More than $2 billion of aid sent between 1950 and 1975.)

1947   Thousands killed in Taiwanese uprising against post-war governor, General Chen Yi.

The World

1840 Britain introduces the first postage stamp.

1846 Beginning of the Mexican War.

1848 Marx and Engels publish the *Communist Manifesto*.

1857 The Indian Mutiny.

1861–65 The American Civil War.

1867 Establishment of the Dominion of Canada.

1869 Suez Canal is completed. First U.S. transcontinental railroad is opened.

1880s The European powers (Germany, Belgium, Britain) seize control of most of central Africa.

1898 The Spanish-American War.

1899 The Boer War begins in southern Africa.

1900 The Boxer Rebellion breaks out in China.

1917 The United States enters World War I. A Jewish home in Palestine is promised by the Balfour Declaration.

1927 Mussolini comes to power in Italy.

1929 The Wall Street crash brings on Great Depression.

1933 President Roosevelt introduces the New Deal. Hitler becomes German Chancellor; the Nazi era begins.

1937 War begins between Japan and China.

1939–45 World War II. In 1941 the United States enters the war after Pearl Harbor; in 1944 the Allies land in Normandy; 1945 brings the defeat of Germany, and the atom bomb is dropped on Japan.

1946–49 Civil war in China.

1947 India and Pakistan gain independence.

Southeast Asia

1947–57	Thailand enters time of political unrest and flux of government policy until finally, in 1957, a state of national emergency is declared; Field Marshal Phibun is ousted and new elections are held.
1947–66	Indonesia's Communist party becomes increasingly powerful, with several coup attempts; in 1965, political tension climaxes with coup that leads to more than 100,000 deaths. Sukarno replaced by Suharto (present-day leader) and Indonesia's Communist Party is banned.
1948–60	Federation of Malaya is proclaimed; Malaya enters 12-year state of emergency as Malayan Communist Party begins widespread terrorist campaign and attacks police stations, plantations, communication facilities; thousands murdered including High Commissioner Sir Henry Gurney in 1951.
1949	With Chaing Kai-shek as president, Taiwan is proclaimed the seat of National Government of the Republic of China (ROC).
1953–57	Ramon Magsaysay elected as president of Philippines; defeats Communist insurgents, the Huks.
1954	United States pledges to protect Taiwan from mainland assault. In hope of presenting a united front to forestall Communist aggression, Southeast Asia Treaty Organization (SEATO) is formed. Singapore's People's Action Party (PAP) is established under leadership of Lee Kuan Yew.
1958–63	Despite dissension among leading politicians, Thailand's economy grows under Generals Sarit Thanarat and Thanom Kittikachorn.
1959	Lee Kuan Yew wins general elections (agreed upon by Great Britain in 1957) and becomes Singapore's first prime minister.
1962–65	The people of Singapore vote heavily in favor of becoming part of Malaysia; after two years Singapore secedes.
1963	Malaysia established, joining together the Federation of Malaya, Singapore, Sabah, and Sarawak. Association of Southeast Asian Nations (ASEAN) is formed.
1965	Ferdinand Marcos takes office as president of the Philippines. Singapore leaves the Federation of Malaysia and becomes independent sovereign state.
1970–80	Martial law, imposed by Philippines' president Marcos, stifles dissent but increases armed insurgency. By mid 1980s the country falls into deep recession.
1973–76	Continual student demonstrations, strikes, and political assassinations occur in Thailand.
1974	Unrest erupts in Indonesia when students state street demonstrations against the visit of Japan's premier.
1975–78	Chiang Kai-Shek dies; in first presidential succession in Republic of China (ROC), his son Chiang Ching-Kuo takes offices.
1977	SEATO is disbanded.
1978	Vietnam invades Cambodia, ousting Pol Pot and Khmer Rouge.

The World

1948 The State of Israel is established.

1950 Beginning of the Korean war.

1953 Death of Stalin.

1954 French defeated in crucial battle in Vietnam. International conference grants independence to North Vietnam and Cambodia.

1956 Suez Crisis; Russia stamps out the Hungarian revolt.

1961 Berlin Wall is constructed. Increased U.S. involvement in Vietnam.

1962 Cuban Missile Crisis.

1963 President Kennedy is assassinated.

1966 Cultural Revolution in China.

1969 First man lands on the moon.

1973 United States abandons the Vietnam War. Britain joins EEC.

1974 President Nixon resigns.

1975 Formation of Socialist Republic of Vietnam.

Southeast Asia

1979 Elections for lower house of bicameral legislature are held in Thailand.

1981 Benigno Aquino, Jr., Philippines' opposition leader, is shot; Marcos's downfall begins.

1984 Great Britain agrees that Hong Kong will revert to Chinese nationality in 1997.

1986 Corazon Aquino, widow of Benigno Aquino, Jr., wins victory as president of the Philippines in spite of Marcos's efforts to curve vote. Taiwan's martial law lifted.

1986 Taiwan's opposition party, Democratic Progess Party, is permitted to function openly; residents of Taiwan are given rights to visit relatives in mainland China.

1987 Chiang Ching-Kuo dies and is succeeded as president and leader of the Kuomintang party (KMT) by Lee Teng-hui, a native Taiwanese.

1989 Burma changes name to Myanmar.

The World

1979–84 The decline of world leaders—the Shah of Iran falls (1979); Yugoslavia's Marshal Tito dies (1980); President Sadat of Egypt is assassinated (1981); President Brezhnev of the U.S.S.R. dies (1982); Indira Gandhi of India is assassinated (1984).

1982 The Falklands War between Argentina and Britain.

1985 Mikhail Gorbachev comes to power in the Soviet Union.

1986 The Chernobyl nuclear reactor disaster.

1988 George Bush elected president of United States.

1989 Japanese Emperor Hirohito dies. Students stage Democratic revolt in China's Tiananmien Square.

Religion in Southeast Asia

In the courtyard of the Temple of the Emerald Buddha two monks wrapped in saffron robes walk with graceful, measured tread over the sun-warmed flagstones. The bright Bangkok sunlight shimmers from the mosaic glass and golden tiles that adorn the facade of the temple. It reflects off the costume and weapons of two ferocious-looking stone guardians, who protect the sacred grounds with stone muskets—meticulous replicas of 18th-century English weapons. The monks ascend the steps of the veranda leading to the temple and remove their sandals. They move past a kneeling woman who is lighting joss sticks to present to the Buddha image. She is dressed in a smartly tailored blue silk suit; diamond and sapphire rings glitter on her fingers. Inside the temple it is cool; the only sound is the soft whirring of two large oscillating fans. The monks (perhaps they are visitors from a remote village) fold themselves quietly into the lotus position and contemplate the Buddha.

Even though it is midwinter it is hot in Singapore, for here the thermometer climbs to the low 90s all year long. Inside the Hindu temple you feel momentarily disoriented, as if you had been transported to South India. The air is heavy with incense; women in bright saris and red *tike* spots (incorrectly called "caste marks") between their eyes stroll by, while children play at their feet. The scene seems oddly casual. Before an altar women light sticks of incense, a priest hurries by on an errand; in front of a smaller altar, a family gathers as a priest blesses offerings of fruit and flowers and prays for a son's success in his university examinations. In a courtyard a crowd of people has gathered to prepare offerings, decorations, and musical instruments. You inquire about what is going on, and are told to come back tomorrow for the Thaipusam festival, when a procession of penitents—some of whom beat themselves with whips or pierce their flesh with nails, giving thanks to Lord Subramaniam for a request granted or a sin pardoned—will wind its way along Tank Road.

Sunday morning. It is cool here in the hills of Sumatra. Lingering wisps of morning fog wreathe distant mountains. The path to the church wanders through terraced rice fields, where newly planted green shoots stretch toward the sun in muddy rich water, past the fields and through the village where the communal longhouses of the Bataks stand in two facing rows. Under the houses pigs and piglets pick through the garbage. Majestic cocks strut from yard to yard while flocks of chicks scamper after the plump mama hens. The people of the village have all gone to church except for a few old folk who doze in the sun. A few rowdy youngsters play a game of ball. Past the village and past the shuttered schoolhouse, the path turns upward toward the sound of a hauntingly familiar melody. The words are strange but the tune of the doxology is unmistakable, even though the church choir has altered its tempo so that it sounds like an operatic overture. Around the last bend of the path is the church itself: a sturdy, whitewashed frame structure with a tall steeple. Through the glassless windows comes the sound of Batak voices soaring in praise of God the Father, Son, and Holy Ghost.

Shafts of light from the setting sun illuminate the towering clouds in the tropical twilight sky in Kuching, Sarawak. In one of the Malay *kampongs* near the river, the early evening is awash with lingering light. At the entrance to the small kampong mosque, men and women gather to chat before evening prayer. The men wear sarongs, and the women don special white prayer robes before entering the mosque. The light fades. Now, inside the mosque—lit from within like a stage setting, the large open windows forming the proscenium—we see the men assemble in neat rows and bow, facing Mecca, to the west. An adjacent window frames the women, completely enveloped in their voluminous white robes, standing behind the men and also facing west. A wall separates the women from the men. The mosque contains no decorations or ornaments; no gilded figures or statues; no multilimbed goddesses wreathed in flowers; no incense to distract worshipers' thoughts from the words of the daily prayer: *La ilah illa 'llah Muhammad rasul Allah* (There is no god but Allah; Muhammad is the messenger of God).

It is a sunny April day on a hillside near the fishing port of Aberdeen, Hong Kong. In the Chinese cemetery the mood is one of festivity and family joy, for this is the month of Ching Ming, when families make their annual outing to clean the ancestral graves, repair any damage done to the stones during the year, and offer paper money to the spirits of the departed. Rice and sweets are ceremoniously offered to the departed; the family consumes the leftovers. The dead have been remembered in an honorable way; spirits have been appeased; the family has renewed its bonds with a day of feasting and picnicking.

Like the shifting patterns in a kaleidoscope, the rituals, ceremonies, prayers, and customs of all the world's major religions meet the eye of a visitor to Southeast Asia in a series of changing scenes. The intrepid tourist will spend many hours "doing temples," and his weary feet will carry him up hundreds of steps and through miles of courtyards. His camera will click unceasingly, recording images of Buddha, of Jesus, of Rama and the pantheon of Hindu and Chinese gods. He will take pictures of mosques with golden domes and of minarets festooned with loudspeakers. Probably he will view at least one procession, perhaps in Bali, where graceful women bear elaborate towers of bamboo and blossoms, baked rice cakes, and colored sugar to the temple. At night, if he is in Malaysia or Indonesia, he may turn on the TV and listen to a Qu'ran-reading competition.

Mosque and church; wat and temple; the wheel and the lotus, crescent and cross; Hindu and Buddhist, Muslim and Christian live side by side in Southeast Asia. All are imported faiths, and each has undergone some subtle changes in transition.

A quick glance at the calendar in Singapore demonstrates the impact of multiple religious faiths on a modern society. The government of multiracial Singapore is basically Chinese. The only holiday when these hardworking people close up shop altogether is Chinese New Year. Nevertheless, the government recognizes holidays sacred to four religions. Not only the Chinese New Year, but also important Buddhist, Islamic, and Hindu occasions are declared public holidays.

Even the date of the year is not the same for everyone. After all, the fact that it is 1,990 years after the birth of Christ is not a meaningful date for most Asians. Muslims date the era from the year of Muhammad's hegira in AD 622. The Buddhist year goes back to 563 BC. Christian dating, like the English language, is used for business, banking, and all international transactions. Many Asian calendars are bilingual, with Arabic numerals and Christian dates on one side and Chinese, Buddhist, or Islamic dates on the other. In Thailand, the cornerstones of important buildings usually carry two dates.

The calendar plays an important part in the lives of the people, because elements of astrology (both Hindu and Chinese) are taken into consideration when making important decisions. Statesmen, kings, and peasants refer to astrologers or *bomohs* or *dukuns* for help. The Chinese and Thai, for example, attach great importance to the year of a person's birth according to a 12-year cycle. Each year is represented by an animal: 1982 was the Year of the Dog, 1983 the Year of the Pig, 1984 the Year of the Rat, and so on. In considering marriage it is wise to know the birth year of your intended, because certain combinations are said to be fraught with difficulties.

In most of Asia, time is regarded as cyclical, whereas for most Occidentals it is linear. For people in the Judaeo-Christian tradition (and in Islam, which evolved from that tradition), each individual life is an entity—a unit—created at a specific moment in time. Death is considered the termination of the physical life of that individual, while the soul may continue to exist through eternity. The conditions of the afterlife, according to Christian and Muslim belief, depend in large part on the behavior of the individual during his earthly sojourn. Christians, according to most dogmas, believe in resurrection, but nowhere do you find any reference to the idea of reincarnation. And here is where the great schism between Eastern and Western thought begins. Hindu and Buddhist beliefs rest on the assumption that life, as well as time, is cyclical. The soul may endure over the course of many lives. Often the conditions of the new life depend on the behavior of the soul in its previous body.

A devout Christian seeks Eternal Life through the teaching of Christ. A devout Buddhist seeks *nirvana*, or eternal nothingness, and follows the teachings of Buddha as set forth in his sermon "Setting in Motion the Wheel of Righteousness."

Buddhism

The cyclical notion of time and the idea of reincarnation were taken over by Buddhists from older Hindu and Vedic beliefs. Indeed, Buddha was born a Hindu prince, and much of his teaching was aimed at a reform of the structure and complexities of Hinduism. For example, Buddha, like another great Indian religious reformer, Gandhi, deplored the Hindu caste system.

The "historic Buddha" (actually the term "buddha" refers to an awakened or enlightened being) was born Siddhartha Gautama about 563 BC near the border of Nepal. A wealthy prince, he lived in luxury, married happily, and had a son. Like many people of his class, he had been protected from viewing the harsher aspects of life. Legend says that one day he went out from the palace and for the first time saw poverty, sickness, and death. Overwhelmed by these realities, he renounced his worldly position and became a wandering mendicant, seeking the meaning of life. After years of fasting, begging, and traveling, he sat down under a bodhi tree and sank into a deep meditation lasting 49 days. At last he achieved enlightenment, and Siddhartha became a Buddha.

The answer he found after his contemplation was that to escape from suffering and misery, human beings must eliminate desire and attachment. In this world, maintains Buddha, evil is caused by desire, which grows from ignorance caused by wrong thought and misdirected action. Thus, in order to achieve nirvana, an individual must extinguish desire by renouncing evil action and atoning for wrongs already done, either in this or in a previous life. Each life an individual goes through is another chance to escape the wheel. If he ignores opportunities for thinking and right action, in his next incarnation he will have to pay for past mistakes. The Five Precepts in Buddhist teaching resemble the Ten Commandments and prescribe guidelines for right living. They are: not to kill, steal, do sexual wrong, lie, or use any intoxicants. Thus, a devout Buddhist should be both a pacifist and a vegetarian.

As it spread from northern India throughout Asia, Buddhism branched into many schools and sects. The basic divisions are Theravada Buddhism (sometimes called Hinayana, or "Lesser Vehicle," Buddhism), Mahayana ("Greater Vehicle") Buddhism, and Tantric Buddhism. The Theravada school is closest to the original Buddhism of Gautama. It emphasizes that each person must seek his or her own salvation through enlightenment, attained by prayer, fasting, and the rigorous avoidance of temptation and evil. Theravada is a monastic religion, and people enter religious communities (the *Sangha*) for mutual guidance and support.

Burma and Thailand are both Buddhist countries, and there religion forms an integral part of life. In Thailand, for example, it is customary for every young man who is able to spend at least three months of his youth as a monk, when he will eat only the food he has received as "merit" offerings by the people early in the morning. The remainder of the day is spent in study, prayer, and meditation. Buddhist monks appear at every official function, whether it be the opening of a village school or the inauguration of a military airfield.

Mahayana Buddhism originated in India but developed most fully in China, Korea, and Japan. The Greater Vehicle is so called because it acknowledges that most people do not have the fortitude to achieve enlightenment on their own. Believers in Mahayana sects such as the Pure Land School call upon the aid of saints to help them to salvation. These saints, called bodhisattvas, are fully enlightened beings who have voluntarily postponed their own entry into nirvana to help others along the way. In Southeast Asia, most Mahayana temples, such as the famous Ayer Hitam Temple in Penang (Malaysia), were founded by Chinese immigrants. These temples are filled with images of Kuan Yin, the Goddess of Mercy, and other bodhisattvas, which have become objects of devotion among the faithful.

Tantric Buddhism is a subsect of Mahayana Buddhism; it in turn has divided into various sects that are found most prominently in Tibet, but also in northern Burma as well as in China and Japan. Tantric Buddhism is also centered on monasteries, and emphasizes secret rituals designed to combat demons and overcome evil.

Buddhism, being a nontheistic religion, is tolerant of other faiths and beliefs. Thus it is that elements of older religions turn up in the practices and customs of Buddhists in Southeast Asia. For instance, in Sri Lanka, where it is believed that the Buddha visited the island three times and where there is evidence of Buddhist beliefs from that early time, the real conversion of the island to Buddhism occurred in 247 BC, when Mahinda, missionary son of Emperor Asoka of India, converted Devanampiyatissa, King of Anuradhapura, to that faith, but it can be seen that the rudiments of demon and cobra worship still survive, along with the Hindu influences.

In Thailand, pre-Buddhist animistic notions are widely held. The most visible is the spirit house, a tiny replica of a temple perched on a pole, which serves as a dwelling place for the Phra Phum or guardian spirit of the land. Every day this spirit, or *phi* as the Thais say, is presented with an offering of food, incense, and candles. On special occasions, such as New Year or the anniversary of the Phra Phum's installation, grander food offerings are made. As resident phi, he helps the family in time of trouble or difficulty.

Not all phi are friendly. Some are ghosts of people who died suddenly and violently or for whom there were no proper funeral ceremonies. Other phi are demons or fairies from other realms who have come to earth to do mischief. These must be appeased. Help comes from angelic beings borrowed from the Hindu pantheon.

Hinduism

Hindu-Brahmanic influence, which can be seen throughout Southeast Asia from Burma to the island of Java in Indonesia, is a relic of historical kingdoms that came under Indian influence in the 6th to 10th centuries. In Thailand some of these Hindu traditions came from the great Khmer kingdom that flourished in the 9th to 12th centuries. (The most spectacular example of the Khmer glories, of course, is the Angkor Wat complex of temples in Cambodia.) Thai royalty retains several court Brahman priests as a holdover from the times when they advised the king on heavenly omens so that he might rule more wisely. In modern times, these priest-astrologers advise only on special matters affecting the royal family and for public ceremonies.

The Hindu influence in Indonesia dates back to the powerful Srivijaya kingdom, which controlled much of Sumatra and the Malay Peninsula in the 10th century. In Java, a succession of empires combined several aspects of Hindu and Buddhist traditions so that in some instances Shiva, the Hindu god of destruction and regeneration, became merged with Buddha—as can be seen in the temple at Prambanan near Jogjakarta.

The grounds of the Prambanan temple provide the setting for performances of a modern dance-drama based on the *Ramayana*, held during the summer months. One of two great Sanskrit epics (the other being the *Mahabharata*), the *Ramayana* narrates the life and adventures of Rama, an incarnation of Vishnu descended to earth in human form to subdue the demon Ravanna. The *Ramayana* theme is present in dance, painting, and sculpture throughout Southeast Asia.

The advent of Islam in the 16th century, and its rapid spread thereafter, extinguished Hinduism in Indonesia except on the island of Bali. Balinese religion, which encompasses all aspects of life from work to play, from birth to death, is a rich mixture of Hindu mythology, animist beliefs, and an underlying awe of nature and God as manifest in the great volcano Gunung Agung. The Balinese, who accept the Hindu concept of Kali Yug—the last of the four great epochs before the end of the world—believe that in such times as these it is imperative to maintain a proper reverence for all the gods and spirits who dwell on the island, for their anger can be very destructive. Many Balinese believe that both the eruption of the volcano in 1963 and the wave of killings during the civil unrest in 1965 occurred because of religious improprieties.

The two most famous local deities of Balinese Hinduism are the witch Rangda and her adversary, the lionlike beast called Barong. The Barong Kris Dance performed daily at Batubulan is a modern, secular version of the very sacred *calonerang* exorcistic dance-drama that is used by the Balinese to protect their villages from evil; calonerang is rarely seen by outsiders, because it is performed at midnight at village crossroads and in graveyards. Both versions depict a struggle between Rangda, the personification of darkness and evil, and the protective Barong; the struggle always ends in a draw, because in the mortal world neither good nor evil can completely triumph.

Balinese Hinduism has absorbed so many local island deities as well as mystic practices from Java that it has very little in common with that observed by other Hindu communities in Southeast Asia. During the 19th century many Indians, especially from the southern part of India, emigrated to the Malay Peninsula and the Indonesian archipelago. They brought their religion with them, but some of its more rigid rules, such as the caste system, were relaxed somewhat in the course of the journey.

Hindu belief in reincarnation forms the basis of religious practice and faith. Unlike the Buddhist concept of nirvana, the Hindu concept is one of attained deliverance. The Hindu dogma teaches that the soul can be released from the wheel of life only by the observance of dharma—doing one's duty according to one's position in life. The aim of each existence is to perform the dharma of that life so correctly that the soul will be rewarded with a higher station in the next life.

The Hindu godhead consists of a holy trinity: Brahma the Creator, Vishnu the Preserver, and Shiva the Destroyer. Each god appears in a number of different forms, or incarnations, and has a consort and many minor deities attached to his worship. Brahma is usually depicted with four heads

to indicate his creativity and intellect. Vishnu is usually
pictured with four arms, stressing his versatility and
strength. His consort is the popular goddess of wealth and
fortune, Lakshmi. Shiva is probably the most popular of the
three, and the most widely worshiped. As he is the god of
both destruction and regeneration, he is thought to be sym-
pathetic to the human condition. In his incarnation as Shiva
Nataraja, Lord of the Dance, he dances continuously to
keep the world in existence. His consort, who is known by
many names and is worshiped in several forms, is a source of
comfort and inspiration. Her more familiar names are Kali,
Parvati, or Dewi. Shiva has two sons: Ganesha, the
elephant-headed god of knowledge and "remover of obsta-
cles," and Subramaniam, god of war. Worship of the deities
takes place daily in the home and in the temple on festival
days. Thaipusam, which pays homage to Subramaniam, is
celebrated widely in Singapore and Kuala Lumpur. The
other major Hindu holiday is Deepavali, the autumn festival of lights.

Islam

Despite its long cultural and historical role, Hinduism is a
minority religion in Southeast Asia today. The reason for
this was the great Islamic expansion during the 15th and
16th centuries, when part of the Malay Peninsula (including
the four southernmost provinces of Thailand), all of the Indonesian archipelago (with the exception of Bali), and the
southern islands of what is today the Philippines became
Muslim.

Islam, which is monotheistic (believing in one god), exclusive, and highly moralistic, came as quite a contrast to the
easygoing pantheism of the Hindu and Buddhist religions it
replaced. With the advent of Islam, the way of life in these
areas changed. Some of the more obvious changes were in
the calendar, the status of women, and the role of the state
in regulating citizens' behavior.

The Islamic calendar is divided into 12 lunar months, as is
the Chinese, so that all festivals move forward every year.
Unlike the Chinese calendar, however, the Muslim lunar
calendar does not attempt to make any accommodation to
the solar year by adding "leap months" (7 months during
the course of every 19 years). Muslim holidays, therefore,
move forward 11 days each year, which explains why Muslims do not celebrate a fixed New Year's Day. Also, this
system ensures that the month of fasting, Ramadan, rotates through the seasons and therefore is never confused
with local planting or harvest festivities, which hark back
to pagan customs and would be considered taboo for orthodox Muslims.

Islam is often seen in the West as a religion that oppresses
women. There is some truth in that view, but the reality is

not so simple. In Islam's Arabian homeland, the laws of the Koran regarding women were designed mainly to protect their personal dignity and legal rights. Women were expected to cover their hair (but *not* necessarily to wear a veil; that is a later development that varies widely in the Islamic world according to local custom) and to be modest in their dealings with outsiders. They were also given the legal right to own property, and protection from arbitrary divorce. Muslim men may have up to four wives, if they can afford them. A man may divorce his wife by saying "I divorce thee" three times, but both law and custom require a waiting period for the divorce to become final, and a woman who has borne a son may not be divorced except for grave, and legally specified, causes.

On the other hand, Islamic law clearly also makes women both separate and inferior. The Koran says: "Men have authority over women because God has made the one superior to the other . . . so good women are obedient." Among some orthodox groups in Southeast Asia, unmarried women are strictly segregated from men in schools and social organizations, and married women are expected to avoid any dealings with men outside their own families. But other groups have adapted Islamic law to local custom; among the Minangkabau of Sumatra and Malaysia, for example, women own most of the property and have a strong voice in community affairs. In other cases, women have received some protection from the strictness of Islamic law through parliamentary women's-rights legislation.

In Southeast Asia, Malaysia and Brunei are avowedly Islamic nations; Indonesia has no official religion, but the population is overwhelmingly Muslim. Government departments include a bureau of religious affairs. Indonesia's constitution requires that every citizen must profess belief in a single deity. This law is inconvenient for the Chinese and Balinese, who have been forced rather artificially to add a "supreme deity" to their elaborate pantheons. In recent years many Chinese have become Christian to avoid harassment.

Islam, like Christianity, is based on a specific holy scripture: the Koran, or Qu'ran, which is a collection of the words of Allah as revealed to his prophet, Muhammad. To a devout Muslim the book is the holy of holies, and much time is spent reading and studying it. The book must be treated with reverence, never handled carelessly, and should never be placed beneath any other books. One should never drink or smoke while the Koran is being read aloud, and it should be heard in respectful silence. In many villages children are taught to memorize great numbers of verses, and Koran competitions are annual events.

The Koran sets forth the Five Pillars of Islam: the Profession of Faith, the Five Daily Prayers, the obligation to fast, the obligation to make the pilgrimage, and the obligation to give alms. The Profession of Faith is the familiar doctrine of the Unity of God, which is heard in every mosque and from every minaret: There is no God but Allah; Muhammad is the messenger of God.

The Five Daily Prayers are made at specific times of day: at dawn, at noon, in the afternoon, at sunset, and at night. The Muslim tradition gives specific instructions on how to say prayers: kneeling and bowing in the direction of Mecca (of course, in this part of the world to "face Mecca" means to turn west, not east). Because the Koran demands cleanliness before prayer (preferably a total bath, but if this is not possible then a ritual cleansing of face, hands, and feet), you will see tanks and basins of water outside all mosques.

The third Pillar of Islam is fasting. The ninth month of the year, Ramadan, is set aside for ritual fasting. For 30 days all adult Muslims are enjoined against taking any food from dawn to dusk. During this month, as one would expect, work efficiency tends to drop, because in addition to being hungry and thirsty, many Muslims are also sleepy because they have stayed up much of the night eating. Adherence to the tradition is quite strict, and in some villages special police prowl the streets looking for secret munchers. The Koran does, however, give dispensation to the sick and to those who must take a meal in the course of their work. The end of Ramadan is the great feast, Hari Raya Puasa. After a morning visit to the mosque, the family returns home for a memorable feast that more than makes up for the month of deprivation.

The fourth Pillar is the duty to make a pilgrimage to Mecca. Obviously for Muslims in Southeast Asia this can be difficult, and therefore the pilgrimage is obligatory only for those who can afford it. Nevertheless, because of the honor and prestige accorded to those who have made the journey and because the pious regard it as a religious duty, every year thousands of men and women, many of them old, board pilgrim ships and planes for the long, arduous journey to the west. Those who return are addressed as Haji (or Hijah for women), indicating that they have fulfilled their obligation. The last Pillar is almsgiving, similar to the Christian custom of tithing. In Malaysia this money is collected by the Department of Religious Affairs and is used for welfare projects for the poor.

Christianity

Because of its claims to universal validity and the simplicity of its faith, Islam swept through the islands of Southeast Asia up to the Philippines, where it ran head-on into the Spanish Catholic Church. With the establishment of Spanish authority in Manila on June 3, 1571, Islam encountered a nearly impenetrable barrier to further expansion.

The Filipinos often pride themselves on having the only Christian country in Asia, as well as the most westernized. Before the 16th century, the myriad islands that make up the Philippines had never reached the advanced stage of civilization of their western neighbors. The Filipinos accepted the Catholic teaching eagerly for a variety of reasons. In the first place, Catholicism did not have to contend with an organized, established religion because most of the indigenous beliefs involved ancestral spirits and nature gods; they offered neither a systematic theology nor a firm promise of salvation. So for the Filipino, acceptance of the new religion did not involve any deep traumatic rejection of old ways. In fact, many of the older customs were absorbed into Catholic ritual. The second factor was the language problem. The islands were a hodgepodge of different languages and dialects. Catholic schools, which taught Spanish as well as the catechism, gave the Spanish colonial authorities a means of unifying the country both religiously and linguistically. Furthermore, the church offered protection from marauding pirates and outlaw gangs—one of the terms for new Christians was "those who live under the bells."

Needless to say, Catholicism acquired many Philippine characteristics, such as the fiesta. Just as the pagan religions had been centered in the home, so was the new one. Even today, in some rural areas, the images of saints carried in procession on festival days are kept in the homes of important or well-to-do members of the community, rather than in the church. Indeed, the focus of a fiesta is often on lavish preparations for the family feast rather than on the religious observance in the church. This is not to say that Filipinos take their religion lightly; only that they have added some facets of their own heritage.

As you travel through the Philippine countryside, you will come across some huge, stark, very un-Roman-looking cathedrals. These are the churches of an indigenous new Christian faith, the Iglesia ni Kristo, which incorporates nationalistic feelings into a Protestant liturgy. It is estimated to have almost a million members.

Elsewhere in Southeast Asia, Christian missionaries, both Catholic and Protestant, followed the colonizing European powers. The lovely churches in Macau, Malacca, and parts of Indonesia and along the coastal regions of Sri Lanka, where nearly all the fisherfolk are Catholic, are remnants of the Portuguese presence.

Missionary work in Southeast Asia did not disappear with the departure of the colonial powers. Indeed, in certain areas proselytizing church groups are more active than ever. Much current missionary effort is directed toward the tribal peoples living in remote mountains and jungles, where pagan practices still prevail. Though Islam is Malaysia's national religion, the East Malaysian states are predominantly Christian.

Changing Times

Within the last few years the world has become much smaller, and more and more of us travel to areas where once only intrepid explorers or dedicated missionaries ventured. The global village, as Marshall McLuhan calls it, now includes formerly remote and exotic lands. Anna and her problems with the King of Siam are a quaint subject for a musical, but the portrait of King Mongkut as a barbarian monarch is outdated. If you visit a Buddhist monastery in Thailand today, you may encounter several European faces among the saffron-robed bikkhus—undergoing the same course of study and meditation that King Mongkut did for 27 years. A former prime minister of Malaysia serves as president of an international Muslim organization, and the pope has visited the Philippines. Yellow-robed Hare Krishna devotees dance and chant on Fifth Avenue in New York and Oxford Street in London.

Religion in Southeast Asia no longer plays the role it once did, when personal identity was established by an individual's spiritual tenets. Educational, national, and professional ties have superseded the bonds that rituals in the home and ceremonies in the community once forged. Overcrowding in the cities has pushed people closer together, sometimes with unfortunate results, when vastly different customs clash with one another. The Call to Prayer, when amplified over a loudspeaker, becomes noise pollution to some ears; the clanging cymbals accompanying a Chinese funeral are equally unwelcome to the ears of others.

In today's universities boys and girls of different faiths study together—and sometimes fall in love! Marriages outside the religious community, while still not as numerous as in the West, have become a reluctantly accepted part of life.

In rural areas change comes more slowly. Nevertheless, modern communication techniques have brought once-remote villages into the 20th century almost overnight. An illiterate old farmer may not understand helicopters and moving-picture shows or the news that man has landed on the moon, but he is aware that these phenomena exist.

But just as people in the West have become aware of the value of tradition, so in the East old customs and rituals are undergoing a reassessment in terms of cultural identity as well as spiritual sustenance. During these transitional times a visitor to Southeast Asia has a unique opportunity to observe and participate in the customs, rituals, and ceremonies of many different religions. He can visit a mosque or a Hindu temple, and he is as welcome in a Buddhist wat as in a Christian church. Old taboos about strangers have been relaxed, so that a visitor may find himself overwhelmed by hospitality. Nevertheless, sensitivity and good manners are essential. Do not persist in trying to enter a religious building if the people within ask you not to. Do not intrude on or photograph people at prayer. Remove your shoes when entering a mosque, and wear a waist sash when entering a Balinese temple. Dress modestly, as you would want strangers to dress if they visited your own church or synagogue.

Throughout Southeast Asia, religion has remained a more important feature of day-to-day social activity than it has in most of the West. Although the form and nature of this religious feeling vary widely within the region, a large proportion of the population is actively involved in it. There is still a strong sense of traditional values, reflected in fundamental social attitudes.

3 Hong Kong

Introduction

Most people's first reaction to Hong Kong is a gasp as their air-plane dips in its final approach to Kai Tak Airport, seemingly missing the rooftops and harbor by a hairsbreadth. At night the territory appears suddenly, in a blaze of a billion lights; during the day there is some warning, from the clusters of new towns in outlying districts and the crisscrossing wakes of countless vessels serving one of the world's busiest ports.

Once on the ground, the visitor has no time to come to terms with the place—he is at once overwhelmed by the sights, sounds, smells, and physical crush of this community of six million. Few arrivals can avoid being swept up in the energy, excitement, and apparent confusion. This vibrancy is just as much a visitor attraction as the tens of thousands of shops selling the world's luxuries duty-free.

The colony (a now unpopular term) consists of 51.5-sq-km (32-sq-mi) Hong Kong Island, the 5.6 sq km (3.5 sq mi) of mainland Kowloon, and the assorted islands and hinterland of the New Territories, which cover about 588 sq km (365 sq mi). Some agricultural areas—with fruit orchards, piggeries, and vegetable and duck farms—can still be found; however, large stretches of rural land have been covered over by multistory factories and vast high-rise housing estates.

The key to Hong Kong's existence, however, remains the port. Here the world's busiest container terminal, with the very latest automation systems, handles a major share of China's trade, as well as the huge shipments of Hong Kong textiles, electronics, toys, watches, and other goods—and does it 24 hours a day.

The deep, sheltered harbor was the reason for Hong Kong's becoming a part of the British Empire in 1841. Previously British traders had their offices in Canton (145 km, or 90 mi, along the coast), where they traded opium and European manufactured goods for tea, silk, and porcelain. The Chinese attempted to ban the import of opium, and a brief war ensued, ending with a British victory and the prize of strategically located Hong Kong.

From the beginning it was an international entrepôt, with a government appointed by London and devoted to the principles of laissez faire, which meant maintaining law and order and a protective garrison while allowing traders and entrepreneurs total freedom to prosper or fail. The multiracial population—Europeans, Americans, Australians, Japanese, Indians, and Southeast Asians, as well as the predominant Chinese—increased from 4,000 in 1841 to 23,000 by 1847 and by 1941 had reached 1.4 million, inflated by floods of refugees who fled to Hong Kong during times of unrest in China. Following the 1949 revolution, the colony found itself swamped with another 2 million people, who brought the capital and skills that created most of Hong Kong's manufacturing industries. The influx has continued, especially during the Cultural Revolution, and today the population (now 98% Chinese) approaches the 6-million mark.

On June 30, 1997, the British government will leave and the territory will revert to Chinese sovereignty, in accordance with the Sino-British Agreement of September 1984. Beijing has promised that Hong Kong will become a Special Administrative Region, with its own economic, educational, and judicial system for a guaranteed 50 years after the handover.

China describes this as its "one country, two systems" policy (to be applied one day perhaps to Taiwan) and is currently putting together—with British government representatives and some Hong Kong citizens—a constitution. Meanwhile, most Hong Kong residents look ahead without enthusiasm. Thousands of skilled young people have emigrated, and many more have applied for visas at the Canadian, American, and Australian consulates. Britain has made it clear that it will not permit Hong Kong passport holders to settle in the United Kingdom. The bulk of the population, however, will remain after 1997, with no great confidence in China's promises or ability to administer a place of Hong Kong's sophistication. Still, the people continue to work hard, invest, obey the law—and hope for the best. In fact, Hong Kong has become a kind of boom town, with frenetic economic and social activity, as people indulge in a last fling before the end of an era.

Arriving and Departing by Ship

See Chapter 1.

Staying in Hong Kong

Getting Around

A helpful guide to the excellent system of public transport linking Hong Kong's islands and its chunk of the Chinese mainland is the leaflet *Places of Public Interest by Public Transport*, published by the Hong Kong Tourist Association (HKTA, *see* Important Addresses and Numbers, below).

By Bus A fast and efficient way to get to and from the airport is to use the **Airbus** (tel. 745–4466), which runs every 15 minutes from 7 AM to 11:30 PM. Route A1 (HK$5) runs through the Kowloon tourist area. Routes A2 and A3 (HK$8) go to Hong Kong Island: A2 serves the Harbour View International House, Furama, Hilton, Mandarin, and Victoria hotels; A3 serves the Causeway Bay hotels.

By Subway The **Mass Transit Railway** (MTR) is a splendid, air-conditioned subway that links Hong Kong Island to the shopping area of Tsimshatsui and outward to parts of New Territories. Trains are frequent, safe, and easy to use. Fares range from HK$2.50 to HK$6; a special **Tourist Ticket** for HK$20 can save you money.

By Taxi Taxis are usually red; a roof-sign lights up when the taxi is available. Fares in the urban areas start at HK$6.50 and go up by HK$.80 per ¼ km. There is a HK$20 surcharge for crossing the harbor through Cross-Harbour Tunnel. The Aberdeen and Lion Rock tunnels carry surcharges of HK$3. Most people give a small tip, either by leaving the odd change or from HK$.50 to HK$1 for a large fare. Taxis are usually reliable in Hong Kong, but if you have a complaint—about overcharging, for example

Hong Kong

0 ____ 2 miles
0 ____ 3 km

PEOPLES REPUBLIC OF CHINA

Deep Bay

Lo Wu

Lok Ma Chau

San Tin

Mai Po

Lau Fau Shan

Yuen Long

Ha Tsuen

Kam Tin
Walled
Village

*Tai Lamn Chung
Reservoir*

Tuen Mun

Shek Kok
Tsui

Tsuen Wan

*Tsing
Yi*

Chek Lap Kok

Peng Chau

Tung Chung

Mui Wo

Lantau Island

*Silver Mine
Bay*

Tai O

*Hei Ling
Chau*

Cheung
Sha

Cheung Chau
Island

JETFOIL
TO MACAU

*Shek Kwu
Chau*

Soko Islands

South China Sea

N

Crooked Island

Sheung
Shut

Fanling

Wu Kau
Lang

Plover Cove
Reservoir

Tolo Channel

Grass
island

Taipo

Kam Shan

Pan
Chung

Tolo Harbour

NEW TERRITORIES

Chek
Keng

Shatin

Sai Kung

Ho chung

Kau Sai
Chau

High Island

Sung Dynasty Village

Chi Kok
usement
Park

Port Shelter

Basalt
Island

KOWLOON

Kai Tak Airport
Kowloon
Bay

Yau Tong

Junk Bay

Tai Wan
Tau

ctoria

Victoria
Harbour

Tei Tong
Tsui

HONG KONG

Tung Lung
Chau

Stanley

Repulse
Bay

Lamma
Island

Stanley
Peninsula

Po Toi
Islands

Subway & Rail Lines

----- Kowloon/Canton
Railway (KCR)

——— Mass Transit
Railway (MTR)

—there is a special hot line (tel. 577–6866). Be sure to get the taxi license number, which is usually displayed somewhere on the dashboard.

By Tram All visitors should take a street tram at least once. Take your camera and head for the upper deck. The trams run along Hong Kong Island's north shore from Kennedy Town in the west, all the way through Central, Wanchai, Causeway Bay, North Point, and Quarry Bay, ending in the former fishing village of Shaukiwan. The destination is marked on the front, and the fare is only HK$.60. Avoid rush hours.

By Peak Tram This funicular railway dates back to 1888 and rises from ground level to **Victoria Peak** (1,305 ft, or 391 m) offering a panoramic view of Hong Kong and five stops en route. The fare is HK$6 one way or HK$10 round-trip. There is a restaurant at the top. The tram runs daily from 7 AM to midnight, every 10–15 minutes. There is a free shuttle bus to and from the Star Ferry.

By Rickshaw Rickshaws are operated by a few old men who take tourists on a token ride and pose for pictures. The scale of charges is supposed to be around HK$50 for a five-minute ride, but the rickshaw men are merciless. A posed snapshot costs from HK$10 to HK$20.

By Train The **Kowloon-Canton Railway** (KCR) has 12 commuter stops on its 34-km (21-mi) journey through urban Kowloon and the new cities of Shatin and Taipo, on its way to the Chinese border. The main station is at Hunghom, Kowloon, where you can catch the express trains to China. Adult fares range from HK$2 to HK$19.50. The crossover point with the MTR is at Kowloon Tong Station (tel. 606–9606).

By Ferry The **Star Ferry** (tel. 844–2288) is one of Hong Kong's most famous landmarks. These double-bowed, green-and-white vessels cross the harbor between Central on Hong Kong Island and Tsimshatsui in Kowloon every few minutes from 6:30 AM to 11:30 PM. The cost for the seven-minute ride is HK$.80, upper deck, and HK$.60, lower deck (children, HK$.50).

Hong Kong Ferry Company (tel. 542–3081) boats leave from the Outlying Islands Pier, about a 10-minute walk west of the Star Ferry Pier on Hong Kong Island, for Lantau, Lamma, Cheung Chau, and Peng Chau islands. There are two- and three-deck ferries; the ones with three decks have an air-conditioned first-class section on the top deck, with access to the outside deck for magnificent views. Round-trip fares vary from HK$9 to HK$24. Most take about an hour and are very scenic. For more information, call 542–3081.

By Helicopter **Heliservices** (tel. 520–2200) offers limited sky-taxi service, at HK$3,240 for 30 minutes, and tours (*see* Guided Tours, below). The helipad is on Fenwick Pier Street, Hong Kong Island.

By Limousine Most of the best hotels have their own limousines. The Mandarin and the Peninsula rent chauffeur-driven Rolls-Royces.

By Car It is unlikely you will want to rent a car in Hong Kong. The driving conditions are difficult, traffic is constantly jammed, and parking is usually impossible. Public transportation is excellent, and taxis are inexpensive. If you do decide to rent a car, take one *with* a driver. Several operators offer such services, which can be arranged through your hotel. Charges begin at

HK$400 for the first three hours, HK$130 for each subsequent hour.

If you are determined to drive yourself, you'll need an international driver's license. Try **Avis** (50 Po Loi St., Zung Fu Car Park, Hunghom, Kowloon, tel. 346–6007), **National Car Rental** (Harbour Crystal Centre, 100 Granville Rd., Tsimshatsui East, Kowloon, tel. 367–1047), and **Fung Hing Hire Co.** (4 Tsui Man St., Happy Valley, Hong Kong, tel. 572–0333).

On Foot If you're not defeated by the heat, it is pleasant to stroll around parts of Hong Kong. On Hong Kong Island, for example, you can enjoy a walk through the very traditional Western district, where life has not changed much over the years. If you are a very keen walker, you can go for a long stroll in New Territories or on Lantau Island. Contact the HKTA for maps.

Important Addresses and Numbers

Tourist Information Information centers are just beyond Customs at the Hong Kong International Airport; on the Star Ferry Concourse in Kowloon, at Shop G2, Royal Garden Hotel (69 Mody Rd., Tsimshatsui East, Kowloon), and in the basement of the HKTA's main office (Jardine House, Central District, Hong Kong Island). These centers stock in-depth fact sheets on specific areas, and a free shopping guide. They also have a monthly official guidebook for HK$10, which is available for free at the hotels.

Consulates and Commissions **U.S. Consulate** (26 Garden Rd., Hong Kong Island, tel. 523–9011). **U.K. Commission** (Overseas Visa Section, Hong Kong Immigration Dept., Upper Basement, Mirror Tower, 61 Mody Rd., Tsimshatsui East, Kowloon, tel. 733–3111). **Canadian Commission** (Tower 1, Exchange Sq., 11th–14th Floors, Connaught Pl., Hong Kong Island, tel. 810–4321).

Emergencies **Police, fire,** or **ambulance** (tel. 999).

Royal Hong Kong Police Visitor Hot Line (tel. 527–7177). English-speaking police officers wear a red shoulder tab.

Business Information Hong Kong makes life as easy as possible for visiting business people. Around the world it operates **Trade Development Council** offices for preplanning and background information. In the Territory the TDC (Great Eagle Centre, Wanchai, tel. 833–4333) can help and advise. You may also find the **Hong Kong General Chamber of Commerce** (United Centre, Central, tel. 529–9229), **American Chamber of Commerce** (Swire House, Central, tel. 526–0165), or **British Chamber of Commerce** (Sing Pao Centre, 8 Queen's Rd., Central, tel. 810–8118) very useful.

Telephones

In January 1990 Hong Kong will drop area prefixes or incorporate them, so that all numbers will have seven digits.

Local Calls A HK$1 coin gives you unlimited time at a pay phone.

International Calls Pay phones have a digital display showing the amount of money remaining from your original deposit. Many hotels offer direct dial, as do many business centers, but always with a hefty surcharge. Dial 013 for assistance in placing a direct-dial long-distance call or 010 for an operator-assisted call. The central telephone offices (with cable, fax, and telex facilities) are located in Exchange Square, Central, and Hermes House, 10 Middle Road, Tsimshatsui, Kowloon.

Information Dial 108 for directory assistance. Operators speak English, but be prepared to spell names. If a number is constantly busy and you think it might be out of order, call 109 and the operator will check the line.

Mail

Postal Rates Postcards and letters under 10 g (0.4 oz) for North America or Europe cost HK$1.80, and HK$.90 for each additional gram. Aerograms are HK$1.40.

Receiving Mail Travelers can receive mail at the **American Express** office (16-18 Queen's Rd. Central, Basement, New World Tower, Central, tel. 843–1888) weekdays 9–5:30.

Currency

The units of currency are the Hong Kong dollar and the cent. There are bills of HK$1,000, HK$500, HK$100, HK$50, HK$20, and HK$10, and coins of HK$5, HK$2, HK$1, HK$.50, HK$.20, and HK$.10. At press time, the exchange rates were HK$7.80 = US$1, HK$6.55 = C$1, and HK$12.10 = £1.

What It Will Cost

Aside from a few guest houses and hostels, lodging prices start at the equivalent of around US$50 a night, plus 15% service charges. It is still possible to go into a small Chinese restaurant and have a bowl of noodles and tea for about US$1, and a splendid dim sum meal can be had for under US$5. Posh Western and Chinese restaurants, of course, are predictably expensive. Foreign-brand clothing is a great bargain at street markets, less so in luxury shopping complexes or hotel arcades.

Sample Prices Cup of coffee, US$1.80–US$2.50 at hotel coffee shop, 45¢ at McDonald's; soft drink, US$2 at hotel bar, 40¢ at McDonald's; beer, US$1.40–US$2.80 at pub or hotel bar, US$2.50–US$6.40 at other bar or hostess club; double room, US$58–US$83 moderate, US$30 budget.

Language

The official languages of Hong Kong are English and Chinese. The most commonly spoken Chinese dialect is Cantonese, but Mandarin is gaining in popularity because it is the official language of China. In hotels, major restaurants, shops, and tourist centers, almost everyone speaks English, but this is not the case with taxi drivers and workers in small shops and market stalls. In a street café, you may find neither an English-language menu nor anyone who speaks English and so you may have to resort to pointing at the food on someone else's table.

Opening and Closing Times

Banks are open at 9:30 or 10 Monday–Saturday and close at 3 or 5 PM weekdays, noon Saturdays. **Shop** hours vary. Small Chinese shops are open daily from 10 until 8 or 9, European department stores Monday–Saturday 9–6, Japanese and Chinese department stores 10–7 or later every day except one weekday. **Museums** are usually open daily 10–6 (some close for one weekday). **Restaurant** hours depend on the cuisine. Typical Chinese restaurants are open 8 AM–10 PM, Western restaurants noon–11.

National Holidays

The following are national holidays (Chinese festival days change each year according to the lunar calendar): Jan. 1; Chinese New Year (3 days in Feb.); Good Friday; Easter Saturday; Easter Monday; Ching Ming (Apr.); Queen's Birthday (June 11); Dragon Boat Festival (June); last Monday in August; mid-Autumn Festival (Sept.); Chung Yeung Festival (Oct.); Dec. 25–26. Offices and banks are closed on these days, but except for Chinese New Year, many shops are open.

Festivals and Seasonal Events

For exact dates and further details about the following events, contact the HKTA.

Mid-Jan.–Feb.: Hong Kong Arts Festival takes place in theaters and halls throughout Hong Kong.
Late Jan.–Feb.: Chinese New Year is a time to visit friends and relatives and wear new clothes, and a time when the city virtually comes to a standstill.
Feb. or Mar.: Spring Lantern Festival is on the last day of Chinese New Year celebrations, when streets and homes are decorated with brightly colored lanterns.
Late Mar. or early Apr.: The Invitation Sevens, a premier event, is a rugby tournament sponsored by Cathay Pacific and the Hong Kong Bank.
Late Apr. or early May: Birthday of Tin Hau, goddess of the sea. Fishermen decorate their boats and converge on seaside temples to honor Tin Hau. Everyone even remotely connected with the sea happily participates, including some commuters who use the Hong Kong ferries. The busiest area is around the Tin Hau Temple in Junk Bay.
Bun Festival on Cheung Chau Island is a three-day spirit-placating rite that culminates in a grand procession with young children taking part in tableaux. Thousands of people converge for the finale.
May or June: Dragon Boat Festival pits dragon-head boats against each other in races to commemorate the hero Ch'u Yuen. The long and many-oared boats are rowed to the beat of a drum. International races, sponsored by the HKTA, follow a week later.
Aug.: Hungry Ghosts Festival is a time when food is set out to placate roaming spirits temporarily released from hell. Offerings are made everywhere.
Sept.: Mid-Autumn and Lantern Festival brings families together. Mooncakes are eaten while the moon rises. More public and spectacular are the crowds with candle lanterns that gather in the park and other open spaces.

Tipping

Hotels and major **restaurants** add a 10% service charge. In many of the more traditional Chinese restaurants, a waiter will bring small snacks at the beginning of the meal and charge them to you, even if you did not order them. This money is in lieu of a service charge. It is customary to leave an additional 10% tip in all restaurants; **taxis** and **beauty salons** are also tipped 10%.

Guided Tours

Those whose time is limited, or who prefer to relax and leave the organization to professionals, can choose from a wide variety of tours. Unless otherwise stated, tours listed here can be booked at major hotels.

Exploring Hong Kong

Highlights for First-time Visitors

Aberdeen Floating Village (*see* Tour 5)
Harbour Cruise (*see* Tour 1)
Ladder Streets of Western District (*see* Tour 1)
Ride on a double-decker tram (*see* Tour 3)
Skyscrapers of Central (*see* Tour 1)
Stanley Market (*see* Tour 5)
Star Ferry (*see* Tour 1)
Victoria Peak by Day (*see* Tour 2)
Victoria Peak by Night (*see* Tour 2)

Tour 1: Hong Kong Island

Numbers in the margin correspond with numbered points of interest on the Tours 1 and 2: Hong Kong and Kowloon map.

Until 1841, when it was ceded by the Chinese, Hong Kong Island was home to a few fishing communities and a haven for pirates. It had no fresh-water source and very little vegetation. Little wonder that, on hearing of this latest addition to the British empire, the foreign minister dismissed it as "that barren island." Today it contains some of the most valuable real estate in the world (much of it on reclaimed land), a population of more than 1.5 million, as well as reservoirs and well-forested hills. Over the years the entire northern coast has become a series of interlocking townships, which are beginning to challenge the preeminence of **Central District** as a place to do business, thanks to lower rents and convenient MTR connections.

Central, as everyone calls it, features some of Hong Kong's most eye-catching skyscrapers. In close proximity they soar to the skyline with steel, stone, and glass of all colors and shapes.

Increasingly, more and more high rises are appearing in **Western District** and **Kennedy Town,** to the west of Central, as they do to the east, where **Wanchai** and **Causeway Bay** grow upward with new blocks containing offices, shops, restaurants, theaters, and hotels.

Central and Western Districts ❶ **Star Ferry** is the logical place to start your tour of Central District. Since 1898, the ferry terminal has been the gateway to the island for visitors and commuters crossing the harbor from Kowloon. In front of the terminal you will usually see a few red rickshaws. Once numbering in the thousands, these two-wheel, man-powered "taxis" are all but gone. Also in front of the terminal is one of the *Tote* (off-track betting offices). To the right, as you face inland, are the main **Post Office** and the towering 66-story **Jardine House.** Formerly named the Connaught Centre, it is easy to spot with its many round windows. It was completed in 1973 and was one of Central's first skyscrapers.

❸ Farther to your right is the futuristic **Exchange Square,** with its gold- and silver-striped glass towers. This complex is home to the Hong Kong Stock Exchange, and contains some of the most expensive rental space on the island. In front is **Blake Pier.** The open-air pink stone café at the far end is one of the best and least expensive spots from which to enjoy the panoramic view of the harbor while eating or drinking.

❹ The **City Hall complex** (Central, between Edinburgh Pl. and Connaught Rd.) faces out over Queen's Pier and the harbor. In addition to municipal offices, it contains a theater, concert hall, museum, exhibition and art galleries, and a library. Many of the events in the annual International Arts and Film Festival are held here.

❺ **HMS *Tamar,*** next to the City Hall Complex, is not a ship but the 28-story headquarters of the British Army and Royal Navy. The area gets its name from a ship once anchored in the harbor.

❻ **Statue Square** is a small oasis of green between Connaught Road Central and Chater Road. Filled with shaded walks and fountains, it is popular with office workers during lunchtime. It is also a favorite gathering spot on weekends for hundreds of housemaids from the Philippines. The square is above the **Central MTR Station,** one of the busiest subway stations in the world, handling almost two million passengers daily.

A modern building bordering the square houses the **Hong Kong Club,** one of the last social bastions of the fading British colonial system. Next door is the **Legislative Council** building, with its domes and colonnades. It formerly housed the Supreme Court and is one of the few remaining grand Victorian buildings left in this area. Right now the Council has a largely consultative role, without any real power. In front of the Council building is the **Cenotaph** monument to all who lost their lives in the two world wars.

The modern glass-and-steel structure at the end of the square is the headquarters of the **Hongkong and Shanghai Bank.** Known simply as The Bank, this is the largest and most powerful financial institution in Hong Kong. It still issues local bank notes and has enormous influence in every field of investment. The building was designed to make a positive statement about the future of Hong Kong and its capitalistic system. To the east of the bank is the even taller headquarters of the **Bank of China,** designed to rival its neighbor in both aesthetic and financial force.

Between these two giant bank towers is the **Hilton Hotel** (2 Queen's Rd., Central), one of the earliest of the post-war luxury hotels and still one of the best in town.

❼ In front of the Hilton is **Chater Garden** (Chater and Jackson Rds.), former home of the Hong Kong Cricket Club.

Tours 1 and 2: Hong Kong and Kowloon

0 — 440 yards
0 — 400 meters

Victoria Harbour

**Distance from
Kowloon to Hong Kong Island
districts has been reduced.
See main map for correct scale.**

Connaught Rd. West
Bonham
Wing Lok St.
Strand
SHEUNG WAN
Bridges St.
Aberdeen St.
Staunton St.
Caine Rd.
Macau Ferry Pier
Connaught Rd. Central
Des Voeux Rd.
Stanley St.
Wellington St.
Queen's Rd. Central
D'Aguilar St.
Wyndham St.
Central
Pedder St.
Blake Pier
Chater Rd.
Garden Rd.
Cotton Tree Dr.
Queensway
Harcourt Rd.
ADMIRALTY
Naval Dockyard

Academy for Performing Arts, **21**
Arts Centre, **20**
Aw Boon Haw (Tiger Balm) Gardens, **23**
Bird Market, **34**
Chater Garden, **7**
City Hall complex, **4**
Convention and Exhibition Center, **19**
Exchange Square, **3**

Food St., **22**
Government House, **16**
HMS *Tamar*, **5**
Hilton Hotel, **14**
Hollywood Rd., **11**
Hong Kong Cultural Centre, **26**
Jardine House, **2**
Kansu St. Jade Market, **33**
Kowloon Park, **31**

The Landmark, **9**
Li Yuen St. East and West, **10**
Man Mo Temple, **12**
Mandarin Oriental Hotel, **8**
Museum of Tea Ware, **15**
Nathan Rd., **30**
Peak Tram, **18**
Peninsula Hotel, **25**

Regent Hotel, **28**
Space Museum, **27**
Star Ferry (HK), **1**
Star Ferry Pier, **24**
Statue Square, **6**
Sung Dynasty Village, **35**
Temple St., **32**
Tsimshatsui, **29**
Upper Lascar Row/Cat St., **13**
Zoological & Botanical Gardens, **17**

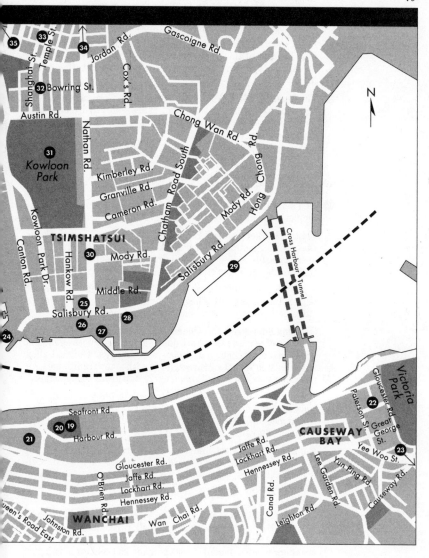

8 On the west side of Statue Square is the **Mandarin Oriental Hotel** (5 Connaught Rd.), one of the finest hotels in the world.

Head west and follow the tracks of the rattling old trams that pass in front of the Hongkong Bank. This will take you along **Des Voeux Road,** which is lined with shops and tall office buildings.

9 **The Landmark** (Des Voeux Rd. and Pedder St.) is an impressive shopping complex, with atrium, cafés, and hundreds of top-name shops. Concerts, cultural shows, and other events are presented here free of charge.

Follow Pedder Street, beside The Landmark, and turn west on **Queen's Road Central,** one of the main shopping arteries. Narrow lanes on either side are filled with tiny shops and stalls filled with goods.

10 **Li Yuen Street East and West,** for example, are bargain alleys for clothing, shoes, costume jewelry, woolens, and handbags.

Central Market (Queen's Rd. Central and Queen Victoria St.) is the city's largest public food market. More than 300 stalls offer every type of food—fish on the first floor, meat on the second, fruits and vegetables on the third.

Wing On Street (off Queen's Rd. Central), a small side street better known as **Cloth Alley,** is worth exploring because of its stalls overflowing with fabrics and sewing accessories.

On **Wing Sing Street** (off Queen's Rd. Central) you will find every type of egg on sale—tiny quail eggs, large goose eggs, and preserved eggs, known as 1,000-year-old eggs. The next alley to the west is **Wing Lok Street,** lined with many traditional Chinese shops selling everything from rattan goods to medicines.

Queen's Road Central now forks to the left, but you should continue straight ahead to Bonham Strand East. **Man Wa Lane** is a tiny street (off Bonham Strand East) where you'll find carvers of chops (engraved seals).

Bonham Strand East and West is an area left relatively untouched by the modern world. The streets are lined with traditional shops, many open-fronted. Among the most interesting ones are those selling live snakes, both for food and medicinal use.

Queen's Road West is filled with embroidery shops selling richly brocaded wedding clothes and all types of embroidered linens, clothing, and household goods. Also along this street are shops where colorful items are made and sold for burning at Chinese funerals. Houses, cars, furniture, and TV sets—all made of paper and bamboo—are among the items necessary to ensure the departed a good life in the hereafter.

11 Funerals are also the theme for some shops along **Hollywood Road.** Here you will find traditional Chinese coffins and more of the elaborate ceremonial items needed for a funeral. Farther along you will find shops selling different grades of rice, displayed in brass-banded wood tubs. Look to the left for a sign saying "Possession Street." This was the place where Captain Charles Elliott of the British Royal Navy stepped ashore in 1841 and claimed Hong Kong for the British Empire. It is interesting to note how far today's harbor is from this area, which was once on the water's edge—the result of a century of massive land reclamation.

Farther east along Hollywood Road are many antiques, curio, and junk shops.

⓬ **Man Mo Temple** is also on Hollywood Road. It is one of Hong Kong's oldest and most important temples and is dedicated to Man, the god of literature, and Mo, the god of war. The statue of Man is dressed in green and holds a writing brush. Mo is dressed in red and holds a sword. To their left is a shrine to Pao Kung, god of justice, whose face is painted black. To the right is Shing Wong, god of the city. Coils of incense hang from the roof beams, filling the air with a heavy fragrance. The temple bell, cast in Canton in 1847, and the drum next to it are sounded to attract the attention of the gods when a prayer is being offered.

⓭ To reach **Upper Lascar Row/Cat Street** from the temple, walk down the steps of **Ladder Street.** In the days before wheeled traffic, most of the steep, small lanes on the hillside were filled with steps.

Continue downhill and you will return to **Queen's Road Central.** Along this section are shops selling many different kinds of tea and traditional Chinese art supplies, including writing brushes, paper, and ink. Here, too, you can buy fans or have a calligrapher write a good luck message for you on an item you purchase.

From Central to the Peak ⓮ The **Hilton Hotel** (2 Queen's Rd. Central) is where you start this tour, which takes you to the Peak. You can picnic at the Peak, so bring or buy lunch.

Queen's Road Central was once the seafront, and site of the old military parade grounds. Most of the important colonial buildings of the Victorian era were within easy reach of this area. Walking around this part of Central is a bit tricky because of pedestrian tunnels and overpasses.

⓯ **The Museum of Tea Ware in Flagstaff House** is easy to reach by walking through the tunnel under Cotton Tree Drive. Built in 1845, Flagstaff House is the city's oldest colonial building and once the official residence of the commander of the British Forces. Since 1984 it has housed the Museum of Tea Ware. The museum displays include everything connected with the art of serving tea, from the 7th century onward. *Cotton Tree Dr., tel. 529–9390. Admission free. Open 10–5. Closed Wed.*

St. John's Cathedral, completed in 1849 and a good example of Victorian-Gothic architecture, is the Anglican cathedral. *Garden Rd., just above the Hilton. Open daily 10–8.*

⓰ **Government House,** a handsome white building up the hill from the cathedral, is the official residence of the governor. It was built in 1891 (Upper Albert Rd.).

⓱ A visit to **The Zoological and Botanical Gardens** is a delightful way to escape the city's traffic and crowds. In the early morning, people come here to practice t'ai chi ch'uan (the ancient art of shadow boxing). The quiet pathways are lined with semitropical trees, shrubs, and flowers. The collection of animals in the zoo is amazingly rich, with such creatures as golden-haired monkeys, lesser pandas, and jaguars. There is also an aviary with more than 300 species of birds, including flocks of cranes and pink-and-white flamingos. *Upper Albert Rd., opposite Government House. Admission free. Open daily 6:30 AM–7 PM.*

⑱ Lower Peak Tram Terminus is where you will find the **Peak Tram,** the steepest funicular railway in the world. It passes five intermediate stations en route to the upper terminal, 550 m (1,805 ft) above sea level, and was opened in 1888 to transport people to the top of Victoria Peak, which is the highest hill overlooking Hong Kong Harbour. Before the tram, the only way to get to the top was to walk or take a bumpy ride up the steep steps in a sedan chair. The tram has two 120-seat cars that are hauled up the hill by cables attached to electric motors. *Between Garden Rd. and Cotton Tree Dr. Fare: HK$6 one way, HK$10 round-trip. Open daily 7 AM–midnight. Trams run every 10–15 min.*

The Chinese name for **Victoria Peak** is *Tai Ping Shan* (Mountain of Great Peace). It might also be called Mountain of Great Views, for the panorama is breathtaking. On a clear day you can see across the islands to the People's Republic of China. The area is a popular picnic spot and filled with beautiful walking paths that circle the peak.

The **Peak Tower Building,** completed in 1972, contains a restaurant, coffee shop, gift shops, and a post office. Just below the summit is a lookout pavilion that was once part of a former governor's residence. The original gardens and country walks remain and are open to the public.

As an alternative to taking the Peak Tram down the hillside, you can catch bus No. 15 or a cab to Central. This will take you on a trip as exciting and beautiful as the one on the tram through the steep roads of the residential areas of Mid-Levels.

Wanchai Wanchai was once one of the five "wan," or areas that the British set aside for Chinese residences. Today, in addition to the old section with its bars and massage parlors made famous in *The World of Suzie Wong,* it is a mixture of office buildings, restaurants, apartment buildings, and shops. The old waterfront is now well inland, and a whole new area occupies the reclaimed harborside.

⑲ It is dominated by the brilliant, new **Convention and Exhibition Centre,** the best-equipped and most modern of its kind in the region.

⑳ ㉑ The **Arts Centre** and the **Academy for Performing Arts** are two adjacent buildings at the heart of Hong Kong's cultural activities. They have excellent facilities for exhibitions and the performing arts. The Academy was financed with money donated by the Royal Hong Kong Jockey Club out of its profits from horse racing. The Arts Centre has an excellent restaurant. One interesting gallery in the Arts Centre is the **Pao Sui Loong Galleries,** which has no permanent collection but hosts international and local exhibitions throughout the year. *2 Harbour Rd. Academy, tel. 823–1500; Arts Centre, tel. 823–0230; Pao Sui Loong: 4th–5th floors, Arts Centre Bldg., tel. 823–0200. Admission free. Open daily 10–8.*

Causeway Bay, Happy Valley, and North Point Causeway Bay is one of Hong Kong's best shopping areas. It can be easily reached from Central by the tram, which runs along Hennessey Road, or by the MTR to Causeway Bay Station.

The **Excelsior Hotel** and **Noonday Gun** are a fun part of any tour of Causeway Bay. "In Hong Kong they strike a gong and fire off a noonday gun," wrote Noël Coward in his song "Mad Dogs and Englishmen." They still fire that gun, exactly at noon each day, in a small enclosure overlooking the Yacht Club Basin and Typhoon Shelter, opposite the Excelsior Hotel and the World Trade Centre. The gun itself, with brasswork polished bright, is a Hotchkiss, dating from 1901.

㉒ Sample the 25 or so restaurants on **Food Street** (between Gloucester Rd. and Kingston St.), where virtually every type of cuisine is available, both Asian and Western. Most restaurants here are reasonably priced, with waiters who speak English.

Victoria Park, reached by passing under the elevated highway at the end of Gloucester Road, offers a delightful escape from the crowds and traffic. Beautifully landscaped with trees, shrubs, flowers, and lawns, it offers recreational facilities for swimming, lawn bowling, tennis, and roller skating. There is even a go-cart track. The Lantern Carnival is held here in midautumn, with the trees a mass of colored lights. Just before Chinese New Year, the park features a huge flower market. In the early morning, the park is filled with people practicing t'ai chi. At other times, the park can be a pleasant place to sit in the sun, stroll, or jog.

The large Japanese department stores, **Sogo, Daimaru, Mitsukoshi,** and **Matsuzakaya,** all have branches on or near **Great George Street,** off the end of Hennessey Road.

Left of Tung Lo Wan Road is **Jones Street,** which has some fine old traditional Chinese houses. From here continue uphill on Tai Hang Road (a 15-minute walk or a brief taxi or No. 11 bus
㉓ ride) to **Aw Boon Haw (Tiger Balm) Gardens.** Built in 1935 with profits from sales of a popular menthol balm, the gardens were the pet project of two Chinese brothers, who also built their mansion here. Eight acres of hillside are covered with grottoes and pavilions filled with garishly painted statues and models of Chinese gods, mythical animals, and scenes depicting fables and moralistic stories. It's a sort of Oriental Disneyland, and great fun to explore, especially for children. There is also an ornate pagoda, seven stories high, containing Buddhist relics and the ashes of monks and nuns. *Tai Hang Rd., Happy Valley. Admission free. Open daily 10–4.*

Tour 2: Kowloon

Kowloon is a peninsula on mainland China, directly across Victoria Harbour from Central. Legend has it that Kowloon was named by a Chinese emperor who fled here during the Sung Dynasty (960–1279). He counted eight hills on the peninsula and called them the Eight Dragons—so the account goes—but a servant reminded him that an emperor is also considered a dragon, and so the emperor called the region *Gau-lung* (nine dragons), which became Kow-loon in English.

Kowloon is where many of Hong Kong's hotels are located. In the Tsimshatsui district is the clock tower of the old Kowloon-Canton Railway station, the YMCA, the Peninsula Hotel, bustling Nathan Road luxury hotels and shopping centers, the Space Museum, and a waterfront esplanade extending to Tsimshatsui East and the new railroad station.

Today visitors can take a taxi through the Cross-Harbour Tunnel from Causeway Bay or Central to Kowloon, or ride the MTR from Central to Kowloon in minutes. The Star Ferry, however, is still unquestionably the most exciting way to cross the harbor.

㉔ **Star Ferry Pier** is a convenient starting place for any tour of Kowloon. Here you will also find the bus terminal, with traffic going to all parts of Kowloon and New Territories. On your left, as you face the bus station, is **Ocean Terminal,** where luxury cruise ships berth. Inside this terminal and in the adjacent **Ocean Centre** are miles of air-conditioned shopping arcades.

To the right of the Star Ferry is the **Clock Tower,** all that is left of the Kowloon-Canton Railway Station, which once stood on this site. The new station, for travel within China, is a mile (1.6 km) to the east.

Head east along **Salisbury Road,** and immediately on your left is **Star House,** where you'll find one of the best branches of the **China Arts and Crafts** department stores. Crossing Canton Road, you'll see a tree-covered hill to your left, headquarters of the **Marine Police** (Canton and Salisbury Rds.). Taking the underpass across Kowloon Park Drive, you will come to the **YMCA** (41 Salisbury Rd.), one of Kowloon's oldest institutional buildings.

㉕
㉖ The next block on the left contains the superb **Peninsula Hotel** (Salisbury Rd.). Outside are its fleet of Rolls-Royce taxis, and doormen in white uniforms. Opposite is the **Hong Kong Cultural Centre,** with theaters, concert halls, museums, and libraries.

㉗ The neighboring dome-shaped **Space Museum** houses one of the most advanced planetariums in Asia. It contains a **Hall of Solar Science, Exhibition Halls,** and a **Space Theatre** with shows on the night sky and space travel. Only some shows are in English but headphones are provided for free simultaneous translations of the Cantonese shows. *10 Salisbury Rd., tel. 721–2361. Space Theater: Admission charge. Open Mon. and Wed.–Sun.; 7 shows daily, weekdays beginning at 2:30; 8 shows Sat., beginning at 1:30; 10 shows Sun., beginning at 11:30. Closed Tues. Exhibition Hall and Hall of Solar Science: Admission free. Open Mon. and Wed.–Fri. 2–9:30, Sat. 1–9:30; Sun. and holidays 10:30–9:30. Closed Tues.*

㉘ Among Hong Kong's finest luxury hotels is the **Regent** (Salisbury Rd.). Its lobby has windows offering panoramic views of the harbor—a good place for a drink at sunset.

㉙ **Tsimshatsui** is part of the land reclamation now occupied by a parade of luxury hotels, restaurants, and entertainment and shopping complexes.

㉚ **Nathan Road,** the "Golden Mile" runs north and is filled with hotels and shops of every description. To the left and right are mazes of narrow streets lined with additional shops crammed with every possible type of merchandise.

㉛ Just off Nathan Road is **Kowloon Park.** The former site of Whitfield Military Barracks is today home of an ultramodern recreation complex and park containing a **Chinese Garden** with lotus pond, streams, a lake, and an aviary with a colorful selection of rare birds. On the south end of the park, near Haiphong

Road entrance, is the **Jamia Masjid and Islamic Centre,** Hong Kong's main mosque, built in 1984 with four minarets, decorative arches, and a marble dome.

The **Hong Kong Museum of History** is housed in two former barracks in the park. Its collection covers local history, archaeology, ethnography, and natural history, with both permanent and changing exhibitions. The museum's photographs of old Hong Kong are of particular interest. *Haiphong Rd., tel. 367–1124. Admission free. Open Sat.–Thurs. 10–6, Sun. 1–6. Closed Fri.*

㉜ Continue north on Nathan Road three blocks to Jordan Road, make a left and another left onto **Temple Street,** which becomes an **open-air market** in the evening filled with street doctors offering cures for almost any complaint, fortune tellers, and, on most nights, Chinese opera. The best time to visit is 8–11 PM.

㉝ North is the **Kansu Street Jade Market.** You'll get there by following Temple Street to Kansu Street and turning left. The daily jade market carries everything from ordinary pendants to precious carvings. The best time to visit is from 10 to noon.

The Yaumatei Typhoon Shelter, opposite Ferry Street, is home to a colorful floating community living on the packed sampans and fishing junks. It is best explored by one of the small boats that ply the harbor. The fishermen and their families still follow their traditional way of life, departing from here each day and returning to unload their catch at local markets.

㉞ Return to Nathan Road, walk north eight blocks to Argyle Street, and turn left. You can hear the **Bird Market** (Hong Lok St., behind Mongkok MTR Station) long before you see it. Though the area is only two blocks long, it is packed with hundreds of caged birds for sale, all singing and chirping at one time. Song birds have always been prized by the Chinese.

㉟ To go back in history hundreds of years, visit the **Sung Dynasty Village,** northwest of Kowloon city. Take the MTR at Mongkok station and go five stops north to Mei Foo station. From here it is a short walk along Lai Wan and Mei Lai Roads. The village recreates the life of a Sung village 1,000 years ago. There are faithful replicas of the houses, shops, restaurants, and temples of the period. You can watch men work at ancient crafts, and see people dressed in costumes of the time. The easiest way to see the village is to take an organized tour, which can be arranged through your hotel tour desk. You can also visit on your own. *Laichikok, tel. 741–5111. Admission charge. Open Sat.–Sun. and holidays, 12:30–5.*

Tour 3: The South Side

The easiest way to tour the south is on an organized bus tour, lasting about four hours, but this will show you only a few highlights. If you have time, take a city bus or taxi from Central, and stop at the following points of interest along the way.

Starting in Central and passing through Western, the first major point of interest will be **Hong Kong University.** Established in 1911, it has about 6,000 undergraduate and 1,700 post-graduate students. Most of its buildings are spread along Bonham Road. In this area you will also find the **Fung Ping Shan Museum,** founded in 1953. It contains an excellent collection of

Chinese antiquities, especially ceramics and bronzes dating from 3,000 BC. There are also some fine paintings, lacquerware, and carvings in jade, stone, and wood. *94 Bonham Rd. Admission free. Open Mon.–Sat. 9:30–6.*

Continuing around the western end of the island, you come to **Pok Fu Lam** and **Wah Fu Estate** overlooking **Lamma Island.** These are two huge housing developments, complete with shops, recreational facilities, and banks. They are typical of Hong Kong's approach to mass housing. From here you ride downhill to Aberdeen.

Aberdeen, named after an English lord, not the Scottish city, got its start as a refuge for pirates some 200 years ago. After World War II, Aberdeen became fairly commercial as the *Tanka* (boat people) attracted tourists to their floating village of sea-going fishing junks. Many still live afloat but others have moved ashore.

You can still see much of traditional Aberdeen, such as the **Aberdeen Cemetery** (Aberdeen Main Rd.), with its enormous gravestones and its glorious view.

An interesting detour is **Apleichau Island,** which can be reached by bridge or sampan. It has a boat-building yard where junks are constructed, as well as some yachts and sampans. Almost all the boats are built without formal plans. From the bridge you can get a superb view of the harbor and its countless number of junks.

East of Aberdeen are **Ocean Park** and **Water World,** two theme parks. Ocean Park is on 170 acres of land overlooking the sea and is one of the world's largest oceanariums, attracting thousands of visitors daily. On the "lowland" site are gardens, parks, and a children's zoo. A cable car, providing spectacular views of the entire south coast, takes you to the "headland" side and to Ocean Theatre, the world's largest marine mammal theater, with seats for 4,000 people. Here, too, is one of the world's largest roller coasters and various other rides. The adjacent, 65-acre Water World is an aquatic fun park with slides, rapids, pools, and a wave cove. *Wong Chuk Hang Rd., tel. 532–2244 or 555–0947. Ocean Park. Admission charge. Open daily. Water World: tel. 555–5222. Admission charge. Open May–Oct.*

Deep Water Bay (Island Rd.) is just to the east of the theme parks. This was the site of the film *Love Is a Many-Splendored Thing.* Its beauty and deep coves are still many-splendored.

The waterside road continues to **Repulse Bay,** named after the British warship HMS *Repulse* (not, as some local wags say, after the pollution of its waters). The famed Repulse Bay Hotel was demolished in 1982, but the **Repulse Bay Verandah Restaurant and Bamboo Bar,** replicas of the restaurant and bar in the old hotel, were opened in 1986 and are run by the same people who operated the original hotel. The hotel gained notoriety in December 1941 when invading Japanese clambered over the hills behind it and entered its gardens, which were being used as headquarters by the British. After a brief battle, the British surrendered. Today, the hillside behind the hotel features a huge development of luxury apartments.

Another reminder of World War II is **Stanley.** It became notorious as the home of the largest Hong Kong prisoner-of-war camp run by the Japanese. Today, Stanley is known for its market, where designer fashions are sold at wholesale prices. Hong Kong has dozens of shops offering similar bargains, but it's more fun shopping for them in the countrified atmosphere around Stanley. You can also find ceramics, paintings, and secondhand books.

Shek O, the easternmost village on the south side of the island, is filled with old houses, great mansions, a superb golf course and club, a few simple restaurants, a pretty beach, and fine views.

From Shek O, the round-island route continues back to the north, to the housing and industrial estate of **Chai Wan** (Chai Wan Rd.). From here you have a choice of a fast journey back to Central on the MTR, or a slow ride to Central on the two-decker tram.

Tour 4: New Territories

The visitor who has taken the trouble to explore Hong Kong and Kowloon should go one step further and spend at least a day in **New Territories.** Here you will not only look across the border into the People's Republic of China, you will also be able to enjoy broad vistas of forested mountainsides and visit some of the many ancient temples that fill the area.

Only about 25 km (15 mi) separate Kowloon's waterfront from the People's Republic of China. New Territories is often referred to as "the land between," because it is the area between Kowloon and the Chinese border. It is called New Territories because it was the last area of land claimed by the British in extending their Hong Kong colony. A day's touring around New Territories will show you yet another face of Hong Kong, a rural one, with small villages, and peasants working in their rice fields and market gardens. You will be surprised at how remote and undeveloped some parts of New Territories are, at the miles of land without a single building, at the forests, and at the hilltops free of high-rise, or even low-rise, buildings. The easiest way to see the region is by taking a six-hour "Land Between" tour organized by the HKTA. *Tel. 524–4191. Departs Queen's Pier, Central, at 8:30 AM, Holiday Inn Golden Mile at 9 AM, and Holiday Inn Harbour View at 9:10 AM. Cost: HK$220 adults, HK$170 children. Weekdays only.*

Ching Chung Koon Taoist Temple is located near the town of Tuen Mun. This huge temple has room after room of altars, all filled with the heady scent of incense burning in bronze holders. On one side of the main entrance is a cast-iron bell with a circumference of about five feet. On the opposite side of the entrance is a huge drum that was used to call the workers back in the evenings. The temple also includes a retirement home, built from donations, which provides a quiet and serene atmosphere for the elderly. The grounds are beautiful, with plants and flowers, hundreds of dwarf shrubs, ornamental fish ponds, and pagodas.

Tuen Mun has a population of 332,000 and is one of Hong Kong's "new towns"—satellite cities created to take the spillover of population from the crowded areas of Kowloon and Hong Kong Island. They provide both industrial areas and living accommodations for the workers and their families. Other new towns are Tsuen Wan, Yuen Long, Shatin, Taipo, Fanling, and Junk Bay.

By 1990 the seven towns are expected to house three million people, or 41% of Hong Kong's projected population of 7.3 million.

Lau Fau Shan is a village famous for its fish market. Here you will find people selling freshly caught fish and shellfish, as well as dried fish and salted fish. Select what you want, pay for it, take it to one of the many restaurants, and have it cooked to order. This is the oyster capital of Hong Kong, but don't eat them raw.

Kam Tin Walled Village, a regular stop on most tours, was built in the 1600s as a fortified village belonging to the Tang clan. There are actually six walled villages around Kam Tin, but Kut Hing Wai is the most popular. The original walls are intact, with guardhouses on the four corners and arrow slits for fighting off attackers. The image of antiquity is somewhat spoiled now by the modern homes and their TV antennas looming over the ancient fortifications.

Next stop is the town of **Lok Ma Chau,** where the big attraction is the view. You can stand on a hill and look down on the Sham Chun River. Across the river, barely a mile (1.6 km) away, is the People's Republic of China. Unless you plan a tour into China, this is as close as you will get. Elderly "models" here demand HK$1 before you can photograph them.

Fanling is a town that combines the serene atmosphere of the Royal Hong Kong Golf Club with the chaos of rapid growth. The nearby **Luen Wo Market** is a traditional Chinese market, well worth visiting.

Taipo means shopping place in Chinese and every visitor here discovers that the town more than lives up to its name. Located in the heart of the region's breadbasket, Taipo has long been a trading and meeting place for local farmers and fishermen. It is now being developed, with new housing and highways everywhere you look.

South of Taipo is the **Chinese University.** The **Art Gallery,** located in the university's **Institute of Chinese Studies** building, is well worth a visit. It has large exhibits of paintings and calligraphy from the Ming period to modern times. *Tel. 695–2218. Admission free. Open Mon.–Sat. 10–4:30, Sun. and holidays 12:30–4:30. Closed between exhibitions and on major holidays.*

Across from the campus is the popular **Yucca de Lac Restaurant** which has outdoor dining facilities. About a 15-minute walk from the University is the starting point for a ferry tour of **Tolo Harbour** and the **Saikung Peninsula.** *Call the Hong Kong Ferry Co. for ferry schedule, tel. 542–3081.*

Whether you enter **Shatin** by road or rail, you will be amazed to find this metropolis in the middle of New Territories. Another of the "new towns," Shatin underwent a population explosion that took it from a town of 30,000 to one of more than 461,000 in 10 years. It is home to the **Shatin Racecourse,** Hong Kong's second largest. Nearby is the huge **Jubilee Sports Centre,** a vast complex of tracks and training fields designed to give Hong Kong's athletes space to train under professional, full-time coaches for international competition. Shatin is also home of **New Town Plaza,** the most extensive shopping complex in New Territories.

You'll need to climb some 500 steps to reach the **Temple of Ten Thousand Buddhas,** nestled among the foothills of Shatin, but a visit is worth every step. Inside the main temple are nearly 13,000 gilded clay statues of Buddha, all virtually identical. They were made by Shanghai craftsmen and donated by worshipers. From this perch you can see the famous **Amah Rock.** Amah means "nurse" in Chinese, and the rock, which resembles a woman with a child on her back, is popular with female worshipers. To the west of the temple is **Tai Mo Shan,** Hong Kong's highest peak, rising 985 m (3,230 ft) above sea level.

Tour 5: The Outer Islands

The outer islands are the "Other Hong Kong," with an unspoiled natural beauty that is as much a part of Hong Kong as Kowloon's crowded tenements or Hong Kong Island's concrete canyons. But most visitors miss the opportunity to see this side of the territory.

In addition to Hong Kong Island there are 235 islands. The largest, Lantau, is bigger than Hong Kong Island; the smallest is just a few square feet of rock. Most of them are uninhabited. A few are gradually being developed.

You can reach the islands by scheduled ferry services operated by the Hong Kong Ferry Company. The ferries are easy to recognize by the large (HKF) letters painted on their funnels.

Try to go on a weekday; on weekends, Hong Kongers flock to them and pack the ferries. *Leave from the Outlying Districts Services Pier and Government Pier, Central. Tel. 542–3081 for schedule. Round-trip fare: HK$9–$22.*

The biggest of the islands, **Lantau,** covers 88 sq km (55 sq mi) and is almost twice the size of Hong Kong Island. However, Lantau's population is less than 17,000, compared with Hong Kong Island's 1.5 million. Lantau is well worth a full day's visit, even two. The ferry will take you to **Silvermine Bay,** which is being developed as a commuter's suburb of Hong Kong Island.

Safe, sandy beaches, such as those of **Cheung Sha,** stretch along southern Lantau's shoreline. The island's private bus services link the main ferry town, **Mui Wo** in Silvermine Bay, with **Tung Chung,** which has a Sung Dynasty fort, and **Tai O,** the capital of Lantau. Tai O, an ancient fishing village, is divided into two parts connected by a rope-drawn ferry. In the mountainous interior of the island you will find a tea plantation with a horseback riding camp, and a Buddhist monastery. The monastery, **Precious Lotus Monastery,** is near **Ngong Ping** and has one of the world's largest statues of Buddha. The statue, on Lantau Peak, 915 m (3,000 ft) above sea level, has a red flashing light for warning aircraft. The monastery, gaudy and exuberantly commercial, is famous for its vegetarian meals served in the temple refectory, as well as for the giant Buddha.

Time Out Allow time to stop for a meal at either of Lamma's two ferry villages: **Sok Kwu Wan** and **Yung Shue Wan.** In both villages, lines of friendly, open-air harborside restaurants, some with amazingly diverse wine lists, offer feasts of freshness that put many restaurants on Hong Kong Island to shame.

Dining out is a major joy on **Cheung Chau Island,** which lies south of Lantau. Almost every Western visitor's favorite Hong

Kong island, it has dozens of good, open-air cafés on either side of its crowded sand-bar township—both on the **Praya Promenade** along the waterfront and overlooking the main public beach on **Tung Wan.**

Cheung Chau is Hong Kong's most crowded outlying island, with 30,000 or more people, most of them living on the sand bar that connects the dumbbell-shape island's two hilly tips. It has a Mediterranean flavor to it that has attracted artists and writers. The entry into Cheung Chau's harbor, through lines of fishing boats, is an exhilarating experience. There is also history on Cheung Chau—ancient rock carvings, pirate caves, and a 200-year-old temple built to protect the islanders from the twin dangers of plagues and pirates.

With the opening of the island's first hotel, **Cheung Chau Warwick Hotel** on Tung Wan Beach, it is now possible to stay on the island in reasonable comfort.

What to See and Do with Children

City Plaza (Taikooshing) has roller-skating and ice-skating, plus a new "World of Whimsy," a playground with rides and games.

Cultural shows, featuring acrobats and fire-eaters, are held in the late afternoon on various days in Ocean Terminal, the New World Centre, Tsimshatsui Centre, the Landmark, and Cityplaza (tel. 568–8665).

Two of the best places to take children are the **Ocean Park** and **Water World** theme parks (south side of Hong Kong Island). The Headland section of **Ocean Park,** reached by an exciting cable-car ride, has the **Ocean Theatre,** with performing dolphins and a killer whale; a wave cove, where you can watch seals, penguins, and other marine creatures frolic; and Atoll Reef, a giant aquarium with hundreds of fish, including sharks. Also in the Headland is the "Dragon," one of the world's longest roller-coaster rides. The Golden Pagoda has goldfish, a large-screen theater, and bird and animal shows. There is also a huge, walk-through aviary. **Water World** (open May–October) is a water play park adjacent to Ocean Park with swimming pools and water slides. *Ocean Park: tel. 555–0947. Open daily 10–6. Water World: tel. 555–6055. Opening and closing times vary.*

Pokfulam Riding School, run by the Royal Hong Kong Jockey Club, has riding facilities for children, with all levels of instruction. *75 Pokfulam Reservoir Rd., Hong Kong Island, tel. 550–1359. Cost: HK$150 for 45 min. on horses, HK$120 for ponies.*

Space Museum (*see* Tour 2).

Sung Dynasty Village (*see* Tour 2).

Toys "R" Us (tel. 730–9462), the largest toy shop in the world, occupies most of the basement of Ocean Terminal. It has over a million toys in stock, and an infant-care center.

Shopping

Is Hong Kong still a "shoppers' paradise" and the world's bargain basement? The answer is a qualified yes. On the credit side, goods such as cameras, sound systems, computers, precious gems and metals, fabrics, and furs are brought into the territory, in large quantities, free of import duties. Another plus is the high standard of craftsmanship found in Hong Kong, which accounts for its being the manufacturer of fashion garments and jewelry, under license, for the world's leading houses as well as local stores.

On the debit side, shop rents in Hong Kong have soared in recent years, and wages have risen, forcing up prices, especially in Central and Tsimshatsui. As a result, many smaller stores, and those selling goods with low markups, have moved—usually to be replaced by brand-name boutiques and jewelry stores, most of which seem to survive on infrequent sales of very expensive items.

The best bargains in clothing are found in the increasing number of factory outlets for seconds and overruns (complete details in *The Complete Guide to Hong Kong Factory Bargains* by Dana Goetz, widely available in Hong Kong), in the lanes between Queens Road Central and Des Voeux, on the side streets of Tsimshatsui, and in Stanley market.

Most stores selling cameras, electronics, sound equipment, jewelry, and high fashion accept major credit cards, although not for the best discounts. A little bargaining can be productive in these shops; a lot of bargaining is expected in the lanes and markets. Department stores and larger shops will pack and ship goods overseas.

For bilingual addresses of the territory's most recommended shops, see the HKTA's *Official Guide to Shopping, Eating Out and Services in Hong Kong.*

Shopping Centers
Hong Kong Island

Cityplaza. This is one of Hong Kong's newest shopping centers (above Taikoo Shing MTR Station, Quarry Bay), popular with families because of its ice- and roller-skating rinks, bowling alley, and weekly cultural shows. Many shops feature children's clothing, with labels such as Les Enfants, Crocodile, Peter Pan, and Crystal. With more than 400 shops, there are also plenty of toy shops, and fashion shops for men and women.

The Landmark. One of Central's most prestigious shopping sites, The Landmark (Des Voeux Rd. and Pedder St., above Central MTR Station) is filled with boutiques and galleries. It's a multistory complex featuring names such as Céline, Loewe, D'Urban, Gucci, Joyce Boutique, and Hermès of Paris. There are also art galleries and fine jewelry shops. A pedestrian bridge links The Landmark with shopping arcades at *Swire House* and *Prince's Building.*

Kowloon

New World Centre. The New World Centre (next to the New World Hotel) boasts four floors of fashion and leather boutiques, jewelry shops, restaurants, optical shops, tailors, hi-fi stores, arts and crafts shops, and the Japanese *Tokyo Department Store.* The *Regent Hotel Shopping Arcade*, featuring mostly designer boutiques, can be reached through the center.

Ocean Terminal–Ocean Centre–Hong Kong Hotel–Harbour City. Located next to the Star Ferry Terminal, it is one of the largest shopping complexes in the world; Harbour City alone is Asia's largest shopping, office, and residential complex, with about 140 clothing shops, 36 shoe shops, 31 jewelry and watch stores, and 46 restaurants. It is connected by moving sidewalk to Ocean Terminal and Ocean Centre, which lead into the Hong Kong Hotel Shopping Arcade.

Department Stores

Chinese

The various Chinese-product stores give shoppers some of the most unusual and spectacular buys in Hong Kong—and often at better prices than in China. Whether you are looking for pearls, gold, jade, silk jackets, fur hats, Chinese stationery, or just a pair of chopsticks, you cannot go wrong with these stores. Most are open seven days a week but tend to be very crowded on Saturdays, Sunday sale days, and weekday lunchtimes. These shopkeepers are expert at packing, shipping, and mailing goods abroad. The principal stores are:

Chinese Arts & Crafts for silk-embroidered clothing, jewelry, carpets, and art objects. *There are 7 branches: Star House (tel. 735–4061) and Shell House in Central; New World Centre (tel. 369–7760), Silvercord Bldg. (tel. 722–6655), and 233 Nathan Rd. (tel. 735–4980) in Tsimshatsui; 26 Harbour Rd. in Wanchai; and Whampoa Garden in Hunghom, Kowloon.*

China Products Company offers an excellent selection of goods, including household items. *19–31 Yee Wo St., next to Victoria Park, and 488 Hennessy Rd., both in Causeway Bay, tel. 890–8321 and 577–0222.*

Western

Of the department stores that stock large selections of Western goods at fixed prices, the oldest and largest chains are **Wing On** (9 branches), and **Sincere** (173 Des Voeux Rd., Central, tel. 544–2688, and 83 Argyle St., Kowloon, tel. 394–8233). **Lane Crawford** is the most prestigious department store of all, with prices to match. The main store (70 Queen's Rd., Central, tel. 524–1002) is the best. Branches are in Windsor House, Causeway, Bay and Pacific Place, Central, on Hong Kong Island; 74 Nathan Road, and Ocean Terminal in Kowloon.

Markets, Bazaars, and Alleys

These give you some of the best of Hong Kong shopping—good bargains, exciting atmosphere, and a fascinating setting.

Cloth Alley (Wing On St., west of Central Market) has fantastic bargains in all kinds of fabrics.

Jade Market (Kansu St., off Nathan Rd., Yaumatei) has jade in every form, color, shape, and size. Some trinkets are reasonably priced, but unless you know a lot about jade, don't be tempted into buying expensive items.

Li Yuen Streets East and West (between Queen's and Des Voeux Central Rds.) offers some of the best bargains in fashions, with or without famous brand names. Many of the shops also feature trendy jewelry and accessories. You can also find traditional Chinese quilted jackets. Bags of every variety, many in designer styles, are particularly good buys here. Watch out for pickpockets in these crowded lanes.

Stanley Village Market (take the No. 6 or 260 bus from Central) is a popular haunt for Western residents and tourists looking for designer fashions, jeans, T-shirts, and sportswear, all at factory prices and in Western sizes. **Stanley's Selection** (11B

New St., tel. 813–2662) usually has a good choice of sportswear, as does **Fashion Shop** (53 Stanley Style House, tel. 813–0406), which is always piled high with jeans. Also interesting are the shops selling curios and household items from throughout Asia. **Manor House Collection** (17 Stanley Main St., tel. 813–9882) has a large choice of lacquerware, Korean chests, and Thai carvings. A variety of arts and crafts shops stock mostly Chinese products, such as rosewood boxes, porcelain dolls, and traditional tea baskets. **Oriental Corner** (125A Stanley Main St., tel. 813–2223) has Chinese wedding boxes and other carved items. Stanley Village Market is also a good place to buy linen.

Temple Street, in Kowloon (near the Jordan MTR Station), is a night market filled with a colorful collection of clothes, handbags, electrical goods, gadgets, and all sorts of household items. Cantonese opera competes with pop music, and there's a constant chatter of hawkers' cries and shoppers' bargaining. The market stretches for almost a mile (1.6 km) and is one of Hong Kong's liveliest nighttime shopping experiences.

Factory Outlets For the best buys in designer clothes, visit some of the factory outlets and pick up high fashion (almost indiscernibly damaged seconds or overruns) at a fraction of the normal price. One of the best areas for silks is Man Yue Street in Hunghom, Kowloon (take a taxi to Kaiser Estate, Phase I, II, and III). Here are factories such as **Camberley** (tel. 333–7038), **Four Seasons** (tel. 363–2218), **Vica Moda** (tel. 765–7333), and **Bendini** (tel. 334–2341), all of which produce for the fashion houses of Europe and the United States.

Specialty Stores
Antiques Bargains and discoveries are much harder to find these days than they were a few years ago. If you want to be sure of your purchase, patronize such shops as **Charlotte Horstmann and Gerald Godfrey** (Ocean Terminal, Tsimshatsui, tel. 735–7167), **Eileen Kershaw** (Peninsula Hotel, Tsimshatsui, tel. 366–4083), **Lattices** (38 Hollywood Rd., Central, tel. 545–9921), **Zitan** (43–55 Wyndham St., Central, tel. 523–7584), **Gallery 69** (123 Edinburgh Tower, and The Landmark, both in Central, tel. 868–4365), or **Lane Crawford** (70 Queen's Rd., Central, tel. 524–1002).

For shoppers with more curiosity than cash, **Hollywood Road** is a fun place to visit. Treasures are hidden away among a jumble of old family curio shops, sidewalk junk stalls, slick new display windows, and dilapidated warehouses.

Eastern Dreams (corner of Lyndhurst Terr. and Hollywood Rd., Central, tel. 544–2804) has two floors of antique and reproduction furniture, screens, and curios. **Yue Po Chai Antique Co.** (132–136 Hollywood Rd., Central, tel. 540–4374) is one of Hollywood Road's oldest, and has a vast and varied stock. **Schoeni Fine Arts** (27 Hollywood Rd., Central, tel. 542–3143) sells Japanese, Chinese, and Thai antiques, Chinese silverware, such as opium boxes, and rare Chinese pottery. **Kim's Gallery** (5 Hollywood Rd., Central, tel. 523–7232) is stuffed full of antique and reproduction Korean chests.

In the Cat Street area, **Cat Street Galleries** (38 Lok Ku Rd., Sheung Wan, Western, tel. 541–8908) is a collection of dealers all under one roof. You'll find them tucked away among the high-rise office buildings that are the result of the area's redevelopment.

Cameras and Binoculars Many of Hong Kong's thousands of camera shops are clustered on the Lock Road-lower Nathan Road area of Tsimshatsui, in the back streets of Central, and Hennessy Road in Causeway Bay. Two well-known and knowledgeable dealers are **Williams Photo Supply** (Prince's Bldg., tel. 523–9308, and Furama Inter-Continental Hotel, Central, tel. 522–1268) and **Photo Scientific Appliances** (6 Stanley St., Central, tel. 522–1903).

If in doubt about where to shop for such items, stick to the HKTA member shops. Pick up its *Official Guide to Shopping, Eating Out & Services* at any of its information centers and authorized dealers. All reputable dealers should give you a one-year, worldwide guarantee.

Carpets and Rugs Regular imports from China, Iran, India, Pakistan, Afghanistan, and Kashmir make carpets and rugs a very good buy in Hong Kong. There are also plenty of carpets made locally. For Chinese carpets, branches of **China Products** and **Chinese Arts & Crafts** shops give the best selection and price range. For locally made carpets, **Tai Ping Carpets** (Shop 110, G/F, Hutchinson House, 10 Harcourt Rd., Central, tel. 522–7138) is highly regarded, especially for custom-made rugs and wall-to-wall carpets.

Computers All of the big names—Apple, Sinclair, Osbourne, IBM, BBC/Acorn—sell in Hong Kong. If you are going to buy, make sure the machines will work on the voltage in your country—an IBM personal computer sold in Hong Kong will work on 220 volts, while the identical machine in the United States will work on 110 volts. Servicing is a major concern, too.

The real bargains in computers are the locally made versions of the most popular brands. But be forewarned: Even though the prices are lower than in Europe and the United States, you may have trouble getting your Hong Kong computer past customs on your return.

The Asia Computer Plaza (Silvercord, Canton Rd., Tsimshatsui) has 40,000 square feet devoted to everything connected with computers. Most big names have outlets here. There are also three shopping centers into which are crammed dozens of small computer shops. On Hong Kong Island, the most accessible are the **Ocean Shopping Arcade** (140 Wanchai Rd.) and the **Hong Kong Computer Centre** (54 Lockhart Rd., Wanchai, tel. 861–3118). The **Golden Shopping Centre** (Shamshuipo, Kowloon) is more difficult to reach. Take the MTR to Shamshuipo Station, and use the Fuk Wah Street exit.

Furniture and Furnishings Home decor has boomed tremendously in Hong Kong in recent years, and manufacturers of furniture and home furnishings have been quick to expand their activities. **Design Selection** (39 Wyndham St., Central, tel. 525–8339) has a good choice of Indian fabrics. **Interiors** (38 D'Aguilar St., Central, tel. 525–0333) and **Furniture Boutique** (3 Tin Hau Temple Rd., Causeway Bay, tel. 578–1039) stock imported and local goods. **The Banyan Tree** (Prince's Bldg., Central, tel. 523–5561; World Finance Centre and Harbour City, Tsimshatsui, tel. 735–2359 and 735–7425) sells ready-made or made-to-order rattan furniture and some antique Chinese, Korean, and Filipino pieces. Queen's Road East, in Wanchai, has several furniture shops specializing in rattan.

Rosewood furniture is a very popular buy in Hong Kong. Queen's Road East, in Wanchai, the great furniture retail and manufacturing area, offers everything from full rosewood dining sets in Ming style to furniture in French, English, or Chinese styles. Custom-made orders are accepted in most shops on this street. **Choy Lee Co. Ltd** (1 Queen's Rd. East, tel. 527–3709) is the best known.

Furs It seems bizarre that Hong Kong, with its tropical climate, should host so many fur shops. But furs are a good buy here, with high-quality skins, meticulous tailoring, excellent hand-finishing, and competitive prices. Some of the largest and most popular shops are **Siberian Fur Store** (21 Chatham Rd., Tsimshatsui, tel. 366–7039, and 29 Des Voeux Rd., Central, tel. 522–1380); **Stylette Models** (L2–38B New World Centre, Tsimshatsui, tel. 366–2382; the Excelsior Hotel at Causeway Bay, tel. 890–2666), and **Jindo Fur Salon** (Harbour City, Tsimshatsui, tel. 730–9208), which offers a wide range at factory prices.

Handicrafts The traditional crafts of China include a fascinating range of
and Curios items: lanterns, temple rubbings, screen paintings, paper cuttings, seal engravings, and wooden birds. The HKTA publishes a useful pamphlet, *Arts and Crafts and Museums*, listing places where you can buy these specialty items; it is available at all HKTA information centers.

The Welfare Handicrafts Shop (Jardine House, Central, tel. 524–3356) stocks a good collection of inexpensive Chinese handicrafts for both adults and children. All profits go to charity. For contemporary gifts, T-shirts, dolls, posters, and hats, try **Startram (HK) Ltd.** (Star House, by Kowloon Star Ferry, tel. 730–5038; Regal Meridien Hotel, Tsimshatsui, tel. 723–7362; and Peak Tower, on the Hong Kong side, tel. 849–6876).

Mountain Folkcraft (12 Wo On La., Central, tel. 525–3199) offers a varied collection of fascinating curios. **The Forms Folkcrafts** (1/F, 37 Wyndham St., Central, tel. 523–6357) is worth a visit if you like goods from China, Nepal, and Tibet. More can be found in **Tribal Arts & Crafts** (41 Wyndham St., Central). For Filipino goods, visit **Collecciones** (61 Wyndham St., Central, tel. 523–2745); for Indonesian goods, **Vincent Sum Designs Ltd.** (5A Lyndhurst Terr., Central, tel. 542–2610); for Thai crafts, **Thai Shop** (Silvercord, Haiphong and Canton Rds., Tsimshatsui, tel. 722–0963), and for New Zealand products, **Kiwi Shop** (166 Wanchai Rd., Hong Kong Island).

Hi-Fis, Stereos, Hennessy Road in Causeway Bay has long been the mecca for
Tape Recorders finding hi-fi gear, although many small shops in Central's Queen Victoria and Stanley streets and in Tsimshatsui's Nathan Road offer a similar variety of goods. Be sure to compare prices before buying, as they can vary widely. Also make sure that guarantees are worldwide and applicable in your home country.

Jewelry Jewelry is the most popular item among visitors to Hong Kong. It is not subject to any local tax or duty, so prices are normally much lower than they are in most other places of the world. Turnover is fast, competition fierce, and the selection fantastic.

If you are not a gemologist, shop only in reputable outlets— preferably one recommended by someone who lives in Hong

Kong or listed in *The Official Guide to Shopping, Eating Out and Services in Hong Kong*. Hong Kong law requires jewelers to indicate on every gold item displayed or offered for sale both the number of carats and the identity of the shop or manufacturer.

As one of the world's largest diamond-trading centers, Hong Kong offers these gems at prices that are at least 10% lower than world-market levels. When buying diamonds, check the "Four C's": color, clarity, carat (size), and cut. *For information or advice on diamonds, call the Diamond Importers Association, Hong Kong Island, tel. 523–5497.*

Pearls, another good buy, should be checked for color against a white background. Colors vary from white, silvery white, light pink, darker pink, to cream. Cultured pearls usually have a perfectly round shape, semi-baroque pearls have slight imperfections, and baroque pearls are distinctly misshapen.

Jade is Hong Kong's most famous stone, but beware. Although you will see "jade" trinkets and figurines everywhere in Hong Kong, the good jade is rare and expensive. Its quality is determined by the degree of translucency and by the evenness of color and texture.

If you are wary of spending your money at the Jade Market, (*see* Markets, Bazaars, and Alleys, above), visit **Jade House** (Regent Hotel Shopping Arcade, tel. 721–6010) or **Jade Creations** (Lane Crawford House, Queen's Rd., Central; Shop 110 in Ocean Terminal, Tsimshatsui, tel. 522–3598).

Famous international jewelers with shops in Hong Kong include **Van Cleef & Arpels** (Landmark in Central, and Peninsula Hotel in Tsimshatsui, tel. 522–9677), **Cartier** (Peninsula Hotel, tel. 368–8036; Prince's Bldg. in Central, tel. 522–2964), and **Ilias Lalaounis** (Regent Hotel lobby, in Tsimshatsui, tel. 721–2811, and Landmark, tel. 524–3328). For modern jewelry with an Oriental influence, take a look at the fabulous designs by **Kai-Yin Lo** (Peninsula Hotel in Tsimshatsui, Central, tel. 723–3722).

Kung-Fu Supplies The two most convenient places to buy your drum cymbal, leather boots, sword, whip, double dagger, studded wrist bracelet, Bruce Lee kempo gloves, and other kung-fu exotica are **Kung Fu Supplies Co.** (188 Johnston Rd., Wanchai, tel. 891–1912) and **Shang Wu Kung Fu Appliance Centre** (366 Lockhart Rd., Wanchai, tel. 893–3756).

Leather From belts to bags, luggage to briefcases, leather items are high on the list for the Hong Kong shopper. The best and most expensive leather goods come from Europe, but locally made leather bags in designer styles go for a song on Li Yuen streets East and West, in Central, and in other shopping lanes. The leather-garment industry is a growing one, and although most of the production is for export, some good buys can be found in the factory outlets in Hunghom, Kowloon.

Linens, Silks, Embroideries Pure silk shantung, silk and gold brocade, silk velvet, silk damask, and printed, silk crepe de chine are just some of the exquisite materials available in Hong Kong at reasonable prices. The best selections are in **Chinese Arts & Crafts**.

Irish linens, Swiss cotton, Thai silks, and Indian, Malay, and Indonesian fabrics are among the imported cloths available in

Hong Kong. Many of them can be found on Wing On Lane in
Central. **Vincent Sum Designs** (5A Lyndhurst Terr., Central,
tel. 542–2610) specializes in Indonesian batik. Thai silks are
about the same price in Hong Kong as they are in Bangkok. Attractive fabrics from India are available from **Design Selection**
(39 Wyndham St., Central, tel. 525–8339) and **The Thai Shop**
(Silvercord, Canton Rd., Tsimshatsui, tel. 722–0968).

The best buys from China are hand-embroidered and ap-
pliquéed linens and cottons. You can find a magnificent range of
tablecloths, place mats, napkins, and handkerchiefs in the **China Products** and **Chinese Arts & Crafts** stores, and in linen
shops in Stanley Market. The art of embroidery is said to have
originated in Swatow, a port city in China's Guangdong Province. A shop named after this city, **Swatow Drawn Work** (G2–3
Worldwide House, Central, tel. 522–2860) sells some of the
best examples of this delicate art form.

Optical Goods There are a vast number of optical shops in Hong Kong, and
some surprising bargains, too. Soft contact lenses, hard lenses,
and frames for glasses go for considerably less than in many
other places. **The Optical Shop** (branches throughout Hong
Kong) is the fanciest and probably the most reliable store.

Tailor-Made For a suit, overcoat, or jacket, give the tailor plenty of time—at
Clothing least three to five days, and allow for a minimum of two proper
fittings plus a final one for finishing touches. Shirts *can* be done
in a day, but again you will get better quality if you allow more
time. Some shirtmakers like to give one fitting.

There are a number of reputable and long-established tailors in
Hong Kong for both men and women. **Sam's** (Burlington House,
94 Nathan Rd., Kowloon, tel. 367–9423) has been in business
since 1957. Another tailor is **Cheng and Cheng** (Regal Meridien
Hotel, 71 Mody Rd., Tsimshatsui, tel. 723–9151). **Ascot Chang**
(Peninsula and Regent hotels, Kowloon, tel. 721–2080 and 367–
8319; and Prince's Bldg., Central, tel. 523–3663) has special-
ized in shirtmaking since 1949.

TVs and Video Color TV systems vary throughout the world, so it's important
Recorders to be certain the TV set or video recorder you purchase in Hong
Kong has a system compatible to the one in your country. Hong
Kong, Australia, Great Britain, and most European countries
use the *PAL* system. The United States uses the *NTSC* system,
and France and Russia use the *Seacam* system. The HKTA has
a useful brochure called *Shopping Guide to Video Equipment*.

Watches You will have no trouble finding watches in Hong Kong. Street
stalls, department stores, and shops overflow with every variety, style, and brand name, many of them with irresistible
gadgets. (But remember Hong Kong's remarkable talent
for imitation. A super-bargain gold "Rolex" may have hidden
flaws—cheap local or Russian mechanisms, for instance, or
"gold" that rusts). Stick to officially appointed dealers carrying the manufacturers' signs.

Sports and Fitness

Participant Sports

Golf Three clubs welcome visitors, with reciprocal rights from a club at home or introduced by a member (or the concierges of major hotels).

The **Royal Hong Kong Golf Club** allows visitors to play on its nine-hole course at Deep Water Bay, Hong Kong Island, or on its three 18-hole courses at Fanling, New Territories. *Fanling, tel. 670–1211 for bookings, 670–0647 for club rentals. Deep Water Bay, tel. 812–7070. Weekdays only.*

The **Clearwater Bay Golf and Country Club** in New Territories has tennis, squash, badminton, table tennis, and a health spa, in addition to golf. The Hong Kong Tourist Association (HKTA) and this club run a Sports and Recreation Tour for visitors *(see* Tours). *Clearwater Bay Rd., Saikung Peninsula, tel. 719–1595. HKTA tour, tel. 524–4191.*

The **Discovery Bay Golf Club** on Lantau Island is open to visitors on weekdays. *Tel. 987–7271. Take hoverferry from Blake Pier in Central.*

Hiking The **MacLehose Trail,** named after a former governor, stretches 100 km (60 mi) and links eight of the area's most beautiful parks. The trail starts at **Pak Tam Chung** on the Saikung Peninsula and is split into 10 sections, ranging from 5 to 16 km (3–9 mi), each graded according to difficulty. Most parts of the trail can easily be reached by public transportation. From **Pak Tam Chung to Long Ke** is an 11-km (7-mi) hike. At Long Ke you can either return on a circular route (about 18 km or 11 mi), or continue along the coast until you reach **Pak Tam Au**—24 km (15 mi) of hard walking. The scenery is magnificent, with dramatic coastline and sweeping landscapes, and views all the way to China. *No. 5 bus from Star Ferry to Choi Hung; change to No. 92, which takes you to Saikung; pick up No. 94 to Pak Tam Chung; take first section of the trail to Long Ke.*

Squash **Squash** is very much a club activity in Hong Kong. However, there are public courts at the **Hong Kong Squash Centre,** where you'll need a passport to make a booking, and the **Harbour Road Indoor Games Hall,** both on Hong Kong Island; and at Laichikok Park, in Kowloon. *Hong Kong Squash Centre, tel. 869–0611. Laichikok Park, tel. 745–2796. Harbour Rd. Indoor Games Hall, tel. 893–7684.*

Tennis You will probably have to make arrangements with a private club if you want to play tennis. Although there are a limited number of public tennis courts, they are heavily booked in advance. To book a public tennis court you will need identification such as a passport. *Victoria Park, tel. 570–6186; Bowen Rd., tel. 528–2983; Wongneichong Gap, tel. 574–9122; and Kowloon Tsai Park, tel. 336–7878.*

Water Sports **Junking**—dining on the water aboard large *junks* (flat-bottom Chinese fishing boats) that have been converted to pleasure craft—is unique to Hong Kong. This type of leisure has become so entrenched in the colony that there is now a fairly large junk-building industry that produces highly varnished, upholstered, and air-conditioned junks up to 80 feet long.

These floating rumpus rooms serve a purpose, especially for citizens living on Hong Kong Island who need to escape by spending a day on the water. Because so much drinking takes place, the junks are also known as "gin palaces," commanded by "weekend admirals." They also serve as platforms for swimmers, waterskiers, and snorkelers. If anyone so much as breathes an invitation for junking, grab it. To rent a junk, call **Detours Ltd.** (tel. 311–6111) or **Simpson Marine Ltd.** (tel. 555–8377). The junks, with crew, can hold up to 45 people and cost HK$2,500 per day or HK$150 per person for a 90-minute harbor tour.

To **waterski** you will need a speedboat and equipment. Contact the **Waterski Club** (tel. 812–0391) or ask your hotel front desk for names and numbers.

Windsurfing is certainly not unique to Hong Kong, but the territory has welcomed it with open sails. A company called Kent operates four **Windsurfing Centres** throughout the territory, offering lessons and board rentals. The cost for lessons is about HK$250 for four hours (spread over two days). Cost for a windsurfing board is around HK$40 per hour. The centers are at **Stanley Beach** (tel. 566–0320 or 566–0425); **Tun Wan Beach** on Cheung Chau Island (tel. 981–8316 or 981–4872); **Tolo Harbour,** near Taipo in New Territories (tel. 658–2888); and **Sha Ha Beach,** in front of the Surf Hotel, Kowloon (tel. 792–5605).

Swimming is extremely popular with the locals, who have dozens of beaches to choose from (*see* Beaches, below).

To go **sailing** you must belong to a yacht club that has reciprocal rights with one in Hong Kong. Contact the Royal Hong Kong Yacht Club (tel. 832–5972) to make arrangements.

A number of clubs have **scuba diving** trips almost year-round, but it is usually difficult for visitors to join them unless introduced by a friend. However, **Bunn's Diving Equipment Corporation** offers Sunday outings for qualified divers. *188 Wanchai Rd., Hong Kong Island, tel. 891–2113. Cost: HK$250 for outings, HK$160 per dive for equipment rental.*

Spectator Sports

Horse Racing and Gambling

Horse racing is the nearest thing in Hong Kong to a national sport. It is a multimillion-dollar-a-year business, employing thousands of people and drawing crowds that are almost suicidal in their eagerness to rid themselves of their hard-earned money.

The Sport of Kings is run under a monopoly by the Royal Hong Kong Jockey Club, one of the most politically powerful entities in the territory. Profits go to charity and community organizations. The season runs from September or October through May. Some 65 races are held at two race courses—**Happy Valley** on Hong Kong Island and **Shatin** in New Territories. Shatin's race course is only a few years old and is one of the most modern in the world. Both courses have huge video screens at the finish line so that gamblers can see what is happening each foot of the way.

Races are run at one track on Wednesday nights, and at both tracks on either Saturday or Sunday. Even if you're not a gambler, it's worth going just to see the crowds.

Tourists can view races from the Members' Stand at both tracks by showing their passports and paying HK$50 for a badge.

In a place where gambling has developed into a mania, it may come as a surprise to learn that most forms of gambling are forbidden. Excluding the stock market, which is by far the territory's biggest single gambling event, the only legalized forms of gambling are horse racing and the lottery. Nearby Macau is another story—there you can get your fill of casino gambling *(see* Macau Excursion).

Dining

by Jack Moore

Jack Moore is the restaurant columnist for the South China Morning Post's *weekly* T.V. & Entertainment Times *magazine and a regular contributor to* Epicure *magazine.*

Nowhere in the world is the cooking more varied than in this city, where Cantonese cuisine (long regarded by Chinese gourmets as the most intricate and sophisticated in Asia) is augmented by cookery from many other parts of China and virtually every other culinary region on earth. Indeed, among Hong Kong's thousands of restaurants you'll even find such unexpected fare as Dutch, Caribbean, Sri Lankan, and regional American. Be advised, however, that while Hong Kong contains some of Asia's best restaurants, it also contains some of the worst, so don't expect just any old neighborhood restaurant to turn out to be a gourmet's dream.

One hint: While in Hong Kong, you *must* try two things: Peking duck (nowhere will you find better) and dim sum—tasty hors d'oeuvres served as a meal between breakfast and late afternoon.

Highly recommended restaurants are indicated by a star ★.

Category	Cost*
Very Expensive	over HK$500 (US$64)
Expensive	HK$300–HK$500 (US$38–US$64)
Moderate	HK$100–HK$300 (US$13–US$38)
Inexpensive	under HK$100 (US$13)

per person plus 10% service charge

American
Expensive–Moderate

San Francisco Steak House. For more than 20 years, this mock-Barbary Coast eatery has been pleasing both locals and traveling Americans with a combination of down-home atmosphere (if your home runs to dark paneled walls, red flock wallpaper, and replicas of Powell Street cable cars) and American fare. The clam chowder is an original Boston recipe. Steaks are Angus beef and are treated with the respect good meat deserves. The California-style *cioppino* (seafood stew) comes straight from Fisherman's Wharf. Also excellent is the Canadian salmon, served as a whole baked baby coho. *101 Barnton Court, Harbour City, 9 Canton Rd., Tsimshatsui, Kowloon, tel. 735–7576. Reservations advised. Dress: informal. AE, DC, MC, V.*

Chinese
Very Expensive

Eagle's Nest. Atop the Hilton Hotel, this tourist-oriented eatery offers a spectacular view of Hong Kong harbor, a fine selection of Cantonese and other Chinese regional dishes, splendid premises in the best American hotel style, and first-rate service. A full-size band provides dinner and dancing music. The menu features mostly well-known specialties—Peking duck, beggar's chicken, barbecued pork with plum sauce. Bird's-nest, shark's-fin, and abalone soups are available but costly. Fresh seasonal seafood dishes are always a specialty, along with an excellent "Lotus Vegetable Platter." *Hongkong Hilton, 2 Queen's Rd., Central, Hong Kong Island, tel. 523–3111. Reservations recommended. Jacket and tie suggested. AE, DC, MC, V.*

Moderate
★
Yung Kee. Once rated by *Fortune* magazine as one of the world's 15 best restaurants, this multistory eatery offers very good Cantonese food amid riotous Chinese decor featuring writhing golden dragons. The restaurant attracts clientele from office workers to visiting celebrities, and all receive the same cheerful high-energy service. Roast goose is the specialty, with the skin beautifully crisp. Seafood fanciers should try the sautéed fillet of pomfret with chili and black bean sauce. *Wellington St., Central, Hong Kong Island, tel. 523–1526. Reservations advised. Dress: casual. AE, DC, MC, V.*

Moderate–
Inexpensive
Great Shanghai Restaurant. Do not come for the decor unless you're really fond of dingy restaurants. This is, however, an excellent spot both for culinary adventurers and for those serious about Shanghai food, which tends to feature more blatant flavors than does Cantonese. You may not be quite ready for the sea blubber or braised turtle with sugar candy, but do try one of the boneless eel dishes, Shanghai-style yellowfish soup, and excellent spiced and soyed duck. *26 Prat Ave., Tsimshatsui, Kowloon, tel. 366–8158 or 366–2683. Reservations strongly recommended. Dress: casual. AE, DC, MC, V.*

Inexpensive
★
American Restaurant. Despite the name, the cuisine here is from Peking, which means hearty, stick-to-the-ribs fare suitable for the chilly climate of northern China. A typically overdecorated Chinese restaurant full of red and gold fixtures, the 40-year-old American is noted for its hot-and-sour soup, fried and steamed dumplings, and noodle dishes. Some insist the Peking duck is the best in town; this is also an excellent place to sample beggar's chicken, cooked in clay and lotus leaves. Don't confuse this place with The American Cafe, which has branches all over town and is merely a fast-food chain. *20 Lockhart Rd., Wanchai, Hong Kong Island, tel. 527–7277 or 527–7770. Reservations recommended, essential on weekends. Dress: informal. No credit cards.*

Continental
Very Expensive
★
Hugo's. The Hyatt hotel's showpiece since it opened in 1969, Hugo's is a big space that still manages to make diners feel cozy. Done in warm colors and filled with lots of activity (including wandering Filipino minstrels), this is a place locals favor for celebratory dinners. The food is renowned, for very good reasons. The lobster bisque and U.S. prime rib are exceptional. More distinctive, however, is the baked rack of lamb in an onion-and-potato crust with juniper-berry cream, and the salmon and scallops baked in flaky pastry with mango and spinach. *Hyatt Regency, 67 Nathan Rd., Tsimshatsui, Kowloon, tel. 311–1234. Reservations recommended. Jacket and tie required. AE, DC, MC, V.*

Moderate
★
Jimmy's Kitchen. Probably the most famous (and still one of the best) of the territory's restaurants, this China Coast institu-

0   440 yards

0   400 meters

Victoria Harbour

Macau Ferry Pier

Connaught Rd. West

Bonham

Wing Lok St.
Strand

Connaught Rd. Central

SHEUNG WAN

Des Voeux Rd.

Bridges St.

Aberdeen St.

Staunton St.

Caine Rd.

Wellington St.

Stanley St.

Queen's Rd.

D'Aguilar St.

Wyndham St.

Central

Pedder St.

Central

Chater Rd.

Naval
Dockyard

Harcourt Rd.

ADMIRALTY

Garden Rd.

Cotton Tree Dr.

Queensway

Dining

American Restaurant, **9**

Bentley's Seafood Restaurant and Oyster Bar, **5**

Chesa, **17**

Chili Club, **11**

Eagle's Nest, **8**

Gaddi's **16**

Great Shanghai, **25**

Hugo's, **21**

Jimmy's Kitchen, **4**

Sagano Restaurant, **24**

San Francisco Steak House, **19**

Tandoor Restaurant, **3**

Yung Kee, **2**

Lodging

China Merchants, **1**

The Excelsior, **13**

The Hong Kong Hilton International, **7**

Hyatt Regency, **20**

Kowloon, **22**

Mandarin Oriental, **6**

Omni Hong Kong Hotel, **18**

Park Lane Radisson, **12**

Peninsula, **15**

Ramada Inn Hong Kong, **10**

Regal Riverside, **27**

The Regent, **14**

Ritz, **26**

Shangri-La, **23**

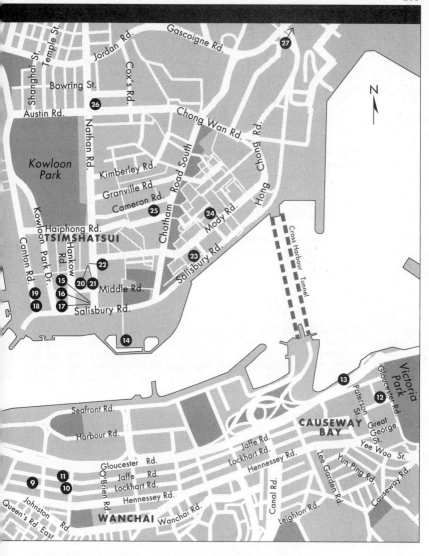

tion first opened for business in 1928 and has been catering to a devoted clientele in one Hong Kong location or another ever since. A well-kept and comfortable old restaurant with booths, dark woodwork, lattice partitions, and brasswork on the walls, Jimmy's serves equally old-fashioned dishes, like corned beef and cabbage. Other specialties include borscht, stroganoff, and goulash. *South China Bldg., 1 Wyndham St., Central, Hong Kong Island, tel. 368-4027; Kowloon Centre, 29 Ashley Rd., Tsimshatsui, Kowloon, tel. 526-5293 or 368-4027. Reservations necessary. Jacket and tie or smart casual. AE, DC, MC, V.*

English
Very Expensive

Bentley's Seafood Restaurant and Oyster Bar. Here, in the basement of an office building, you'll find an exact copy of a well-known swank London restaurant, with cream-colored walls, floral carpet, Dickensian prints, and the overall feel of an exclusive English club. There are even oysters from Colchester in season—and from many other places in the world as well—served up raw or cooked as oysters Kilpatrick, with tomato, chili, and bacon; oysters Imperial, with champagne sauce; or oysters Bentley, with tomato and curry sauces. The Dover sole is the best in town, grilled simply with lemon and butter, and the fish pie is classic English cooking at its rare best. *Prince's Bldg. (enter off Statue Square), Central, Hong Kong Island, tel. 868-0881. Reservations necessary. Jacket and tie recommended. AE, DC, MC. Closed Sun.*

French
Very Expensive
★

Gaddi's. The classiest lunch or dinner venue in Hong Kong for the past 40 years, Gaddi's is a Rolls-Royce among restaurants. The decor includes huge chandeliers made in Paris and salvaged from wartime Shanghai, ankle-deep Tai Ping carpets that exactly match the napery, and a priceless coromandel screen, made in 1670 for the Emperor's Summer Palace in Beijing. The service is never less than superlative, and the menu changes frequently. The soufflés are exquisite; a favorite one is liberally laced with Grand Marnier. *The Peninsula Hotel, Salisbury Rd., Tsimshatsui, Kowloon, tel. 366-6251, ext. 3989. Reservations essential. Dress: the best you have, black tie if possible. AE, DC, MC, V.*

Indian
Expensive–Moderate

Tandoor Restaurant, This upstairs eatery, one of the classiest venues in town for Indian food, is exotically decorated with mirrors, Indian paintings, colorful cloth hangings, and musical instruments. A glass-fronted kitchen allows you to watch the chef at work. There's a rose for every lady and a cheroot for every gentleman after dinner, which is likely to be superb. There are almost 100 dishes to choose from, but don't miss the tandoor specialties, the roast lamb *sagwalla* (covered with tasty spinach), and the lamb *rogan josh*, swimming in Kashmiri spices. Also featured are no fewer than 14 kinds of Indian bread, all worth tasting. *Carfield Commercial Bldg., 75-77 Wyndham St., Central, Hong Kong Island, tel. 521-8363. Reservations essential. Dress: smart casual. AE, DC, V.*

Japanese
Very Expensive

Sagano Restaurant. Probably the most popular Japanese restaurant in Hong Kong, the Sagano features remarkable food, impeccable service, and a panoramic view of the constant activity in Hong Kong harbor. The main offering of the house is Kansai cuisine, from Kyoto, which features light sauces and absolute freshness. Sushi and sashimi are prepared from fish imported from Japan. Save some room for the special house dessert, plum sherbet. *Hotel Nikko Hong Kong, 72 Mody Rd., Tsimshatsui, Kowloon, tel. 739–1111. Reservations absolutely necessary. Dress: smart casual. AE, DC, MC, V.*

Swiss
Expensive

Chesa. Lovingly fostered by a succession of Swiss hotel managers over 25 years, this is a perfect reproduction of an Alpine country tavern, with wood beams, tiny windows, hand-painted butter molds, and real Swiss linens. Sample the *tassette Suisse*, an aromatic beef broth with bone marrow, morels, and fresh herbs under a light pastry crust; the pan-fried fillet of lake trout with roast almonds; or the deep, rich oxtail stew with red wine. Fondues for two and a good selection of esoteric and excellent Swiss wines are on offer. *Service is impeccable. Peninsula Hotel, Salisbury Rd., Tsimshatsui, Kowloon, tel. 666–251. Reservations strongly advised. Dress: smart casual/ business suit. AE, DC, MC, V.*

Thai
Moderate
★

Chili Club. This place is arguably the most popular—and most excellent—Thai restaurant in a city where this cuisine is very popular indeed. It's above one of Wanchai's main thoroughfares, although there are no windows that show you the neighborhood. The dining room is Spartan, clean, and cramped. A must-try is the spicy-sour shrimp soup with an overriding taste of lemongrass, and don't miss the squid salad, filled with tiny bits of chili pepper. If you like tastes that linger, try the durian ice cream for dessert. *68 Lockhart Rd., Wanchai, Hong Kong Island, tel. 527–2872. Reservations essential. Dress: casual. MC, V.*

Lodging

by Linda Miller

As one might expect in one of the world's most important financial centers, Hong Kong caters to the convenience of business executives. Deluxe hotels—including some of the world's best—have business centers that provide secretarial services, translators, easy access to telex and fax machines, and libraries of local publications. In fact, the city's top hotels provide the best all-around hotel services of any city in the world. They also contain some of Asia's finest restaurants.

In the busy period—spring and fall—advance bookings are strongly recommended. Even with the rash of new hotels (another 7,600 rooms will be added by the end of 1990), rooms can prove scarce March through June and September through early December.

The Hong Kong Tourist Association publishes a *Hotel Guide* listing member hotels and their rates, services, and facilities (the brochure is published twice a year, so it is usually one price hike behind) but it does not make reservations. The **Hong Kong Hotel Association** (HKHA) does, at no charge, through its reservations office at Kai Tak International Airport.

Choosing where to stay in Hong Kong depends on the purpose of your visit. Thanks to the harbor tunnel and the subway, it no longer matters whether you stay "Hong Kong–side" or "Kowloon-side." Either side of the harbor is only minutes away by MTR.

Highly recommended hotels are indicated by a star ★.

Category	Cost*
Very Expensive	over HK$1,500 (US$192)
Expensive	HK$1,000–$1,500 (US$128–US$192)
Moderate	HK$700–$1,000 (US$90–US$128)
Inexpensive	under HK$700 (US$90)

*All prices are for a standard double room; add 15% for service charge and tax.

Hong Kong Island People who need to be near the city's financial hub prefer the Central district on Hong Kong Island. Central is as busy as New York's Manhattan Island on weekdays but quiet at night and on weekends. Wanchai, east of Central, was once a sailor's dream of "Suzie Wongs" and booze. Although it is still one of the city's more entertaining nightlife areas, land reclamation has given it an array of new harbor-front skyscrapers. Causeway Bay, farther east, is ideal for those who like to try lots of different restaurants or are on shopping trips; Happy Valley is near the racetrack.

Very Expensive **The Hong Kong Hilton International.** Excellent business facilities, six executive floors, and a Central district location make this elegant hotel an attractive choice for business travelers. The hotel also boasts a 110-foot brigantine that makes regular lunch, cocktail, and dinner cruises and is available for weekend island picnics or private hire. Rooms are pastel, modern, and well-appointed. *2 Queen's Rd., Central, tel. 523–3111. 668 rooms, 83 suites. Facilities: health club with heated outdoor pool, tennis courts, business center, 9 restaurants, 2 nonsmoking floors, beauty salon, barbershop, gift shop, shopping arcade, florist. AE, CB, DC, MC, V.*

★ **Mandarin Oriental.** Much touted by travel writers as "one of the world's great hotels," the Mandarin speaks of elegance from the moment you enter the vast lobby, decorated with antique gilded Chinese wall sculpture. Guest room walls are decorated with antique maps and prints, and there's always fresh fruit on hand. Centrally located next to the Star Ferry concourse, the hotel is a place to spot visiting celebrities and VIPs—for more than 25 years it has catered to the well-to-do and business travelers with hefty expense accounts. *5 Connaught Rd., Central, tel. 522–0111 or 800/526–6566. 489 rooms, 58 suites. Facilities: health club with heated indoor pool, business center, 4 restaurants, beauty salon, barbershop, gift shop, shopping arcade, florist. AE, CB, DC, MC, V.*

Expensive **The Excelsior.** In Causeway Bay overlooking the Royal Hong Kong Yacht Club marina, the Excelsior offers a good selection of restaurants and entertainment. Jazz evenings in the basement bar and rooftop disco add to the hotel's appeal. Eighty percent of the rooms have harbor views. Sports-minded guests will appreciate the hotel's tennis courts and the jogging track in the adjacent park. Business travelers like the many services and the proximity to the World Trade Centre, only a short walk away through an air-conditioned walkway. *281 Gloucester Rd., Causeway Bay, tel. 576–7365. 903 rooms, 22 suites. Facilities: business center, 4 restaurants, nonsmoking areas, beauty salon, barbershop, gift shop, shopping arcade, florist. AE, CB, DC, MC, V.*

Park Lane Radisson. This elegant hotel, opposite Victoria Park and in the midst of small shops and department stores, is at the center of Hong Kong Island's busiest shopping, entertainment, and business areas. *320 Gloucester Rd., Causeway Bay, tel. 890–3355 or 800/333–3333. 850 rooms, 25 suites. Facilities: health club, business center, 3 restaurants, beauty salon, shopping arcade, florist. AE, CB, DC, MC, V.*

Moderate **Ramada Inn Hong Kong.** Within walking distance of the new Convention and Exhibition Centre, this hotel appeals to the budget-conscious business traveler. The lobby is bright and modern but small: If you want to sit and rest, you will have to use the adjacent café. *61-73 Lockhart Rd., Wanchai, tel. 861–1000 or 800/272–6232. 284 rooms, 2 suites. Facilities: indoor heated pool, business center, restaurant. AE, DC, MC, V.*

Inexpensive **China Merchants.** Located in the island's waterfront district, west of the Central business core, this three-year-old, medium-size hotel is part of a chain that includes 10 properties in the People's Republic of China. (Trips to China are easily arranged here.) As the name indicates, the hotel was built to cater to visiting business people; the rooms are small, clean, comfortable, and entirely functional. Features include bidets, a location handy to the China and Macau ferry piers, and views of Victoria Harbour or The Peak (depending on which side your room is on). *160–161 Connaught Rd. W, tel. 559–6888. 285 rooms, 3 suites. Facilities: health club, business center, 3 restaurants, nonsmoking areas, limited shopping arcade. AE, DC, MC, V.*

Kowloon Most of the hotels in Hong Kong are situated on the Kowloon peninsula. The fabled shopping "Golden Mile" of Nathan Road runs through "old" Tsimshatsui. Back streets are filled with restaurants, boutiques, stores, and hotels.

Tsimshatsui East is a grid of modern office blocks (many with restaurants or nightclubs) and luxury hotels. This area has been created on land reclaimed from the harbor in the last decade, so none of these hotels is very old.

There are three luxury hotels (all members of the Omni chain) in Harbour City, on the western side of the Tsimshatsui promontory—Asia's largest air-conditioned shopping and commercial complex. Northern Kowloon contains more of the smaller, older hotels, most on or near Nathan Road. These are probably the best bets for economy-minded visitors.

Very Expensive **Peninsula.** "The Pen," the grand old lady of Hong Kong hotels,
★ was built in 1928, when travelers took many weeks (and trunks) to reach Hong Kong by boat and train from London. Almost a British colonial institution, with a lobby reminiscent of Europe's great railway lounges, this is the ultimate in colonial class. The Pen's glory as a monument to good taste and Old World style is in evidence everywhere: the columned and gilt-corniced lobby; the fleet of Rolls-Royces; large, high-ceilinged bedrooms; attentive room valets; French soaps and daily newspapers. Gaddi's, the hotel's French restaurant, is perhaps Hong Kong's most distinguished gourmet restaurant. *Salisbury Rd., tel. 366–6251. 190 rooms, 20 suites. Facilities: business services, 6 restaurants, beauty salon, barbershop, gift shop, shopping arcade, florist. AE, DC, MC, V.*

★ **The Regent.** Built in 1980, this elegant modern hotel on the southernmost tip of Tsimshatsui offers luxurious guest rooms with spectacular harbor views. The view can also be enjoyed from the restaurants or the cocktail lounge, where windows rise 12 m (40 ft) above the polished granite floor. Those who want the best and are prepared to pay for it will appreciate such Regent features as fine Oriental art displays and computerized guest histories to store information about guests' preferences. *Salisbury Rd., tel. 721–1211 or 800/545–4000. 530 rooms, 70 suites. Facilities: health club with heated oversize outdoor pool, massage, business center, 4 restaurants, beauty salon, barbershop, shopping arcade, florist. AE, CB, DC, MC, V.*

Shangri-La. Billed as one of the top 10 hotels in the world, this Westin waterfront hotel focuses on the international business traveler. The executive floor offers 24-hour services, personalized stationery, and complimentary breakfast and cocktails. The modern, pastel rooms are large by Hong Kong standards and have views either of Victoria Harbour or of the city. A range of live entertainment, including string quartets and harp and piano music, is available at bars, restaurants, and nightclubs throughout the hotel. Located on the eastern shore of Tsimshatsui, the hotel is convenient to shopping and 15 minutes from the airport. *64 Mody Rd., tel. 721–2111 or 800/228–3000. 689 rooms, 20 suites. Facilities: health club with indoor pool, business center, 5 restaurants, bar, nightclub, lounges, nonsmoking floor, barbershop, gift shop. AE, CB, DC, MC, V.*

Expensive **Hyatt Regency.** Major renovations in 1987 have given the Hyatt
★ a dramatic marble-and-teak lobby and plush, earth-tone guest rooms. The hotel—which boasts a gallery of Oriental antiques and an award-winning Chinese restaurant—is five minutes away from the Star Ferry and steps from the MTR. *67 Nathan Rd., tel. 311–1234 or 800/228–9000. 706 rooms, 17 suites. Facilities: business center, 4 restaurants, nonsmoking rooms, beauty salon, barbershop, gift shop, shopping arcade, florist. AE, CB, DC, MC, V.*

★ **Omni Hong Kong Hotel.** The largest and most luxurious of the three Omni hotels on the western side of Tsimshatsui (the others are the Omni Marco Polo and the Omni Prince). All are part of the enormous Ocean Centre–Harbour City hotel, entertainment, and shopping complex. The location has made the hotels favorites—the Star Ferry and bus terminals are next door, and old Tsimshatsui is a short walk away. *Harbour City, tel. 736–0088 or 800/THE OMNI. 670 rooms, 84 suites. Facilities: heated outdoor pool, business center, 7 restaurants, nonsmoking floor, beauty salon, barbershop, shopping arcade, florist. AE, DC, MC, V.*

Moderate **Kowloon.** A shimmering mirrored exterior and a chrome,
★ glass, and marble lobby reflect the Kowloon's aims for efficiency and high-tech amenities. It is on the southern tip of Nathan Road's Golden Mile, just minutes from the Star Ferry and even closer to the MTR. Hotel guests have direct access to the facilities of the Peninsula, across the street, and the Repulse Bay restaurants and can charge expenses to their hotel accounts. *19 Nathan Rd., tel. 369–8698. 704 rooms, 34 suites. Facilities: business center, 2 restaurants, nonsmoking rooms, beauty salon, barbershop, gift shop, shopping arcade, florist. AE, CB, DC, MC, V.*

Inexpensive
★
Ritz. Located north of the Tsimshatsui area of Kowloon and near the Jordan MTR, this hotel provides the basics in Oriental surroundings. Live entertainment and bars can be found about a mile south. *122 Austin Rd., tel. 369–2282. 60 rooms. Facilities: restaurant. AE, DC, MC, V.*

New Territories With the massive redevelopment in the New Territories north of Kowloon has come the introduction of some international-standard hotels. When it opens in late 1990, the Panda Kowloon will be the biggest in Hong Kong, with 950 rooms. Accommodations are limited on the outlying islands, although some of them (such as Cheung Chau Warwick), have a booming business in rooms to rent—look for the photographs of them on placards that line the waterfront opposite the ferry pier. Those wishing to escape the main tourist-hotel areas or on a tight budget might consider these areas. You might also contact the Trappist Monastery on Lantau Island (Trappist Haven, Lantau Island, Box 5, Peng Chau, Hong Kong); rooms are available to those who apply well in advance.

Moderate **Regal Riverside.** This large, modern hotel overlooks the Shing Mun River in the foothills of Shatin. Be prepared to spend at least 20 minutes getting to the Kowloon shopping district. The city-resort atmosphere comes not only from its location but from such features as Hong Kong's largest hotel disco and a health club with Hong Kong's only float capsule (purported to soothe away the day's pressures). *Shatin, tel. 718–0333 or 800/543–4300. 389 rooms, 11 suites. Facilities: business center, 3 restaurants, nonsmoking floors, beauty salon, barbershop, shopping arcade. AE, DC, MC, V.*

The Arts and Nightlife

The best daily calendar of cultural events is the *South China Morning Post*, which has a daily arts and culture page. The *Hong Kong Standard* also lists events. Weekly listings are in the *TV and Entertainment Times*. The government radio station, RTHK 3567 AM, announces events during the 7 AM–10 AM "Hong Kong Today" program.

City Hall has posters and bulletin boards listing events and ticket availability, and booths where tickets can be purchased. The monthly *City News Urban Council* newspaper, which also lists events, is free and available at City Hall.

Performance Halls **City Hall** (Edinburgh Pl., by Star Ferry, Central, tel. 522–
Hong Kong Island 9928). This complex has a large auditorium, a recital hall, and a theater. Classical music, legitimate theater, and films are presented here.
Hong Kong Arts Centre (2 Harbour Rd., Wanchai, tel. 823–0200). Here you will find 15 floors of auditoriums, rehearsal halls, and recital rooms.
Hong Kong Fringe Club (2 Lower Albert Rd., Central, tel. 521–7251). Locally run, this has some of Hong Kong's most interesting visiting and local entertainment and art exhibitions.
Queen Elizabeth Stadium (18 Oi Kwan Rd., Wanchai, tel. 575–6793). Although this is basically a sports stadium with a seating capacity of 3,500, it frequently presents ballet, orchestra concerts, and even disco.
Hong Kong Academy for Performing Arts. (1 Gloucester Rd., Wanchai, tel. 823–1500). This arts school has two major thea-

ters seating 1,600 people, plus a 200-seat studio theater and
outdoor theater.

Kowloon **Hong Kong Coliseum.** (Hung Hom Railway Station, Hunghom,
tel. 765–9234). This stadium has seating capacity for more than
12,000 and presents everything from basketball to ballet.
Isimshatsui Cultural Centre (Salisbury Rd. near Star Ferry).
Opening late 1989 with theaters, concert halls, etc. Details
were unavailable at press time.

New Territories **Tsuen Wan Town Hall** (tel. 414–0144; take the MTR to Tsuen
Wan Station).
Shatin Town Hall (tel. 694–2510), a 5-minute walk from the
KCR at Shatin, is an impressive building attached to an enor-
mous shopping arcade.

Festivals and **Hong Kong Arts Festival** (Jan.–Feb.) includes four weeks of mu-
Special Events sic and drama from around the world. Information abroad can
be obtained through HKTA offices.
Hong Kong Fringe Festival (Jan.–Feb.) Runs simultaneously
with the Arts Festival.
Hong Kong International Film Festival (Apr.). This includes
two weeks of films from virtually every country in the world.
Brochures are available at City Hall. *Tel. 573–9595 for information.*
Festival of Asian Arts (Oct.–Nov.). Perhaps Asia's major
cultural festival, this draws over 150 artistic events from as far
afield as Hawaii, Bhutan, and Australia.

Performing Arts **Hong Kong Philharmonic Orchestra.** More than 100 artists
Ensembles from Hong Kong, the United States, and Europe perform
everything from classical to avant-garde to contemporary mu-
sic by Chinese composers. *Tel. 832–7121 for ticket information.*
Hong Kong Chinese Orchestra. Created in 1977 by the Urban
Council, this group performs only Chinese works.

Chinese Opera Like Japanese kabuki, Chinese opera entertains with colorful
costumes, painted faces, acrobatics, comic routines, and an incredible range of stylized movements. The stories and
characters, from Chinese history or Confucian parables, are
well known to the audience, who applaud an especially well-
executed gesture (there are no less than 107 for the hands
alone), a firm falsetto trill, a clever bit of swordplay, or a humorous mime.

Peking opera is the most stylized form of the art. It features
masklike makeup, elaborate headdresses, and a variety of
regional dialects. It is performed in Hong Kong by Beijing companies during festivals or on special tours (check daily
newspapers). **Cantonese opera** is rather less formal but just as
colorful. It is performed by local troupes during festivals (such
as the Feast of the Hungry Ghosts) or at night markets like that
on Shanghai Street. Many Westerners find it noisy and incom-
prehensible. For more information, contact the HKTA
Information Department (tel. 524–4191).

Nightclubs and **Eagle's Nest** (Hilton Hotel, 2 Queen's Rd., Central, tel. 523–
Cabaret 3111) is a 25th-floor aerie with marvelous views and an excellent band with vocalists for easy listening and romantic
dancing. Prices are fairly upmarket. **Golden Crown** (66 Nathan
Rd., Kowloon, tel. 366–6291) is one of the older Chinese
nightclub-restaurants. Families (including small children) and

couples are found here enjoying Cantonese meals or dancing late into the night.

Pubs and Bars   **The Galley** (basement of Jardine House, Connaught Rd., Central, tel. 526–3061) is not only one of Central's best-value restaurants, it is a favorite haunt at night for drinking, playing darts, and listening to the Filipino band. **Jockey Pub** (Swire House, Chater Rd., tel. 526–1478) is another congenial, reasonably priced rendezvous for local residents. For music while you drink, **Rick's Cafe** (4 Hart Ave., Kowloon, tel. 367–2939) has probably the best jazz in town, played by a resident group or visiting players.

Discos   **Canton** (World Finance Centre, Harbour City, Canton Rd., Kowloon, tel. 721–0209) continues to set the trend for Hong Kong discos. It has two floors for high-energy, high-decibel dancing. Sometimes international stars perform here. Entrance fees are about HK$100, which includes two drinks. Next door is **Hot Gossip** (Harbour City, Canton Rd., Kowloon, tel. 723–7908), with separate cocktail lounges, which appeals to a slightly more conservative crowd.

Topless and   **Bottoms Up** (14 Hankow Rd., Kowloon, tel. 721–4509), immor-
Girlie Bars   talized in a James Bond movie, isn't really risqué at all—the topless barmaids serve men accompanied by their wives and girlfriends. Surviving Wanchai girlie bars such as **Pussycat** (17 Fenwick St., tel. 527–1347) and the **Suzie Wong Club** (21 Fenwick St., Wanchai, tel. 527–7461) cater to visiting sailors and local tired businessmen.

Hostess Clubs   **Club Cabaret** (New World Centre, Kowloon, tel. 369–8431), is a small, reasonably priced club, whereas **Club Volvo** (Mandarin Plaza, Tsimshatsui East, tel. 369–2883) earned notoriety by introducing a Rolls-Royce to take guests to their VIP rooms, and offering vast sums to attract over 1,000 hostesses. If you have to ask the price, you don't belong here.

Macau

Introduction

by Shann Davies

British writer Shann Davies has lived and traveled in many countries, but she always comes back to Macau, which she first visited in 1962. She is the author of Viva Macau!, Chronicles in Stone, *and* Macau *(Times Editions).*

Macau, like Hong Kong, was settled by Westerners engaged in trade with China. It too is a modern capitalist community with a predominantly Chinese population. In most other respects, however, the two territories are very different, which makes Macau especially appealing as an excursion from Hong Kong.

The Portuguese set up shop, home, and church in Macau, with tacit permission of the Chinese, in 1557. At that time direct trade between China and Japan was banned and the merchants of Canton, as well as those of Kyushu in southern Japan, saw the Portuguese as the ideal entrepreneurs.

For almost a century Macau was an entrepôt for cargoes of Chinese silk, porcelain, and tea; Japanese silver; East Indian spices; Indian muslin; Persian gems; African ivory; Brazilian foodstuffs; and European manufactures. At the same time the city became missionary headquarters for Jesuit scholars who took Christianity and Western science to Japan and China.

Macau lost its prime importance when Japan closed its doors and the Dutch captured Portugal's sea-lanes. It reemerged as a summer home for American and European traders in the 18th century, only to sink again into obscurity when Hong Kong was settled in 1841 to become the major port on the South China coast.

Today a great deal of Macau's multinational history is still in evidence. An astonishing number of historic sites have survived as everyday working buildings—within a few short blocks a visitor can find a 16th-century Buddhist temple, 17th-century European fort, 18th-century baroque church, 19th-century colonial mansion, and 20th-century skyscraper. Dozens of small restaurants offer fine Macanese, European, and Asian food at prices far below those of Hong Kong. Another main attraction is gambling, which is available in casinos, at horse and greyhound races, and in the jai alai fronton.

Some visitors combine a visit to Macau with a day trip across the border to China, which is today open to tourists, vegetable sellers, businessmen, and technicians engaged in joint ventures and overseas Chinese visiting ancestral homes. (But *see* Excursions in Guided Tours, above, regarding potential difficulties.) China will resume its sovereignty over Macau on December 20, 1999, under an agreement similar to Hong Kong's 1997 takeover.

Macau has a population of about half a million, most of whom live in the 6.5-sq-km (2.5-sq-mi) mainland city. The rest make up communities on the predominantly rural islands of Taipa and Coloane. About 95% are Chinese, and 7,000 are Portuguese or Eurasian Macanese.

Important Addresses and Numbers

Tourist Information
In Macau, the **Department of Tourism** has an office at the Arrivals terminal (on the wharf), open daily 9–6. There is also an office on Avenue Amizade (tel. 561167, open daily 9–6), around the corner from the Sintra Hotel.

Probably more useful is the **Macau Tourist Information Bureau** (MTIB) in Hong Kong (tel. 540–8180 or 540–8196, open weekdays 9–5, Sat. 9–1), on the same floor of the Shun Tak Centre as the wharf entrance. Two other branches may be helpful—in Australia (449 Darling St., Balmain, NSW 2041, tel. 555–7548), and in Britain (22A Devonshire St., London W1N 1RL, tel. 01/224–3390). In addition, there is a Macau information desk at Hong Kong's Kai Tak Airport, just outside the Arrivals Hall (open daily 8 AM– 10 PM).

National Holidays

Macau celebrates all major Catholic holidays, Chinese New Year, other important festival days, plus historic occasions, such as Portuguese Republic Day (October 5) and Independence Day (December 1). Offices and banks close for these holidays, but most shops stay open.

Festivals and Seasonal Events

June: The **Dragon Boat Festival** derives from an ancient Chinese festival in which fishing communities would compete in long, shallow boats with dragon heads and tails, in honor of a poet who drowned himself to protest official corruption. (His friends took to boats and pounded their oars in the water while beating drums to scare away the fish who would have eaten the poet's body.) The races are held in the Outer Harbour, where the waterfront provides a natural grandstand. Teams from all over the world compete in gaily decorated boats, accompanied by drum beating and firecrackers.

Nov.: The **Macau Grand Prix** takes place on the third or fourth weekend in November. From the beginning of the week, the city is shattered with supercharged engines testing the 6-km (3.8-mi) Guia Circuit, which follows the city roads along the Outer Harbour to Guia Hill and around the reservoir. The Grand Prix was first staged in 1953 and the standard of performance has now reached world class. Today cars achieve speeds of 224 kph (140 mph) on the straightaways, with the lap record approaching 2 minutes, 20 seconds. The premier event is the Formula Three championship, with cars brought in from around the world. Hotel bookings during the Grand Prix are made far in advance; the weekend should be avoided by anyone not interested in motor racing.

What It Will Cost

Prices in Macau for hotels, restaurants, and shopping are between a third and a half lower than in Hong Kong.

Passports and Visas

Visas are not required by Portuguese citizens or nationals of the United States, Canada, the United Kingdom, Australia, New Zealand, France, West Germany, Austria, Belgium, the Netherlands, Switzerland, Sweden, Denmark, Norway, Italy, Greece, Spain, Japan, Thailand, the Philippines, Malaysia, Brazil (up to a six-month stay), or Hong Kong.

Currency

The official currency unit in Macau is the pataca, which is divided into 100 avos. Bank notes come in five denominations: 500, 100, 50, 10, and 5 patacas; coins are 5 and 1 patacas and 50, 20, and 10 avos. The pataca is pegged to the Hong Kong dollar, which circulates freely in Macau but not vice versa. At press time, the exchange rate was 7.80 patacas to the U.S. dollar.

Language

Portuguese is the official language, though since 95% of Macau's residents are Chinese, most speak Cantonese. English is widely understood.

Mail

The **General Post Office** (Largodo Senado, tel. 574491) and most hotels supply stamps—much in demand by collectors—and provide telex, cable, and facsimile services. Airmail letters cost from 3.30 patacas, postcards and aerograms 2.50 patacas.

Receiving Mail Macau's General Post Office offers Poste Restante, but there are no American Express or other mail holding offices.

Telephones

Telephone service is a bit erratic, with numbers constantly being changed; however, international calls are handled efficiently. Macau's country code is 853.

Information Call 121 for directory assistance. Operators speak English.

Arriving and Departing from Hong Kong

Travel agents and most Hong Kong hotels can arrange for tickets for the 64-km (40-mi) Hong Kong–Macau crossing. **Ticketmate** computer-booking outlets in Exchange Square (Central, Hong Kong Island) and the major Mass Transit Railway (MTR) stations sell tickets up to 28 days in advance for the Jetfoils. It's best to get the return ticket at the same time because it can be inconvenient to do so in Macau. Tickets can also be booked in Hong Kong by phone and with credit cards (Jetfoil, tel. 859–3288, AE, DC, V; hydrofoils and Jetcats, tel. 523–2136, AE, V). There is a HK$15 departure tax from Hong Kong, none from Macau.

By Plane At press time, helicopter service between Hong Kong and Macau was scheduled to begin in 1989. Contact MTIB (tel. 540–8180) for more information.

By Sea The vast majority of sailings for Macau use the Macau Terminal in the Shun Tak Centre (200 Connaught Rd.), a 10-minute walk west of Hong Kong's Central District. In many cases information is hard to obtain over the phone; it's best to call the MTIB (tel. 540–8180).

A fleet of Boeing **Jetfoils** provides the most popular service between Hong Kong and Macau. Carrying about 260 passengers, these craft ride comfortably on jet-propelled hulls at 40 knots and make the trip in about an hour. Jetfoils depart at least every half hour from 7 AM to dusk. The top deck of each vessel is first class, and there are nonsmoking sections on both decks. Fares for first class are HK$75 on weekdays, HK$80 on weekends and public holidays, and HK$95 on the night service. Lower-deck fares are HK$65, HK$70, and HK$85.

The **regular ferry service** is a pleasant, leisurely way of getting to Macau and takes about three hours. The fares range from HK$30 for aircraft-type seats to HK$150 for a VIP cabin.

Hong Kong Macau Hydrofoil Company (HMH) operates a fleet of **hydrofoils** that take about 75 minutes and make 22 round-trips a day between 8 AM and dusk. Fares are HK$46 weekdays, HK$58 weekends and holidays. HMH also operates three jet-propelled catamarans called **Jetcats,** which carry 215 passengers and make the trip in about 70 minutes, with 10 round-trips a day. Fares are HK$46 on weekdays, HK$58 on weekends.

The newest vessels on the Macau run are **High Speed Ferries,** which take about an hour and a half on five round-trips daily between 8 AM and 10:30 PM. These sleek, comfortable craft have a sun deck and first-class lounge. Fares are HK$46 first class, HK$38 economy class weekdays, HK$57 weekends, and HK$45 holidays.

Another relatively new service is by Sealink's **hover-ferries.** They carry 250 passengers and take about an hour. Fares are HK$45 weekdays, HK$56 weekends and holidays.

Getting Around

In the old parts of town and shopping areas, walking is the best means of transportation. Here the streets are narrow, often under repair, and invariably crowded with vehicles weaving between sidewalk vendors and parked cars, so that pedestrians often make the fastest progress.

By Pedicab This tricycle-drawn, two-seat carriage has been in business as long as there have been bicycles and paved roads in Macau, and a few look like originals. They cluster at the wharf, and their drivers hustle for customers, usually offering guide services. To appreciate the pedicab, especially on a sunny day, take one along the Praia Grande and admire the avenue of ancient trees and the seascape of islands and fishing junks. The city center is not a congenial place for pedicabs, and the hilly districts are impossible. Of course you have to haggle, but you shouldn't pay more than HK$15 for a short trip.

By Taxi There are usually plenty of taxis at the wharf, outside hotels, and cruising the streets. All are metered and most are air-conditioned and reasonably comfortable, but the cabbies speak little English, so it's best to carry a bilingual map or name card in Chinese. Flag-fall is 4.50 patacas for the first 1,500 m (about 1 mi), 60 avos for each additional 250 m (¼ mi). Drivers don't expect more than small change as a tip. For trips to Taipa there is a five-pataca surcharge, and to Coloane 10 patacas.

By Bicycle Bicycles are available for rent at about 10 patacas an hour from shops on Avenida Dom Joao 1V in the city and near the Taipa bus station.

By Hired Car Self-drive Jeeplike minivehicles called mokes are more expensive but fun and ideal for touring. International and most national driving licenses are valid. Rates are HK$250 weekdays, HK$280 a day weekends; special packages in conjunction with hotels are available. For Macau mokes contact tel. 543–4190 or Ticketmate in Hong Kong, or the office at the wharf in Macau (tel. 378851). For Avis mokes call tel. 542–2189 in Hong Kong, or their office in the Mandarin Oriental (tel. 567888, ext. 3004).

Guided Tours

Regular and customized tours, for individuals and groups, by bus or car, are easily arranged in Macau, and provide the maximum amount of sightseeing in a short space of time.

There are two basic tours. One covers mainland Macau with stops at the Chinese border, Kun Iam Temple, St. Paul's, and Penha Hill. It lasts about 3½ hours. The other standard tour consists of a two-hour trip to the islands across the bridge, to see old Chinese villages, temples, beaches, the trotting track, and the University of East Asia.

The most comfortable way to tour is by chauffeur-driven car. For a maximum of four passengers it costs HK$100 an hour. Taxis can also be rented for touring.

Most people book tours with Macau agents while in Hong Kong or through travel agents before leaving home. If you do, the cost will include transport to Macau. There are many licensed tour operators in Macau. Among those specializing in English-speaking visitors, and who have offices in Hong Kong, are **Able Tours** (8 Connaught Rd. W, tel. 545–9993), **Estoril Tours** (Macau Wharf, tel. 559–1028), **International Tourism** (143 Connaught Rd., tel. 541–2011), **Macau Tours** (287 Des Voeux Rd., tel. 542–2338), and **Sintra Tours** (Macau Wharf, tel. 540–8028).

Exploring Macau

Numbers in the margin correspond with points of interest on the Macau map.

Tour 1: The Outer Harbor

The history of Portuguese Macau almost came to an end at the ❶ **Outer Harbor** in 1622, when the Dutch fleet landed a large invasion force to capture the rich port. From here the troops attacked Guia and Monte forts, only to be defeated by a ragtag army of Jesuit priests, Portuguese soldiers, and African slaves.

Today the harbor is designed to welcome all arrivals. On the 1.6-km (1-mi) avenue from the wharf are the Mandarin Orien- ❷ tal, Presidente, and Lisboa hotels, the **Jai Alai Stadium** and its ❸ casino, the new **Macau Forum** for conferences and sports events, and the grandstand for the annual motor and motorcycle Grand Prix events.

❹ Overlooking the harbor are the slopes of **Guia Hill,** embossed with new homes, a convent, and a hospital, and topped with a fort and the oldest lighthouse on the China coast, built in 1865 and still a beacon for ships.

Tour 2: Downtown

For a relatively straightforward introduction to the many-layered and often contradictory character of the city, you can ❺ stroll the main street, **Avenida Almeida Ribeiro,** generally known by its Chinese name, **Sanmalo.** It begins a short walk from the Lisboa and ends at the floating casino in the inner harbor. Within this short distance you find colonial Portugal, traditional China, and modern Asia locked in an architectural and social embrace.

Like a European city, the focal point of this downtown is a large square with a fountain and plaza surrounded by several impres- ❻ sive buildings. The **Leal Senado** (Loyal Senate) has a classically simple facade, garden courtyard, and Edwardian council chambers. The Senate acts as a municipal government, taking care of parks, garbage collection, and the police force. The library in the Leal Senado, a superb copy of a classic Portuguese library, contains possibly the best collection of books in English about China's history, society, economy, and culture. *Open Mon.–Sat. 1–7.*

❼ The Senate president is by tradition the president of the **Santa Casa da Misericordia** (Holy House of Mercy), the oldest Chris-

Macau

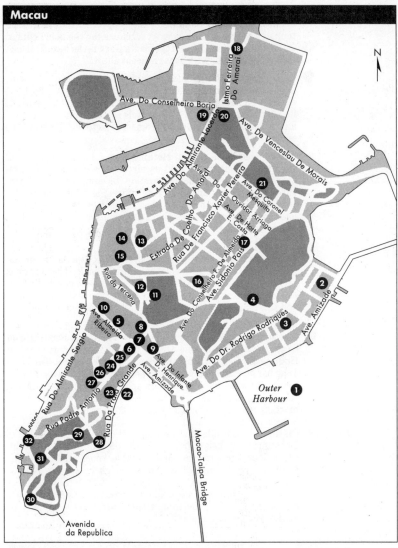

A-Ma Temple, **31**

Avenida Almeida Ribeiro, **5**

Bela Vista Hotel, **28**

Bishop's Palace, **29**

Camões Grotto and Garden, **14**

Camões Museum, **13**

Canidrome, **19**

Dom Pedro V, **24**

Guia Hill, **4**

Jai Alai Stadium, **2**

Kun Iam Temple, **21**

Leal Senado, **6**

Lin Fung Miu, **20**

Lou Lim Ieoc Garden, **16**

Macau Forum, **3**

Maritime Museum, **32**

Memorial Home of Dr. Sun Yat-Sen, **17**

Monte Hill, **11**

Old Protestant Cemetery, **15**

Outer Harbour, **1**

Palacio, **23**

Portas do Cerco, **18**

Post Office, **9**

Pousada de São Tiago, **30**

Praia Grande, **22**

Rua Cinco do Outubro, **10**

St. Augustine, **25**

St. Lawrence, **27**

St. Paul's, **12**

Santa Casa da Misericordia, **7**

São Domingos Church, **8**

Seminary of St. Joseph's, **26**

tian charity on the China Coast. Its headquarters occupy a handsome baroque building in the square, and its offices administer homes for the elderly, kitchens for the poor, clinics,

8 and a leprosarium. Behind the Santa Casa is the beautiful **São Domingos** church, with a magnificent altar.

9 The central **Post Office** and telephone exchange, as well as some handsome old commercial buildings with arcades at street level, are also in the square. The São Domingos produce market, its narrow streets packed with stalls selling fruit, vegetables, and wholesale-price clothing from local factories, leads off the square.

Sanmalo has some regular clothing stores, but the majority of shoppers come here for gold jewelry, watches and clocks, Chinese and Western medicines, brandy, biscuits, and salted fish. Interspersed are banks, lawyers' offices, and the Central Hotel. Now a rather dingy, inexpensive place to stay, the Central used to contain the city's only casinos, where the *fan tan* (button game) attracted the high rollers and the top-floor brothel did a thriving business.

The heart of the old red-light district was Rua da Felicidade ("Street of Happiness"), which runs off Sanmalo. The area does preserve the atmosphere of a prewar China-coast community, especially in the evening. After sunset, food stalls with stools and tiny tables are set out. Lights blaze from open-front restaurants, laundries, tailor shops, and family living rooms.

10 Another side street off Sanmalo worth a detour is **Rua Cinco do Outubro,** which contains one of the best-looking traditional Chinese medicine shops anywhere. The Farmacia Tai Ning Tong has an elaborately carved wood facade and a cavernous interior, its walls lined with huge apothecary jars of medicinal roots, deer horn, and other assorted marvels. In a corner are mortars and pestles for making potions to order.

Time Out On the opposite side of the street is the **Lok Kok teahouse.** It looks undistinguished from the outside, but climb up to the third floor and discover an incredible room with pyramid-vaulted wood ceilings, skylights, brightly carved pillars, stained-glass windows, and walls hung with scrolls and mirrors. It is open from 4 AM to mid-afternoon and caters to a wide cross-section of the population, from wharf workers to bankers, market porters to students.

Tour 3: The Old Citadel

11 The most remarkable early buildings in Macau were on **Monte Hill.** Built by the Jesuits, they included a fort, a college, and the collegiate church of the Mother of God, commonly known as

12 **St. Paul's.** By the early 17th century, the college had become a university for scholar-missionaries en route to the courts of China and Japan. The church was declared the most magnificent in Asia, and a small town of merchants, clerics, and craftsmen grew up around the Monte.

Today this area is the heart of old Macau for visitors and is easily reached from Senate Square via Rua da S. Domingos. The college was destroyed in a fire in 1835, and the ruins of the fort now form a quiet belvedere. Of the church, only the great stone facade remains, but it is less a ruin than a dramatic symbol of Macau and certainly the leading attraction.

Traditional craftsmen, still in business carving camphorwood chests and family shrines, hand-beating metal utensils, making barrels and mattresses, and weaving bird cages, occupy the jumble of narrow streets below the church. Tercena and Estalagens are the most interesting streets.

⑬ Following either Rua de S. Paulo or Tercena, you reach Praça Luis de Camões and the former **Camões Museum.** Named for Portugal's greatest poet, the building—constructed in the 1770s—is a superb example of Iberian colonial architecture, with spacious, high-ceilinged rooms and tall windows shaded by louvered shutters. In the late 18th and early 19th centuries it was rented by the British East India Company as a residence for the men who controlled much of the China trade of their time. Camões Museum is being renovated to house the local cultural Foundation, and a new museum is being planned.

⑭ Next to the old museum is the **Camões Grotto and Garden,** frequented from dawn to dusk by people practicing t'ai chi ch'uan (shadowboxing), men carrying their caged songbirds for a country walk, young lovers, students, and groups huddled over games of Chinese chess.

⑮ The **Old Protestant Cemetery,** a "corner of some foreign field" for over 150 Americans and British, is opposite the entrance to the garden. It is a well-kept and tranquil retreat, where tombstones recall the troubles and triumphs of Westerners in 19th-century China. Some of the names are familiar, including Captain Henry Churchill, great granduncle of Sir Winston; Joseph Adams, grandson of John Adams, the second U.S. president; Robert Morrison, who translated the Bible into Chinese; and Thomas Beale, the opium king.

Tour 4: Restoration Row

Conservation and common sense don't always go together, but there is an outstanding example of such a match in Macau's Restoration Row, a row of houses built in the 1920s in symmetrical arcadian style, on the **Avenida do Conselheiro Ferreira de Almeida,** a block or so from the Royal and Estoril hotels. The owners of the houses were persuaded to forgo huge profits and sell to the government. The houses were then converted into homes for the Archives, the National Library, the Education Department, and university offices. The exteriors were extensively repaired and the interiors transformed.

⑯ Continuing along the avenue, you come to Estrada de Adolfo Loureiro and the **Lou Lim Ieoc Garden,** a classic Chinese garden modeled on those of old Soochow. Built in the 19th century by a wealthy Chinese merchant, the enclosed garden is a miniaturized landscape with forests of bamboo and flowering bushes, a small lake filled with lotus and golden carp, and a traditional nine-turn bridge.

⑰ Another place of interest in this area is the **Memorial Home of Dr. Sun Yat-Sen.** Dr. Sun, father of the 1911 Chinese revolution, worked as a physician in Macau from 1892 to 1894, and some of his family stayed here after his death. The memorial home, in strange mock-Moorish style, was built in the mid-1930s. It contains photographs, books, and souvenirs of Sun and his long years of exile in different parts of the world. *1 Rua Ferreira do Amaral. Admission free. Open Mon. and Wed.–Fri. 10–1, weekends 3–5.*

Tour 5: On the Doorstep of China

The date 1849 and a solemn quotation from Camões are inscribed on the stone gate—**Portas do Cerco**—that leads to China. The gate is closed at night, but throughout the day it sees a steady stream of two-way traffic. From China come farmers carrying morning-fresh produce in bamboo baskets or on trucks, along with Chinese officials involved in joint business ventures and Macau and Hong Kong residents returning from visits with their families. From Macau the traffic consists of busloads of tourists and groups of business people.

Close by the border are two very different attractions. On one side is the **Canidrome,** where greyhound races are enthusiastically followed. On the other side of the road is the **Lin Fung Miu,** or Temple of the Lotus, once used to provide overnight accommodations for mandarins traveling between Macau and Canton. Today it is visited for its exquisite facade of clay bas-reliefs and classic architecture.

The Buddhist **Kun Iam Temple,** nearby on the Avenida do Coronel Mesquita, should not be missed. It has a wealth of statuary and decoration, and in the courtyard is a stone table where the first Sino-American treaty was signed in 1844 by the Viceroy of Canton and President John Tyler's envoy, Caleb Cushing.

Tour 6: Peninsula Macau

The narrow, hilly peninsula stretching from the main street to Barra Point and the Pousada de Sao Tiago is quintessential Macau, very Portuguese and very Chinese, ancient and uncomfortably modern. It is bounded on one side by the **Praia Grande** and its extension, Avenida da Republica, a graceful, banyan-shaded boulevard where people fish from the seawall or play Chinese chess.

The cargo and fishing wharfs of the inner harbor, with their traditional Chinese shophouses—the ground floors occupied by ship's chandlers, net makers, ironmongers, and shops selling spices and salted fish—are on the opposite side of the peninsula. In between there are several areas of historic or scenic interest. One is Largo de Sto. Agostinho, or St. Augustine Square, which is reached by climbing the steep street next to the Senate, or from the Praia Grande and the pink-and-white **Palacio,** which houses government offices.

Taking the Travessa do Paiva to the right of the Palacio, you pass the trimly restored headquarters of the Department of Tourism. Beyond is the dimple-stone ramp to the square, which looks as if it came all of a piece from 19th-century Portugal. To the left is the **Dom Pedro V** theater, built in 1859 and modeled after a European court theater. Opposite is the imposing church of **St. Augustine,** and next door is Casa Ricci, offices for one of the most active Catholic charities in Macau. Across the square is the **Seminary of St. Joseph's,** home of preeminent local historian and living legend Father Manuel Teixeira and a collection of religious art by 17th-century European and Japanese painters.

Retracing your steps down the ramp and continuing along the Rua de São Lourenco, you reach the elegant twin-tower church
㉗ of **St. Lawrence** and the Salesian Institute, a technical school that stands on part of the site of the headquarters of the British East India Company. From here you can take the Rua do Pe.
㉘ Antonio to the **Bela Vista Hotel** or return to the Praia Grande and follow it to the Calcada do Bom Parto. Either way, you'll want to stop and visit the Bela Vista, a century-old landmark hotel.

Farther up the hill is one of the best lookouts in Macau, the
㉙ courtyard of the **Bishop's Palace** and Penha Chapel. The palace is always closed, and the chapel is opened only on the feast day of Our Lady of Penha, patroness of seafarers, and on the Feast of Fatima.

㉚ At the far end of the peninsula is Barra Point, with the **Pousada de São Tiago,** a Portuguese inn built into the ruined founda-
㉛ tions of a 17th-century fort; the **A-Ma Temple,** Macau's oldest and most venerated place of worship (which gave its name to
㉜ Macau); and the new **Maritime Museum.** This gem of a museum has been a consistent favorite since its doors opened at the end of 1987. It is ideally located—where the first Chinese and later first Portuguese made landfall—and is housed in an imaginatively restored colonial house facing the harbor. The old number-one wharf was restored to provide a pier for a fishing junk, tug, dragon boat, sampan, Vietnamese refugees' boat, and a copy of one of the "flower boat" floating pleasure palaces that once sailed along the China coast. Inside are displays on the local fishing industry, models of historic vessels, charts of great voyages by Portuguese and Chinese explorers, navigational aids, and much, much more. *Tel. 595481. Admission free. Open Wed.–Mon. 10–6.*

Tour 7: Taipa Island

Linked to the city by the graceful 2.5-km (1.6-mi) bridge, Taipa can be reached by bus (including a double-decker with open-top roof deck) or taxi. Some residents jog over it daily.

Taipa and Coloane, its neighbor, are Macau's New Territories, having been ceded by China only in 1887. Until the building of the bridge, both islands led a somnolent existence, interrupted only by occasional pirate raids. Taipa's economy depended on the raising of ducks and the manufacture of firecrackers. There are still some duck farms to be seen, as well as some firecracker factories, which look like ancestral Chinese villages but now produce fireworks for the American and European markets.

The **village of Taipa** is a tight maze of houses and shops in the traditional mold. It is changing, due to the island's new prosperity, and now boasts banks, a two-story municipal market, air-conditioned shops, and several excellent restaurants. Below the church of Our Lady of Carmel is the **Taipa House Museum.** This finely restored 1920s mansion contains authentic period furniture, decorations, and furnishings that recapture the atmosphere and lifestyle of a middle-class Macanese family in the early part of the century. *Taipa Praia, tel. 327088. Admission free. Open Tues.–Sun. 9–5.*

Another restored building worth a visit is the **Pou Tai Un Temple,** a short walk from the Hyatt Regency. It is famed for its vegetarian restaurant (the vegetables are grown in an adjoining garden), and has been embellished with a new yellow tile pavilion and statue of the Buddhist goddess of mercy.

For Buddhists, Taoists, and Confucians, Taipa is a favored, last, earthly address. They are buried or their bones stored in the massive **United Chinese Cemetery,** which covers the cliff on the northeastern coast of the island. It is lavishly decorated with colored tiles and assorted religious images.

The northeast section of Taipa provides a stunning contrast, thanks to a recent building boom. Just across the bridge is the luxurious Hyatt Hotel and the hilltop **University of East Asia.** On the western side of the island is the raceway of the **Macau Horse Racing Club,** 50 acres of reclaimed land with an ultra-modern, five-story grandstand, and a track that is scheduled to open for flat racing in September 1989.

Tour 8: Coloane Island

Situated at the end of a 2.4-km (1.5-mi) causeway from Taipa, the larger, hillier island of Coloane has so far been spared from development. About a 25-minute drive from the city, it is generally considered to be remote. This makes it a popular spot for relaxed holidays, especially at the attractive 22-room **Pousada de Coloane.** There is a long beach below the Pousada and another at **Hac Sa** (Black Sands). Both are clean, although the water is Pearl River ocher. There are plenty of cafés for food and drink.

The village of Coloane, with its old tile-roof houses, the Tam Kong Temple, and the **Chapel of St. Francis Xavier,** are interesting to overseas visitors. The picturesque chapel, with its cream-and-white facade and bell tower, was built in 1928. Outside its door is a monument surrounded by cannonballs commemorating the local defeat of a pirate band in 1910, Macau's last encounter with old-style pirates. There are some important relics inside the chapel. The most sacred is an arm bone of St. Francis Xavier, who died in 1552 on an island 80 km (50 mi) from here while waiting to begin his mission in China.

Other relics are the bones of the martyrs of Nagasaki and those of Vietnamese Christians executed in the early 17th century. By a strange irony, although it is not so strange for Macau, Coloane has a sizable Vietnamese community of boat people who fled their country and now await resettlement in a large, open camp administered by the Catholic church.

Coloane Park, on the west coast of the island, is the newest of Macau's natural preserves. Its centerpiece is a walk-in aviary containing more than 200 species of birds, including the rare Palawan peacock and the crested white pheasant. Nearby is a pond with black swans, a playground, a restaurant, a picnic area, and a nature trail around the hillside. Developed by the Forestry Department, the park has an impressive collection of exotic trees and shrubs. *Tel. 569684. Admission charge. Open daily 9–7.*

Spectator Sports

Greyhound Racing Races are held in the scenic, open-air Canidrome, close to the Chinese border. Most dogs are imported from Australia. The 10,000-seat stadium has rows and rows of betting windows and stalls for food and drink. *Ave. General Castelo Branco, tel. 574413. Races held weekends and holidays at 8 PM.*

Horse Racing The raceway, built for Asia's first trotting track, is located on reclaimed land close to the Hyatt Regency Hotel. The Macau Trotting Club spared no expense: The five-story grandstand accommodates 15,000 people, 6,000 of them in air-conditioned comfort. There are restaurants, bars, and some of the most sophisticated betting equipment available. Unfortunately, trotting races did not bring in sufficient revenue and the track was converted for flat racing in mid-1989. Tel. 327211.

Jai Alai Played in a custom-built stadium opposite the ferry pier, jai alai has never really caught on in Macau. Local cynics claim that human players can't be trusted the way horses and dogs can. *Games weeknights 7–midnight, Sat. and Sun. 2 PM.*

Stadium Sports A variety of sporting events are held at the **Macau Forum**'s multipurpose hall, including the world table tennis championships. Call the Macau Forum (tel. 568711), or the Tourism Department for a schedule of events.

Dining

By the time the Portuguese arrived in Macau, they had adopted many of the ingredients grown and used in the Americas and Africa—peanuts, green beans, pineapples, lettuce, sweet potatoes, shrimp paste, a variety of spices from Africa and India—and brought them to China. In China, the Portuguese discovered tea, rhubarb, tangerines, ginger, soy sauce, and the Cantonese art of quick-frying to seal in the flavor.

A good example of Macanese food is called Portuguese chicken: chunks of chicken baked with potatoes, coconut, tomato, olive oil, curry, olives, and saffron. Extremely popular family dishes include *minchi* (minced pork and diced potatoes panfried with soy), pork baked with tamarind, and duckling cooked in its own blood, all of which are served with rice.

The favorites of Portuguese cuisine are regular menu items. The beloved *bacalhau* (codfish) is served baked, boiled, grilled, deep fried with potato, or stewed with onion, garlic, and eggs. Portuguese sardines, country soups such as *caldo verde* and *sopa alentejana*, and dishes of rabbit are on the menus of many restaurants. Sharing the bill of fare are colonial favorites: from Brazil come *feijoadas*, stews of beans, pork, spicy sausage, and vegetables; Mozambique was the origin of African chicken, baked or grilled in fiery *piri-piri* peppers. In addition, some kitchens prepare baked quail, curried crab, and the delectable Macau sole that rivals its Dover cousin. And then there are the giant prawns that are served in a spicy sauce—one of Macau's special dining pleasures.

Not surprisingly, Chinese restaurants predominate in Macau. In addition, several restaurants offer excellent Japanese, Thai, Korean, Indonesian, and even Burmese meals. One of the best bargains in Macau is wine, particularly the delicious Portuguese *vinho verde*, a slightly sparkling wine, and some reds and whites, such as the Dao family of wines.

Dress is informal, and nowhere are jackets and ties required. The Department of Tourism's brochure "Eating Out in Macau" is very useful.

Highly recommended restaurants are indicated by a star ★.

Category	Cost*
Expensive	over 150 patacas (US$19)
Moderate	50–150 patacas (US$6.50–US$19)
Inexpensive	under 50 patacas (US$6.50)

per person, including service and half a bottle of wine

Macanese-Portuguese
Expensive

Fortaleza. The setting of this exquisite restaurant would be reason enough to dine here. Located in the traditional Portuguese inn in the 17th-century Barra fortress, it offers views of an idyllic seascape of green islands and sailing junks. The decor and atmosphere recall the days of the Portuguese empire, with crystal lamps, hand-carved mahogany furniture, blue and white tiles, and plush drapes. The food is almost as marvelous, with a good selection of classic Macanese dishes, such as baked codfish, quail, and spicy prawns as well as Continental dishes. *Pousada de Sao Tiago, Ave. Republica, tel. 78111. Reservations recommended for evenings. Dress: informal. AE, DC, MC, V.*

Moderate
★

A Galera. This is an elegant, handsomely decorated restaurant, with blue-and-white-tile wall panels, black-and-white-tile floors, pearl-gray table linen, Wedgwood dishware, a bar with high-back armchairs, and views of the S. Francisco fortress. The atmosphere and menu indicate high prices, but in fact this is not so. Main courses include *bacalhau a bras* and squid stuffed with spiced meat; also try the rich, homemade soups and dessert souffles. *Lisboa Hotel, 3rd floor of new wing, tel. 577666, ext. 1103. Reservations not necessary. Dress: informal. AE, DC, MC, V.*

Afonso's. One of the most attractively designed restaurants in Macau, Afonso's is horseshoe shaped, with Portuguese tiles on the wall, floral cushions on the rattan chairs, spotless table linen, and dishware made to order in Europe. Picture windows frame the gardens outside. The menu is imaginative and the prices incredibly reasonable. The menu is a good balance of Macanese favorites and regional Portuguese dishes, including *açorda* bread, seafood soup, and *frango na pucara*, chicken in a clay pot. There is an excellent wine list and the service is cheerful and efficient. *Hyatt Regency Hotel, Taipa Island, tel. 321234. Reservations recommended. Dress: informal. AE, DC, MC, V.*

Fat Siu Lau. Opened in 1903, this is the oldest European restaurant in Macau and one which has maintained the highest standards of food and service. Years ago it looked like the average Chinese café, but now each of its three floors is elegantly furnished and decorated. The top two are perfect for romantic candle-lit dinners; the ground floor seems to have been transported from Portugal. The walls of bare brick are partly covered with white stucco, blue tiles, and green vines. There is also a false half-roof with Cantonese tiles. The menu is tried and true. Regulars automatically order the roast pigeon Fat Siu Lau made famous. Other favorites are African chicken, sardines, and ox breast with herbs. *64 Rua da Felicidade, tel. 573585. Reservations not necessary. Dress: informal. No credit cards.*

Galo. This new restaurant proves what can be done with flair and dedication. A traditional Taipa village house was gutted, then decorated in bright Iberian colors and Macanese touches, such as Chinese rattan hats for lamp shades and big porcelain plant pots. The food is also country-style. One specialty is from Madeira and consists of chunks of orange-flavored lamb on a suspended skewer; others include rice with chicken in a hot sauce, codfish salad with tomatoes and green olives, and curry crabs. Topping off the pleasure of dining here are scenes of village life viewed through the lattice windows. *47 Rua do Cunha, Taipa Island, tel. 327423. Reservations not necessary. Dress: informal. No credit cards.*

Henri's Galley. Situated on the banyan-lined waterfront (with some tables on the sidewalk), this is a favorite with local residents and visitors from Hong Kong. The decor reflects owner Henri Wong's former career as a ship's steward: There is a complete "alphabet" of signal flags strung from the ceiling, pictures of old ships on the walls, and red and green lights to keep passengers on an even keel. The food is consistently good, with probably the biggest and best spicy prawns in town, delicious African and Portuguese chicken, Portuguese soups, and fried rice, complete with hot Portuguese sausage. *4 Avenida da Republica, tel. 76207. Reservations recommended, especially on weekends. Dress: informal. MC, V.*

Pinocchio's. Until the opening of the Hyatt Hotel, the only reason most visitors went to Taipa was to eat at this restaurant. The courtyard is covered with a corrugated tin roof and lighted with harsh fluorescent strips. The simple café chairs and tables are rickety, and service can be very casual, especially on busy weekends. Neither is much English spoken. However, there's no better place for curry crabs, baked quail, and steamed shrimp. Other specialties are superlative leg of lamb and roast suckling pig, which have to be ordered in advance. *4 Rua do Sol, Taipa Island, tel. 327128. Reservations essential on weekends. Dress: informal. Closed first Mon. and Tues. of the month. No credit cards.*

Pousada de Coloane. This is 20 minutes by car from the city, by Macau standards a long, long way to go for a meal, but many residents and Hong Kong regulars consider it well worth the trip. The setting is fine, with a large, open terrace. When the weather is good, an alfresco lunch overlooking the beach and water is marvelous. For indoor dining, the restaurant is reminiscent of many in Lisbon, with dark wood panels, colorful tile floors, and folk art decorations. Service can be rather haphazard, but the food is usually excellent. Among the specialties are feijoadas, grilled sardines, and stuffed squid. Best of all is the Sunday buffet, with a great selection of Macanese dishes for only 70 patacas per person. *Praia de Cheoc Van, Coloane Island, tel. 328144. Reservations not necessary. Dress: informal. MC, V.*

Lodging

Highly recommended hotels are indicated by a star ★.

Category	Cost*
Expensive	500–900 patacas (US$64–US$115)
Moderate	300–500 patacas (US$38–US$64)
Inexpensive	under 300 patacas (US$38)

*All prices are per standard double room; add 10% service and 5% tax.

Expensive

★ **Hyatt Regency and Taipa Island Resort.** Opened in 1983, the Hyatt is the first hotel in Asia with guest rooms that were fully prefabricated (in the United States) and shipped as modules. They conform to Hyatt Regency's high standards, with all the modern conveniences and attractive furnishings. The public areas were built in Macau and combine the best of Iberian architecture and Chinese decor. The foyer is a spacious lounge with white arches, masses of potted plants, and fabulous Chinese lacquer panels. A small casino is located off the lobby. The Taipa Resort, which adjoins the hotel, has a complete health spa, sporting facilities, a large pool and botanical garden, a jogging track, and a marvelous Macanese restaurant. *Taipa Island, tel. 321234, in Hong Kong 559–0168, elsewhere Hyatt Hotels Reservations. 365 rooms. Facilities: restaurants, bars, casino, health spa, outdoor pool, 2 squash courts, 4 tennis courts, sauna, whirlpool, gym, massage, beauty parlor/barber, baby-sitting, car rental, tours, shuttle bus service to wharf. AE, DC, MC, V.*

Mandarin Oriental. Built on the site of the old Pan Am seaplane terminal, with views of the Pearl River and islands, this is a beautifully designed and furnished hotel. Its lobby features reproductions of Portuguese art and antiques, the Grill Room has a wood ceiling inlaid with small oil paintings, and the Cafe Girassol could have been transported from the Algarve. Guest rooms have marble bathrooms and teak furntiure. *Avenida da Amizade, tel. 567888, in Hong Kong 548–7676, elsewhere Mandarin Oriental reservation offices. 438 rooms. Facilities: restaurants, bars, casino, 2 outdoor pools, 2 tennis courts, 2 squash courts, gym, sauna, massage, beauty parlor, car rental, tours, shuttle bus to wharf. AE, DC, MC, V.*

★ **Pousada de Sao Tiago.** This is a traditional Portuguese inn that was built, with enormous imagination and dedication, into the ruins of a 17th-century fortress. For instance, the ancient trees that had taken over the fort were not cut down but incorporated into the design. A classic European fountain plays over the site of the old but still operative water cistern. Furnishings, made to order in Portugal, include mahogany period furniture, blue-and-white-tile walls, and crystal lamps, plus terra-cotta floor tiles from China and carpets woven in Hong Kong. The entrance is the original entry to the fort, and natural springs have been trained to flow down the rocky wall in tile channels on either side of the staircase. Each of the rooms, complete with four-poster beds and marble bathrooms, has a balcony for great views with breakfast or cocktails. *Avenida da Republica, tel. 78111, in Hong Kong 810–8332. 23 rooms. Facilities: restau-*

rant, bar, terrace, outdoor pool, chapel, car rental. AE, DC, MC, V.

Ritz. This new, exclusive hotel stands on a rise behind the Bela Vista and occupies a commanding view of the bay and islands. *Rua Comendador Kou Ho Neng. 46 rooms. Facilities: indoor pool, health club, café, restaurant.*

Royal. The Royal has an excellent location, with fine views of Guia, the city, and Inner Harbour. The marble-clad lobby boasts a marble fountain and lounge, plus some excellent shops. *2 Estrada da Vitoria, tel. 552222, in Hong Kong 542–2033, elsewhere Dai-Ichi Hotels reservation offices. 380 rooms. Facilities: restaurants, sing-along bar, lounge, indoor pool, squash court, health club, sauna, gym, shuttle bus to wharf and casino. AE, DC, MC, V.*

Moderate **Beverly Plaza.** Opened in 1989, this twin-tower hotel is almost next door to the Lisboa and close to the wharf and Macau Forum. It is designed to appeal to business people with spacious, attractive rooms. *Avenida do Dr. Rodrigo Rodrigues, tel. 337755. 300 rooms and suites. Facilities: 2 restaurants, bar, shuttle bus to wharf, China tours. AE, DC, MC, V.*

Estoril. In the residential district, this hotel caters primarily to Hong Kong Chinese and patrons of the Paris Nightclub, on the ground floor. It has a good Chinese restaurant and elaborate sauna. *Avenida Sidonio Pais, tel. 572081. 89 rooms. Facilities: restaurant, sauna, nightclub. DC, MC, V.*

Guia. Built by Chinese interests on the hill above the Royal Hotel, and just below Guia Hill, Guia was originally designed to be an apartment block until its award-winning architect was asked to convert it to a small hotel. It opened in March 1989. *Estrada do Engenheiro Trigo, tel. 513888, in Hong Kong 770–9303. 89 rooms. Facilities: restaurant, café, sauna. AE, DC, MC, V.*

Lisboa. Rising above a two-story casino, with walls of mustard-color tiles, frilly white window frames, and a roof shaped like a giant roulette wheel, the main tower of the Lisboa has, for better or worse, become one of the popular symbols of Macau and is an inescapable landmark. A new wing houses the Crazy Paris Show, the superb A Galera restaurant, a disco, billiards hall, and raucus children's game room. *Avenida da Amizade, tel. 577666, in Hong Kong 559–1028. 750 rooms with bath. Facilities: restaurants, bars, casino, game rooms, disco, theater, bowling center, sauna, outdoor pool, tours, shuttle bus to wharf. AE, DC, MC, V.*

Metropole. This centrally located hotel is managed by the China Travel Service, and it contains an office where bookings can easily be made for trips to China. It has pleasant, comfortable rooms and an excellent Portuguese-Macanese restaurant. *63 Rua da Praia Grande, tel. 88166, in Hong Kong 540–6333. 109 rooms. Facilities: restaurant, China tour arrangements. MC, V.*

Pousada de Coloane. This small, delightful resort inn features a huge terrace overlooking a good sandy beach, a pool, and a superb restaurant serving excellent Macanese and Portuguese food. The rooms have good-size balconies and stocked refrigerators. *Praia de Cheoc Van, Coloane Island, tel. 328144, in Hong Kong 369–6922. 22 rooms with bath. Facilities: restaurant, bar, terrace, outdoor pool, shuttle bus to wharf. MC, V.*

Presidente. The Presidente has an excellent location and is very popular with Hong Kong visitors. It offers an agreeable lobby lounge, European and Chinese restaurants, the best Korean food in town, a sauna, and a great disco with a skylight roof. *Avenida da Amizade, tel. 553888, in Hong Kong 526–6873, elsewhere Utell International reservations offices. 340 rooms. Facilities: restaurants, sauna, nightclub/disco. AE, DC, MC, V.*

Sintra. A sister hotel of the Lisboa, the Sintra is quieter, with few diversions apart from a sauna and European restaurant and bar. It is ideally located, overlooking the Praia Grande bay and within easy walking distance of the Lisboa and downtown. *Avenida Dom Joao 1V, tel. 85111, in Hong Kong 540–8028. 236 rooms. Facilities: restaurant, bar, tours, shuttle bus to casino. AE, DC, MC, V.*

Inexpensive   **Bela Vista.** One of Macau's great delights is to sit on the spacious balcony of the Bela Vista and have tea or cocktails while enjoying the panoramic view. The rooms are big and usually in need of redecoration, the food quality varies from excellent to awful, and service can be very slow, but no one will deny the appeal of the atmosphere here. *8 Rua Comendador Kou Ho Neng, tel. 573821, in Hong Kong 540–8180. 25 rooms. Facilities: restaurant, bar. AE, DC, MC, V.*

Central. In the heart of town, this was once the home of Macau's only legal casino and best brothel. Now it is a budget hotel with clean but basic rooms and an excellent Chinese restaurant. *Avenida Almeida Ribeiro, tel. 77730. 160 rooms. Facilities: restaurant. AE, MC, V.*

Nightlife

According to old movies and novels about the China coast, Macau was a city of opium dens, wild gambling, international spies, and slinky ladies of the night. It might come as a letdown to find the city fairly somnolent after sunset. Most people spend their evenings at the casinos or over long dinners.

Theater   **Lisboa Theater.** Apart from a few concerts by visiting performers or shows by local artists, theater in Macau means the Crazy Paris Show at the Lisboa, first staged in the late 1970s. The stripper-dancers come from Europe, Australia, and the Americas, while the choreographer and director are Parisian professionals. The show is very sophisticated and cleverly staged. *Lisboa Hotel, 2nd floor, new wing, tel. 377666, ext. 195. Daily shows at 8:30 and 10 PM, with additional shows on weekends and holidays at 11:30 PM. Admission: HK$90 weekdays, HK$100 weekends and holidays. Tickets available at hotel desks, Hong Kong and Macau ferry terminals, and the theater.*

Discos   The **Green Parrot** is both elegant and fun, with a good selection of music and a professional disc jockey. *Hyatt Regency Hotel, tel. 321234. Admission: 52 patacas weekdays, 72 patacas weekends and holidays; includes one drink. Open 9 PM–4 AM.*

The **Skylight** is a disco and nightclub, with floorshows by English strip-tease artists. *Presidente Hotel, Ave. da Amizade, tel. 533888. Admission: 48 patacas; includes one drink. Open 9 PM–4 AM.*

The **Mikado** disco is a bright, brassy place with high-tech lighting and a lively crowd. *Lisboa Hotel, new wing, tel. 577666. Admission: 50 patacas; includes one drink. Open 9 PM–4 AM.*

The **Paris Nightclub** is the most popular in Macau among locals and Hong Kong visitors. Like other clubs in the city, it has Thai and Filipino hostesses and good music. It also has an attractive decor, a good dance floor, and an excellent band. *Estoril Hotel, Ave. Sidonio Pais, tel. 568317. The minimum charge is 33 patacas weekdays, 45 patacas weekends and holidays. Open 9:30 PM–4 AM.*

Casinos   There are casinos in the **Lisboa, Mandarin Oriental,** and **Hyatt Regency** hotels, the **Jai Alai Stadium,** and the **Palacio de Macau,** usually known as the floating casino. No one under 18 is allowed in, although identity cards are not checked. Betting limits are posted, but high rollers are not discouraged by such things. There are 24-hour money exchanges, but most gamblers use Hong Kong dollars.

4 Indonesia

*by Nigel Fisher
and Lois
Anderson*

The sheer size of Indonesia is mind boggling. The nation consists of 13,677 islands (more than half of them uninhabited) stretching for 5,120 km (3,200 mi) from the Pacific to the Indian Ocean. From north to south, the islands form a 1,760-km (1,100-mi) bridge between Asia and Australia.

The size and diversity of Indonesia are what make the country so fascinating. A visitor has the option of relaxing in one of Bali's luxury resorts or taking a river trip through the jungles of Borneo. Since tourism is a new priority for Indonesia, infrastructure is sporadic. Only in areas slated for tourist development can travelers expect to find services approaching international standards. Elsewhere, expect only modest accommodations and casually scheduled transport. Patience is a key to enjoying Indonesia.

Because of its fertile lands, Java has supported some of Indonesia's mightiest kingdoms. For the same reason, the island has become overpopulated, accounting for 60% of the nation's population. At least 13 million people live in and around Jakarta, the capital. Jakarta already has a range of international hotels, and more are under construction. Efforts are being made to improve the museums, whose displays do not do justice to their wealth of treasure. Resort parks have been built, and a new marina is being planned. Offshore, in the Java Sea, Pulau Seribu (Thousand Islands) has resort hotels. Excursions are available to Krakatau (Krakatoa), the island whose volcano erupted with such violence in 1883. Within a two-hour drive of Jakarta are hill towns offering an escape from the tropical heat, tea plantations, botanical gardens, and the volcanic crater of Tangkuban near Bandung, a pleasant university town in the mountains.

As a tourist destination, Jakarta doesn't hold a candle to the rest of the country, but it serves as a convenient gateway to other Indonesian destinations. Central Java, for example, has the architectural wonders of the 9th-century Buddhist Borobudur and Hindu Prambanan temples. Both are within a short drive of Jogjakarta and Solo (Surakarta), towns rich in culture and handicrafts.

Across a 2-mile strait from East Java is the magical island of Bali, with a proud, smiling people whose religion is a unique form of Hinduism blended with Buddhism and animism. Here, distinctive architecture and holy mountains compete for attention with surf-swept beaches and the luxury and comfort of sophisticated hotels.

From Bali, islands stretch eastward like stepping stones, all waiting to be explored. There is Lombok, offering virgin beaches and the hospitality of Balinese Hindus and Sasak Muslims. The tiny island of Komodo—home to the world's largest reptile, the Komodo dragon—is part of the Lesser Sundas island group, which includes the predominantly Catholic island of Flores, with wonderfully unspoiled physical beauty and crystal-clear waters.

Northeast of Bali is Sulawesi, home to the Bugis, who for centuries have sailed their stout *prahus* (boats) on the Java Sea among the islands. Part of the island is inhabited by the Toraja, whose unique animist culture celebrates death as the culmination of life.

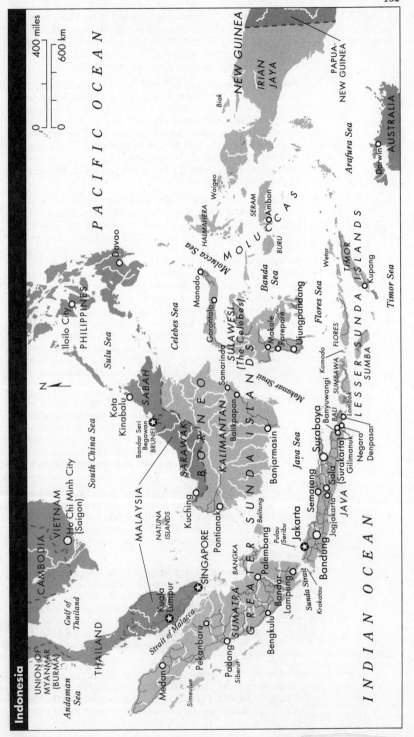

Indonesia

132

West of Sulawesi is Kalimantan, which shares the island of Borneo with Brunei and the Malaysian states of Sabah and Sarawak. Home to the Dayaks, tribal peoples whose generous hospitality is shadowed only by their recent past as headhunters, Kalimantan is for the most part traversed by river.

Farther west is Sumatra, with the popular resort at Lake Toba, where on Samosir Island, the Batak people have ornately carved traditional houses built on poles, with high, saddleshape roofs. To the south, around Bukit Thinggi, a quiet hill town north of Padang, the Minangkabau live in distinctive houses with buffalo-horn-shape roofs.

East of Sulawesi are the Moluccas, a group of islands no less fascinating and beautiful than the rest, with jungle-clad volcanoes, beaches, and coral gardens, but virtually ignored by tourists. From the Moluccas, it is less than an hour's flight to Irian Jaya, former Dutch New Guinea. Irian Jaya is rough and mountainous but offers anyone willing to hike along narrow paths from one village to the next the rare opportunity of meeting primitive cultures confronting the 20th century.

From Jakarta's tall steel-and-glass office buildings to Irian Jaya's thatched huts, Indonesia embraces an astonishing array of cultures. The national motto—Unity in Diversity—reflects the proud individualism of the many ethnic groups, who continue to preserve their culture. Today Indonesia's 174 million people—Asmats, Balinese, Bataks, Dayaks, and on down through the alphabet—speak as many as 300 languages, though a national language, Bahasa Indonesia, is officially recognized as a means of binding the population together. Maintaining a unified Indonesian nation is understandably a major task.

The history of the Indonesian archipelago goes back at least 250,000 years, as evidenced by the discovery in central Java of so-called Java Man, the "missing link," and the earliest-known direct ancestor of modern man. The first Indonesian empire arose with the development of a maritime trade with India. By the 5th century, there were several powerful Indianized Hindu kingdoms in Indonesia. By the 7th century a Buddhist kingdom, Srivijaya, had arisen in Sumatra, and for the next 600 years, the Srivijayans ruled the seas, establishing an empire that stretched from Malacca (in Malaya) south to the Java Sea. For 100 years around the turn of the 9th century the Buddhist Sailendras controlled central Java, building the fabulous Buddhist monument at Borobudur and other Buddhist temples. The Sailendras were defeated by a vassal Hindu state, the Sanjayan, which has left us the majestic temples at Prambanan, less than 100 km (62 mi) from Borobudur.

Java's next great kingdom, the Majapahit, emerged in the late 13th century, and by the time it reached its zenith in the mid-14th, it controlled the entire archipelago as well as the Malay Peninsula. Today Indonesians look upon this short-lived empire as their most glorious. The rise of new Islamic powers, especially in Malacca, weakened the Majapahit empire until it was finally defeated by the new Islamic state of Demerak, based on Java's north coast. The Hindu Majapahits took refuge on Bali, and their legacy contributes to the unique development of culture on the island today.

Islam crept through most of Indonesia, less by the sword than through trade. The political alliances of Islamic kingdoms were shattered when the Portuguese took Islamicized Malacca in 1511, leaving the doors wide open for the Dutch. The Dutch presence in Indonesia began in 1596 with an expedition under the command of Cornelis de Houtman, who was seeking spices to bring back to Europe, where they were in great demand. In 1602 the United Dutch East India Company was formed to establish a Dutch monopoly on the spice trade. The company met with only moderate success until a series of military operations forced the issue. In order, for example, to secure control of the five tiny nutmeg- and mace-producing Banda islands, most of the 15,000 inhabitants were rounded up and killed. Slaves were then imported to work the plantations.

By the end of the 17th century, the Dutch had the spice trade sewed up and were raking in the profits. In the 18th century the bottom fell out of the market and continual Indonesian uprisings proved so costly to the Dutch East India Company that it had to declare bankruptcy in 1799. The Dutch government then took control. During the Napoleonic Wars, Britain's Sir Thomas Raffles invaded Java and assumed control from 1811 to 1816. The Dutch returned but in the late 1820s were nearly evicted by the guerrilla tactics of a charismatic Muslim prince from a Javanese ruling family, Pangeran Diponegoro. The cost of this war was 8,000 Dutch and 200,000 Javanese deaths, many from starvation and cholera.

This rebellion crushed, Holland instituted a system whereby taxes were paid in labor, so that Dutch colonials could grow crops to sell in Europe. Reducing the local population to virtual serfdom did wonders for Dutch coffers. Further outbreaks of rebellion on the part of Indonesians were put down with wholesale slaughter. Some of the most infamous incidents occurred in Bali, where in 1894, 1906, and 1908 Balinese rulers and courtiers rushed headlong into Dutch gunfire, armed only with ceremonial daggers, rather than suffer the humiliation of Dutch rule.

In this way the Dutch destroyed the indigenous kingdoms and brought the whole of the archipelago under Dutch rule, paving the way for a unified Indonesian nation. By the mid-1920s, the movement to independence had begun in earnest, and the Japanese occupation in World War II moved things along considerably. At first the Japanese were seen as liberators—key positions once held by Dutch were given to Indonesians, and the Dutch language was banned—but it soon became clear that they were simply another race of exploiters. Uprisings were put down ruthlessly, one Indonesian remarked that the cruelty inflicted in the four years of Japanese occupation equalled that of 350 years of Dutch rule.

Three days after the Japanese surrendered, the Indonesian nationalist leaders, of whom Sukarno was one, proclaimed independence, but it was not to be achieved so easily. The Dutch sent in troops to reclaim their colony, and while they were able to control the cities, the makeshift Indonesian army held the countryside. In 1949 the United Nations Security Council ordered the Dutch to withdraw, and Indonesia's sovereignty over the former Dutch East Indies was recognized on December 29, 1949.

A new nation had to be built. A Western-style parliamentary government was adopted, but with more than 30 parties, coalition governments rapidly rose and fell. The economy was in shambles. In the 16th century Indonesia had been a comparatively rich country. Four centuries of colonial exploitation had not only stopped its development but left it without sufficient resources to feed a burgeoning population. The crisis came to a head in the 1950s, when disaffected groups in Sumatra, northern Sulawesi, and western Java tried to secede. Terming this a national emergency, Sukarno and the army in 1959 declared a system of "guided democracy."

Blaming Western imperialism for Indonesia's ills, he threw out the capitalists, turned to socialist reforms, and began to ally himself with the strongest civilian political party, the Communist PKI. The economy further deteriorated, and by 1965, inflation was running at 680%.

In the early hours of October 1, 1965, rebel officers kidnapped six generals from their homes and executed them. Other rebel units occupied the national radio station and took up positions around the presidential palace. By the evening of the same day, the rebels were ousted. The Communist PKI, seen as the instigator of the attempted coup, was banned and communism was outlawed.

Directed by General Suharto and with the support of the moderate Muslim population, the army swept through the country, slaughtering every communist or suspected communist they could lay their hands on. The wave of killings continued through 1966. A conservative estimate of deaths is put at 200,000; thousands more were imprisoned. Indonesia's Chinese suffered most, in part because the People's Republic of China was thought to be supporting the communists. Even today the Chinese are on the fringes of Indonesian society (no Chinese-language newspapers are allowed into Indonesia), but because of their wealth and business acumen—which tend to surpass that of the indigenous Indonesians—the government accommodates them.

With the extensive power handed him by Sukarno in 1966, Suharto (formally installed as Indonesia's second president in 1968) engineered a 180-degree turn in Indonesia's economic and political policies. All relations with the People's Republic of China were severed, and investment from the West was sought.

In the past two decades the nation has made rapid strides. One of Suharto's greatest achievements is having turned his country from a rice importer to a rice exporter. Increases in oil production and the development of petrochemicals have established Indonesia as the world's fifth-largest OPEC producer. At the moment oil accounts for 70% of the country's foreign revenues, but because of volatile oil prices, the move is on to diversify, and Indonesia is now the world's leading exporter of liquid natural gas.

The new nation, the third great Indonesian empire, is Java-based or, more correctly, Jakarta-based. The guiding hand is Suharto, whose third term expires in 1993, for the most part benevolent, so long as he is not criticized. Political dissent is not tolerated, and media censorship is a way of life. Within these parameters, Indonesia has become a progressive and stable republic, taking on an ever-increasing presence in the socioeconomic development of Southeast Asia.

Staying in Indonesia

Getting Around

By Plane **Garuda Indonesia Airways** serves every major city by jet. **Merpati Airlines** flies to some big cities and many provincial towns, often using propeller craft. **Bouraq** flies propeller planes to the smaller towns not served by the other airlines. **Continental** has service to Denpasar (Bali) via Guam.

Reservations are strongly advised on popular routes—between Jakarta and Jogjakarta, for example. Expect delays, especially during the monsoon rains, which can make air travel impossible. You can save up to 60% on domestic flights by buying your tickets in Indonesia instead of overseas. However, if you don't use these tickets, you will not receive a full refund.

By Train Only Java has a useful passenger railroad, running east–west across the island. It offers three travel classes, with air-conditioned sleepers available for trips between Jakarta and Jogjakarta. Southern Sumatra has train service between Panjang and Palembang. Except for the Jakarta–Jogjakarta express, trains can be slow, and they're not always air-conditioned. You can get schedules and tickets at hotel travel desks, travel agencies, or train stations; schedules are also available at tourist offices.

By Bus The main means of land travel in Indonesia, buses offer varying degrees of comfort. Long-distance expresses are air-conditioned and have reclining seats; some even show video programs. Local buses can be crowded and steaming hot. It's an inexpensive means of transport—the 14-hour trip between Jakarta and Jogjakarta, for instance, costs Rp 13,500 on an air-conditioned express. Tickets and schedules are available from terminals, travel desks, or travel agencies. Tourist offices also provide schedules. For Java and Sumatra, contact **Antar Lintas Sumatra** (Jln. Jati Baru 87A, Jakarta, tel. 021/320970). For Java, Bali, and Sumatra, **PT. ANS** (Jln. Senen Raya 50, Jakarta, tel. 021/340494).

By Boat Ferries run between many of the islands. Hotel travel desks and travel agencies have schedules; you buy your tickets at the terminals. For longer trips, **Pelni,** the state-owned shipping company, serves all the major ports with ships accommodating 500 to 1,000 passengers in four classes. First-class cabins are air-conditioned and have private bathrooms. Schedules and tickets are available from Pelni's head office (Jln. Angkasa 18, Jakarta, tel. 021/416262) or at travel agencies.

By Car Self-drive rental cars are available only in Jakarta, Jogjakarta, *Rentals* and Bali—and only for use in the vicinity. You'll need an international driver's license. Elsewhere, and for long-distance trips, your rental car includes a driver. A helpful hint: Indonesians love to talk. If your driver gets too involved in chatting with you, feign sleep so he'll concentrate on the road. But do talk to him occasionally or suggest rest stops to keep him awake and alert.

Road Conditions Indonesia's main roads are in fairly good condition, but side and back roads can be poor. Tourist areas often get very congested, with small trucks, bemos, scooters, bicycles, and pedestrians adding to car traffic.

Rules of the Road Driving is on the right, as in the United States. Road signs reading *hati hati* mean "warning."

Gasoline Gas prices are comparable to those in the United States. Stations are few and far between, so don't set out with less than a quarter tank.

By Taxi Registered taxis and hired cars may be hailed on city streets—look for the yellow, number plates. Except in Jakarta and Surabaya, you negotiate the fare with the driver before setting out. Most hotels have taxi stands.

By Bajaj Popular in Jakarta, this three-wheeled, two-passenger motor vehicle is less comfortable and less expensive than a taxi but can be faster, since it can scoot amid the traffic. They are hailed on the street, and you negotiate the fare.

By Becak These three-wheeled pedicabs are useful for short distances. In Jakarta they are permitted only in the outlying neighborhoods, but elsewhere in Indonesia they are plentiful. Becak drivers are tough bargainers, but if one doesn't meet your price, another may.

By Horse Cart Horse-drawn carts are disappearing fast, but they remain popular in Padang and other tourist areas. The cost depends on your bargaining skill.

Telephones

Jakarta's telephone system has improved, and most business establishments have phones, but the rest of the country is less well endowed. In most cases you are best off using hotel phones despite the small surcharges; that way you don't need to amass quantities of coins, and an operator can help with translation and information.

Local Calls Public phones take only Rp 50 coins, which are not easy to find. Three minutes costs Rp 100. For calls outside the locality, dial the area code before the number.

International Calls Major Indonesian cities are now hooked into the International Direct Dialing (IDD) system via satellite. If you want to avoid using hotel phones, the most economical way to place an IDD call is from the nearest **Kantor Telephone & Telegraph** office. For towns without the IDD hookup, go through the operator (in tourist destinations many speak English). You may make collect calls to Australia, Europe, and North America; for other countries, you need a telephone credit card. Reduced rates on international phone calls: 9 PM–6 AM daily.

Information For operator and directory assistance dial 104 in Jakarta, 100 elsewhere. Most local operators, however, do not speak English.

Mail

Postal Rates Two kinds of airmail are available: regular *(pos udara)* and express *(kilat)*. Kilat rates to the United States or the United Kingdom are Rp 600 for postcards and Rp 1,550 for 1g (.035 oz) letters.

Receiving Mail In Jakarta, have letters sent to the main post office (open Mon.–Thurs. 8–4, Fri. 8–11 AM, Sat. 8 AM–12:30 PM) addressed to you c/o Central Post Office, Jalan Pos Utara, Jakarta, and marked *poste restante*. Your surname should be written in underlined capitals, with only the initial of your given name, to avoid misfiling. Major post offices outside Jakarta also accept *poste restante*.

Travelers can also use the services of **American Express** (Arthaloka Bldg., Jl. Merdeka Selatan 17, Jakarta, tel. 021/ 5703310). The office is open weekdays 8:10 AM–midnight, Saturday 8:15 AM–11 PM. You should be a cardholder or be using American Express traveler's checks.

Currency

Indonesia's unit of currency is the rupiah. Bills come in denominations of 100, 500, 1,000, 5,000, and 10,000 Rp, coins in 5, 10, 25, 50, or 100 Rp. Exchange rates at press time were Rp 1,650 = US $1, Rp 2,736 = £1.

What It Will Cost

Prices in Indonesia depend on what you're buying: The basic cost of living is low and domestic labor is cheap, but you pay a premium for anything imported. Thus, renting a car is expensive, hiring a driver is not; camera film is expensive, food is not. Regionally, costs rise in direct relation to tourism and business development. Prices in Bali and Jakarta are relatively high, particularly at deluxe hotels and restaurants. Sumatra and Sulawesi, by contrast, are bargains. In general, Indonesia's prices are comparable to Malaysia's and lower than Thailand's.

Taxes **Hotels** and formal **restaurants** add a 5.5% government tax and a 10% service charge to their bills. Departing passengers on international flights pay an **airport departure tax** of Rp 9,000. For domestic travel, airport taxes vary from Rp 2,500 to Rp 3,500.

Sample Prices Continental breakfast at hotel, $3; bottle of beer at hotel, $2.50; bottled water, 75¢; Indonesian dinner at good restaurant, $15; 1-mile taxi ride, 75¢; double room, $50–$75 moderate, over $115 very expensive.

Language

Although some 300 languages are spoken in Indonesia, Bahasa Indonesia has been the national language since independence. English is widely spoken in tourist areas.

Opening and Closing Times

Banks are open from either 8 or 8:30 AM to noon or 2 PM. Bank branches in hotels stay open later. **Government offices** are open Monday–Thursday 8–3 and Friday 8–11:30 AM. Some are also

open on Saturday 8–2. **Business offices** have varied hours; some
are open weekdays 8–4, others 9–5. Some offices work a half
day on Saturday. Most **museums** are open Tuesday–Thursday
and weekends 9–2 (although some larger museums stay open
until 4 or 5), Friday 9–noon. Most **shops** are open Monday–
Saturday 9–5.

National Holidays

The following are national holidays (some are tied to the Muslim or Buddhist calendar, hence the dates vary from year to
year): New Year's Day, Jan. 1; Ascension Day, 40 days after
Easter; Lebaran, the last two days of Ramadan (May); Waicak,
Birth of Buddha, variable (May); Haji, commemorating Mecca
pilgrimages, variable (July); Independence Day, Aug. 17;
Birth of Mohammed, variable (Oct.); Christmas Day, Dec. 25.

Festivals and Seasonal Events

Festival dates depend on the calendar prevalent in the region
where they take place. Most of Indonesia uses the Islamic calendar; the Balinese use a lunar calendar. The **Indonesia Calendar of Events,** with listings for the entire archipelago, is
available at Garuda airline offices, or contact the tourist information offices.

Early spring: Galungan, Bali's most important festival, celebrates the creation of the world, marks a visit by ancestral
spirits, and honors the victory of good over evil. Celebrants
make offerings in family shrines and decorate their villages. On
the 10th and last day they bid farewell to the visiting spirits
with gifts of *kuningan,* a saffron-yellow rice.

Around Mar. 22: Nyepi, the Balinese New Year, falls on the vernal equinox. New Year's Eve is spent exorcising evil spirits,
which are first attracted with offerings of chicken blood, flowers, and aromatic leaves, then driven away with noise as
masked youths bang gongs and tin pans. On Nyepi the island
falls silent: No fires or lamps may be lit, and traffic is prohibited.

May: Waicak Day, a public holiday throughout Indonesia, celebrates the Buddha's birth, death, and enlightenment.

May: Idul Fitri, two days marking the end of Ramadan (a month
of fasting during daylight), is the most important Muslim holiday. Festivals take place in all the villages and towns of Muslim
Indonesia.

May–Oct: The **Ramayana Ballet Festival** is held at the Prambanan temple near Jogjakarta during the full-moon week each
month. A cast of 500 performs a four-episode dance-drama of
the *Ramayana* epic.

Aug. 17: Independence Day is celebrated throughout Indonesia
with flag-raising ceremonies, sports events, and cultural performances.

Mid-Oct.: The town of Pamekasan on Java holds **bull-racing fi-
nals.** A jockey stands on skids slung between two yoked bulls.
The animals are decorated, and there's mass dancing before
they run. The winner is judged by which bulls' front feet cross
the finish line first.

October: Sekaten commemorates the birth of Mohammed. In
Jogjakarta the sultan's antique *gamelan*—a unique Indonesian
ensemble of soft percussion instruments—is played only on

this day. The concert is performed in the gamelan pavilion of the *kraton*, the sultan's palace complex. Then the celebrants form a parade, carrying enormous amounts of food from the kraton to the mosque, where they distribute it to the people.

Dec.–Jan.: Kesodo ceremonies are held by the Hindu Tenggerese at the crater of Mt. Bromo on Java.

Tipping

Most **hotels** add a 10% service charge. Some **restaurants** do as well; if not, tip 10%. **Porters** at the airport should receive Rp 500 per bag. **Taxi drivers** are not tipped except in Jakarta and Surabaya, where Rp 300, or the small change, is the minimum. For a driver of a **hired car,** Rp 1,000 for half a day would be the minimum tip. **Private guides** expect a gratuity, perhaps Rp 5,000 per day.

Shopping

Arts and crafts in Indonesia are bargains by U.S. standards. From **Java** the best buys are batik cloth and garments, traditional jewelry, leather *wayang* puppets, and leather accessories. In **Bali,** look for batiks, stone- and woodcarvings, bamboo furniture, ceramics, silverwork, traditional masks, and wayang puppets. **Sumatra** is best for thick handwoven cotton cloth; carved-wood panels and statues, often in primitive, traditional design; and silver and gold jewelry. From **Sulawesi,** there's filigree silverware, handwoven silks and cottons, handcarved wood panels, and bamboo goods. Be aware that machine-produced goods are sometimes sold to tourists as hand-crafted.

Bargaining   Major cities have shopping complexes and department stores where prices are fixed. At small shops, bargaining is necessary. Offer half the asking price (25% in more touristy areas). You will finish with a price somewhere in between. Shops with higher-quality merchandise are likely to take credit cards, but payment in cash puts you in a better bargaining position.

Sports and Beaches

Swimming pools, health clubs, tennis, badminton, and sometimes squash and racquetball are available at the major hotels. There are golf courses near the larger cities. Special adventure tours can be arranged through tour operators.

Scuba Diving   Scuba diving is becoming popular, and licensed diving clubs have sprung up around the major resort areas. Flores and North Sulawesi have some of the world's best diving; there is diving also at Pulau Seribu, off Jakarta. For information, call the Indonesian diving organization **Possi** (Jln. Prapatan No. 38, Jakarta, tel. 021/348685).

Spectator Sports   Traditional sports include **bull races** in Madura, Java; **bullfights** (bull against bull) at Kota Bharu, near Bukit Thinggi, Sumatra; and **cockfighting** (though it is illegal) in Java, Bali, and Sulawesi.

Beaches   **Bali, Lombok, Flores,** and **North Sulawesi** have some of the most beautiful beaches in the world. Bali's Kuta Beach is popular with surfers.

Dining

Warungs are Indonesian street food stalls, sometimes with benches and tables in the open, under canvas, or sheltered by a sheet of galvanized tin. The food here—usually rice dishes and *soto ayam*, the native chicken soup—varies from drab to tasty but is always cheap: You can eat well for Rp 1,000. Warungs are often clustered together at a *pasar malam*, or night bazaar.

Rumah makans are just like warungs, only with fixed walls and roofs. Another step up is the *restoran*, a very broad category. Most are Chinese-owned and serve both Indonesian and Chinese cuisine. The dining rooms of tourist hotels generally offer Chinese, Indonesian, and Western fare; the native specialties are usually toned down. If you enjoy spicy food, you'll be happier at more authentic eateries.

Rice *(nasi)* is the staple of the Indonesian diet. It's eaten with breakfast, lunch, and dinner, and as a snack. But it normally serves as a backdrop to an exciting range of flavors. Indonesian food can be very hot. Your first sample might be *sambal*, a spicy relish made with chilis that is placed on every restaurant table. Indonesians cook with garlic, shallots, turmeric, cumin, ginger, fermented shrimp paste, soy sauce, lime or lemon juice, lemongrass, coconut, other nuts, and hot peppers.

Naturally, fresh fish and shellfish abound throughout Indonesia. Fish *(ikan)* is often baked in a banana leaf with spices, grilled with a spicy topping, or baked with coconut. Shrimp come cooked in coconut sauce, grilled with hot chilis, made into prawn-and-bean sprout fritters, or, in Sulawesi, with butter or Chinese sweet-and-sour sauce.

For dessert, Indonesians eat fresh fruit: papaya, pineapple, rambutan, salak, and mangosteen. Because this is a mostly Muslim country, wine and alcohol are expensive additions to a meal; beer is your best bet.

Even in Jakarta, you will see well-dressed Indonesians eating with their fingers. Most food comes cut into small pieces, and finger bowls are provided. Tourists normally receive forks and spoons.

Drink only bottled water, and avoid ice in any beverage. It's best to steer clear of raw, unpeeled fruits and vegetables.

Throughout this chapter, the following restaurant price categories apply:

Category	Cost*
Expensive	over Rp 43,750 (US $25)
Moderate	Rp 17,500–Rp 43,750 (US $10–US $25)
Inexpensive	under 17,500 (US $10)

per person, not including tax or service

Lodging

Most Indonesian towns offer a range of hotels and three types of rooming houses: *penginapan, losmen,* and *wisma*. Theoretically, the penginapan is cheapest, with thin partitions between rooms, and the wisma most expensive, with thicker walls. The term "losmen" is often used generically to mean any small rooming house. Facilities vary widely: Some Bali losmen are comfortable and social, others dingy and dirty.

The government classifies hotels with star ratings, four stars being the most luxurious. Its criteria are somewhat random, though. No hotel without a garage gets four stars, for example, and most Indonesian tourists don't need a garage. In general, upkeep and cleanliness correlate with room rates.

You'll find superb resorts—such as the Bali Oberoi and Mandarin Oriental in Jakarta—that cost half what you would expect to pay in Europe. At the bottom range in the less touristed areas, you get a clean room with shower and Asian toilet for less than $2.50 a night.

Category	Cost*
Very Expensive	over Rp 201,250 (US $115)
Expensive	Rp 131,250–RP 201,250 (US $75–US $115)
Moderate	Rp 87,500–Rp 131,250 (US $50–US $75)
Inexpensive	under Rp 87,500 (US $50)

double room; subject to 5.5% tax and 10% service charge

Jakarta

Introduction

Indonesia's capital is a place of extremes. Modern multistory buildings look down on shacks with corrugated-iron roofs. Wide boulevards intersect with unpaved streets. Elegant hotels and high-tech business centers stand just a few blocks from overcrowded kampongs. BMWs accelerate down the avenues while pedicabs plod along the back streets.

Although the government is trying to prepare for the 21st century, Jakarta has trouble accommodating the thousands who flock to it each year from the countryside. Because of the number of migrant workers who come to the city each day, it is difficult to accurately estimate the city's population. The census puts Jakarta's population at 7 million, but the true number is closer to 13 million. The crowds push the city's infrastructure to the limit. Traffic grinds to a standstill, and a system of canals, built by the Dutch to prevent flooding in below-sea-level Jakarta, cannot keep pace with the heavy monsoon rains, so the city is sometimes under water for days. The heat and humidity take getting used to. But air-conditioning in the major hotels, restaurants, and shopping centers provides an escape. Early morning and late afternoon are the best times for sightseeing.

Arriving and Departing by Plane

Airports and Airlines Jakarta's airport, **Soekarno Hatta,** is a modern showpiece, with glass-walled walkways and landscaped gardens. While most of the area is not air-conditioned, it's breezy and smartly clean. There is a small duty-free shopping area. A Visitor Information

Center outside the International Arrivals Hall is open 8–10, closed Sunday and when they feel like it.

The major international carriers serving Jakarta are **Garuda Indonesia Airways,** the national carrier (tel. 021/588707), **Singapore Airlines** (tel. 021/587441), **Thai International** (tel. 021/ 320607), and **Qantas** (tel. 021/326707). Garuda flies to all of Indonesia's 27 provinces; **Merpati** (tel. 021/348760) also has domestic flights.

Between the Airport and Center City The airport is 35 km (20 mi) northwest of Jakarta. A toll expressway takes you three-quarters of the way to the city quickly, but the rest is slow going. New road construction may alleviate some of the airport traffic by the end of 1990. Until then, allow a good hour for the trip.

By Taxi Taxis *from* the airport add a surcharge of Rp 2,300 and the road toll (Rp 2,700) to the fare on the meter. The surcharge does not apply on taxis going *to* the airport. **Blue Bird Taxi** (tel. 021/ 325607) offers a 25% discount on the toll charge either way. The average fare to a downtown hotel is Rp 17,000.

By Bus Air-conditioned buses operate every 20 minutes between the airport and six points in the city, including the Gambir Railway Station, Rawamangun Bus Terminal, and Pasar Minggu Bus Terminal and cost Rp 2,000.

Hotels have stopped offering transfer service, but a **shuttle bus** leaves from the airport to most of the larger hotels. If you are not staying at one of them, catch the shuttle to the hotel nearest yours and take a taxi for the remaining distance. Shuttle bus cost is Rp 4,000.

Arriving and Departing by Train and Bus

By Train Use the **Tanah Abang Railway Station** (Jln. KH Wahid Hasyim, southwest of Merdeka Sq., tel. 021/340048) for trains to Sumatra. All other trains—to Bogor and Bandung or to the east Java cities of Semarang, Jogjakarta, Solo, Surabaya, Madiun, and Malang—start from the **Kota Railway Station** (Jln. Stasiun Kota, south of Fatahillah Square, tel. 021/678515 or 021/ 679194) or the **Gambir Railway Station** (Jln. Merdeka Timur, on the east side of Merdeka Sq., tel. 021/342777 or 021/348612).

Tickets may be purchased at the station or from travel agencies, including **Carnation** (Jln. Menteng Raya 24, tel. 021/ 344027) and **P.T. Bhayangkara** (Jln. Kebon Sirih 23, tel. 021/ 327387).

By Bus All three bus terminals are off Merdeka Square. **Pulo Gadang** (Jln. Perintis Kemerdekaan, tel. 021/489–3742) serves Semarang, Jogjakarta, Solo, Surabaya, Malang, and Denpensar. Use **Cililitan** (Jln. Raya Bogor, tel. 021/809–3554) for Bogor, Sukabumi, Bandung, and Banjar. **Kalideres** (Jln. Daan Mogot) is the depot for Merak, Labuhan, and major cities in Sumatra. Buy tickets at the terminals or at travel agencies.

Getting Around

By Car Though self-drive rental is available, it is not advised. Traffic congestion is horrendous and parking is very difficult. Cars may be rented from **Avis** (Jln. Doponegoro 25, tel. 021/341964),

Hertz (Hotel Mandarin, Jln. Thamrin, tel. 021/371208), or **National** (Hotel Kartika Plaza, Jln. Thamrin 10, tel. 021/332849).

By Taxi A cheap and efficient way of getting around, Jakarta's metered taxis charge Rp 500 (29¢) for the first kilometer (.62 mi) and Rp 250 (15¢) for each additional kilometer. Air-conditioned cabs cost Rp 600 (34¢) and Rp 300 (17¢), respectively. Both types may be flagged on the streets, and most hotels have taxi stands. For a radio-dispatched taxi, call **Blue Bird Taxi** (tel. 021/325607).

By Bus Non-air-conditioned public buses charge a flat Rp 250; the (green) air-conditioned buses charge Rp 500. All are packed during rush hours, and pickpockets abound. The routes can be labyrinthine, but you can always give one a try and get off when the bus veers from your desired direction. For information, contact these companies: **Hiba Utama** (tel. 021/413626 or 021/410381), **P.P.D.** (tel. 021/881131 or 021/411357), or **Mayasari Bhakti** (tel. 021/809–0378 or 021/489–2785).

By Chauffeured Car Air-conditioned, chauffeur-driven cars can be hired for a minimum of two hours, at hourly rates of Rp 11,375 for a small Corona or Rp 21,000 for a Mercedes. Daily charters cost Rp 105,000 and Rp 210,000, respectively. Try **Blue Bird** (tel. 021/325607).

By Bajaj, Becak, and Bemo: *See* Getting Around in Staying in Indonesia, above.

Important Addresses and Numbers

Tourist Information The **City Visitor Information Centre** has brochures and maps locating city sights and hotels. You can also get information here on bus and train schedules to other Java destinations. *Jakarta Theatre Bldg., Jln. M.H. Thamrin 9, tel. 021/354094; open Mon.–Thurs. 8–3, Fri. 8–11:30 AM, Sat. 8–2.*

The more comprehensive Falk City Map of Jakarta is available at bookstores for Rp 9,000.

Embassies Most nations are represented in Jakarta, including the United States (Jln. Medan Merdeka Selatan 5, tel. 021/360360, open weekdays 8–2), United Kingdom (Jln. M.H. Thamrin 75, tel. 021/330904, open weekdays 8:15–4), and Canada (Jln. Jend. Sudirman Kav. 29, 5th floor, Wisma Metropolitan 1, tel. 021/510709, open weekdays 8–2:45).

Emergencies Consult your hotel concierge, if possible, for advice in English. Call 110 for **police,** 119 for **ambulance service,** 118 in **traffic accidents.** For emergency transport, however, **Blue Bird Taxi** (tel. 021/325607) may be a more reliable source to call.

Doctors English-speaking staff are available at the 24-hour clinic and pharmacy **SOS Medika Vayasan** (Jln. Prapanca Raya 32–34, tel. 021/771575 or 021/733094). A group practice clinic, **Bina Medica** (Jln. Maluku 8–10, tel. 021/344893) provides 24-hour service, ambulance, and English-speaking doctors. **Doctors-on-Call** (tel. 021/683444, 021/681405, or 021/514444) has English-speaking doctors who make house calls. Payment in cash is required.

Dentists Dental services are provided at the **Metropolitan Medical Centre** (Wisata Office Tower, 1st floor, Jln. Thamrin, tel. 021/

320408) and **SOS Medika Clinic Service** (Jln. Prapanca Raya 32–34, Kebayoran Baru, tel. 021/733094).

English-Language Bookstores Major hotel shops carry magazines, newspapers, paperbacks, and travel guides in English. For a larger book selection, try **PT Indira** (Jln. Melawi V/16, Blok M, tel. 021/770584, open Mon.–Sat. 8 AM–8:30 PM or the **Family Book Shop** (Kemang Club Villas, Jln. Kelurahan Bangka, tel. 021/799–5525, open daily 9:30–8:30).

Late-Night Pharmacies **SOS Medika Vayasan** (Jln. Prapanca Raya 32–34, tel. 021/771575 or 021/733094) is open 24 hours.

Travel Agencies Travel agencies arrange transportation, conduct guided tours, and can often secure hotel reservations more cheaply than you could yourself. **Natourin** (18 Buncit Raya, Jakarta 12790, tel. 021/799–7886) has extensive facilities and contacts throughout Indonesia. Three large government-owned travel agencies with branch offices at most Indonesian tourist destinations are **Nitour** (Duta Merlin, Jln. Gajah Mada 3–5, tel. 021/346346), **Pacto** (Jln. Surabaya 8, tel. 021/332634), and **Satriavi** (Jln. Prapatan 32, tel. 021/380–3944).

Guided Tours

Hotel tour desks will book the following tours or customize outings with a chauffeured car. **Gray Line** (tel. 021/639–0008) covers most of Jakarta and surrounding attractions.

Orientation **City Tour.** This six-hour tour covers the National Monument, Pancasila Monument, Beautiful Indonesia in Miniature Park, and Museum Indonesia.

Indocultural Tour. This five-hour tour visits the Central Museum, Old Batavia, the Jakarta Museum, and a batik factory.

Beautiful Indonesia Tour. This three- to four-hour afternoon tour takes you by air-conditioned bus through the Beautiful Indonesia in Miniature Park (*see* Tour 3), where the architecture and customs of different regions are displayed.

Jakarta by Night. This five-hour trip around the city includes dinner, an Indonesian dance performance, and a visit to a nightclub.

Excursions Tours beyond Jakarta include the following: a nine-hour trip to **Pelabuhanratu,** a former fishing village that is now a resort; an eight-hour tour to the **safari park** at **Bogor** and the **Botanical Garden,** 48 km (30 mi) south of Jakarta at a cool 183 m (600 ft) above sea level, and to **Puncak Mountain Resort;** and a two-day tour into the highlands to visit **Bandung** and its volcano, with stops at **Bogor** and **Puncak.**

Highlights for First-time Visitors

Beautiful Indonesia in Miniature Park (*see* Tour 3)

Dreamland (*see* Tour 3)

Fatahillah Square (*see* Tour 1)

Merdeka Square, with the National Monument and National Museum (*see* Tour 2)

Pasar Ikan and Sunda Kelapa Harbor (*see* Tour 1)

A shadow puppet performance at the Museum Wayang (*see* Tour 1)

Exploring Jakarta

At Jakarta's center is the vast, parklike Merdeka Square, where Sukarno's 433-foot Monas Monument is topped with a gold-plated flame symbolizing national independence. Wide boulevards lining the square, and the Presidential Palace (Suharto does not live here), army headquarters, City Hall, Gambir Railway Station, National Museum, and other government buildings have addresses here.

The square and the area immediately south along Jalan M.H. Thamrin (*jalan* means "street"), is known as the Menteng district. This is the downtown of new Jakarta, home to most banks, large corporations, and international hotels. New Jakarta extends southwest, continuing through the district known as Kebayoran to Bloc M, where many expatriates live.

North and west of Merdeka Square, around the port of Sunda Kelapa at the mouth of the Ciliwung River, is the Kota area. This is "old town," where the Portuguese first arrived in 1522. A century later, in 1619, the Dutch secured the city, renamed it Batavia, and established the administrative center for their expanding Indonesian empire.

Dutch rule came to an abrupt end when, in World War II, the Japanese occupied Batavia and changed its name back to Jayakarta. The Dutch returned after Japan's surrender, but by 1949 Indonesia had won independence and, abbreviating the city's old name, established Jakarta as the nation's capital.

We deal with the old and the new areas as separate tours, followed by exploration of Jakarta's parks, offshore islands, and other attractions within easy reach.

Numbers in the margin correspond with numbered points of interest on the Jakarta map.

Tour 1: Old Batavia

❶ The heart of the old city, or Kota as it is known, is **Fatahillah Square,** which is cobbled with ballast stones from old Dutch trading ships. The fountain at its center is a reproduction of one originally built in 1728. This was the last object seen by the criminals who were beheaded in the square while their judges watched from the nearby Town Hall balconies. Just to the north is an old Portuguese cannon whose muzzle tapers into a clenched fist. The clenched fist is a Javanese fertility symbol, and childless women have been known to straddle the cannon.

Around the square are three noteworthy museums, to which we will return. For now, walk up Jalan Cengken, the street leading
❷ off from the north side of the square, to the **Pasar Ikan** (fish market). This market is in full swing early in the morning. It's colorful, noisy, smelly, and slimy, and if you can take it, there are great photo opportunities.

Walk through the back of the fish market onto the wharf of **Sunda Kelapa Harbor,** and save the entrance fee, or walk out of

Beautiful Indonesia in
Miniature Park, **14**

Dreamland
(Taman Impian
Jaya Ancol), **15**

Fatahillah Square, **1**

Glodok, **7**

Istiqlal Mosque, **11**

Jakarta Cultural
Center (TIM), **12**

Jakarta Fine Art
Gallery, **6**

Maritime Museum, **3**

Museum of Old
Batavia, **4**

National Monument, **8**

National Museum, **9**

Pasar Ikan, **2**

Presidential Palace, **10**

Puppet Museum, **5**

Textile Museum, **13**

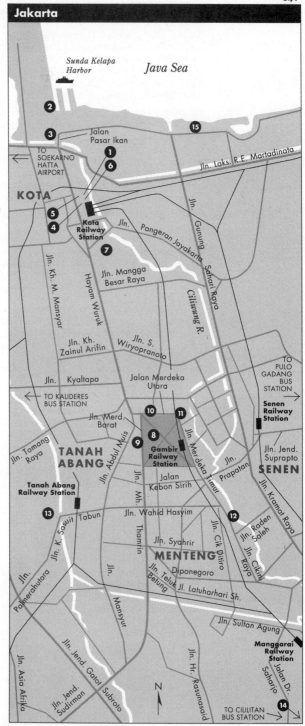

Jakarta

the market and enter the port through the main gate. Lined up at oblique angles to the piers are Makassar and Bugis sailing ships (called *prahus*). They look like beached whales, but they sail the Indonesian waters as they have for centuries, trading between the islands. Because the government plans to develop a tourist marina here and moor the trading ships elsewhere, this scene may soon change. *Admission charge to enter the port. Open daily 8–4.*

On the way back to Fatahillah Square on Jalan Pasar Ikan are two former Dutch East Indies warehouses that have been restored to house the **Maritime Museum** (Museum Bahari). One warehouse contains ancient maps and documents that tell the history of the spice trade; the other is devoted to models of Indonesian sailing vessels. Neither exhibit is very thorough. *Jln. Pasar Ikan 1, tel. 021/669–3406. Admission charge. Open Tues.–Thurs. 9–2, Fri. 9–11, Sat. 9–1, Sun. 9–3.*

Once in Fatahillah, you'll notice on the south side of the square the old Town Hall, built by the Dutch in 1707. Preserved as a historical building, it's now the site of the **Museum of Old Batavia** (Museum Sejarah Jakart). The history of Batavia is chronicled with antique maps, portraits, models of ancient inscribed Hindu stones, antique Dutch furniture, weapons, and coins. Unfortunately, the exhibits have few explanations in English, and the museum is rather gloomy. Beneath the halls are the dungeons where criminals once awaited trial. Prince Diponegoro, the Indonesian patriot who nearly managed to evict the Dutch from Java in 1830, was imprisoned here on his way to exile in Menado. All you see of them are the double-barred basement windows along Jalan Pintu Besar. *Jln. Taman Fatahillah No. 1, tel. 021/677424. Admission charge. Open Tues.–Thurs. 9–2:30, Fri. 9–noon, Sat. 9–1, Sun. 9–3.*

On the west side of Fatahillah Square, in a former Protestant church, is the **Puppet Museum** (Museum Wayang). It contains an extensive collection of traditional Indonesian *wayang kulit* (intricately cut leather shadow puppets used to perform stories from the Hindu epics *Ramayana* and *Mahabarata*) and *wayang golek* (wood puppets used to play Arabic folk tales or stories of prince Panji, a legendary Javanese prince associated with the conversion of Java to Islam), as well as puppets from Thailand, China, Malaysia, India, Kampuchea, and elsewhere. Also on display are puppets used for social education, including wayang kulit used in the Jogjakarta Family Planning program. *Jln. Pintu Besar Utara No. 27, tel. 021/679560. Admission charge. Open Tues.–Thurs. and Sun. 9–2, Sat. 9–1.*

On the east side of the square is the **Jakarta Fine Art Gallery** (Belai Seni Rupa Jakarta), in the former Palace of Justice, built between 1866 and 1870. The permanent collection includes paintings by Indonesia's greatest artists; contemporary works, such as wood sculptures; and the Chinese ceramic collection of Adam Malik, a former Indonesian vice-president. (A museum in the southeast of the Menteng district, the **Adam Malik Museum,** Jalan Diponegoro No. 29, tel. 021/337400 or 021/337388, has a larger display of his collection.) *Jln. Taman Fatahillah No. 2, tel. 021/676090. Admission charge. Open daily 9–2.*

Time Out The **Fatahillah** café (Jln. Taman Fattahillah No. 14, tel. 021/ 23842), on the north side of the square, is a friendly place for Indonesian hors d'oeuvres or ice cream and has interesting bric-a-brac for decor.

Behind the Old Town Hall, on Jalan Pangeran Jayakarta opposite the Kota Railway Station, is the oldest church in Jakarta. The exterior is plain, but inside you'll see 17th-century carved pillars, copper chandeliers, solid ebony pews, and plaques commemorating prominent Dutch administrators.

7 **Glodok** is Old Batavia's Chinatown. Much of this district has been demolished. But wander around Glodok Plaza (a shopping center and office building—the landmark of the area), and you can still find small streets crowded with Chinese restaurants and shops selling Chinese herbal medicines. Glodok is also a night entertainment district, but unless you know your way around, it's better left to the locals.

Tour 2: New Jakarta

8 Modern Indonesia is celebrated by Merdeka Square and the towering **National Monument** (Monumen Nasional, or Monas). Local wags call it "Sukarno's last erection," and many have scoffed at this Russian-built phallic symbol commemorating Indonesia's independence. The World Bank supplied funds for 77 pounds of pure gold to coat the "flame of freedom" atop the column while most Indonesians starved. But the monument now stands for Indonesia's impressive economic development. For the visitor it serves as a useful landmark. Take its interior elevator up to just below the flame for a bird's-eye view of the city. *Admission charge.*

In the basement of the monument is the **Museum of National History,** with a gallery of 48 dioramas illustrating Indonesia's history and struggle for independence. The Hall of Independence contains four national treasures: the flag raised during the independence ceremony in 1945; the original text of the declaration of independence; a gilded map of the Indonesian Republic; and the Indonesian coat of arms, which symbolizes the five principles of the Indonesian Republic: belief in one supreme god; a just and civilized humanity; unity of Indonesia; concensus arising from discussion and self-help; and social justice. *Jln. Silang Monas, tel. 021/681512. Admission charge. Open daily 9–5; closed last Mon. of each month.*

9 On the west side of Merdeka Square stands the **National Museum** (Museum Nasional), recognizable by the bronze elephant in front—a gift from the King of Thailand in 1871. The museum has the most complete collection of Indonesian antiquities and ethnic artwork in the country. There are five sections: Hindu and Buddhist stone carvings from the 7th to 15th centuries; an exhibit of prehistoric skulls, weapons, and cooking utensils dating back 4,000 years; Indonesian ethnic crafts; a treasure room with gold trinkets, jeweled weapons, and Buddhist statues; and one of the largest collections of Chinese ceramics outside China. If you can time your visit to coincide with one of the free tours given in English—Tuesday, Wednesday, and Thursday at 9:30 AM—you'll appreciate the museum a thousand times more. To the right, as you face the museum, is the Museum Shop, selling artifacts such as wayang golek or wayang kulit (made for tourist sale, but of good quality), and books on Indonesia. *Jln. Merdeka Barat No. 12, tel. 021/360976. Admission charge. Open Tues.–Thurs. and Sun. 8–2, Fri. 8–11, Sat. 8–1.*

From the museum, you may want to make a circle around the square in a taxi. Traveling clockwise, you'll pass the **Presidential Palace** on the northwest corner; the **Istiqlal Mosque** (Jln. Veteren), Indonesia's largest mosque (guided tours are available); and **Emmanuel Church** (Jln. Merdeka Timor 10), a classical Dutch Protestant church built in 1835.

Keep the taxi and continue south down Jalan Cikini Raya to the **Jakarta Cultural Center** (Taman Ismail Marzuki), or TIM. (If you walk, it is about 15 minutes from the south side of the square.) There is something happening here from morning to midnight. Most evenings, either the open-air theater or the enclosed auditorium stages some kind of performance, from Balinese dance to imported jazz, from gamelan concerts to poetry readings. Your hotel will have a copy of the monthly program. Two art galleries display paintings, sculpture, and ceramics. Also within the complex are an art school, an art workshop, a cinema, a planetarium, and outdoor cafés. *Taman Ismail Marzuki, Jln. Cikini Raya No. 73, tel. 021/342605. Admission charge. Open daily 8–8. Shows at the planetarium are Tues.–Sun. 7:30, and Sun. 10, 11, and 1.*

Directly west from TIM and about 10 minutes by taxi is the **Textile Museum** (Museum Tekstil), with a collection of more than 327 kinds of textiles made in Indonesia. It will give you an idea of what to expect by way of design and quality in the fabrics you'll come across when traveling in the country. *Jln. K. Sasuit Tubun No. 4, tel. 021/365367. Admission charge. Open Tues.–Thurs. 9–2, Fri. 9–11, Sat. 9–1, Sun. 9–2.*

Tour 3: Green Parks

About 12 km (7 mi) southeast of Merdeka Square and 30 minutes by taxi is the **Beautiful Indonesia in Miniature Park** (Taman Mini Indonesia Indah). Its 250 acres holds 27 full-size traditional houses, one from each Indonesian province. The Batak houses of North Sumatra, the Redong longhouses of the Kalimantan Dyaks, the cone-shape huts of Irian Jaya, and the Toraja houses of South Sulawesi are all represented. There are even miniature Borobudur and Prambanan temples.

Other attractions include a 30-minute movie, *Beautiful Indonesia,* shown daily from 11 to 5; the Museum Indonesia, with traditional costumes and handicrafts; a stamp museum; the Soldier's Museum, honoring the Indonesian struggle for independence; the Transportation Museum; and Museum Asmat, highlighting the art of the master carvers of the Asmat people of Irian Jaya. The park also has an orchid garden, an aviary, a touring train, cable cars, horse-drawn carts, paddleboats, and places for refreshment. English-speaking guides are available, if you call in advance. *20 km (12 mi) south of central Jakarta, off Jagorawi Toll Rd., tel. 021/849525. Admission charge. Museums open daily 9–3; outdoor attractions open daily 9–5.*

North of Kota and along the bay stretching east is **Dreamland** (Taman Impian Jaya Ancol), on 1,360 acres of land reclaimed in 1962. Billed as Southeast Asia's largest recreation area, it provides entertainment round the clock. A village unto itself, it has hotels, nightclubs, shops, and amusement centers, including an oceanarium with dolphin and sea lion shows, a golf course, a race car track, swimming pools and water slides. Here Africa is represented by a comedy of mechanized monkeys, America by a Wild West town, Europe by a mock Tudor house, and Asia by buildings from Thailand, Japan, India, and Korea. Rides, shooting galleries, and food stalls surround these attractions. Because Ancol is near Kota, you may want to spend the afternoon here after touring Old Batavia. Avoid coming on weekends, however, when it is thronged with Jakarta families. *Tel. 021/681512. Admission charge. Open daily 24 hrs.*

Short Excursions from Jakarta

The Highlands You can explore some of the lovely countryside around Jakarta in a day trip. The sprawling, smoky city of **Bogor,** 60 km (36 mi) south of the capital, hides several attractions. Travel agents *(see* Guided Tours, above) can arrange a visit of the former **presidential palace.** Behind the white-porticoed building are the **Botanical Gardens,** founded in 1817 by the first English governor-general of Indonesia, maintained by the Dutch, and adopted by Sukarno. The 275-acre garden has 15,000 species of plants, hundreds of trees, an herbarium, cactus gardens, and ponds with enormous water lilies. *Admission charge. Open daily 9–5.*

The road from Bogor winds through tea plantations and rain forests, past waterfalls and lakes. This is the **Puncak** region, where on clear days you'll get views of the Gede, Pangrango, and Salak mountains. At the **Safari Park,** 75 km (46 mi) from Jakarta on the road to Puncak, you can fondle lion cubs, ride elephants, and watch other animals roam around. *Admission charge. Open daily 9–5.*

Krakatau You'll need to make an overnight trip to see the famous **Krakatau** (Krakatoa) volcano, in the Sunda Strait between Sumatra and Java. This Krakatau is actually the son of the volcano that erupted in 1883, killing 36,000 people and creating marvelous sunsets seen around the world for the next two years. The **Carita Krakatau Beach Hotel** at Carita Beach, 150 km (95 mi) west of Jakarta, will arrange trips to the volcano and is a destination in itself *(see* Beaches, below).

What to See and Do with Children

Beautiful Indonesia in Miniature Park *(see* Tour 3). **Fantasy World** (Dunia Fantasi) at Dreamland *(see* Tour 3). The **planetarium** at the Jakarta Cultural Center *(see* Tour 2) has astronomy shows. *Jln. Cikini Raya No. 73, tel. 021/342605. Admission charge. Show times Tues.–Sun. at 7:30 PM, Sun. also at 10 AM, 11 AM, and 1 PM.*

Shopping

Markets **Jalan Surabaya Antiques Stalls** (Pasar Barang Antik Jalan Surabaya), the "flea market" of Jakarta, has mundane goods at either end, but in the middle you might find delftware, Chinese porcelain, old coins, old and not-so-old bronzes, and more. You *must* bargain. Open daily 9–6.

Pasar Melawai (Blok M, Jln. Melawai) is a series of buildings and stalls with everything from clothing to toys, cosmetics, and fresh foods. English is spoken. Open daily 9–6.

Specialty Stores
Antiques For serious antique shopping, try Jalan Paletehan I (Kebayoran Baru), Jalan Maja Pahit and Jalan Gajah Mada (Gambir/ Kota), Jalan Kebon Sirih Timur and Jalan H.A. Salim (Mentang), and Jalan Ciputat Raya (Old Bogor Rd.). Some reliable shops are **NV Garuda Arts, Antiques** (Jln. Maja Pahit No. 12, Kota, tel. 021/342712), **Madjapahit Art and Curio** (Jln. Melawai III/4, behind Sarinah Jaya Department Store, tel. 021/715878), **Alex Papadimitiou** (Jln. Pasuruan No. 3, Meteng, no sign, tel. 021/348748).

Textiles **Batik Mira** (Jln. MPR Raya No. 22, tel. 021/761138) has expensive but excellent-quality batik. Its tailors will do custom work, and customers can ask to see the factory at the rear of the store.

Batik Srikandi (Jln. Melawasi VI, 6A, Blok M, tel. 021/736604) has top-quality batik with many unusual designs. **Batik Danar Hadi** (Jln. Raden Saleh No. 1A, tel. 021/342748) carries a large selection of batik. **Bin House** (Jln. Panarukan No. 33, tel. 021/335941) carries Indonesian handwoven silks and cottons, including ikat, plus antique textiles and objets d'art. Iwan Tirta is a famous designer of batik fabrics and clothing for men and women. His company and shop go by the name **PT Ramacraft:** (Jln. Panarukan No. 25, tel. 021/333122).

Handicrafts The **Sarinah** department store's third floor is devoted entirely to handicrafts (Jln. M.H. Thamrin 11, Menteng, tel. 021/ 323705).

Sports and Fitness

Diving **Jakarta Dive School and Pro Shop** (Hilton Hotel, Bazaar Shop No. 32, Jln. Jend. Sudiman, tel. 021/583051, ext. 9008) offers open-water lessons and equipment rental. **Dive Indonesia** (Borobudur Hotel, Jln. Lapangan Banteng Selatan, tel. 021/ 370108) specializes in underwater photography and arranges trips to Flores and Sulawesi islands. On Pulau Sepa is the **Thousand Island Resort and Diving Center** (Jln. Kalibesar Barat 29, tel. 021/678828).

Golf Jakarta has two well-maintained 18-hole golf courses open to the public, both extremely crowded on weekends: the **Ancol Golf Course** (Dreamland, tel. 021/682122), with pleasant sea views, and **Kebayoran Golf Club** (Jln. Asia-Afrika, Pintu No. 9, tel. 021/582508).

Health and Fitness Centers You can get a good workout in Jakarta whenever you need one. The **Clark Hatch Physical Fitness Center** has two facilities with up-to-date equipment plus massage, heat treatment, sauna, and whirlpool (Hotel Borobudur Intercontinental, Jln. Lap. Banteng Selatan, tel. 021/370108, and Jakarta Hilton Hotel, Jln. Gatot Subroto, tel. 021/583051). Other gyms include the **Medical Scheme** (Setiabudi Bldg. L., Jln. H.R. Rasuda Said, Kuningan, tel. 021/515367), **Pondok Indah Health and Fitness Centre** (Jln. Metro Pondok Indah, tel. 021/764906), and **Executive Fitness Centre** (ground floor, south tower, Kuningan Plaza, Jln. H.R. Rasuda Said, tel. 021/578–1706).

Jogging The **Hash House Harriers/Harriettes,** an Australia-based jogging club, has a chapter in Jakarta. Men run Monday at 5 PM, women Wednesday at 5 PM, and there's socializing in between. For meeting places and running routes, write to Hash House Harriers/Harriettes (HHH Box 46/KBY, Jakarta, tel. 021/799–4758).

Racquetball The **Borobudur Hotel** (Jln. Lapangan Bateng Selatan, tel. 021/370108) has courts.

Squash Nonguests can play squash at three top hotels when the courts are not fully booked: **Borobudur Intercontinental Hotel** (Jln. Lapangan Banteng Selatan, tel. 021/370108), **Jakarta Hilton International** (Jln. Jend. Gatot Subroto, tel. 021/583051), and **Mandarin** (Jln. M.H. Thamrin, tel. 021/321307).

Swimming Most of Jakarta's tourist hotels have pools. **Dreamland** has a four-pool complex, including a wave pool (*see* Tour 3).

Beaches

The Thousand Islands North of Jakarta in the Java Sea are the little **Pulau Seribu,** or Thousand Islands—a misnomer, because there are only 250 of them *(pulau* means island). Their white-sand beaches, covered with coconut palms, offer a retreat from the heat and bustle of the capital. For a day trip, you can hop over to **Kepulauan Seribu** by motorboat from Marina Jaya Ancol (tel. 021/681512), or take a hovercraft (the port is at Jln. Donggala 26A, Tanjun Priok, tel. 021/325608). Several islands have rustic getaways, such as the Kotok Island Resort, with 42 unspoiled acres of coconut groves and tropical foliage, plus good scuba diving and snorkeling *(see* Lodging, below). Accommodations are also available on Pulau Patri, Pulau Melinjo, Pulau Bidadari, and Pulau Onrust.

For island bookings, contact **PT Pulau Seribu Paradise** (Setiabudi Bldg. 1, ground floor, block C1, tel. 021/515884), **PT Seabreeze** (Marina Ancol, tel. 021/680048), **PT Sarotama Prima Perkasa** (Jln. Ir. H. Juanda III/6, tel. 021/342031), or **Pulau Seribu Marine Resort PT Pantara** (Wisata Jaya Rm., 6/7 Hotel Borobudur, Jln. Lapangan Banteng Selatan, tel. 021/370108).

Carita Beach Quiet and unspoiled, Carita Beach lies 150 km (95 mi) west of Jakarta. The **Carita Krakatau Beach Hotel** has equipment for all water sports and arranges trips to the Krakatau volcano, a four-hour boat ride away *(see* Short Excursions from Jakarta, above). Air-conditioned buses leave daily from the hotel's reservation office in Jakarta (ground floor arcade, Hotel Wisata International, Jln. Thamrin, tel. 021/320252 or 320408, ext. 125). Those who take the bus get a 25% discount on their first night's stay at the hotel.

Dining

Introduction All the major hotels have Western and Indonesian restaurants; many of the Indonesian restaurants also offer Chinese food. Outside the hotels, dining options range from restaurants providing formal atmosphere to inexpensive street stalls.

The following terms appear frequently on Indonesian menus:

bakmi goreng—fried noodles with bits of beef, pork, or shrimp, tomatoes, carrots, bean sprouts, cabbage, soy sauce, and spices

dendeng ragi—thin square of beef cooked with grated coconut and spices

gudeg—chicken with jackfruit

ikan—fish

kelian ayam—Sumatran chicken curry

nasi champur—steamed rice with bits of chicken, shrimp, and vegetables with sambal

nasi goreng—fried rice with shallots, chilies, soy sauce, and catsup; at breakfast, likely to be topped with a fried egg; at other meals, may include pork (in Bali), shrimp, onions, cabbage, mushrooms, or carrots

nasi rames—a miniature rijstaffel

rijstaffel—literally, "rice table"; steamed rice with side dishes such as sayur lodeh, gudeg, or kelian ayam

sambal—a spicy, chili-based relish

satay—grilled skewered *ayom* (chicken), *babi* (pork), *daging* (beef), *kambing* (lamb), or ikan, served with a spicy peanut sauce

sayur lodeh—a spicy vegetable stew

soto ayam—chicken soup, varying from region to region but usually including shrimp, bean sprouts, spices, chilies, and fried onions or potatoes.

Expensive
Chinese
★
The Spice Garden. The Taiwanese chef at this elegant, high-ceilinged restaurant prepares 160 spicy Szechuan specialties, including sliced braised chicken with hot pepper oil and abalone soup with fermented black beans. The crimson-and-gold decor includes batik wall hangings by Indonesia's renowned designer Iwah Tirta. *Mandarin Oriental Hotel, Jln. M.H. Thamrin, tel. 021/321307. Reservations advised. Dress: dressy. AE, DC, MC, V.*

Continental
Oasis. The Oasis serves international cuisine as well as a traditional rijstaffel. A specialty is medallions of veal Oscar, in a cream sauce with mushrooms, crabmeat, and asparagus. The atmosphere lives up to the cuisine in this lovely old house decorated with tribal art and textiles. A combo alternates with Batak singers to provide music nightly. *Jln. Raden Saleh No. 47, tel. 021/326397. Reservations necessary. Dress: dressy. AE, DC, V. Closed Sun.*

French
Le Bistro. Candlelit and intimate, with checked tablecloths and copper pots, the decor here puts you in the mood for the classic Provençal menu—simple food, prepared with herbs, from the south of France. Try the roast chicken with rosemary and thyme. At the back of the dining room is a circular piano bar where you can have an after-dinner liqueur and maybe persuade one of the hostesses to sing. *Jln. K.H. Wahid Hasyim 75, tel. 021/364272. Reservations recommended. Jacket and tie suggested. AE, DC, V.*

Japanese
Tora-Ya. Some say this is Jakarta's best Japanese restaurant. The several attractive small dining rooms, each with a clean, spare decor, reflect the Japanese aesthetic. The service is low-key and very good. Both sushi and *kaiseki* (banquet) cuisine are offered. *Jln. Gereja Theresia No. 1, tel. 021/310–0149. Reservations suggested. Jacket and tie required. AE, DC, V.*

Moderate
British
The George and Dragon. For a change from rice dishes, try this restaurant for fish and chips or steak, kidney, and mushroom pie. The atmosphere is informal, and the bar, the first British pub in Jakarta, is very friendly. The decor is warm and cozy,

with lots of wood. **George's Curry House** next door is under the same management and serves Indian, Sri Lankan, and Sumatran curries. Specialties include *tandoori murk*, chicken marinated in yogurt and spices, then charcoal-roasted. *Jln. Teluk Betung No. 32, tel. 021/325625. Reservations advised for weekends at George's Curry House. Dress: casual. AE, V.*

Mexican **Green Pub.** The Green Pub is recommended not only for its Mexican food but for the live country-western music on Saturday and jazz on Thursday. The decor is an attempt at Western saloon style, and the burritos and enchiladas are quite authentic. *Jakarta Theatre Bldg., Jln. M.H. Thamrin 9, tel. 021/359332, or Jln. H.R. Rasuna Said, Setia Budi Bld. 1, tel. 021/517983. No reservations. Dress: casual. AE, V.*

Indonesian **Handayani.** This is a true neighborhood restaurant, with friendly service and some English-speaking help. Decor is not its strong point—lines of tables and chairs in a bare room. But Handayani is popular with locals for its Indonesian food. The extensive menu offers such dishes as chicken bowels steamed in banana leaves, beef intestine satay, and goldfish fried or grilled, along with lobster-size king prawns cooked in a mild chili sauce. The *nasi goreng handayani* is a special version of the Indonesian staple. *Jln. Abdul Muis No. 35E, tel. 021/373614. Reservations not necessary. Dress: casual. DC, V.*

In the Streets of Jakarta. Around the pool on Friday night, the Hilton hotel creates a completely "safe" version of the food stalls found throughout the city, with satays, Indonesian fried chicken, and various rice dishes. Since the Hilton is in the expatriate district, you'll see many Europeans dropping in for Friday night dinner. *Jakarta Hilton International, Jln. Jend. Gatot Subroto, tel. 021/583051. Reservations advised for Fri. night. Jacket and tie suggested. AE, DC, MC, V.*

Mira Sari. Regional Indonesian specialties are served in the air-conditioned dining room, in the garden, or on the terrace. Comfortable rattan chairs with soft pillows, fresh flowers on the tables, and warm, friendly service make this a congenial spot. The menu includes a very good version of Indonesian chicken soup, excellent spiced grilled fish, prawns grilled with spices and chilies, and roast or fried spiced chicken. *Jln. Patiunus 15, tel. 021/771621. Reservations required. Jacket and tie suggested. No credit cards.*

★ **Sari Kuring.** This restaurant near Merdeka Square serves very good Indonesian seafood, especially the grilled prawns and fried Thailand fish "à la Sari Kuring," marinated in spices, then quickly fried. The restaurant is large, but on many levels connected by stone steps, so there is a feeling of some intimacy. *Jln. Silang Monas Timur 88, tel. 021/352972. Reservations suggested. Dress: casual. AE, V.*

Multinational **Vic's Viking.** Centrally located (near the Hotel Indonesia and the Mandarin Oriental, Vic's offers a vast buffet of Indonesian, Chinese, and some European dishes. This is a restaurant for tourists and does get a little hectic, with groups of people picking their way down the buffet line, but if you are starving or simply want to sample many dishes, it is a good choice. *Jln. M.H. Thamrin No. 31, tel. 021/322452. Reservations suggested. Jacket and tie suggested. V.*

Vietnamese **Paregu.** Paregu has the best Vietnamese food in town, a simple decor with Oriental embellishments, and top-notch service.

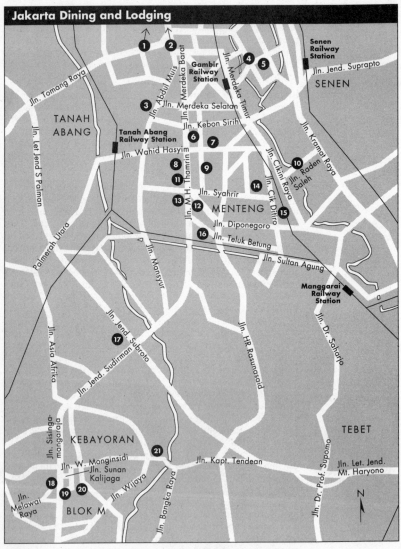

Jakarta Dining and Lodging

Dining

The George & Dragon/George's Curry House, **16**
Green Pub, **6**
Handayani, **3**
In the Streets of Jakarta, **17**
Le Bistro, **7**
Mira Sari, **18**
Oasis, **10**
Omar Khayyam, **15**
Paregu, **19**
Sari Kuring, **4**
The Spice Garden, **12**
Tora-Ya, **9**
Vic's Viking, **8**

Lodging

Hotel Borobudur Intercontinental, **5**
Hotel Indonesia, **13**
Interhouse, **20**
Jayakarta Tower, **2**
Kebayoran Inn, **21**
Kotok Island Resort, **1**
Mandarin Oriental, **12**
Marcopolo, **14**
President Hotel, **11**

Try the Vietnamese version of spring rolls; fried rice with scrambled eggs, chicken, shrimp, and a blend of herbs and spices; and the herbed seafood. *Jln. Sunan Kalijaga No. 64, tel. 021/774892. Reservations suggested. Dress: casual. No credit cards.*

Inexpensive Indian **Omar Khayyam.** In addition to an Indian buffet lunch, there is an extensive menu of specialties, including very good curries and tandoori dishes. The restaurant's decor gives homage to the eponymous Persian poet: Some of his poetry is inscribed on the walls. Try the chicken *tikka makhanwalla,* boneless tandoori chicken with tomato, butter, and cream sauce; or the marinated fish, wrapped in a banana leaf and deep-fried. *Jln. Antara No. 5–7, tel. 021/356719. No reservations. Dress: casual. No credit cards.*

Lodging

Jakarta has some world-class accommodations, with all the modern amenities. Most tourist hotels are south of Merdeka Square. In 1990 and 1991 several new hotels, including a Hyatt, will open along Jalan M.H. Thamrin. If you book your hotel through a travel agency, you will probably receive a better rate than if you make reservations directly with the hotel *(see* Travel Agencies in Important Addresses and Numbers, above).

Very Expensive **Hotel Borobudur Intercontinental.** The hotel's marble reception area has a carved-stone reproduction of a relief panel from the Borobudur temple for which it is named. Teak and batiks are used to create an opulent Indonesian atmosphere. Billed as "your country club in Jakarta," this large, modern hotel complex boasts 23 acres of landscaped gardens and excellent facilities. Floor-to-ceiling windows at the back of the Pendopo Lounge look out onto the tropical gardens, which makes the lounge a delightful place for afternoon tea, cocktails, or snacks. The guest rooms are spacious, with Javanese accents, and have all the amenities: minibar, color TV with in-house movies and satellite channels, IDD telephone. The Garden Wing, has suites with kitchens. The Music Room disco has the feel of a private club. Restaurants include the Toba Rotisserie for Continental cuisine, the Keio Japanese Restaurant, the Nelayan Seafood Restaurant, and the Bogor Brasserie for informal meals and snacks. *Jln. Lapangan Banteng Selatan, Box 329, Jakarta 10710, tel. 021/370108. 852 rooms, including 140 suites in the Garden Wing. Facilities: 4 restaurants, tea/cocktail lounge, disco, 24-hr room service, Olympic-size pool, 8 tennis courts, 5 squash courts, racquetball, badminton court, jogging track, minigolf course, fitness center, business center, children's play area, conference and banquet facilities. AE, DC, MC, V.*

★ **Mandarin Oriental.** This is the most sophisticated hotel, with the best service, in Jakarta. The circular, elegant lobby has three tall, beautifully carved Batak roofs, each housing a Sumatran statue. An open mezzanine above the lobby provides comfortable seating for tea or cocktails and some elegant shops, including a gallery for Ide Bagus Tilem, Bali's master woodcarver. The guest rooms are spacious and have top-quality furnishings: thick russet carpeting, floral bedspreads, offwhite draperies on the picture windows, and dark wood furniture. Thick terry bathrobes hang in the marble bathrooms, and rooms have minibars and color TV. Complimentary afternoon tea and hors d'oeuvres are delivered to your room. Restaurants include the Club Room, with classic French cuisine, Spice Garden (*see* Dining, above), the Clipper Lounge for light meals, the Pelangi Terrace for breakfast or buffet lunch by the pool, and the Captain's Bar for cocktails and music in a nautical atmosphere. *Jln. M.H. Thamrin, Box 3392, Jakarta, tel. 021/321307. 455 rooms. Facilities: 4 restaurants, cocktail bar, 24-hr room service, health center, outdoor pool, sauna, business center, meeting and conference rooms. AE, DC, MC, V.*

Expensive　**Hotel Indonesia.** Built for the Asia Games in 1962, the Hotel Indonesia was Jakarta's first high rise. Recently refurbished, it offers comfort, if not luxury. Room decor is modern, with spare hotel furniture, but with Indonesian-patterned bedcovers and framed batik on the walls. The rooms are utilitarian, with color TV and minibar. *Jln. M.H. Thamrin, Box 54, Jakarta, tel. 021/320008. 666 rooms. Facilities: 2 restaurants, bar, large outdoor pool, conference facilities. AE, DC, MC, V.*

Kotok Island Resort. On 42 unspoiled acres of coconut groves, this resort two hours from Jakarta by boat owns all the island except the eastern tip, which belongs to a private Japanese club. The resort has 22 bungalows with bamboo walls and basic bamboo furniture, plus a tiled shower bathroom. Eight units are air-conditioned, but thanks to the sea breezes, the rest are comfortable with just an overhead fan. This is a back-to-nature environment, and the accommodations are rustic, with primitive plumbing. The dining room—an open-air pavilion over the water—serves well-prepared Indonesian specialties, especially grilled fresh fish. Licensed instructors give scuba diving courses. There's informal entertainment in the evening, and the hostess/manager is highly knowledgeable about Southeast Asian culture. The resort provides a launch service from Jakarta. *The reservation office is at the Duta Merlin Shopping Arcade, 3rd floor, Jln. Gajah Mada 3–5, Jakarta, tel. 021/362948. 22 rooms. Facilities: restaurant, bar, boutique, diving center (diving packages available). No credit cards, unless you book through a travel agent.*

President Hotel. Like many other hotels in the Japanese Nikko Hotel group, the President has a spare, utilitarian atmosphere but is equipped with all the modern amenities. Guest rooms are simple, with blue-and-navy striped fabrics and plain wood furniture. The bathrooms, as in Japan, are small. The President offers good Japanese food at its Ginza Benkay restaurant, Japanese and Indonesian at the Kahyangan, and Chinese at the Golden Pavilion. *Jln. M.H. Thamrin 59, Jakarta 10350, tel. 021/320508. 354 rooms. Facilities: 3 restaurants, cocktail lounge, coffee shop, banquet and conference facilities. AE, DC, MC, V.*

Moderate　**Jayakarta Tower.** This tourist-class hotel is within walking dis-
★　tance of Kota. The marble lobby is accented with hand-blown chandeliers and carved-wood panels. The coffee shop's menu includes Western and Indonesian specialties, but ask to see the special Thai menu. Guest rooms are spacious. Each has a double or two twin beds, with Javanese patterned spreads, plus a table and two chairs and a vanity/desk. Only executive rooms have minibars. Restaurants include the Munakata, a branch of a Tokyo restaurant; and the Dragon, a Chinese restaurant with a separate Thai menu—the better choice. Next door, and affiliated with the hotel, is the Stardust Discotheque. *Jln. Hayam Wuruk 126, Box 803, Jakarta 11001, tel. 021/629–4408. 435*

rooms. Facilities: 2 restaurants, coffee shop, 24-hr room service, disco, large outdoor pool, health center, meeting and banquet rooms. AE, DC, MC, V.

Inexpensive **Interhouse.** Centrally located in Kebayoran—the expatriate neighborhood and shopping district—this hotel offers comfortable, though not large, air-conditioned rooms with pleasant, homey furnishings and usually a pastel decor. *Jln. Melawai Raya No. 18–20, Box 128/KBYB, Jakarta, tel. 021/716408. 130 rooms. Facilities: restaurant. AE, V.*

Kebayoran Inn. Just south of the center of Jakarta, this is a quiet, residential-type lodging. The clean, air-conditioned rooms are simply decorated, with an Indonesian batik or ikat here and there. *Jln. Senayan 87, Jakarta, tel. 021/775968. 61 rooms. Facilities: restaurant. AE, V.*

Marcopolo. This basic and economical hotel caters to Asian business travelers. Its air-conditioned rooms have private baths, but hot water is available only in the morning and evening. The rooms are relatively clean, though plainly decorated. *Jln. T. Cik Ditiro 19, Jakarta, tel. 021/325409. 181 rooms. Facilities: restaurant/coffee shop, outdoor pool, nightclub. AE, V.*

The Arts

For information on Jakarta art events, good sources to check are the *Indonesian Observor* or contact the City Visitor Information Center (tel. 021/354094).

Plays, music and dance performances, art shows, and films are held at the **Taman Ismail Marzuki** arts center. Monthly schedules of events are distributed to hotels. *Jln. Cikini Raya No. 73, tel. 021/342605.*

Jakarta Hilton Cultural Program (Indonesia Bazaar, Hilton Hotel, Jln. Jend. Sudirman, tel. 021/583051). Programs of regional dance are offered weekly.

At the **Bharata Theater** (Jln. Kalilio, no tel.), regular performances of traditional *wayang orang* (dance-dramas), depicting stories from the *Ramayana* or *Mahabharata* epics, are staged from 8:15 to midnight every night but Monday and Thursday. Sometimes the folk play *Ketoprak*, based on Javanese history, is also performed.

Wayang kulit (leather shadow-puppet plays, depicting stories from the *Ramayana* or *Mahabharata)* or wayang golek (wood puppet plays, usually depicting Islamic legends) are performed twice a month at the **Museum Nasional** (Jln. Merdeka Barat No. 12, tel. 021/360976).

The **Wayang Museum** (Jln. Pintu Besar Utara No. 27, tel. 021/ 679560) also offers puppet performances. Check with the museum for dates and times.

Beautiful Indonesia in Miniature (off Jagorawi toll rd. tel. 021/ 849525) offers various regional dances on Sunday and holidays from 10 to 2. (*Also see* Tour 3 in Exploring Jakarta, above).

Batik Berdikari (Jln. Masjid in Palmerah, southwest of Merdeka Square, tel. 021/5482814), a shop with a factory on the premises, presents various types of Indonesian batik, and displays the ways batik is made, either hand-drawn or printed. Open daily 9–4.

Nightlife

Across from the Sarinah department store, the long-established **Jaya Pub** has a piano bar with lively music and vocalists at night. Very popular with expatriates and Indonesians alike. *Jln. M.H. Thamrin No. 12, tel. 021/327508. Open daily noon–2AM.*

The dimly lit **Tanamur** has good jazz and soft rock and is usually pretty crowded. *Jln. Tanah Abang Timur 14, tel. 021/353947. Open nightly 9–2.*

The **Pit Stop** nightclub/disco is a favorite. *Hotel Sari Pacific, Jln. M.H. Thamrin, tel. 021/323707. Open nightly 9–2.*

The **Ebony Videotheque** is a lively, posh two-floor disco with a large screen for viewing old movies and a Saturday-night floor show. *Kuningan Plaza, Jln. Rasuna Said No. C11–14, tel. 021/513700. Open Sun.–Thurs. 9 PM–2 AM, Fri. and Sat. 9 PM–3AM.*

The **Stardust**, housed in a former theater, claims to be Asia's largest disco. *Jayakarta Tower Hotel, Jln. Hayam Wuruk 126, tel. 021/629–4408. Open nightly 9 PM–2 AM.*

Central Java

Introduction

Central Java nurtured some of Indonesia's great Indian kingdoms in the 8th and 9th centuries, including the Buddhist Sailendras, who built the Borobudur temple, and the Hindu Sanjayans, who made Prambanan their religious center. Today tourists use Jogjakarta as a base for visiting these temples, the best-known architectural and cultural sites of Indonesia. Jogjakarta, a city of some 300,000 on a fertile plain in the shadow of three volcanoes, has many hotels, restaurants, and shops. The ancient city of Solo, 64 km (40 mi) to the east, is quieter and less commercial, but also a cultural center.

Arriving and Departing by Plane

Airports and Airlines From Jakarta's Soekarno-Hatta Airport, **Garuda** (Jakarta tel. 021/334425, Jogjakarta tel. 0274/4400–5184) offers several daily flights to **Adisucipto Airport,** 10 km (6 mi) east from Jogjakarta. Flights take about 45 minutes. They fill up quickly, so reservations are essential. There are also flights into Jogja from Denpasar (Bali) and Surabaya (Java).

Between the Airport and Center City A minibus runs until 6 PM from the Adisucipto Airport to the terminal on Jalan Senopati for Rp 250; from there you can catch a becak to your hotel. Taxis to or from downtown charge Rp 5,000. The major hotels send their own minibuses to the airport.

Arriving and Departing by Car, Train, and Bus

By Car The distance between Jakarta and Jogjakarta is 618 km (371 mi). Although the scenery may be beautiful, the drive is slow going and service areas are few and far between. It is advisable to hire a driver when traveling through Indonesia.

By Train Trains from the Gambir and Kota railway stations in Jakarta leave several times daily for Jogja. The trip takes seven–12 hours and costs Rp 6,700–Rp 21,500, depending on whether the train is an express or a local and on the class of ticket. The most comfortable trip is via the *Bima Express*, which leaves Gambir at 4 PM and arrives in Jogja at 1:15 AM. The train has sleeping compartments, and you can have someone from your hotel meet you at the station.

There are also daily trains from Bandung (an eight-hour trip) and from Surabaya (seven hours).

By Bus Night buses from Jakarta take about 14 hours and cost about Rp 12,250. Buses also run from Denpasar on Bali (12 hours), Bandung (seven hours), and Surabaya (eight hours). (*See* Getting Around by Bus in Staying in Indonesia, above). **Antar Lintas Sumatra** (Jln. Jati Baru 87A, Jakarta, tel. 021/320970) or **PT. ANS** (for Java, Bali, and Sumatra), Jln. Senen Raya 50, Jakarta, tel. 021/340494.

Getting Around

By Becak Jogja has 25,000 becak, and they are the main form of public transportation.

By Taxi Catch taxis in front of the larger hotels, such as Garuda or Mutiara; in general, they do not cruise the streets. Taxis are not metered; there are hourly charges, averaging Rp 5,000 per hour within the city, with a two-hour minimum. There's little bargaining leeway within Jogja; drivers will negotiate more for out-of-town trips.

By Bicycle Bicycles may be rented for Rp 1,000 a day from the **Hotel Indonesia** (Sosromenduran IV), the **Restaurant Malioboro** (Jln. Malioboro 67), and from other shops.

By Motor Scooter These cost about Rp 8,000 a day and may be rented from **Yogya Rental** (Jln. Pasar Kembang 86) and **A.A. Rental** (Jln. Pasar Kembang 25, tel. 0274/4489).

Important Addresses and Numbers

Tourist Information Jogjakarta's **Tourist Information Office** (Jln. Malioboro 16, tel. 0274/3543) has maps, schedules of events, bus and train information, and a helpful staff. Open Mon.–Sat. 8–8. In Solo, the Tourist Information Office is at Jalam Slamet Riyadi 235, tel. 0271/6508. Open Mon.–Sat. 8–5.

Emergencies Police, tel. 110; **fire,** tel. 113; **ambulance,** tel. 118, for Solo and Jogjarkarta..

Travel Agencies Jogja and Solo's three main companies are **Nitour** (Jln. K.H.A. Dahlan 71, tel. 0274/3165), **Pacto** (Jln. Malioboro 72, tel. 0274/88195), and **Satriavi** (c/o Hotel Ambarrukmo Palace, Jln. Adisucipto, tel. 0274/88488).

Guided Tours

Hotels and travel agencies can arrange the following tours, either in a private chauffeured car or as a group tour by bus:

Jogja City A three-hour tour including the sultan's palace, Sono Budoyo Museum, Kota Gede silverworks, and batik and wayang workshops.

Borobudur	An eight-hour tour of Jogjakarta, the countryside, and the Borobudur, Mendut, and Pawon temples.
Prambanan	A three-hour tour of the temple complex.
Jogja Dieng Plateau	A 10-hour tour of the Dieng Plateau, with its spectacular scenery, sulfur springs, and geysers, plus a visit to Borobudur.
Art and Handicrafts	A five-hour tour of the local craft centers for leather puppets, woodcarving, silverwork, batik, and pottery.

Exploring Central Java

Numbers in the margin correspond with points of interest on the Central Java map.

Tour 1: Jogjakarta

1 Every Indonesian has a soft spot for **Jogjakarta,** or Jogja. It is in many respects the heart of Indonesia. Students from Jogja's Gajah Mada University account for some 20% of the city's population. Dance and choreography schools, wayang troupes, and poetry workshops make it an artist's mecca. Every evening classical drama and dance performances are staged somewhere in the city. Leading Indonesian painters and sculptors display their work in numerous galleries, and craft shopping is a major preoccupation. The batik here and in Solo is said to be superior even to Bali's.

Jogja sprawls. Unless you stay at the Garuda or one of the less expensive city hotels, chances are you will be a few kilometers from Jalan Malioboro. This thoroughfare is where the action is, day and night. It is the main shopping street, not only for established shops but also sidewalk stalls. These set up cardboard stands selling handicrafts until about 9 PM, then convert to food stalls serving Jogja's specialties: *nasi gudeg* (rice with jackfruit in coconut milk) and *ayam goreng* (marinated fried chicken). Malioboro is a fascinating street to stroll, and if you arrive by 8 PM, you can catch both the shops and the food.

At the southern end of Malioboro stands the *kraton,* or Sultan's palace. The large, grassy square in front of the kraton is the **Alun-alun,** where the townspeople formerly gathered to trade, gossip, and hear the latest palace news.

The Jogja kraton has special significance to Indonesians as the bastion against Dutch colonialism. During the War of Independence 1945–1949, Jogja's Sultan Hamengku Buwono allowed the Indonesian freedom fighters—including guerrilla commander Suharto, now the nation's president—to use the kraton as a military base. Built in 1756, it is a vast complex of pavilions and buildings, part of which—strictly off-limits to the public—is home to the present sultan. The complex is protected by 400 guardians (in blue shirts) and 1,000 servants (in red shirts).

At the center of the green-trimmed white palace is the **Golden Pavilion** (Bengsal Kengono), an open hall with carved teak columns and a black-and-gold interior, where weddings, cremations, and coronations are held. The complex includes a gallery exhibiting a collection of gamelan instruments. Try to time your visit to catch the Sunday classical dance rehea

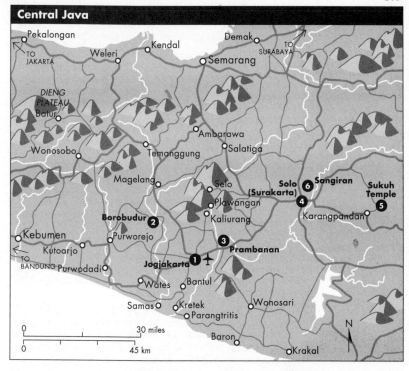

Central Java

crowns above the frame were mistresses, not wives). In yet another pavilion is a collection of sedan chairs. The last one was used in
1877; now a Rolls-Royce transports the sultan on ceremonial occasions. *No phone. Admission charge. Open Sun.–Thurs.*
8:30–1, Fri. and Sat. 8:30–11:30.

Behind the kraton is the recreational **Water Palace** (Taman
Sari), constructed by the same sultan who built the kraton. A
large artificial lake, sunken bathing pools, underground pas-
sageways, and towers where gamelan orchestras serenaded
the royalty were all part of this noble retreat. It was abandoned
in the 18th century and fell to ruin; the restored sections
give a sense of what pleasure the privileged enjoyed. Visit the
ornate bathing pools used by the princesses, the underground
mosque, and climb the tower from which the sultan watched his
concubines lounge by the water. *No phone. Admission free.*
Open daily 8–5.

Of Jogja's several museums, the most interesting and well-
maintained is the **Sono Budoyo Museum** on the square before
the kraton. Inside this traditional Javanese-style building is a
collection of crafts and batiks from Java and Bali. Its archaeological treasures include a small gold Buddha, and the display
of wayang golek, the wood puppets used in Muslim theater, is
charming. *Tel. 0274/2775. Admission charge. Open Tues.–*
Thurs. 8–1, Fri. and Sun. 8–11, Sat. 8–noon.

Out toward the airport, about 8 km (5 mi) southeast of Jogja, is
the **Affandi** museum, the home and studio of Indonesia's best-
known painter. A permanent collection of his works, along with

paintings by young artists, is exhibited in an oval, domed extension to the traditional paddy-field house. *Jln. Laksda, Adisucipto 67, no. tel. Admission free. Open daily 9–5.*

Sasono Wirotmo was the residence of Prince Diponegoro, who rebelled against the Dutch occupation and led a bloody guerrilla battle in the Java War (1825–30). The house is now a museum, displaying the prince's krises, lances, and other revered possessions. *Tegalrejo (4 km west of Jogjakarta), tel. 0274/3068. Donation. Open by appointment only.*

Tour 2: Borobudur

You can take guided coach tours from Jogja hotels or hire a minibus and guide (usually more informed) from a Jogja travel agency. Or take the public bus toward Samarung, then change at Muntilan for the Ramayana bus to **Borobudur.**

That it took perhaps 10,000 men 100 years to build it becomes credible the moment you set eyes on the cosmic structure of Borobudur, in the shadow of the powerful volcanoes that the Javanese believe are the abode of God. Borobudur is about 42 km (26 mi) from Jogjakarta. Try to go early in the morning— plan to end your two- to three-hour visit before noon—while the temperature is still relatively cool.

Borobudur was abandoned soon after completion (AD 850), and the forest moved in. The man who founded modern Singapore, Thomas Stamford Raffles (then the English lieutenant-governor of Java), and his military engineer, H.C.C. Cornelius, rediscovered the temple in 1814. A thousand years of neglect had left much of it in ruins, and the temple has undergone two mammoth restorations, first from 1907 to 1911, and then from the 1960s with the help of UNESCO and US$25 million. The second restoration took two decades to complete.

The temple is a giant stupa: Five lower levels contain 1,500 relief carvings depicting the earthly life of Siddhartha in his passage to enlightenment. Start at the eastern staircase on the first level and walk clockwise around each gallery to follow the sequence of Lord Buddha's life.

Above the reliefs are 432 stone Buddhas. Even higher, above the square galleries, are three circular terraces with 72 latticed stupas that hide statues depicting the Buddha's departure from the material world and existence on a higher plane. The top stupa symbolizes the highest level of enlightenment. Looking out at the surrounding mountains from the upper level of Borobudur, you feel some of the inspiration that created this grand monument. If you go around each of the nine galleries, you will have walked 4.8 km (3 mi) closer to heaven. On weekends the complex is fairly crowded—another reason to come early. *No phone. Admission charge. Open daily 6:15–5.*

About 1.5 km (1 mi) east of Borobudur, on the way back to the main road, is the small temple Candi Pawon, built around the same time as Borobudur. It is thought that worshipers purified themselves here on their way to Borobudur. Another kilometer or so farther east is the small 9th-century temple Mendut. The exterior of this friendly temple is superbly carved with some 30 large relief panels depicting scenes from the Buddha's previous incarnations. Inside stands a magnificent 3-m (10-ft) statue of

Buddha, flanked by the bodhisattvas Avalokitesvara and Vajrapani. *No phone. Admission charge. Open daily 9–5.*

Tour 3: Prambanan

③ Prambanan is a half-hour drive (16 km, or 10 mi) from Jogjakarta via the Solo road. If you book through a tour agency, you can combine a visit to Prambanan with a visit to Borobudur, or you can combine Prambanan with a trip to Solo, 46 km (29 mi) farther from Jogja. Minibuses go out to Prambanan from the Jalan Solo terminus in Jogja.

When the Sanjayan kingdom evicted the Buddhist Sailendras, the Sanjayans wanted to memorialize the return of a Hindu dynasty and, supposedly, undermine Borobudur. Toward this end, they built Prambanan. When the 9th-century complex was rediscovered in 1880, it had fallen into ruin from centuries of neglect and enveloping vegetation. In 1937 reconstruction began, and the work continues today.

The temple was built with an outer stage for commoners, a middle stage for high-ranking nobility, and main temple area for royalty. Of the original 244 temples, eight major and eight minor temples are still standing, in the highest central courtyard of the Prambanan plain.

The center temple, dedicated to Shiva the Destroyer, is the highest (47 m, or 155 ft) and the best-restored; Vishnu's is to the north, and Brahma's, to the south. Originally they were painted—Shiva's red, Brahma's white, Vishnu's a dark gray—but only traces of the paint remain. To the east of these temples are three smaller ones, which contained the "vehicles" of each god: Shiva's bull, Vishnu's elephant, and Brahma's goose. Only the bull is extant.

In part because the complex was dedicated to Shiva, and in part because Shiva's temple is the best-restored, this is where you will want to focus. Over the entrance is the head of Kali, a protection against evil from land. On the balustrade, the *naga* (serpent) guards against evil from the sea. The base is decorated with medallions with lions (an imported figure) or half-bird, half-human figures flanked by trees of good hope. Above these, on the outer balustrade, are carvings of classical Indian dancers and celestial beings.

The inner wall of the balustrade is carved with lively, sometimes frivolous, reliefs telling the story of the *Ramayana*. From the east gate, walk around the temple clockwise to follow the story in sequence. The reliefs show free-flowing movement, much humor, and a love of nature. In contrast to Borobudur's, these carvings combine a celebration of the pleasures and pains of earthly life with scenes from Hindu mythology. They are more fun to look at (monkeys stealing fruit and bird-women floating in air), but the drama they portray—the establishment of order in the cosmos—is just as serious.

In the main chamber, at the top of the east stairway, a four-armed statue of Shiva the creator and destroyer stands on a lotus base. In the south chamber, Shiva appears as divine teacher, with a big beard and big stomach. The statue in the western chamber is Ganesha, Shiva's elephant-headed son. And in the northern chamber, Shiva's consort, Durga, kills the demon buffalo. *No phone. Admission charge. Open daily 6–5.*

The numerous other Buddhist and Hindu temples between Jogja and Prambanan are in various states of ruin but merit at least a day of exploring. A great way to see them is to rent a bike and pack a lunch. Signs on the Jogja–Solo road point the way to the temples. Most are off the road, down small paths.

Tour 4: Solo

Minibuses leave for **Solo** throughout the day (7–5) from Jogjakarta's Terminal Terban (Rp 1,500) or may be caught along Jalan Sudirman or Jalan Solo. From Solo's **Gilligan bus terminal,** you take a bemo (Rp 300) or a becak (Rp 750) the 3 km (1.8 mi) into town. A shared taxi from Jogja to Solo costs Rp 2,500 per person. The train from Jogja takes one hour; third-class fare is only Rp 500.

Just 60 km (38 mi) east of Jogjakarta, Solo (also known as Surakarta or Sala) is less Westernized—and has fewer tourists—than Jogja. Solo has its own traditional batik designs and its own style of dance. And while its people are devoutly Muslim, their daily life is less religious.

There are two kratons, or sultan's palaces, in Solo. On the west side of town is the **Mangkunegaran Palace,** home of Prince Mangkunegoro, a complex of carved, gilded teak pavilions. The outer center pavilion, or *pendopo,* serves as the audience hall and is typical of a Javanese royal building. The Italian marble floor, laid in 1925, guardian lions from Berlin, and 50-ft roof supported by teak pillars make the pendopo very grand. Its ceiling is painted with a flame motif bordered by symbols of the Javanese zodiac, designed with the eight mystical colors (yellow to ward off sleep, green to subdue desire, purple to keep away bad thoughts, etc.). The effect is gaudy but dramatic.

The museum, in the ceremonial pavilion just behind the main pendopo, displays dance ornaments, masks, jewelry, chastity belts for men and women, and wayang kulit and wayang golek puppets. At center stage is the enclosed bridal bed (originally a room reserved for offerings to the rice goddess). To the left of the museum are the official reception rooms: a formal dining room, with a Javanese-style stained-glass window (made in Holland) and an ivory tusk carved with depictions of the wedding of Arjuna, one of the heroes of the Mahabharata; a mirrored parlor area; and a "bathing" room for royal brides. *No phone. Admission charge. Open Mon.–Thurs. and Sat. 9– noon, Fri. 9–11 AM.*

From the palace, return to Solo's main street, Jalan Slamet Riyadi, via Jalan Diponegoro. Just off Diponegoro is Pasar Triwindu, Solo's flea market, where hundreds of stalls sell everything from junk to old coins to batik. Bargain like crazy! *Open daily.*

Walk north about five blocks and take a left onto Gladak to reach Solo's other palace, **Kraton Kasuhunan** (sometimes called Kraton Solo). This kraton suffered terrible damage from a fire in 1985 that gutted the elaborate ceremonial pavilion. Now the palace is being rebuilt. The museum—one of Central Java's best—was unharmed by the fire. It contains a priceless collection of silver and bronze Hindu figures and Chinese porcelain, but the real treat is three royal carriages given to the sultanate by the Dutch in the 18th century. The English-speaking guide will greatly help you appreciate the collection. *No phone. Admission charge. Open Sat.–Thurs. 9–noon.*

Excursions from Solo
⑤

Sukuh Temple stands 35 km (21 mi) east of Solo. A hired car (cost: Rp 15,000) is the most convenient way to get there; the journey takes a good hour along winding, hilly roads. You can also reach it by bus, but it requires three changes: At Tertomoyo catch the bus to Tawangmangu, then get off at Karangpandan for a minibus to Sukuh.

Sukuh contains elements of Hinduism, Buddhism, and animism. Looking like an abbreviated pyramid, the delightful temple is full of cult symbols and objects with erotic suggestions. Though the temple was built in the 15th century, no one knows by whom or what cults were celebrated. Because few tourists make it here, the place has a mystical atmosphere, enhanced by the lush surrounding rice terraces. *Admission charge. Open daily 9–4.*

⑥ **Sangiran** is where Eugene Dubois discovered Java Man (or *Homo erectus*, as his species is now known) in 1891. The museum contains a replica of Java Man's cranium and models of *Homo sapiens'* ancestors who lived some 250,000 years ago, plus fossils of other forms of life, such as now-extinct elephants. You can get to Sangiran, 15 km (9 mi) north of Solo, by taking a bus to Kaliso, then walking 30 minutes to the site; or have a taxi take you from Solo for Rp 10,000 round-trip. *No phone. Admission charge. Open Mon.–Sat. 9–4.*

Shopping

Jogjakarta and Solo are a shopper's dream, but be selective—there's a lot of tacky merchandise alongside the treasures—and bargain gracefully. After you have offered your next-to-last price, walk away. You will probably be called back.

Shopping Streets

Jalan Malioboro in Jogja is lined with shops; the handicraft stalls turn into food stalls around 9 PM. Most of the merchandise is junk, but it's worth picking through. This is a convenient area to buy T-shirts or shorts.

Solo's main shopping street is **Jalan Secoyudan.** In addition to a score of goldsmiths, you'll find antiques stores selling curios from the Dutch colonial days, as well as krises and other Javanese artifacts. **Jalan Slamet Riyadi** also has antiques shops.

Specialty Shops
Batik

The patterned Indonesian textiles called batik—made by drawing on fabric with wax, then dyeing the unwaxed parts—can be found in all the stalls in Jogjakarta. Many prints with batik design are machine-made, however, so beware. Before you buy, try to visit the batik factories, where you can watch the process and shop in the showrooms. One such place is Jogja's **Batik Plentong** (Jln. Tirtodipurun No. 28, tel. 0274/2777), whose showroom has everything from yard goods to pot holders and batik clothing, hand-stamped and hand-drawn.

Solo has its own batik style, often using indigo, brown, and cream, as opposed to the brighter colors of Jogja's batiks. Prices are better in Solo, and you have some 300 batik factories to choose from. Aside from the shops along Jalan Secoyudan, visit **Pasar Klewer,** a huge batik market just outside the Kraton Solo with a fine selection of goods on the second floor. An established shop that sells batik and demonstrates the batik-making process is **Dinar Hadi Batik Shop** on Jalan Dr. Rajiman (no tel.).

Handicrafts Handicrafts in Jogjakarta include batik "paintings," batik-patterned T-shirts and other apparel or household items, small hand-tooled leather goods, pottery (items decorated with brightly colored elephants, roosters, and animals from mythology are made in Kasongan, just south of Jogja), and wayang kulit (leather) and wayang golek (wood) puppets. All the shops and stalls on Jalan Malioboro and around the kraton sell puppets and other handicrafts. The **Jogjakarta Handicrafts Center** on Jalan Adisucipto (no tel.), not far from the Ambarrukmo Palace Hotel, sells work by disabled craftsmen.

Leather Leather is a great buy in Jogjakarta. The shops and stalls on Jalan Malioboro offer a wide variety of goods, but you'll get better quality and design at **Kusuma** (Jln. Kauman 50, parallel to Malioboro, tel. 0274/5453). There's room for modest bargaining, but no credit cards are accepted.

Silver Many silversmiths have workshops and salesrooms in **Kota Gede**, 6 km (3 ½ mi) southeast of Jogja. The largest, **Tom's Silver** (Jln. Kota Gede 3-1 A, tel. 0274/3070 or 0274/2818), offers quality workmanship. Also try **MD Silver** (Jln. Keboan, tel. 0274/2063).

Dining

Jogjakarta **The Floating Restaurant.** This restaurant looks Moroccan, with
Expensive a pavilion overlooking gardens, and low tables—with ikat-covered floor cushions—as well as Western-style tables. At the center is a copious buffet of Indonesian specialties, which may include *gudeg* (chicken with jackfruit), the most famous dish of central Java, and *pepes ikan* (marinated fish baked with coconut). An Indonesian singer and instrumentalist provide background music. The place also has a barbecue buffet with Western dishes such as pasta carbonara, as well as Indonesian specialties, accompanied by native dance drama. *Ambarrukmo Palace, Jln. Laksda Adisucipto, tel. 0274/88488. Reservations are advised. Dress: casual. AE, DC, MC, V.*

Pesta Perak. Smartly decorated with wrought-iron furniture and a sultan-costumed maître d', Pesta Perak has excellent Javanese cuisine. Its rijstaffel includes satays, gudeg, and fish wrapped in banana leaves. *Jln. Tentura Rakyat Mataran 8, tel. 0274/86255. Reservations optional. Dress: smart casual. MC, V.*

Moderate **Sintawang.** Though the tables are Formica, the restaurant is clean and offers a wide range of outstanding seafood, either cooked Javanese-style or grilled for Western palates. Try the udang bakar (marinated and grilled prawns), *pais udang* (prawns spiced and grilled in a banana leaf), or *ikan asam manis* (fish in a sweet-and-sour sauce). *Jln. Magelang 9, tel. 0274/2901. No reservations. Dress: casual. AE, DC.*

Kasuma Sahid. Without a doubt this is the place to dine in Solo. Part of the Prince Hotel, this formal restaurant is light and airy, with white linen and polished silver. The menu, offering Indonesian specialties, features chicken with jackfruit and fish wrapped in banana leaves, with the restaurant's own special blend of spices. Western dishes with a nouvelle French influence and Indonesian accent are features as well. *Jl. Sugiyo-*

pranoto 22, Solo, tel. 0271/6356. No reservations. Dress: casual. AE, DC, MC, V.

Inexpensive **Ny Suharti.** People come here for the best fried chicken in Java,
★ perhaps in all of Indonesia. Order one for two people, with rice
on the side. The chicken is boiled, marinated in spices, then
fried to a crisp. Forget charm or atmosphere. *Jln. Lakada
Adisucipto Km 7, tel. 0274/5522. No reservations. Dress: casual. No credit cards.*

Lodging

Jogjakarta Although there are some full-service hotels in Jogjakarta and
Solo that meet international standards, many hotels and guest
houses do not have such facilities as private bath and air-conditioning. When lodging in this area it is recommended that you
stay in an accommodation that offers these amenities.

Expensive **Ambarrukmo Palace.** Jogjakarta's premier hotel—its only
★ international-class accommodation—is built on the grounds of
the former royal country retreat. The lobby is spacious. Guest
rooms are large, decorated with light gay Indonesian-
patterned fabrics with mahogany furniture, and equipped
with all the amenities, including color TV and minibars. The
best have balconies overlooking the gardens. *Jln. Laksda
Adisucipto, Jogjakarta, tel. 0274/88488. 266 rooms. Facilities:
3 restaurants, bar, 24-hr room service, large outdoor pool,
travel agencies, shopping arcade. AE, DC, MC, V.*

Moderate **Hotel Garuda.** This imposing old hotel, with its private court-
★ yard in the center of town, has a modern annex behind the
colonial main building, which once housed several government
ministries. Some suites in the main building have high-
ceilinged sitting rooms overlooking the courtyard. The
standard guest rooms are plainly furnished but have all the latest conveniences, including color TV with video and minibar.
The restaurant offers Indonesian and Western food. *Jln.
Malioboro No. 72, Jogjakarta, tel. 0274/86353. 120 rooms. Facilities: restaurant, coffee shop, bar, 24-hr room service,
outdoor pool, poolside bar. AE, DC, MC, V.*
Sahid Garden Hotel. Many tour groups use this hotel, though it
is overpriced and in serious need of refurbishing. The cottage
rooms are the oldest and dowdiest. The new tower is an im-
provement, but you still can't be sure of hot water. The staff,
however, is very friendly. *Jln. Babasari, Jogjakarta, tel. 0274/
87078. 142 rooms. Facilities: restaurant, bar, 24-hr room service, outdoor pool, travel desk. AE, DC, MC, V.*

Inexpensive **Batik Palace Hotel.** For modest accommodation in the center of
Jogjakarta, this hotel offers worn but clean rooms with twin
beds, table, and chair. The lobby, decorated with batiks and
crafts, is a comfortable place to relax. *Jln. Mangkubumi 46,
Box 115, Jogjakarta, tel. 0274/2229. 38 rooms. Facilities: restaurant, outdoor pool. V.*
Mutiara. This downtown hotel has two buildings. The rooms in
the older one are somewhat worn and musty. The newer building has fresher rooms that, in spite of their pale green and
orange-flecked decor, are worth the extra $5. *Jln. Malioboro
18, Jogjakarta, tel. 0274/4531. 109 rooms. Facilities: restaurant, coffee shop, outdoor pool and pool bar, 24-hr room
service. AE, DC, MC, V.*
Rose Guest House. The rooms here are very modest but do have

private baths and either air-conditioning or overhead fans. The tariff includes breakfast and airport transfer, so this hotel is an extremely good value. *Jln. Prawirotaman 22, Jogjakarta, tel. 0274/27991. 29 rooms. Facilities: small restaurant, outdoor pool. No credit cards.*

Solo
Moderate
★

Kusuma Sahid Prince Hotel. Three two-story buildings and outlying bungalows are set on 5 acres of landscaped gardens. The lobby veranda—the original *pendopo agung* (prince's courtyard)—is a wonderful place for tea or a cooling drink. Most guest rooms have twin beds, a couple of upholstered chairs, and a writing desk; the best overlook the pool. The bathrooms are pristine, and hot water is usually available. The dining room offers excellent Indonesian and Western food at reasonable prices. *Jln. Sugiyopranoto 22, Solo, tel. 0271/6356. 103 rooms. Facilities: restaurant, bar, 24-hr room service, large outdoor pool, travel desk, drugstore and shops, banquet/ meeting rooms. AE, DC, MC, V.*

Inexpensive

Mangkunegaran Palace Hotel. Adjacent to the palace and owned by the prince, this hotel has great potential, but it desperately needs renovation. If you don't mind cracked plaster and a musty smell, the Mangkunegaran is the least expensive palace you are ever likely to stay in. The most appealing room is the dining room, which has a batik-painted ceiling just like the palace's. *Istara Mangkunegaran Solo, tel. 0271/5683. 50 rooms. Facilities: restaurant, outdoor pool, free admission to the palace. AE, DC, MC, V.*

The Arts

Eight-hour wayang kulit performances of the full *Ramayana* or *Mahabharata* are usually held every second Saturday of the month at **Sasono Hinggil,** just south of Jogja's kraton. These plays begin at 9 PM and last until dawn. Inquire at the Tourist Information Center.

Actors perform stories from the *Ramayana* nightly at the **People's Park** (Taman Hiburan Rakyat; Jln. Brig. Jen. Katamso, Jogjakarta). Shows last about two hours.

At the **Jogjakarta Crafts Center,** called Ambar Budaya, hour-long wayang kulit performances take place every Monday, Wednesday, and Saturday at 9:30 PM (Jln. Laksda Adisucipto, Jogjakarta, opposite the Ambarrukmo Palace Hotel).

The *Ramayana* ballet is performed outdoors before the Prambanan temple complex on four successive full-moon nights between May and October (weather permitting). Hotel tour desks can arrange tickets and transportation. This is an elaborate presentation with scores of dances, a full-blown orchestra, and armies of monkeys strutting around the stage. At the covered theater in the complex, traditional dancing is performed every Thursday evening 7:30–10. *Jln. Raya Jogja-Solo Km 16, Prambanan, Jogjakarta, tel. 0274/88544.*

At Solo's **Mangkunegaran Palace,** a gamelan orchestra performs each Saturday from 9 to 10:30 AM. Dance rehearsals are held on Wednesday from 10 to noon and on Monday and Friday afternoon.

Bali

Introduction

The "magic" of Bali has its roots in the fact that the island is religiously distinct from the rest of Indonesia: Unlike their Muslim neighbors, the Balinese are Hindus. Their faith also contains elements of Buddhism and of ancient animist beliefs indigenous to the archipelago. To the Balinese, every living thing contains a spirit; when they pick a flower as an offering to the gods, they first say a prayer to the flower. All over the island, from the capital city of Denpasar to the tiniest village, plaited baskets filled with flowers and herbs lie on the sidewalks, on the prows of fishing boats, and in markets. These offerings are made from dawn till dusk, to placate evil spirits and honor helpful ones. Stone figures guard the entryways to temples, hotels, and homes. The black-and-white-checked cloths around the statues' waists symbolize the balance between good and evil. Maintaining that harmony is the life work of every consolidated Balinese.

Indian culture came to Bali as early as the 9th century; by the 14th century, the island was part of the Hindu Majapahit empire of east Java. When that empire fell to Muslim invaders, Majapahit aristocrats, scholars, artists, and dancers fled to Bali, consolidating Hindu culture and religion there.

Although the island is only 140 km (84 mi) long by 80 km (48 mi) wide, a week would not be enough to appreciate Bali's beaches, temples, volcanoes, and towns. With Indonesia's most developed tourist infrastructure, Bali has three main beach areas on the southern coast where 90% of its visitors stay. Each has its distinctive appeal, and the three are within easy reach of one another.

Kuta has one of the world's most splendid golden-sand beaches. It was the first resort to be developed on Bali and is now extremely commercial—and somewhat tawdry. It appeals mainly to young Australians on package holidays that even with airfare cost less than a beach vacation at home. Kuta's main street, just two blocks from the beach, is crammed with boutiques, Western fast-food chains, bars, and discos. But the sunsets are as spectacular as ever, and as you walk east along Kuta to Legian, the beach becomes less crowded. Legian Beach is a little quieter than Kuta and has some beach hotels, but its main shopping street is also noisy and crowded. Kuta and Legian are for 24-hour partying, not for a peaceful vacation.

Sanur Beach, 9 km (5 mi) east of Denpasar, was Bali's second beach resort. Its hotels, restaurants, and shops are more spread out, so the pace here is less hectic than in Kuta. The beach is less dramatic, too: Instead of wild waves, there's a coral reef that keeps the water calm—especially appealing to windsurfers.

Nusa Dua, a former burial ground, consists of two tiny islands linked to the mainland with a reinforced sand spit. Unlike Kuta and Sanur, this is an entirely planned resort, with no indigenous community. Its large, self-contained hotels include a Club Med, soon to be joined by Hyatt and Sheraton. Visitors who stay here must travel inland to see the real Bali, but Nusa Dua's beaches are wide and peaceful and its hotels luxurious.

Few tourists miss the sunset at Tanah Lot, on the southwest coast. This pagodalike temple sits on a small, rocky islet, surrounded by water at high tide and otherwise accessible by a ramp. Though it's packed with visitors and souvenir stalls, the temple is still venerated as a holy site; it is believed to be guarded by snakes in the rock holes. Despite the commercialism, few sights anywhere match the view of the sun dropping behind the sea and silhouetting the temple.

Another popular destination is Ubud, an artists' colony that has grown into a center of art galleries and craft shops. Ubud offers several good hotels for those who come here more for Balinese culture than for the beaches. It's also cooler here than to the south.

Most of Bali's cultural attractions are inland, to the north and east of Denpasar. Tourists do not normally stay in the capital, a busy market town of about 20,000 people. But Denpasar is worth a half-day visit.

Important Addresses and Numbers

Tourist Information **Dipardi Bali** (Jln. S. Parman, Niti Mandala, Denpasar, tel. 0361/22387 or 0361/26313).

Emergencies **Police,** tel. 110; **ambulance,** tel. 118; **fire,** tel. 113.

Pharmacies **Bali Farma Apotik** (Jln. Melatig, Denpasar, tel. 0361/22878) and **Indonesia Farma Apotik** (Jln. Diponegoro, Denpasar, tel. 0361/27812) provide reliable service and advice.

Arriving and Departing by Plane

Airport and Airlines Bali's airport, **Ngurah Rai,** is 13 km (8 mi) southwest of Denpasar, at the southern end of the island between Kuta and Sanur. **Garuda Indonesia** is the main carrier, with flights from Los Angeles. **Continental Airlines** also flies to Bali, with connections in Guam. **Qantas** flies to Bali from Australia. Departure tax is Rp 9,000 for international flights, Rp 2,000 for domestic.

Between the Airport and Hotels Some hotels will send a car to the airport if you inform them of your flight number. Otherwise, order a taxi at the counter outside customs; the fixed fare varies from Rp 5,000 to Rp 10,000, depending on the location of your hotel.

Arriving and Departing by Boat and Bus

Ferries make the 35-minute crossing frequently between Ketapang in eastern Java and Gilimanuk in western Bali. Inquire at the pier.

Buses from Jogjakarta to Denpasar (16 hours) use the ferry; an air-conditioned bus costs Rp 16,500. Bus service is available also from Jakarta and Surabaya. Tickets may be purchased through any travel agent.

Two ferries a day make the 3½-hour crossing from Lembar, south of Ampenan in Lombok, to Padangbai, east of Denpasar. Bemos provide transport from Padangbai to Denpasar. The major travel agencies will be able to tell you about schedules.

Getting Around

By Taxi Taxis are available in the main tourist areas. They are unmetered, but fares within the Kuta–Sanur–Nusa Dua area are fixed. The 15-minute ride from Kuta to Nusa Dua, for example, is Rp 9,000; from Sanur to Nusa Dua, Rp 15,000. Taxis hailed in the street usually charge less than those hired at a hotel. For longer journeys, rates are more negotiable—count on about Rp 15,000 per hour.

By Bemo Bemos ply the main routes from Denpasar to Sanur and Kuta.

By Car Renting cars or jeeps in Bali is convenient and popular. Daily rates vary from $50 at Avis to $20 at a small operator, including insurance (with a $300 deductible) and unlimited mileage.

Two companies to try are **Lina Biro Jasa** (Jln. Bakungsari, Kuta, tel. 0361/51820) and **Avis** (Jln. Veteran 5, Denpasar, tel. 0361/24233; also at the Bali Hyatt, Sanur, tel. 0361/8271; Nusa Dua Beach Hotel, tel. 0361/71210; and Sanur Beach Hotel, tel. 0361/8011).

Guided Tours

The best way to explore Bali is with a private car and knowledgeable guide. Without a guide, you may miss much of what is so intriguing about Bali. A car, driver, and guide can be hired from most travel/tour agencies or from your hotel travel desk. The following standardized tours take groups in buses or vans virtually every day:

Denpasar City Tour (three hours) includes the Art Centre and the Bali Museum. **Kintamani Tour** (eight hours) includes the Barong and kris dance performance; silversmith-and-goldsmith, wood-carving, and painting villages; the sacred spring at Tampaksiring; and Kintamani, with its view of Batur volcano and Lake Batur.

Sangeh and Mengwi Tour (four hours) visits the Bali Museum in Denpasar, Sangeh and the sacred monkey forest, and the Pura Taman Ayun temple at Mengwi. **Ubud Handicraft Tour** (five hours) visits the handicraft villages north of Denpasar; Ubud, the artists' center; the museum in Ubud; and Goa Gajah, the elephant cave.

Besakih Temple Tour (seven hours) offers fantastic views on the way to the temple on the slopes of Mt. Agung, and includes the ancient hall of justice in Klungkung and the bat cave. A full-day (10-hour) tour includes Besakih and Kintamani, the handicraft villages, Ubud, and other temples.

Afternoon Tanah Lot Sunset Tour (five hours) includes the monkey forest, the temple at Mengwi, and sunset at Tanah Lot.

Turtle Island Tour (four hours) goes by fishing boat from Suwung, near Benoa harbor, to Serangan, an island just off the coast of Sanur, to watch the giant sea turtles.

One established company is **Satriavi Tours & Travel** (Jln. Veteran 7, Denpasar, tel. 0361/24385); it also maintains a desk at the Nusa Dua Beach Hotel (tel. 0361/971210, ext. 719). Other reliable tour operators include **Nitour** (Jln. Veteran 5, Denpasar, tel. 0361/22593) and **Pacto** (Jln. Tanjung Sari, Sanur, tel. 0361/

8247). For a personal guide, contact **I Made Ramia Santana** (Jln. Planet No. 9, Denpasar, tel. 0361/25909).

Exploring Bali

Numbers in the margin correspond with points of interest on the Bali map.

Tour 1: Denpasar

You can book city tours through your hotel, or you can see Denpasar on your own, by taxi or bemo. A good place to begin is **Pasar Banjung,** the liveliest market in town. It is busiest in the early morning but continues until early afternoon. The large, two-story covered market, near the bridge off Jalan Gajahmada, is packed with spice vendors and farmers selling vegetables, meats, and flowers. The little girls who volunteer to guide you around the market get commissions from any vendor you patronize; of course, your price is raised accordingly.

If you come to Denpasar in the evening, head for the **night market** in the riverside car park of the multilevel shopping center at Kusumasari. The market is a gathering place for locals, who come to chat, shop, and feast on Balinese food.

At the center of the crossroads where Jalan Gajahmada intersects with Jalan Veteran is a large statue of Brahma. Its four faces look in the cardinal directions. To the left on Jalan Veteran is the **Hotel Bali** (Jln. Veteran 3, tel. 0361/5681), in a building dating from the Dutch colonial period.

Continue through this intersection past Puputan Square—a park on the right-hand side, with its Sukarno-inspired heroic statue of the common man—to reach **Pura Agung Jagatnatha,** Bali's state temple. To find the entrance, go right at the end of the park onto Jalan Letkol, and it's on your left.

The temple's center stupa is surrounded by a moat and rises eight levels; at the top is a statue of Shiva with flames coming out of his shoulders. The stupa is supported by the cosmic turtle (on whose back the real world symbolically sits) and protected by a huge carved face with a red-cloth tongue. *Nagas* (serpents) entwine the base; around the bottom are relief carvings.

You must wear a sash to enter any Balinese temple; one can be rented on-site for a few rupiah. As shorts are considered improper temple attire, avoid them or borrow a sarong when visiting any holy place.

Farther down Jalan Letkol is the **Bali Museum,** with Balinese art dating from present times back to the prehistoric. The buildings are excellent examples of Balinese temple and palace architecture. *Jln. Letkol. Wisnu, tel. 0361/2680 or 0361/5362. Admission charge. Open Tues.–Thurs. and Sun. 8–2, Fri. 8–11 AM, Sat. 8AM–12:30 PM.*

Another Denpasar attraction is **Abiankapas,** a large art complex. In the summer, dance performances are held in its auditorium. During the rest of the year, it offers temporary exhibits of modern paintings, batik designs, and woodcarvings. *Jln. Abian Kapas, no tel. Admission charge. Open daily 10–4.*

Tour 2: Inland to Ubud

The main route leading north to Ubud from Denpasar passes through several villages, each known for a different craft. None is more than 8 km (5 mi) from the next. Ubud itself gained fame as an art colony and has since become a popular shopping area and base for exploring the interior of Bali. To the east are important Hindu temples and the holy mountain of Agung.

❶ The first village out of Denpasar is **Batubulan,** famous for the stone carvers whose workshops and displays line the road. Their wares range from the classic guardian figures that stand before Balinese temples and houses to smaller statues. At 9:30 each morning, dance-dramas are performed at the theater (*see* The Arts, below).

❷ Next comes **Celuk,** the village of the silver- and goldsmiths,
❸ then **Suka Wati,** the cane-weaving village. Both have lots of
❹ workshops and salesrooms. **Batuan,** farther north, is a weaving and painting village. An excellent art gallery here, **Jati,** carries a vast array of Balinese arts (*see* Shopping, below).

Before leaving Batuan for the next village, Mas, visit the 10th-century **temple of Brahma** (Pura Puseh Pura Desa). The brick-and-sandstone temple has three parts. You enter the outer courtyard through a classic Balinese split gate. The bell tower, in the second courtyard, is hung with the ubiquitous black-and-white checked cloth. In the main courtyard, a stone screen protects the temple from bad spirits: Because a bad spirit can't turn a corner, it can't go around the screen.

In one corner of the main courtyard is a shrine to Brahma, here a hermaphroditic figure is guarded by two nagas. Nearby, another shrine has three roofs representing the god's three manifestations. The face over the gate entrances, known as Boma, guards against evil from the earth, the nagas against evil from the sea.

❺ Just before Mas, you'll come to the village of **Kemenuh,** where the **home of Ida B. Marka,** a famous woodcarver, is open to the public. The sales showroom is in front; there is no pressure to make a purchase. Behind is a courtyard and a cluster of buildings that serve as the family complex. The centerpiece is the building used for weddings and other rites of passage; here is where the oldest family member sleeps. Other structures include the family temple, a granary, and a cooperative workshop where other villagers help carve and polish. This is a rare opportunity to look inside a Balinese home.

❻ The next stop is **Mas,** the woodcarvers' village. **Ida Bagus Tilem,** often called Bali's top woodcarver, lives here. His work, which has been exhibited internationally, is sold in his small shop.

After Mas, take a right turn on the road toward Pejeng and Gianyar. A car park on the right indicates the entrance to the
❼ **Elephant Cave** (Goa Gajah). Discovered in 1923 by a farmer cultivating his field, the cave temple is thought to have been built in the 11th century. In the courtyard, water spouts from the hands of six stone nymphs into two pools. It is believed that worshipers would purify themselves here before passing through the mouth of the giant Boma face carving on the entrance.

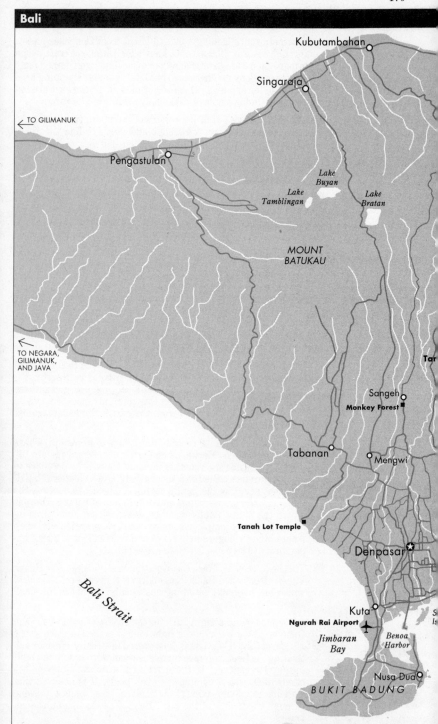

Bali

Kubutambahan

Singaraja

TO GILIMANUK

Pengastulan

Lake Buyan

Lake Tamblingan

Lake Bratan

MOUNT BATUKAU

TO NEGARA, GILIMANUK, AND JAVA

Tar

Sangeh

Monkey Forest

Tabanan

Mengwi

Tanah Lot Temple

Denpasar

Bali Strait

Kuta

Ngurah Rai Airport

Jimbaran Bay

Benoa Harbor

S Is

Nusa Dua

BUKIT BADUNG

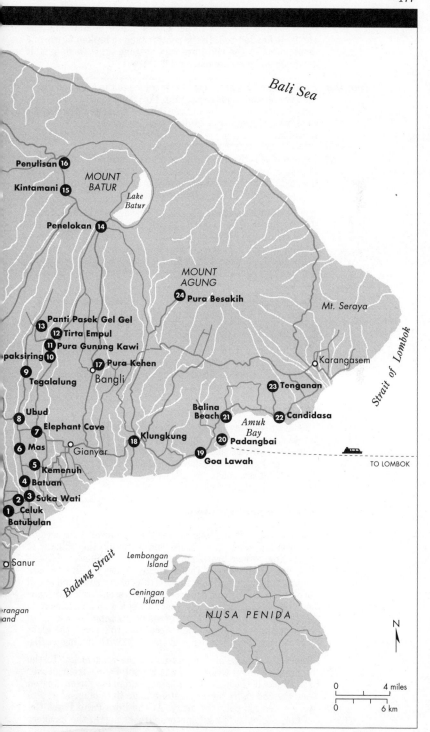

The cave itself is pitch dark—hope that your guide has a flashlight. To the left is a niche with a statue of Ganesha, the elephant-headed god. In the center stands a broken figure of a demon, and to the right are carved-stone *linga* (male phallic symbols) and *yoni* (female forms).

Time Out At the top of the hill, near the entrance to the area and above the cave, is a pleasant restaurant, **Puri Suling** (no tel., no credit cards). A terrace looks out over the rice fields and down to the cave area. In addition to dull Western food, the restaurant serves excellent Indonesian specialties.

8 Beyond Mas is the artist-colony town of **Ubud.** For an overview of Balinese and Indonesian painting, visit the **Neka Gallery,** at the east end of the main street; it also shows works by Western artists who have lived in Bali. *Open daily 9–4.*

The **Puri Lukisan Museum**—set in a garden at the west end of the main street, with rice paddies and water buffalo in the background—exhibits only modern Balinese art. The sculptures and paintings are arranged chronologically, so you can follow the development from formal religious art to more natural, realistic depictions of dances, festivals, and rice harvesting.

Ubud's main street is lined with shops selling art, textiles, clothing, and other handicrafts. On most days you'll also find a street market. In the center of town is **Puri Saren,** a prince's palace that is also a hotel (*see* Lodging, below). The complex is beautiful, but not very well kept up. You enter through a split gate. The prince's living quarters are at the end of the courtyard; guest accommodations are in surrounding buildings. One contains an old tiger costume from the Barong dance, and a peacock walks the grounds. On Monday and Friday dances are performed in the courtyard; the dancers rehearse on Sunday.

Walk down Monkey Forest Road, across from Puri Saren, to the **Monkey Forest,** where a small donation will get you a close-up view of monkeys accustomed to tourists and to the peanuts they buy to feed them. A path winds through the tall trees. All around Ubud are roads or trails that lead through the countryside to other artisans' villages.

Tour 3: Inland from Ubud

The road north from Ubud passes through lovely countryside patchworked with rice fields and through the village of
9 **Tegalalung,** whose craftsmen carve intricate flower designs
10 into wood. In the town of **Tampaksiring,** follow the sign to **Pura**
11 **Gunung Kawi,** a monument to an 11th-century ruler and one of the oldest in Bali. From the access road, a stone stairway leads down to a lush green valley. Pass through a stone archway to the canyon floor and two rows of memorial temples, carved in niches in the face of two cliffs. According to legend, the giant Kebo Iwa carved these niches in one night with his fingernails.

Beyond the village of Tampaksiring, the road forks. To the
12 right is the famous **temple at Tirta Empul.** People from all over Bali come to bathe in the holy spring, said to have been created when the god Indra pierced a stone to produce magical waters
13 that revived his poisoned army. At the **Pura Panti Pasek Gel Gel holy spring,** a few kilometers farther north, the hawkers

are less demanding, and fewer tourists interrupt the sanctity of the temple. The temple is dedicated to Vishnu, whose many responsibilities include water and irrigation. The main shrine appropriately stands in the center of a pool filled with holy water and fat goldfish. Bathing pools are segregated by sex and age.

North of Sebatu, the vanilla- and clove-bordered road climbs quickly. Roadside stalls sell fruits and vegetables, replacing the souvenir and handicraft kiosks of the lower altitudes.
⓮ Penelokan, a village at the edge of the old crater of 1,450-m (4,757-ft) Mt. Batur, affords a great view of the lake inside the vast crater, where a new volcano has arisen.

Time Out Except when the low clouds move in, as they often do later in the day, two restaurants offer superb views of the crater: **Puri Salera,** (tel. 0361/88226, no credit cards), about a kilometer out of Penelokan toward Batur, and the **Batur Garden** in Batur. The local fare is reasonably good, but you pay for the view.

Along the road on the rim of the crater are two other villages,
⓯ Kintamani—a quiet town whose losmen are used by hikers—
⓰ and **Penulisan.** Here, an old stairway leads up a hill to the ancient temple **Pura Sukawana.** Most of the decaying sculptures are from the 11th century, but look closely and you will find older, pagan phallic symbols. The view, which stretches across Bali to the Java Sea, is breathtaking, especially at sunrise.

The drive south from Penelokan to Bangli is a quick run downhill. On the outskirts of Bangli is an S-curve; here take a left,
⓱ and at the foot of the hill is **Pura Kehen,** a 12th-century temple dedicated to Shiva. A great flight of steps leads up to this terraced temple. In the first courtyard is a giant holy banyan tree with a bell tower used to summon the villagers for ceremonies and other events. The entrance to the inner courtyard is up two steep, parallel flights of steps. At the top center are the "closed gate" and the Boma face, blocking evil spirits. Within the inner courtyard, the main shrine sits on a cosmic turtle entwined by nagas.

Besakih, on the slopes of Mt. Agung, is about a 40-minute drive northeast from Bangli. But you may want to call it a day at this point and return to Ubud or the beach. We have combined Besakih with Klungkung in the next excursion.

Tour 4: Eastern Bali

To the southeast of the main road between Ubud and Denpasar
⓲ is **Klungkung,** a former dynastic capital. In the center of town stands the **Hall of Justice,** built in the late 18th century. The raised platform in the hall supports three thrones—one with a lion carving for the king, one with a dragon for the minister, and one with a bull for the priest. The accused brought before this tribunal could look up at the painted ceiling and contemplate the horrors in store for convicted criminals.

Heading east out of Klungkung, the road drops south to run along the coast and through the area of Kusamba, speckled with the thatched roofs of salt-panning huts. Just beyond is
⓳ Goa Lawah, the bat cave. Unless you long to see thousands of bats hanging from the ceiling, you may not want to subject yourself to the aggressive hawkers, postcard sellers, and

young girls who throw you a flower, then angrily demand payment when you leave. The cave is said to lead all the way to Mt. Agung.

20
21 Continuing east along the coast will take you to **Padangbai**— the port for the ferry to Lombok—and then to **Balina Beach,** a quiet area with a deserted strand and small hotel complexes offering sport-fishing and diving facilities.

22 **Candidasa,** once a budget traveler's escape from Kuta, now boasts a dozen small hotels and restaurants. The waters here are gentle because of a reef 270 m (300 yd) offshore—good for snorkeling—but at high tide the sea swallows the beach.

23 On the western side of Candidasa, a road turns inland to **Tenganan,** an ancient walled village of the Balinese who preceded the Majapahit. The village consists of two parallel streets lined on either side with identical walled compounds. Inside the compounds, houses face each other across a grassy central strip, where the public buildings stand. Tenganan keeps to its traditions—it is, for example, the only place in Indonesia where double ikat is still woven—and people seldom marry outside the village.

Return to the main coast road at Candidasa, where a left turn leads to Amlapura. Here the road splits; take the road to Rendang, then turn right to climb the 11 km (7 mi) to Besakih.

24 **Pura Besakih,** known as the mother temple of Bali, is the most sacred of them all. Situated on the slopes of Mt. Agung, the complex has 30 temples—one for every Balinese district—on seven terraces. It is thought to have been built before Hinduism reached Bali and subsequently modified. The structure consists of three main parts, the north painted black for Vishnu, the center white for Shiva, and the south red for Brahma. You enter through a split gate.

Much of the temple area was destroyed in 1963 when Mt. Agung erupted, killing 1,800 believers, but diligent restoration has repaired most of the damage. Visitors are not allowed into the inner courtyard, but there is enough to see to justify the 2 km- (1 mi)-long walk from the parking lot through souvenir stands and vendors. From Besakih, return the 8 km (5 mi) back to the main road, then either continue straight to Klungkung or go right for Bangli. Denpasar is 60 km (35 mi) away.

Tour 5: Lombok

The island of Lombok lies 45 km (27 mi) east of Bali. You can take a 20-minute flight to the island, spend the day exploring, and return by nightfall—though Lombok really deserves more time. Several Merpati flights leave Denpasar daily for Lombok's Mataram airport (cost: Rp 17,000 one-way). Two daily ferries make the 3½-hour crossing from Padangbai, Bali to Lembar, Lombok (first class, Rp 4,800; second class, Rp 3,350). Bemos and taxis are available on Lombok.

For those who find Bali overpopulated and commercial, Lombok is an alternative. It has a mix of Balinese Hindus and Muslims. Most of the Hindus live on the western side of the island around Ampenan, Mataram, and Cakranegara; this is where you'll find most of the temples and palaces. At **Suranadi,** a cool hill resort, Hindu pilgrims take the holy waters. **Lingsar temple** is unique in that Hindus and Muslims make joint offerings to ensure rain for a bountiful harvest.

Lombok has some beautiful virgin beaches, and its climate is drier than Bali's—an advantage during the rainy season. The Cakranegara area is known for handwoven textiles, Sukarare for ikat, and Penujak for pottery.

Though tourism is still in its infancy on Lombok, there are guest houses all over the island. The major hotel is **Senggigi Beach Hotel,** on a promontory overlooking the sea and 20 minutes out of Mataram. Try to get to Lombok before the government builds the huge hotel complex it has planned.

Shopping

Though there are countless stores in Kuta, Sanur, and Ubud, the best places for shopping are the craft villages north of Denpasar, where you usually buy right at the workshop. Workshop prices should be better, but you must always bargain: The tourist asking price is at least 25% higher than normal. Also remember that most guides get a commission on your purchases. If your guide stops at every shop along the road though you are not an inveterate shopper, speak up—there is too much to see in Bali to spend all your time this way. For shopping in Lombok, *see* Tour 5.

Art   For the best of Batuan—Bali's painting center—ask any local to direct you to the studios of **Mokoh, I. Made Budi,** or **Wayan Darmawan.** The **Jati Art Gallery** (Batuan Sukawati Gianyar) sells paintings and artifacts, including antique wayang kulit, old masks and temple ornaments, handwoven ikat, batiks, woodcarvings, and new puppets.

In Ubud, first visit the **Neka Art Gallery** (*see* Tour 2, above) to get an overview of Balinese fine art, then get directions to the workshops of **A.A. Gd. Sobart, Gusti Ketut Kobot, I.B. Made Poleng, Mujawan, Sudiarto,** or **I. Bagus Nadra.**

Baskets and Cane   The village of **Sukawati** is known for its cane weaving and for wind chimes. Stalls lining the road sell baskets, hats, and some furniture.

Batik   Balinese batiks tend to be more colorful than the traditional Javanese style, and the designs are more floral than geometric. You'll find selections all over Kuta, Sanur, and Ubud. A good source of hand-drawn batiks is **Popiler** (tel. 0361/36498) in Tohpati village, just north of Batubulan. If you pay cash instead of using a credit card, you may increase your bargaining power by around 20% for the yard goods, paintings, garments, and household items here. Behind the shop, you're invited to watch girls outlining the designs with wax.

Ikat   The town of **Tenganan** (*see* Tour 4, above) is the only place in Indonesia where double ikat fabric is still woven. The design is dyed on individual threads of both the warp and the filling before being woven (in single ikat, the dye goes only on the warp threads).

Silver and Gold   **Celuk,** north of Denpasar, is the gold- and silversmiths' village. In the workshops behind the shops, you can watch boys working the silver and setting semiprecious stones. As a rule, the jewelry you find here is 90%–92% silver, the tableware 60%–70%. If you have time, you can custom-order pieces.

One shop with a large selection is **Dewi Sitha** (no phone), on the left side of the road going north. Remember that with a smile and a murmur you might drive the cost of a $125 bracelet down to $80. Especially where price tags are in dollars, bargaining is the rule.

Stone Carving   **Batubulan,** the first village on the road north from Denpasar, is the source of virtually every guardian figure in Bali. On each side of the road you'll see workshops where boys chip at the soft sandstone, and sculptures are for sale out front. Most workshops make small carvings for tourists. **I. Made Sura** is one of the better shops; it also carries some woodcarvings, old wood ornaments, and carved doors.

Wayang Kulit

The hand-cut, painted shadow puppets for sale on Bali are usually new. You can buy antiques at the **Jati Art Gallery** in Batuan (*see* Art, above) and at the **Mega Art Gallery** in Denpasar (Jln. Gajahmada), which also sells new puppets, wood carvings, and paintings.

Wood Carving

Just outside the wood-carving village of Mas are the home and studio of **Ida B. Marka,** where you can see works in progress and buy finished examples (*see* Tour 2, above). In Mas, visit the home of **Ida Bagus Tilem,** Indonesia's most famous woodcarver (tel. 0361/6414–*also see* Tour 2). Mask-carvers have shops in the back lanes; the masks, which make great wall hangings, range in price from $2 to $50, depending on their size and complexity.

Sports, Fitness, Beaches

Beaches   The tourist enclaves at Kuta/Legian, Sanur, and Nusa Dua all boast very different beaches (*see* Introduction, above, for complete descriptions). Off the beaten track, try **Balina Beach** and **Candidasa** in eastern Bali (*see* Tour 4, above).

Boating   For yacht charters, contact **Jet Boat Tours** (Jln. Pantai Karang 5, Sanur, tel. 0361/839). Sanur's **Bali Hyatt** has two deep-sea fishing boats.

Cockfighting   Although cockfighting is technically illegal in Indonesia, the Balinese incorporate the sport into their temple ceremonies, and many men keep cocks for playing and betting. These rituals are not meant for tourists, but any local you befriend will know where the next fight is scheduled.

Golf   The 18-hole **Bali Handera Golf Course**—possibly the only course anywhere that's set in a volcanic crater—is at Bedugul, one hour north of Denpasar. Daily greens fees are $45 on weekends and $30 during the week. The **Bali Hyatt** in Sanur (tel. 0361/8271) has a three-hole course. A 36-hole course is planned for Nusa Dua.

Tennis and Squash   Several hotels have tennis courts; the **Nusa Dua Beach** also has squash courts.

Water Sports Personnel at all beach hotels can direct you to facilities for surfing, diving, windsurfing, and deep-sea fishing. The **Balina Diving Association** (Balina Beach, tel. 0361/80871) also arranges dives. You can get scuba equipment and a ride out to the reef at Sanur from **Bali Aquatic Sports** (La Barong Bar, Kuta), **Gloria Maris** (Jln. Airport, Kuta), or **Nusa Lembongan Tours** (Happy Restaurant, Kuta). Windsurfers can be rented at the beach market in Sanur.

Nusa Lembongan, the island opposite Sanur beach and next to Nusa Penida, offers surfing and diving. But for the best surfing, head to Ulu Watu, on the eastern side of the Bukit Peninsula at Bali's southern tip.

Dining

Kuta and Sanur offer a fairly wide range of restaurants. In Nusa Dua, most of the dining is at hotels. Western food abounds in Kuta, though mostly of the fast-food variety. Hotels offer better Western cooking.

Kuta/Legian **Oberoi.** In an open pavilion with a bamboo ceiling, you dine
Expensive around a pool with a fountain surrounded by trees and flowers. A Swiss chef and Balinese sous-chef turn out both an Indonesian buffet and an à la carte menu with a Continental flair. Try the crepe "le Oberoi," with its filling of crabmeat, cream, onions, and white wine, or the coconut-breaded shrimp, deep-fried and served with a ginger cream sauce. The Oberoi also prepares Indian specialties. *Legian Beach, Jln. Kayu Aya, tel. 0361/51061. Reservations suggested during busy season. Jacket suggested. AE, DC, MC, V.*

Moderate **Indah Sari.** On Kuta's main drag, this seafood-and-barbecue restaurant serves fresh, well-prepared dishes, from prawns to grouper, that you can order either spicy or bland. The open-fronted restaurant can get boisterous and is probably best for dining in small groups. *Jln. Legian, Kuta, tel. 0361/51834. No reservations. Dress: casual. AE, MC, V.*

Nusa Dua **Kertosa Restaurant.** This formal Continental restaurant has
Expensive the atmosphere of a European hotel, despite the Balinese stone sculptures on pedestals. The menu is international with a French flavor, and there's even a wine list—a costly luxury in Bali. *Nusa Dua Beach Hotel, tel. 0361/7120. Reservations suggested. Jacket suggested. AE, DC, MC, V.*

Sanur **Fisherman's Place.** This open-air restaurant, set in the garden
Expensive by the pool of the Bali Hyatt, serves only the freshest seafood and grills it over hot coals. If you go deep-sea fishing on the hotel's boat and get lucky, the restaurant will cook your catch and charge you for just the trimmings. *Bali Hyatt, Box 392, Sanur, tel. 0361/88271. Reservations suggested. Jacket suggested. AE, DC, MC, V.*

★ **Spice Islander.** The elegant Balinese decor, with gilded table bases and heavy rattan chairs, is a great setting in which to get acquainted with Balinese cuisine. A rijstaffel buffet with no fewer than 30 dishes—all labeled with their ingredients—is laid out on a lotus altar in the center of the room. Among the delicacies: *crancam ayam* (chicken soup with ginger), *kalio hati dengan kentang* (spicy chicken livers with potato), *opar sapi* (beef in coconut curry sauce), *satay lilit* (skewered pork and beef), and *gudeg yogya* (a dish made of jackfruit). *Bali*

Hyatt, Sanur, tel. 0361/88271. Reservations suggested during busy season. Jacket suggested. AE, DC, MC, V.

Telaga Naga. With a name meaning "dragon's pond," this is the best Chinese restaurant in Bali. Two lily ponds create a floating pavilion atmosphere, and the Singaporean chef specializes in Cantonese and Szechuan cuisine. Try the minced chicken with chili and cucumber as an appetizer, followed by fried lobster with chili and black bean sauce. *Near the Bali Hyatt, Sanur, tel. 0361/88271. Reservations required. Jacket suggested. AE, DC, MC, V.*

Moderate **Le Gong.** The gong hangs in a central garden, and while the restaurant is on Sanur's main street, its woven bamboo walls and set-back tables give it a relaxing atmosphere. To make the most of the traditional Balinese menu, order a few dishes and share them. Some suggestions: soto ayam, prawns in butter sauce, fish grilled with spices, and nasi goreng. Fresh papaya or pineapple makes a refreshing dessert. *Jln. Legong, Semawang-Sanur, tel. 0361/88066. Reservations suggested. Dress: casual. No credit cards.*

Penjor Restaurant. Set back from the main street, this bamboo-walled restaurant surrounds an open courtyard where tables are laid in fine weather. Each night a different Balinese dance-drama is presented, in view of the diners, and the set menu rotates Balinese, Indonesian, Chinese, and Indian dinners. Owner Ida Bagus Ketut Oka speaks English fluently and loves to chat with his guests. *Batu Jumbar, Sanur, tel. 0361/88226. Reservations optional. Dress: casual. AE, DC, MC, V.*

Ubud **Kupu Kupu Barong.** Perched on a terrace in the hotel of the
Expensive same name, this restaurant overlooks the spectacular green
★ valley of the Ayung River. Marble-top tables, rattan chairs, and milk glass–and–brass lamps add charm. The menu includes Indonesian and international fare. Try the smoked duck with Balinese side dishes. *Kedewatan, Ubud, tel. 0361/23172. Reservations suggested during busy season. Jacket suggested. AE, V.*

Moderate **Ananda Cottages.** Part of the Ananda Cottages hotel, this open-air restaurant is surrounded by rice paddies. Its menu lists Western dishes and Indonesian specialties, including *satay pusut* (grilled skewered meat in a spicy peanut sauce) and *betutu bebek* (Balinese duck). *Ananda Cottages, Box 205, Denpasar, tel. 0361/8001. No reservations. Dress: casual. No credit cards.*

Lodging

As Bali's tourist industry grows, more hotels open every year in its popular areas. The following are just some of the many options for travelers. Mailing addresses are given, rather than street locations.

Kuta/Legian **Oberoi.** Among the luxurious Oberoi's assets is its location, at
Very Expensive the far western end of Legian Beach away from the crowds. Its
★ 33 acres offer tranquillity and privacy, with thatched cottages and private villas spaced among gardens of bougainvillea, hibiscus, and frangipani. The lobby and lounge building, with a coral exterior and polished stone floors inside, faces the sea. Rooms are beautifully furnished in dark wood, with ikat bedcovers and draperies. Each cottage has its own veranda; the

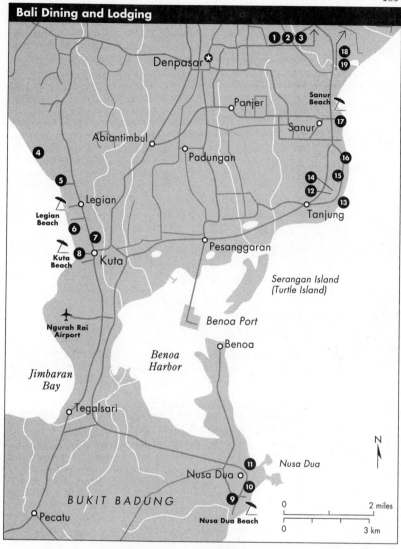

Dining
Ananda Cottages, **3**
Fisherman's Place, **13**
Indah Sari, **7**
Kertosa, **11**
Kupu Kupu Barong, **1**
Le Gong, **12**
Oberoi, **4**
Penjor, **15**
Spice Islander, **13**
Telaga Naga, **14**

Lodging
Ananda Cottages, **3**
Bali Hyatt, **13**
Balina Beach, **18**
Buala Club, **9**
Kul Kul Beach
Resort, **6**
Kupu Kupu Barong, **1**
Kuta Palace Hotel, **5**
Nusa Dua Beach
Hotel, **11**
Oberoi, **4**
Puri Buitan
Cottages, **19**

Putri Bali, **10**
Sari Yasa Samudra
Bungalows, **8**
Segara Village, **17**
Tandjung Sari, **16**
Tjampuhan, **2**

villas have balconies and garden courtyards. Service is personal and friendly, and Balinese dance is performed on most evenings in an amphitheater. *Box 451, Denpasar 80001, tel. 0361/51061. 63 cottages, 12 villas. Facilities: restaurant (see Dining), beachfront café, poolside bar, water sports, tennis, 24-hr room service, jeep rental, shopping arcade, laundry service. AE, DC, MC, V.*

Expensive **Kul Kul Beach Resort.** Opened in 1989, Kul Kul is architectural-
★ ly the most interesting and attractive hotel on Kuta beach. Its design makes clever use of a small property: From a cocktail deck over the car port, guests can watch the sunset or sip an after-dinner liqueur. The sun deck is built over rocks on one side of the pool, and you clamber down boulders to have a dip or get a drink. Accommodations consist of modern bungalows that include sitting rooms and bedrooms furnished in Balinese style with rattan and bamboo and with deluxe bathrooms. *Jln. Pantai Kuta, Legian Kelon, Kuta, tel. 0361/51952. 52 rooms. Facilities: European/Indonesian restaurant, poolside bar, disco. AE, MC, V.*

Moderate **Kuta Palace Hotel.** Set on 11 acres on Legian beach, this hotel consists of two-story buildings surrounding a courtyard with gardens and pools. Rooms are simply but pleasantly decorated in Balinese-patterned fabrics and a cream-and-rust color scheme. All have air-conditioning, refrigerators, and views. *Box 244, Denpasar, tel. 0361/51433. Facilities: restaurant, outdoor pool, 24-hr room service, tennis, laundry service. AE, DC, MC, V.*

Inexpensive **Sari Yasa Samudra Bungalows.** Across the road from Kuta beach, this collection of cottages offers bare-bones accommodations with ceiling fans and only limited hours of hot water in the private baths. It's virtually without aesthetic appeal but cleaner and newer than its sister property, Yasa Samudra, next door. *Box 53, Denpasar, tel. 0361/51562. 31 rooms. Facilities: restaurant, bar, pool. No credit cards.*

Nusa Dua **Nusa Dua Beach Hotel.** Even among those who like extrava-
Very Expensive gant hotels, some may feel that this one goes overboard. From the enormous floodlit Balinese split gate to the open, four-story lobby, everything here is done on a big scale. The long guest wings overlook gardens, waterfalls, and stone sculptures. Rooms are furnished in dark wood and light cane, with Balinese paintings, TV, and minibar. The hotel presents classical dance-dramas in the evening. *Box 1028, Denpasar, tel. 0361/71210. 425 rooms, 25 suites. Facilities: 4 restaurants, 4 bars, 2 outdoor pools, tennis, squash, water sports, shopping arcade, business center, health center. AE, DC, MC, V.*

Expensive **Buala Club.** At the southern end of Nusa Dua beach, this quiet hotel offers an all-inclusive vacation, with free activities and personalized service. Accommodations are in a two-story Balinese-style building surrounded by gardens. Rooms are simple but pleasant, with ikat-patterned fabrics; all have a private balcony or veranda. *Box 6, Nusa Dua, tel. 0361/71310. 50 rooms. Facilities: 3 restaurants, bar, outdoor pool, private beach, horseback riding, water sports, boutique, drugstore, conference rooms. AE, DC, MC, V.*
Putri Bali. The Putri Bali has a private beach and specializes in water sports. Each room is cheerfully decorated in red and gold, with patterned fabrics, balcony, and minibar. *Box 1,*

Nusa Dua, tel. 0361/71020. 425 rooms. Facilities: 5 restaurants, 2 bars, outdoor pool, tennis, squash, health club, shopping arcade, convention facilities. AE, DC, MC, V.

Sanur
Very Expensive
Bali Hyatt. The queen of Sanur, this hotel sits on 36 acres of gardens along the beach. Though the hotel is large, it strives to maintain a Balinese atmosphere. The open lobby building has a soaring roof thatched with elephant grass; from the ceiling hang chandeliers of gilded carved coconut. Stone sculptures decorate the lounge, where a gamelan orchestra plays in the early evening. Rooms are decorated in pastel colors with teakwood furniture, handwoven fabrics, and Balinese paintings. The gardens contain many unusual trees and flowers, and one pool replicates the famous Elephant Cave—but adds a waterfall. *Box 392, Denpasar 80001, tel. 0361/8271. 387 rooms. Facilities: 5 restaurants, 4 bars, disco, 2 outdoor pools, boating, golf, tennis, water sports, function rooms. AE, DC, MC, V.*

Expensive
★
Tandjung Sari. This unique hotel on Sanur beach is a peaceful "village" of Balinese-style bungalows set in tropical gardens that hide small stone temples and statues. The lobby is an open pavilion decorated with wood and stone carvings. Bungalows have split bamboo walls and are furnished with handwoven fabrics, an antique or two, and a minibar. Most of the bathrooms have skylights. *Box 25, Denpasar, tel. 0361/8441. 24 bungalows. Facilities: restaurant, private beach, beach bar, outdoor pool, water sports. No credit cards.*

Moderate
Segara Village. At the north end of Sanur Beach, this small hotel offers Balinese-style thatch-roof cottages. The open lobby houses both restaurants, so it can be busy. Rooms are air-conditioned and have a balcony or veranda and private bath. Decor is very simple. *Box 91, Denpasar, tel. 0361/8407. 40 rooms. Facilities: 2 restaurants, 4 bars, room service 6 AM–10 PM, 2 outdoor pools, tennis, game room, drugstore, bike rental. AE, DC, MC, V.*

Ubud
Very Expensive
★
Kupu Kupu Barong. The loveliest of Bali's country lodgings, this beautiful and intimate hotel sits on the precipice of a deep valley, with glorious views of rice terraces and the Ayung River below. You approach the reception area via a path trellised with banana leaves, hibiscus, and clove trees. The bungalows are individually designed to blend with the hilly landscape, with woven rattan or stone-face walls and unique crafted furnishings. Six more bungalows are nearing completion. Children, however, are not permitted. *Jln. Kecubung 72, Denpasar, tel. 0361/23172. 48 rooms. Facilities: restaurant, outdoor pool, tennis. AE, DC, MC, V.*

Moderate
Tjampuhan. On the main road just out of Ubud, atop a ravine overlooking a holy river, Tjampuhan was once an artists' colony and still includes the former house of German painter Walter Spies. The lobby is no more than an open terrace off the road, with paths leading to the bungalows. These have carved and gilded wood doors, woven bamboo walls, bamboo furniture, and handwoven fabrics and batik as decorations. Unfortunately, the rooms are somewhat damp and musty. You ring for breakfast with bamboo bells. *Box 15, Denpasar, tel. 0361/28871. 40 bungalows. Facilities: restaurant, bar, outdoor pool, tennis, car and bike rental. MC, V.*

Inexpensive
★
Ananda Cottages. This friendly, relaxed hotel is set in the rice paddies in Campuhan, up the hill outside Ubud. The open-air lounge and lobby surround a central garden; the "cottages" are thatch-roof, brick bungalows with two units above and two below. Room decor is simple, with rattan furniture and ikat bedcovers. The upper rooms have better views and baths. *Box 205, Denpasar, no tel., telex 35428 Ubud IA. 30 rooms. Facilities: restaurant, bar, outdoor pool. No credit cards.*

Balina Beach/
Candidasa
Inexpensive
Balina Beach. Popular among scuba and snorkel enthusiasts for its diving club, this hotel has one- and two-story thatched cottages scattered near the sandy beach 3 km (1.8 mi) west of Candidasa. The best rooms, upstairs in the two-story bungalows, have sitting rooms and porches. All have private baths and ceiling fans; their rattan decor is simple. *Partai Buitan, Manngis Karang Asem, tel. 0361/8777. 41 rooms. Facilities: restaurant, bar, diving club. V.*

Puri Buitan Cottages. Opened in late 1988, the Puri Buitan has recently added to its bungalow capacity. The beach here is very quiet, and a reef keeps the sea perfect for swimming. Rooms are simple and clean, with the first-floor units good for families. *Box 464, Denpasar 80001, no tel. 34 rooms. Facilities: restaurant, outdoor pool. V.*

The Arts

One of Bali's chief charms is that the arts are everywhere. Temple ceremonies, dances, and village festivals go on all the time; all you need is a good source of current information. Check the monthly *Bali Guide to Events*, available at any hotel or tour office, for listings.

Perhaps the most popular attraction is the traditional dance-drama. The show is high drama, exciting, and colorful. The plot revolves around the eternal fight between good and evil. Good is represented by the mythological animal character Barong, danced by two men in a costume with the famous flashy tiger mask; evil is represented by the mythological monster Rangda, with a wild man, long fingernails, and a mask with sharp teeth. No less colorful, and certainly more beautiful, are the female dancers, and for humor and sadness, there is the beguiling monkey.

The dance is accompanied by the traditional gamelan orchestra consisting of gongs, a type of xylophone with bronze bars, drums (most beaten by the hand), two different string instruments, and a flute. As Balinese dancing is much livelier and more exuberant than the more restrained Javanese dancing, so the Balinese gamelan is sharper with more crescendo. Attending a performance can be arranged through your hotel or through a travel agent, or you can go by yourself.

Every morning in **Batubulan,** dancers and actors perform the classical Barong and Kris Dance on an open-air stage (seating is covered). Arrive by 9 AM, as the theater fills quickly and you will want seats near the stage for a much better view. The lively dancing is accompanied by exciting gamelan music. *Pemaksan Barong Denjalan, Batubulan–Gianyar. Admission charge. Daily at 9:30 AM.*

In the summer, dance performances are held in the auditorium in **Abiankapas,** a large art complex in Denpasar. Especially during the art festival, held every year from mid-July to mid-August, the modern-style Balinese buildings make an attractive setting for cultural performances.

Other performances are offered with or after dinner at the large hotels, including the Bali Hyatt, Hotel Bali Beach, Bali Seaside Cottages, and Sanur Beach Hotel in Sanur; Nusa Dua Beach Hotel in Nusa Dua; and the Bali Oberoi in Legian. **Penjor Restaurant** (tel. 0361/88226) on Sanur's main street, Batur Jumbar, offers dinner with traditional Balinese dance nightly at 9 PM on an outdoor stage. At the end of the performance, the audience is invited onstage.

The **Wisata Budaya** arts center in Bangli regularly presents wayang performances and art exhibits.

Outside Ubud, the prince's palace complex (*see* Tour 3, above) has a courtyard where traditional Balinese dances are performed every Monday and Friday, and rehearsed on Sunday. *Show times 6-7.*

Nightlife

Life on Bali focuses on sightseeing and beach activities; by late evening, most areas quiet down, with one exception: Kuta Beach. Here the activity begins with drinks at cafés (one of the most consistently popular is **Poppies,** Poppies Gang, Kuta, tel. 0361/23059) in the early evening, which may continue well into the night or shift to the discos. Most of these have a modest cover charge of Rp 2,000 to Rp 3,000 and start rolling at 9 PM, closing at 2 AM.

Gado-Gado (open Tues., Thurs., and Sat.) is an open-air disco near the ocean. **Kayu Api** (no phone), at the intersection of Jalan Legian and Jalan Melasti, has live music, often of international caliber. **Koala Blu** (Jln. Kuta) attracts mostly Australians. The popularity and life span of the other Kuta/Legian discos swings like a pendulum. Two recent favorites are **Sand Bar** on Jalan Legian and **Peanuts** across the road. **Rum Jungle** on Jalan Pura Bagus draws a mostly younger crowd, as does **Teruna** on Jalan Legian, just beyond the center of Legian Beach.

The newest area night spot is at the **Kul Kul Beach Resort** (tel. 0361/51952) on Jalan Pantai Juta at the boundary of Kuta and Legian townships. Here, on an open-sided stage, a small band plays the top 20 interspersed with large-screen video. A delightful veranda lounge offers a lower noise level.

In Sanur, most hotels have some form of entertainment with a live band. The liveliest spots are the Bali Hyatt's plush **Matahari** and the **Sobek** disco on Jalan Batujimat. In Nusa Dua, the hotels all offer evening entertainment, either Balinese dance or a live band playing current international favorites.

Sulawesi

To the north and east of Bali and Java is the island of Sulawesi, formerly called the Celebes. Four long peninsulas radiate from a central mountainous area, so some say the island is orchid-shape. Its geography is dramatic—from rice fields to rain forests and mountains to hidden bays, from which Bugis pirates once raided merchant ships. As if cast off in some strange upheaval, Sulawesi has become the last home of such unique animals as the babirusa (a pig-deer with upward-curving tusks) and the anoa (a pygmy buffalo).

Sulawesi has the potential to become a vacationer's paradise. Miles of empty beaches and superb scuba diving in crystal-clear waters await discovery on the north coast around Manado. Hunting and camping areas spread down the southeastern peninsula. The rivers of west-central Sulawesi wind through small ikat-weaving towns, and islands with isolated fishing villages line the southern coast. But Sulawesi is virtually unspoiled, and its tourist infrastructure is confined mostly to the main city, Ujung Pandang, and to Tanatoraja (Torajaland).

The Toraja live in the northern mountains of south Sulawesi, practicing an ancient animist religion alongside Christianity. With their traditional clan houses—the carved and painted *tongkonans*—built on piles and topped by a massive roof shaped like a ship or buffalo horns, and their public sacred rituals, the Toraja offer the visitor a fascinating glimpse of Indonesia's multifaceted population.

The Toraja comprise only a small minority of Sulawesi's inhabitants. The Makassars and the Bugis are more numerous, and the journey from Ujung Pandang to Tanatoraja passes through Bugis country. Though many now have settled on land to cultivate rice, the seafaring Muslim Bugis still ply the Asian seas in their sailing ships, called *prahus*, trading among Indonesia's islands.

Most visitors fly into Ujung Pandang and use it as a starting point for travel in Sulawesi. The city, called Makassar by the Dutch, is a bustling commercial center. But although it's the fifth-largest Indonesian city, Ujung Pandang has little to hold the tourist's attention.

The Toraja people are Sulawesi's prime attraction. Tourism has affected the Toraja, but their customs, rituals, and social structure have survived the centuries. Perhaps the only obvious change in the last 500 years is that now buffalo and pigs are sacrificed instead of humans.

Tanatoraja's two main towns are Makale, the administrative center, and Rantepao, the commercial and tourist center with the best selection of hotels. You'll need at least three days to visit Tanatoraja, plus two to get there and back. Plan on a longer stay if you want to get off the beaten track to the remote villages. The best time for a trip is at the beginning or end of the dry season, April through October. Vast numbers of Europeans descend in June and July, so try to avoid those months.

Because the country between Ujung Pandang and Rantepao is fascinating, the ideal way to visit Tanatoraja is to make the outbound journey by road and return by air.

Arriving and Departing by Plane

Airports and Airlines **Garuda** flies to Ujung Pandang from Jakarta and Surabaya on Java, and from Denpasar on Bali. Garuda also has service from Ambon, **Biak**, and Jayapura. The smaller **Merpati, Bouraq,** and **Mandala** also serve Ujung Pandang.

Merpati Airlines flies between Ujung Pandang and Rantepao's simple airport three times a week. The runway can become unserviceable in the rainy season, causing frequent flight cancellations. The airport is 24 km (15 mi) from town.

Between the Airport and Downtown Taxis from the Ujung Pandang airport cost about Rp 9,000. Purchase a coupon inside the terminal, next to the baggage claim. In Rantepao, a cab to town costs Rp 15,000.

Arriving and Departing by Ship

Pelni ships from Surabaya (tel. 031/21041) or Ambon (tel. 0311/3161–2049) pass through Ujung Pandang every seven days and disembark at Pelabuhan Hatta Harbor, a short becak ride from the center of town. Because Ujung Pandang is the gateway to eastern Indonesia, many other shipping companies take passengers from here aboard freighters to the Moluccas and other eastern islands and to Kalimantan, on Borneo. Pelni also has a subsidiary, Perintis, which serves many of the outer ports of Indonesia. For information, contact Pelni at one of the above numbers, or call the head office in Jakarta (tel. 021/416262).

Getting Around

By Taxi You can hail cruising cabs in Ujung Pandang or find them waiting outside hotels. Taxis are unmetered; you negotiate the fare. Two large companies are **Mas. C.V.** (tel. 0411/4599) and **Omega** (tel. 0411/22679).

By Bus A large company, with currently the newest buses serving towns outside Ujung Pandang is **Liman Express** (tel. 0411/5851).

The bus to Tanatoraja from Ujung Pandang takes nine hours, plus an hour lunch break. There are morning and evening departures in both directions. At Rp 12,500, it's an economical way to go. Since the countryside is not to be missed, make sure to make one trip during daylight. Liman Express has the newest buses.

By Bemo In Ujung Pandang, bemo minivans run along Jalan Jend. Sudirman/Ratulangi; Jalan Hasnuddin/Cendrawash; and Jalan Bulusaraung/Mesjid Raya to Maros (sometimes detouring to the airport). Public minibuses to towns outside Ujung Pandang leave from Jalan Sarappo whenever they're full.

By Becak For journeys less than 3¼ km (2 mi), bicycle rickshaws are the popular means of transport. Bargain hard. A trip in town should cost about Rp 500, even if the driver begins by asking Rp 2,000.

By Car Self-drive rental cars are not available—or permitted—on Sulawesi.

By Tour Bus Travel agencies either take clients one way from Ujung Pandang to Rantepao by minibus and fly them back, or go both ways by minibus. The advantage is the guide. (*See* Guided Tours, below, for tour companies in Ujung Pandang.)

Important Addresses and Numbers

Tourist Information In Ujung Pandang, **South Sulawesi Tourist Office** (Jln. Sultan Alauddin 105 B, tel. 0411/83897) is open Mon.–Thurs. and Sat. 7–2, Fri. 7–11 AM.

Emergencies **Police,** tel. 110 or 7777; **ambulance,** tel. 118.

Guided Tours

Ramayana Tours (Jln. Anuang 94, tel. 0411/83676) is particularly good for tours into Torajaland because many of its guides come from there. It also offers excursions to the southeast peninsula, famous for boatbuilding and a reclusive Muslim village, and arranges customized tours, such as a jeep trip across the island and a canoe visit to the weavers of Galumpang in central Sulawesi.

Other agencies include **Nitour Tours and Travel** (Jln. Lamaddukellang 2, tel. 0411/7723) and **Pacto Ltd.** (Jln. Jend., Sudirman 56, tel. 0411/83208).

Exploring Ujung Pandang

The principal site is **Fort Rotterdam,** now officially called Benteng ("fort") Ujung Pandang, though most people still use its old name. Located by the harbor in the center of the old city, it began as a fortified trading post for the Sulawesi Goanese dynasty and a defense against pirates. The fort was first captured and rebuilt by the Portuguese in 1545, then captured by the Dutch in 1608 and reinforced again. On Saturday night at 8, dance performances are often held here. Personnel at your hotel should know whether any are scheduled. *Fort admission free. Open daily 7–6.*

The fort includes the **Galigo Museum,** divided into ethnology and history sections. The ethnographic museum is the more interesting, with a large collection of artifacts from different areas of Sulawesi. *Admission charge to each museum. Open Tues.–Thurs. 8–1, Fri. 8–10 AM, weekends 8–noon.*

Just 3¼ km (2 mi) north of Ujung Pandang is Paotare, a harbor where the Bugis prahus come to unload their cargo, mend their sails, and prepare for their next passage. The pier has missing planks and gaping holes, so watch where you step.

Excursion to Tanatoraja

The four-hour drive north to Pare Pare, halfway between Ujung Pandang and Rantepao, is through flat countryside of rice fields, with the Strait of Makassar on the left. The area is inhabited by Bugis, whose houses, on stilts and with crossed roofbeams, line the road. In some you'll see fish hanging from the rafters, curing in the sun. **Pare Pare** is a city of 90,000 and Sulawesi's second-largest town. From its port, boats cross the Makassar Sea to Kalimantan. There is little to see in Pare Pare, but it has two decent restaurants.

Time Out **Bukit Indah** is a smart restaurant with six hotel rooms and a view of the bay. Perched on a hill, it catches a breeze, and everything is pristinely clean. To reach Bukit Indah, take a right turn up the hill from the main street just before entering downtown Pare Pare. The crab and corn soup is delicious, as are the fried frogs' legs.

Sempurna, on the main street (149 Jln. Bau Massepe, tel. 0421/ 21573), is a clean, Formica-furnished, air-conditioned restaurant in the center of town for tasty Indonesian and Chinese food. Try the sweet-and-sour shrimp.

From Pare Pare the road twists and turns inland, leaving the sea to the west as it climbs into limestone hills forested with tropical pine and palms. Shimmering in the distance are the steely blue mountains that locked out intruding cultures for centuries. Not until 1980 was the road paved. Before then, the rutted, stony track took hours to cover. Dominated by Bamba Buang mountain, the scenery becomes increasingly dramatic. According to legend, the souls of the Torajan dead assemble here to journey to the "gate of God." As the road continues into the mountains of Tanatoraja, look to the right across the small valley and you'll recognize the **"Lady Mountain,"** where two ridges split off, to suggest a woman's legs. In the distance is **Rura,** said to be the very first Toraja village.

Time Out Located 248 km (153 mi) from Ujung Pandang and 54 km (32 mi) before Makale is a roadside restaurant, **Puntak Lakawan,** with a terrace affording spectacular views—an exciting introduction to Tanatoraja. Travelers stop here for the views, the strong coffee, and the "tourist only" Western toilet facilities— not for the food.

Finally, the road leads through carved gates, announcing the entrance into Tanatoraja. Bypass Makale and head straight for Rantepao, the center of tourist travel and the hub of the network of roads that peel off into the countryside to the Toraja villages.

Numbers in the margin correspond to points of interest on the Torajaland map.

❶ **Rantepao** is a small, easygoing market town. Its big event occurs every sixth day, when the "weekly" market at the town crossroads attracts just about everyone from the surrounding villages. Even on off days, the market shops sell wood carvings, cloth, and other Toraja-crafted goods. Rantepao also has small restaurants and inexpensive hotels. The more comfortable accommodations are a few kilometers out of town, however, either back on the road to Makale or on the road east toward Marante.

If you have time, the ideal way to experience Tanatoraja is by hiking through the hills along small paths from one village to the next. Visiting them by bus is possible, with short hikes, but it is slow going. You can also hire a minivan or four-wheel-drive jeep with a guide. Wear strong, ankle-supporting shoes, because you'll do some walking over rutted tracks or roads.

Each tour guide has his favorite villages for visiting. He should be able to learn about any scheduled ceremonies. Encourage him to do so, for witnessing one is an event you won't forget.

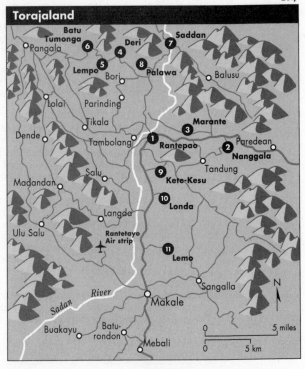

Torajaland

The **funeral ceremony** is the most important event in the life of a Toraja. Though families traditionally gave as lavish a funeral as possible to demonstrate the prestige of the dead to the gods, a competition for status has now entered the ceremony. Wealth is measured in buffalo: The more buffalo sacrificed at the funeral, the more honor to the dead, the family, and the clan. Even Toraja who have converted to Christianity continue the funeral ritual to show prestige, keep tradition, and make sure the dead have plenty of influence with the gods.

When a clan erects a new tongkonan, there's a large **house-warming** ceremony with the whole clan present, which may mean hundreds of people. Buffalo and pigs are sacrificed—again to display prestige.

Of the hundreds of villages in Tanatoraja, the following are some of the more accessible. To varying degrees, they give the visitor a chance to see aspects of animist culture and architecture. Most villages on the regular tourist route require a donation of Rp 1,500 or more. In theory, this helps the villagers maintain their buildings.

② To the east of Rantepao is **Nanggala**. This is a quiet village and one of the best examples of a traditional Toraja life. The tongkonan and other houses are built on poles with soaring prow-shape roofs, lined up facing north (whence the ancestors came), and *lumbung* (granaries or rice barns, smaller than the houses but similar in shape) opposite. The tongkonan is cared for by the clan leader. A noble clan may decorate all the walls with carved and painted designs symbolizing the buffalo, the sun, and important crops. A middle-ranking clan is permitted to decorate only the front gable. When you see a wood buffalo head or the horns of sacrificed buffalo affixed to the front pole of the house, you're looking at the house of a noble clan.

3 Also to the east of Rantepao is **Marante,** where you'll find burial caves in a limestone cliff. The remnants of poles in the cliff used to support hanging coffins, and some old carved coffins remain. There is also a funeral bier shaped like a traditional house—a ship to carry the deceased to the next life. At one end of the village is a modern home with a prow projecting from the roof, and a wood buffalo head attached to its front post—a fabulous anachronism.

4 5 6 A drive north from Rantepao to **Deri, Lempo,** and **Batu Tumonga** provides spectacular scenery—mountains, rice terraces, and rain forest. A right turn off the road to Deri leads to **7** the weaving center of **Saddan** (a blue sign points the way). Here, Toraja women weave and sell their colorful designs, which use mainly primary colors in geometric patterns. You can also purchase the beautiful vegetable-dyed ikat textiles from Galumpang, an area north and west of Tanatoraja known for its weaving.

8 On the road back to Rantepao from Saddan is the very old village of **Palawa,** where hundreds of horns of sacrificed buffalo hang on the houses and where eight traditional homes contain shops selling Toraja carvings, textiles, old coins, and junk.

9 The more heavily traveled tourist villages such as **Kete-Kesu,**
10 11 **Londa,** and **Lemo,** lie south of Rantepao. Some are the sites of limestone burial caves with *tau taus*, wood effigies carved for noble Toraja and placed on a balcony at the cave. The spirit of the ancestor honored thus will help the descendants enjoy a better life.

These are just a few of the villages nestling in the valleys throughout Tanatoraja. The farther you go from Rantepao and Makele, the fewer tourists the inhabitants have seen, and the more welcoming they are. If you have time and spirit, head into the northwestern or eastern part. These areas are the least infiltrated. Most of the inhabitants will know a few words of Bahasa Indonesian, but no English.

Evening entertainment is minimal in Rantepao. Some hotels offer cultural shows, but they are generally a waste of time and money.

Dining

The Makassarese and Bugis are famous seafarers, so you can expect good seafood in Sulawesi, but the best kitchens are often run by local Chinese.

Rantepao **Pondok Torsina.** Located in the rice fields a few kilometers
Inexpensive south of Rantepao, this small hotel-and-restaurant serves good Indonesian food on a veranda overlooking the paddies. Try the asparagus soup, shrimp in spicy butter sauce, and grilled fish. The Toraja owner is very helpful in filling in the information gaps left by your guide. *Tikunna Malenong, tel. 0423/21293. No reservations. Dress: casual. No credit cards.*

Restaurant Rachmat. Near the traffic circle with a model of a Toraja house, this Chinese-operated restaurant offers tasty Indonesian and Chinese dishes. *Jln. Diponegoro 10. No reservations. Dress: casual. No credit cards.*

Ujung Pandang
Moderate

Restaurant Surya. Super Crab, as this restaurant is called, serves some of the best seafood in Ujung Pandang. The proprietor, Jerry, speaks English, so you won't have any problem with the menu. The large, bright room has no decor or atmosphere, but the crab-and-asparagus soup is delicious, as are the gigantic prawns. *Jln. Nusakambangan 16, tel. 0411/7066. No reservations. Dress: casual. No credit cards.*

Lodging

Rantepao
Moderate
★

Hotel Misiliana. Make sure to book rooms in the new part, where a courtyard garden has a row of traditional houses with rice barns opposite. Guest rooms surround the courtyard in two- or four-unit bungalows designed to complement the houses. The rooms are spotless, furnished with twin beds in colorful native covers, and have modern, tile bathrooms. The dining room and lobby building have Toraja-carved motifs. Breakfast and dinner are included in the tariff, and both meals offer a fixed menu—Europeanized Indonesian fare of no distinction. There usually is a cultural show in the evening—not worth the entrance fee. *Jln. Rantepao, Box 01, tel. 0423/21212. 100 rooms. Facilities: restaurant, art shop. AE, DC, V.*

★

Toraja Cottages. Just 3 km (2 mi) east of Rantepao, and set among tropical gardens, this hotel consists of rows of attached cottages terraced around the main building. The guest rooms, with twin beds, are small but clean. Westernized Indonesian food is served in an open veranda restaurant with rattan furniture, and, amusingly, a model of the Statue of Liberty on a corner table. A smaller, more formal dining room does not serve tour groups. A small bar off the lobby functions as a gathering place. At press time, the hotel was planning to add 100 rooms. *Kamp. Bolu, tel. 0423/21369. Reservations and information: Jln. Johar 17, Jakarta Pusat, Jakarta, tel. 021/321346; or Jln. Somba Opu 281, Ujung Pandang, tel. 0411/84146. 63 rooms. Facilities: 2 restaurants, bar, outdoor pool. V.*

Inexpensive

Pondok Torsina. This small hotel, set in the rice fields, is very utilitarian but clean. Its owner is knowledgeable about Toraja culture, and the restaurant serves good Indonesian food. *Rantepao Tikunna Maenong, tel. 0423/21293. Reservations: Elly 6, Tondirerung, Do. S. Tangka 19, Ujung Pandang, tel. 0411/4985. 10 rooms, 6 with private bath. Facilities: restaurant. No credit cards.*

Ujung Pandang
Expensive
★

Makassar Golden Hotel. This hotel at the harbor sports Toraja-style roofs on its main building. Most rooms face the sea and have wall-to-wall carpeting, with beige decor and red-and-natural woven bedcovers in a Toraja design. Makassar also has cottages facing the sea. All rooms have private bath, minibar, and TV with video programs. The elegant Losari Restaurant serves French food. *Jln. Pasar Ikan 50, tel. 0411/22208. 115 rooms. Facilities: 2 restaurants, banquet hall, conference hall, disco, art shop, Olympic-size outdoor pool. AE, DC, MC, V.*

Moderate　**Makassar City Hotel.** Toraja-style carved-wood panels are the theme here. The hotel is centrally located, and its lounge has crushed-velvet sofas and soft leather chairs. The coffee shop serves Western and Indonesian dishes. Rooms are spacious, with sitting areas, king-size beds, color TV, and minibar. *Jln. Khairil Anwar 28, tel. 0411/7055. 100 rooms. Facilities: restaurant, bar, outdoor pool, conference room. AE, DC, MC, V.*

Inexpensive　**Hotel Ramayana.** Between the airport and Ujung Pandang, this place is clean but purely utilitarian. It's conveniently across the street from the Liman Express office, which runs buses to Torajaland. *Jln. G. Bawakaraeng 121, tel. 0411/22165. 35 rooms. Facilities: restaurant, travel desk. No credit cards.*

5 Malaysia

Introduction

by John W. English

John English, who teaches journalism at the university in Athens, Georgia, has lived and worked in Malaysia.

Malaysia is, for one thing, an extraordinary olfactory experience. In the cities, the acrid smell of chilies frying in street-vendor stalls mingles with the sweetness of incense wafting out of Indian shops, the pungency of curry powders from spice merchants, the delicate scents of frangipani and other tropical flowers that bloom everywhere, and the diesel fumes from taxis and buses. The jungle has a heavy, damp, fermenting aroma that will haunt your imagination long after you've returned to comfortable, everyday life at home.

Malaysia is composed of two parts. East Malaysia comprises the states of Sabah and Sarawak on the island of Borneo, which includes the Indonesian state of Kalimantan as well as the republic of Brunei. West Malaysia, the southern portion of the Malay Peninsula (which also includes part of Thailand), is also called peninsular Malaysia or Malaya, as the country was known before the addition of the East Malaysian states in 1963.

Though East Malaysia has a larger land mass, it is mostly jungle, and 80% of the nation's population lives on the peninsula. This population—some 15.6 million—is about 56% indigenous Malays, 34% ethnic Chinese, 9% Indians, and 1% others, including the Kadazan, Dayak, and other tribes of East Malaysia. While Malaysia is officially a Muslim country, some Malays remain animists, the Chinese are mostly Buddhists and Christians, and most Indians are Hindu. The East Malaysian states are primarily Christian, thanks to the 20th-century missionaries who helped develop the areas.

This mix of cultures is one of Malaysia's main fascinations. It confronts visitors especially in the cities, where, interspersed with businessmen in Western garb and teenagers in T-shirts and jeans, you'll see Malay women in floral-print sarongs, Muslim women with traditional head coverings, Chinese in the pajama-type outfits called *samfoo*, and Indian men in dhotis. It manifests itself in a lively and varied street-food scene, with a proliferation of vendors selling everything from exotic fruits and juices to Hokkien noodles to Malay satay to fish grilled with pungent Asian spices. And it proclaims itself joyously in the street festivals and religious ceremonies that these different cultures celebrate throughout the year.

Malaysia is also topographically diverse, offering some of the world's best coral reefs, long stretches of white-sand beaches (both developed, with plenty of water-sports facilities, and deserted), the highest mountain in Southeast Asia, hill resorts that provide recreation and escape from the tropical sun, spectacular limestone outcroppings (at Ipoh), vast areas of primary jungle, and networks of rivers perfect for white-water rafting.

On the west coast of the peninsula is Kuala Lumpur, Malaysia's capital and the gateway through which most visitors enter the country. It is a sprawling, clamorous, modern city that nevertheless retains many reminders of the past, though perhaps not a lot of charm. The island of Penang, on the other hand, is an exciting combination of beach resort area and university town, with charm to spare. It is a wonderful place to tool around on a bicycle through streets with lively shops and graceful colonial architecture on days when you're not sunning on exceptional beaches. For a sense of Malaysia's colonial history, a visit to

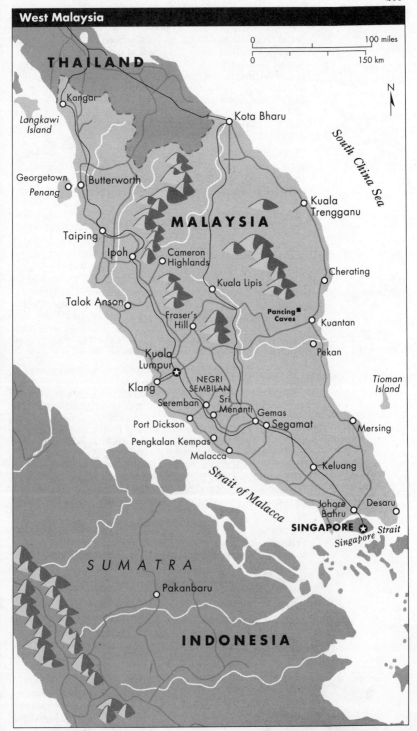

THAILAND

Kangar

Langkawi
Island

Kota Bharu

Georgetown
Penang

Butterworth

Kuala
Trengganu

MALAYSIA

Taiping

Ipoh

Cameron
Highlands

Cherating

Kuala Lipis

Talok Anson

Pancing
Caves

Fraser's
Hill

Kuantan

South China Sea

Kuala
Lumpur

Pekan

Klang

NEGRI
SEMBILAN

Tioman
Island

Seremban

Sri
Menanti

Port Dickson

Gemas

Segamat

Mersing

Pengkalan Kempas

Malacca

Keluang

Strait of Malacca

Johore
Bahru

Desaru

SINGAPORE

Singapore Strait

SUMATRA

Pakanbaru

INDONESIA

0   100 miles
0   150 km

N

Malacca, with ruins and restored buildings from successive European colonizers, is a must.

The peninsula's east coast is less developed, allowing a glimpse of a quieter Malaysia. The area around Kuantan offers excellent beaches and some first-rate resorts; Mersing, to the south, is the jumping-off point for Tioman Island, where the film *South Pacific* was shot. The scenery is as idyllic today as it was then, and a resort hotel offers a perfect base for a water-sports and jungle-hiking island vacation. Much of the rest of the peninsula is covered with rubber estates, oil palm plantations, and cool hill stations.

Sabah and Sarawak, on Borneo, deliver all the adventure that the word *Borneo* promises, including trips through dense jungle by backpack and longboat to visit the descendants of headhunters at their longhouses, where you can stop over for the night—a rare opportunity to learn about a culture so very different from what you've left at home.

A Brief History The earliest inhabitants of the Malay Peninsula were neolithic Negrito peoples whose descendants—the Orang Asli—still live simply in jungle uplands. Several waves of progressively more Mongoloid groups brought Iron and Bronze cultures to the peninsula and spread out over the entire archipelago. Later, with the emergence of the Java-based Majapahit, the Malay Peninsula came under the influence of a Hindu-Javanese empire that exerted little political control but strong cultural influence. This can be seen in the *wayang kulit* (shadow puppet) plays—a form of oral story-telling—still performed in villages, and many ceremonies and customs that remain in practice.

In the 15th century, Islam entered Malaya from northern Sumatra and became the official religion of the powerful state of Malacca during the reign of Sultan Iskandar Shah. Islam solidifed the system of sultanates, in which one person and his family provided both political and religious leadership. (Today Malaysia still has nine sultans; every five years one is elected to serve a term as constitutional monarch. The head of government in this parliamentary democracy is the prime minister.)

For the next 200 years the peninsula was a hornets' nest of warring sultanates, marauding pirate bands, and European adventurers who, searching for spice and gold, introduced guns and cannons. The Portuguese conquered Malacca, followed by the Dutch, who established a stronghold in Java and outposts in Sumatra and Malacca. British settlements in the Straits of Malacca, Singapore, and Penang flourished. In 1824 a treaty with the British separated Malaya from Dutch-held Sumatra, and the two regions, so similar in historical development, cultural traditions, and religious customs, began to split and follow the lead of the new European colonists.

In the middle of the 19th century, millions of Chinese fled from war and famine in their homelands and sought employment in Malaya's rapidly expanding tin industry. Soon after their arrival, another new enterprise developed: rubber. Rubber requires intensive labor, and workers were again brought in from outside—this time from India. Other groups left India to trade, open shops, or lend money. The British in India had also trained many civil servants and professionals, and they, too, came to Malaya to practice.

The Indian community maintained strong ties with home. Even today it is not unusual for an Indian to request a bride or groom from his or her ancestral village—many marriages are still arranged—and Indians often return to their native land at retirement, something the Chinese can no longer do.

These patterns of life in Malaya were well-established until World War II. Malays continued their traditions in *kampongs*, or communal villages, where time flowed slowly. The sultans prospered under British protection, combining the pleasures of East and West. The Chinese, growing ever more numerous and powerful, became the economic backbone of the peninsula, with the Indians performing various middleman roles. The British maintained a benevolent rule. Each community flourished separately, with little cultural interchange.

The war had little impact on life in Malaya until the Japanese attack on Pearl Harbor and subsequent invasion of Malaya threw the complacent population into turmoil. Japanese forces landed in the northern state of Trengganu and moved rapidly down through the jungle, taking Singapore in March 1942. Life on the Malay Peninsula changed overnight.

The British, of course, had furthest to fall. Many women and children were evacuated to Australia, but the men remained. Former planters, bankers, executives, and soldiers were suddenly thrust from a life of ease into hardship or jail. Many prisoners perished constructing the infamous "Death Railway" in Siam. The survivors had to endure the indignities of captivity, which completely undermined their image as "superior" whites.

The Chinese received particularly harsh treatment from their Japanese conquerors. They faced constant harassment from Japanese forces, who jailed and executed thousands. Many Chinese fled to the jungle, where, aided by remnants of the British army, they formed guerrilla bands. As in Europe, those most adept at underground organization were Communist-trained. By the end of the war, Communist influence among the Chinese was much enhanced by the years spent in the jungle fighting the Japanese.

The war left the people floundering in economic uncertainties. Until independence under a federation of Malayan states was declared in 1957, politics consisted mostly of jockeying for power between the two major racial groups. The Malays, realizing that independence would remove British protection and leave the Chinese in control, became politically active. The Chinese, despite their economic clout and with their ranks decimated by the occupation, failed to organize politically. Thus, the years of separatism took their toll on national unification and development. Bitter disputes raged among the local leadership. In 1948 the Chinese guerrilla forces began a campaign of terrorism, harassing plantation workers, owners, and managers. Travel along the jungle roads was hazardous, and many Malays and British were killed in ambush. The insurgents were gradually pushed back into the jungle, and in 1960 the emergency was lifted.

Such ethnic factionalism plagued the new federation until 1963, when the nation of Malaysia was created. It included two British protectorates in northern Borneo—Sabah and Sarawak—that were to serve as an ethnic balance against the power of the Chinese in Singapore. Indonesia, however, viewed Malaysia as a threat, and President Sukarno declared Confrontation—a sort of miniwar that finally fizzled out in 1967.

Today Malaysia's racial and political power balance is still delicate. In spite of legislation to promote "Bumiputra," or numerically dominant ethnic Malay interests, the Chinese still control much of Malaysia's commerce and industry. Much has been done to defuse tensions among the ethnic groups, but pressures continue.

Staying in Malaysia

Getting Around

By Plane **Malaysia Airlines** flies to 35 towns and cities in Malaysia. Domestic flights are relatively inexpensive and often fully booked, especially during school holidays and festivals. You must confirm reservations a day or so beforehand.

By Train **Malayan Railways,** known as KTM, offers cheap and relatively comfortable service on the peninsula. Beginning at Singapore, one branch leads northwest to Butterworth, the Penang station, via Kuala Lumpur; at Butterworth, a connection can be made with the International Express to Bangkok (runs thrice weekly) or a local train to Haadyai, Thailand. Another branch leads to Kota Bharu, at the northeast tip of peninsular Malaysia; at Pasir Mas, a trunk line connects KTM with the Thai railway, 23 km (14 mi) to the north. Both express and local service, and both air-conditioned and non-air-conditioned cars, are available. Passengers with tickets for distances over 200 km (124 mi) can stop off at any point on the route for one day per 200 km traveled: *the stationmaster must endorse the ticket immediately upon arrival at the stopoff station.* On long trips movies are shown, but the passing scenery is always more interesting. In some sections the route goes through jungle and you may see wild monkeys. Sleepers are available on overnight service for a supplemental charge. Dining-car food is simple, cheap, and tasty. For information on the rail line in Sabah, *see* Getting Around By Train in East Malaysia, below.

Rail Passes A foreign tourist can buy the KTM Railpass, permitting unlimited travel for 10 days (M$85) or 30 days (M$175), at main railway stations in Malaysia and in Singapore.

By Bus Bus service is extensive and cheap, but only coaches traveling between major cities are air-conditioned. Local buses are usually crowded, noisy, and slow, but it's a great way to people watch and sightsee at the same time.

By Boat **Feri Malaysia** (tel. 03/238–8899) operates the cruise ship *Muhibah* between Kuantan (on the east coast of peninsular Malaysia), Singapore, Kuching (Sarawak), and Kota Kinabalu (Sabah). The ship offers air-conditioned cabins and suites, restaurants, a cinema, a disco, a gym, and a swimming pool. In port cities there's regular **ferry service** to the islands. To get to Pangkor, catch the ferry in Lumut; for Langkawi, in Kuala Perlis or Penang. Launches serve Tioman Island from Mersing and Pulau Gaya from Kota Kinabalu.

By Taxi Taxi operators near bus terminals call out destinations for long-distance, shared-cost rides; drivers leave when they get four passengers. Single travelers who want to charter a taxi pay four times the flat rate and leave whenever they want. The quality of service depends on the condition of the vehicle and bravado of the driver. In general, the cost is comparable to that of a second-class train ticket or non-air-conditioned bus fare.

City taxis are plentiful and relatively cheap. Rates in peninsular Malaysia are metered. Those in Sabah and Sarawak are not—set the fare with the driver in advance. Air-conditioning or late-night rides cost 20% more than what's on the meter.

By Car Rentals The largest operation in Malaysia, **Avis** has offices all over the mainland; rates range from M$40 to M$125 a day with unlimited mileage. Special three-day rates are available. The main office is in Kuala Lumpur (40 Jln. Sultan Ismail, tel. 03/242–3500). **Budget** (tel. 03/255–1044) has offices in Kuala Lumpur and counters at Subang and Penang airports. **Hertz** (tel. 03/261–1136) has offices in Kuala Lumpur, Penang, and Johore Bahru. **Mayflower** (tel. 03/261–1136) is part of Acme Tours, with a counter at the Ming Court Hotel in Kuala Lumpur.

Road Conditions The only superhighway in the country runs from Kuala Lumpur to Malacca, and it is lightly traveled because of the tolls. The two-lane trunk road between Kuala Lumpur and Penang has heavy traffic day and night. Slow-moving trucks, motorcycles, and bicycles make it somewhat treacherous. Back roads are narrow but paved, and the pace is relaxed—you'll weave around dogs sleeping in the road. Mountain roads are often single-lane, and you must allow oncoming cars to pass.

Rules of the Road Tourists are urged to get an international driver's license in addition to a valid permit from home. Seat belts are compulsory for drivers and front-seat passengers, and stiff fines are imposed on those caught without them. Driving is on the left side of the road. Some common traffic signs: *AWAS* (caution), *jalan sehala* (one way), *kurangkan laju* (slow down), and *ikut kiri* (keep left). Directions are *utara* (north), *selatan* (south), *timur* (east), and *barat* (west).

Parking In the cities, on-street parking is plentiful, and meters are closely monitored. Public lots are also available. In some areas of Kuala Lumpur, you are expected to pay young hoodlums to "protect" your car while you are away; if you don't do it, they may vandalize your car. Locals believe it's worth a few coins for such insurance.

Gas Stations charge about M$5 per gallon and offer full service. Except for a few 24-hour stations in cities, most places are closed at night.

Breakdowns Car-rental agents in most cities will assist with problems. The **Automobile Association of Malaysia** (Hotel Equatorial, KL, tel. 03/261–3713 or 03/261–2727) can also offer advice in case of a roadside emergency.

Telephones

Local Calls Public pay phones take 10-sen coins (time unlimited on local calls).

International Calls You can direct-dial overseas from many hotel-room phones. If you want to avoid the hotel charges, local phone books give pages of information in English on international calling, rates, and locations of telephone offices.

Information Dial 104 for directory information.

Mail

Postal Rates Stamps and postal information are generally available at hotel front desks. To the Americas, **postcards** cost 55 sen, **airmail letters** M$2.20 (½ oz). **Aerograms** are the best value of all, at 40 sen.

Receiving Mail **American Express** (Bangunan MAS, 5th floor, Jln. Sultan Ismail, KL) will hold cardholders' mail for 30 days at no charge.

Currency

Malaysian ringgit, also called Malaysian dollars, are issued in denominations of M$1, M$5, M$10, M$20, M$50, M$100, M$500, and M$1,000. The units are called sen and come in coins of 1, 5, 10, 20, and 50 sen. Exchange rates at press time were M$2.70 = US$1 and M$4.80 = £1.

What It Will Cost

The Malaysian ringgit is worth about 8% less than in 1988, and since prices have remained relatively stable, Westerners get more for their money. At press time the exchange rate was M$2.70 = US$1. As might be expected, prices in the cities are higher than elsewhere, Kuala Lumpur being the most expensive.

Taxes A 5% tax is added to **hotel** and **restaurant** bills, along with a 10% service charge, in a system that the locals call "plus plus." (You'll see the "++" symbols where this applies.) **Airport departure taxes** vary depending on destination. For domestic flights it's M$3; for flights to Singapore and Brunei, M$5; for other international flights, M$15.

Sample Prices Cup of tea in hotel coffee shop, $1.30; cup of tea in open-air *kedai*, 60¢; Chinese dim sum breakfast, $2.16; hotel breakfast buffet, $4.45; bottle of beer at a bar, $1.50; bowl of noodles at a stall, $1.10; 1-mile taxi ride, 75¢; typical bus fare, 19¢; double room, $28 budget, $41 moderate, $67 luxury.

Language

The official language is Bahasa Malaysia, but English is widely spoken in government and business and is the interracial lingua franca. The Chinese speak several dialects, including Cantonese, Teochew, Hakka, and Hokkien. The Indians are primarily Tamil speakers. In the countryside, most people use a kampong version of Malay, even in Sabah and Sarawak, where native languages (Kadazan and Iban) predominate.

Opening and Closing Times

Shops are generally open 9:30 AM–7 PM; **department stores** and **supermarkets,** 10–10. Many places are closed Sunday, except in the states of Johor, Kedah, Perlis, Kelantan, and Terengganu, where Friday is the day of rest. **Banks** are open weekdays 10–3 and Saturday 9:30 to 11:30 AM. **Government office hours** are Monday–Thursday 8–12:45 and 2–4:15, Friday 8–12:45 and 2:45–4:15, and Saturday 8–12:45.

National Holidays

The major national public holidays include Chinese New Year, February 17–18; Labor Day, May 1; Hari Raya Puasa, usually mid-May; King's Birthday, June 1; Hari Raya Haji, usually late July; Maal Hijrah, August 14; National Day, August 31; Prophet Muhammad's Birthday, October 23; Deepavali, November 8; and Christmas, December 25. Museums and government offices may be closed on state holidays as well.

Festivals and Seasonal Events

Malaysia's multiracial society celebrates numerous festivals, since each ethnic community retains its own customs and traditions. The dates of some holidays are fixed, but most change according to the various religious calendars.

Jan.–Feb.: During **Chinese New Year,** Chinese families visit Buddhist temples, exchange gifts, and hold open house for relatives and friends.

Jan.–Feb.: The Hindu festival **Thaipusam** turns out big crowds for a street parade in Penang and a religious spectacle at the Batu Caves near Kuala Lumpur. Indian devotees of the god Subramaniam pierce their bodies, cheeks, and tongues with steel hooks and rods.

Mid-May: The **Kadazan Harvest Festival** is celebrated in Sabah with feasting, buffalo races, games, and colorful dances in native costumes.

May–June: Gawai Dayak, a week-long harvest festival, is celebrated in Sarawak with dances, games, and feasting in the longhouses.

Early June: The **Dragon Boat Festival** features boat races off Gurney Drive in Penang.

June 3: Every state marks the **King's Birthday** (Yang Di-Pertuan Agong) with parades. In Kuala Lumpur's Merdeka Stadium, a trooping of the colors is held.

May–Aug.: Hari Raya Puasa, a major holiday, whose date varies according to the Muslim lunar calendar, marks the end of Ramadan, the fasting month. It is a time of feasting and rejoicing and often includes a visit to the cemetery, followed by mosque services. Tourists are welcome at the prime minister's residence in Kuala Lumpur during open-house hours.

Aug. 31: Merdeka Day is Malaysia's Independence Day. Arches are erected across city thoroughfares, buildings are illuminated, parades are arranged, and in Kuala Lumpur there is a variety show in Lake Gardens.

Aug.–Sept.: On **All Soul's Day,** or the **Feast of the Hungry Ghosts,** Chinese honor their ancestors by burning paper objects (for the ancestors' use in the afterlife) on the street. Chinese opera is performed in various locations in Penang and other cities.

Oct.–Nov.: During **Deepavali,** the Hindu festival of lights, celebrating the triumph of good over evil, houses and shops are brightly decorated.

Late Dec.: During the **Chingay Procession,** Malaysian Chinese parade through the streets of Penang and Johore Bahru doing stunts with enormous clan flags on bamboo poles, accompanied by cymbals, drums, and gongs. It's a noisy, colorful, folksy pageant.

Dec. 25: Christmas is widely celebrated, with decorations, food promotions, music, and appearances of Father Krismas.

Tipping

Tipping is usually unnecessary, since a 10% service charge is automatically added to restaurant and hotel bills. You'll know that's the case when you see the ++ symbol on menus and rate cards. Tip porters one ringgit per bag. It would be insulting to tip less than 50 sen. Malaysians usually tip **taxi drivers** with their coin change. Otherwise, when you want to acknowledge fine service, 10% is generous—not expected.

Shopping

For an overview of Malaysian goods, check out the Central Market and the Karyaneka Handicraft Centre in Kuala Lumpur.

Malaysia's hand-printed batiks, with layers of rich colors and elaborate traditional designs, have become high fashion worldwide. Shirts and simple skirts and dresses can be purchased off the rack in most sizes, or you can buy lengths of fabric and have garments made at home.

Pewter is another Malaysian specialty, since it's made from one of the country's prime raw materials, tin. The best-known manufacturer is Selangor Pewter, which markets its goods through its own showrooms as well as department stores, gift shops, and handicraft centers throughout the country.

Malaysian handicrafts, especially those from Sarawak in East Malaysia, are well made and appealing, such as rattan baskets in pretty pastels and hand-woven straw goods and handmade silver jewelry from Kelantan. The Dayak people in Sarawak create weavings called *pua kumbu*, which use primitive patterns and have a faded look like that of an antique Persian carpet. Tribal sculptures have an allure similar to their African counterparts. Perhaps the most unusual handcrafted material is *kain songket*, an extraordinary tapestrylike fabric with real gold threads woven into a pattern.

Prices in most shops and larger stores are fixed, but you can discreetly ask for a discount. In street markets, flea markets, and antiques stores, bargaining is expected.

Sports and Beaches

Beaches and Water Sports The best beaches in Malaysia are along the Batu Ferringhi strip on Penang Island. The resort hotels that line most of the beachfront offer rental equipment for windsurfing, sailing, waterskiing, and parasailing. Pangkor and Langkawi islands, off the northwest coast, have good golden-sand beaches and are not yet as developed, although both do offer resorts and watersports facilities. On the east coast, Kuantan, Desaru, and Tioman Island offer resort life; north of Kuantan, miles of quiet and lovely sandy beaches and picturesque villages await those willing to swap luxuries for a more traditional Malay experience. In East Malaysia, the Damai is the best beach in

Sarawak, and the pristine islands off Kota Kinabalu in Sabah offer fine snorkeling and beaches.

Diving Sipadan Island, off Sabah's east coast in the Celebes Sea, is the best dive spot in Malaysia, and one of the best in the world. Coral reef and green sea turtles are among the attractions. Tioman Island is located on coral fringes and has diving facilities. *See also* Group Tours, for diving tours.

Golf Golf is part of the British legacy in Malaysia, and you'll find excellent courses throughout the country. Among the best are the **Royal Selangor Golf Club** in Kuala Lumpur and the **Bukit Jambul Golf and Country Club** in Penang. Ask the TDC for its *Golf Handbook*.

Hiking The best climb in Southeast Asia is Mt. Kinabalu in Sabah. Paths through a park at its base offer rewarding but less arduous walking. Jungle trekking can be arranged in Taman Negara, a national park north of Kuala Lumpur. For leisurely hikes in cooler temperatures, try the hills of the highland resorts (ask the TDC for its hill resorts booklet).

East Malaysia specializes in hiking, either full-scale backpacking through dense jungle or shorter hiking trips combined with road and river transport.

River Rafting Sabah's scenic white-water rivers guarantee exciting outdoor adventures.

Dining

Surprisingly, "real" Malay food is not as widely available in Malaysia's restaurants as Chinese or even American fast-food fare, including Kentucky Fried Chicken and A&W. Restaurants in major hotels offer a range of international dining styles, including Japanese, Korean, French, Italian, and Continental. Kuala Lumpur and Penang are Malaysia's culinary stars, with excellent restaurants and a wide variety of cuisines.

Street food is a main event throughout Malaysia; locals share tables when it's crowded. Look at what others are eating, and if it looks good, point and order. One favorite is the *popiah*, a soft spring roll filled with vegetables. The *meehon* and *kweh teow* (fried noodles) are especially tasty and cheap. Pay each provider for the individual dish he or she makes. Be cautious with the *nasi kandar*, a local favorite, for the chilies rule the spicy prawns and fish-head curry.

As a general rule, food handlers are inspected by health-enforcement officers, but the best advice is to patronize popular places: Consumers everywhere tend to boycott stalls with a reputation for poor hygiene.

Because fruit is so plentiful and delicious, Malaysians consume lots of it, either fresh from the ubiquitous roadside fruit vendors or fresh-squeezed—try especially star fruit or watermelon juice. Mangoes, papayas, rambutans, mangosteens, and finger-size bananas are widely available. The "king" of fruits is the durian, but be prepared: The smell is not sweet, even though the taste is. Hotels have strict policies forbidding durians in guest rooms, so most buyers select a fruit, have the seller cut it open, then eat the yellow flesh on the spot (it's sort of like vanilla pudding).

Category	Cost*
Very Expensive	over M$62.50 (US$25)
Expensive	M$37.50–M$62.50 (US$15–US$25)
Moderate	M$15–M$37.50 (US$6–US$15)
Inexpensive	under M$15 (US$6)

per person without tax, service, or drinks, based on 3 dishes shared between 2 people

Lodging

In the cities you will find international-class hotels affiliated with such global chains as Hilton, Holiday Inns, and Regent. Regional and local hotel groups, such as Merlin and Ming Court, also run luxury operations. Beach resorts at Penang's Batu Ferringhi, Pangkor and Langkawi islands off the peninsula's west coast, and Port Dickson near Kuala Lumpur also range from quiet and simple to world-class facilities. Cheraning, on the quieter east coast, has a Club Med (tel. 800/258–2633 in the U.S.).

Nightlife in Malaysia revolves around the major hotels, which may offer cultural shows, lounges and bars with live entertainment, discos, and restaurants from coffee shops to supper clubs. Many now staff fully equipped business centers and health clubs.

Bathrooms in the city generally offer Western-style commodes, whereas squat Asian-type facilities are common in rural areas. Better hotels have in-house movies available on color television.

Inexpensive Chinese hotels abound in Malaysia, though they are often a bit down at the heel. Rest houses, a British legacy in which government bungalows are rented out to officials on duty in the area, are available to tourists at low rates when government officers aren't using them, but they are difficult to book in advance, and you can count on their being full during school holidays. To check their location and availability, write or visit any Tourist Development Corporation office. **Youth Hostels Association** (Box 2310, 9 Jln. Vethavanam, off 3½-mi Jln. Ipoh, KL, tel. 03/660872) operates hostels throughout Malaysia. For a complete list of accommodations, ask the TDC for a copy of its Hotel List. Also, Utell International (tel. 800/44–UTELL) represents more than 30 hotels in Malaysia.

Throughout the chapter, the following hotel price categories will apply.

Category	Cost*
Very Expensive	over M$160 (US$60)
Expensive	M$130–M$160 (US$48–US$60)
Moderate	M$75–M$130 (US$28–US$48)
Inexpensive	under M$75 (US$28)

All prices are for a double room; add 5% tax and 10% service charge.

Kuala Lumpur

Introduction

Kuala Lumpur (KL) is a city of contrasts. Gleaming new skyscrapers sit next to century-old, two-story shophouses. On six-lane superhighways, rush hour traffic often appears to be an elongated parking lot, but nearly a quarter of the population still lives in *kampongs* within the city, giving KL as much a rural feel as urban.

KL was founded by miners who discovered tin in this spot where the Kelang and Gombak rivers formed a broad delta. Those pioneers were a rough, hardy lot, and the city retains some of that early boomtown character. Despite its bustling, cosmopolitan style, KL is at heart an earthy place, where people sit around the *kedai kopi* (coffee house) and talk about food, religion, and business. It also is the center of the federal government, and since government is dominated by Malays and business by Chinese, the tone of the city is as much influenced by the easygoing Malays as by the hyperactive Chinese.

While not one of the world's great destination cities, KL does offer first-rate hotels, excellent and varied cuisines, a lively blend of cultures, a rich mix of architectural styles from Moorish to Tudor to International Modern, a generally efficient infrastructure, and the lowest prices of any major Asian city.

Arriving and Departing by Plane

Airports and Airlines   **Subang Airport,** 26 km (16 mi) southwest of downtown, is the gateway to Malaysia. In addition to international flights, domestic routes are served by **Malaysia Airlines** (MAS). Among the many other airlines that serve Subang are **British Airways** (tel. 03/242–6177), **Northwest Orient** (tel. 03/238–4355), **Qantas** (tel. 03/238–9133), **Royal Brunei** (tel. 03/242–6511), **Singapore Airlines** (tel. 03/292–3122), and **Thai International** (tel. 03/293–7100).

Between the Airport and Downtown
By Taxi   Taxi service to city hotels runs on a queue-and-coupon system. You buy the coupon from a counter near the queue, paying by zone; prices range from M$15 to M$20 to the downtown area. Beware of unscrupulous drivers trying to lure you into private "taxis"—before you get in, look for a license posted on the dash of the passenger side and a meter.

By Bus   Public bus No. 47 runs between the airport and the central bus station downtown, where you can catch another bus to your final destination. Fares are cheap, but the "hourly" service is erratic and not available after midnight, when international flights often arrive. Buses to the airport start running at 6 AM. Travel time is about 45 minutes, depending on traffic conditions.

Arriving and Departing by Car, Train, and Bus

By Car   The roads into and out of KL are clearly marked, but traffic jams are legendary. It's best to avoid the morning and late-afternoon rush hours if possible.

By Train All trains from Butterworth and Singapore deposit passengers at the main railway station (tel. 03/274–7435), which is on Jalan Sultan Hishamuddin, a short distance from the city center. There are always cabs at the taxi stand.

By Bus Regional buses bring passengers to the main **Pudu Raya terminal** on Jalan Pudu, across from the new Maybank skyscraper, where you can get a taxi or local bus to your city destination.

Getting Around

Walking is the best way to get around the city center's three main areas, called the Golden Triangle. For short distances you can always hop a minibus or hail a taxi.

By Bus Bus service covers most of the metropolitan area. Fares are based on distance, 20 sen for the first kilometer and 5 sen for each additional 2 kilometers. Just tell the conductor where you want to go, and have small change ready, because ticket sellers don't like to break large bills. Minibuses charge 50 sen for rides of any distance. Before you get on ask the driver whether his route serves your destination. Bus stops are usually marked. Bus companies serving KL include **Foh Hup** (tel. 03/238–2132), **Sri Jaya Kenderaan** (tel. 03/442–0166), and **Toon Foong** (tel. 03/238–9833). The two major bus stations are **Pudu Raya** on Jalan Pudu and the **Kelang** terminal on Jalan Sultan Mohamed.

By Taxi Taxis are plentiful in KL. You can catch them at stands, hail them in the street, or request them by phone (pickup costs extra). Radio-dispatch taxi companies include **Kuala Lumpur Taxi Assn.** (tel. 03/221–4241), **Comfort Radio Taxi** (tel. 03/733–0495), and **Teletaxi** (tel. 03/221–1011). Taxis are metered. Air-conditioned cabs charge 20% more (M$1 first kilometer, 40 sen each additional). You can hire a cab by the hour for M$12 the first hour and M$8 per hour afterward. A 50% surcharge applies between midnight and 6 AM, and extra passengers (more than two) pay an additional 10 sen each per ride. Luggage is charged at 10 sen per item. Most taxi drivers speak passable English, but make sure they understand where you want to go and know how to get there before you get in. Be sure the meter is activated when you take off so there won't be any dispute over the fare when you arrive.

Important Addresses and Numbers

Tourist Information The **KL Visitors Centre** (3 Jln. Hishamuddin, tel. 03/230–1369) is open weekdays 8–4:15, Saturday 8–12:45 PM. It supplies city maps, directions, and assistance in finding hotels. The **Tourist Development Corporation** (TDC, 26th floor, Menara Dato Onn, Putra World Trade Centre, Jln. Tun Ismail, tel. 03/293–5188) has information on all of Malaysia. It is open Monday–Thursday 8–12:45 and 2–4:15, Friday 8–noon and 2:30–4:15, and Saturday 8–12:45 PM.

Embassies **Australia High Commission** (6 Jln. Yap Kwan Seng, tel. 03/242–3122). **British High Commission** (Wisma Damansara, 5 Jln. Semantan, tel. 03/247–7122). **Canadian High Commission** (Plaza MBF, 5th floor, Jln. Ampang, tel. 03/261–2000). **United States Embassy** (376 Jln. Tun Razak, tel. 03/248–9011).

Emergencies For **police, ambulance,** and **fire,** dial 999.

Doctors
: The telephone directory lists several government clinics, which treat walk-in patients for a cash fee; these are open during normal business hours.

English-Language Bookstores
: Because English is widely used in Malaysia, reading material is easy to find, especially on Jalan Tuanku Abdul Rahman, in the 100-block area, and in the Sungei Wang Plaza on Jalan Sultan Ismail.

Travel Agencies
: **American Express** (MAS Bldg., 5th floor, Jln. Sultan Ismail, tel. 03/261–0000). **Thomas Cook** (Wisma Bouftead, Jln. Raja Chulan, tel. 03/241–7022). *Also see* Guided Tours, below.

Guided Tours

The TDC maintains a list of all licensed tour operators; you can also get brochures in most hotel lobbies and information from local travel agents. One of the biggest operators is **Mayflower Acme Tours,** with a main office at 18 Jalan Segambut Pusat (tel. 03/626–7011) and a desk at the Ming Court Hotel lobby (tel. 03/261–1120). The other major tour operator is **Reliance** (3rd floor, Sungei Wang Plaza, Jalan Sultan Ismail, tel. 03/248–0111).

Highlights for First-time Visitors

National Museum
National Art Gallery
Lake Gardens
Central Market
Sultan Abdul Samad building and Selangor Club
Coliseum Cafe
Karyaneka Handicraft Centre
Pudu Prison mural
Bank Bumiputra building

Exploring Kuala Lumpur

In this walking tour, we cover the area known as the Golden Triangle. The walk can be done in a couple of hours, but you'll get more out of it if you linger along the way. Don't hesitate to talk to the locals—they are, by and large, open and friendly.

Numbers in the margin correspond with numbered points of interest on the Kuala Lumpur map.

❶ The ideal place to begin is Malaysia's **National Museum** (Muzim Negara), a short walk from the Visitors Centre. The museum's distinctive architecture makes it easily identifiable; the building is modeled after an old-style Malay village house, enlarged to institutional size. On its facade are two large mosaic murals depicting important moments in history and elements of Malay culture.

A number of exhibits are located behind the museum. The **transportation shed** displays every form of transport used in the country, from a Malacca bullock cart, with its distinctive upturned roof, to pedaled trishaws, still in use in Penang, to the newest symbol of national pride, the Malaysian car called the Proton Saga, coproduced with Japan's Mitsubishi Motor. Don't miss the Malay-style house, called **Istana Satu** ("first palace"). Built on stilts, the simple little wood structure is open and airy—perfectly adapted for the tropics—and features decorative wood carvings. Burial totem poles from Sarawak line the path to the museum.

The cultural gallery, to the left as you enter the museum, emphasizes Malay folk traditions. One exhibit explains *wayang kulit*, the shadow plays performed with puppets cut out of leather and manipulated with sticks. You can see how a simple light casts the images on the screen, though the exhibit doesn't capture the theatrical magic the storyteller creates as he spins out rich folk legends. You'll also see a tableau of an elaborate Malay wedding ceremony and exhibits on etiquette, top spinning, Islamic grave markers, colorful cloth headdresses, and a martial-arts form called *silat*. Chinese culture in Malaysia is highlighted at the far end of the gallery. A model Nonya (Peranakan, or straits-born Chinese) home shows classical Chinese furniture, such exquisite antiques as carved canopy beds, and a table-and-chair set with pearl inlay.

The historical gallery has models of regional-style homes and a collection of ceramic pottery, gold and silver items, and other artifacts, plus traditional costumes, now seen only at festivals or on hotel doormen. Exhibits trace the stages of British colonization from the old East India Company in the late 18th century to its withdrawal in the mid-20th. Photos and text outline the Japanese occupation during World War II and Malaysia's move toward federation status in 1948 and independence in 1957. A natural-history exhibit upstairs is devoted to indigenous animals, with stuffed flying lemurs, birds, insects, and poisonous snakes. *Jln. Damansara, tel. 03/238–0255. Admission free. Open daily 9–6; closed for Fri. prayers, 12:15–2:45 PM.*

2 Behind the museum are the scenic **Lake Gardens,** where you can enjoy a leisurely stroll and join city dwellers relaxing, picnicking, and boating on the lake. Also in the park is the **National Monument,** a bronze sculpture dedicated to the nation's war dead, and an **orchid garden** with more than 800 species.

3 Next door to the Visitors Centre is the **National Art Gallery.** The four-story building was the old Majestic Hotel until its conversion into a museum in 1984. The permanent collection serves as an aesthetic introduction to Malaysia and its people. It also reflects native artists' visions and concerns. They tend to work in contemporary modes—conceptual pieces, pop images, bold sculptures, humorous graphics, and realistic landscapes. The gallery is a bit funky, with its ceiling fans, linoleum-covered floors, and some dimly lit rooms, but it's still a treat. The museum shop sells witty posters, prints and cards, and artsy T-shirts at reasonable prices. *1 Jln. Sultan Hishamuddin, tel. 03/230–0157. Admission free. Open daily 10–6, except for the Fri. prayer break.*

The imposing Moorish structures next door and across the **4 5** street are the **main railway station** and the administrative **offices of KTM** (Kereta-api Tanah Melayu), the national rail system. Built in the early 20th century and renovated since, they were designed by a British architect to reflect the Ottoman and Mogul glory of the 13th and 14th centuries. The KTM building blends Gothic and Greek designs and distinctive, wide exterior verandas.

Kuala Lumpur

0 ——— 1 mile
0 ——— 1 km

N

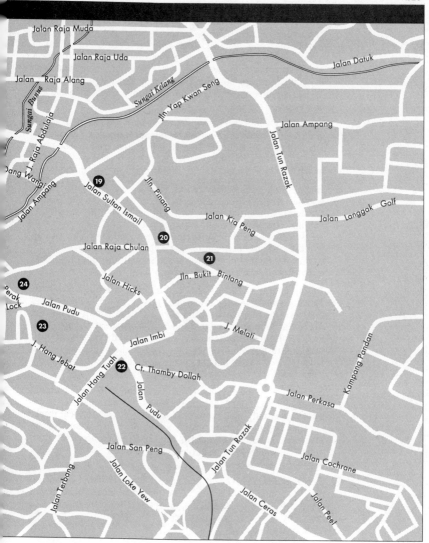

Jalan Raja Muda

Jalan Raja Uda

Jalan Raja Alang

Jalan

Sungai Bunus

Jn. Raja Abdulaja

Sungai Kelang

Jln. Yap Kwan Seng

Jalan Datuk

Jalan Ampang

Dang Wangi

Jalan Ampang

19

Jalan Sultan Ismail

Jln. Pinang

Jalan Tun Razak

Jalan Kia Peng

Jalan Langgak Golf

Jalan Raja Chulan

20

21

Jalan Hicks

Jln. Bukit Bintang

24

Perak
Lock

Jalan Pudu

23

J. Hang Jebat

Jalan Imbi

J. Melati

Jalan Hang Tuah

22

Ct. Thamby Dollah

Jalan Pudu

Kampang Pandan

Jalan Perkasa

Jalan San Peng

Jalan Tun Razak

Jalan Cochrane

Jalan Terbang

Jalan Loke Yew

Jalan Ceras

Jalan Peel

6 Up Jalan Sultan Hishamuddin is the **National Mosque** (Masjid Negara), currently undergoing restoration and expansion. Its contemporary architecture features a towering minaret spire, purple roof, and geometric-patterned grillwork. The entrance is on Jalan Lembah Perdana. Signs remind visitors to dress modestly and to remove their shoes when entering, and that certain areas are off-limits, especially during prayer times. The mosque complex also houses a library and a mausoleum. *Open Sat.–Thurs. 9–6, Fri. 2:45–6.*

7 At Jalan Cenderasari, go under the road via the pedestrian walkway to the impressive **Dayabumi Complex** (Kompleks Dayabumi). Constructed in 1984, it has three parts—the main post office building, the spectacular gleaming white office tower with its lacy Islamic motif, and the plaza connecting the two.

In the post office, philatelists can buy colorful and exotic stamps. Around the corner from the main lobby is a tiny **Stamp Museum** (Galeri Setem), which will be opened for viewing if you ask. Inside, series of stamps spotlight native musical instruments, animals, butterflies, and orchids. The stamp exhibit also promotes nationalistic spirit, with early series focusing on historical events, royalty, and the military. *Post office open weekdays 8–6, Sat. 8–noon.*

At the center of the two-level plaza area is a huge fountain. From the upper level, you can get a good view of the commercial district. One landmark on the horizon is the Hindu temple **Sri Mahamariamman**, in Jalan Bandar. The ornate structure, with images of numerous deities in tile, gold, and precious stones, was rebuilt in 1985 by craftsmen from India and houses a tall silver chariot that is part of a procession to the Batu Caves each Thaipusam.

Stroll through the glistening red marble lobby of the Dayabumi tower, whose major tenant is Petronas, the national oil company. Occasionally, art exhibits in the lobby feature local work. On the shopping-arcade level is a host of shops, including the **Pasaraya Supermarket** and the trendy **Rupa Gallery** (lot 158), which specializes in architectural artworks (*see* Shopping, above).

8 Across the plaza in the other direction is the **British Council,** on a hill beyond the main road. The public reading room has all sorts of English books and magazines and is a pleasant place to rest. *Jln. Bukit Aman, tel. 03/298-7555. Open Tues.–Fri. 10–6:30, Sat. 10–4:45.*

9 On the town side of the plaza, cross the pedestrian bridge to the **Central Market,** a lively bazaar in the heart of KL. Housed in a renovated art deco building that used to be the city's produce market, it was converted into a series of stalls and shops in 1986. Now the 50-year-old market, painted apricot and baby blue, is the commercial, cultural, and recreational hub of downtown from 10 to 10 daily. Some 250 tenants do business within the two-story, block-long market. Demonstrations of such disappearing arts as batik block printing, Kelantan silversmithing, and the weaving of *kain songket*—a lush (and expensive) fabric made with gold threads—draw crowds to an area called the kampong. Cultural programs are presented daily, highlighting such Malaysian fare as wayang kulit, gamelan orchestras, Chinese opera, lion dances, and traditional Malay dances. Major festivals always include programs here. Free shows are held outdoors on a stage next to the Klang River most nights (*see* The Arts and Nightlife, below).

The Central Market gives visitors a chance to study the whole gamut of Malaysian goods. It has local cakes called *kuih*, herbal products used as medicines and for cooking, Malaysian kites, batik clothing, jewelry, antiques, copper relief pictures, rattan baskets, and wood and bamboo crafts. Young artists produce watercolors of rustic village life, and tile painters will custom-make a tile for you in pop or romantic designs. The portrait corner, where artists do both caricatures and realistic sketches in colored charcoal, always attracts a crowd.

In addition, some 40 food vendors serve Malaysian dishes at reasonable prices. This is a great place to sample dishes you have never tried before.

Exit either the way you came in or via the other side door onto a street called Leboh Pasar Besar, which means "big market." Cross the river and go up a block to the corner, where you will **⑩** see the padang, or playing field, of the **Selangor Club,** a private club in a rambling Tudor-style building. The padang covers an underground parking lot for the central business district.

⑪ The massive **Sultan Abdul Samad building,** constructed in 1897 with Moorish arches, copper domes, and clock tower, is considered the center of the old city. Preservationists fought to have it restored in the early 1980s. Its original occupant was the state secretariat (Dewan Bandaraya); it now houses the judicial department and high courts, along with a handicrafts museum called **Infokraf Malaysia,** a branch of the national handicrafts center. *Corner of Jln. Tun Perak Museum, tel. 03/293–4929. Admission free. Open Sat.–Thurs. 9–6.*

Three major religious centers surround the old Dewan, as the **⑫** building is called. **St. Mary's Anglican Church,** pristine with its red tile roof and manicured grounds, offers services in Tamil **⑬** and English. **Masjid Jamek Bandaraya,** on a point where the Kelang and Gombak rivers flow together, is the city's oldest mosque. Its two minarets are only slightly taller than the coconut palms on the grounds. A vendor beside the main gate sells **⑭** tape recordings of those hypnotic prayer chants. **Masjid India,** a modern Indian Muslim mosque, is the centerpiece of Little India. One attraction here is the street vendors selling local *ubat* (medicine) or *jamu* (cosmetics) with all the theatricality of old carnival barkers and snake-oil salesmen. They lure potential customers with elaborate stories and "magic" acts in which audience members participate.

Heading north up Jalan Tuanku Abdul Rahman, note the few remaining turn-of-the-century, two-story shophouses, with decorative flourishes along the roofline. Walking through these often-crowded streets and peeking into the shops is exciting, but there are many steps to negotiate, and the pavement is uneven and can be treacherous.

At Jalan Melayu, an Indian vendor runs a tidy **newsstand** that reeks of incense. A fun souvenir is a Malay comic book called *Gila Gila* ("crazy"), a local version of *Mad* magazine.

Along this strip of "Batu Road," as the locals call Jalan Tuanku Abdul Rahman, are a number of colorful sari shops, bookstores, stationery shops, Indian Muslim restaurants, and stores of an indeterminate nature. If you enjoy seeing local

⓯ films when you travel, drop by the **Coliseum Theatre,** which showcases the best of Malaysian and Indonesian cinema. Tickets are inexpensive, and all seats are reserved. Note that the cheap seats are downstairs in front and first class is in the balcony—the reverse of what you might expect. These movies usually have only Chinese subtitles, but you can usually figure out what's going on because they are quite action-oriented. Around the theater's parking lot are public toilets *(tandas)*, near the traffic signal, and a number of American fast-food outlets, where the homesick can gorge on burgers, fries, and fried chicken.

Across the road from the theater on Jalan Bunus, lots of little shops and vendors press on in the shadow of the bustling Mun Loong department store. Outside Mun Loong is a bank of telephones.

Time Out The **Coliseum Cafe** (100 Jln. Tuanku Abdul Rahman, tel. 03/292
⓰ –6270; *see* Dining, below) is another city landmark. Built in 1921, the Coliseum is known for two things: It has the best steak in town, and it's the favorite watering hole for rowdy locals. The unpretentious atmosphere exudes history, so with a little imagination you can conjure up visions of British rubber planters in the 1930s ordering a *stengah*, or half-pint of ale. A sizzling steak with all the trimmings costs about US$5, a great value. The place is usually crowded and doesn't take reservations, but waiting in the pub can be an event in itself.

Coliseum owners Wong Chin-wan and Loi Teik-nam sit behind the bar working and chatting with customers: young Europeans traipsing around Asia on a student budget, and regulars—a mix of Chinese, Indians, and Malays, including a number of journalists and a cartoonist nicknamed Lat. Lat is an institution: His cartoons—which appear in the *New Straits Times* and have been collected into nearly a dozen books— often reflect the national mood.

Walking north on Batu Road, you can stop for a frosty mug of root beer at the **A&W** or a bowl of steaming noodle soup at one of the open-air coffee shops with marble-top tables and bentwood chairs. In the daytime, shopping families fill the streets while a troupe of blind musicians with bongo drums and electric piano entertains passersby. After midnight the street life changes dramatically, as *pondans* (transvestites) chat up men who cruise by in cars.

Farther along Batu Road is the **Peiping Lace Shop** (No. 217), which features Chinese linens, lace, jewelry, and ceramics. **China Arts,** next door, is a branch of Peiping Lace that sells furniture; the rambling shop is filled with decorative coromandel screens, carved writing desks, teak and camphor chests, and antique vases.

⓱ The **Selangor Pewter showroom** (No. 231) has a full range of pewter products, which have been made in Malaysia for more than 100 years. Most designs are simple and of superior quality. A few items, such as a photo frame encrusted with Garfield the Cat, are pure kitsch. In its Heritage Collection, Selangor has replicas of *caping*, fig leaf-shape "modesty discs" that nude children once wore to cover their genitals; now teenagers wear them on chains as pendants. In the back of the shop you can see a demonstration of the process of pewter making.

At the meeting of Jalan Dang Wangi and Jalan Tuanku Abdul Rahman, the Odeon Theatre occupies one corner, and the huge **18** **Pertama Kompleks** another. Pertama ("first") is typical of most town shopping centers: clothing, shoe, appliance, and record shops, plus several recreational spots, including a video-games room, a pool hall, and a nightclub.

Continue up Jalan Dang Wangi and turn left onto Jalan Ampang, where the auto dealership shows various models of the Proton Saga. Turn right at the next corner and you'll see **19** the **Merlin Hotel,** whose coffee shop and lobby lounge are popular meeting spots. In front of the hotel, in the early morning, a makeshift stand hawks Malaysia's favorite breakfast dish, *nasi lemak*—a bundle of rice with salt fish, curry chicken, peanuts, slices of cucumber, and boiled egg—for one ringgit.

The next stretch of "gold coast," with its high-rise luxury hotels and modern skyscraper offices, argues convincingly that Malaysia is a nation emerging into modernity. Another confirmation of that fact comes when you get into a taxi and the driver tells you that you can make a local phone call for about a quarter—and hands you a mobile phone.

Caution: Watch your handbag or shoulder bag while walking in this district. Snatch thieves on motorcycles are known to ride up alongside strollers, snatch their goods, and buzz off. Police advise walkers to carry bags under the arm, on the side away from the street, to forestall such incidents.

Turn left on Jalan Raja Chulan. In the next block you'll see a row of outdoor food stalls along Jalan Kia Peng, just behind the Hilton Hotel in the car park. Locals insist that this hawker **20** area, **Anak Ku,** is among the best in the city.

21 The **Karyaneka Handicraft Centre** is a campus of museums and shops that sell regional arts and crafts. Each of 13 little houses is labeled with the name of a Malaysian state. Inside, goods from that area are on display and demonstrations are conducted by local artisans. The main building, shaped like a traditional Malay house, stocks goods from the entire country, including a wide selection of rattan baskets and straw purses and mats; batik-design silk shirts, dresses, scarves, and handkerchiefs; delicate silver jewelry; native sculpture from Sarawak; and lengths of kain songket. *186 Jln. Raja Chulan, tel. 03/243–1686. Admission free. Open Sun.–Fri. 9–6, Sat. 9– 6:30.*

Behind the center, across a little stream, are two small museums. The **Crafts Museum** has changing exhibits. The **International Crafts Museum** nearby has a modest collection of work from other parts of the world. The **botanical gardens** that border the little stream offer a quiet spot to rest and reflect.

As you leave the center, turn left and head for the next block, which is Jalan Bukit Bintang, then turn right. A couple of blocks along on the left you'll find the **Kuala Lumpur Shopping Centre,** and across the street, the new **Regent Hotel.** Two shopping complexes at the next intersection, the **Bukit Bintang Plaza** in front and the **Sungai Wang Plaza** behind it, form one of the largest shopping areas in the city. Among the tenants are boutiques, bookshops, and the **Metrojaya** and **Parkson** department stores, possibly the city's finest. The atrium area almost always has an exhibition of some sort—comic books, fitness equipment, whatever.

Outside, across from the taxi stand, are racks of a strange green produce that more resembles a porcupine than a fruit: the Malaysian durian, which grows in the jungle and is prized highly by city dwellers (*see* Dining in Staying in Malaysia, above). Hereabouts, as elsewhere, hawkers contribute to the atmosphere with the pungent smell of chilies frying and peanuts steaming. At night, crowds often gather around a pitchman selling medicines.

Jalan Bukit Bintang is a jumble of modest hotels, goldsmiths and other shops, and finance companies. Past the Federal Hotel, in front of the Cathay and Pavilion cinemas, the vendors hawk the usual candies and some unusual drinks, such as coconut water—ask the vendor to drop in a little ice—or crushed sugarcane juice, pressed as you wait.

㉒ Head east up Jalan Pudu one block. On the corner at Jalan Imbi stands the **Pudu Prison** with its beautifully painted tropical-landscape wall—topped with barbed wire. The mural, painted by inmates, is the longest in the world, according to the *Guinness Book of World Records.* You'll also note a warning that death is the mandatory sentence for drug trafficking in Malaysia, and the news reports will confirm that the law is enforced. Turn around and head back down Jalan Pudu.

㉓ The **Pudu Raya bus station** has all the rough-and-tumble of any big-city bus station. The area is beset by a severe litter problem, despite government fines. Air pollution, too, can be a problem because of the incessant traffic jams and the continued practice of using leaded gasoline.

㉔ On the imposing hill just ahead is the new **Maybank Building,** designed to resemble the handle of a *kris* (an ornately decorated dagger), the national emblem. Up the escalators, you can enter and walk around the soaring five-story bank lobby during banking hours. Of special interest is the new **Numismatic Museum,** which exhibits Malaysian bills and coins from the past, can supply information on the nation's major commodities, and adjoins a gallery of contemporary art. *Tel. 03/280–8833, ext. 2023. Museum admission free. Open daily 10–6.*

Beyond Pudu Raya, Jalan Pudu becomes Jalan Tun Perak, with several of the ubiquitous kedai kopi offering simple, refreshing snacks. Beyond Leboh Ampang you'll come again to the Kelang **㉕** River. To your right is the **Bank Bumiputra,** built in the shape of a kampong house. On the other side of Jalan Tun Perak is **㉖** Wisma Batik, with the **Batik Malaysia Berhad** (BMB) on the first and second floors. This shop has a wide selection of batik fabrics, shirts, dresses, and handicrafts upstairs. At the next intersection the loop of our tour is completed.

㉗ A unique attraction about 11 km (7 mi) north of the city is the **Batu Caves,** vast caverns in a limestone outcrop. The caves are approached by a flight of 272 steps, but the steep climb is worthwhile. A wide path with an iron railing leads through the recesses of the cavern. Colored lights provide illumination for the stalagmites and other unique features and formations. It is here that the spectacular but gory Thaipusam festival takes place in its most elaborate form. In the main cave is a Hindu Temple dedicated to Lord Subramaniam. Behind the Dark

Cave lies a third cave called the Art Gallery, with elaborate sculptures of figures from Hindu mythology. The caves are staggering in their beauty and immensity: The Dark Cave is 366 m (1,200 ft) long and reaches a height of 122 m (400 ft). For information on tours, *see* Guided Tours, above.

Off the Beaten Track

Near the Turf Club's old racetrack on Jalan Ampang is a little arts and design center called **10 Kia Peng.** In the renovated stables of an old mansion there, 14 prominent sculptors, painters, woodcarvers, calligraphers, and printers hold workshops and sell their art at reasonable prices. A gallery has regular exhibitions, and hawker stalls provide snacks. *Off Jln. P. Ramlee and Jln. Pinang, tel. 03/248–5097. Open daily 10–6.*

Shopping

Malaysia offered few bargains until duty-free shopping reduced prices a few years ago. Now most quality radios, watches, cameras, and calculators are slightly cheaper in KL than in Singapore. Look for a duty-free sticker in shop windows.

If you can't find a particular product or service, call **Infoline** (tel. 03/230–0300), a telemarketing company that will try to steer you in the right direction. It also gives advice on restaurants and night spots.

Many of the following shops and centers are discussed in greater detail in Exploring, above.

Shopping Centers Recently opened, **The Mall** on Jalan Putra is the largest in Southeast Asia. Its anchor tenant is the **Yaohan** department store, but it has numerous specialty shops as well. **The Weld** on Jalan Raja Chulan is one of the decidedly upscale malls in KL: It has a marble interior and an atrium, and its shops include Crabtree & Evelyn, Benetton, Bruno Magli, and Etienne Aigner.

The most popular shopping centers are the **Bukit Bintang Plaza, Sungai Wang Plaza,** and **KL Plaza,** all in the same vicinity on Jalan Bukit Bintang and Jalan Sultan Ismail. All have major department stores, such as **Metrojaya** and **Parkson,** plus bookstores, boutiques, and gadget shops. Also worth a visit are **Yow Chuan Plaza,** on Jalan Tun Razak and the **Pertama Kompleks** at Jalan Tuanku Abdul Rahman and Jalan Dang Wangi (*see* Exploring, above).

Street Markets At KL's street markets, crowded hawker stalls display everyday goods, from leather handbags to pocketknives to pop music cassettes. Bargaining is the rule, and only cash is accepted. Two major night markets operate daily. The largest is on **Petaling Street** in Chinatown; the other is **Chow Kit** on upper Jalan Tuanku Abdul Rahman. On Saturday night, between 6 and 11, **lower Jalan Tuanku Abdul Rahman** near the Coliseum Theatre is closed for a market, where you'll find everything from the latest bootleg tapes to homemade sweets. In the **Kampung Baru** area on Sunday, another open-air bazaar (called *pasar minggu*) offers Malay handicrafts and local food.

Specialty Stores For Nonya antiques, try **Le Connoisseur** in Yow Chuan Plaza.
Antiques The shop is open only in the afternoon, but call Mrs. Cheng to

visit at other times (tel. 03/241–9206). For Chinese arts and crafts, look in at **Peiping Lace Co.** (217 Jln. Tuanku Abdul Rahman, tel. 03/292–9282) or **China Arts** next door (tel. 03/292–9250).

Art The **Rupa Gallery** (Dayabumi Shopping Centre, tel. 03/755–9142) specializes in architectural artwork, including delightful watercolor-print notecards of shophouses and line-drawing prints of KL landmarks by Victor Chin. Watercolors and portraits finished or in progress can be found at the **Central Market.**

Handicrafts The best buys are Malaysian handicrafts, which are simple and attractive. For rattan baskets, straw handbags, woodcarvings, Kelantan silver jewelry, and batik fashions, try **Karyaneka Handicrafts Centre** on Jalan Raja Chulan (tel. 03/241–3704). The stalls of the **Central Market** (Jln. Cheng Lock, tel. 03/274–6542) offer handicrafts as well as a wide range of other souvenirs, including portraits, painted tiles, jewelry, and antiques. The best selection of batik fabric and fashions is at **Batik Malaysia Berhad** on Jalan Tun Perak (tel. 03/291–8606).

Traditional and modern pewterware designs are available at the **Selangor Pewter** showrooms (231 Jln. Tuanku Abdul Rahman, tel. 03/298–6244). Other fine gift shops are at **Metrojaya** in Bukit Bintang Plaza and **Plaza Yow Chuan** on Jalan Ampang. You can also visit the **Selangor Pewter Factory,** a few miles north of the city. In its showroom, visitors can see how pewter is made from refined tin, antimony, and copper and formed into products such as pitchers and candelabras. Duty-free souvenirs can be bought here, too. *4 Jln. Usahawan 6, Setapak, tel. 03/422–3000. Open Mon.–Sat. 8:30–4:45, Sun. 9–4.*

Jewelry Try **Jade House** on the ground floor of KL Plaza (tel. 03/241–9640) or **Jewellery by Selberan,** with showrooms in KL Plaza (tel. 03/241–7106) and Yow Chuan Plaza (tel. 03/243–6386).

Sports and Fitness

Golf Hotels can make arrangements for guests to use local courses, including the **Selangor Golf Club,** which enjoys the best reputation.

Jogging Two popular places to run are the **parcourse** in Lake Gardens and around the **racetrack area** on Jalan Ampang.

Spectator Sports

The sports pages of the newspapers list many sporting events at **Merdeka Stadium** (on Jalan Stadium).

Horse Racing Malaysians, especially the Chinese, have a passion for horse racing, and a regional circuit includes race days in KL, Penang, Ipoh, and Singapore. Races are held on Saturday and Sunday year-round.

Martial Arts In some cultural shows (*see* The Arts and Nightlife, below), you can see men performing *silat,* a traditional Malay form of combat and self-defense.

Beaches

The nearest beach to KL is at Port Dickson, about an hour and a half away. Intercity buses from KL's Pudu Raya station take passengers to the terminal in Port Dickson; local buses there will drop you off anywhere you want along the coast road. The beach stretches for 16 km (10 mi), from the town of Port Dickson to Cape Rachado, with its 16th-century Portuguese lighthouse. A good place to begin a beach walk is the fifth milestone from town. On the coast road stalls offer fruits of the season.

Dining

by Eu Hooi Khaw

Eu Hooi Khaw has worked as a journalist and restaurant reviewer in Malaysia for many years.

Though KL is not a coastal city, it reaps the ocean's benefits. Seafood is the rage among locals, who wash it down with ice-cold beer, and outdoor restaurants serving both have sprung up in the city and on its fringes.

The lack of purely Malay restaurants is offset by the hotels, which serve Malay buffets and à la carte dishes. Food festivals featuring regional specialties from the different Malaysian states are also frequently held. Three styles of Indian cooking— southern Indian, Mogul, and Indian Muslim (a blend of southern Indian and Malay)—can be found in KL. Eating Indian rice and curry with your hands on a banana leaf, as is done in the southern Indian restaurants, is an experience to be savored.

Thai and Japanese restaurants are legion, and the cuisine of the Nonya, or straits-born Chinese—a combination of Malay, Chinese, and Thai tastes—is gaining popularity. A few restaurants, such as Nonya Heritage, distinguish themselves through their authenticity: Their cooking methods are traditional and laborious, but the result is outstanding eating.

The increasingly affluent city population is growing fond of fine Continental restaurants, found mostly in the four- and five-star hotels. Traditional steakhouses, such as the Coliseum Cafe, also draw crowds. But for some of the best Chinese and other cuisines, you may want to venture out of KL into Petaling Jaya, a suburb 12 km (7.5 mi) southwest and just 20 minutes by cab.

Eating out almost anywhere is informal. Jackets and ties are seldom worn, except at the swankiest five-star hotels. Most places accept credit cards. The more expensive restaurants add a 10% service charge and 5% sales tax, and tipping is not necessary. Lunch is normally served from 11:30 AM to 2:30 PM, dinner from 6:30 to 11. Seafood restaurants are usually open from 5 PM to 3 AM.

The following terms appear throughout this section:

asam—sour, a reference to the sourness of the *asam* fruit, used in some curries

dim sum—Chinese snacks, eaten at breakfast or lunch, made with meat, prawns, or fish and usually steamed or deep-fried

garoupa—a local fish with tender flesh and a sweet flavor

green curry—a Thai curry with fewer chilies than Indian, made with small green *brinjals* (eggplants) and meat

ice kacang—shaved ice heaped over red beans, jelly, sweet corn, and green rice-flour strips, flavored with syrup or coconut sugar

kacang (pronounced "ka-chang")—signals the presence of beans or nuts

kaya—a jam made from steaming a mixture of eggs, sugar, and coconut cream

kerabu—a hot-and-sour Thai salad of chicken, jellyfish, mango, squid, beef, or almost anything else, dressed with onions, lemongrass, lime juice, and small chilies

Nonya—Chinese born in Malaysia who have assimilated and adapted Malay customs

rendang—meat simmered for hours in spices, chilies, and coconut milk until nearly dry

roti—bread

sambal—a thick, hot gravy of chilies, local roots and herbs, and shrimp paste

tandoori—meat or seafood roasted in a clay oven, northern-Indian style

tomyam—Thai soup cooked with seafood or meat in asam juice, sometimes very hot and sour

Very Expensive
French

Lafite Restaurant. Named for France's finest vineyard, Lafite serves classic, Provençal, and nouvelle French cuisine in a romantically lit setting with pastel-hued wallpaper and upholstery. Oil paintings and fine crystal are on display, and an impressive wine cellar is the dining room's centerpiece. Specialties include rabbit loin with figs and port wine, trio of seafood in yellow-pepper sauce, and poached pear with almond cream. The Table Surprise Lafite is a lavish Continental dinner buffet. *Shangri-La Hotel, 11 Jln. Sultan Ismail, tel. 03/232–2388. Reservations advised. Jacket and tie preferred. AE, DC, MC, V.*

Expensive
Continental

Terrace Garden. Soothing shades of green and gray, white walls, black-framed windows, and pale green trellis dividers blend well in this restaurant converted from a house. Dolly Lim runs the place sweetly and efficiently; Dolly Augustine sings evergreen numbers for entertainment. The chef recommends U.S. tenderloin stuffed with spinach leaves and smoked salmon; the lobster Thermidor is the best around. Finish with mocca Bavaria, a three-layer cream custard with Tía Maria sauce, or the blueberry pie. On Friday and Saturday there's a barbecue in the open-air extension. *308 Jln. Ampang, tel. 03/457–2378. Reservations advised on weekends. Dress: informal. AE, DC, MC, V.*

Japanese

Chikuyo-tei. In the basement of an office complex, Chikuyo-tei—the oldest Japanese restaurant in the city—has a warmly lit, woody interior with tatami rooms and sectioned-off dining areas. It serves an excellent *unagi kabayi* (grilled eel) and is well-known for its special *nigirisushi*, a variety of sushi made with tuna, herring, salmon eggs, and squid. The *teppanyaki*—meat, seafood, and vegetables sliced, seasoned, and cooked on a hot plate in front of you—is popular. *See Hoy Chan Plaza, Jln. Raja Chulan, tel. 03/230–0714. Reservations advised. Dress: informal. AE, DC, MC, V. No lunch Sun.*

Moderate
Chinese Seafood

Happy Hour Seafood Restaurant. Strings of lights drape the front of this restaurant, and its tables spill out onto the walkway, which has a little more atmosphere than the brightly lit, functional room indoors. Steamed, baked, or fried crabs filled with rich red roe are the specialty. Other good choices are the prawns steamed with wine and ginger, and the deep-fried garoupa. *53 Jln. Barat, off Jln. Imbi, tel. 03/248–5107. Reservations not necessary. Dress: informal. AE, DC, V. Dinner only.*

★ **Restoran Makanan Laut Selayang.** This excellent restaurant is very plain: Food, not decor, is the point. You can eat outside, under a zinc roof, or in a simple air-conditioned room that seats 30 at three large, round tables. One great dish here is black chicken—a small Malaysian bird with black skin and white feathers—steamed in a coconut. Also good are the deep-fried soft-shell crabs and the prawns fried with butter, milk, and chilies. Adventurous diners can try steamed river frogs and soups of squirrel, pigeon, or turtle. The house specialty is *fatt thieu cheong* ("monk jumps over a wall"), a soup of shark's fin, sea cucumber, dried scallops, mushrooms, and herbs, which must be ordered in advance. *Lot 11, 7½ mi Selayang, tel. 03/ 627–7015. Reservations not necessary. Dress: informal. AE, V.*

Continental **Coliseum Cafe.** The aroma of sizzling steak—the house specialty—clings to the walls of this old café established before World War II. A nostalgic, British colonial ambience prevails, though the waiters' starched white jackets are a bit frayed at the seams. Steaks are served with brussels sprouts, chips, and salad. Another favorite here is crab baked with cheese. The Sunday lunch of light curry dishes, or *tiffin*, is not to be missed. *Also see* Exploring, above. *98 Jln. Tuanku Abdul Rahman, tel. 03/292–6270. No reservations. Dress: informal. No credit cards.*

Indian Muslim **Restoran Sri Pinang.** All that's hot and spicy is served in an air-conditioned, bright, somewhat stark room in an office complex. Dig into fish-head curry, prawns *sambal*, and rice with raisins. Or try the deep-fried fish roe and stuffed squid. For dessert, the ice kacang here can't be beat. *Lower ground floor, Menara Aik Hua, Changkat Raja Chulan, tel. 03/230–6170. Reservations necessary for lunch. Dress: informal. AE, MC, V. Closed Sun. and holidays.*

Malay **Yazmin.** Yazmin has moved from a shopping complex to a white
★ colonial bungalow on shady, sprawling grounds. Guests dine in an airy upstairs hall whose front windows overlook a bamboo grove. Evocative black-and-white photographs taken by a sultan grace the walls, and the owner/hostess is Raja Yazmin, a Malay princess. Especially recommended are the *rendang tok* (beef simmered with spices and coconut), *roti canai* (unleavened bread), and *rendang pedas udang* (prawns cooked in coconut, chilies, and herbs). If you prefer, you can have your buffet lunch or dinner on a cozy, village-style timber terrace with a dried-palm roof. High tea is served daily, there's a Sunday brunch, and traditional Malay dances are performed every night. *6 Jln. Kia Peng, tel. 03/241–5655. Reservations advised. Dress: informal. AE, DC, MC, V. Closed 4 days at end of Ramadan.*

Nonya **Nonya Heritage.** White lace curtains and ethnic woodcarvings grace this cozily lit restaurant, which serves hot-and-sour, spicy, and rich cuisine. The Nonya Golden Pearl, a deep-fried ball of minced prawns and fish with a salted egg yolk in the middle, is a good start. Then try the spicy fried rice in a pineapple, the *melaka sotong* (squid) with chilies, the asam fish-head curry, or the kerabu. *44–4 Jln. Sultan Ismail, tel. 03/243–3520. No reservations. Dress: informal. AE.*

Kuala Lumpur Dining and Lodging

Dining
Ala'din, **2**
Chikuyo-tei, **24**
Coliseum Cafe, **7**
Happy Hour Seafood Restaurant, **22**
Kedai Makanan Yut Kee, **8**

Lafite Restaurant, **10**
Lotus Restaurant, **5**
Nonya Heritage, **16**
Restoran Makanan Laut Selayang, **1**
Restoran Sri Pinang, **12**
Satay Anika, **18**
Teochew Restaurant, **21**
Terrace Garden, **27**
Yazmin, **25**

Lodging
Equatorial, **13**
Federal Hotel, **19**
Holiday Inn City Centre, **4**
Holiday Inn on the Park, **14**
Kuala Lumpur Hilton, **15**

Merlin, **9**
Ming Court, **26**
P. J. Hilton, **6**
Pan Pacific, **3**
Park Avenue, **20**
Regent, **17**
Park Royal of Kuala Lumpur, **23**
Shangri-La, **11**

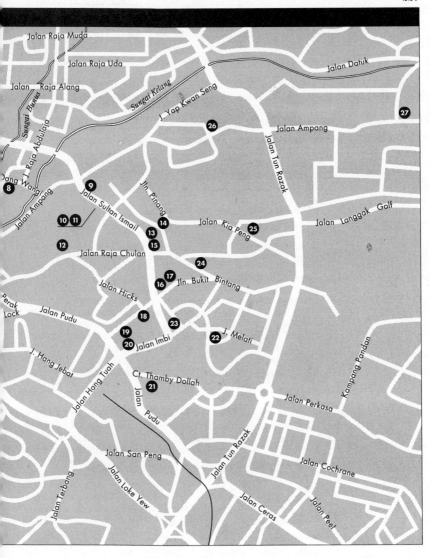

Northern Indian **Ala'din.** The deep pink table settings in this cozy place contrast with creamy white walls; trellis screens separate the tables; sitar music soothes the senses. The curries (with yogurt and cream, rather than coconut) are served with various Indian breads, and the chicken, crab, and rabbit tandooris are popular. Another winner is mutton *karai*—meat simmered in a clay pot with coriander, black pepper, and capsicums. For dessert there's *rasmalai*, a rich custard with semolina and almonds. *6 Jln. Telwai Empat, Bangsar Baru, tel. 03/255–2329. No reservations. Dress: informal. AE, DC, MC, V.*

Southern Indian **Lotus Restaurant.** The fun here is eating from a banana leaf with your hands. Heaped on the leaf are rice, pickles, and such spicy goodies as chili-hot crabs and mutton curry. Try also the *dosai*, a thin, crisp Indian pancake with a hint of sourness. *Badam halva*, an almond-and-milk drink, takes away the curry sting, as does the restaurant's cool cream-and-sky-blue interior. Mind how you close up the banana leaf after eating: Folding it toward you means you enjoyed the meal, folding it away from you shows you were displeased. *15 Jln. Gasing, Petaling Jaya, tel. 03/792–8795. No reservations. Dress: informal. No credit cards. Open 7 AM–11 PM.*

Teochew Chinese **Teochew Restaurant.** Spanning two shop buildings, this restaurant is soothingly decorated in cream and brown, with well-spaced tables and screened-off private dining rooms. It's popular on weekends and holidays, when 100 varieties of dim sum are served for breakfast and lunch. Typical Teochew specialties include noodles made entirely of fish; sea cucumber stuffed with scallops, crab, mushrooms, and water chestnuts; and sizzling prawns. Try also the *oh wee*, a sweet yam dessert with gingko nuts, served with tiny cups of bitter Teochew tea. *270–272 Jln. Changkat Thamby Dollah, off Jln. Pudu, tel. 03/241–5851. Reservations advised. Dress: informal. MC, V.*

Inexpensive **Kedai Makanan Yut Kee.** This 60-year-old family-run coffee
Hainanese shop/restaurant is one of the few that has not been torn down in
★ the name of progress. Big and airy but rather noisy from the city traffic, the place boasts marble-topped tables and regular customers who insist on their favorite seats. Recommended are *roti babi*, a sandwich with pork filling dipped in egg and deep-fried, and asam prawns. The black coffee is the best around, and the Swiss roll filled with kaya makes a fine dessert. *35 Jln. Dang Wangi, tel. 03/298–8108. No reservations. Dress: informal. No credit cards. Open 7 AM–6 PM. Closed Mon.*

Satay **Satay Anika.** Meat marinated with spices, threaded on sticks like a kebab, grilled over charcoal, and served with a nutty, spicy sauce used to be a delicacy found only in street stalls. Now you can enjoy it in the cool comfort of a restaurant in KL's busiest shopping complex. Plainly furnished and well-lit, Satay Anika is owned by a family that has been cooking satay for four generations. A portion of beef, mutton, chicken, or beef liver satay is 10 sticks. Wash it down with Malaysian fruit juices, and try the ice kacang for dessert. *Lower ground floor, Bukit Bintang Plaza, Jln. Bukit Bintang, tel. 03/248–3113. Reservations advised. Dress: informal. No credit cards.*

Lodging

Almost all the tourist hotels are north of the train station, with the best concentrated near the intersection of Jalan Sultan Ismail and Jalan Bukit Bintang, the heart of the commercial district and one corner of the Golden Triangle. For a map pinpointing locations, *see* Dining, above.

Very Expensive   **Kuala Lumpur Hilton.** KL's first high-rise luxury hotel still maintains its world-class standards for service and quality. The mood of crisp elegance is set in the lobby, with fresh flowers and glowing chandeliers. The pastel-decorated rooms have bay windows, sitting areas, and desks. The 36th-floor Paddock Room offers bird's-eye vistas of the city. The Aviary Bar, just off the lobby, is a popular meeting lounge, and the Melaka Grill features gourmet dining. The Hilton's cosmopolitan reputation is enhanced by an English pub and Chinese, Japanese, and Korean restaurants. *Box 10577, Jln. Sultan Ismail, 50718 KL, tel. 03/242–2122 or 800/HILTONS. 581 rooms, including executive suites. Facilities: 24-hr coffee shop, shopping arcade, squash and tennis courts, fitness center, pool, conference facilities. AE, DC, MC, V.*

Ming Court. Opened in 1984, this 13-story hotel is locally owned. Its unusual structure, U-shaped and tiered, is an attraction apart from the usual amenities. Rooms are decorated in yellow and green; those with a balcony offer great city views. The second-floor pool area is tropically landscaped and features a bar, cabanas, and a wading pool for children. The service is fine, but some public areas could use a little sprucing up. *Box 11295, Jln. Ampang, 50740 KL, tel. 03/261–8888 or 800/44–UTELL. 447 rooms. Facilities: pool, coffee house, bar, 3 restaurants, banquet and conference facilities, business center. AE, DC, MC, V.*

Pan Pacific. New in 1986, this hotel is next to the Putra World Trade Centre and across from The Mall shopping complex. Its multilevel lobby includes exposed-glass elevators in an atrium space and live music in the lounge. The rooms are richly appointed with comfortable furniture; some are decorated in dark colors. The VIP floor has butler service. *Box 11468, 50746 KL, tel. 03/442–5555 or 800/937–1515. 600 rooms, with executive floor and suites. Facilities: 24-hr coffee shop, 3 restaurants (Chinese, Japanese, Continental), health club, pool, business center. AE, DC, MC, V.*

Park Royal of Kuala Lumpur. This 21-story hotel, formerly called the Regent, was renamed in early 1989. The 14-year-old hotel's luxury accommodations were recently renovated. Given its location near the shopping district, the hotel is a popular meeting place, especially the serene garden lounge off the lobby. *Jln. Sultan Ismail, 55100 KL, tel. 03/242–5588 or 800/421–0536. 360 rooms. Facilities: 3 restaurants, shopping arcade, business center, health club. AE, CB, DC, MC, V.*

P.J. Hilton. Located in Petaling Jaya near the industrial zone, this luxury hotel caters to visiting executives—the IBM crowd. Its rooms and public areas are less grand than the KL Hilton's, but the accommodations are quite spacious. The sedate lobby lounge is as comfy as a living room. *2 Jln. Barat, 46200 Petaling Jaya, tel. 03/755–9122 or 800/HILTONS. 398 rooms. Facilities: 3 restaurants, fitness center, squash, tennis, golf, pool, disco. AE, DC, MC, V.*

Regent. This brand-new hotel, located across from the KL Plaza Shopping Centre, is scheduled to open in late 1989. Its owners, Regent International, which formerly ran a hotel in the next block, say all the guest rooms will have marble bathrooms and excellent city views. Not much else was known at press time, but given this company's reputation, expect everything to be done with great style, elegance, and care. *126 Jln. Bukit Bintang, 55100 KL, tel. 03/248–9500 or 800/545–4000. 454 rooms. Facilities: pool, 7 food and beverage outlets, health club, sauna, Jacuzzi, squash courts, business center, meeting and function rooms. AE, CB, DC, MC, V.*

★ **Shangri-La.** This centrally located hotel is new, large, and luxurious. Its sedate and spacious lobby sees a lot of activity. Businesspeople can keep up with stock prices and Reuters news with a Beriteks interactive videotext unit near the newsstand. Shangri-La boasts the largest guest rooms in KL, superbly decorated and equipped with every amenity. *11 Jln. Sultan Ismail, 50250 KL, tel. 03/232–2388 or 800/44–UTELL. 722 rooms. Facilities: health club, pool, squash, tennis, English pub, disco, convention ballroom accommodating 2,000, 13 function rooms, 24-hr business center, 3 restaurants (Cantonese, Japanese, French), garden coffee shop. AE, DC, MC, V.*

Expensive **Equatorial.** This 16-story hotel is near the KL Hilton. Its basement café serves a "hawker" buffet of authentic local dishes. Rooms have been pleasantly refurbished: The deluxe rooms are spacious and equipped with such amenities as a hair dryer and telephone in the bathroom. *Jln. Sultan Ismail, 50250 KL, tel. 03/261–2022 or 800/44–UTELL. 300 rooms. Facilities: 4 restaurants (Swiss, local, Chinese, Japanese), pool, business center, shopping arcade, ballroom, function rooms. AE, DC, MC, V.*

Federal Hotel. This Nikko hotel in the heart of the shopping district is distinguished by a revolving rooftop restaurant and an 18-lane bowling alley downstairs. The front of the hotel, with its street-level coffee shop, is decidedly urban, but the landscaped pool area is tropical in atmosphere. The guest rooms have large windows and the usual amenities. *35 Jln. Bukit Bintang, 55100 KL, tel. 03/248–9166 or 800/44–UTELL. 450 rooms, including executive and VIP suites. Facilities: pool, disco, Chinese restaurant, poolside buffet, coffee shop, shopping arcade, convention halls. AE, CB, DC, MC, V.*

Holiday Inn on the Park. Just off the main drag, this 14-story hotel is surrounded by trees. Upper floors overlook the nearby Turf Club. Many guest rooms are decorated in corporate green-and-white, but they do offer complimentary extras such as in-room movies and coffee- and tea-making facilities. One of its restaurants, called the Satay Station, is created from an old railway coach. *Box 10983, Jln. Pinang, 50732 KL, tel. 03/248–1066 or 800/HOLIDAY. 200 rooms. Facilities: small pool, shopping arcade, 4 restaurants (Thai, Italian, pizza, coffee shop), fitness room, sauna, tennis court. AE, DC, MC, V.*

Holiday Inn City Centre. Alongside the Gombak River, the front of this 18-story hotel faces a major thoroughfare, so the atmosphere is urban. Its central location is a prime asset. The hotel's lobby is compact and busy. Guest rooms have refrigerators and minibars, along with the usual amenities. *Jln. Raja Laut, Box 11586, 50750 KL, tel. 03/293–9233 or 800/HOLIDAY. 250 rooms. Facilities: business center, shopping arcade, pool,* *health center, squash court, Chinese restaurant, local coffee shop, bar. AE, DC, MC, V.*

Park Avenue. Formerly the Prince, this high-rise hotel is near the major shopping district. Its rooms were renovated when the hotel changed hands in 1989. An 18th-floor restaurant serves Western fare. *Jln. Imbi, 55100 KL, tel. 03/243–8388. 300 rooms. Facilities: 3 restaurants (Chinese, Western, coffee shop), business center, pool, disco. AE, MC, V.*

Moderate   **Merlin.** Centrally located, this older hotel could use a little spif-
★   fing up, but the rooms and service are a good value. Its spacious pool is one of the best. Dim sum in the Golden Dragon is first-rate. *2 Jln. Sultan Ismail, 50250 KL, tel. 03/242–0033 or 800/44–UTELL. 700 rooms. Facilities: 24-hour coffee shop, live music in Scot's Bar, pool, health center, shopping arcade, convention and banquet rooms. AE, CB, DC, MC, V.*

The Arts

A free monthly guide called "This Month," published by the Kuala Lumpur Tourist Association, is available at hotels and TDC offices. The Metro Diary column in the daily *The Star* also lists cultural events, including films, seminars, and nightclub activities.

Most government-sponsored cultural events are in the folk vein rather than the fine arts. Traditional culture is regularly presented on Friday evening from 8 to 9 on Level 2 of the Putra World Trade Centre. Free performances are held nightly at 7:45 at the **Central Market's** outdoor stage. The offerings are sometimes as contemporary as fashion shows or jazz concerts. The schedule of events is published in a monthly brochure distributed to hotels.

Nightlife

Hotel Lounges   At the lounges and clubs of the major hotels, the atmosphere is international, the tabs pricey. Most have entertainment nightly except Sunday. The **Aviary Lounge** at the KL Hilton (Jln. Sultan Ismail, tel. 03/242–2222) becomes darkly romantic when its quiet jazz combo plays. The **Lobby Lounge** of the Pan Pacific Hotel (Jln. Putra, tel. 03/442–5555) has a piano bar with singer. The **Federal Hotel** (35 Jln. Bukit Bintang, tel. 03/248–9166) features nostalgic tunes in its **Sky Room Supper Club** and live popular music in its **Lobby Bar.** The **Casablanca Club** at the Holiday Inn City Centre (Jln. Raja Laut, tel. 03/293–9233) has pop singers. The **Blue Moon Lounge** of the Equatorial Hotel (Jln. Sultan Ismail, tel. 03/261–7777) offers a live combo.

Pubs and Bars   Pubs are modeled after their British counterparts, while bars are American-style, with country-and-western, blues, jazz, or pop bar bands. The main problem with either type is location, which is frequently in the suburbs and difficult to find, even for taxi drivers. In the Damansara vicinity, the **Eighty Eight Pub** (84 Jln. SS21/39, Damansara Utama, tel. 03/717–5403) has live music nightly; and the **DJ Pub,** part of the Executive Club (37 Jln. SS22/19, Damansara Jaya, tel. 03/717–0966), opens at 4:30 PM and often has bands. The quirkiest spot may be the **Anglers Pub** (22 Jln. SS2/67 in Petaling Jaya), which shows fishing videos in the early evening, with musical entertainment afterward. A number of the major hotels have pubs—they are more expensive, of course.

Discos Action at the discos cranks up around 11 PM. Some discos have live bands as well as platter-spinning. Some places have a cover and others may have a drink minimum. Ask locals which discos are hot at the moment, but at press time the KL Hilton's **Tin Mine** (Jln. Sultan Ismail, tel. 03/242–2222), long a hot spot for Malaysian film, TV, and fashion celebrities, remains the premier spot. Its main competitors are **Club Oz** at the Shangri-La Hotel (Jln. Sultan Ismail, tel. 03/232–2388) and **Reflections** at the PJ Hilton (Jln. Barat in Petaling Jaya, tel. 03/755–9122). The **Hippodrome** (tel. 03/261–2562), on the roof of the Ampang Park Shopping Complex, has a floor show with Chinese singers from Taiwan, live music, high-tech lighting, and a seating capacity of 2,500.

Nightclubs and Cabarets *Kelab malam*, as these places are known, seem stuck in the 1950s, with variety acts, floor shows, and bands with singers. The two best-known nightclubs are **Pertama,** in the Pertama Complex (Jln. Tuanku Abdul Rahman, tel. 03/298–2533) and the **Shangri-La** (tel. 03/232–1174) at Pudu Raya.

Excursions from Kuala Lumpur

Malacca

Once the most important trading port in Southeast Asia, Malacca (Melaka) is now a relatively sleepy backwater. Created as the capital of a Malay sultanate, it was captured in 1511 by the Portuguese, who built fortifications and held it until 1641, when the Dutch invaded and took possession. The British took over in Victorian times and remained in control until Malay independence was declared in 1957. In this, Malaysia's most historic town, you'll find impressive buildings and ruins dating from all these periods of colonial rule. These sights are brought to life nightly in a new sound-and-light show, in which the city's history is told to the accompaniment of Malay music, sound effects, and illuminated monuments. (Admission charge to outdoor seating area. Narration in Bahasa Melayu, 8:30 PM; in English, 10:30 PM.)

Tourist Information The **Melaka Tourist Information Centre** is in the heart of the city on Jalan Kota (tel. 06/236538).

Getting Around By Car The superhighway between KL and Johore Baru has an exit for Melaka, which is about 147 km (91 mi) south of KL.

By Train Malacca does not have a train station, but train travelers can get off in Tampin, 38 km (24 mi) north of the city. From Tampin, take a taxi to Malacca (about M$3). For information, call the KTM office in Malacca (tel. 06/223091) or the train station in Tampin (tel. 06/411034).

By Bus Express bus service from KL to Malacca is offered by **Jebat Express** (tel. 03/282202 in KL or in Malacca, 06/222503) for M$6.50. You can take other buses from Malacca to Port Dickson (Barat Express, tel. 06/249937), Butterworth (Ekspress Nasional, tel. 06/220687), or Singapore (Melaka–Singapore Express, tel. 06/224470).

By Taxi Local taxis will take you to KL from Malacca for double the regular fare (tel. 06/223630).

Guided Tours

The best-known travel guide in Malacca is Robert Tan Sin Nyen (256-D Jln. Parameswara, 75000 Melaka, tel. 06/244857). His firm is **A1 Tours** (tel. 06/239103). You can take a river tour of the city (45 or 90 minutes) from the dock (tel. 06/236538) on Jalan Quayside, behind the information center.

Exploring

One of the oldest of Malacca's Portuguese ruins, dating from 1521, is **St. Paul's Church,** atop Residency Hill. In 1753 the site became a burial ground. The statue at the summit commemorates St. Francis Xavier, who was buried here before being moved to his permanent resting spot in Goa, India, where he began his missionary career. The **Church of St. Peter**—built in 1710 and now the church of the Portuguese Mission under the jurisdiction of the bishop of Macao—is interesting for its mix of Occidental and Oriental architecture. It is about a half mile east of the city center, on Jalan Bendahare.

The only surviving part of the 1511 Portuguese fortress, **A Famosa,** is the impressive Porta de Santiago entrance gate, which has become the symbol of the state of Malacca. Near the gate, the **Muzium Budaya,** a museum with collections on Muslim culture and royalty, is housed in a re-creation of a traditional wood palace. *Admission charge.*

The Dutch influence in Malacca is more palpable today. **Christ Church** was built in 1753 of bricks brought from Zeeland (Netherlands) and faced in red laterite. Across the street is the imposing **Stadthuys,** thought to be the oldest remaining Dutch architecture in the Orient. This complex of buildings was erected between 1641 and 1660 and used until recently for government offices. Now it houses the **Malacca Historical and Literary Museums,** whose exhibits include Dutch furniture, Chinese and Japanese porcelain, Straits Chinese embroidery, and numerous photographs. *Tel. 06/220769. Admission charge. Open daily 9–6.*

Malacca's history, of course, predates the arrival of the Western colonialists. Six centuries ago, a Ming emperor's envoy from China set up the first trade arrangements in the ancient Malay capital; a daughter of the emperor was sent to Malacca as wife to Sultan Mansor Shah. She and her 500 ladies-in-waiting set up housekeeping on **Bukit China** (Chinese Hill). The early Chinese traders and notables who lived and died in Malacca were buried on this hill, and their 17,000 graves remain, making Bukit China the largest Chinese cemetery outside China.

The **Chinese quarter**—narrow streets lined with traditional shophouses, ancient temples, and clan houses (note the intricately carved doors)—reflects the long Chinese presence. **Cheng Hoon Teng Temple** is one of the city's oldest temples; you'll recognize it by its ceremonial masts, which tower over the roofs of the surrounding old houses, and by the porcelain and glass animals and flowers that decorate its eaves.

Don't miss **Baba Nyonya Heritage,** two 19th-century mansions in the straits-born Chinese style, whose intricate woodwork is as impressive as their elegant antique Chinese furnishings. Built by a Chinese millionaire named Chan, the museum is today run by a fifth-generation family member. *48 Jln. Tun Cheng Lock, tel. 06/231272. Admission charge. Open daily 10–12:30 and 2–4:30.*

Near the **Padang Pahlawan** (where you'll find Malacca-style bullock carts that you can ride in or pose beside, for a fee), in a building that was once the old Malacca Club, the **Proclamation of Independence Memorial** documents events leading up to the nation's independence with photographs, maps, and more. *Tel. 06/241231. Open Tues.–Sun. 9–6 (except closed Fri. noon–3).*

Several attractions are near the 810-acre **Ayer Keroh Recreational Forest** (Utan Rekreasi, tel. 06/328401), with cabins and camping. **Mini-Malaysia Cultural Village,** 15 km (9 mi) from Malacca, showcases 13 model houses built in styles representing different states and decorated inside with regional arts and crafts. Cultural shows and native games are performed outdoors. *Tel. 06/328498. Admission charge. Open weekdays 10–6, weekends and holidays 9–7.*

Adjacent to Ayer Keroh Lake is the open-plan **Melaka Zoo,** with species from Southeast Asia and Africa displayed in environments approximating their native habitats. (At the nearby **Melaka Reptile Park,** you can see snake races as well as exhibits.) *Tel. 06/324054 or 06/228229. Admission charge. Open daily 10–6.*

Shopping

A number of antiques shops line **Jonker Street** (now known as Jln. Hang Jebat). For local souvenirs, try the row of stalls just behind the restaurants along Jalan Taman, which used to be the waterfront road before land reclamation.

The most unusual souvenir in town is a pair of little three-inch brocade slippers made by **Yeo Sing Guat** (92 Jln. Hang Jebat, no phone), for Chinese women whose feet were bound when they were children to create tiny "lotus feet," a symbol of beauty during the Ming dynasty. Mr. Yeo says only a handful of elderly women still wear his shoes; most of his purchasers are tourists. A pair costs about M$50.

Dining

It would be a shame to leave the city without trying some of its spicy cuisine, both Nonya and Portuguese fare. If you visit Portuguese Square, where descendants of the original community still live (a cultural show is held here at 7:30 each Saturday night), try any of the three restaurants there.

Summerfield's Coffee House. This 24-hour café, a popular meeting place, serves both Western and local dishes. Snacks range from a bowl of noodles to an ice cream sundae. *Ramada Renaissance, Jln. Bandahara, tel. 06/248888. No reservations. Dress: casual. AE, DC, MC, V. Moderate.*
Trading Post. Try the daily buffet of spicy local dishes, such as rendang, at this garden restaurant. Barbecues by the pool are held in the evening. *Malacca Village Resort, Ayer Keroh, tel.*

*06/323600. No reservations. Dress: casual. AE, DC, MC, V.
Moderate.*

Nyonya Makko Restaurant. This modest restaurant has such
Nonya specialties as curried fish. For dessert, cool off with
gula Melaka, a sago pudding with coconut milk and palm syrup. *123 Taman Melaka Jaya, tel. 06/240737. No reservations.
Dress: casual. No credit cards. Inexpensive.*

Lodging

Malacca Village Resort. Located on seven acres just off the superhighway between KL and Singapore, this luxury resort is
lushly landscaped and well-equipped. Its distance from the city
may be a problem for those without a car, but it is within walking distance of the zoo, Mini-Malaysia, and the forest.
Recreational facilities are plentiful, including a small lake
across the road and nearby golf course. Rooms have a tropical
atmosphere, with tile and shutters. *Ayer Keroh, 75450 Malacca, tel. 06/323600 or 800/44–UTELL. 160 rooms. Facilities: 3
restaurants, 2 bars, boating. AE, DC, MC, V. Expensive.*
Ramada Renaissance. Businessmen choose this 24-story hotel,
built in 1984, for its central location, its spacious rooms
equipped with refrigerators, and its many amenities. *Jln.
Bendahara, Box 105, 75720 Melaka, tel. 06/248888 or 800/228–
9898. 295 rooms, including 16 suites. Facilities: 4 restaurants,
2 lounges, disco, large pool, gymnasium, Jacuzzi, squash
courts, billiards, convention facilities, nearby golf course.
AE, DC, MC, V. Expensive.*
Merlin Melaka. Rooms here are a trifle tatty, but the Malaysian
chain-operated facility offers full service and good value. *Jln.
Munshi Abdullah, 75100 Melaka, tel. 06/240777. 243 rooms
and suites. Facilities: pool, billiards, squash, roller skating,
shopping center next door, 2 restaurants, lounge, disco. AE,
DC, MC, V. Moderate.*

Penang

Introduction

Called the Pearl of the Orient for its natural beauty as well as
for its charming and graceful colonial architecture, Penang is a
city that respects tradition but is not stodgy or sleepy. The island's beaches—in particular the glorious stretch at Batu
Ferringhi—may have made it justly famous as a beach-
vacation destination, but its capital city, Georgetown, is a vibrant university town that is the intellectual center as well as
the conscience of the country, a place where ideas are gener-
ated and venerated. It is also a great place to tour on foot, by
bicycle, or by trishaw, stopping off frequently to sample the
many fun shops and world-famous cuisine that are found around
every corner.

The population is primarily Chinese, with a sizable Indian community living downtown and Malays residing in the
countryside. Batu Ferringhi has all the resort activity you
could wish for, yet is never overcrowded.

Arriving and Departing by Plane

Airports and Airlines The **Penang International Airport** (tel. 04/831373), located in Bayan Lepas, about 18 km (11 mi) from Georgetown, is served by **MAS, Singapore Airlines, Garuda, Cathay Pacific,** and **Thai Airways.** All departing passengers pay an airport tax: M$15 for international flights, M$5 to Singapore, and M$3 for domestic destinations. Penang is about a 40-minute flight from KL.

Between the Airport and Hotels Airport taxis use a coupon system with fixed fares. A one-way ride into the city costs M$13.50; to Batu Ferringhi it's M$20.20.

By Bus A public bus (Yellow No. 66) just outside the airport entrance will take you to the terminal in city center for less than a ringgit. Buses run hourly at night, more frequently during the day.

Arriving and Departing by Car, Train, and Bus

By Car You can either drive across the Penang Bridge from Butterworth (M$7 toll) or bring your car across on the ferry (M$4–M$6, depending on the size of your vehicle; passengers pay 40 sen). The ferry operates 24 hours, but service after midnight is infrequent.

By Train The train station serving Penang is at the ferry terminal on the Butterworth side. You can buy a ticket at the **Butterworth station** (tel. 04/347962) or at a booking station at the **ferry terminal** (Weld Quay, tel. 04/610290). It's not a long walk from Butterworth station to the ferry, but you'll have to carry your own luggage. On the Penang side, porters and taxi drivers will help.

By Bus The **main bus station** (tel. 04/344928) for intercity service is also on the Butterworth side near the ferry terminal. Coach service to Singapore can be booked through **MARA Express** (tel. 04/361192) or **Hosni Express** (tel. 04/617746).

Getting Around

You can walk to most places in downtown Georgetown.

By Taxi Taxi stands are located near most hotels. Two taxi companies are **Syarikat Georgetown Taxi** (tel. 04/613853) and **Island Taxi** (tel. 04/625127).

By Bus Five bus companies operate in the Penang area. Each is identified by a different bus color and serves a different route. All buses operate out of a central terminus on Jalan Prangin, a block from Komtar. Passengers buy tickets from conductors on the bus and pay according to the distance traveled. For information on routes and schedules, call 04/629357.

By Car **Avis** (tel. 04/373964 or 04/811522), **Hertz** (tel. 04/374914), and other major companies have counters at the airport. **Sintat** (tel. 04/830958) has an airport counter only.

By Trishaw Not just tourists but some city residents, mainly elderly Chinese women, rely on trishaws—large tricycles with a carriage for passengers and freight—for transport around town. The pace is pleasant, and it's a relatively inexpensive way to sightsee. Negotiate the route and fare before you get in. A short trip is likely to cost only 5 ringgits. If you want to hire one for longer, the usual hourly rate for one person riding on a nice day would be about M$10. The driver will, of course, ask for more, but negotiate.

Important Addresses and Numbers

Tourist Information   The **Penang Tourist Association** distributes information from centers on level 3 of the Komtar building (tel. 04/614461) and downtown near Fort Cornwallis, at the intersection of Leboh Pantai and Leboh Light (tel. 04/616663). The **TDC** has a counter at the airport (tel. 04/830501; open weekdays 8:30–4:45, Sat. 8:30–1) and an office in Komtar (tel. 04/620066).

Emergencies   For **police, fire,** or **ambulance** service, dial 999. The **Penang Adventist Hospital** (tel. 04/373344) also sends ambulances.

Doctors   Contact the **Hospital Besar** (tel. 04/373333), on Jalan residency at Hospital Road, on the edge of downtown; or the **Specialists Centre** (tel. 04/368501) at 19 Jalan Logan.

English-Language Bookstores   The **Times Bookstore** is on the first floor of the Penang Plaza shopping complex (126 Jln. Burma, tel. 04/23443). Bookshops on Leboh Bishop include **City Book Center** (No. 11, tel. 04/51593) and **Academic** (No. 23, tel. 04/615780).

Travel Agencies   **American Express** (8 Greenhall, 3rd floor, tel. 04/368317). **Thomas Cook** (1 Pengkalan Weld, tel. 04/610511).

Guided Tours

Local companies offer a number of general tours. The most popular is a 73-km (45-mi), 3½-hour drive around the island. It departs from Batu Ferringhi and goes through Malay kampongs, rubber estates, and nutmeg orchards, stops at the Snake Temple, cruises past the Universiti Sains Malaysia campus and through Georgetown; and returns via the beach road.

Major guided-tour companies are **Tour East** (Golden Sands Hotel, Batu Ferringhi, tel. 04/811662, or Penang Plaza, 4th floor, tel. 04/363215) and **Mayflower Acme Tours** (Shangri-La Inn on Jln. Magazine, tel. 04/623724 or Tan Chong Building, 23 Pengkalan Weld, tel. 04/628196).

Both will arrange private car or limousine tours at additional cost and offer side trips to Langkawi Island, Cameron Highlands, and Pangkor Island.

Boat Tours   Tour agents can arrange harbor cruises with **Waterfront Sdn. Bhd.**, which runs a sunset dinner cruise, a waterfront and Penang Bridge trip, and a Monkey Beach excursion.

Special-Interest Tours   The principal tour companies offer such excursions as Penang Hill and Temples, City and Heritage, and Penang by Night, in addition to trips to the world's largest butterfly farm (at Telok Bahang), and the Botanical Gardens.

Exploring Penang

Numbers in the margin correspond with numbered points of interest on the Georgetown map.

❶ Just in front of the Tourist Information Office, near the Swettenham Pier, stands a **Victorian clock tower,** donated to the city by a Penang millionaire to commemorate the diamond

238

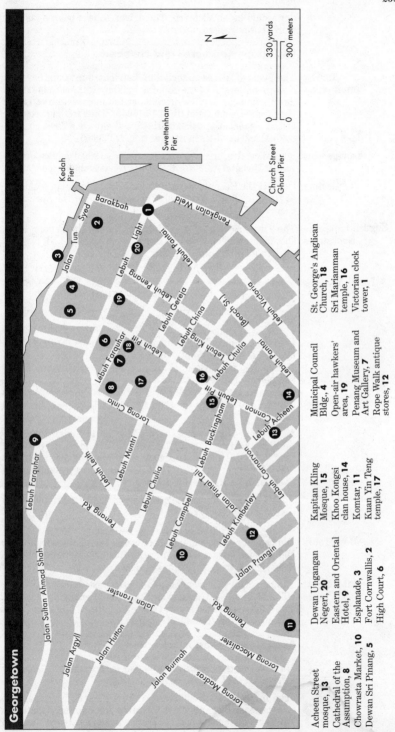

Georgetown

Victorian clock tower, **1**

Fort Cornwallis, **2**

Esplanade, **3**

Municipal Council Bldg., **4**

Dewan Sri Pinang, **5**

High Court, **6**

Penang Museum and Art Gallery, **7**

Cathedral of the Assumption, **8**

Eastern and Oriental Hotel, **9**

Chowrasta Market, **10**

Kuan Yin Teng temple, **17**

Rope Walk antique stores, **12**

Acheen Street mosque, **13**

Khoo Kongsi clan house, **14**

Kapitan Kling Mosque, **15**

Sri Mariamman temple, **16**

Kuan Yin Teng temple, **17**

St. George's Anglican Church, **18**

Open-air hawkers' area, **19**

Dewan Ungangan Negeri, **20**

Kuantar, **11**

N

0   330 yards
0   300 meters

jubilee of Queen Victoria. The tower is 60 feet tall, one foot for every year of her reign up to 1897. Head from the tower up

❷ Jalan Tun Syed Barakbah past **Fort Cornwallis,** the harborside site where city founder Sir Captain Francis Light of the British East India Company first landed on the island in 1786. On the outside, the 1810 compound's moss-encrusted ramparts and cannons give the impression of a mighty fortress, but it never saw any real action. On the inside are an open-air amphitheater, shade trees, and public toilets, as well as some annoying local hustlers offering to serve as guides.

❸ The **Esplanade**—an open, grassy field next door—is a pleasant site for a stroll, especially in the evening, when the sea breezes roll in and the hawkers set up their mobile stands. The padang is often used for recreational sports and festival events. A monument surrounded by palms honors soldiers who died in World War I.

Penang's center used to be Beach Street near the ferry terminal, the heart of the banking district. But since the construction of the Penang Bridge in the mid-1980s reduced pedestrian traffic, the city center has gravitated toward Komtar,

❹ the tallest building in Malaysia. The **Municipal Council Building,** a stately turn-of-the-century structure with arched windows, no longer houses the city government, which moved to Komtar several years ago. The building is now used for special

❺ exhibitions. The **Dewan Sri Pinang** next door is the city's major auditorium, seating some 1,300 for concerts, theater, and other events. Coming cultural activities are posted on a billboard out front. The **Penang Library** is on the first floor.

❻ The colonial structure across the street houses the **High Court.** Malaysia uses the British legal system, and the courts conduct much of their business in English. Cases are open to the public, and visitors are free to wander in and immerse themselves in a local legal drama. Inside the compound is a marble statue dedicated to James Richardson Logan, a lawyer and newspaper editor who devoted his life to public service, advocating freedom of speech, law, and order.

❼ Behind the High Court, on Lebuh Farquhar, is the **Penang Museum and Art Gallery.** The statue outside the 1821 building, which was used as the Penang Free School for more than a century, is of Sir Francis Light. On the first floor is a small museum packed with old photographs, maps, and relics of the city's past. An art gallery upstairs constantly changes exhibits, which range from contemporary works to traditional Malaysian art. *Admission free. Open daily 9–5 (closed Fri. 12:15–2:45).*

❽ Next door is the **Cathedral of the Assumption,** one of the oldest Roman Catholic churches in Malaysia. Past the City Bayview

❾ Hotel is the **Eastern and Oriental Hotel,** commonly known as the E&O. Its reputation as one of Asia's early grand hotels, in the tradition of the Raffles in Singapore and the Oriental in Bangkok, has long since faded, but it's still a pleasant place to visit. The palm-shaded poolside garden is right on the waterfront, a delightful spot to stop for a rest and a cool drink. The outward-facing cannons are reminders of the city's colorful history.

The E&O entrance looks down Penang Road, the city's main shopping area. In the first block is a series of handicraft and antique shops, all carrying a variety of Asian jewelry and gift items such as Thai and Indonesian woodcarvings. In the next block, in front of the Continental, Malaysia, and Ambassador hotels, you'll find a number of trishaws, whose drivers—mostly older men—will solicit you aggressively. A suggested trishaw sightseeing route: Head up Lebuh Muntri past some of the city's best examples of traditional architecture, turn left onto Love Lane, up to Farquhar Street again, then turn left onto Leboh Leith past the 18th-century Cheong Fatt Tse Mansion, one of the oldest remaining Chinese homes in Asia.

At Lebuh Chulia, you'll see lots of young European, Australian, and American travelers of the nouveau hippie genre, who seek out the cheap hotels and seedy bars in this area. The next street in Lebuh Campbell, another main drag for shopping. The shops here sell fabrics, shoes and clothing, costume jewelry, and inexpensive bags and luggage.

⑩ The next block of Penang Road takes you to the **Chowrasta Market,** an indoor wet market selling all sorts of local produce. In front of the entrance, shops sell more produce, plus pickled and dried nutmeg, papaya and mango, and candies made from gingerroot, coconut, and durian. The durian cake, called *dodol*, is sold in little triangular pieces or foot-long rolls.

Time Out Near the market, across the road from the Choong Lye Hock movie theater, is an old-fashioned coffee shop with marble-top tables. The **Teik Hoe Cafe** is nearly hidden by the souvenir vendor who works the sidewalk out front. Although the place looks scruffy, it's a great spot to people-watch over a cup of local coffee (pronounced "ko-pee" in Malay). The blend is strong, with a smooth mocha flavor. The parade of shoppers and passersby makes fine entertainment.

In the labyrinth of stalls in the alley next door to the **Penang Bazaar** (a dry-goods market), you'll find such basics as underwear, belts, and handbags. At the corner, a street hawker sells *chendol*, a local dessert that looks bad—wormlike strands of green jelly served in coconut milk over ice—but tastes good.

Across the plaza, in front of the Capitol Theatre, street vendors peddle luxury knockoffs. Fake Gucci watches sell for about US$9; ersatz Polo cologne and Chanel No. 5 perfume go for half that. Pirated pop and country cassette tapes sell for a little more than US$1 each. The concession stand for the theater is outside, so the confections Asians enjoy are available: Try the dried cuttlefish, called the chewing gum of the Orient. And the young portrait artist who often works here does good charcoal likenesses for just over US$10.

⑪ The Tower of the East, as **Komtar** was dubbed, is now the second-tallest building in the ASEAN region (recently surpassed by the OUB Plaza tower in Singapore), and totally out of scale with the diminutive neighboring buildings. The long flight of stairs you see leads up to a food court on the fifth floor. On the lower levels is a shopping complex named after the country's second prime minister, Tun Razak. At **Chin's Art Gallery,** next to an MAS office, you can have a stone chop (seal) engraved with your initials for US$20–US$50, depending on the stone size and quality. Among the tower's busiest tenants are hip young tailors in trendy haircuts and smart outfits who scurry about fitting customers with garments cut from the bolts of fabric they stack up in every corner of their tiny shops.

Their creations have original flourishes, even on such common items as jeans or military-style shirts. They often toil late at night, long after the rest of the shopkeepers have gone home.

In the center of the mall are a number of fast-food outlets serving hamburgers, fried chicken, and pizza. One of the best Chinese restaurants in the city, Supertanker, is on the upper level (*see* Dining, below).

A two-lane street and pedestrian walkway runs through the ground floor of Komtar. Here you'll notice the **Centre Point** pool parlor—not your typical smoke-filled dive. These teenage boys are practicing for tournaments, when they dress in black bow ties and vests and compete before hushed, well-mannered crowds.

⓬ Around **Rope Walk,** on Jalan Pintal Tali, a number of antiques stores have congregated. Turn right onto Lebuh Kimberly, then, past a row of highly decorated shophouses with elaborately carved doors, turn left onto Carnarvon Street, then right on Acheen. At the next corner is the **Tang Lee Trading Co.,** which manufactures the cheap summer sandals called flip-
⓭ flops. On the right is the **Acheen Street mosque,** the oldest in Penang. To enter, you must get permission from officials. Turn left and you'll be on Cannon Street.

On the right, look for a small sign posted above an entrance to
⓮ an alley, which announces the **Khoo Kongsi clan house,** a complex of structures that may be the most elaborately decorated in Malaysia. Recently restored, the **Leong San Tong** (Dragon Hall) temple is a showcase of Chinese architecture and art, constructed by 19th-century master craftsmen from China. Virtually no surface is unadorned. Notice the relief sculptures depicting Chinese legends and the heavily gilt dragons. The open theater across the square is used for opera performances. Visitors are welcome weekdays 9–5, Saturday 9–1. Permission to enter must be obtained from the office.

Pitt Street is often called the street of harmony, because all four major religions are represented along its few blocks. The
⓯ **Kapitan Kling Mosque** is at the Lebuh Buckingham intersection. Built in the early 1800s, the mosque has been recently renovated and continues to serve the Indian Muslim community. You need permission to enter.

Along this section of Pitt Street is a row of small jewelry shops. The Indians who run them deal in gold and semiprecious stones. Many are also licensed money-changers. These street bankers can handle almost any type of foreign currency and work much longer hours than regular banks. Some also are numismatists, who sell to collectors.

Past the gates of the **Teochew Association house,** on the corner
⓰ of Pitt and Lebuh Chulia, is the **Sri Mariamman temple** on Queen Street, in the heart of the Indian district. The entranceway is topped by a *gopuram,* or tower covered with statues of Hindu deities. Inside, the ceiling features the symbols for the planets and signs of the zodiac. The most prized possession of the faithful is a statue of Lord Subramaniam, which is covered with gold, silver, diamonds, and emeralds. The statue is paraded about during the Thaipusam festival. Visitors can enter the temple, with permission.

⓱ The **Kuan Yin Teng temple,** dedicated to the goddess of mercy, Kuan Yin, is the busiest in the city, perhaps because it's associated with fertility. Built in 1800, this temple serves the Cantonese and Hokkien communities. In the next block, on
⓲ Farquhar Street, is stately **St. George's Anglican Church,** with its gracious flowering trees and gazebo. Built in 1818 by convicts and still a symbol of the British role in Penang's early history, the church is now attended mostly by Indians.

Turn right at Bank Negara on the corner of Lebuh Light. At
⓳ King Street, at an **open-air hawkers' area,** old Chinese men often bring their caged pet birds when they come for a cup of coffee and a breath of morning air. In this area, you may also note elderly men writing letters on old portable typewriters. These public scribes serve clients who need help dealing with a bureaucracy or illiterates who simply want to write a friend.

At Penang Street and Lebuh Light is **Pashnis Restaurant,** one of the few places to get Malay food in this Chinese city. Try a satay snack: charcoaled strips of beef, chicken, or goat dipped in a peanut sauce.

⓴ On the right you'll see the **Dewan Ungangan Negeri,** a majestic colonial building with massive columns. This is the state assembly, and the luxury cars parked out front belong to its illustrious members. You're now across from Fort Cornwallis again—near the ferry if you're hopping back to the mainland and a waterfront cab ride away from the beach hotels.

What to See and Do with Children

At the **Penang Botanical Gardens,** about 8 km (5 mi) from the city center on Jalan Waterfall, relatively tame monkeys live amid the tropical plants. *Admission free. Open daily 10–6.*

The **Penang Bird Park,** located in Perai near Butterworth on the mainland, makes another fine outing. Take the ferry across the harbor and a taxi to the park; a ride of about 13 km (8 mi). A huge walk-in aviary contains all sorts of exotic fowl and beautiful flowers. *Tel. 04/399899. Admission charge. Open daily 10–7.*

Off the Beaten Track

Kek Lok Si is reputedly the largest and most beautiful Buddhist temple in Malaysia. It's worth the trip to the suburb of Air Itam to absorb the temple's serene atmosphere, especially when the monks chant their morning prayers. The century-old hilltop pagoda blends Chinese, Thai, and Burmese architectural influences. The shopping stalls along the route to the temple offer some excellent bargains.

In Air Itam, joggers or walkers may also want to explore the **track** around the reservoir, where Penang gets its drinking water. The path cuts through a tropical forest and across the dam. There is no bus service up to the area, so getting there is a workout in itself. It's best as an early morning outing.

Shopping

Don't hesitate to bargain, but remember—shopkeepers play the game full-time. You'll see signs for duty-free prices on certain goods. Most shops are open 10–10.

Shopping Districts **Penang Road** is the main shopping area, with Leboh Campbell and Jalan Burma as offshoots. Look for antiques and junk in the **Rope Walk** district, now listed on maps as **Jalan Pintal Tali.**

Department Stores **Yaohan, Super Komtar,** and **Pulau Pinang** are in the Komtar complex. **GAMA** is across the road on Jalan Dato Keramat, and **Super** is a couple of blocks up Jalan Burmah.

Markets The **Chowrasta Market** on Penang Road (*see* Exploring, above) is an indoor wet market with shops and stalls outside. On Sunday morning, a **flea market,** offering a mixture of junk and antiques, is held on Jalan Pintal Tali.

Specialty Stores The **Saw Joo Ann** antiques shop, on the corner of Lebuh Hong
Antiques Kong, has high-quality Malaysian artifacts. If it's not open during normal business hours, ask at the coffee shop next door and someone will come to let you browse.

Crafts On Upper Penang Road, shops sell crafts from Malaysia, Thailand, Indonesia, China, and India. **Selangor Pewterware** (tel. 04/366742) has a showroom next to the E&O Hotel on Lebuh Farquhar. The best selection of batik is at the **BMB** shop (tel. 04/621607) in Komtar.

Sports and Fitness

Beaches and The **Batu Ferringhi Beach,** with fine, golden sand shaded by
Water Sports casuarina and coconut trees, has made Penang one of the best-known holiday islands in Southeast Asia. Public facilities, such as showers and changing rooms, are nonexistent. Hotel guests can use hotel lounge chairs on the beach.

Biking Several small bicycle-rental firms operate across the road from the major hotels in Batu Ferringhi, but be aware that the traffic often drifts quite close on the narrow roads.

Golf Penang has two 18-hole golf courses open to the public—**Batu Gantung** and **Bukit Jambul.** For information, fees, and tee-off times, call the golf section of the Penang Turf Club (tel. 04/27070) or the Bukit Jambul Country Club (tel. 04/838552).

Hiking For jungle hiking, the best bet is the Recreational Forest (called Rima Rekreasi in Malay), 1½ km (1 mi) past the village of Telok Bahang. The tropical forest also has a museum, a children's playground, and picnic tables. A **Malayan Nature Society brochure** with six other treks around the hills of Penang is available at tourist information centers.
tators.

Dining

Expensive **Brasserie.** Candles and fresh flowers on the tables soften the so-
Continental phisticated French decor of wood-paneled walls, lace curtains,
★ and black-and-white floor tiles. The menu takes the nouvelle approach to European gourmet cooking, with small, attractive portions of lamb, duck, steak, or tiger prawns. Try the frog-leg ravioli and the sherbet with cassis. *Shangri-La Inn, Jln. Mag-*

azine, tel. 04/622622. Reservations suggested. Dress: formal. AE, DC, MC, V.

Italian **Il Ritrovo.** This Italian bistro, cozily decorated with travel posters and candles in wine bottles, draws locals and tourists alike: Its excellent three-course meal is good value. Chef Luciano does a perfect *antipasti tutti mare* (seafood antipasto), followed by an impressive range of pasta, veal, lamb, and chicken dishes and classic Italian *dolci*. A Filipino band enhances the atmosphere by playing requests. *Casuarina Beach Hotel, Batu Ferringhi, tel. 04/811711, ext. 766. Reservations suggested. Dress: casual. AE, DC, MC, V. Closed Mon.*

★ **La Farfalla.** The island's most elegant restaurant, Farfalla's swank decor includes a white grand piano and a different ice sculpture every night. It overlooks the pool and sea, but the place is so pretty you may not notice the view. Try the *carpaccio d'agnello con zucchine* (thin strips of lamb with zucchini) or the *saltimbocca alla Romana* (veal stuffed with cheese and ham). *Mutiara Beach Resort, Telok Bahang, tel. 04/812828. Reservations suggested. Dress: formal. AE, DC, MC, V.*

Seafood **Eden Seafood Village.** This open-air, beachfront restaurant caters to tourists with a nightly cultural show. Its Chinese-style specialties include crab cooked in a spicy chili-tomato sauce, steamed prawns dipped in ginger sauce, lobster, and fried squid. *Batu Ferringhi, tel. 04/811852. Reservations suggested. Dress: casual. AE, DC, MC, V.*

Moderate **Prosperous.** This busy restaurant serves some 200 Cantonese
Chinese and Hainanese dishes. Specialties include barbecued pork ribs and sweet-and-sour fish. *25 Jln. Gottlieb, tel. 04/27286. Reservations not necessary. Dress: casual. AE, DC, MC, V.*
Supertanker. The noise and crowds at Supertanker are its testimonials: Locals love the food and the prices. Favorites on its Teochew menu are the crisp roast suckling pig and the porridges. *Komtar, tel. 04/616393. Reservations not necessary. Dress: casual. AE, MC.*

European **Eden.** A downtown restaurant with a funky decor, Eden makes
★ fresh oxtail soup every day and does a magnificent Tunisian saddle of lamb. The lunch menu caters to Westerners, with sandwiches, salads, and ice cream sundaes. *15 Jln. Hutton, tel. 04/377263. Reservations not necessary. Dress: casual. AE, DC, MC, V.*

Nonya **Dragon King.** People come here for the food, not the atmosphere or modest decor. This is a good place to sample Nonya cuisine, a spicy local blend of Malay and Chinese food. Try the spicy curried chicken and the kerabu salad. *9 Lebuh Bishop, tel. 04/618035. Reservations not necessary. Dress: casual. AE, MC, V. Closes at 9 PM.*

Inexpensive **E. T. Steamboat.** At this restaurant named after the do-it-
Chinese yourself Chinese stew, waiters bring to your table vegetables, seafood, tofu, and a fondue pot full of rich broth; you custom-cook your own dinner. For variety, try *lowbak* (pork rolls) or *tom yom*, a spicy Thai soup. *Two locations: Komtar and 4 Jln. Rangoon, tel. 04/366025. Reservations not necessary. Dress: casual. AE, MC.*

Indian Muslim **Hameediyah.** This simple downtown restaurant excels with its *nasi kandar* (rice with mutton), fish and chicken curry, or *murtabak*, an Indian-style pizza filled with spicy mutton and onions. *164 Lebuh Campbell, tel. 04/611095. No reservations. Dress: casual. No credit cards. Closed Fri.*

Malay **Golden Phoenix.** Once you claim your table in this hawker-stall area, remember its number so the different vendors will know where to deliver your food. The open-air accommodations are somewhat primitive, but the food is authentic and you get a fine sea breeze from across the road. Try *laksa asam* (a sour soup made with local fish), *or chien* (a fried oyster omelet), or the crisp roast duck. You can wash it down with juices made from starfruit and watermelon. *Gurney Dr., no tel. No reservations. Dress: casual. No credit cards. Open nightly until 2 AM.*

★ **Minah.** This simple, open-air restaurant is out in Minden, near the university. You fill your plate by pointing to what you want as it goes by: curry dishes, satay, beef rendang, or sambal. Try the *goreng pisang* (fried bananas) for dessert. *Glugor Rd., tel. 04/881234. No reservations. Dress: casual. No credit cards.*

Lodging

New hotels in Penang have increased the choices dramatically in the last couple of years. Still, the two main locations for tourist accommodations are Georgetown and the beach, either at Tanjung Bungah or farther out at Batu Ferringhi.

Very Expensive **Equatorial Hotel.** Opened in 1989, this hotel is close to the airport, the industrial zone, and the golf course—but far from town and the beaches. Its unique feature is a 10-story atrium garden with bubble elevators. *1 Jln. Bukit Jambul, 11900 Bayan Lepas, Penang, tel. 04/835133 or 800/223-9868. 415 rooms and suites. Facilities: 3 restaurants, coffee shop, tennis, squash, health club, ballrooms, function rooms. AE, DC, MC, V.*

★ **Penang Mutiara.** This luxury resort at the end of Batu Ferringhi beach opened in late 1988 and has set a new standard of excellence in Malaysia. All rooms have an ocean view and are decorated with rattan furniture, batik wall prints, and Malay-pattern rugs. Balconies, ceiling fans, and shutters give additional tropical flavor. The sparkling-white marble lobby features fountains and waterfalls. *Jln. Teluk Bahang, 11050 Penang, tel. 04/812829 or 800/44–UTELL. 443 rooms. Facilities: 2 swimming pools, health club, tennis, water sports, 5 restaurants, 2 lounges, disco. AE, CB, DC, MC, V.*

Shangri-La Inn. This 18-story hotel is next to the Komtar complex in downtown Georgetown. Its efficient rooms are comfortably decorated and offer great views of the city. The Shang Palace serves dim sum daily. *Magazine Rd., 10300 Penang, tel. 04/622622 or 800/44–UTELL. 426 rooms, 16 suites. Facilities: 3 restaurants, coffee shop, lobby lounge, business center, health club, pool, disco. AE, DC, MC, V.*

Expensive **Golden Sands Hotel.** Extensively renovated in 1988, the beachfront Golden Sands has lush tropical landscaping around the two pools and the open-air lounge and café, with a spectacular indoor-outdoor garden effect. Each room is decorated in soft pastels accented with cane and has a private balcony with a view of sea or hills. Activities such as jungle walks and sandcastle-building competitions are arranged, and special poolside events such as Chinese buffet dinners or barbecues are held most nights. *Batu Ferringhi Beach, 11100 Penang, tel. 04/811911 or 800/44–UTELL. 310 rooms. Facilities: 2 restaurants,*

24-hr coffee shop, 2 pools, outdoor Jacuzzi, children's pool with slide, bar, poolside bar, water sports. AE, DC, MC, V.

Merlin Penang. The impressive gray marble facade of this hotel, which opened in 1985, gives it architectural distinction, but the effect of the grand staircase in the lobby is diminished by the coffee shop right under it. The rooms are done in pastel colors. *126 Jln. Burmah, 10050 Penang, tel. 04/376166 or 800/44–UTELL. 283 rooms and suites. Facilities: restaurant, lounge, buffet, pool, disco, convention rooms. AE, DC, MC, V.*

Rasa Sayang Hotel. Penang's premier beach resort for 15 years, this Shangri-La International hotel was partially renovated in 1989, and its grounds and facilities are first-rate. The hotel has programmed activities day and night. Popular with Japanese tourists, it offers a restaurant with teppanyaki, sushi bar, and tempura. *Batu Ferringhi Beach, 11100 Penang, tel. 04/811811 or 800/457–5050. 320 rooms. Facilities: 2 restaurants; disco; bar; 24-hr coffee shop; putting green; water sports; tennis; squash; volleyball; fully equipped fitness center with sauna, massage, and steam room; convention facilities. AE, CB, DC, MC, V.*

Moderate   **Casuarina Beach Hotel.** Large, cozy rooms, a low-key pace, and attentive service make this established resort a favorite. Named for the willowy trees that mingle with palms along the beach, this hotel has a pleasant pool area and offers champagne brunches and country-and-western music nights. *Batu Ferringhi, 11100 Penang, tel. 04/811711 or 800/44–UTELL. 179 rooms. Facilities: 3 restaurants, lounge, pool bar, water sports. AE, DC, MC, V.*

★   **Eastern & Oriental Hotel.** This century-old hotel, known as the E&O, is small but laid-back and appealing. Renovation some years ago removed much of its original tropical charm, but the rooms are well maintained and the waterfront pool area is still a jewel. *10 Farquhar St., tel. 04/375322. 100 rooms. Facilities: pool, 1885 Grill, Anchor Bar. AE, DC, MC, V.*

Holiday Inn Penang. This seven-story hotel surrounds a large pool right on the beach. Popular with Australians, it offers such activities as bike rides and jungle walks, snooker and ping-pong tournaments, and tennis and windsurfing lessons. Day rates available. *Batu Ferringhi Beach, 11100 Penang, tel. 04/811601 or 800/HOLIDAY. 54 rooms. 3 restaurants, 3 bars. AE, DC, MC, V.*

Inexpensive   **Bellevue.** Located atop Penang Hill, this little hotel is reachable only by funicular railway. Its attractions are spectacular vistas, an aviary and pretty gardens, cool air, and privacy. *Bukit Bendera, 11300 Penang, tel. 04/892256. 12 rooms. Facilities: restaurant, bar. No credit cards.*

Lone Pine. The best bargain on the beach is a bit scruffy, with no pool and few amenities, but its beachfront area is shaded and pleasant. The air-conditioned rooms are spacious if Spartan; all have bath, TV, and fridge. Rates include breakfast and morning tea. *97 Batu Ferringhi Beach, 11100 Penang, tel. 04/811511. 54 rooms. Facilities: restaurant, bar. AE, DC, MC, V.*

Malaysia. All the rooms in this hotel, conveniently located downtown on upper Penang Road, have bath, fridge, and TV. *7 Penang Rd., 10000 Penang, tel. 04/363311. 130 rooms. Facilities: coffee house, bar, disco. AE, MC, V.*

The Arts

Eden Seafood Village (tel. 04/811852) in Batu Ferringhi holds a cultural show for diners most evenings. The show features gentle Malay dancers, Indians laden with bells, and noisy Chinese lion dancers.

Arts events held at the City Hall auditorium downtown are advertised with posters and in the newspapers. Festivals include street events, such as Chinese opera.

Nightlife

Penang's nightlife revolves around the major hotels, where discos cater to the trendy set and sedate lounges host those who enjoy listening to live music while chatting over a drink. Combos tend to stick to such tunes as "Candy Man" and "Feelings," so you may get the impression you are back in an earlier era.

Lounges One favorite spot is the Merlin's uptown **Sri Pinang Lounge** (Jln. Larut, tel. 04/376166), where a singer and band entertain. The Mutiara Beach Resort's serene **Palmetto Lounge** (Telok Bahang, tel. 04/812828) has a resident pianist. In the downtown Shangri-La Inn's **Lobby Lounge** (Jln. Magazine, tel. 04/622622), a string quartet—playing everything from classical pieces to waltzes to pop—alternates evenings with a Latin combo. For a drink with a panoramic city view, head for the revolving restaurant atop the **City Bayview Hotel** (Farquhar St., tel. 04/23301). For listings of who is playing where, check the Nightspots column in *The Star.*

Discos The **Cinta** in the Rasa Sayang Hotel (Batu Ferringhi, tel. 04/811811, ext. 1151) draws an international crowd nightly. **Juliana's** in the Shangri-La (Jln. Magazine, tel. 04/622622) features the latest lighting effects and sound equipment from London, with special events most nights.

Bars Downtown Georgetown still has seedy bars, with dim lights and ladies of indeterminate age and profession. Try the **Hong Kong Bar** on Lebuh Chulia (tel. 04/619796), or ask the young hippies who flock to the cheap Chinese hotels in the vicinity.

East Malaysia: Sabah and Sarawak

Introduction

Sabah and Sarawak, Malaysia's eastern states, share the northern third of the island of Borneo with Brunei, sandwiched between them. Each state has a large land mass—much of it primary jungle, with majestic tropical forests and abundant wildlife—and a relatively small population. Borneo's forbidding interior made it far less attractive to early traders and explorers than neighboring countries. Sabah and Sarawak remained uncolonized by the British until the mid-19th century, and they were annexed to the independent state of Malaysia only in 1963. Thus the native peoples—the Iban, Bidayuh, Kadazan, and other tribes—have little in common with West

Sabah and Sarawak

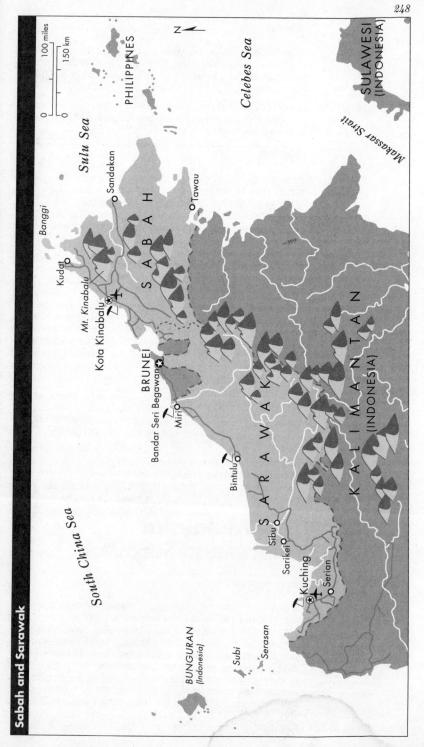

Malaysians, who absorbed much European and Chinese culture. The ancient languages, arts and crafts, and social customs of Sabah and Sarawak remain relatively intact. Some tribes still live in traditional longhouses, communal bamboo structures that house from 10 to 40 families under one roof.

Borneo is among the last wildernesses in Southeast Asia. Rain forest and jungle, threaded by numerous rivers and rapids, cover most of the land, and intrepid travelers explore it on foot, by jeep, or by longboat. Because the tourist industry is only now being developed, you won't trip over other tourists, and native lifestyles are for the most part uncorrupted and authentic. You can trek through the jungle interior, ride a longboat upriver, and stay overnight in a tribal longhouse. At the same time, the capital cities and beach resorts offer considerable luxury, with gourmet restaurants, water sports, and tennis courts.

A visitor taking a trip up one of the rivers for a night or two in a longhouse will find the "forest primeval." Insects hum, invisible creatures bark and grunt, water gurgles and sighs. Equally mysterious are the groaning and screeching of trees that, burdened by age and debris, finally crash through the jungle growth.

Sabah, known as the Land Below the Wind because it lies below the typhoon belt, occupies the northern tip of the island. Its primary resource is its vast timber operations, on which fortunes have been built. With an area of some 7,700 sq km (30,000 sq mi), the state has about 1 million people, of which the Kadazans are the largest ethnic group. The Bajaus, who live along the west coast, are seafarers; many also farm and raise ponies. Chinese make up about a quarter of the population. Most Sabahans are Christians, so there is some religious tension between the Islamic state and its citizens. Sabah's capital, Kota Kinabalu, is a relatively new town, built and expanded after the Second World War. It contains little to interest the tourist but serves as a jumping-off point and transportation hub for exploring the state.

Most travelers to Sabah visit Mount Kinabalu, the legendary mountain in the primitive interior. This is the highest peak in Southeast Asia, at 4,100 m (13,500 ft). From a national park at its base, climbers can make the ascent in two days. For beachcombers, the seas around Sabah offer a kaleidoscope of marine life: You can snorkel, scuba dive, or putter about the reefs in glass-bottom boats.

Sarawak's modern history began in 1846, after Sir James Brooke settled a dispute between the local rajah and the Sultan of Brunei. Establishing peace and bringing relief from marauding pirate bands, Rajah Brooke instituted a benevolent family regency that lasted more than a century, until the arrival of the Japanese. Their intrusion was deeply resented by the tribal people, who eagerly resumed their practice of headhunting, which had been banned by the Brooke rajahs. But Sarawak has otherwise remained for the most part peaceful, unspoiled, and serene.

Sarawak is bigger and poorer than Sabah, with some 1.5 million people inhabiting its 125,000 sq km (48,250 sq mi). About 360,000 live around the capital city of Kuching, a pleasant and fairly modern town that still has a sleepy pace and atmosphere. About 80% of Sarawak's population is Chinese or Malay; as in Sabah, Christians outnumber Muslims.

Sarawak's principal tourist attractions are the Dayak and Iban longhouses, upriver from Kuching. The guided trips give travelers a sense of river life as well as the richness and power of the jungle. You can visit longhouses for a day or stay over for a night or more, sharing communal meals and admiring native dances. Another fascinating destination is the Niah Caves, which have yielded a wide range of archaeological finds, including human remains believed to date from 40,000 years ago.

Important Addresses and Numbers

Tourist Information
Sabah Tourist Association (Level 1, International Airport, Kota Kinabalu. tel. 088/224911, ext. 335). **TDC** (Block L, Lot 4, Bangunan STPC, Bandaran Sinsuran, Box 136, 88675 Kota Kinabalu, tel. 088/211698).

Sarawak Tourist Association (Lot 244, Level 2, Sarawak Plaza, Kuching, tel. 082/240620; airport counter, tel. 082/456266). **TDC** (AIA Building, 2nd floor Jln. Song Thian Cheok, Kuching, tel. 082/246575).

Emergencies Dial 999.

Arriving and Departing by Plane

Note: Sabah and Sarawak have separate immigration-control systems from those in West Malaysia. American visitors need valid passports but are not required to get a visa. Travelers on business or with student passes can stay up to three months.

Airports and Airlines
Malaysia Airlines is the primary carrier to Sabah and Sarawak. In addition, **Royal Brunei** flies into both the new **Kota Kinabalu (KK) International Airport** (tel. 088/54811) and Sarawak's **Kuching International Airport** (tel. 082/454242) and **Philippine Airlines, Singapore Airlines,** and **Cathay Pacific** fly into KK.

Between the Airport and Center City
A taxi ride from the Kota Kinabalu airport to city center costs M$10.20. Kuching's spacious airport is about 11 km (7 mi) south of town, and the unmetered taxis charge M$14 for the trip.

Arriving and Departing by Ship

The cruise ship *Muhibah* (contact **Feri Malaysia,** Menara Utama UMBC, Jln. Sultan Sulaiman, 5000 Kuala Lumpur, tel. 03/238–8899) makes regular runs to these eastern states from Port Klang and Kuantan in West Malaysia.

Getting Around

By Car Four-wheel-drive vehicles are recommended for driving in the interior. Drivers can be hired, too. For rentals in KK, try **Avis** (tel. 088/56706), **Kinabalu** (tel. 088/23602), or **E&C** (tel. 088/57679). In Kuching, local rental companies have counters at the airport; Avis and Hertz are not represented.

By Train **Sabah State Railways** (tel. 088/54611) runs a scenic rail line from Kota Kinabalu south to Tenom. The 49-km (31-mi) stretch between Beaufort and Tenom passes through the spectacular Crocker Range and Padas Gorge, takes 1½–2 hours, and costs

M$8.35 first class, M$2.75 economy. Sarawak has no rail service.

By Taxi In KK you can always find a cab near the Hyatt downtown; in Kuching, drivers gather in front of the Holiday Inn. Outside these cities, taxis are not plentiful. Ask personnel at your hotel to call one for you, or inquire in the street about the location of the nearest taxi stand. Summoning cabs by telephone isn't very reliable, as you'll be calling a taxi stand, but you can try 088/51863 or 088/25669 in KK.

Cabs are more expensive here than in peninsular Malaysia, and they are unmetered. Ask at your hotel to get an idea of usual fares to various destinations; agree on the price with your driver before setting out.

By Bus Public bus companies serve the cities and the countryside, but poor road conditions make intercity travel rough. Kota Kinabalu's main terminal is in front of the port. **Leun Thung Transport Co.** (tel. 088/762655) goes from city center to Tanjung Aru, and **Tuaran United Co.** (tel. 088/31580) stops at all the villages along the road to Tuaran.

In Kuching, the main terminal is at Mosque Road, where a posted map displays the routes. Among the companies serving the area are **Kuching Matang Transport** (tel. 082/422814) and **Sarawak Transport** (tel. 082/242579).

Other Transportation Shared taxis and minibuses congregate near the bus terminals, and boat taxis and chartered launches have kiosks along the waterfront.

Guided Tours

Sabah Tour operators in Kota Kinabalu include **Api Tours** (Bandaran Berjaya, tel. 088/221230), **Bakti** (Hyatt Hotel, Jln. Datuk Salleh Sulong, tel. 088/534426), and **Discovery** (Jln. Haji Saman, tel. 088/57735). The **Marina** (Tanjung Aru Beach Hotel, tel. 088/214215) specializes in island trips and water sports.

Orientation A KK city tour covers its highlights in just two hours (note that the mosque and Sabah Museum are closed Friday). A countryside tour stops at a fishing village, driving past rice fields and rural kampongs to the town of Tuaran. Other excursions include the Sunday market at Kota Belud, a day trip to Tenom, and the orangutan sanctuary.

Diving Trips The diving season lasts from mid-February to mid-December; in August and September, the green sea turtles come ashore to lay their eggs. **Borneo Divers** (Bag 194, KK, tel. 088/421371) arranges dive excursions to Sipadan and the reefs of Tunku Rahman National Park; the company also offers packages with Malaysia Airlines.

Rafting and Jungle Treks **Api** and **Discovery** have white-water rafting as well as hiking safaris into the interior, including visits to native villages.

Sarawak Four travel agencies in Kuching offer a variety of tours throughout the state. You'll find the itineraries and prices comparable at **Interworld Travel Service** (110 Green Rd., tel. 082/252344), **Sarawak Travel** (70 Padungan Rd., tel. 082/243708), and **Borneo Island Tours** (Jln. Borneo, tel. 082/423944). **Borneo Adventure** (1st floor, Panungan Arcade, Jln. Song Thian Cheok, tel. 082/245175) specializes in backpacking tours but has longhouse and hotel-based excursions as well.

Orientation It takes about three hours to cover Kuching's historic sites, including a drive past the central market and a Malay village, with a stop at the Sarawak Museum.

Nature You can take guided nature walks to the orangutan sanctuary, a crocodile farm, or the Bako National Park and Matang area. Tour organizers also arrange backpacking and spelunking excursions into mountain regions, national parks, and ancient caves.

Exploring Sabah

Kota Kinabalu The capital, called Jesselton when Sabah was the British crown colony of North Borneo, was razed during World War II, thus its local name Api-Api ("fires"). It got its new name in 1963, when Sabah and Sarawak joined independent Malaysia. Little of historic interest remains, because the oldest part of the city is vintage 1950s. The multistory shophouses sell hardware and other practical goods; the upper floors are residences. The central market on the waterfront sells produce and handicrafts, but most of these goods are Philippine rather than local.

KK's main draw is the **Sabah Museum,** on a hilltop off Jalan Penampang about 3 km from city center. The building resembles a traditional longhouse, and its contents are a good introduction to local history, archaeology, botany, and ethnography. One exhibit features the innumerable varieties of the large ceramic *tajau,* a household jar common throughout Asia. Another displays the many ingenious uses of bamboo in toys, animal traps, musical instruments, and farm tools. A third gallery is devoted to headhunting. *Bukit Istana Lama, tel. 088/ 53199. Admission free. Open Sat.–Thurs. 9–6.*

Excursions A favorite destination is **Mt. Kinabalu National Park,** 113 km (68 mi) or two hours from KK. Nature lovers can walk miles of well-marked trails through jungle dense with wild orchids, carnivorous pitcher plants, bamboo, mosses and vines, and unusual geologic formations. The wildlife is shy, but you are likely to see exotic birds and possibly a few orangutans.

For some, the main event is scaling **Mt. Kinabalu,** the highest mountain in Southeast Asia—and thus a place of spiritual significance for the Kadazan people. Climbers can reach the peak in two days without too much exertion, and the view from the summit on a clear morning is worth every step. Mountain guides are equipped with mobile telephones, and the park has a helipad.

Three seas converge at the northern tip of Borneo, and their shores are all easily accessible from KK. You can make a day trip to picnic and snorkel among the coral reefs at the little park on **Pulau Gaya,** in the South China Sea, or join a boat excursion to a **turtle park** and **crocodile farm** off the east coast, in the Sulu Sea. Scuba divers will find some of the world's richest reefs off **Sipadan Island** in the Celebes Sea farther south.

The small coastal trading town of Sandakan, reached by sea or air, is 21 km (13 mi) from the **Sepilok Orang Utan Rehabilitation Centre**—an almost unique jungle habitat for these near-human primates. (From Sandakan, buses go to the sanctuary several times a day—you'll have to walk 2 km (1.2 mi) from the entrance to the center. For schedules, tel. 088/215106.) Here, illegally captured animals are prepared for a return to the wild. There's no guarantee that you'll see the apes in this vast forest, but there's enough to make the trip worthwhile if you don't— including waterfalls, cool streams for swimming, and other rain forest wildlife. *Tel. 089/214179 or 660811. Admission free. Open daily 9–4.*

Arrange any of these trips through one of the tour companies listed under Guided Tours, above.

Exploring Sarawak

Kuching suffered little damage during the Second World War, and a walk around town will give the visitor some feeling for its history. Its oldest building is the 1840s **Tua Pek Kong** Chinese temple, downtown on Jalan Tuanku Abdul Rahman and Padaungan Road. You can watch worshipers lighting incense and making paper offerings to the god of prosperity. Among the colonial buildings worth seeing is the **Court House,** the former seat of the British White Rajahs, with its portico and romanesque columns (the clock tower was added in 1883). This remains the venue for any event of pomp and circumstance. Behind the Court House on Jalan Tun Haji Openg stands the **Pavilion building,** where, beneath an elaborate Victorian facade, the Education Department now does its business.

Across the river is **Fort Margherita,** built in 1879 by Rajah Charles Brooke. Today it serves as a police museum, displaying cannons, rifles, and other colonial weapons. The nearby **Astana** was the Brooke palace, built in 1870—three bungalows, complete with military ramparts and tower. Today Astana is the official residence of Sarawak's head of state and is not open to the public.

The highlight of the city is the **Sarawak Museum,** one of the best in Southeast Asia—comprehensive and beautifully curated. In addition to exhibits of local insects and butterflies, sea creatures, birds, and other wildlife, there are displays on Dayak body tattoos, burial rites, face masks, and carvings. In the new building across the road is a delightful exhibit on cats *(kuching* means "cat" in Malay), a model of the Niah Caves showing how nests are gathered, a movie theater, an art gallery, and a crafts shop. *Jln. Tun Haji Openg, tel. 082/24231. Admission free. Open Mon.–Thurs. 9:15–5:30, Sat. and Sun. 9:15–6.*

Excursions Few tourists come this far without making a trip to a tribal **longhouse.** Some are as close as a 1½-hour drive from Kuching; others involve longer rides and boat trips. You can visit for a day or stay over for as long as a week. Either way, your hosts welcome you with a mixture of hospitality and polite indifference. While accommodations are spartan, guest quarters usually include mosquito netting, flush toilets, and running water. The attraction here is seeing—and sharing—a lifestyle that has changed little in centuries. Tour operators give advice on dress and comportment.

One overnight trip goes to the **Skrang River.** A car or bus takes you through pepper plantations, run mostly by Chinese families, to the town of Serian, where you board a canoe for a beautiful ride through the jungle on the clear, green river. A longhouse awaits you at the end of the journey.

The **Niah Caves,** an archaeologist's mecca, are 109 km (68 mi) from the port town of Miri, a 40-minute flight from Kuching. (A taxi from Miri costs M$20.) The caves contain stone, bone, and iron tools; primitive paintings and drawings; and Chinese ceramics. The caves were occupied for thousands of years and are still used as a commercial resource by the local people, who gather guano from the cave floors for fertilizer and collect birds' nests from the ceilings for bird's-nest soup—a Chinese delicacy. Adventurous travelers can go through the caves with a guide. To reach the caves you must walk over a long path of 10-inch-wide boards. This trip is not for the lazy, but greatly rewarding. In the Niah National Park, there's a hostel (contact the National Parks Office, tel. 085/33361 or 36637).

About 22 km (14 mi) from Kuching is the **Semonggok Wildlife Rehabilitation Centre,** where orangutans, other monkeys, honey bears, and hornbills formerly in captivity are prepared for return to their natural habitat. You can get a visitor's permit through the Forestry Department (Mosque Rd., Kuching, tel. 082/248739). *For tour arrangements, tel. 082/423111, ext. 1133. Admission charge. Open weekdays 8–4:25, Sat. 8–12:45.*

Shopping

Sarawak The handicrafts in Sarawak are among the most fascinating in the world. Especially distinctive are the handwoven blankets, or *pua kumbu,* whose intricate tribal designs have ceremonial significance. Baskets, hats, and mats are made from a combination of rattan, palm leaves, and reeds; their designs vary according to ethnic group. The woodcarvings of Sarawak often bear the motif of the hornbill, the national emblem. Pottery designs show a Chinese influence, as do brassware and silver objects. The crafts shop next to the **Sarawak Tourist Information Center** in Kuching has a large selection of all kinds of handicrafts, and other shops around the city stock similar goods.

A **Sunday market** in the car park of Bank Bumiputra on Jalan Satok sells everything from fruit to heirlooms. For antiques, try along Wayang Street, Temple Street, and the Main Bazaar. Bargaining is expected.

Sabah Sabah handicrafts are less elaborate than Sarawak's, but they do have character. Two KK shops specializing in local products are **Borneo Handicrafts** (ground floor, Lot 51 Jln. Gaya, tel. 088/714081) and **Sabah Handicraft Centre** (ground floor, Lot 49 Bandaran Berjaya, tel. 088/221230). Borneo Handicrafts also has an outlet at the airport (tel. 088/230707).

For other shopping in KK, cruise through **Kompleks Karamunsing** off Jalan Kolam or the **Matahari Superstore** (tel. 088/214430) in the Segama district near the Hyatt. For jewelry, try **Ban Loong** (tel. 088/217126) or **Yun On Goldsmiths** (tel. 088/219369) in the Wisma Merdeka building.

The **night market** in Kota Kinabalu usually sets up about 7 PM in front of the central market. One portable souvenir is mountain-grown Sabah Tea.

Sports, Fitness, Beaches

Sabah Beaches The best bet is the islands of the **Tuanku Abdul Rahman National Park,** a 15-minute speedboat ride from the pier in downtown KK. Here serenity and privacy prevail. Pretty coral formations and exotic marine life attract snorkelers and divers. Tour operators will arrange a picnic lunch for an outing. Some camping facilities and a few cabins are available for overnights.

Golf Kota Kinabalu has two private golf courses that can be used by visitors who make arrangements in advance through their hotels. The 18-hole course at **Bukit Padang** is run by the Sabah Golf and Country Club; the 9-hole course at **Tanjung Aru** is under the auspices of the Kinabalu Golf Club.

Health and Fitness Centers The **Likas Sports Complex** is a 300-acre facility behind Signal Hill, a few kilometers east of KK on Jalan Kompleks Sukan, with an Olympic-size pool, a track, eight tennis courts, and a weight-training gym. Also open to the public are the **International** in Bandaran Berjaya (tel. 088/212586) and **Merigaya** at the Hyatt Hotel (tel. 088/210407).

Water Sports You can snorkel, scuba dive, windsurf, and sail off the beach at **Tanjung Aru,** only a few minutes from KK, and on small islands accessible through the major hotels.

Sarawak Beaches Idyllic **Damai Beach** is about 20 km (12 mi) northwest of Kuching, at the foot of Santubong Mountain. The Holiday Inn resort there provides facilities for water sports such as windsurfing, catamaran sailing, kayaking, and waterskiing.

Other picturesque but undeveloped beaches in Sarawak include **Brighton Beach** and **Tanjong Lobang** in Miri, and **Tanjong Batu** and **Tanjong Kidurong** in Bintulu.

Boating Recreational boating is available at the **Holiday Inn Damai Beach** resort (tel. 082/411777).

Golf The **Sarawak Golf and Country Club** (tel. 082/23622) at Petra Jaya is open to guests of major hotels. The **Holiday Inn Damai Beach** (tel. 082/411777) has a new 18-hole course.

Jogging Runners in Kuching use the **Holiday Inn course** or head to the stadium at Petra Jaya. Australia's **Hash House Harriers** (tel. 082/411133) have open runs on Tuesday for men and on Wednesday for women.

Squash The **Sarawak Golf and Country Club** has squash courts; make arrangements through your hotel.

Swimming There's a public pool on Padungan Road (tel. 082/51354).

Dining

Kota Kinabalu **Gardenia.** This elegant restaurant has a Western-style menu listing lobster as well as New Zealand lamb with mint sauce. Business travelers and government officials eat here. *55 Jln. Gaya, tel. 088/54296. Reservations required during holidays. Dress: smart casual. AE, DC, MC, V. Expensive.*
Kasturi Terrace. You can eat indoors in air-conditioned comfort or outdoors on the terrace overlooking the pool and gardens. Fare at the daily international-style buffets includes local rice and noodle dishes and Western-style salads and desserts. Fresh seafood is a specialty. *Tanjung Aru Beach Resort, Jln.*

Aru, tel. 088/58711. No reservations. Dress: casual. AE, DC, MC, V. Expensive.

Nam Hing. The locals who patronize this Chinese restaurant order the tasty seafood dishes—chili crab, squid, and prawns. The noise and gusto of the clientele provide a lively distraction from the bland decor. *32 Jln. Haji Saman, tel. 088/51433. No reservations. Dress: casual. No credit cards. Moderate.*

Noodle Inn. Across from the Capitol Theatre, the inn features 30 types of noodle dishes, some in soups, some dry, and others fried. Also on the menu are 20 varieties of *congee* (rice porridge) and three delicious creamy dessert puddings—peanut, almond, and sesame. *56 Bandaran Berjaya, tel. 088/219734. No reservations. Dress: casual. AE, DC, V. Inexpensive.*

Kuching **Lok Thian.** This large restaurant, located near the Dewan Mesayakat, is renowned for its Cantonese barbecue. *319 Jln. Padungan, tel. 088/3130. No reservations. Dress: casual. AE, DC, V. Moderate.*

Meisan Szechuan. This gaudily decorated Chinese restaurant overlooks the Sarawak River. Waiters deliver 23 varieties of dim sum—all you can eat. *Holiday Inn Kuching, Jln. Tuanku Abdul Rahman, tel. 082/423111. Reservations suggested on Sun. morning. Dress: casual. AE, DC, MC, V. Moderate.*

Tsui Hua Lau. Cantonese and Szechuan dishes grace an extensive menu at this brightly lit, two-story restaurant. The unusual entrées include braised turtle, sea cucumber, and bird's nest soup (a bowl for 10 costs M$100). The barbecued duck and Szechuan-style shredded beef meet high standards. *22 Ban Hock Rd., tel. 082/414560. No reservations. Dress: casual. AE, DC, V. Moderate.*

Waterfront Cafe. On the river, this serene ground-floor coffee shop has a good view of the wharf and the water traffic. Its menu features Malay, Chinese, and Indian favorites plus Western specialties. The noodle dishes are delicious; the service is fine. *Kuching Hilton, Jln. Tuanku Abdul Rahman, tel. 082/248200. No reservations. Dress: casual. AE, DC, MC, V. Moderate.*

Lodging

Sabah **Hyatt Kinabalu.** The Hyatt appeals especially to business travelers and shoppers. Rooms are spacious and comfortable; many have views of the port and nearby islands. The downtown hotel's 24-hour coffee shop is a magnet for late-night revelers. *Jln. Datuk Salleh Sulong, 88994 KK, tel. 088/221234 or 800/228-9000. 350 rooms, including 50 suites. Facilities: business center, 2 bars, 3 restaurants, pool. AE, DC, MC, V. Very Expensive.*

★ **Tanjung Aru Beach Hotel.** This premier luxury resort, opened in 1983 and run by Shangri-La International, is near the airport and 10 minutes from downtown. The dark, open lobby, with aquariums showcasing tropical marine life, establishes a tranquil tone. Rooms are tastefully decorated with wicker furniture, and each has a private balcony overlooking the hotel's 23 landscaped acres and the sea and islands beyond. The leisure center teaches and arranges windsurfing, scuba diving, waterskiing, sailing, white-water rafting, and glass-bottom boat rides. For dining, the buffet of local specialties at the Kasturi Terrace (*see* Dining) is delectable. *Locked Bag 174, 88999 KK, tel. 088/58711 or 800/457-5050. 300 rooms and* *suites. Facilities: French restaurant, lounge, disco, 4 lighted tennis courts, golf course nearby, business center, fitness center, pool, Jacuzzi. AE, DC, MC, V. Very Expensive.*

Hotel Perkasa. This international-style resort hotel is located on a hilltop facing Mt. Kinabalu, to which excursions can be arranged. Its rooms offer a mountain view as well as heaters—a rarity in the tropics—to warm the brisk mountain air. *W.D.T. 11, 89300 Ranau, tel. 088/889511. 74 rooms. Facilities: restaurant and lounge, secretarial service, sightseeing desk, tennis court, fitness center, golf nearby. AE, DC, MC, V. Moderate.*

Sarawak **Holiday Inn Kuching.** The first international hotel on the river seems to bustle all the time, perhaps because it's next door to a major shopping arcade. A new wing has been added, and the old wing extensively renovated. The rooms are compact but nicely decorated and are replete with all the amenities. *Jln. Tuanku Abdul Rahman, Box 2362, 93100 Kuching, tel. 082/423111 or 800/HOLIDAY. 320 rooms, including executive suites. Facilities: 24-hr coffee house, 2 restaurants, bake shop, bar, disco, sauna, fitness center, lighted tennis court, pool, business center, children's playground. AE, DC, MC, V. Very Expensive.*

★ **Kuching Hilton.** This 15-story luxury hotel opened in late 1988 and offers superlative accommodations. On the Sarawak River, just across from Fort Margherita, it has quickly become a landmark for quality service and fine dining. The bleached furniture in its spacious rooms includes a desk with a view. One "Penthouse Floor" and two executive floors offer special amenities: separate check-in, a personal butler, and private lounge. All the restaurants have views that enhance any meal. *Jln. Tuanku Abdul Rahman, Box 2396, 93748 Kuching, tel. 082/248200 or 800/HILTONS. 322 rooms and 3 floors of suites. Facilities: 5 restaurants, cocktail lounge, fitness center, pool, executive business center, convention and banquet rooms. AE, DC, MC, V. Very Expensive.*

Holiday Inn Damai Beach. The only beach resort in Sarawak, this hotel is located about 24km (15 mi) from Kuching on a lovely stretch of beach on the South China Sea. (A shuttle bus connects the two Holiday Inn properties.) The word *damai* means "harmony and peace," and that's available on this 90-acre spread in a tropical rain forest. But the hotel also offers water sports, jogging, and jungle treks among its plentiful opportunities for recreation. Rooms are large and well furnished, with an outdoorsy feeling created by glass patio doors. *Box 2870, 93756 Kuching, tel. 082/411777 or 800/HOLIDAY. 202 rooms, including suites, studios, and chalets. Facilities: 2 restaurants, disco, 2 tennis courts, 2 squash courts, 18-hole Trent Jones–designed golf course, minigolf, large pool, poolside snack bar, water-sports equipment, bicycle rental, sauna, fitness center, game room, business center, convention and banquet rooms, children's playground with minizoo, aviary, child-care center. AE, DC, MC, V. Expensive.*

Aurora. A well-located Asian hotel, clean, and a good value. Its large rooms are cheaply furnished but have air-conditioning, TV, phone, and private bath. *McDougall Rd., Box 260, Kuching, tel. 082/20281. 86 rooms. Facilities: coffee house, 2 restaurants, terrace. No credit cards. Moderate.*

The Arts and Nightlife

The international hotels offer East Malaysia's most sophisticated entertainment. Local culture is most evident during harvest festivals—May in Sabah and June in Sarawak.

Sabah   A year-round opportunity to see Kadazan culture and taste its food is planned for a **folk village** at **Karambunai,** about 16 km (10 mi) out of KK via the Tuaran Road, scheduled to open early in 1990. Cultural shows at the model kampong will be presented by the Kadazan Cultural Association (tel. 088/713696). The **Tanjung Aru Beach** hotel's Garden restaurant (tel. 088/58711) has cultural shows every Saturday at 8:30 PM. At the Sunday **market** in **Kota Belud,** visitors can watch Bajau dancing, pony riding, and cockfights.

Among the modern nightclubs recommended in KK are the **Mikado** (Hyatt Hotel lower level, tel. 088/219888), **Tiffany Disco and Music Theatre** (9 Jln. Karamunsing, tel. 088/210645), and the **Bistro Showcase and Discotheque** (Wisma Budaya, Jln. Tuanku Abdul Rahman, Kg. Air, tel. 088/225877). Most night spots are small, seedy, dark rooms with disco music blaring through megawatt sound systems. On occasion the pace slows down and local dances—such as the Kadazan *sumazou*—are requested. Most places have hostesses to chat and dance with; you are expected to buy them drinks in return for their company.

Sarawak   The new **Cultural Village and Heritage Centre** at Damai runs twice-weekly programs of such folk arts as dancing, kite flying, and handicraft production. Plans are in the works for a restaurant serving local dishes with longhouse-style accommodations for tourists. The Sarawak Economic Development Corporation directs the project, but call the Damai Beach Resort (tel. 082/411777) for details.

The Holiday Inn Kuching has a minicultural show every Monday, Thursday, and Saturday evening at 7:30. A troupe of gong players and pretty female dancers perform a variety of dances from the state's different ethnic groups.

For nightlife in Kuching, the most popular local clubs include White Swan, Silver Star, Starlight Disco, and the Aquarius in the Holiday Inn.

Brunei

Introduction

Nestled between Sabah and Sarawak is a tiny nation different from any other in Southeast Asia. Since 1929, when oil was discovered off its shores, the sultanate of Brunei Darussalam—no larger than the state of Delaware, and with a population of only 235,000—has developed into the second-richest country in the world. While Brunei shares with its neighbors a blend of Malay and Muslim traditions, a tropical climate, and a jungle terrain, its people enjoy a standard of living unmatched except by that in Kuwait. In the 16th century Brunei dominated an empire reaching as far south as Manila, but the nobility was cruel and unpopular, and its power was gradually eroded by internal politics and revolts. Partly to protect the primitive tribes of the

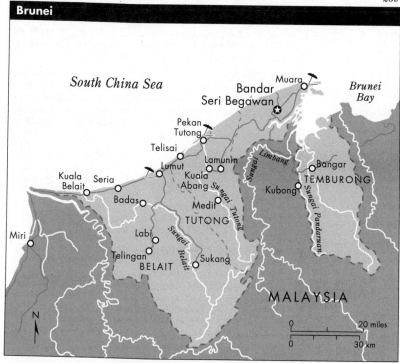

interior—and partly to exploit the weakness of the Brunei throne—the first British White Rajah, James Brooke, took over the region in 1839. Brunei became a British protectorate in 1888, and the money started flowing when the oil did, about 40 years later. Britain helped quell a rebellion against the sultanate in 1962; political stability followed, and Brunei was granted full independence in 1984.

Passports and Visas

Americans need a visa to enter Brunei. Canadian and British citizens, and those from neighboring Asian countries, can visit for two weeks without a visa.

Currency

Brunei dollars are issued in notes of B\$1, B\$5, B\$10, B\$50, B\$100, B\$500, and 1,000. Coins come in denominations of 1, 5, 10, 20, and 50 cents. The Brunei dollar is at par with the Singapore dollar, which also circulates in Brunei; at press time B\$1.95 = US\$1.

Language

The official language is Bahasa Malaysia, but English and the Hokkien Chinese dialect are widely spoken.

Telephones

You can direct-dial international calls from the major hotels or from the Central Telegraph Office on Jalan Sultan. The country code for Brunei is 673; no city codes are used.

Brunei's 29th sultan has ruled since 1967, when his father abdicated. Like his predecessors, he takes seriously his role as a guardian of Islamic values. For instance, he mandated whippings for criminals convicted of crimes ranging from vandalism to rape. His fabulous wealth also makes him a major player in global politics: His US$10 million contribution to the Nicaraguan rebels linked his name with the Iran-Contra arms scandal. Bragging about the 42-year-old sultan's extravagance —his passion for polo ponies, Italian sports cars, and London fashions—is a national pastime. He is famous also for his beneficence. His government spends its oil revenues on public education, health care, and cultural programs. And his investments abroad have ensured that Brunei's prosperity will continue long after its oil and gas are exhausted.

Because the country doesn't need foreigners' hard currency and generally disdains foreign values and customs, tourism is not a highly developed industry, but visitors can be comfortably accommodated in the modern capital, Bandar Seri Begawan (BSB). The city, situated on a wide, lovely river, and the Kampung Ayer (water village), where many of its citizens dwell in houses built on stilts, are well worth a stop for the traveler to Asia.

Important Addresses and Numbers

Tourist Information Brunei has no official agency to handle visitors. The **Economic Development Board** (State Secretariat Office, BSB, tel. 31794) can provide general information, and a booth at the airport distributes city maps and hotel brochures.

Emergencies Dial 22333 for **police,** 22366 for an **ambulance,** and 22555 in case of **fire.**

When to Go

Brunei's tropical temperatures don't vary much from one season to the next: It's hot and humid year-round, and the equatorial sun is fierce. Even during the December–January monsoon, be prepared for blasts of heat between downpours. There is no peak tourist season.

Festivals and Seasonal Events

The widely observed Muslim religious holidays vary according to the Islamic calendar. Chinese, Hindu, and Christian holidays are also observed, some on fixed dates. (*See* this section at the beginning of the Malaysia chapter.) In addition, Brunei celebrates **National Day** (Feb. 23), the **anniversary of the Royal Brunei Army** (May 31), and the **sultan's birthday** (July 15).

What It Will Cost

Sample Prices Breakfast of toast, eggs, and coffee, $5–$8; taxi ride, $2 for first mile, $1 per mile thereafter; double room, $120 expensive, $50–$75 moderate.

Mail

Receiving Mail The only means of receiving letters in Brunei is at your hotel. American Express and Thomas Cook do not have offices, and the GPO will not hold mail.

Arriving and Departing by Plane

Airport and Airlines The national carrier, **Royal Brunei Airlines** (tel. 29438), has routes throughout Southeast Asia. **Malaysia Airlines** flies from Kuching in Sarawak and Kota Kinabalu in Sabah, though not daily. **Singapore Airlines, Cathay Pacific,** and **Thai International** also serve Brunei.

Brunei International Airport, near Bandar Seri Begawan, is sleek, modern, and efficient. Departing passengers pay an airport tax of B$12 on international flights, B$5 to Singapore or Malaysia.

The only way to get downtown from the airport is via taxi. There are unmetered, and you must negotiate the fare in advance—B$15 is average for the 4-km (2½-mi) ride.

Arriving and Departing by Car, Bus, and Boat

A road that's not yet entirely paved links Kuala Belait, 112 km (70 mi) southwest of BSB, with the Malaysian town of Miri in Sarawak. It's slow going and involves two river crossings by ferry and two immigration-control stops. Taxis charge about B$30 for the ride. Brunei's **Sharikat Berlima Belait** runs daily buses on this route; fare is B$16.

You can get to Brunei from Limbang in northern Sarawak via a riverboat that takes half an hour and costs about B$7. A ferry also runs from the island of Labuan in Sabah in two hours; fare is B$15.

Getting Around

By Car Two rental agencies have counters at the airport—**Avis** and **Sharikat Yuran.**

By Taxi You can hire a private taxi for sightseeing, but drivers often speak a minimum of English. Hotels will arrange such service for B$45 an hour.

By Bus Bus service in Bandar Seri Begawan is erratic. Buses leave only when full, so there may be a long wait. The central bus terminal is behind the Brunei Hotel on Jalan Pemancha—also where you catch the bus to Seria.

By Boat Water taxis—small, open boats—to the Kampung Ayer areas are available near the market off Jalan Sungai Kianggeh. Bargain with drivers for fares; a complete hour tour should cost between B$20 and B$25.

Guided Tours

The **Travel Centre/Borneo** (56 Jln. Sultan, Teck Guan Plaza, tel. 29601) offers three half- or full-day city tours. The company also arranges trips to the oil fields at Seria, a longhouse in the interior, and Kuala Balai, where a primitive skull house contains the handiwork of former headhunters.

Exploring Bandar Seri Begawan

Unlike most Asian cities, where imposing modern offices and hotels dominate the skyline, Brunei's capital city has a traditional look. Its buildings are appealing and well landscaped, but few are more than three stories tall. This low profile makes the mosque's stately minarets and huge golden dome—the first thing you see as you drive into BSB—all the more impressive. You can easily walk to the main attractions of this clean little city in a day: Most are near the mosque in the central district.

The **Sultan Omar Ali Saifuddin Mosque** is considered the most beautiful in Southeast Asia. This superb example of modern Islamic architecture was built in 1959 of imported white marble, gold mosaic, and stained glass—all made possible by petrodollars. It's partly surrounded by a lagoon, where a religious stone boat called the **Mahaligal** floats year-round, as elegant and ornate as the mosque itself. *Cor. Jln. Elizabeth II and Jln. Stoney. Open to the public daily except Thurs. afternoon and all day Fri.*

Across from the mosque on Jalan Elizabeth II, note the mosaic mural on the facade of the **Language and Literature Bureau,** depicting scenes from village life. Walk away from the mosque to Jalan Sultan, where a left turn will take you past the **Parliament House,** a heavily gilted and tiled building now used mainly for ceremonial purposes, and to the **Churchill Memorial** at city center.

The late sultan, educated at Sandhurst in Britain, revered Winston Churchill and built this memorial to instill the statesman's values in the children of Brunei. The museum here houses the largest collection of Churchilliana outside Britain, including a series of hats symbolizing his many roles: soldier, patriot, scholar, and polo player. Other exhibits are memorabilia from the last days of Britain's Far Eastern empire, displays and videos commemorating Brunei's independence, and documents tracing the history of its constitution. The museum complex also has a tropical aquarium. *Jln. Sultan, tel. 25354. Admisison free. Open Wed.–Mon. 9:30–4:30.*

Backtrack on Jalan Sultan and turn left toward the river on Jalan Cator. Along the riverbank here is the town market, where women come daily to buy and sell fresh produce and other necessities. Merchandise is spread on mats on the ground, and everybody bargains. Walking along the riverfront, you'll come to Jalan Residency and the **Arts and Handicrafts Centre** (tel. 40676). The new, eight-story building, shaped like the scabbard of a kris, contains workshops for silversmithing, brassmaking, weaving, and basketware. The silver goods—including such oddities as miniature cannons and boats—are exquisitely made. Crafts are for sale in the showroom, but prices are steep. *Open daily 9:30–4:30.*

On the river near the Brunei Hotel, you can hop a boat for a tour of the Kampong Ayer (*see* Getting Around by Boat, above). More than a third of the city's population lives in these river communities, in modern homes built on stilts in the water. Schools, clinics, and small mosques stand among the houses, which all sport TV antennae. Craftsmen such as boatbuilders, weavers, and brassworkers earn their living in these communities, but most residents commute by water taxi or private boat to work on terra firma. And while most women shop at the market across the river, you'll still see the older generation in paddleboats on the water selling food and household goods.

Two attractions lie at short distances from the central district of BSB. The **sultan's palace** (called Istana Nural Iman, or "Palace of Righteous Light") is about 3 km (2 mi) west on Jalan Tutong. Although the palace is officially closed to the public, impromptu tours are sometimes given if you ask, and there's a three-day open house during the Hari Raya Puasa festival in October. Built in the shape of a Borneo longhouse at a cost of US$500 million, this is the largest and most opulent home in the world. The sultan, his two wives, and their children actually inhabit the palace, which boasts 1,788 rooms and a throne room that seats 2,000. If you can't visit the interior, drive by just to glimpse the massive arched roofs, gold domes, and expanses of imported marble. Near the palace wall is a sculpture garden, a permanent ASEAN exhibit that features modern works from neighboring countries, all based on the theme "Harmony in Diversity."

About 6 km (4 mi) from town on the Kota Batu road is the **Brunei Museum,** set on 120 acres near the river. The brassware, silver, Chinese bronzes, ivory, and gold collections are magnificent. A natural history gallery displays stuffed animals and mounted insects; another exhibit showcases ancient ceramics, traditional tools and weapons, and other artifacts of Borneo life. The museum has an entire section, sponsored by Shell Petroleum, devoted to the local oil industry. A new building nearby houses the **Museum of Malay Technology,** which emphasizes native ingenuity in coppersmithing, loom weaving, hunting, fishing, and extracting juice from sugarcane. *Jln. Subok, tel. 44545. Admission free. Open Tues.–Sun. 9:30– 5:30.*

Shopping

The showroom at the **Brunei Arts and Handicrafts Centre** (*see* Exploring BSB, above) has the best selection of local work, but its prices—especially for the finely worked silver—are high.

Gold jewelry (24-karat) is popular among Brunei's citizens, so goldsmiths offer a wide selection. Try **Chin Chin Goldsmith** (33 Jln. Sultan, tel. 22893) or **Million Goldsmith & Jewelry** (Mile 1, Teck Guan Plaza, Jln. Sultan, tel. 29546).

The newest shopping complex is the **Plaza Abdul Razak** on Jalan Tutong (tel. 41536), which is anchored by the **Yaohan** department store. Less than a kilometer from city center, the high-rise structure includes office units, apartments, a music center, restaurants, and shops. Stores close at 9:30 PM.

Sports and Fitness

The Sheraton Utama publishes a jogger's guide, which features a 20-minute run, up to Tasek Park to see the waterfall, or a 35-minute hilly route through Kampong Kianggeh. Joggers are urged to run early in the morning to avoid the heat and traffic.

Dining

Bandar Seri Begawan is not a great place for eating out, although it has a few noteworthy restaurants. Hotel coffee shops are popular with locals as well as visitors. Restaurants close at 10:30 PM. If you enjoy low-cost hawker food, visit the **open-air stalls** near the Edinburgh Bridge and along the river on Jalan Kianggeh, near Jalan Pemancha.

The Heritage. Brunei's finest Western-style restaurant serves French nouvelle cuisine in subdued surroundings, with flowers on the table, modern art on the walls, and waiters in tuxedos. The European chefs offer such standards as prime rib or fantail shrimp, plus an innovative dish or two nightly. *Sheraton Utama Brunei, Jln. Sungai Kianggeh, tel. 44272. Reservations recommended. Jacket required for dinner. AE, DC, MC, V. Expensive.*

Chempaka Cafe. This no-frills coffee shop serves Chinese, Malay, and local dishes. Try the Brunei noodles, which are topped with beef, prawns, and a tangy chili sauce with lime. *Ang's Hotel, Jln. Tasek Lama, tel. 43443. No reservations. Dress: casual. AE, DC, MC, V. Moderate.*

The Grill Room. Located next to the multistory car park, this restaurant with a warm English decor serves huge steaks with french fries, broiled tomatoes, and freshly baked bread. Morning pastries are a treat. *22 Jln. Sultan, tel. 24908. Reservations recommended for dinner. Dress: casual. AE, V. Moderate.*

Mabuhay. Brunei's only Filipino restaurant serves such specialties as chicken adobo, sizzling deer meat, and tiger prawns. The decor is meant to remind you of Manila. *Jln. Gadong, tel. 40538. Reservations recommended. Dress: casual. AE, MC, V. Moderate.*

The Regents Rang Mahel. A cozy room with red tablecloths and a room-length, carved-wood screen, The Regents serves northern Indian cuisine, Muslim-style. Among the specialties are dishes from the tandoori ovens. *Jln. Tutong, tel. 28489. No reservations. Dress: casual. AE, V. Moderate.*

Lodging

Because Brunei is ambivalent toward tourists, accommodations are not plentiful and advance reservations are advised. Apart from the Sheraton, most hotels are plain, clean, and comfortable. All listed here have a private bath, air-conditioning, and a TV in each room.

Sheraton Utama. For many business travelers, this is the *only* place to stay in Brunei. It maintains international standards and its location is convenient. Rooms are well appointed with minibar, refrigerator, and closed-circuit movie channel. *Box 2203, BSB, tel. 44272. 158 rooms. Facilities: business center, pool, 2 restaurants and bar, gift shop. AE, DC, MC, V. Very Expensive.*

Ang's Hotel. The Chinese furniture in the lobby tips you off to the primary clientele of this centrally located, five-story hotel. Rooms were renovated a few years ago and fitted with queen-size beds. Some have kitchens for long-term guests. *Box 49, BSB, tel. 43553. 80 rooms. Facilities: pool, Western-style restaurant, café and pub, business center, beauty salon. AE, DC, MC, V. Expensive.*

6 Philippines

Introduction

by Luis H. Francia

Luis H. Francia was born and raised in Manila. Now a New York resident, he is a poet and playwright, film critic/curator, and a freelance writer for such publications as the Village Voice, Asiaweek, *and the* Far Eastern Economic Review.

Filipinos are often referred to as the "Latins of the East," and indeed this archipelago of 7,100 islands extending between Taiwan to the north and Borneo to the south sometimes seems like a misplaced Latin American country. While the dominant racial stock is Malay—akin to the indigenous populations of Indonesia, Borneo, and Malaysia—people's names are Hispanic and their faith Roman Catholic (the Philippines is the only Christian nation in Asia). To add to this cultural mix, English is widely spoken here, making the Philippines the fourth-largest English-speaking nation in the world after the United States, the United Kingdom, and India. Furthermore, the government is headed by a democratically elected president. These features reflect four centuries of Spanish and American colonization. As a celebrated Filipino writer put it, the Philippines spent more than 300 years in a convent and 50 in Hollywood.

Historically, this cultural potpourri began around the 8th to the 10th century, when the native Malays intermarried with Arab, Indian, and Chinese merchants who came to trade. Then, in 1521, Ferdinand Magellan, landing on the island of Cebu, claimed the country for Spain. The intrepid Portuguese navigator was killed shortly thereafter by Lapu-Lapu, a native chieftain. Spanish rule was uneasy, periodically interrupted by regional revolts that culminated in 1896 in a nationwide revolution, the first of its kind in Asia. Nationalist aspirations were aborted, however, as the United States, after defeating Spain in the Spanish-American War, took over in 1898 but not without a bitter, five-year guerrilla war.

American rule lasted until July 4, 1946, when Manuel Roxas took over as the first postcolonial president. At press time, in spite of political unrest, the freely elected government of Corazon C. Aquino holds office. The administration succeeded 14 years of Ferdinand Marcos's dictatorial rule, from 1972 to 1986, when he was ousted by the bloodless, four-day "People Power" revolution. The country has since had a new constitution and national elections for the revived bicameral legislature.

Because of its colonial history and its people's innate warmth, the Philippines today is a country open to strangers and tolerant of cultural idiosyncrasies. Filipinos are a gregarious, fun-loving people whose hospitality is legendary. "No" is a word frowned upon; a Filipino will find countless ways to decline a request without sounding negative, smoothing over a potentially disruptive moment. Westerners should be aware that insistent straightforwardness is not necessarily prized and can be counterproductive.

Filipinos love to joke and tease and have an innate sense of the absurd. These qualities come in handy in a society full of paradoxes and contradictions, such as Catholic values coexisting with tropical hedonism; a freedom-loving people still contending with such feudal practices as private armies; and poverty amid sunshine and rich natural resources.

A 22-year-old nationwide Communist insurgency—with its roots in agrarian unrest and social injustice—has been compounded by a Muslim secessionist movement in southern Mindanao. However, no Beirut-like scenarios exist here. Ex-

The Philippines

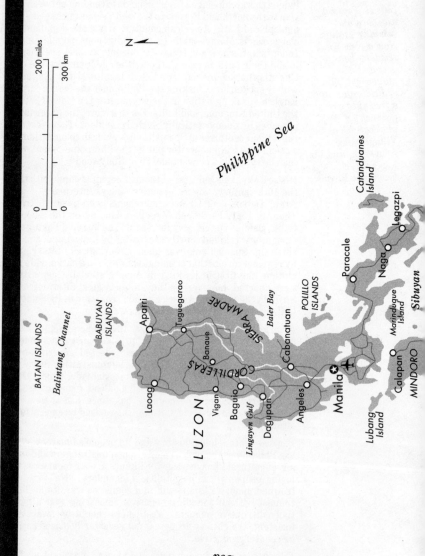

cept for some remote areas, the chances of being caught in a cross fire are virtually nil.

The Philippines, with three island groupings—Luzon (the largest), the Visayas, and Mindanao—has twice the coastline of the continental United States and offers diverse attractions. Luzon has cosmopolitan, historic Metro Manila—with its vibrant nightlife—the breathtaking mountain ranges to the north, and Spanish-era architecture and churches. The Visayas have some of the country's best beaches, charming cities, and music-loving inhabitants, while Mindanao has a number of minority tribes, a sizable Muslim population, and rare flora and fauna. All three regions have warm, translucent seas, inviting tropical beaches, highland treks, and unusual physical features. And the traveler will find in all three that dining well, especially on seafood, is an inexpensive treat.

The Philippines may not have world-class museums or a monumental ruin at every turn, but the outstanding beauty of the land, the many picturesque towns and villages, and the hospitality, music, and gaiety of its people more than compensate.

Staying in the Philippines

Getting Around

By Plane   Philippine Air Lines (PAL), the nation's flag carrier, serves 42 cities and towns in the archipelago. **Manila Domestic Airport** is the country's biggest hub; next is Cebu City's **Mactan International Airport,** used mainly for domestic flights and chartered international flights from Tokyo.

PAL changes its flight schedule every quarter, though the changes don't usually affect major routes. It's always wise to confirm your flight at least two days in advance. The 24-hour PAL reservation line in Manila is 832–3166.

There are smaller, privately owned charter companies, such as **Aerolift** (tel. 817–2361 or 819–4223) and **Pacific Air** (832–2731, 832–2732, or 833–2390). These have regular flights to some cities and resorts, mainly in the south. Both offer light-aircraft and helicopter charters.

By Train   Only Luzon has a railway system, the **Philippine National Railways** (PNR, tel. 210–011), which has seen better days. Lines run to San Fernando in Pampanga Province, north of Manila, and as far south as Iriga, Camarines Sur in the Bicol region. Rail passes are not available, and the upkeep of the carriages leaves much to be desired. Fares are slightly lower than those for bus travel, and trips take longer.

By Bus   The Philippines has an excellent bus system, with 20 major bus lines covering the entire archipelago. Service between major destinations is frequent, often on an hourly basis. This is a cheap way to travel, and it's generally a safe way to get around. It's possible to go island-hopping through a combination of bus and island ferries. These routes are usually limited to islands close together, though today one can get from Manila in Luzon to Davao City in Mindanao, on the Philtranco line, in 44 hours.

Outside Manila, most bus terminals are adjacent to the public markets. In Manila, the most convenient terminals are along the Epifanio de los Santos Highway. Bus companies serving major routes have coaches with or without air-conditioning. The former offer films on videotape, but the quality is hideous. Some of the bigger bus lines are **Philtranco** (tel. 833–5061 to 5064), **Pantranco** (tel. 997–091 to 098), and **Victory Liner,** (tel. 833–0293, 833–5019, or 833–5020).

By Boat Much of the local populace travels by boat, the cheapest way to get from island to island. Rates for a huge, luxurious suite from Manila to Cebu City (a 24-hour trip) are $30 one way per person, while third-class (as economy is referred to in the Philippines) can be as low as $11. The same trip via PAL costs $50 but takes only an hour and five minutes.

Speed, reliability, and safety vary from line to line: The **Negros Navigation** (tel. 272–930), **William** (tel. 219–821), and **Aboitiz** (tel. 217–339) lines generally have well-kept ships and good records. **Sulpicio** (tel. 201–781) and **Gothong** (tel. 213–611) lines have lesser reputations. Possibly the worst maritime disaster in modern history occurred when the Sulpicio Line's *Doña Paz*, with about 4,000 passengers on board (way above the limit), sank in 1987. Most drowned.

By Car
Road Conditions Road conditions vary from excellent, with smooth cement or asphalt highways (generally around metropolitan areas like Manila, Cebu, and Baguio), to bad, where "road" is a euphemism for a dirt track, dusty in the summer and muddy during the rainy season.

While highway signs display speed limits—60 mph maximum and 35 mph minimum—they are not enforced, so on the open road you can go as fast as you dare. Use prudence in populated areas and where children or farm animals are nearby.

Rules of the Road Driving is on the right, and you must be over 25 and have a valid driver's license to rent a car. Here you must drive defensively. This is not a car culture, so driving rules tend to be honored in the breach.

Parking Parking is not a problem, even in congested Manila. In the Tourist Belt and in Makati, there's a P5 fee for parking, collected in advance, with no time limit. Major hotels have free parking for their guests.

Gas A liter costs P10.50.

Breakdowns There are no road-service organizations, but if you do break down, passing motorists and townsfolk will gladly lend a hand.

Telephones

Local Calls Local calls are untimed, except for those made on a pay phone, which costs three 25-centavo coins for the first three minutes or so. For domestic long-distance calls, you'll need to go through an operator by dialing 109 (there are no area codes, though direct dialing is slowly being introduced), on a person-to-person or station-to-station basis.

International Calls A few of the big hotels have direct overseas dialing. Otherwise, dial 108. Whether or not the party is at the other end, a connection fee of about $1 is charged. Overseas rates person-to-person to the United States and the United Kingdom are $12 for the first three minutes and $2.90 for each additional minute; station-to-station, it's $9 for the first three minutes, $2.90 for each additional minute.

Information For directory assistance, dial 114. All operators speak English.

Mail

Postal Rates To most Western countries, stamps are 30¢ for a letter, 20¢ for a postcard, and 25¢ for an aerogram.

Receiving Mail Letters sent to you c/o Poste Restante at the General Post Office in Manila (Plaza Lawton, Manila, tel. 471–411) will be held. Or have your mail addressed to you c/o American Express, Ground Floor, PhilamLife Building, United Nations Avenue, Ermita, Manila.

Currency

The unit of currency is the peso, made up of 100 centavos. Bills come in denominations of P2, P10, P20, P50, and P100. Coins range from 5 centavos to P2. The exchange rate at press time is P21=$1; P34=£1.

What It Will Cost

The Philippines remains a bargain, with low inflation. Predictably, Metropolitan Manila is the most expensive destination. Other urban areas, such as Cebu City in the Visayas and Baguio in northern Luzon, are less expensive, and the surrounding provincial areas are cheapest of all.

Taxes Airport departure tax is P200. Hotels add a 10% service charge (as do most restaurants) and a government tax of 13.7%. Sales tax is 6%.

Sample Prices Cup of instant coffee, 20¢; fresh-brewed native coffee, 25¢–50¢; bottle of beer, 35¢–80¢; Coca-Cola, 20¢; hamburger, $1.50–$2.50; one-mile cab ride, $1.50; double room, $3–$15 budget, $16–$55 moderate, $60–$145 luxury.

Language

The Philippines is an English-speaking country, a legacy of its years as a U.S. colony. Communicating is rarely a problem, either in the cities or in the countryside. A second lingua franca is Pilipino, which is based on the regional language of Tagalog.

Opening and Closing Times

Banks are open 9–4; **supermarkets,** 9:30–7:30; **public markets,** dawn to dusk; **museums,** 9–noon and 1–5.

National Holidays

New Year's Day, Jan. 1; Holy Week, Maundy Thursday through Easter Sunday; Labor Day, May 1; Day of Valor, May 6; Independence Day, June 12; Philippine-American Friendship Day, July 4; All Saints' Day, Nov. 1; Andres Bonifacio Day, Nov. 30; Christmas, Dec. 25; José Rizal Day, Dec. 30. Most shops remain open during holidays, though banks close. Museums vary.

Festivals and Seasonal Events

The most spectacular festivals are in honor of Jesus Christ, either as the Holy Infant (Santo Niño) or the martyred Son of God, and the Virgin Mary.

Jan.: Three orgiastic, dancing-in-the-streets carnivals take place this month: the **Ati-Atihan** (third weekend, Kalibo, Aklan), the **Sinulog** (third weekend, Cebu City), and the **Dinagyang** (last weekend, Iloilo City). In all three, the Holy Infant is the object of veneration. Kalibo's Ati-Atihan, the oldest and most popular, is the noisiest and most crowded, as competing town bands thump enthusiastically night and day. All three cities get crammed to the gills, and plane, ship, and room reservations must be made two or three months in advance. In contrast, on January 9, the **Black Nazarene** procession of the Quiapo district in Manila is a more somber but equally intense show of devotion, as the faithful compete to pull the carriage holding a statue of Christ that is believed to be miraculous.

Late Mar.–early Apr.: Christ's final sufferings are remembered during the last week of Lent, Holy Week. In the provincial towns of Bulacan and Pampanga, in central Luzon, masked and bleeding flagellants atoning for their sins are a common sight in the streets. Small groups of old women and children gather at makeshift altars and chant verses describing Christ's passion. The **Turumba** in Pakil, Laguna (held the second Tuesday and Wednesday after Holy Week) honors Our Lady of Sorrows. Devotees dance through the streets trying to make her smile.

May: All over the country, the **Santacruz de Mayo** commemorates St. Helen's discovery of the Holy Cross in 1324. The celebrations include gay, colorful processions, complete with floats of each town's patron saint, beautifully gowned young women acting as May queens, and local swains dressed in their Sunday best. One of the more unusual Santacruzan feasts is in Lucban, Quezon Province, where multicolored rice wafers, called *kiping*, are shaped into window ornaments, usually in the form of fruits and vegetables.

Sept.: The **Peñafrancia** (third weekend in September) is the biggest festival in the Bicol region, drawing as many as 10,000 spectators to Naga City in southern Luzon. A procession of floats on the river honors the Virgin of Peñafrancia.

Tipping

Tipping is now an accepted practice, and 10% is considered standard for waiters, bellboys, and other hotel and restaurant personnel; many restaurants and hotels tack on a 10% service charge. When there is a service charge, tipping becomes optional, but it is customary to leave loose change. At Ninoy Aquino International Airport, **porters** expect P5 for each piece of luggage (in addition to P5 per piece paid to the porter office). **Hotel doormen** and **bellboys** should get about the same. For **taxi drivers,** P4 is fine for the average 1½-mile ride.

Shopping

The Philippines can yield great bargains if you know what to look for and where. There are handicraft stores all over the country, usually located near the public market in small- to medium-size cities and towns and in shopping centers in such large urban areas as Manila, Cebu, and Baguio. Because Manila is the commercial capital of the country, regional goods are available there, though prices are not usually advantageous. It makes sense to focus on handicrafts special to the region you're visiting, for example: handwoven rattan baskets and backpacks from northern Luzon; handwoven cloth from northern Luzon, Iloilo City, and southern Mindanao; shellcraft from Cebu City and Zamboanga City; handwoven pandan mats with geometric designs from Zamboanga City and Davao City; brassware from southern Mindanao; bamboo furniture from central Luzon; gold and silver jewelry from Baguio City and Bulacan province; and cigars from Baguio City and the Ilocos region.

Bargaining is an accepted and potentially profitable way of shopping in public markets, flea markets, and small, owner-run stores. Department stores and big shopping areas have fixed prices.

VAT   A new VAT tax of 10% is charged by all businesses.

Sports and Beaches

Beaches and Water Sports   The Philippines has an abundance of beaches, from pebble-strewn coastlines and black volcanic stretches to brilliant white expanses. The advantage of being on a tropical archipelago (remember, 7,100 islands!) is that you're never far from the sea.

The tropical waters are ideal for a variety of water sports, from snorkeling to waterskiing. A number of resorts in different regions offer equipment and facilities. Some of the loveliest beaches are on the smaller islands, particularly in the Visayas region, such as Boracay, Sicogon, Iloilo, Bohol, and Cebu. Palawan is possibly the least developed island and the wildest in terms of flora and fauna.

Diving   The country has some of the best dive sites in the world, with more than 40 known spots, most concentrated around Palawan and the Visayas. Many more wait to be discovered. Most resorts rent out snorkeling equipment; the tonier ones have scuba gear as well. Philippine Airlines allows divers an extra 30 kilos free of charge on domestic flights. It will issue a permit card good for two years. For more information, contact the Philippine Commission on Sports Scuba Diving (tel. 585–857 or 503–637).

Golf   There are 26 golf courses in the country, 13 in Luzon alone.

Mountain Climbing/Trekking   The Cordilleras, Mt. Mayon in southern Luzon, and Mt. Apo in Mindanao are all good sites for mountain climbing and trekking. For more information, call the Department of Tourism (tel. 588–358) or PAL Mountaineering Club (tel. 586–712).

Surfing   Surfers have recently discovered the Philippines, though there are still only a handful of surf centers. Most are on the island of Catanduanes off southern Luzon, on the Pacific coast.

Dining

For a discussion of Philippine cooking in general, see the introduction to Manila's Dining section, below. Also, as prices vary

widely from area to area, see the Dining sections of cities and
regions, below, for price charts.

Lodging

Manila and the larger cities offer accommodations ranging from
luxury hotels to Spartan lodgings. The major establishments
routinely add a 10% service charge. All add a government tax of
13.7%.

During the peak season, from October through April, prices
quoted are prices charged. In the off-season, however, some of
the higher-priced hotels in the big cities offer discounts ranging from 30% to 50%. In other regions, prices are firm—and
low anyway.

As prices vary widely from location to location, see the Lodging section of cities and regions, below, for price charts.

Manila

The urban sprawl that is Metropolitan Manila (made up of the
cities of Manila, Makati, Pasay, Quezon, Caloocan, plus 13
towns) is a fascinating, even surreal, combination of modernity
and tradition. In Manila's streets you'll see horse-drawn
calesas, or carriages, alongside sleek Mercedes Benzes, Japanese sedans, passenger buses, and the ubiquitous passenger
jeepneys—usually converted World War II jeeps.

It is also a city of stark contradictions and a microcosm of Philippine society. At the upper end of the scale is Makati, the
country's financial center, with its wide, well-kept boulevards,
high-rise apartment and office buildings, ultramodern shopping centers, and the well-guarded residential walled enclaves
(complete with security guards) of the often fabulously rich. In
contrast to the Makati mansions—whose aesthetics range from
the sublime to the ridiculous—is the large slum of Tondo, dominated by a huge pile of garbage known as "Smoky Mountain"
for the endless burning of trash fires. Here the poor live in cardboard shanties and scavenge for a living.

For all that, the "noble and ever loyal city"—as Manila was described by its Spanish overlords—and its 10 million inhabitants
have a joie de vivre that transcends their day-to-day battles for
survival. The fortuitous blend of Latin and Southeast Asian
temperaments makes for an easygoing atmosphere, where
having fun is as important as doing business. Manilans bear
their burdens with humor and a casual grace. If, like
New Yorkers, they love to complain about their considerable
hardships, it doesn't prevent them from crowding the city's
myriad restaurants, bars, and clubs. The nightlife here
may well be Asia's liveliest. Manila has discotheques, coffeehouses, nightclubs, massage parlors, topless bars, music
lounges, and beer gardens. Certainly its bands—rock, Latin,
or jazz—have the reputation for being the finest in Southeast
Asia.

The city was built by the Spanish conquistadors in 1571 as
Intramuros, a fortified settlement on the ashes of a Malay
town. Manila spread outward over the centuries, so that the
oldest districts are those closest to Intramuros. Yet very few
buildings today attest to the city's antiquity, since it suffered

extensive destruction during World War II. Among the older districts are Ermita and Malate. Fronting Manila Bay, they make up the so-called Tourist Belt because of their central location and the density of hotels, clubs, restaurants, boutiques, and coffee shops.

Like most other Third World cities, Manila has its share of congestion, pollution, haphazard planning, and poverty. But its flamboyance and spontaneity can be insanely marvelous.

Arriving and Departing by Plane

Airports and Airlines Metropolitan Manila is served by the **Manila Domestic Airport** (tel. 832–3566), cheek-by-jowl with **Ninoy Aquino International Airport** (tel. 832–1961). In light traffic, it's a 15-minute ride to Makati's hotels; getting to the Tourist Belt takes 20 minutes to half an hour. The domestic airport is used almost exclusively by **PAL.**

Between the Airport and Downtown

Manila Domestic Airport This is essentially a one-building affair, with cabs lined up on the driveway. Fares to the Tourist Belt will cost about P100; to Makati, P50. These are prearranged prices. If you wish to save, just walk to the busy Domestic Airport Road 6m (20 ft) away and hail a passing cab, which will charge according to the meter.

Ninoy Aquino Airport The major hotels provide shuttles to and from the international airport, so look around for one before using another means of transport.

By Taxi Normally a metered cab ride to Makati should cost no more than $2, and to the Tourist Belt in Manila, $3. But taxi drivers at the airport prefer an agreed-upon price. Some will want payment in dollars. It's best to go to the departure area on the third level and flag a taxi that has just brought in departing passengers.

By Limousine Inquire at the arrival hall booth.

By Car **Hertz, Avis,** and **National** have booths in the arrival area.

By Bus To the right of the airport building at the end of the driveway are stops for public buses, such as the **Love Buses** (tel. 951–203), that pass by the Tourist Belt via Makati. Though inexpensive, they're not recommended if you have a lot of luggage. And expect many stops.

Arriving and Departing by Car, Train, and Bus

By Car The best routes for leaving or entering the city are the Epifanio de los Santos Highway (EDSA), the South Expressway, and the EDSA-North Diversion link. EDSA is the main artery connecting Pasay, Makati, Quezon, and Caloocan. The North Diversion begins in Caloocan, at a junction of EDSA, and leads to points north. The South Expressway originates in Manila, passes through Makati with EDSA as a junction, and leads to points south.

By Train The main terminal, **Tutuban Station** (tel. 210–011), is in the Tondo district of Manila. There is one other station in the Paco district.

By Bus There are about 20 major bus companies in the Philippines and almost as many terminals in Manila. Those closest to downtown Manila and Makati can be found at Plaza Lawton (now called Liwasang Bonifacio, but bus signboards still use "Lawton") and along a portion of EDSA in Pasay City, not far from Taft Avenue.

Some companies: **Philtranco** (EDSA cor. Apelo Cruz St., Pasay City, tel. 833–5061 to 5064); **Victory Liner** (EDSA, Pasay City, tel. 833–0293, 833–5019, or 833–5020); **BLTB** (EDSA, Pasay City, and at Plaza Lawton, tel. 833–5501); **Pantranco** (325 Quezon Blvd. Ext., Quezon City, tel. 997–091 to 098); and **Dangwa** (1600 Dimasalang, Sampaloc, tel. 731–2859). The only way to get tickets is to go to the terminal; you can purchase tickets in advance.

Getting Around

Manila isn't a city for walking, though you can do so within certain areas, particularly in the Tourist Belt and in some parts of Makati. Sidewalks are generally narrow, uneven, and sometimes nonexistent. The tropical sun discourages the kind of walking you can do in Tokyo or Hong Kong anyway. Instead, choose from a vast array of transportation, public and private, from horse-drawn carriages to elevated rail.

By Car Between the frustration and the smoke emissions, the traffic jams in Manila can reduce drivers to tears. If you don't have to drive within the city, don't. Public transportation is plentiful and cheap.

If you do drive, improvisation—such as sudden lane changing—is the rule rather than the exception. Many of the nonarterial roads are narrow and become clogged during morning (7:30–10) and afternoon (3:30–7) rush hours. On the other hand, a car gives you flexibility, parking isn't a problem, and you don't have to deal with cabs whose meters may run faster than a speeding bullet. Some car-rental agencies: **Avis** (tel. 741–0907, 830–2088, or 878–497), **Hertz** (tel. 817–2761, 868–685, or 831–9827), **National** (tel. 818–8667, 815–4508, or 833–0648).

By Elevated Railway The **Light Rail Transit** (LRT, tel. 832–0423) is an elevated, modern railway, with 16 stops on a north–south axis. It's the fastest, cleanest, and safest mode of transport in the city. The southern terminal is at Baclaran in Pasay City, the northern at Monumento in Caloocan City. Most stops are in Manila. Operations commence at 4:30 AM and shut down at 10:30 PM. Fare between any two stations going one way is P4. Each station displays a guide to the routes.

By Bus and Jeepney Public bus and jeepney routes crisscross Metropolitan Manila and, for areas not served by the LRT, are the cheapest way of getting around. The average fare ranges from 10¢ to 25¢. An excellent means of transport is the **Love Bus** (tel. 951–203), a fleet of air-conditioned coaches that make fewer stops than the regular, non-air-conditioned ones. Fares average P8. Buses make sense for longer trips, while jeepneys are best for short ones. For example, a bus is recommended to get to Quezon City from Ermita, but within Ermita, or from one district to the next, take a jeepney. The latter can accommodate 10 to 12 passengers and is perhaps the city's most colorful form of public transport, gaudily decorated and with the driver's favorite English slogan emblazoned in front.

By Taxi Not as cheap as other means of public transport but still cheap; a metered 2-mile cab ride should cost about $2. However, while rates are theoretically standard, a number of cab companies routinely tolerate their drivers' tampering with the meters. **Golden Taxicab** (tel. 596–701) and **Metro Manila Corporation** (tel. 951–203) have a reputation for reliability and honesty. If you feel the fare registered is exorbitant, say so politely. Often the driver will allow you to pay less than what's shown.

Try to take a taxi from the better hotels, where cabs are always waiting. Some hotels have their doormen note down the taxi number, useful in case of problems.

By Limousine The major hotels have limousine service and use mostly Mercedes Benzes. The following car-rental agencies also provide limo service: **Qualitrans** (tel. 832–5114) has a booth at the NAIA and 16 years of experience. It provides service to all points in Luzon and has air-conditioned, spacious, and well-maintained cars and neat, courteous, and prompt drivers. Rates in Manila are $50 for the first three hours and $15 for each additional hour. **Filipino Transport** (tel. 833–9122) provides similar service at somewhat lower rates: in Manila, $60 for eight hours, $7.50 for each additional hour; Outside Manila, rates vary. For instance, Manila to Baguio overnight costs $175, and $60 per additional day. At least 24-hour notice is required.

By Caretela or Calesa Good for short hops within a neighborhood are the horse-drawn carriages called *caretelas* (the larger size) and calesas. They are available mostly in the older neighborhoods, such as Chinatown, and very inexpensive (about P4 per ride).

By Pedicab These motorcycles with attached cabs are found everywhere, and are also good for inexpensive (P1–P2) short hops.

Important Addresses and Numbers

Tourist Information The **Department of Tourism** has a Tourist Information Center on the ground floor of its main offices at the Tourism Building (Agrifina Circle, Rizal Park, Manila, tel. 502–384 or 501–703). Other counters: mezzanine and arrival mall at Ninoy Aquino International Airport (NAIA; tel. 832–2964); Manila Domestic Airport (tel. 832–3566); Nayong Pilipino Reception Unit at the Nayong Pilipino Complex (tel. 832–2367 or 832–3768), Airport Rd., NAIA. The Tourist Security Division (tel. 501–728 or 501–660) can assist in cases of theft, missing luggage, or other untoward incidents.

Embassies **Australia** (16th floor, Bank of the Philippine Islands, cor. Ayala Ave. and Paseo de Roxas, Makati, tel. 817–7911). **Canada** (9th floor, Allied Bank Center, 6754 Ayala Ave., Makati, tel. 815–9536 to 9541). **United Kingdom** (Electra House, 115–117 Esteban St., Makati, (tel. 853–002 to 009). **United States** (1201 Roxas Blvd., Manila, tel. 521–7116).

Emergencies **Manila police,** tel. 599–011 or 594–344; **fire,** tel. 581–176 or 483–734. **Makati police,** tel. 816–0495 or 816–1322; **fire,** tel. 816–2553.

Emergency Rooms **Makati Medical Center** (2 Amorsolo St., cor. De La Rosa, near Ayala Ave., tel. 815–9911 to 9943). **Manila Doctors' Hospital**

(667 United Nations Ave., Ermita, near the UN stop on the LRT, tel. 503–011).

Dental Clinics Call Dr. Juanito Obal, executive director of the Philippine Dental Association (tel. 816–6144), for referrals.

Medical Clinics Call the **Philippine Medical Association** (tel. 974–974 or 992–132) for referrals.

Late-Night Pharmacies **Mercury Drug Store,** a citywide chain, has 24-hour branches in Cubao, Quezon City (tel. 781–746); Quiapo, Plaza Miranda (tel. 401–617); and Guadalupe Commercial Center Makati, (tel. 864–327). **College Pharmacy** (1458 Taft Avenue, tel. 593–683) is also open 24 hours.

English-Language Bookstores **National Book Store** is a chain with 18 outlets. In the Tourist Belt, try the branch at Harrison Plaza (cor. M. Adriatico and Vito Cruz Sts., tel. 572–179); in Makati, try the Quad Arcade at the Makati Commercial Center (tel. 865–766 or 865–771). **Solidaridad** (531 Padre Faura, Ermita, tel. 586–581) is frequented by Manila's literati and offers political, literary, and popular titles.

Travel Agencies In addition to **American Express** (ground floor, PhilamLife Bldg., United Nations Ave., tel. 506–480 or 521–9492) and **Thomas Cook** (Ayala Ave., Makati, tel. 816–3701 or 818–5891), you might try **Baron Travel Corp.** (Pacific Bank Bldg., Ayala Ave., Makati, tel. 817–4926) and **Turismo Filipino** (BF Condominium Bldg., Aduana St., Intramuros, tel. 48–622).

Guided Tours

Orientation The average city tour takes three hours and can be arranged by any of the tour agencies listed above.

Boat Take a 2½-hour sunset-and-moonlight cruise in Manila Bay, arranged by **Windjammer Cruises** (Ramon Magsaysay Ctr., 1680 Roxas Blvd., tel. 502–050, ext. 23). There is also a morning boat tour to Corregidor—the famous World War II battle site and island fortress at the mouth of Manila Bay—offered by **Maglines** (tel. 506–611) on Tuesday, Thursday, and weekends. Boats leave from the dock at Rizal Park at 7:30 AM.

Personal Guides English-, Spanish-, Japanese-, French-, Italian-, German-, Indonesian-, and even Hebrew-speaking guides are available. The Department of Tourism will provide a list. Guides charge P135 for a minimum of two hours, P220 for a three-hour city tour.

Highlights for First-time Visitors

Bamboo Organ (*see* Tour 3)
Coconut Palace (*see* Tour 2)
Intramuros (*see* Tour 1)
Malacañang Palace (*see* Tour 1)
Pagsanjan Falls (*see* Tour 3)
Quiapo Church (*see* Tour 2)
Rizal Park (*see* Tour 1)
Villa Escudero (*see* Tour 3)

Exploring Manila

Orientation Metropolitan Manila is roughly crescent-shape, with Manila Bay and the scenic Roxas Boulevard, which runs along it, forming the western boundary. Forming the eastern border is the Epifanio de los Santos Highway (EDSA). The Pasig River bisects the city into north and south, with the oldest districts, including the ancient walled city of Intramuros, near where the river empties out into Manila Bay.

By using Roxas Boulevard and Taft Avenue as the western and eastern limits, respectively, and Intramuros and Vito Cruz Street as the north and south parameters, a visitor should get a pretty good idea of Ermita and Malate, or the Tourist Belt. On the boulevard are nightclubs, the Cultural Center of the Philippines complex, hotels, restaurants, apartment buildings, the huge Rizal Park, and Intramuros. On Taft Avenue are the LRT, universities, shops, retail stores, and several hospitals. In between are bars and cocktail lounges, the infamous go-go joints (especially on M.H. Del Pilar and A. Mabini streets), massage parlors, coffeehouses, more restaurants and hotels, office buildings, boutiques, and shopping malls.

Numbers in the margin correspond with numbered points of interest on the Manila and Intramuros maps.

Tour 1: Historic Manila

❶ We begin at **Malacañang Palace,** former seat of the Spanish governor-generals and the colonial American administrators. Today it is the official residence of Philippine presidents—the Philippine White House—though Corazon Aquino prefers to live in the guest house, a symbolic gesture meant to disassociate her from the dictatorial Ferdinand Marcos. Now open to the public, Malacañang's colonial Spanish architecture and interior decor are worth seeing, especially the three chandeliers in the reception hall, the beautiful hardwoods used for the grand staircase, the portraits of former presidents, and the exquisite music room. For a touch of contemporary history, visit the bedrooms of Ferdinand and Imelda Marcos. His is rather spare, dominated by a hospital bed and a dialysis machine. Hers is cavernous, with a gargantuan canopied bed, a baby grand piano, and a lounge area. The bedrooms are rather gloomy: The Marcoses feared for their safety and distrusted windows. The basement is where Imelda's infamous horde of shoes can be seen, along with rows and rows of designer dresses, fur coats, and a bulletproof bra. *J.P. Laurel St., tel. 621–321. Admission charge. Open Mon. and Tues. 8:30–11, 1–3, Thurs. and Fri. 8:30–11, noon–3, Sat. 8:30–3. Closed Wed., Sun., holidays.*

❷ A half-hour drive from Malacañang Palace on the other side of the Pasig River is **Paco Park.** At the intersection of San Marcelino and General Luna streets, this petite but beautiful circular park of moss-covered stone—with a picturesque chapel in the middle—was a cemetery until it was declared a national park in 1966. Its two concentric walls served as burial niches for the Spanish elite. No burials have been performed here since 1912. *Tel. 502–011 or 590–956. Admission charge. Open daily 8–5.*

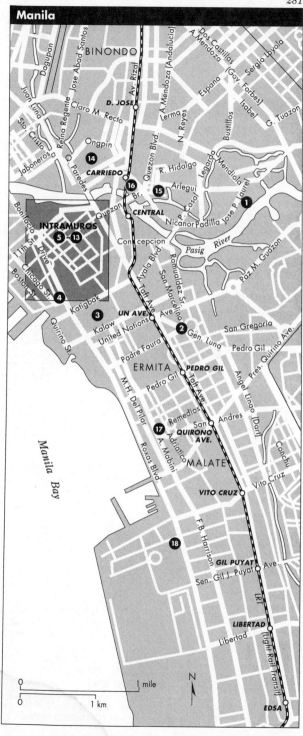

Binondo, **14**
Coconut Palace, **18**
Intramuros, **5-13**
Malacañang Palace, **1**
Malate Church, **17**
Manila Hotel, **4**
Paco Park, **2**
Quiapo Church, **15**
Quiapo Public Market, **16**
Rizal Park, **3**

③ West of Paco Park and 30 minutes away by foot is **Rizal Park,** named after the national hero José Rizal. He was, among other things, a doctor, linguist, botanist, novelist, poet, educator, and fencer. Executed by the Spanish in 1896 because of his reformist views, he was originally buried at Paco Park but now lies under the Rizal Monument, designed by Swiss artist Richard Kissling and erected in 1912. Rising above the statue is a stately 50-foot obelisk. The 24-hour guards, like honor guards everywhere, try to be as impassive as possible. A nearby marble slab set into an octagonal wall is inscribed with Rizal's poem *Mi Ultimo Adios*, composed just before his death, in the original Spanish and in several other languages including English.

④ A short stroll from the monument is the doyen of Philippine hotels, the **Manila Hotel** (Rizal Park, tel. 470–011), built in 1912. This is where General Douglas MacArthur lived during much of the American colonial era (Ernest Hemingway also stayed here once). The lobby is spacious without making you feel lost, and gracious in that Old World style. Note the ceiling and woodwork, made entirely of precious Philippine hardwoods, the floors of Philippine marble, and the mother-of-pearl and brass chandeliers.

Time Out The hotel's coffee shop, **Cafe Ylang Ylang** (tel. 470–011) has an excellent buffet for about $10, complete with soup to seafood to dessert.

⑤ Across from the hotel is **Intramuros,** Manila's ancient walled city. Built by the Spaniards in the 16th century on the site of a former Malay settlement, Intramuros is a compact 3 sq. mi. Within were churches, schools, convents, offices, and residences. In its heyday it presented a magnificent sight to visiting galleons. The walls are still formidable, 9m (30 ft) thick, with cannon emplacements and a strategic location facing the bay. It had seven drawbridges and an encircling moat, filled in by the Americans and now used as a golf course.

Exploring Intramuros on foot should take about 2½ hours. Or you can rent a caretela for about $5 to take you around. Key **⑥** points to see are **Fort Santiago,** off Aduana Street, a stone fort used by the Spanish, Americans, and Japanese and now a **⑦** pleasant park good for promenades; **Plaza Roma** where bull-**⑧** fights were once staged; and the Romanesque **Manila Cathedral** (a reconstruction of the original 1600 structure). Three arched doorways form an imposing facade: The middle one is made of bronze, with eight panels portraying the cathedral's history. Inside, the clerestory's stained-glass windows depict the history of Christianity in the Philippines. Underneath the main altar is a crypt where the remains of the former archbishops are en-**⑨** tombed. On General Luna Street is **San Agustin Church,** the second-oldest stone church in the country, with 14 side chapels and a trompe l'oeil ceiling. Up in the choir loft, note the hand-carved 17th-century seats of molave, a beautiful tropical hardwood. Adjacent to the church is a small museum run by the Augustinian Order, featuring antique religious vestments and religious paintings and icons.

Time Out Across from San Agustin is the **Barrio San Luis Complex,**
⑩ which houses the restaurant **Muralla.** The place has a good but

Barrio San Luis
Complex, **10**
Casa Manila, **11**
Fort Santiago, **6**
Manila Cathedral, **8**
Plaza Roma, **7**
Puerta Isabel, **12**
Puerta Real, **13**
San Agustin Church, **9**

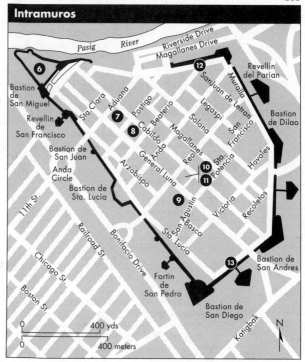

limited Philippine menu; the period furniture and waiters
dressed in *barong Tagalog* (the traditional long-sleeved blouson
worn as formal attire) are perfectly in keeping with the history
that surrounds you.

⑪ In the complex also are several shops and the splendid **Casa Manila,** a re-creation of a 19th-century Spanish patrician's three-
story domicile, complete with carriage entrance, inner courtyard, and grand stairway.

Be sure to explore the walls and the fortified gates—the
⑫ **Puerta Isabel,** whose chambers house a display of baroque
⑬ floats bearing statues of saints, and the **Puerta Real,** are fine
examples—or you'll miss what makes Intramuros Intramuros.
Gray, stately, defiant, the walls give you a feeling of invincibili-
ty. *Tel. for Intramuros: 487–325 or 461–195. Admission free to
Puerto Isabel. Casa Manila, tel. 496–793 or 487–754. Admission: P10, P5 students. Open Tues.–Sun. 9–6.*

Tour 2: Colorful Neighborhoods and a Palace

Forbidden by the Spanish from living in Intramuros, Chinese
merchants and their families settled north of the Pasig River,
⑭ and a sizable community—now known as **Binondo,** Manila's
Chinatown—grew up here in the 18th century. Bounded by the
river, Claro M. Recto Avenue, Del Pan Street, and Avenida
Rizal, the district is a jumble of narrow streets packed with
jewelry shops, sporting-goods and clothing stores, apothecar-
ies, kung fu schools, movie houses showing Hong Kong flicks,

magazine stalls, seedy hotels, brothels, and restaurants that usually offer Amoy and Fukienese cuisine. The thing here is simply to stroll about, especially on Ongpin, the main street. Or, if you wish, stop a calesa and have the driver take you around.

West of Binondo, not far from the foot of Quezon Bridge and fronted by Plaza Miranda, is **Quiapo Church**. The church (built in the 16th century and later enlarged) and its crowded environs are as close to an authentic Philippine neighborhood as you can get in Manila. The church is home to the famed **Black Nazarene,** a dark statue of Jesus of Nazareth made by a Mexican craftsman and brought from Mexico in the 18th century. Its devotees claim that praying to the statue can produce miracles. It isn't unusual to see supplicants crawling on their knees from the entrance to the altar.

In Plaza Miranda, orators of varying skills and persuasions harangue passersby. Toward Quezon Bridge and the river is the **Quiapo Public Market.** Here, especially in the sections below Quezon Bridge, one can find handicrafts, from handwoven mats to rattan baskets and straw brooms, at bargain prices.

Moving south across the river and into the **Malate** district, you'll come to **Malate Church,** on the corner of Remedios and M.H. Del Pilar streets. The gray stone church is an intriguing mixture of Romanesque and Baroque styles. Photographers love to shoot its picturesque and well-kept facade. Its interior, however, is unremarkable. Between the church and Roxas Boulevard is **Rajah Sulayman Park,** whose centerpiece is a statue of Rajah Sulayman, a pre-Spanish (16th-century) ruler of Manila.

Time Out   Around Malate Church you'll find innumerable places for lunch. You can walk on Remedios Street, flanking Malate Church, eastward—i.e., away from the bay—and choose from several cafés around Remedios Circle. **Cafe Adriatico** (1790 Adriatico St., tel. 584–059) serves good hamburgers and Continental or Philippine entrées. **Penguin Cafe** (Remedios St., cor. Bocobo St., tel. 521–2088) has a nice outdoor patio and serves homemade pasta, salads, and Viennese-style desserts. The 24-hour **Aristocrat** (Roxas Blvd., cor. San Andres St., tel. 507–671) is a popular choice with everyone from gangsters to businessmen; prices are reasonable and the food is decent.

A 10-minute drive from the church south on Roxas Boulevard is a $10 million project of former first lady Imelda Marcos, the **Coconut Palace,** so named because more than 70% of the construction materials were derived from the coconut tree. This grandiose structure, located within the Cultural Center Complex, faces Manila Bay and was constructed for Pope John Paul's visit in 1981 (he refused to stay there). Each of the seven (the Marcoses' lucky number) palatial suites is named and styled after a different region of the country. The Ilocos Room, for instance, has chairs with mother-of-pearl inlay and a coffee table laminated with tobacco leaves, while the Zamboanga Room features brassware and hand-woven mats. Many of the bathroom fixtures are 24-karat gold. Several of Imelda's jet-set friends stayed here at one time or another, among them Van Cliburn, Cristina Ford, and Brooke Shields. *Cultural Center*

*Complex, tel. 832–0223. Admission charge. Open Tues.–Sun.
9–11:30 and 1–4:30.*

Short Excursions from Manila

Tagaytay Ridge and the Bamboo Organ
A 60-km (37 mi) drive that begins on the South Expressway and takes you along tree- and flower-lined roads, with rice fields on either side, brings you to Tagaytay Ridge, 750 m (2,500 ft) above sea level. Here you can view what may be the world's smallest volcano, Taal Volcano, actually a volcano within a volcano. With cool temperatures and scenic vistas, Tagaytay provides welcome relief from Manila's heat and congestion. On the way you may want to detour to Las Piñas to view the world's only bamboo organ, housed in the 18th-century San José Church. The organ, built in 1795, has 121 metal pipes, 832 bamboo pipes, 22 registers, and a five-octave manual.

To get to San José Church, go south on Roxas Boulevard, turn left on Airport Road, turn right on Quirino Avenue, and continue until you get to Las Piñas. For Tagaytay, backtrack to Roxas, go north, turn right after Baclaran Church on to Redemptorist Road. This will take you to EDSA. Take the South Expressway, and get off at the Carmona exit. From there, clearly marked signs will take you to Tagaytay.

Pagsanjan Falls
About an hour and a half southeast of Manila, the town of Pagsanjan was used by Hollywood director Francis Ford Coppola for his epic film *Apocalypse Now* (the older residents complain the town hasn't been the same since). It is known for its river rapids and the numerous waterfalls that empty into the Magdapio River, with the last, the Magdapio Falls, cascading from a height of about 30 m (100 ft). Visitors begin downstream, in small boats guided through the rapids by skillful oarsmen. A raft trip under the Magdapio Falls into a cave caps off the ride. It's exhilarating, and it also offers a glimpse of rural life: villagers bathing and laundering in the river, and an occasional water buffalo (*carabao* in Pilipino) cooling off. Be sure to dress appropriately, and wrap your camera and watch in plastic. Life preservers aren't provided, so you might want to think twice about bringing children along. The round-trip takes 2½–3 hours. The fee is $5 per passenger when two are in a boat or $10 for a single passenger. The boatmen expect to be tipped, and they generally get about $2.50 each. To get to Pagsanjan, take the South Expressway to the end, then turn left to Calamba (there will be signs). Turn right at the first major intersection. There are signs indicating the way to Pagsanjan.

Villa Escudero
If the sight of smiling children in traditional dress serenading you with native instruments doesn't warm your heart, nothing will. These friendly kids greet visitors to Villa Escudero, a working 1,600-acre rice-and-coconut plantation with its own river and man-made falls, only a 90-minute drive from Manila. After being serenaded you can explore the **Escudero Museum,** with an eclectic and colorful collection that includes war memorabilia (such as cannons and tanks, which children always seem to enjoy), antique religious artifacts and altars, paintings, stuffed animals, and celadon. Once you're through, you can tour the plantation on a water buffalo–drawn cart and see demonstrations of coconut harvesting. There's a river for swimming

and fishing afterward. A buffet lunch is served at the base of a man-made waterfall, where tables are set in the shallows. *Admission charge.*

To drive to Villa Escudero, start on the South Expressway and go all the way to the end. Turn right toward Lucena City, and bear left at the Santo Tomás intersection. You will be on the road to San Pablo City, passing through Alaminos. As soon as you approach the archway signaling the end of Laguna Province and the start of Quezon Province (where Villa Escudero is), slow down. The entrance to Villa Escudero is immediately after the archway, on your left.

What to See and Do with Children

Manila Zoo. This small zoo in the Tourist Belt has the usual assortment of wild animals, including local species such as the tamaraw (a peculiar water buffalo), the rare mouse deer, and the Palawan pheasant. *Quirino Ave., cor. Adriatico St., tel. 586–216. Admission charge. Open daily 7 AM–6 PM.*

Matorco Ride. This is a scenic drive by Manila Bay in open-air, double-decker buses on Roxas Boulevard that starts and ends at the Rizal Monument. *Tel. 597–177 or 711–1585. Admission: P3 one-way. Buses run late afternoon–10 PM.*

Off the Beaten Track

A ride on the LRT. The Light Rail Transit (LRT) is an excellent means of getting city views beyond the usual tourist sights. For only P4, you can take in the heart of Manila. Begin at the Baclaran Terminal, not far from Baclaran Church, which is packed with devotees for special services every Wednesday. From Baclaran, there are 15 stops; a round-trip takes about 1¼ hours. You pass through congested neighborhoods and can often peer into offices, apartments, and backyards. Keep an eye out for the remarkable Chinese Cemetery near the Abad Santos stop. The mausoleums are virtual mansions with ornate, pagoda-style architecture, a reminder that wealth makes a difference even in death. At the last stop, Monumento, walk a short distance to the monument marking the spot where Filipino revolutionaries began the struggle against Spain. *LRT hours: 4:30 AM–10:30 PM.*

The Tabacalera Tour. La Flor de Isabela, Companía General de Tabacos de Filipinas (Flower of Isabela, General Company of Philippine Tobacco), with a well-deserved reputation for fine cigars, will show visitors the time-honored process of making a cigar. Cigars and humidors can be purchased and even personalized. Call the factory in advance for a free tour. *936 Romualdez St., cor. United Nations Ave., tel. 508–026, loc. 273 or 274. Open Sun.–Fri. 8–5.*

Cockfights. This national pastime, in which two cocks equipped with razor-sharp spurs fight to the death, can involve betting sums ranging from the petty to the astronomical. A fight can last less than a minute if uneven, longer if the combatants are well-matched. This is obviously not for animal lovers. Sometimes the winner may be barely alive at the end and will wind up, like the loser, on the owner's dinner table. The prefight ceremonies are fascinating: Odds makers patrol the noisy and often cigarette smoke–filled cockpit taking bets, and handlers prepare their feathered charges with time-honored methods.

In the metropolitan area, cockfights are usually held on Sunday. The big arenas are La Loma Cockpit (68 Calavite St., tel. 731–2023) and the Pasay Arena (Dolores St., Pasay City, tel. 861–746).

Shopping

Manila, as the nerve center of the country, has all the shopping options, from sidewalk vendors and small retail stores to market districts and shopping centers. Both local and foreign goods are readily available in different precincts of the city.

Nothing beats shopping in the market districts for color, bustle, and bargains—in a word, for atmosphere. Here haggling is raised to a fine art. Located in the older areas of the city, each encompasses several blocks and is a neighborhood unto itself. Crowds can be intense, and as in any urban area, they include pickpockets. Don't be paranoid, just alert. Shopping malls, on the other hand, are found in relatively newer areas, such as Makati's commercial center, and in Quezon City. The malls are better-organized and easier to get to, making up in convenience what they lack in charm. Prices are fixed here, so bargaining is pointless.

Market Districts
Divisoria   North of Binondo, this is the largest district, with everything from fresh produce, fruit, and cooking utensils to hardware, leather goods, and handicrafts. Savvy Manilans and bargain hunters come to browse among the assorted stalls, emporia, and department stores until they see what they want at the right price.

Baclaran   On Roxas Boulevard near Baclaran Church, the many stalls here specialize in ready-to-wear. Prices are supposedly lowest on Wednesday, when the weekly devotions to Our Lady of Perpetual Help are held at the church. The disadvantages of Wednesday shopping are the crowds and worse-than-usual traffic jams.

San Andres Market   In the Tourist Belt, this market is noted for its tropical and imported fruits. Bright and neatly arranged, the piles of mangoes, watermelons, custard apples, and jackfruit are above average. It's pricey, but you can bargain.

Shopping Malls
Pistang Pilipino   Innumerable stalls here sell all types of Philippine handicrafts, from woven rattan baskets and woodcraft to brassware, shellcraft, and tribal clothing and jewelry. If you're traveling to other parts of the country, it might be a good idea to look at that region's goods here to get an idea of what's available and the price range. Crafts are bound to be cheaper in their region of origin. And you can always come back once you return to Manila. *Ermita, M.H. Del Pilar St., cor. Pedro Gil. Open daily 8–8.*

Harrison Plaza   This huge center has department stores, supermarkets, jewelers, drugstores, boutiques, record and electronics shops, video rentals, restaurants and snack bars, and four movie houses. *In the Tourist Belt, adjacent to the Century Park Sheraton, on Adriatico and Vito Cruz Sts. Opening hours vary, but all*

*shops close at 7:30 PM, except the fast-food shops, which are
open till 8:30.*

Shopping Centers
*Makati Commercial
Center*

Bounded by Makati Avenue on the west, Ayala Avenue on the
north, Epifanio de los Santos Highway on the east, and Pasay
Road on the south, this is the biggest such center in the country, including several shopping malls and such gigantic
department stores as Shoemart and Landmark, two hotels,
sports shops, money changers, etc. There are small plazas
where the weary can rest and watch humanity stream by. For a
good ice-cream parlor, try Magnolia's Dairy Bar, right beside
the Quad movie theaters and not far from the Manila Garden
Hotel. And for a Spanish-style *merienda*, or snack, try Dulcin-
ea in the arcade right near the corner of Makati and Ayala
avenues. *Opening hours vary, but most shops close at 8 PM.
Restaurants close at 10.*

Specialty Stores

For antiques and small handicraft stores, a good street for
shopping is A. Mabini in the Tourist Belt. Some of the more
reputable stores are: **Bauzon Antiques** (1219 A. Mabini, tel.
504–542), **Goslani's** (1571 A. Mabini, tel. 507–338), **Terry's Antiques** (1401 A. Mabini, tel. 588–020), **Tesoro's** (1325 A. Mabini,
tel. 503–931), and **Via Antica** (1411 A. Mabini, tel. 507–726).

Sports and Fitness

Golf

Golf courses in the metropolitan area open to the public include
Capitol Hills Golf Club, Quezon City, 18 holes (tel. 883–402);
Intramuros Golf Club, Intramuros, 18 holes, right beside the
historic walls of Intramuros (tel. 478–470); and **Puerto Azul
Beach and Country Club,** Ternate, Cavite, a championship 18-
hole course in a tropical resort by the sea and a 45-minute drive
from Manila (tel. 815–3993 or 815–3999).

Jogging

The best places to go jogging in the city are in the Tourist Belt
along Roxas Boulevard, by the sea wall; in Rizal Park; and on
the grounds of the Cultural Center Complex.

Swimming

All the major hotels have swimming pools open to nonguests for
a fee. Other public pools are at **Pope Pius X Catholic Center**
(United Nations Ave., Ermita, tel. 573–806 or 590–484) and
Rizal Memorial Sports Complex (Vito Cruz St., Malate, tel.
509–556, 585–909, or 582–136).

Tennis

The city's numerous tennis courts include **Club Intramuros**
(Intramuros, tel. 477–754), **Philippine Plaza Hotel** (Cultural
Center Complex, tel. 832–0701), **Rizal Memorial Stadium** (Vito
Cruz St., Malate, tel. 583–513), and **Velayo Sports Center** (Do-
mestic Airport Rd., tel. 832–2316).

Spectator Sports

Basketball

Basketball is the Philippines' premier sport, an enduring legacy of the American colonial era. Tournaments are held by the
professional Philippine Basketball Association (tel. 872–720)
as well as by the NCAA, the University Athletic Association of
the Philippines (UAAP), and the Philippine Amateur Basketball League (PABL). The major courts are at the Ultra Center
in the town of Pasig and at Rizal Coliseum in Malate.

Cockfights

See Off the Beaten Track, above.

Horse Racing There are two tracks, the Santa Ana Race Track (tel. 879–951) and the San Lazaro Hippodrome (tel. 711–125), with races on Tuesday and Wednesday evenings and Saturday and Sunday afternoons.

Beaches

In spite of its magnificent bay, Manila has no beaches to speak of. There are, however, several beach areas from 1½ to 5 hours' drive from the city.

Puerto Galera Located on the nearby island of Mindoro, five hours away by bus and ferry, this is very popular with Western travelers, especially single men, many of whom bring along bar girls (*see* Nightlife, below). At times the scene here is overly commercial and crowded, but the approach by ferry is beautiful, with coconut-tree-lined shores and dramatic inlets. There are about six beach areas; La Laguna, Talipanan, and White Beach are best for swimming and snorkeling along the small reefs. Accommodations in general are basic, with prices for cottages ranging from $3.50 to $15 per day.

Hundred Islands North of Manila on the west coast of Luzon, this aggregate of small islands (the largest being Governor's and Quezon)—part of the Hundred Islands National Park—has good to spectacular beaches and some good snorkeling. There are no commercial establishments, so bring food and refreshments. Some of the islands have no shade, and some have snakes; the boatmen will know which ones are which. You board boats in the town of Lucap, a 4½-hour drive from Manila.

Dining

by Reynaldo G. Alejandro

Reynaldo Alejandro is a chef, cooking teacher, and author of several books, including The Philippine Cookbook.

Philippine cooking, declared a visiting writer, "has a unique and intriguing personality that can surprise a stranger without stunning him." There's a good reason for this mix of the exotic and the familiar: Centuries of interaction with other cultures brought a wide range of foreign influences—not least on the local food. The Malay settlers, Chinese traders, and Spanish and American colonists all left their mark on Philippine cuisine.

The early Filipinos used simple cooking methods: open-fire broiling, boiling, and roasting. Two beloved native dishes are direct descendants of this Malay heritage. *Adobo* is chunks of chicken and pork marinated in palm vinegar, crushed garlic, bay leaves, salt, and peppercorns, then broiled, grilled, or—the preferred method—boiled. In *sinigang*, a lightly boiled dish of shellfish, meat, or vegetables, the distinctive sour taste is provided by tomatoes, lime juice, and tamarind.

Two other national favorites with a strong Malay flavor are *kare-kare*, a vegetable stew with oxtail, pig's legs, beef, or tripe with a sauce of crushed peanuts and ground toasted rice; and *guinataan*—vegetables, pork, or chicken cooked in coconut milk.

A must at every fiesta, *lechon*, or roast suckling pig, is one of the many Chinese legacies on the Philippine menu. It's served with a variety of sauces, of which liver may be the most opulent.

Of course the Chinese also brought the egg roll. Its Philippine version, the *lumpia*, dipped in soy sauce, vinegar, and garlic, is sometimes sprinkled with powdered peanuts. And native cooks adopted the Chinese noodle so thoroughly that almost no region is without a *pansit* of its own.

Rice, that Asian staple, is ubiquitous—but in the Philippines it is also ground into flour and baked into a variety of unusual sweets. *Bibingka* is a delicacy no visitor should miss: A rice-flour cake made with coconut milk, sugar, and eggs, it's baked in a clay oven over charcoal and topped with fresh grated coconut, salted duck's egg, or native white cheese.

When the Spanish arrived in 1521, they brought standard fare whose Eastern adaptations are now considered among the best dishes in Asia. The rice-based *paella* evolved into a native specialty, and chicken *relleño*—a whole chicken stuffed with boiled eggs, pork, sausage, and spices—is popular for special occasions. Many restaurant menus feature *cocido*, a boiled stew of meat and vegetables, and *callos*, a rich combination of meat, chicken, sausage, and vegetables.

Spain ceded the islands to the United States in 1898, and sandwiches, salads, and new desserts arrived with the Americans. Thus, you will see fried chicken on so many menus—but Philippine-style: marinated in soy sauce, lemon or vinegar, and garlic.

Regional specialties tend to reflect outside influences, too. The spicy dishes of the Bicol region owe their bite to the neighboring Indian and Muslim cuisines, which favor chilis and other hot seasonings. In fact, the diet of Philippine Muslims in the south is similar to Sumatran cooking—with the addition of such local delicacies as turtle eggs. Try the Bicol *pinangat*, chopped taro-type leaves cooked with coconut milk, ginger, onion, garlic, and chili and flavored with *bagoong*, a salty paste made of brine-fermented shrimp and fish. (This sauce shows up in the north, too, where the Ilokanos prize their pungent *pinakbet*—the Philippine interpretation of ratatouille, liberally doused with bagoong.)

Finally, the food of the Pampanga and Tagalog provinces will remind you of nouvelle cuisine: light, simple dishes based on fresh ingredients. Tomatoes, vinegar, tamarind, the cucumberlike *kamias*, and the lime-flavored *calamansi* fruit are generously used, for a cool, sweet-and-sour bouquet.

Every nuance of Philippine cooking can be sampled in Manila, so you can have an exciting culinary adventure without leaving the capital. As in every other city and town, turo-turo flourish here, and they may be the best sources of traditional food. Some are stationary kiosks at marketplaces, bus stops, schools, and other crowded locales, luring passers-by with *puto* (sweet rice cakes), *taho* (mashed bean curd with caramel), *tocino* (cured beef, eaten for breakfast like bacon), *turon* (a banana fritter), *lugao* (rice porridge), pansit, or a hearty adobo for lunch or dinner.

As anywhere else, trends come and go: One innovation of the 1970s, *kamayan* dining, popularized the habit of eating with one's fingers. Filipinos like the style because it reminds them of fiestas; foreigners like it because it reminds them of picnics. Food is served on wood plates covered with banana leaves, which give the homely practice a certain chic.

While reservations are recommended in many restaurants, most operate on a first-come, first-served basis. During holidays or conventions, book in advance. Dress is rarely formal: Jackets or *barong*, the traditional shirt, suffice for men even in the most expensive establishments. Lunch hours are normally noon to 2:30, dinner from 8 to 10:30. Restaurants in Manila apply a 4.2% tax on food and an 8.7% tax on alcoholic beverages. Finally, most restaurants do not add a service charge, so expect to leave a 10%–15% tip.

Highly recommended restaurants are indicated by a star ★.

Category	Cost*
Very Expensive	over P400 ($20)
Expensive	P240–P400 ($12–$20)
Moderate	P120–P240 ($6–$12)
Inexpensive	under P120 ($6)

per person without tax, service, or drinks

Very Expensive

★ **Maynila.** This four-level restaurant boasts stained-glass windows and a hand-painted ceiling some 12m (40 ft) high. A stunning chandelier made of shells and "twinkle stars" that appear behind the French windows add to the nighttime elegance. The world-renowned Bayanihan Dance Troupe provides entertainment. The Likha menu is a collection of nouvelle Philippine dishes, including *manok sa biringhe,* an oven-roasted boneless squab seasoned with coconut cream and garnished with leeks. The *lomo basilan*—tenderloin stuffed with lobster, mushrooms, and native cheese—is a standout. *Manila Hotel, Rizal Park, Manila, tel. 470–011, loc. 1358 or 1360. Reservations suggested. Jacket or barong required. AE, DC, MC, V. Closed Sun.*

Prince Albert Rotisserie. The repertoire of French and Continental grilled meat and seafood here includes *endouillette de lapu-lapu*—scallops, prawns, and mussels in a honey-and-orange sauce—and lamb fillet with goat cheese, hazelnuts, and chives. The setting is plush Victorian, accented with an opulent colored-glass ceiling, royal burgundy colors, and a copper kitchen. *Hotel Inter-Continental Manila, 1 Ayala Ave., Makati, Metro Manila, tel. 815–9711, loc. 7247. Reservations advised. Jacket or barong recommended. AE, DC, MC, V. No lunch weekends.*

Expensive **Patio Guernica.** One of three restaurants owned by an art collector and his German-born wife, this former Opus Dei study center is decorated with fine wood paneling and wrought-iron grills, reminiscent of turn-of-the-century architecture. On the ground floor, once a chapel, a small tabernacle with an ornate door is still visible. A favorite dish from the Spanish-food menu is steak à la Pobre (smoldered in olive oil and topped liberally with fried minced garlic), first introduced by chefs in the 1950s. Strolling musicians serenade diners. *1856 J. Bocobo St., Remedios Circle, Malate, Manila, tel. 521–4415, 521–4417, or 581–228. Reservations advised. Dress: casual. AE, DC, MC, V. Closed Good Fri. No lunch Sun. or holidays.*

Peacock Restaurant. The original Peacock introduced its esteemed clientele to Peking duck and succulent Cantonese fare.

Manila Dining and Lodging

Dining

Aling Asiang Specialty Restaurant, **14**

Aristocrat Restaurant, **8**

Bistro Remedios, **6**

Flavours and Spices, **13**

Gene's Bistro, **21**

Kamayan Restaurant, **12**

The Landmark Food Center, **15**

Maynila, **1**

Patio Guernica, **5**

Peacock Restaurant, **9**

Prince Albert Rotisserie, **17**

Sea Food Market and Restaurant, **20**

Tempura-Misono, **11**

Lodging

Admiral Hotel, **7**

Century Park Sheraton, **9**

Malate Pension, **4**

Mandarin Oriental, **19**

Manila Hotel, **1**

Manila Midtown Hotel, **3**

Manila Peninsula, **18**

Nikko Manila Garden, **16**

Philippine Plaza, **10**

Pope Pius XII Catholic Center, **2**

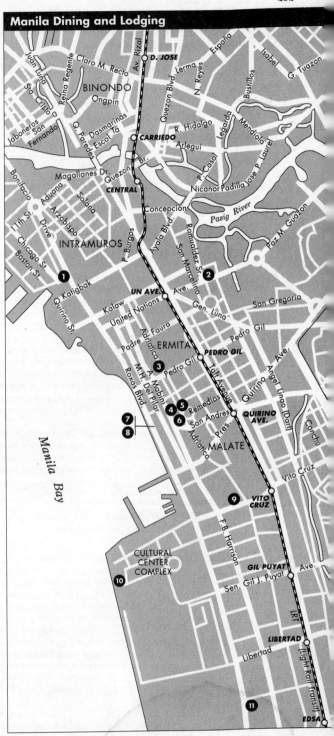

The restaurant now has three branches: at the Century Park Sheraton, in Greenhills, and at the Makati Greenbelt Center. The largest branch, in Greenhills, boasts a rich Oriental setting, created by cool chartreuse tones, Chinese crafts, and paintings. Dividers allow for privacy. The other locations have similar decor. *Front Row Junction, Greenhills Shopping Ctr., San Juan, Rizal, Metro Manila, tel. 775–317 or 775–324. Century Park-Sheraton, Vito Cruz, Manila, tel. 582–228. Greenbelt, Makati, Metro Manila, tel. 857–352 or 857–370. For all: Reservations advised. Jacket or barong required. AE, DC, MC, V. Closed holidays.*

★ **Sea Food Market and Restaurant.** Get a cart, shop for your ingredients, and the cooks will prepare them in this bright, open setting. The Makati branch is four times the size of the Ermita location, and both are very popular. Notable dishes from an international menu include steamed lapu-lapu with soy sauce, coconut crab with chili sauce, lobster salad, and mixed vegetables with oyster sauce. *7829 Makati Ave., Makati, Metro Manila, tel. 815–4237, 850–361, and 862–107; 1190 J. Bocobo St., Ermita, Manila, tel. 521–4351 or 505–761. Reservations required. Dress: casual. AE, DC, MC, V.*

Tempura-Misono. The designers here took the Japanese reverence for nature seriously. The ambience is traditionally Japanese, with a carp pool, bamboo, and sand art. A sushi bar, a teppanyaki area, and private dining rooms complete the effect. Manager Albert Seeland is famous for his highly colored, refreshing drinks, for his piquant chicken wings (made with vinegar, mirin wine, sugar, and spring onions), and for two beautifully served menu creations: Pandora's Box is beef amiyaki, abalone mushrooms, jumbo prawns, and bean sprouts in a maroon-black lacquer box. Love Boat is steak, shrimp tempura, oysters, abalone mushrooms, and bean sprouts served in a lacquer Japanese boat. *2702 Roxas Blvd., Pasay, Metro Manila, tel. 831–2611, loc. 8184 or 8139. Reservations advised. Dress: casual. AE, DC, MC, V.*

Moderate **Aling Asiang Specialty Restaurant.** Philippine fare is prepared with care and presented with élan in a sumptuous beige-and-salmon interior accented by etched glass and hanging leaves and rattan. Blue marlin bellies, charcoal-broiled tuna jaw, and chicken in yams are among the specialties. *Merienda*—a mid-morning or mid-afternoon repast—is served here. *Plaza Bldg., Greenbelt Center, Makati, Metro Manila, tel. 819–0006 or 817–2207. Reservations suggested. Dress: casual. AE. Closed Good Fri.*

Bistro Remedios. Philippine regional cooking is presented here in an understated setting accented with artifacts and paintings of Philippine landscapes. A favorite hangout for the food cognoscenti and literary circle, this restaurant serves pork knuckles fried in garlic sauce and deep-fried frogs stuffed with minced pork and spices. *1903 Adriatico St., cor. Remedios St., Malate, Manila, tel. 521–8097. Reservations suggested. Dress: casual. AE, CB, DC, MC, V. No lunch on Sun.*

Flavours and Spices. Originally an exotic-spice store, this casual Thai eatery can now accommodate 88—the "lucky number" of owner Add Lim. At one end of the soft green room, accented with Thai objets d'art, shelves are stacked with bottles of aromatic spices, bundles of garlic, chilis, and other condiments flown in from Bangkok. The authenticity of the food is attested to by the daily presence of Thai embassy officials. Exquisite dishes are delightfully flavored with lemongrass and spices, some cooked with fresh coconut milk. A specialty is *tom khagai*—chicken soup with ginger, lemongrass, tomatoes, and coconut milk. *Garden Sq., Greenbelt Commercial Center, Makati, Metro Manila, tel. 815–3029 or 819–1375. Reservations advised. Dress: casual. AE, DC, MC, V.*

★ **Kamayan Restaurant.** Set in an antique Philippine house with wood tables, narra chairs (narra is a smooth, hard Philippine wood), and waiters in traditional Philippine garb, this restaurant is named for the practice of eating with one's bare hands. Your food arrives on wood plates garnished with banana leaves, and you take it from there. Try the whole roast suckling pig; *asadong alimango*, crab sautéed in oil with its roe, onion, and garlic; and *kinulob na kitang*, deep-fried fish wrapped in banana leaves and flavored with onions and tomatoes. *47 Pasay Rd., Makati, Metro Manila, tel. 815–1463 or 883–604. Reservations advised. Dress: casual. AE, DC, MC, V. Closed Good Fri.*

Inexpensive   **Aristocrat Restaurant.** This fourth-generation family-style eatery has been serving Philippine food for 52 years. It is an unassuming, spacious place with an indoor patio and marble-and-tile dining areas, some facing Manila Bay, that seat up to 200. Noted dishes are chicken barbecue, with fried Java-style rice (in a tomato sauce with spices), sate sauce, and papaya pickles; and *pancit luglog,* "fat" rice noodles with traditional toppings over a rich duck-egg sauce. *Roxas Blvd. cor. San Andres, Malate, Manila, tel. 521–8147, 521–8138, or 507–671. Reservations advised, especially for parties of 12 or more. Dress: casual. No credit cards. Open 24 hrs a day, year-round.*

★ **Gene's Bistro.** Manila's "high priest of nouvelle cooking," Gene Gonzalez has given an innovative Western twist to Pampango specialties, with turn-of-the-century flair. This Gonzales restaurant (he has seven in Metro Manila) is full of greenery and Philippine antiques, and there is a courtyard for alfresco dining. Inspired entrees include steak Hector, done with sweetbreads and wine sauce, and lapu-lapu au gratin. The seven-course menu is complemented by a coffee list with 56 selections. *243 Tomas Morato St., Quezon City, tel. 921–5193. Reservations suggested, especially on weekends. Dress: casual. AE, DC, MC, V.*

The Landmark Food Center. Can turo-turo go upscale? It does here, in a spacious open-air food mall with tables and busboys to clear them. The stalls include **Wei-Chuan,** where you eat steaming Chinese noodles with oyster sauce, cashew nuts, quail eggs, or black mushrooms; **West Villa,** for hearty Chinese cuisine, such as hot spare ribs, sweet-and-sour pork, or dim sum; **Bangusan,** which prepares a local fish any number of ways; **Kimchi,** a Korean enclave for dishes of marinated chicken, pork, beef, and bean sprouts; **Elar's** for crackling roast pig; **Digman,** which specializes in Philippine desserts; **Ulam Ni San Pedro,** which offers Philippine fast food, such as homemade sausages and pickled vegetables; the **Grill Spot,** where everything is broiled to spicy perfection; **Sinangag Plaza,** for a native breakfast; and, for those who miss pizza and Italian hero sandwiches, **Greenwich Pizza** and **Birdhouse.** *Makati Commercial Center, Makati, Metro Manila, tel. 810–9990. No reservations. Dress: casual. No credit cards. Closed holidays.*

Lodging

Manila has lodgings for every type of traveler, from the hedonist with deep pockets to the backpacker who must count his pennies. Almost all the hotels are in two areas: the so-called Tourist Belt (Malate and Ermita districts) in downtown Manila, and Makati, Manila's Wall Street and fashionable residential enclave. The former has more lodging options, while Makati has mainly upscale hotels.

Unless otherwise noted, rooms in all listed hotels have private bath. For a map pinpointing hotel locations, *see* Dining, above.

Highly recommended hotels are indicated by a star ★.

Category	Cost*
Very Expensive	over P2,000 ($100)
Expensive	P1,600–P2,000 ($80–$100)
Moderate	P700–P1,600 ($35–$80)
Inexpensive	under P700 ($35)

*All prices are for a standard double room; add 10% service charge and 13.7% government tax.

Ermita/Malate The advantages of staying in the Tourist Belt are Manila Bay, with its fabled sunsets, and the assortment of restaurants, bars, clubs, coffee houses, and shops. The Cultural Center of the Philippines is right on Roxas Boulevard, the scenic main road flanking the bay.

Century Park Sheraton. The sunny, six-story lobby brings the outdoors in, with an aviary and artfully arranged tropical foliage. A string quartet serenades lobby loungers every evening from 4 to 8. The hotel seems popular with Asian guests. The rooms, done in muted but cheery tones, are spacious. Best are those facing the bay; worst are those with a view of the adjacent parking lot and shopping complex, although you still see part of the bay. *Vito Cruz, cor. Adriatico St., tel. 501–201 or 506–041. 500 rooms. Facilities: 8 restaurants, a coffee shop, deli, nightclub, bar, fitness center, business center, grand ballroom, outdoor swimming pool. AE, DC, MC, V. Very Expensive.*

Manila Hotel. The doyen of Manila's hotels, this is where General MacArthur made his headquarters before World War II. Other luminaries have stayed here, from Ernest Hemingway to Douglas Fairbanks. The magnificent lobby exudes an Old World feeling, with floors of Philippine marble, narra and mahogany hardwood ceilings, and mother-of-pearl and brass chandeliers. The MacArthur Club, reached by private elevator, serves complimentary breakfast. Room decor re-creates the colonial era. Best rooms face the bay and the pool. *Rizal Park, tel. 470–011. 570 rooms. Facilities: outdoor pool, 2 tennis courts, grand ballroom, 7 restaurants, bar, business center, gym. AE, DC, MC, V. Very Expensive.*

★ **Philippine Plaza.** Luxurious and grand, a veritable resort sans beachfront, the Plaza has an enormous lobby with two levels, the lower one graced by a carp pool and a waterfall. The huge circular swimming pool, with slides for the kids and a snack bar smack in the middle, is reputed to be one of Asia's best. All rooms have terraces with views of Manila Bay. The decor is bright but not gaudy, with contrasting dark wood paneling. *Cultural Center Complex, Roxas Blvd., tel. 832–0701. 673 rooms. Facilities: outdoor pool with bar/restaurant, 4 tennis courts, minigolf course, ballroom and function rooms, 24-hr fitness center, 8 restaurants, nightclub, lounge, business center. AE, DC, MC, V. Very Expensive.*

Manila Midtown Hotel. Its spacious lobby strains neither for grandeur nor grandiosity. Room decor is perfunctory, but the lamps are native-style. The location is right beside the Robinson's shopping complex. If you have an early morning appointment, leave yourself a little extra time: Elevators for some reason are slow then. *Pedro Gil and Adriatico Sts., tel. 522–2629. 600 rooms. Facilities: outdoor pool, 5 restaurants, deli, nightclub, disco, bar, business center, gym. AE, DC, MC, V. Expensive.*

Admiral Hotel. Fronting the bay, this businesslike place is unpretentious but efficient, with a lobby that looks like that of an office building. Rooms are air-conditioned, neat, and modern but a bit small. Best are those with a view of the bay. The staff is friendly and attentive. *2138 Roxas Blvd., tel. 572–081 to 093. 110 rooms. Facilities: pool, disco, restaurant, coffee shop. AE, DC, MC, V. Moderate.*

Malate Pension. This is a favorite with backpackers and budget travelers, nondescript, except for a nice garden at the rear, but safe and very near the Tourist Belt's more interesting coffeehouses. Try the fruit shakes. *1771 Adriatico St., Malate, tel. 593–489. 39 rooms, 9 with bath. Facilities: garden, coffee shop, baggage storage. No credit cards. Inexpensive.*

Pope Pius XII Catholic Center. No pretensions, very similar to a YMCA, clean and comfortable. *1175 United Nations Ave., Paco, tel. 573–806. 88 rooms. Facilities: outdoor swimming pool, coffee shop. No credit cards. Inexpensive.*

Makati This district, the business capital of the country and neighbor to the airport, is relatively new and uncongested. The streets and sidewalks are wide, making it easier than elsewhere to walk around, and the hotels are concentrated around the gigantic Makati Commercial Center, which has everything from movie houses to money changers.

Mandarin Oriental. The ambience here is discreet and elegant, with a small but stately lobby done in black marble with a cut-crystal chandelier, and luxurious room decor. A favorite with businessmen. *Makati Ave. and Paseo de Roxas St., tel. 816–3601. 470 rooms. Facilities: outdoor pool, ballrooms and function rooms, 4 restaurants, bar/nightclub, bake shop, gym, business center. AE, DC, MC, V. Very Expensive.*

★ **Manila Peninsula.** The Pen, as Manilans call it, exudes an informal elegance, expressed in the wide lobby—divided by a grand aisle with floral decor—and the understated furnishings and color schemes of the well-kept and spacious rooms that are more like suites. *Makati and Ayala Aves., tel. 819–3456. 535 rooms. Facilities: outdoor pool, 4 restaurants, nightclub, bar, deli, business center. AE, DC, MC, V. Very Expensive.*

Nikko Manila Garden. Smack in Makati Commercial Center, with snack bars, restaurants, bookstores, cinemas, boutiques, and department stores, the Manila Garden has an uninspired and somewhat cluttered lobby but extremely helpful staff. Rooms are a bit cramped; the decor is modern and cheerful. The Japanese restaurant here is among Manila's best. *Makati Commercial Center, tel. 857–911. 523 rooms. Facilities: outdoor*

pool, gym, 5 restaurants, nightclub, bar, 6 banquet and confer-
ence rooms, business center, medical and dental clinic. AE,
DC, MC, V. Expensive.

The Arts

A good guide to the city's cultural life is *What's on in Manila*, a
biweekly publication distributed free by major hotels and tourist information centers. Check the entertainment pages of the
dailies, particularly the Sunday editions.

At the entrance to the offices of the Cultural Center of the Philippines complex (tel. 832–1125 to 1139), you can pick up a
monthly calendar of the center's offerings. The government-
run center emphasizes music, theater, dance, and the visual
arts and has a resident dance company and theater group. The
center also hosts internationally known artists and musicians,
sometimes in cooperation with the various cultural arms of the
foreign embassies. The center's two art galleries display figur-
ative and abstract art.

Theater The oldest professional theater group is **Repertory Philippines**
(tel. 865–211), which regularly stages Broadway hits and musicals in English. Shows are usually at the Insular Life
Auditorium (tel. 817–3051) or at the Rizal Theater (tel. 862–
020), both in Makati.

Concerts Free concerts are given at Rizal Park on Sundays beginning at
4:45 PM, usually with a program of popular Western and Philippine music. Often the prestigious Manila Symphony Orchestra or
a well-known singer or musician is featured. Paco Park offers similar programs on Friday evenings.

Dance The Cultural Center of the Philippines has a resident dance
company: **Ballet Philippines** (tel. 832–3675) and provides offices
for **Bayanihan Dance Company** (tel. 832–3688). The latter is a
world-famous folk-dance group. The ballet company is the Philippines' best, with guest dancers from around the world.
Fabella-Elejar (tel. 862–020), a modern-dance group, performs
at different venues.

Film Metro Manila has many cinema houses, but most of the
English-language films are the substandard B type.

The **Goethe House** (687 Aurora Blvd., Quezon City, tel. 722–
4671) and the **Thomas Jefferson Library** (395 Buendia Ave.
Ext., tel. 818–5484) regularly offer free film screenings, ranging from silent classics to contemporary movies. During the
two-week **Metro Manila Film Festival** in December, only Philippine films are shown in the cinemas.

Art Galleries Of Manila's many galleries, the best include **Ateneo de Manila
Gallery** (tel. 998–721) in Loyola Heights, Quezon City, with
modern art; **Heritage Gallery** (tel. 799–484) in Cubao, Quezon
City, which exhibits both traditional and nontraditional art;
Luz Gallery (tel. 882–558), on EDSA in Makati, a famous venue
for well-established modern artists; and **Pinaglabanan Galleries** (tel. 705–318) in San Juan, which focuses on avant-garde
artists.

Nightlife

Manila is a pleasure-seeker's paradise with a catholic array of night activities, from the soothing to the sinful. You can listen to jazz or rock, have a drink at a bar while ogling topless female dancers, dance madly at a disco, or have a snack and cappuccino in one of the lively coffeehouses.

Cafés   The largest concentration is in the Malate district, in and around Remedios Circle. **Penguin Cafe** (Remedios and Bocobo Sts., tel. 521–2088), which doubles as an art gallery, has the best outdoor patio, an artistic crowd, and good homemade pasta. **Cafe Adriatico** (1790 Adriatico St., tel. 584–059) features classical music, Philippine food, and a more subdued atmosphere. **Hard Rock Cafe** (Adriatico St. near Remedios Circle, tel. 584–059) has a young crowd, music videos, and raucous rock.

Folk Houses   **Your Father's Mustache** (2144 M.H. Del Pilar St., tel. 50–0742) and **Hobbit House** (1801 A. Mabini St., tel. 506–573 or 521–7604) feature a regular roster of folk singers. Freddie Aguilar, who's famous throughout Southeast Asia, performs twice weekly at the Hobbit House, where midgets wait on you.

Discos   Manila discos tend to be cavernous. The beat is generic and follows Western fashions. Some of the trendier ones are **Altitude 49** (Manila Garden Hotel, tel. 857–911); the **Billboard** (7838 Makati Ave., tel. 876–727), a favorite of expatriates; **Euphoria** (Hotel Intercontinental, Ayala Ave., tel. 815–9711), a hangout for yuppies; **Pulse** (1030 Pasay Rd., tel. 818–5288); **Stargazer** (Silahis Hotel, Roxas Blvd., tel. 573–811), which appeals to a mixed crowd; and the **Cellar Disco** (Century Park Sheraton Hotel, Vito Cruz, tel. 501–201).

Bars and Lounges   There are really two types of bars: those with skimpily attired dancers and those without. The former play disco music, while the latter have more varied fare. The largest concentration of "girlie" bars is found along M.H. Del Pilar and A. Mabini streets in the Tourist Belt, between Padre Faura and R. Salas streets. Customers can engage the dancers in conversation, pay for their drinks, and, if they wish to take them out, pay the bar owner a "bar fine" of about $8. Try **Firehouse** (1406 M.H. Del Pilar, tel. 521–9431); **Blue Hawaii** (1427 M.H. Del Pilar, tel. 595–482), with a nice restaurant at the rear serving burgers and fries; and **New Bangkok** (1314 M.H. Del Pilar, tel. 522–4170).

Nongirlie bars and music lounges are spread out in Makati and the Tourist Belt. In the Tourist Belt try **Playboy Club** (Silahis Hotel, tel. 573–811), **Tap Room** (Manila Hotel, tel. 470–011), **Siete Pecados** (Philippine Plaza Hotel, tel. 832–0701), **Oar House** (A. Mabini St., cor. Remedios, tel. 595–864), **Remembrances** (1795 A. Mabini, tel. 521–7605), and **Guernica's** (1856 Bocobo St., Malate, tel. 521–4415). In Makati, try **Nina's Papagayo** (1 Anza St., tel. 887–925), **Sirena** (Manila Peninsula, Ayala Ave., tel. 819–3456), **Chez Moi** (5347 General Luna St., tel. 885–038), and **Intramuros Bar** (Manila Garden Hotel, tel. 857–911).

Nightclubs   Manila nightclubs offer floor shows that vary from performances of well-known bands and cultural presentations to highly choreographed "model" shows, in which a lot of skin is bared. **Pistang Pilipino** (Pedro Gil, cor. Mabini, tel. 521–2209) and **Zamboanga** (1619 Adriatico St., tel. 572–835) serve Philippine cuisine and present regional folk dances. **Lost Horizon** (Philippine Plaza, tel. 832–0701) usually has a lively pop band, while **Top of the Century** (Century Park Sheraton, tel. 522–1011) and **La Bodega** (Manila Peninsula, tel. 819–3456) are more intimate, with well-known jazz singers and ensembles.

Casinos   **Silahis International Hotel** has a government-run, 24-hour casino (tel. 573–811). It occupies the whole mezzanine of the hotel and has a room reserved for high rollers. There's another government-run casino at the **Manila Pavillion Hotel** (United Nations Ave., tel. 573–711).

Northern Luzon

Introduction

The Philippines is justly acknowledged for its beautiful waters and beaches, though the fact that the country is essentially mountainous is sometimes overlooked. In northern Luzon are the rugged Cordillera and the Sierra Madre ranges, with breathtaking vistas at elevations of 3,000 to 9,500 feet, and the narrow but beautiful coastal plains of the Ilocos region. It can be chilly at night, especially from November through February. Rains are torrential during the wet season (mid-June through October) and can cause rock slides and impassable roads.

This is where one finds the ancient highland cultures—referred to collectively as Igorots and less modernized than their lowland counterparts—whose origins can be traced to migratory groups older than the Malays. Over the centuries there has been the inevitable intermingling of highland and lowland cultures through commerce, religion, education, and conflict. Nowhere is this more evident than in the charming city of Baguio: A good number of its inhabitants are lowlanders (business people, retirees, artists), so you're as likely to hear Pilipino as Ilocano, the regional tongue. The city also has several universities, attracting students from all over Luzon. Sitting at 1,500 m (5,000 ft) above sea level among pine-covered slopes, Baguio is a lovely respite from the lowland heat and serves as a base from which to explore the rice terraces of Banaue or the towns and churches of the Ilocos region—especially the area around Vigan and Laoag. A combination of rugged terrain and coastal plains, Ilocos is known for its neat towns; its hardworking, thrifty natives; and its gorgeous Spanish-era churches.

Important Addresses and Numbers

All the places noted here are in Baguio City, unless otherwise specified.

Tourist Information   **Department of Tourism** (Governor Pack Rd., tel. 442–5415, 442–5416, or 442–6858).

Emergencies   **Police,** tel. 21–11; **fire,** tel. 311–3222.

Hospitals   **Benguet General Hospital,** La Trinidad (tel. 221–06). **St. Louis University Hospital** (Assumption Rd., tel. 442–5701).

Late-Night **Mercury Drug Store** (Session Rd., tel. 442–4310) is open until
Pharmacies 10 PM.

Arriving and Departing by Plane

Airports **Philippine Air Lines** (tel. 832–3166) has daily 45-minute flights
and Airlines from Manila Domestic Airport to Loakan Airport in Baguio,
and daily one-hour flights to Laoag Airport, farther north.

Arriving and Departing by Car and Bus

By Car From Manila it's a smooth 4½- to 5-hour drive to Baguio via the
North Diversion highway, which begins at EDSA, links up to
the MacArthur Highway and leads to the zigzagging Kennon
Road.

By Bus A number of bus companies run daily trips from Manila to Baguio on an hourly basis, plus numerous daily trips to Vigan and
Laoag. Among them are **Pantranco** (tel. 997–091 to 098), **Victory** (tel. 835–5019), **Dangwa** (tel. 731–2859), and **Philippine
Rabbit** (tel. 711–5811).

Getting Around

By Car On the coastal plains and around the cities of Baguio, Vigan,
and Laoag, the roads range from good to excellent. Northeast
of Baguio, however, deeper into the Cordilleras, they can be
very bad, and public transportation is a better bet.

By Bus Buses are used to get from one town to the next, and they are
numerous and cheap. Terminals are located near the public
markets. Baguio has two terminals, one in front of the public
market on Magsaysay Avenue and the other on Governor Pack
Road near the corner of Session Road.

By Taxi The region's only cabs are in Baguio. They are small Japanese
models, and cheap: Rides within the central part of town cost
less than $1.

By Jeepney Plentiful and good for short routes, jeepneys begin and end
their routes at or near the public market. They can also be hired
for out-of-town trips.

Guided Tours

Manila travel agents can arrange northern tours *(see* Guided
Tours, above). In Baguio, consult the Department of Tourism
(tel. 442–5415 or 442–5416) for local operators. The **Hyatt Terraces Hotel** (tel. 442–5670) also offers several tour packages.

Exploring Northern Luzon

Tour 1: Baguio

*Numbers in the margin correspond with numbered sights on
the Northern Luzon map.*

❶ Billed as the "summer capital of the Philippines," **Baguio** was
developed during the American colonial administration and is
now the commercial, educational, and recreational hub of the
Cordilleras. The air here—at 1,500 m (5,000 ft) above sea level
—is crisp, invigorating, and laden with the fragrance of pine

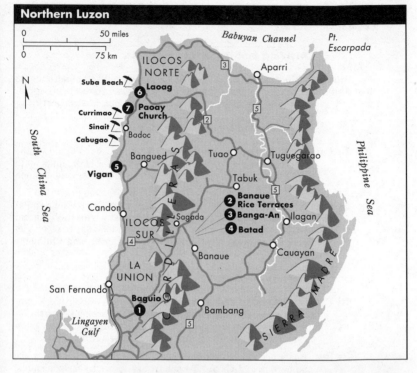

Northern Luzon

Babuyan Channel

Pt. Escarpada

0 — 50 miles
0 — 75 km

N

ILOCOS NORTE

Suba Beach

6 **Laoag**

7 **Paoay Church**

Currimao

Sinait

Cabugao

Badoc

Bangued

Vigan **5**

Candon

ILOCOS SUR

Sagada

Banaue

LA UNION

San Fernando

Baguio **1**

Lingayen Gulf

Bambang

South China Sea

Aparri

3

5

2

Tuao

Tabuk

Tuguegarao

2 Banaue Rice Terraces

3 Banga-An

4 Batad

5

Ilagan

Cauayan

CORDILLERAS

SIERRA MADRE

Philippine Sea

4

5

trees. Avoid the city during the Christmas holidays and Easter week, when the population of 150,000 (and prices) practically double. A day tour could begin at the Department of Tourism (*see* Important Addresses and Numbers, above), where you can pick up maps and suggestions. A small adjacent museum houses artifacts from the area.

A 10- to 15-minute drive from Session Road, the city's main downtown artery, is **Mines View Park,** a promontory from which you can gaze at the surrounding mountains and abandoned silver mines. (Below the promontory, children wait for you to toss coins.) Souvenir stalls sell woodcarvings, brassware, walking sticks, jewelry, native blankets, and bamboo flutes.

A short drive from the park, back toward the city center, is **Mansion House,** built in 1908 as the summer residence of the American governor-generals and now the getaway of Philippine presidents. Visitors enter through gates that replicate those of Buckingham Palace in London. Across the road is the **Pool of Pines,** a carp pool 100 m (109 yd) long that's bordered by pine trees. From the vine-covered stone trellis at the far end, steps lead down to **Wright Park,** where horses can be rented. You can ride out of the park to different parts of the city, but only with a guide.

A stroll away is **Imelda Park,** named after you-know-who. Here you will find sculptures of *anitos* (native gods) and examples of dwellings used by the different highland ethnic groups. For a

small fee, natives dressed in traditional tribal finery will pose
for photos.

On to **Baguio Cathedral,** just off Session Road, which may be
the world's only cathedral painted a light, cheery pink. With its
hints of Norman architecture, the cathedral won't inspire
raves, but it is a good perch from which to get a panoramic view
of Baguio and of Mt. St. Tomás, its highest peak. On one side of
the cathedral is a long flight of steps leading to **Session Road,**
downtown Baguio's mile-long main street, with bazaars, restaurants, movie houses, offices, and cafés.

South of Session Road is **Burnham Park.** Named for American
landscape architect Daniel Burnham, the park's spacious
grounds are perfect for an idyllic stroll. There's boating on the
artificial lake, and bicycles can be rented. North of the park
and at the bottom of Session Road is the **Baguio Public Market.**
Set between a hill and Magsaysay Avenue, the market is an in-
dispensable part of the Baguio experience. A series of alleys
with stalls on either side, it has sections devoted to fish and
meat; fresh vegetables and strawberries, for which Baguio is
famous; dry goods, from Igorot blankets and loincloths to army
surplus; regional handicrafts, with an emphasis on rattan
backpacks, silver jewelry, and tribal ornaments; tailor shops;
and antiques. The money changers here give a better rate than
you'll find at hotels or banks.

Tour 2: Banaue

❷ The **Banaue Rice Terraces** are spectacular, man-made rice paddies terraced into the mountainsides of Mayaoyao and Carballo
by the Ifugaos, a highland tribe, more than 2,000 years ago.
Looking like giant steps to the sky, these terraces would extend for 22,500 km (14,000 mi) if placed end to end, or halfway
around the world. Banaue is an eight-hour drive from either
Baguio or Manila. The area is also good for trekking, and
guides can be hired at fees ranging from P40 to P160.

Some of the terraces can be seen from Banaue itself, but the
best views are in the countryside. Start at **Viewpoint,** a 1½-
hour trek (ask for directions) or a 20-minute drive from the
town proper. This promontory offers a panoramic view of the
terraces. Wizened Ifugao women in native dress will pose for a
little money.

❸ Even more spectacular Ifugao villages are **Banga-An** (an hour's
❹ drive away on rough roads, or three hours on foot) or **Batad**
(1½-hour drive, four to five hours on foot), both set among the
terraces. Along the way you'll see pine-covered slopes, green
valleys dwarfed by clouded peaks, far-off, pyramid-shape
Ifugao huts improbably perched on crags, and mountain
streams irrigating the terraces. You can't drive into these villages; to get close, you must walk. There life goes on pretty
much as it has for centuries: Rice is still planted in age-old rituals and plowed regularly with the help of the ubiquitous water
buffalo. Dogs, pigs, and ducks wander about and under the native huts, which are elevated on wooden posts. Handicrafts—
rattan backpacks, baskets, and ornaments—are sold for low
prices.

Tour 3: Vigan and Laoag

The respective capitals of the Ilocos Sur and Ilocos Norte provinces, these small, coastal cities date to the early years of Spanish colonization. Both—but especially Vigan—have some of the best-preserved Spanish-influenced architecture in the country, suggesting what Manila's Intramuros would have looked like had it not been destroyed during World War II. The towns between these two cities are noteworthy for their ancient churches and bell towers.

⑤ In **Vigan,** a 3½-hour scenic drive from Baguio City, you can explore the old quarter in a couple of hours. The **Ayala Museum** (Burgos St.; open Tues.–Sun. 9–noon, 1–5; admission charge) is a collection of dioramas, artifacts, and paintings relating to the area's history. From there it's about a 10-minute walk to the town's main landmark, the 16th-century **Vigan Cathedral** (also known as the Cathedral of St. Paul), a massive, whitewashed brick-and-wood structure with a tile roof. Chinese lions guard the portals and the gleaming silver altar within. It's a short stroll northwest of the cathedral to the old quarter. The buildings have whitewashed brick walls, tile roofs, sliding *capiz* (mother-of-pearl) windows, and lofty interiors. **General Luna, Crisologo, De los Reyes,** and **Bonifacio streets** have row upon row of these edifices—perfect for Philippine Westerns or gothic films, for which, in fact, they have been used.

⑥ **Laoag** (a 1½-hour ride from Vigan) isn't as interesting as Vigan, though the **Laoag Cathedral** and its **Sinking Bell Tower** are worth visiting. The 17th-century cathedral is heavily buttressed (a protection against earthquakes), with two exterior stone stairways, urn ornamentation, and foliate capitals. North of the church is a bell tower that has sunk about 1 m (1.09 yd), so that its portal is barely visible.

Between Vigan and Laoag are towns whose churches are fine examples of what a local writer once termed Filipino Baroque—unique, even rococo combinations of Western and Asian styles. The most impressive of these, and one of the few Catholic churches designed by Filipinos during the Spanish era, is **⑦** the majestic **Paoay Church** in **Paoay,** a sleepy town about 15 minutes south of Laoag. The frontal crenellations and turrets, massive curlicued buttresses, exterior stairways, and niches give the impression of a Javanese temple. Beside this splendid fusion of styles is a belfry made of limestone, which was used as an outpost during the revolution of 1896 and by guerrillas during the Japanese occupation in World War II.

Off the Beaten Track

Sagada, northeast of Baguio, is a small, tightly knit community deep in the central Cordilleras among the rice terraces. A favorite with adventurous backpackers, the town has several burial caves with hanging coffins, an underground river, waterfalls, limestone formations, and hiking trails. There are no cinemas, no discos, no shopping malls, and no pollution. This is a wonderful place to visit, but be respectful of local customs. The trip from Baguio is a dusty, eight-hour bus ride on narrow winding roads but is more than compensated for by breathtaking mountain vistas. Dangwa buses (tel. 442–4150 or 442–2449) leave in the early morning from the terminal in front of the Baguio public market.

Shopping

Baguio   Check out the handicraft section of the **Baguio Public Market** and the antiques shops right above it. For items made of *ikat* (an indigenous woven cloth), try **Narda's,** with shops at the Hyatt Terraces (tel. 442–5670) and Camp John Hay (tel. 442–2101). At **Munsayac's Handicraft** (21 Leonard Wood Rd., tel. 442–2451), good woodcarvings, brass, and silverware can be found. All along **Session Road** are various shopping arcades and boutiques.

Banaue   Besides the town market, souvenir stands at the most popular scenic spots carry local handicrafts, including tribal spears.

Vigan/Laoag   Other than the town markets, there's the *burnay*, or potters' district, of Vigan, about a 15-minute walk from the cathedral, where jars and urns can be bought for low prices from the potters themselves. Ask for directions, or take a pedicab.

Beaches

The route between Baguio and Vigan consists mainly of a coastal highway by the South China Sea. Numerous small resorts dot the coast, especially in the province of **La Union,** the first province you enter descending from Baguio via Naguilian Road. Accommodations tend to be basic. Between Vigan and Laoag are good beaches—most of which have no resorts—near the towns of **Cabugao, Sinait, Currimao,** and **Pangil.** Sinait's beach, **Pug-os,** is a picture-pretty white-sand beach used by local fishermen to store their boats and nets. Right outside Laoag is **Suba Beach,** a long, black volcanic-sand beach that is bare of tourists and protected by dunes.

Dining and Lodging

Dining. On the Ilocos coast, seafood dishes are the specialty. Try fried squid, fresh shrimp marinated in vinegar and peppers, and grilled catch of the day. In the Cordilleras, vegetables and meat, particularly pork and chicken, are favored. Try *lechon* (pork roasted in an earthen pit) and *pinakbet*, a vegetable dish with bits of pork and tiny shrimp, flavored with *bagoong*, a salty paste (also used as a condiment).

Restaurants in the region are open every day and do not require reservations or formal dress. However, most do not tolerate shorts or sandals. Highly recommended restaurants are indicated by a star ★.

Category	Cost*
Very Expensive	over P300 ($15)
Expensive	P160–P300 ($8–$15)
Moderate	P60–P160 ($3–$8)
Inexpensive	under P60 ($3)

*per person; add 6% sales tax; 10% service charge usually added

Lodging. Baguio City has a wide range of accommodations, from a five-star hotel to pension-style lodgings. The other cities offer mostly family-run hotels, short on amenities but generally well-maintained and clean, with the staff invariably courteous and helpful. Highly recommended hotels are indicated by a star ★.

Category	Cost*
Very Expensive	over P120 ($60)
Expensive	P800–P120 ($40–$60)
Moderate	P400–P800 ($20–$40)
Inexpensive	under P400 ($20)

All prices are for a double room; add 10% service charge and 13.7% government tax.

Baguio Dining

★ **Copper Grill.** An elegant restaurant with a salad bar, the Copper Grill serves Continental cuisine from roasts to grilled seafood. Service is performed with flair as a quartet serenades you. *Hyatt Terraces, South Dr., tel. 442–5670. AE, DC, MC, V. Very Expensive.*

Mario's. Popular with young couples because of its dim lighting, Mario's serves very good steaks, and its Caesar salad is first-rate. *Session Rd., tel. 442–4241. AE, DC, MC, V. Expensive.*

Wok Inn. Through a glass enclosure in this well-lighted, spacious place, you can watch the kitchen staff prepare such Chinese dishes as spicy shrimp with green peppers and steamed fish in black bean sauce. *21 Calderon Rd., tel. 442–2331. No credit cards. Moderate.*

★ **Cafe by the Ruins.** An airy place with a patio setting, this café serves excellent home-cooked Philippine cuisine, including delicious tiny fried fish and vegetables stewed in coconut milk. *23 Chuntug St., no phone. No credit cards. Inexpensive.*

Cafe Amapola. Divided into a lounge and a café, this cozy place serves good hamburgers, pasta, and European-style desserts. *Governor Pack Rd., cor. Session Rd., tel. 442–2455. AE, V. Inexpensive.*

Lodging

★ **Hyatt Terraces.** This is Baguio's sole luxury hotel. The soaring, light-filled lobby has a rice-terrace motif. The brightly furnished rooms have terraces and views of the surrounding greenery. Service here is uniformly excellent. *South Dr., tel. 442–5670. 291 rooms. Facilities: pool, ballroom, 7 function rooms, 4 restaurants, 2 bars, disco, deli, casino. AE, DC, MC, V. Expensive.*

Burnham Hotel. The rooms in this small hotel near Session Road, the heart of downtown Baguio, are clean and wood-paneled. The comfortable lobby is reminiscent of a hunting lodge, complete with fireplace. *21 Calderon Rd., tel. 442–2231 or 442–5117. 18 rooms. Facilities: restaurant, room service. No credit cards. Moderate.*

Munsayac Inn. This is a small, family-run hotel with good ambience. Long patronized by missionaries, the inn will appeal to those who like their lodgings on the quiet side. *124 Leonard Wood Rd., tel. 442–2451. 20 rooms. Facilities: restaurant, handicraft shop, lounge. AE, DC, MC, V. Moderate.*

★ **Casa Amapola.** Located in a quiet neighborhood, this pension—once a family residence—retains a family-style informality.

What was once the living room is now a lounge where guests meet informally, and there's a terrace where you can breakfast while watching the fog lift from the surrounding hills. In addition to the regular rooms, three three-story chalets with verandas and kitchens are available for those who like more privacy. *46 First Rd., Quezon Hill, tel. 442–3406. 13 rooms, 3 chalets. Facilities: dining room, garden. AE, V. Inexpensive–Moderate.*

Banaue
Dining
★

Banaue Hotel Restaurant. This is an informal but excellent restaurant serving both Continental food and such Philippine regional dishes as *pinakbet* (vegetable stew with pork in a salty sauce). The room is large and airy, with bright red decor, native wall hangings, and a view of the hotel gardens. Service is superb. *Banaue Hotel, Banaue, no tel. AE, DC, MC, V. Expensive.*

Lodging

Banaue Hotel. Each room at this semiluxury hotel has a good view of the town and valley, a terrace, and decor reminiscent of a country lodge. *Banaue, Manila, tel. 818–8949. 90 rooms. Facilities: outdoor pool, restaurant, handicraft shop. AE, DC, MC, V. Very Expensive.*

Sanafe Lodge. Near the city market, Sanafe is a combination dormitory and hotel. The small lobby overlooks rice terraces; the rooms are small but clean. Dorm rooms—which sleep eight—are Spartan but also clean, and cheaper. The resident manager is a gold mine of information concerning the area. *Banaue, Manila tel. 721–1075. 14 rooms (8 with bath) and 2 dorms. Restaurant. No credit cards. Inexpensive–Moderate.*

Laoag
Dining
★

Pamulinawen. Wood-paneled and spacious, Pamulinawen serves very good Philippine cuisine, including *pinakbet* and beef *tapa* (cured, dried strips of meat served with a vinegar-and-garlic sauce), and some Continental dishes. *Fort Ilokandia Hotel, near Laoag Airport, tel. 221–166. AE, DC, MC, V. Expensive.*

Lodging
★

Fort Ilokandia. This sprawling hotel is made up of several two-story buildings whose style and room decor suggest Vigan's old residences. Tiled walkways connect the buildings, which are nestled among sand dunes. The hotel has a good black-sand beach. *Near Laoag Airport, tel. 221–166 to 170. 250 rooms. Facilities: restaurant, pool, banquet rooms, disco, bar, gift shops. AE, DC, MC, V. Expensive.*

Vigan
Dining

Cordillera Inn. The setting here is bare, the Philippine food unpretentious but tasty. *Cordillera Inn, General Luna St., cor. Crisologo St., tel. 722–3133. No credit cards. Inexpensive.*

Lodging

Cordillera Inn. This is a colonial-era building with broad stairways and good views of the old quarter. The rooms are Spartan but clean. *Gen. Luna St., cor. Crisologo St., tel. 722–3133. 23 rooms. Facilities: restaurant, handicraft shop. No credit cards, but traveler's checks accepted. Moderate.*

Vigan Hotel. The place may be unprepossessing, but it's right in the old quarter, and the staff is helpful and friendly. *Burgos St., tel. 722–3061. 15 rooms. Facilities: restaurant. AE, DC, MC, V. Inexpensive.*

The Arts

The only venues for the arts in the region are the handicraft stores, the museum in Vigan, and the **Juan Luna Museum**—the home of a well-known 19th-century Filipino artist—in the sleepy town of Badoc, near Laoag (no tel., admission charge, open 9–noon and 1–4). Festivals are occasions for traditional performances, including native dances. The **Banaue Hotel** puts on a free cultural show of Ifugao dances for its guests nightly at 8, or after dinner. After the performance, the dancers try to get the guests to join in for an impromptu session.

Nightlife

Baguio has some nightclubs (concentrated mainly on Abanao Street, not far from the public market), a disco, and a casino. Vigan closes down around 8 PM, while Laoag has a disco and a casino.

Bannatiran. At this cocktail lounge, the clientele is given to singing along to taped instrumental music. *Fort Ilokandia Hotel, Laoag City, tel. 221–166.*
Cafe Amapola. A live band with a vocalist performs nightly. *Governor Pack Rd., cor. Session Rd., Baguio City, tel. 442–2455.*
Casino. A medium-size outlet for gamblers, the place opens in the evening, but one-armed bandits are available 24 hours. Even when the casino is packed, the tables are unnaturally quiet. *Hyatt Terraces, South Dr., Baguio City, tel. 442–5670.*
Gold Mine Disco. Favored by Baguio's young and fashionable set, Gold Mine has an infectious party atmosphere. *Hyatt Terraces, South Dr., Baguio City, tel. 442–5670.*

The Visayas and Southern Philippines

Introduction

Geographically, the Visayas are the center of the Philippines. Bound on the north by Luzon and on the south by Mindanao, this group of islands has some of the best beaches and resorts in the country, unusual natural attractions, and Muslim and other non-Hispanicized minority cultures.

The land and seas are especially fertile, so while northerners are known for their industriousness and frugality, southerners are easygoing, gregarious, and musical (the best guitars come from this area). Yet some of the worst pockets of poverty are also found here, arising out of centuries-old feudalism, an overdependence on cash crops, and the often tragic effects of militarization in areas where the New People's Army is active. It bears repeating that travelers need not worry about being caught up in the conflict: Armed clashes almost always occur in remote rural areas.

Except for Cebu City, there isn't much nightlife in the region. To really enjoy the south, one has to appreciate the affectionate, fun-loving ways of its people, explore the beaches and beautiful scenery, and take in the charm of small towns and cities just by strolling around.

Cebu City, the "Queen City of the South" and capital of Cebu Island, is where Ferdinand Magellan claimed the country for Philip of Spain in 1521. The first Philippine settlement colonized by the Spanish, Cebu is the oldest city in the country.

This small but strategically important port has the advantages of a big city—with restaurants, shops, lodgings, schools, and businesses—but few of its drawbacks. Pollution so far isn't a problem.

Cebu City's airport provides a crucial link between Manila and Mindanao and between the western and eastern parts of the Visayas. It makes sense to use Cebu as a focal point for exploring the southern Philippines. Most regional destinations—such as charming Iloilo City, rich in old mansions and baroque churches—are only a 30-minute flight away. Zamboanga City, only 45 minutes away by plane, is an intriguing mix of Christian and Muslim cultures.

Important Addresses and Numbers

All numbers are in Cebu City unless noted otherwise.

Tourist Information
: **Department of Tourism.** Cebu City: Fort San Pedro, tel. 965–18 or 915–03. Iloilo City: Sarabia Hotel, General Luna St., tel. 787–01 or 754–11. Zamboanga City: Lantaka Hotel, Valderosa St., tel. 32–47 or 39–31.

U.S. Consulate
: Fourth floor, IBAA Building, Gorordo Avenue, tel. 795–10, 520–44, or 707–25.

Emergencies
: **Police and medical:** tel. 956–76 or 746–42.

Arriving and Departing

By Plane
: **Philippine Air Lines** (tel. 832–3166) has daily flights from Manila to major cities in the region, with six to Cebu City's **Mactan International Airport** (on Mactan Island and 45 minutes from the city proper), five to Iloilo City, and two to Zamboanga. In the summer, PAL also has flights from Tokyo to Cebu, and Lufthansa has plans to operate charter flights to Cebu from Frankfurt. Smaller **Lahug Airport**—30 minutes from Cebu City—is used by charter lines such as **Aerolift** (tel. 928–54) and **Varona Aero Services** (tel. 702–29). Flights are available from Mactan Airport to most cities in the region, including Iloilo, Zamboanga, and Davao.

By Ship
: Cebu is a busy port and a primary stop for interisland ships. All the major lines have trips to and from Cebu to ports all over the archipelago. The Cebu–Manila voyage takes 21 hours; Cebu–Davao, 12 hours. Some Cebu offices: **Aboitiz Shipping** (Osmeña Blvd., tel. 754–40 or 930–75; in Manila, tel. 217–339), **Escaño Lines** (Reclamation Area, tel. 772–53 or 621–22), and **Negros Navigation** (Port Area, tel. 943–07; in Manila, tel. 272–930).

Getting Around

By Car
: Roads in the urban areas, especially in Iloilo City, are in good shape. While having a car gives you freedom and privacy, rates for taxis and jeepneys are inexpensive, and local drivers know the area better than you do. Car rental agencies in Cebu: **Avis** (tel. 746–11, 998–23), **Sultan** (tel. 744–54), and **Hamilcars** (tel. 924–31).

By Bus
: As elsewhere in the Philippines, this is the main form of transport between towns. Buses usually begin and end their routes in the vicinity of the public market. Get to the market early in

the morning to secure a good seat. Most buses are not air-conditioned.

By Taxi Taxis have no meters; fares are agreed upon beforehand. Rates for short trips within the city vary from $1 to $2.50. Longer trips—to the airport, for example—cost from $3 to $5.

By Jeepney Jeepneys also begin and end their trips at the public market. Fares are very low: A 2-mile ride within Cebu City, for example, costs only 10¢.

Guided Tours

Tours can be arranged in Manila (*see* Guided Tours, above). You can also consult the local Department of Tourism office (*see* Important Addresses and Numbers, above) for suggestions and a list of guides. The larger hotels usually house tour operators.

Exploring the Visayas and Southern Philippines

Tour 1: Cebu City

Numbers in the margin correspond with points of interest on the Visayas and the Southern Philippines map.

1 In **Cebu City,** the country's oldest—founded by the Spanish conquistador Miguel Lopez de Legaspi in 1571—little is left of the original settlement. Combined with other attractions, though, there's enough for a fascinating and rewarding daylong tour. Most of the historical sights are within walking distance of one another, located in the downtown area near the ports.

We begin at **Fort San Pedro,** the oldest and smallest fort in the country, built in 1565. The Department of Tourism office is located here. You may want to drop in first, ask questions, and pick up maps before exploring the fort and the city. The three bastions with turrets for cannon give the fort its triangular shape. The parapets afford a good view of the sea—a necessity in the days when the settlement was a target of pirate raids. *Port Area, tel. 965–18. Admission charge. Open daily 8–noon and 1–5.*

From the fort it's a 10-minute walk to **Magellan's Cross,** brought over by the famed Portuguese navigator in 1521. You won't see the original; because residents believe the cross is miraculous and used to take slivers from it, it has been encased (for protection) in a hollow wooden cross that is suspended from the ceiling of an open-sided domed pavilion on Magallanes Street.

Opposite the cross are the **Santo Niño** and **Basilica Minore.** The 18th-century basilica (closed daily noon–2 PM), done in typical Spanish baroque style, houses the oldest Catholic image—that of the Holy Infant or Santo Niño—brought over by Magellan and presented to Queen Juana of Zebu. Enshrined in glass and ornamented with gold and precious stones, the icon stands atop a side altar, venerated by a constant stream of devotees. Outside the church stand candle-bearing middle-aged women who, for a donation, will pray and dance to the Santo Niño on your behalf.

A short stroll from the basilica is the oldest street in the country, named after Cristóbal Colón, otherwise known as Christopher

The Visayas and Southern Philippines

Romblon
Odiongan
Tablas Island
Sibuyan Island
Masbate
Uson
Balud
MASBATE
Catarman
Laoang
Palapag
SAMAR
Calbayog City
Catbalogan
Biliran Island

Boracay Island
Kalibo
THE VISAYAS
Visayan Sea
Culasi
Roxas City
PANAY
Sicogon Island
Bantayan Island
Cadiz City
Escalante
LEYTE
Burauen
Ormoc City
Baybay
Leyte Gulf
Passi
Silay City
Talisay
Hilongos
Dinagat Island
Iloilo City
②
Bacolod City
San Carlos City
CEBU
Matcan Island
Maasin
Miagao
Guimaras Island
Strait
① *Cebu City*
Strait
Panaon Island
Panay Gulf
Naga
Carcar
Surigao City
Kabankalan
Moalboal
BOHOL
Chocolate Hills
Mindanao Sea
Cauayan
Sipalay
NEGROS
Bais City
Tanjay
Tagbilaran City
Panglao Island
Hinob-an
Bayawan
Santa Catalina
Dumaguete City
Siquijor Island
Camiguin Island
Cabadbaran
Butuan City
Dapitan City
Dipolog City
Oroquieta City
Gingoog City
Cagayan de Oro City
Iligan City
MINDANAO
Sulu Sea
Marawi City
Valencia
Lake Lanao
Zamboanga Peninsula
Pagadian City
Quezon
Tagum
Parang
Sultan Kudarat
Cotabato City
Mt. Apo
Davao City
④ Taluksangay
Moro Gulf
Dinaig
Pikit
Magpet
③ Zamboanga City
Santa Cruz Island
Kidapanan
Davao Gulf
Lamitan
Isabela
Basilan Island
Polomolok
Malita
Celebes Sea
General Santos City
Glan

0 — 100 miles
0 — 150 km

N

Columbus. Formerly the heart of the Parian District (or Chinatown), **Colón Street** is now downtown Cebu's main drag. Here modernity crowds in on you in the form of movie houses, restaurants, department stores, and other commercial establishments.

Time Out Of the many eateries on Colón Street, try **Snow Sheen** (tel. 767–69) or **Dim Sum Gaisano.** Both are busy, unpretentious, and serve inexpensive but tasty Chinese food.

From the eastern end of Colón Street, it's a short walk to **Casa Gorordo,** former residence of Cebu's first bishop, Juan Gorordo. Now restored, the century-old wood house has a tile roof, mother-of-pearl windows, a wide veranda, and a fine collection of household furnishings from the last century. *Lopez Jaena St., tel. 945–76. Admission charge. Open daily 9–noon and 2–6.*

From Casa Gorordo it's a 20-minute walk to the **University of San Carlos Museum,** which has an extensive collection of anthropological relics: local prehistoric stone and iron tools, burial jars, and pottery. Another section focuses on traditional clothing and ornaments of various tribal minorities. *Cor. Rosario and Junquera Sts., tel. 724–10. Admission charge. Open 9–noon and 3–6, weekends and holidays by appt.*

Incongruously located in an expensive suburb known as Beverly Hills is the **Taoist Temple,** dedicated to the teachings of the 600 BC Chinese philosopher Lao-Tse. You can get here by taxi (referred to as a P.U., for "public utility") for about $2. A flight of 99 steps leads to it from the road. Come for the panoramic views of the city, the colorful and ornate Chinese architecture, and to have your fortune read. *Beverly Hills, tel. 936–52. Admission free. Open daily until dark.*

Tour 2: Iloilo City

This city, capital of Iloilo Province on the island of Panay, is a half-hour flight from Cebu City, with Iloilo airport just 10 minutes from the center. A small and gracious aggregate of six districts, **Iloilo** (pronounced *"ee-lo-ee-lo"*) has a genteel air and loads of southern charm. As always, it's a good idea to visit the Department of Tourism office (at the Sarabia Hotel) to pick up maps, brochures, and tips.

In the city and surrounding area are several churches worth visiting. In the city itself are **Molo Church** and the **Jaro Cathedral.** The former, a twin-spired gothic structure erected in the late 19th century, sits in a pleasant park and has an intricate facade, with a kind of domed pergola, complete with Greek columns, facing it. The larger Jaro Cathedral also shows Gothic influences. In front is an open-air balcony with a statue of the Virgin Mary that locals consider miraculous. Across the street is the church's reconstructed belfry. Take some time to walk around the district and look at the grand, colonial-type residences, with their intricate grillwork and mother-of-pearl windows.

The 200-year-old **Miagao Fortress Church,** 8 km (5 mi) south of the city, has two differently designed bell towers—erected by two different friars—that also served as watchtowers against invasions by Muslim pirates. If you promise to be careful, the bell ringer will let you climb one of the towers. The sandstone facade depicts, amid floral designs, St. Christopher planting a coconut tree.

Time Out Try the seafood or Continental dishes at the breezy **Sunset Terrace** at Hotel Del Rio (M.H. Del Pilar St., tel. 755–85 to 87), by the broad Iloilo River. Note the bamboo fish pens on the water.

Closer to the city center and across from the provincial capitol building is the **Museo Iloilo.** The museum has an excellent collection of pre-Hispanic artifacts dug up mainly on Panay Island. These include fossils, Stone Age flake tools, and gold death masks. Other exhibits focus on liturgical art and the treasures of a British frigate shipwrecked nearby in the 19th century. *Bonifacio Dr., cor. General Luna St., tel. 729–86. Admission charge. Open daily 8–noon and 1–5.*

Tour 3: Zamboanga City

③ A 45-minute plane ride from Cebu, **Zamboanga City** is famous for its bright flowers (its early name, Jambangan, meant "land of flowers"), which grow profusely in every garden. The roadsides are lined with bougainvillea and the bright-red-flowered *gumamela* bushes. It is also a city with a sizable Muslim population, made up mainly of the Yakan, Badjao, Samal, and Tausug tribes.

It's probably best to begin exploring the city at **Plaza Pershing,** named after "Blackjack" Pershing, the first American governor of the region formerly known as Moroland. It's a pleasant spot for a stroll. Two blocks southeast of the square is **City Hall** on Valderrosa Street. Built by the Americans in 1907, it's a curious combination of Arabic and baroque styles.

Heading east on Valderrosa Street you'll come to **Ft. Pilar,** an old Spanish fort not far from the Lantaka Hotel, where the Department of Tourism has its field office (tel. 32–47 or 39–31). Beyond the fort is **Rio Hondo,** a small riverine Muslim village with its own mosque. Many of the houses are on stilts. Men wear white skullcaps, and women wear the distinctive *malong,* brightly decorated wraparound clothing.

Time Out **Alavar's** (R.T. Lim Blvd., tel. 79–40), run by a husband-and-wife team (he cooks, she manages), serves wonderful seafood. The specialty is *curacha* crabs in a creamy, sweet-spicy sauce that is the chef's secret. Down your food with refreshing *buko* (young coconut) juice.

④ A bigger Muslim village on the coast is **Taluksangay,** about 16 km (10 mi) from Zamboanga. At the back of the town's distinctive red-and-white mosque is a prominent Muslim family's burial plot. The community is made up of seaweed gatherers; everywhere piles of seaweed dry in the sun. Stroll along the many catwalks and watch as women weave and sell mats. Remember to bargain; prices quoted at first will be high. On the way back to the city, stop by **Climaco Freedom Park** (named after a beloved mayor slain some years ago) and **Pasonanca Park.** The former's attraction is the Ecumenical Holy Hill: 14 Stations of the Cross on a roadside cliff leading to a giant white cross at the top, where you get good views of the city. The unique offering in Pasonanca is the **Pasonanca Treehouse,**

which is available for one or two nights' (bathroomless) lodging if prior notification is given the city—a fun Tarzan-and-Jane experience for couples young at heart.

Off the Beaten Track

Chocolate Hills, Bohol Island. These are about 50 striking limestone hills, with an average height of 36 m (120 ft), that look like overturned teacups sans handles. About a two-hour bus ride from the market in Tagbilaran City—a half-hour flight from Cebu City—the hills turn chocolate-brown during the dry months (February through May). In July they become green again, their grasses nourished by rain.

Mt. Mayon. Legazpi City near the tip of southern Luzon—an hour's flight from either Cebu or Manila—has what may be the world's most symmetrical (and still active) volcano, towering 2,457 m (8,189 ft) over the Bicol countryside. Aside from the lure of the two- to three-day climb, Mt. Mayon has a volcanology/seismography station at about 750 m (2,500 ft.), with a resthouse offering panoramic views of the volcano and the surrounding terrain. The station has geological displays relating to volcanoes, earthquakes, and tidal waves. You can also see a seismograph in operation. Just 5 km (3 mi) from Legazpi City are the **Cagsawa Bell Tower and Ruins.** They are remnants of a church buried by an 1814 eruption along with more than 1,000 people who had sought refuge there. The best time to view the peak from the city is early morning, before the clouds obscure it. The Department of Tourism office in the city is at Peñaranda Park, Albay District (tel. 4492 or 4026).

Palawan. Looking like a long dagger, this is the archipelago's westernmost island and one of its most isolated and least developed, with unpaved roads outside the capital of Puerto Princessa. There are beautiful beaches throughout, excellent snorkeling and diving spots, and the world's longest known underground river, **St. Paul's Underground River.** Palawan has flora and fauna not found elsewhere in the country, such as the tamaraw (a smaller and wilder version of the water buffalo); giant turtles; peacocks; mouse deer; scaly anteaters; and seven-color doves. Perhaps the most secluded luxury resort in the Philippines is **El Nido** in northern Palawan (in Manila, tel. 857–911 or 892–622), reachable only by private plane or boat. Food, transportation, and lodging are all included in the price, which must be prepaid.

As the island has malaria-bearing mosquitoes, take preventive medication at least two weeks before making the 90-minute flight from Cebu City or Manila. There is a tourism counter at the airport and a field office at City Hall (tel. 21–54).

Shopping

Cebu City **Colón Street** is a good shopping street, with a number of **Gaisano** department stores, part of a regionwide chain. At the **Carbon public market** (Briones and Calderon Sts.), locals shop for handicrafts, fruit, food, flowers, and household items. One of the best handicraft stores in the city is the **Cebu Display Center** (11–13 Magallanes, at Lapu-Lapu St., tel. 522–23 or 522–24), which has an excellent collection of regional crafts, particularly shellcraft. Prices aren't inflated for tourists.

Iloilo City At **Asilo de Molo** (Avancena St., Molo, tel. 774–17), an orphanage for girls, the skills of fine embroidery, especially for church vestments, are taught by nuns. Embroidered gowns, dresses, and exquisite *Barong Tagalogs* are sold at firm prices. **Sinamay Dealer** (Osmeña St., Arevalo, tel. 42–21) is a weaving store where fine cloth is spun from pineapple fiber. Shirts and dresses are made from the cloth, then hand-embroidered. For shellcraft, try **Iloilo Shellcraft Industry** (M.H. Del Pilar St., Molo, tel. 774–73).

Zamboanga City The **City Market** (Alano St., dawn to dark) is one of the most colorful in the country. The fish section has displays of unusual-looking fish, while the handicraft section, especially Row C, has the woven mats Zamboanga is noted for, along with brassware, antiques, shellcraft, batik from Indonesia, and tribal weavings. For tribal weavings prized by Philippine designers, visit the **Yakan Weaving Village,** 5 m (3 mi) from the city on the west coast. The weave is so fine it takes at least a week to finish a meter of cloth. Zamboanga is also famous for shells; the pickings are good at **Zamboanga Home Products** (San José St. at Jaldon, tel. 28–74), **San Luis Shell Industries** (San José Rd., tel. 24–19), and **Rocan** (San José Rd., tel. 24–92).

Beaches

Santa Cruz Island, Zamboanga City. Rent a motorized *banca*, a native canoe fitted with outriggers, from the **Lantaka Hotel** tel. 39–31 or 39–34) for the 20-minute trip to Santa Cruz Island. (Rates are officially set at $5 round-trip.) The small island has a wonderful pink coral beach and a lagoon in the middle. Open-air sheds can be rented for a minimal fee. Be sure to bring water and refreshments, as there are no food or beverage stands. At the beach's eastern end is a Muslim burial ground, ornamented with stars, crescents, and tiny boats—to provide passage to the next life. *Tel. 32–47 or 39–31. Admission charge. Open daily 7–4.*

Moalboal, Cebu. About 72 km (45 mi) southwest of Cebu City is this tiny town with an excellent white-sand beach, **Panagsama,** and coral reefs. Inexpensive accommodations, restaurants, and night spots dot the place.

Panglao, Bohol. This isle is connected by a bridge to Tagbilaran City on Bohol Island, a 20-minute flight from Cebu, and has three beautiful beach areas: **Bikini Beach, Bolod,** and **Alona Beach.** Bolod has the pricey Bohol Beach Club (Manila tel. 522–2301), complete with private beach, cabanas, water sports, pool, and bar. Inexpensive accommodations are available at the other two beaches.

Boracay Island. Famous among Europeans, this bow-tie-shape island off the coast of Panay has one of the Philippines' most beautiful beaches, with sands as fine and smooth as refined sugar. It has accommodations ranging from the expensive to the basic—a few too many, in fact—and is crowded from November to May. Charter flights are available from Cebu or Manila via **Aerolift.**

Sicogon Island. On this privately owned island off northern Panay is a resort offering accommodations in wood-and-thatch cottages, all with private bath and lanai (in Manila, tel. 317–1163). The best of the uncrowded white-sand beaches here are

Bantili and Buaya, and coral reefs provide good snorkeling. Mt.
Upao, (300 m, or 1,000 ft) has trails leading to the peak, which
offers magnificent views of Sicogon and other islands. Thickly
wooded, the island has colorful species of birds and gray and
brown monkeys.

Guimaras Island. A 45-minute boat ride from Iloilo City, this
lush island, famous for mangoes, has a couple of simple, inexpensive resorts, **Isla Naburot** (tel. 766–16) and **Tatlong Pulo**
(tel. 782–97). Isla is the bigger of the two; Tatlong Pulo has just
six cottages. Both resorts have water sports and diving facilities. Tatlong Pulo's mother and daughter owners make you feel
like a member of the family.

Dining and Lodging

Dining. This region has several specialties, particularly in seafood. *Sinugba* is a Cebu method of grilling fish and shellfish
over coals. Zamboangeños like raw fish marinated in vinegar
and hot green peppers, steamed crabs, and barbecued meats.
Iloilo is well known for its *pancit molo* (pork dumplings in noodle soup), *la paz batchoy* (a tripe stew), and pastries. At all
establishments listed, dress is casual and reservations unnecessary. Highly recommended restaurants are indicated by a
star ★.

Category	Cost*
Very Expensive	over P260 ($13)
Expensive	P160–P260 ($8–$13)
Moderate	P65–P160 ($3–$8)
Inexpensive	under P65 ($3)

add 6% sales tax; most places add 10% service charge

Lodging. Cebu City, the second-biggest city in the Philippines,
has a full range of accommodations, while Iloilo and Zamboanga
have mainly mid-range and medium-size hotels. All hotels
listed have private baths, unless otherwise noted. Highly recommended hotels are indicated by a star ★.

Category	Cost*
Very Expensive	over P1,100 ($55)
Expensive	P880–P1,100 ($40–$55)
Moderate	P300–P880 ($15–$40)
Inexpensive	under P300 ($15)

*All prices are for a standard double room; add 10% service
charge and 13.7% tax.*

Cebu City
Dining
★

Lantaw Seafoods Restaurant. You can feast on a splendid, well-
priced buffet—including seafood—in an open-air, garden setting while enjoying a folk-dance show and scenic views of the
city. Seating at long tables is available for groups. *Cebu Plaza,
Nivel Hills, Lahug, tel. 924–31 to 39. AE, DC, MC, V. Expensive.*

Camarin. Good Cebu dishes, particularly grilled seafood, are served by a friendly staff in this tropical-motif restaurant with palmy greenery and waiters in colorful shirts. *Magellan International Hotel, Lahug, tel. 746–21. AE, DC, MC, V. Moderate.*

Ding How Dimsum. Good light Chinese meals are served here. *Colón St., tel. 937–70. No credit cards. Inexpensive.*

★ **Vienna Kaffehaus.** Run by an Austrian, the place tries to recreate the ambience of a Viennese coffeehouse, complete with Viennese food, newspapers, and magazines. *Manros Plaza, Maxilom Ave., tel. 526–20. No credit cards. Inexpensive.*

Lodging **Cebu Plaza.** A luxurious hotel, the Cebu Plaza has panoramic
★ vistas, sprawling grounds, and a clientele consisting mainly of Japanese and Chinese tourists. The best rooms are those that have a view of the city. *Nivel Hills, Lahug, tel. 924–31 to 39. 417 rooms. Facilities: outdoor pool, restaurants, bars, disco, shops, tennis courts, function rooms. AE, DC, MC, V. Very Expensive.*

Magellan International Hotel. You'll feel comfortable in this well-maintained establishment with its air of breezy informality. Rooms are done in muted, restful colors. *Gorordo Ave., Lahug, tel. 746–21. 180 rooms. Facilities: pool, restaurants, bar, pelota courts, travel agencies, airline offices. AE, DC, MC, V. Expensive.*

Montebello Villa. Located in a quiet neighborhood, this hotel has nice gardens and cheerfully decorated rooms. *Banilad, tel. 85–07. 142 rooms. Facilities: restaurants, pool, tennis courts, casino, convention rooms, tour offices, gift shop. AE, DC, MC, V. Moderate.*

Iloilo City **Sunset Terrace.** For the money, you get excellent seafood (try
Dining the blue marlin and *tanguigue,* or local salmon), plus scenic
★ views of the river and (if you time it right) a sunset to boot. *Hotel del Rio, M.H. Del Pilar St., tel. 755–85. AE, DC, MC, V. Moderate.*

Ihawan. A down-home atmosphere prevails in this friendly place serving good chicken barbecue and other grilled meats. *Yulo St., tel. 768–34. No credit cards. Inexpensive.*

Tree House. Built around a real tree house and favored by backpackers, this cafeterialike eatery offers good Philippine food. *General Luna St., tel. 720–47. DC, V. Inexpensive.*

Lodging **Casa Plaza.** A cross between a hotel (rooms are spacious, with private bath) and a pension (rates include breakfast, Philippine-style or Continental), Casa Plaza occupies the third floor of an office building. Laundry facilities are available. *General Luna and Iznart Sts., tel. 769–64 and 734–61 to 67. 15 rooms. No credit cards. Moderate.*

★ **Hotel Del Rio.** The place is modest but quiet, appealing, and well run. The spacious, clean rooms get breezes from the Iloilo River, which flows right beside it. *M.H. Del Pilar St., tel. 755–85. 57 rooms. Facilities: outdoor pool, restaurants, disco, bar, gift shop. AE, DC, MC, V. Moderate.*

Sarabia Manor. Recently renovated, this hotel has a cosmopolitan feel to it and a friendly, well-informed staff. Rooms are well kept and spacious, but ceilings are rather low. *General Luna St., tel. 727–31. 100 rooms. Facilities: outdoor pool, restaurants, cocktail lounge, disco, gift shop. AE, DC, MC, V. Moderate.*

Family Pension House. A reconverted family residence with a tree house, this friendly and lively place seems to be a favorite among young travelers. *General Luna St., tel. 720–47. 25* *rooms. Facilities: restaurants, music lounge. DC, V. Inexpensive.*

Zamboanga City
Dining
★

Alavar's. Justifiably famous for his seafood, the owner/chef creates delicious sauces for crabs. Prawns, clams, blue marlin—this place serves it, in what was once a rambling house. *R.T. Lim Blvd., tel. 79–40. No credit cards. Moderate.*

Palmeras. Dine pleasantly in a shaded terrace set in a garden. Service is a bit slow, but the barbecued meats are good. *Santa Maria Rd., no phone. No credit cards. Inexpensive.*

Lodging
★

Lantaka. In the heart of the city and right by the waterfront, Lantaka has well-appointed rooms and gracious service. The terrace abuts the sea, where Badjaos, a tribe of sea gypsies, sell mats and seashells. Watch the sunset and the sea from the open-air, lovely Talisay Bar. *Valderrosa St., tel. 39–31 to 34. 112 rooms. Facilities: pool, restaurants, bar, conference room, travel offices, handicraft shop. AE, DC, MC, V. Moderate.*

Zamboanga Hermosa Hotel. The rooms are small but comfortably furnished. *Mayor Jaldon St., tel. 20–71. 33 rooms. Facilities: restaurant, laundry service. DC. Inexpensive.*

The Arts

The ground floor of **Casa Gorordo** in Cebu City (Lopez Jaena St., tel. 945–76) is used as an art gallery for contemporary works by Filipino artists. Iloilo has two galleries, the **Iloilo Society of Arts Gallery** (2nd floor, B & C Square, Iznart St., tel. 710–26) and **Galeria de Madia-as** (Washington St., Jaro, Department of Tourism, tel. 787–01 or 745–11), both of which display works by contemporary artists.

Nightlife

Cebu City is the only place in the region with nightlife to speak of. Iloilo City has a few discos and bars. Zamboanga has a few bars. All the following are in Cebu City.

Excellent pop bands perform at the very popular **Alindahaw Bar** (Cebu Plaza Hotel, Nivel Hills, Lahug, tel. 924–31). The city's fashionable set dances at the strobe-lit **Bai Disco** (Cebu Plaza Hotel, Nivel Hills, Lahug, tel. 924–31). At the **Cebu Casino** (Nivel Hills, Lahug, tel. 743–61), not far from Cebu Plaza, the action at the tables goes from 5 PM to 5 AM. **Love City** (Osmeña Blvd., tel. 940–77) is a raucous downtown bar with a mostly male clientele who come for beer and the go-go dancers. **St. Gotthard** (Fulton St., Lahug, tel. 753–76) is a lively disco with waitresses on roller skates. Europeans favor the friendly, informal **St. Moritz Bar** (Gorordo Ave., Lahug, tel. 612–40), part of a hotel of the same name.

7 Singapore

Introduction

by Nigel Fisher

Nigel Fisher is the editor of the monthly travel publication Voyager International. *He has traveled extensively throughout Asia and the world.*

As you are efficiently processed through Changi International Airport, then whisked away in a taxi or air-conditioned coach along a park-lined expressway to your high-rise hotel, don't let first impressions lead you to write Singapore off as just another modern international city. Though it may no longer be the richly exotic and romantic city so vividly documented by Conrad and Kipling, Singapore is yet a unique city where the flavor, spirituality, and gentle manners of the East peacefully co-exist with the comforts, conveniences, and efficiency of the West.

Here you'll find some of the world's most luxurious hotels, offering incomparable service and all the amenities, from fitness centers with computer-monitored exercise equipment to thick terry-cloth bathrobes. On Orchard Road, smartly dressed shoppers browse among glittering shop windows before heading into the dozens of huge side-by-side shopping complexes, jam-packed with boutiques carrying the latest Paris fashions or Japanese electronics at irresistible prices. And in elegant French restaurants, with gleaming silver and crystal and elaborate displays of orchids and roses, tuxedoed waiters serve some of the best cuisine this side of the Seine.

Here you'll also find ethnic neighborhoods, built up around mosques and temples, where Chinese or Indian or Malay merchants dressed in traditional garb hawk the herbal medicines or spices or batiks that spill out of their small shops onto the narrow streets. At the many food centers that dot the city, Teochew and Hokkien, Tamil and Malay cooks in adjacent open-front stalls whip up authentic and delicious dishes whose recipes have been handed down in their families for generations.

To arrive in Singapore is to step into a world where the muezzin call to prayer competes with the bustle of capitalism; where old men play mah-jongg in the streets and white-clad bowlers send the ball flying down well-tended cricket pitches; where Chinese fortune tellers and high-priced management consultants advise the same entrepreneur.

This great diversity of lifestyles, cultures, and religions thrives within the framework of a well-ordered society. Singapore is a spotlessly clean—some say sterile—modern metropolis, surrounded by green, groomed parks and populated by 2.7 million extremely polite, well-mannered people.

Malays, who have the oldest historical claim to Singapore, today account for 14.9% of its population. Their faith in Allah and their orientation to family and service to the community provide a more relaxed, peaceful, and communal flavor and act as a counterpoint to the entrepreneurial vigor of the Chinese.

Though the Chinese make up approximately 76% of the population, their ranks comprise at least half a dozen different ethnic groups—Hokkien, Teochew, Cantonese, Hakka, Fukien, Hainanese—each with its own language, mythology, and especially cuisine. They came as impoverished immigrants in the 19th century and now hold the economic and political strings of the island nation.

Singapore's Indian population, who also descend from 19th-century immigrants, are almost as ethnically diverse as the Chinese. While the majority are Hindu Tamils from South India, there are also Muslims from South India and, in smaller numbers, Bengalis, Biharis, Gujeratis, Marathis, Kashmiris, and Punjabis. From Sri Lanka come other Hindu Tamils and the Sinhalese (often mistaken for Indians), who are neither Hindu nor Muslim but follow the teachings of Hinayana Buddhism.

Today, Indians, who account for 7% of Singapore's population, remain deeply tied to their community and traditional customs. Hinduism remains a powerful force—Singapore has more than 20 major temples devoted to Hindu gods—and some of the Tamil Hindu festivals, such as Thaipusam, are expressed with more feverish ritualism than in India. Indian food, too, remains true to its roots; it has been said that one can eat better curries in Singapore than in India.

While the Malays, Chinese, and Indians account for 97% of Singapore's population, other ethnic groups—from Eurasians to Filipinos, from Armenians to Thais—contribute significantly to the nation's cultural mix. Understandably, the British and the heritage of their colonial stay is profoundly felt even though Singapore became an independent nation in 1967.

In a part of the world where histories tend to be ancient and rich, Singapore is unique in having almost no history at all. Modern Singapore tends to date its history from the early morning of January 29, 1819, when a representative of the British East India Company, Thomas Stamford Raffles, stepped ashore at Singa Pura (Sanskrit for "lion city"), as the island was then called, hoping to establish a British trading settlement on the southern part of the Malay Peninsula. The two sons of the previous sultan, who had died six years earlier, were in dispute over who would inherit the throne. Raffles backed the claim of the elder brother, Tunku Hussein Mohamed Shah, and proclaimed him sultan. Offering to support the new sultanate with British military strength, Raffles persuaded him to grant the British a lease allowing them to establish a trading post on the island in return for an annual rent; within a week the negotiations were concluded. (A later treaty ceded the island outright to the British.)

Thus began the continual rapid changing and adapting that characterizes Singapore to this day: Within three years, the small fishing village, surrounded by swamps and jungle and populated by only tigers and 200 or so Malays, had become a boomtown of 10,000 immigrants, administered by 74 British employees of the East India Company.

As Singapore grew, the British erected splendid public buildings, churches, and hotels, often using Indian convicts for labor. The Muslim, Hindu, Taoist, and Buddhist communities—swelling rapidly from the influx of fortune-seeking settlers from Malaya, India, and South China—built mosques, temples, and shrines. Magnificent houses for wealthy merchants sprang up, and the harbor became lined with *godowns* (warehouses) to hold all the goods passing through the port.

It was certainly an exotic trade that poured through Singapore. Chinese junks came loaded with tea, porcelain, silks, and artworks; Bugis (Indonesian) schooners carried in cargos of precious spices, rare tropical hardwoods, camphor, and produce from all parts of Indonesia. These goods, and more like them from Siam, the Philippines, and elsewhere in the region, were traded in Singapore for manufactured textiles,

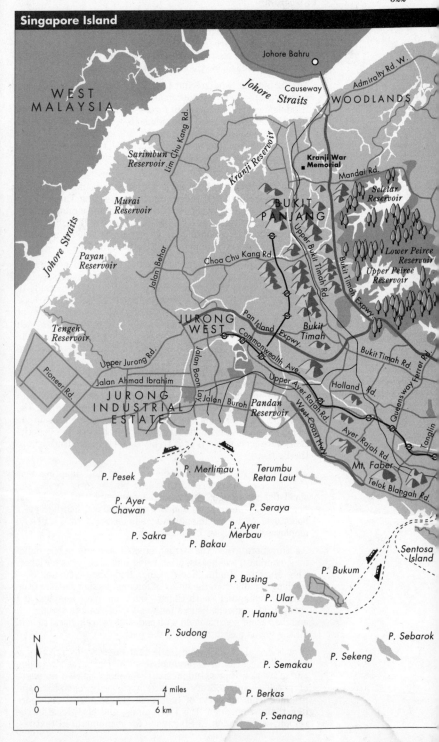

Singapore Island

322

West Malaysia

Johore Bahru
Causeway
Johore Straits
Admiralty Rd. W.
WOODLANDS

Sarimbun Reservoir
Lim Chu Kang Rd.
Kranji Reservoir
Kranji War Memorial
Mandai Rd.
Seletar Reservoir

Murai Reservoir
BUKIT PANJANG
Upper Bukit Timah Rd.
Lower Peirce Reservoir
Upper Peirce Reservoir

Payan Reservoir
Johore Straits
Jalan Behar
Choa Chu Kang Rd.
Bukit Timah Expwy.

Tengeh Reservoir
JURONG WEST
Pan Island Expwy.
Commonwealth Ave.
Bukit Timah
Bukit Timah Rd.

Upper Jurong Rd.
Jalan Boon Lay
Upper Ayer Rajah Rd.
Holland Rd.
Queensway
Ferrer Rd.

Pioneer Rd.
Jalan Ahmad Ibrahim
Jalan Buroh
Pandan Reservoir
West Coast Hwy.
Ayer Rajah Rd.
Tanglin

JURONG INDUSTRIAL ESTATE

P. Pesek
P. Merlimau
Terumbu Retan Laut
Mt. Faber
Telok Blangah Rd.

P. Ayer Chawan
P. Seraya

P. Sakra
P. Ayer Merbau
P. Bakau
Sentosa Island

P. Busing
P. Bukum
P. Ular
P. Hantu

P. Sudong
P. Sebarok
P. Sekeng
P. Semakau

N

0   4 miles
0   6 km

P. Berkas
P. Senang

WEST MALAYSIA

TO DESARU MALAYSIA

P. Seletar

Johore Straits

TO P. TEKONG

P. Serangoon

P. Ubin

P. Ketam

Serangoon Harbour

Yishun Ave. 2

Sembawang Rd.

Bukit Rd.

Yio Chu Kang Rd.

PONGGOL

S. Serangoon

Ponggol Rd.

CHANGI

Changi Airport

SERANGOON

S. Serangoon

Upper Thomson Rd.

Central Expwy

Upper Serangoon Rd.

Tampines Rd.

Loyang Ave.

U. Changi Rd.

MacRitchie Reservoir

Paya Lebar Rd.

Serangoon Rd.

Pan Island Expressway

BEDOK

New Upper Changi Rd.

Changi Rd.

Airport Blvd.

Changi Coast Rd.

Sims Ave.

Geylang Rd.

East Coast Rd.

Rd.

Orchard Rd.

Kallang Rd.

Nicoll Hwy.

KATONG

Mountbatten Rd.

East Coast Parkway

National Stadium

World Trade Centre Ferry Terminal

P. Brani

Buran Darat

P. Tekukor

P. Renggit

Kusu Island

Lazarus Island

St. John's Island

Sister's Islands

Strait of Singapore

Subway & Rail Lines

- - - - North-South MRT line
———— East-West MRT line
———— Railroad lines
⊖ Subway stop

coal, iron, cement, weapons, and machinery and other fruits of Europe's industrial revolution. Another major product traded here by the British was opium, grown in India and sold to mainland China.

By the turn of the century, Singapore had become the entrepôt of the East, a mixture of adventurers and "respectable middle classes." World War I hardly touched the island, although its defenses were strengthened to support the needs of the British navy, for which Singapore was an important base. When World War II broke out, the British were complacent about the impregnability of Singapore, expecting that any attack would come from the sea and that they were well prepared to meet such an attack. But the Japanese landed to the north, in Malaya. The two British battleships that had been posted to Singapore were sunk, and the Japanese land forces raced down the peninsula on bicycles.

In February 1942 the Japanese captured Singapore. Huge numbers of Allied civilians and military were sent to Changi Prison; others were marched off to prison camps in Malaya or to work on the notorious "Death Railway" in Thailand. The 3½ years of occupation was a time of privation and fear for the civilian population; up to 100,000 deaths are estimated during this period. The Japanese surrendered on August 21, 1945, and the Allied military forces returned to Singapore. However, the security of the British Empire was never again to be felt, and independence for British Southeast Asia was only a matter of time.

In 1957 the British government agreed to the establishment of an elected 51-member legislative assembly in Singapore. General elections in 1959 gave an overwhelming majority—43 of 51 seats—to the People's Action Party (PAP), and a young Chinese lawyer named Lee Kuan Yew became Singapore's first prime minister. In 1963 Singapore became part of the Federation of Malaysia, along with the newly independent state of Malaysia.

Mainly due to Malays' anxiety over a possible takeover by the ethnic Chinese, the federation broke up two years later and Singapore became an independent sovereign state. The electorate has remained faithful to Lee Kuan Yew and the PAP. Today there is only one opposition member in Parliament, though, at the last election, the PAP's popular majority was the lowest it has ever been. Singaporeans don't necessarily like the fact that Lee Kuan Yew's will substantially decides their future, but they recognize that it is largely as a result of his firm control and acumen that Singapore is a safe, clean, comfortable, prosperous nation.

Staying in Singapore

Getting Around Singapore

By Subway The most recent addition to Singapore's public transport system is a superb subway, known as the MRT. Only one line is open, but another is scheduled for completion in 1990; when it opens, the system will include a total of 42 stations along 67 km (42 mi). All cars and stations are air-conditioned, and the trains operate between 5:45 AM and midnight daily.

Tickets may be purchased in the stations from vending machines (which give change) or at a booth. There's a S$2 fine for underpaying, so make sure you buy the right ticket for your destination. Fares start at S$.50 for about two stations; the maximum fare is S$1.10. The fare between Orchard Road Station and Raffles Place Station (in the business district) is S$.60. For information, call 732–4411.

By Bus Buses are much cheaper than taxis and—with a little practice—easy to use. During rush hours, they can be quicker than cabs, since there are special bus lanes along the main roads. Some buses are air-conditioned, and service is frequent—usually every five to 10 minutes on most routes. Even without the excellent *Bus Guide,* available for S$.75 at any bookstore, finding your way around is relatively easy. Bus stops close to sightseeing attractions have signs pointing out the attractions.

The minimum fare is S$.40, the maximum S$.80. Exact change is necessary (conductors cannot give change) and should be deposited in the box as you enter the bus. Bus numbers are clearly marked, and most stops have a list of destinations with the numbers of the buses that service them. Buses run from 5:30 or 6 AM until around 11:30 PM.

The **Singapore Explorer Bus Ticket,** which may be purchased at most major hotels, lets you travel anywhere on the island on any bus operated by Singapore Bus Service (SBS—the red-and-white buses) or Trans Island Bus Service (TIBS—the orange-and-yellow buses). You may embark and disembark as frequently as you like, flashing your pass as you board. A one-day pass costs S$5 and a three-day pass costs S$12. With this ticket you also receive an **Explorer Bus Map** with color-coded routes showing bus stops and all major points of interest. For further details, call the Singapore Bus Service Passenger Relations Center (tel. 287–2727).

Coming from Malaysia, you can board a public bus at the Johore bus station or after the Malaysia checkpoint, at the causeway. You get off the bus on the other side of the causeway at the Singapore checkpoint, then reboard the bus for the ride into the city's center. Since you may not be reboarding the same bus—depending on the line at Immigration—do not leave your belongings behind when you get off.

By Taxi There are more than 10,000 taxis in Singapore, strictly regulated and metered. Many are air-conditioned. The starting fare is S$1.60 for the first 1.5 km (0.9 mi) and S$.10 for each subsequent 300 m (984 ft). After 10 km (6 mi) the rate increases to S$.10 for every 250 m (820 ft). Every 45 seconds of waiting time carries a S$.10 charge.

Several surcharges also apply: There is a charge of S$.50 for each additional person (the maximum is four passengers); S$1 is added for every piece of luggage stored in the trunk; trips made between midnight and 6 AM cost an extra S$.50; rides from, not to, the airport carry a S$3 surcharge; and there are "entrance and exit fees" on taxis and private cars going into and out of the central business district, or CBD. Unless a taxi displays a yellow permit, a S$1 surcharge is added to fares from the CBD between 4 and 7 PM on weekdays, and noon and 3 PM on Saturdays. To the CBD, a S$2 fee applies to rides between 7:30 and 10:15 AM Monday through Saturday.

Taxis may be found at stands or hailed from any curb not marked with a double yellow line. Radio cab services are available 24 hours (tel. 452–5555, 474–7707, or 250–0700); a S$1 surcharge is imposed, and the meter should not be switched on until after you have entered the taxi.

Drivers carry tariff cards, which you may see if you want clarification of your tab. Complaints should be registered with the STPB. However, just threatening to complain usually resolves any difficulty, since drivers can lose their licenses if they break the law.

By Ferry One of the pleasures of visiting Singapore is touring the harbor and visiting the islands. Most of the regularly scheduled ferries leave from the World Trade Centre. On weekdays, departures are at 10 AM and 1:30 PM (cost: S$5 round-trip); but on Sunday and holidays, there are eight scheduled departures. Check the return schedule before leaving for the islands.

By Bumboat Bumboats are motorized launches that serve as water taxis. Sailors use these to shuttle between Singapore and their ships. You can hire bumboats to the islands from Clifford Pier or Jardine Steps. The charge is approximately S$30 an hour for a boat that can comfortably accommodate six passengers.

By Car Hiring a chauffeur-driven or self-drive car is not at all necessary in Singapore. Distances are short, and parking, especially in the central business district, is very difficult. Taxis and public transportation are far more convenient and less expensive. Even to visit attractions out of the downtown area, buses or taxis are nearly as convenient and much more economical. And almost everything worth seeing is accessible by tour bus (*see* Guided Tours, below).

The following are some local branches of international agencies: **Avis:** Changi Airport, tel. 542–8833; Shangri-La Hotel, tel. 734–4169; Liat Towers, Orchard Road, tel. 737–1668. **Hertz:** Changi Airport, tel. 545–8181; Marina Square, tel. 336–5200; Tanglin Shopping Centre, Tanglin Road, tel. 734–4646; Westin Stamford Hotel, tel. 339–5656. **National:** Hong Seh Motors Pte. Ltd., #01-02 Tong Nam Building, 73 Bukit Timah Road, tel. 338–8444. **Sintat/Thrifty:** Changi Airport, tel. 542–7288; Dynasty Hotel, tel. 235–5855.

Rates start at S$90 a day, or S$475 a week, with unlimited mileage. A collision/damage waiver (CDW) insurance premium of S$90 per week will cover you for the initial S$2,000 not covered by the insurance included in the basic charge. There is a surcharge for taking the car into Malaysia: Avis, for example, adds S$50 a day, or S$300 per week, to its base charge for compact cars. The CDW is also higher for cars driven into Malaysia.

If you plan to do an overland drive through Malaysia, you can rent a car from a Singapore agency, but it is significantly less expensive to do so in Malaysia. Take the bus for S$.80 to Johore Bahru and you can save approximately S$50 a day on your car rental. Furthermore, you can make reservations with a rental agency in Johore (for example, Sintat/Thrifty, tel. 03/248-2388) from Singapore, and even be picked up from your Singapore hotel by private car at no extra charge.

Rules of the Road Singapore's **speed limits** are 80 kph on expressways unless otherwise posted, and 50 kph on other roads. One rule to keep in mind: Yield right of way at rotaries. Drive on the left-hand side of the road in both Malaysia and Singapore. Driver's licenses issued in the United States are valid in Singapore. To rent a car, you must be at least 23 years old and have a major credit card.

Gasoline Gas costs S$1.27 per liter in Singapore, significantly less in Malaysia. A new government ruling requires any car passing the causeway out of Singapore to have at least half a tank of gas or be fined; the republic's huge losses in revenue as a result of Singaporeans' driving to Malaysia to gas up cheaply led to the understandably unpopular ruling.

By Train Six trains a day operated by Malay Railways arrive from Kuala Lumpur and points north, such as Ipoh and Butterworth (Penang), at Singapore's **Keppel Road station** (tel. 222–5165). Immigration and Customs are at the station.

Important Addresses and Numbers

Tourist Information The most useful address in Singapore is that of the **Singapore Tourist Promotion Board** (Raffles City Tower, 250 North Bridge Rd., tel. 339–6622). The staff here will answer any question that you may have on visiting Singapore and will attend to legitimate complaints. Open weekdays 8–5, Saturday 8–1.

Should you have questions about your visitor's permit or wish to extend your stay beyond the time stamped in your passport, contact the **Immigration Department** (95 South Bridge Rd., #08-26 South Bridge Centre, tel. 532–2877).

Taxis are available 24 hours a day through the **Taxi Service** (tel. 452–5555 or 250–0700).

Embassies and Missions **Australia High Commission,** 25 Napier Road, tel. 737–9311. Open weekdays 8:30–noon and 2–4. **British High Commission,** Tanglin Road, tel. 473–9333. Open weekdays 9–noon and 2–4. **United States,** 30 Hill Street, tel. 338–0251. Open weekdays 8:30–noon.

Emergencies **Police,** tel. 999; **ambulance and fire,** tel. 995.

Doctors and Hospitals Singapore's medical facilities are among the best in the world, and most hotels have their own doctors on 24-hour call. Some government hospitals accustomed to treating overseas visitors are **Alexandra Hospital** (Alexandra Rd., tel. 473–5222), **Kadang Kerbau Hospital** (Maternity—Hampshire Rd., tel. 293–4044), and **Singapore General Hospital** (Outram Rd., tel. 222–3322).

Pharmacies Pharmaceuticals are available at supermarkets, department stores, and hotels. Registered pharmacists work 9–6. Some pharmacies in the major shopping centers stay open until 10 PM. Prescriptions must be written by locally registered doctors. Hospitals can fill prescriptions 24 hours a day.

Credit Cards For assistance with lost or stolen cards: **American Express** (tel. 235–8133), **Carte Blanche** (tel. 296–6511), **Diners Club** (tel. 294–4222), **MasterCard** (tel. 244–0444), and **Visa** (tel. 532–3577).

English-Language Since English is the lingua franca, all regular bookstores carry
Bookstores English-language books. Should you have trouble finding a
book, try the head office of the **Times Bookstore** (tel. 284–8844),
which will tell you whether any of its branches carries the title
you want.

Travel Agencies It is convenient to have your hotel's concierge handle airplane
reservations and ticket confirmations, but airline tickets are
less expensive if you buy them from a travel agent. Agencies
abound in Singapore and will arrange tours, transportation,
and hotels in Indonesia, Malaysia, and Thailand—or anywhere
else, for that matter.

Two of the better-known international travel agencies are
American Express Travel Services (#02-02/04 UDL Bldg., 96
Somerset Rd., tel. 235–8133) and **Thomas Cook Travel Services**
(#03-05 Sanford Bldg., 15 Hoe Chiang Rd., tel. 221–0222; #02-
04 Far East Plaza, 14 Scotts Rd., tel. 737–0366).

Telephones

Local Calls From a pay phone, the cost is S$.10. To make a call, insert a coin
and dial the seven-digit number. There are free public phones
at Changi airport, just past Immigration.

International Calls Direct dialing is available to most overseas countries. The top
hotels provide direct-dial phones in guest rooms; smaller hotels
have switchboards that will place your calls. In either case, the
service charge can be substantial. You can avoid the hotel
charge by making international calls from the General Post Office (*see* Mail, below) or by using the services at Changi airport.
International cables may also be sent from either of these
places.

The newly introduced Telecoms phone card can be useful if
you'll be making several long-distance calls during your stay in
Singapore. The cards, similar to the Foncards in Great Britain,
can be purchased in denominations of S$10, S$20, and S$50 and
permit you to make local and overseas calls. The price of each
call is deducted from the card total, and your balance is roughly
indicated by the punched hole in the card. The costs will be the
same as if you made the call from the GPO. Phone cards are
available from post offices and Telecoms Customer Services
outlets. Telephones that accept the phone card are found in
shopping centers, post offices, and at the airport. For inquiries, call 288–6633.

The direct-dial prefix for Malaysia is 106. For other international calls, dial 104 and the country code. The country code for
Singapore (for calls from outside the republic) is 65.

Information For directory inquiries, dial 103. An economical way to call
North America or the United Kingdom is to use international
Home Countries Direct phones—USA Direct or UK Direct—
which put you immediately in touch with either an American or
a British telephone operator. The operator will place your call,
either charging your telephone credit card or making the call
collect. These phones may be found at the GPO and at many of
the post offices around the city center, such as the one in the
Raffles City shopping complex.

Mail

Most hotels sell stamps and post guests' letters. In addition, there are 87 post offices on the island, most of them open weekdays 8:30–6 (Wednesday until 8) and Saturday 8:30–1. The airport post office and the Orchard Point post office are open daily 8–8. For postal inquiries, contact the **General Post Office (GPO)** in Fullerton Square, off Collyer Quay (tel. 533–6234).

Postal Rates Postage on local letters up to 20 g (0.8 oz) is S$.10. **Airmail** takes about five business days to reach North America and Great Britain. An airmail postcard costs S$.30 to most overseas destinations. A letter up to 10 g (0.4 oz) is S$.35 within Asia, S$.50 to Australia, S$.75 to Great Britain, and S$1 to North America. Printed **aerogram** letters (available at most post offices) are S$.35.

Shops are normally trustworthy in shipping major purchases, but if you prefer to make arrangements yourself, you will find post office staff helpful and efficient. All branches sell "Postpac" packing cartons, which come in different sizes.

Receiving Mail Mail can be sent to you c/o General Delivery, General Post Office, Fullerton Square, Singapore. American Express cardholders or traveler's-check users can have mail sent c/o American Express International, #14-00 UDL Building, Singapore 0923. Envelopes should be marked "Client Mail."

Currency

The local currency is the Singapore dollar (S$), which is divided into 100 cents. At press time, the following exchange rates applied: US$1 = S$1.96, UK£1 = S$1.21, A$1 = S$1.44. Notes in circulation: S$1, S$5, S$10, S$20, S$50, S$100, S$500, S$1,000, S$10,000. Coins: S$.01, S$.05, S$.20, S$.50, S$1.

What It Will Cost

Compared with other world capitals, Singapore is inexpensive, especially with regard to hotel prices. A deluxe hotel room costs a third what it would in Tokyo or London. A meal can also be very inexpensive if you dine at one of the ubiquitous food outlets, called hawker centers, where a full meal of superb food can be had for as little as $4. Public transportation is clean, efficient, and easy to manage, so visitors can also travel around the city of Singapore and the island very inexpensively.

Taxes There is no sales tax in Singapore. A 3% government tax is added to restaurant and hotel bills; sometimes a 10% service charge is added as well. There is a S$12 airport departure tax (for travelers to Malaysia, the tax is S$5). It is payable at the airport. To save time and avoid standing in line, you can buy a tax voucher at your hotel or any airline office.

Sample Prices Cup of coffee, 50¢; large bottle of beer, $2; lunch at a hawker stand, $4; dinner at an elegant restaurant, $20; full breakfast at a luxury hotel, $9. The cost of a standard double room: moderate, $50–$75; very expensive, over $100.

Language

Singapore is a multiracial society with four official languages: Malay, Mandarin, Tamil, and English. The national language is Malay; the lingua franca is English. English, also the language of administration, is a required course for every schoolchild, and is used in the entrance examinations for universities. Hence, virtually all Singaporeans speak English with varying degrees of fluency. Mandarin is increasingly replacing the other Chinese dialects. However, many Chinese will use SinEnglish, a Singaporean version of English, to converse with other ethnic groups, including other Chinese.

Opening and Closing Times

Businesses are generally open weekdays 9 or 9:30 to 5 or 5:30; some, not many, are also open on Saturday mornings.

Banks Banking hours are weekdays 10–3, Saturday 9:30–11:30 AM. Branches of the Development Bank of Singapore stay open until 3 PM on Saturdays. The bank at Changi airport is open whenever there are flights. Money-changers operate whenever there are customers in the shopping centers they serve.

Museums Many museums close on Monday; otherwise, they are generally open 9–5.

Shops Shop opening times vary. Department stores and many shops in big shopping centers are generally open seven days a week from around 10 AM to 6 PM (later some evenings). Smaller shops tend to close on Sundays, although there is no firm rule now that competition is so intense.

National Holidays

The following are national holidays: Jan. 1 (New Year's Day); Jan. 27, 28 (Chinese New Year); Good Friday (Apr. 13); Hani Raya Puasa (Apr. 26); Labor Day (May 1); Vesak Day (May 9); Hari Raya Haji (July 3); National Day (Aug. 9); Dee'pavali (Oct. 7); Dec. 24.

Festivals and Seasonal Events

Singapore is a city of festivals, from the truly exotic to the strictly-for-tourists. The exact dates vary from year to year according to the lunar or Islamic calendar.

Mid-Jan. During **Ponggal,** the four-day harvest festival, Tamil Indians from South India offer rice, curries, vegetables, sugarcane, and spices in thanksgiving to the Hindu gods. In the evening, the celebration takes place at the temples, where rice is cooked while prayers are chanted to the music of bells, drums, clarinets, and conch shells. The Perumal Temple of Serangoon Road is the best place to view these rites.

Mid-Jan.–Feb. **Thaipusam,** probably the most spectacular—and certainly the most gruesome—festival in Asia, celebrates the victory of the Hindu god Subramaniam over the demon Idumban. After night-long ritual purification and chanting, penitents enter a trance and pierce their flesh with knives, steel rods, and fish hooks, which they wear during the procession. The 8.1-km (5-mi) procession begins at the Perumal Temple on Serangoon

Road, passes the Sri Mariamman Temple on South Bridge Road, and ends at the Chettiar Temple.

Chinese New Year is the only time the Chinese stop working. The lunar New Year celebration lasts for 15 days, and most shops and businesses close for about a week.

Feb. The end of the Chinese New Year is marked by the **Chingay Procession.** Chinese, Malays, and Indians all get into the act for this event. Clashing gongs and beating drums, lion dancers lead a procession of Chinese stilt-walkers, swordsmen, warriors, acrobats, and characters from Chinese myth and legend.

Feb. or Mar. The **Birthday of the Monkey God** celebrates this character greatly loved by the Chinese. His birth is marked with a festival twice a year in Chinese temples—once in the spring and again around September. Mediums, with skewers piercing their cheeks and tongues, go into trances. Chinese street operas and puppet shows are usually performed in temple courtyards, and processions are held at the temples along Eng Hoon and Cumming streets.

Apr.–May **Ramadan** is the month of daytime fasting among the city's Muslim population. Food stalls in Bussorah Street and around the Sultan Mosque sell a variety of dishes at the end of the day's fast.

May or June The **Birthday of the Third Prince** celebrates this child god. The Chinese worship him as a hero and a miracle-worker. A temple in his honor is located at the junction of Clarke Street and North Boat Quay, near Chinatown; on his birthday, it is crowded with noisy worshipers who come to watch the flashy Chinese operas, which begin around noon.

Vesak Day commemorates the Buddha's birth, Enlightenment, and death. It is the most sacred annual festival in the Buddhist calendar. Throughout the day, starting before dawn, saffron-robed monks chant holy sutras in all the major Buddhist temples. Captive birds are set free. Candlelight processions are held around some of the temples in the evening.

June The **Dragon Boat Festival** commemorates the martyrdom of Qu Yuan, a Chinese poet and minister of state during the Chou dynasty (4th century BC), who was exiled for speaking out against court corruption and finally threw himself into the river. On seeing Qu Yuan's final and desperate act, local fishermen thrashed the water with their oars and beat drums to prevent fish from devouring their drowning hero. The anniversary of his death is celebrated with a regatta of boats decorated with dragon heads and painted in brilliant colors.

July During the **Birdsong Festival,** owners of tuneful birds hold competitions to see whose chirps best.

Aug. 9 **National Day,** the anniversary of the nation's independence, is a day of processions, fireworks, folk and dragon dances, and national pride. The finest view is from the Padang, where the main participants put on their best show. Tickets for special seating areas are available through the STPB.

Aug.–Sept. For a month each year, during the Chinese **Festival of the Hungry Ghosts,** the Gates of Hell are opened and ghosts are free to wander the Earth. The unhappy ghosts, those who died without descendants, may cause trouble and must therefore be placated with offerings. Imitation money ("Hell money") and joss sticks are burned, and prayers are said at all Chinese temples and in front of Chinese shops and homes. Chinese-opera *(wayang)* performances are held on open-air stages set up in the streets.

Sept. The **Mooncake Festival,** a traditional Chinese celebration, is held on the night of the year when the full moon is thought to be at its brightest. The Chinese have nighttime picnics and carry lanterns through the streets. Mooncakes—sweet pastries filled with red-bean paste, lotus seeds, nuts, and egg yolks— are eaten in abundance.

Sept.–Oct. During the nine-day **Navarathri Festival,** Hindus pay homage to three goddesses: Parvati, consort of Shiva the Destroyer; Lakshmi, goddess of wealth and consort of Vishnu the Protector; and Sarawathi, goddess of education and consort of Brahma the Creator. On all nights, at the Chettiar Temple on Tank Road, there are performances of classical Indian music, drama, and dancing from 7 to 10. On the last evening, the image of a silver horse is taken from its home in the Chettiar Temple and paraded around the streets.

Oct. The Chinese believe that the deities celebrated in the **Festival of the Nine Emperor Gods** can cure illness, bring good luck and wealth, and encourage longevity. They are honored in most Chinese temples on the ninth day of the ninth lunar month; the celebrations are at their most spectacular in the temples on Upper Serangoon Road and at Lorong Tai Seng.

Oct.–Nov. In the **Thimithi Festival,** Indian Hindus honor the goddess Duropadai by walking on fire. According to myth, Duropadai proved her chastity by walking over flaming coals. Today worshipers repeat her feat by walking barefoot over a bed of red-hot embers. See the spectacle at the Sri Mariamman Temple on South Bridge Road.

Deepavali celebrates the triumph of Krishna over the demon king Nasakasura. All Indian homes and temples are decorated with oil lamps and garlands. In Little India the streets are brilliantly illuminated.

Nov. **Merlion Week** is Singapore's version of Carnival, with food fairs, fashion shows, masquerade balls, and fireworks displays. Brochures of the activities are available in every hotel.

Nov.–Dec. Being a multiracial society, Singapore has taken **Christmas** to its commercial heart. All the shops are deep in artificial snow, and a Chinese Santa Claus appears every so often to encourage everyone to buy and give presents.

Tipping

Tipping is not customary in Singapore, and the government actively discourages it. It is prohibited at the airport and not encouraged in hotels that levy a 10% service charge or in restaurants. Hotel **bellboys** are usually tipped S$1 per bag for handling luggage. **Taxi drivers** are not tipped by Singaporeans.

Guided Tours

A wide range of sightseeing tours cover the highlights of Singapore. They are especially convenient for business travelers or others on a tight schedule and can be easily arranged through the tour desks in hotels. The following are a few of the tour operators providing services through major hotels, but there are many others as well. **RMG Tours** (5001 Beach Rd., #08–12 Golden Mile Complex, tel. 298–3944) organizes nightlife and food tours. **Siakson Coach Tours** (3 Miller St., Siakson Bldg., tel. 336–0268) has daily tours to the zoo and Mandai Gardens, plus excursions to Malaysia. **Tour East** (70 Anson Rd., #12–00 Tunas Bldg., tel. 235–5705) offers a variety of tours in Singapore and excursions to Malaysia and Indonesia. **Elpin Tours and Limousine Services** (317 Outram Rd., #02–23 Glass Hotel, tel. 235–3111) arranges tours of Sentosa Island.

The itineraries offered by the different tour operators are very similar. Tours can take two hours or the whole day, and prices range from S$16 to S$70. Most are operated in comfortable, air-conditioned coaches with guides and include pickup and return at your hotel. Tour agencies can also arrange private-car tours with guides; these are considerably more expensive.

Orientation
City Highlights

These are 2½-hour tours, given in the morning or the afternoon. Itineraries vary slightly, but generally you will be shown some of the major sightseeing and shopping areas, including Orchard Road, the high-rise business district along Shenton Way, and the historic buildings along the Padang. You will also see Chinatown and probably the Thian Hock Keng Temple. A visit to the Sri Mariamman Temple, a stroll through the beautiful Botanical Gardens, a drive up Mount Faber for a panoramic view of the city, and a visit to a handicraft factory are also likely to be included. A morning city tour usually features the "Instant Asia" cultural show.

City and East or West Coast

If the tour covers the east coast, you'll see the city highlights and visit some rural sights, such as a Malay village and/or the Kuan Yin Temple. You may also visit the infamous Changi Prison and drive through the green coastal area. This tour takes 4½ hours. The west-coast tour includes the Chinese and Japanese gardens and the Jurong Bird Park.

Boat Trips

Water Tours (3-A, 1st floor, Clifford Pier, tel. 914–4519) operates motorized junks for cruises in the harbor and to Kusu Island. **J & N Cruise** (24 Raffles Pl., #26–02 Clifford Centre, tel. 533–2733) operates the *Equator Dream*, a catamaran that offers lunch, high tea, and dinner cruises (with disco) around the harbor and to the islands. **Island Cruises** (50 Collyer Quay, #01–27 Overseas Union House, tel. 221–8333) offers breakfast, lunch, teatime, and starlight cruises (with strolling musicians) on the sleek new *Singapore Princess*.

Personal Guides

Some 500 tourist guides, speaking a total of 26 languages and dialects, are licensed by the STPB. Call the **Registered Tourist Guides Association** (tel. 734–6425 or 734–6472) to make arrangements. These guides are knowledgeable, and if they are unable to answer a question, they will seek out the information and satisfy your curiosity later.

Excursions

A number of tour operators arrange trips into Malaysia and Indonesia. These run the gamut: a half-day trip to Johore Bahru for S$19, a full-day trip to Malacca for S$68, a two-day visit to the Riau Islands of Indonesia for S$180, a three-day trip to Tioman Island (off the east coast of Malaysia) for S$370. There are also longer tours, which include Kuala Lumpur and Penang in Malaysia, and Lake Toba on the Indonesian island of Sumatra. Several cruises stopping in at Southeast Asian ports in the area begin and/or end in Singapore (*see* Tour Groups in Chapter 1).

Highlights for First-time Visitors

Chettiar Temple (*see* Tour 5)
Empress Place (*see* Tour 1)
Kuan Yin Temple (*see* Tour 4)
Pioneers of Singapore/Surrender Chambers (*see* Tour 9)
Raffles Hotel (*see* Tour 1)
Singapore Zoological Gardens (*see* Tour 8)
Sri Mariamman Temple (*see* Tour 2)
Sultan Mosque (*see* Tour 4)
Temple of 1,000 Lights (*see* Tour 3)
Thian Hock Keng Temple (*see* Tour 2)

Exploring Singapore

The main island of Singapore is shaped like a flattened diamond, 42 km (26 mi) east to west and 23 km (14 mi) north to south. At the top of the diamond is the causeway leading to peninsular Malaysia (Kuala Lumpur is under six hours away by car). At the bottom is Singapore city, the docks, and, offshore, Sentosa and 57 smaller islands—most of them uninhabited—that serve as bases for oil refining or as playground or beach escape from the city. To the east is Changi International Airport and, between it and the city, a parkway lined for miles with amusement centers of one sort or another. To the west is the industrial city of Jurong and several decidedly unindustrial attractions, including gardens and a bird park. At the center of the diamond is Singapore island's "clean and green" heart, with a splendid zoo, an orchid garden, and reservoirs surrounded by some very luxuriant tropical forest. Of the island's total land area, less than half is built up, with the balance made up of farmland, plantations, swamp areas, and forest. Well-paved roads connect all parts of the island, and Singapore city is served with excellent public transportation.

Tour 1: Colonial Singapore

Numbers in the margin correspond with numbered points of interest on the Tour 1: Colonial Singapore map.

A convenient place to start exploring colonial Singapore is at
❶ Clifford Pier and **Collyer Quay,** where most Europeans alighted from their ships to set foot on the island. Walk up Collyer Quay
❷ toward the Singapore River; **Change Alley**—once the site of a popular old bazaar and row of money changers—will be on your left. In April 1989 the area was closed down to make way for a modern business complex.

❸ Beyond Change Alley is the **General Post Office** (GPO), a proud Victorian building of gray stone with huge pillars that's an anachronism in an area of glass-and-steel high rises. Walk down the short, narrow, tree-lined street alongside the GPO and past the riverbank mini–food center to cross the gracious 1868
❹ iron-link **Cavenagh Bridge,** named after Major General Orfeur Cavenagh, governor of the Straits Settlements from 1859 to 1867.

Tour 1: Colonial Singapore

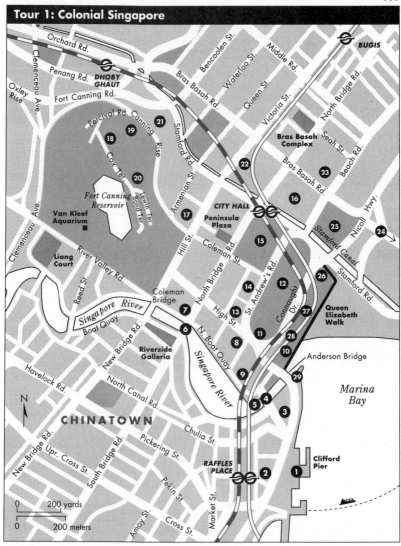

Armenian Church, **17**

Cavenagh Bridge, **4**

Cenotaph War
Memorial, **27**

Change Alley, **2**

City Hall, **14**

Collyer Quay, **1**

Convent of the Holy
Infant Jesus, **22**

Elgin Bridge, **6**

Empress Place, **9**

European cemetery,
19

Fort Canning Park, **18**

General Post Office, **3**

High Street Centre, **7**

Major Gen. Lim Bo
Seng Memorial, **28**

Marina Square, **24**

Merlion Park, **29**

National Museum and
Art Gallery, **21**

Padang, **12**

Parliament House, **8**

Raffles City, **16**

Raffles Hotel, **23**

Raffles statue, **5**

St. Andrew's
Cathedral, **15**

Singapore Cricket
Club, **11**

Supreme Court, **13**

Tomb of Iskandar
Shah, **20**

Victoria Memorial
Hall/Victoria
Theatre, **10**

Victorian fountain, **26**

War Memorial, **25**

Once over the Cavenagh Bridge, take a left onto North Boat Quay. Slightly back from the river is Empress Place, a huge white Victorian building that has been meticulously restored as an exhibition hall. We shall return here shortly, but for now

5 let us proceed a bit farther along the quay to a **statue of Sir Thomas Stamford Raffles,** who is believed to have landed on this spot early on the morning of January 29, 1819. Once this river was the organ of bustling commercial life, packed with barges and lighters that ferried goods from the cargo ships to the docks.

Now all that seeming mayhem is gone, and the river is close to being the sleepy waterway it was when Raffles first arrived. Cargo vessels are banned from entering the river, and the riverfront shops and two-story godowns are empty. Bumboats offer 30-minute **cruises** along the river and into Marina Bay; you can see as much from the shore as from the water, but it's a pleasant ride, and a respite for tired feet. *Dock kiosk, North Boat Quay, tel. 222–2528. Cost: S$5 adults, S$3 children under 12. Operating times: daily 9–7.*

6 Head west along the quay to **Elgin Bridge,** named after Lord Elgin, a governor-general of India. At the bridge, turn right

7 onto North Bridge Road and you'll see the **High Street Centre.** Take the elevator to the top floor of this office-and-shopping complex for one of the best panoramic views of downtown and colonial Singapore—and it's free.

Back at street level, continue on to High Street and turn right to pass under a sheltered, colonnaded walkway lined with mostly open-front shops of Indian merchants. Farther down High Street are graceful old buildings housing the attorney

8 general's chambers and **Parliament House,** designed in 1827 by Irishman George Coleman, the architect of many of Singapore's early buildings. Out front is a bronze statue of an elephant—presented by King Chulalongkorn of Siam during his state visit in 1871.

9 Across from Parliament House stands the neoclassical **Empress Place** building seen earlier. Constructed in the 1860s as the new courthouse, it has had four major additions and housed nearly every government body. Now, after a S$22 million renovation, Empress Place has a new lease on life as a cultural exhibition center. Its vast halls, high ceilings, and many columns give a majestic drama to exhibitions from around the world. Through 1994, the major exhibit will be a series of art collections from China. *1 Empress Place, tel. 336–7633. Admission charge. Open daily 9:30–9:30.*

10 The adjacent **Victoria Memorial Hall,** built in 1905 as a tribute to Queen Victoria, and the **Victoria Theatre,** built in 1862 as the town hall, are the city's main cultural centers, offering regular exhibitions, concerts, and theatrical performances of all types. In front of the clock tower is a **bronze statue of Raffles** by Thomas Woolner. (The Raffles statue by the river is a copy of this).

11 Across the road from the theater is the old **Singapore Cricket Club.** Founded during the 1850s, it became the main center for the social and sporting life of the British community. The club is not open to passing sightseers, but you can sneak a quick look at the deep, shaded verandas around back, from which members still watch cricket, rugby, and tennis matches. The

12 **Padang** (Malay for "field" or "plain")—the playing field on which these matches take place—was originally only half its present size; it was extended through land reclamation in the 1890s. Once called the Esplanade, it was where the colonial gentry strolled, exchanging pleasantries and gossip.

Looking out over the Padang are two splendidly pretentious, ⑬ imperial-looking gray-white buildings: the **Supreme Court** and ⑭ **City Hall.** The Supreme Court was completed in 1939, replacing the famous Hôtel de l'Europe, where Conrad used to prop up on the bar eavesdropping on sailors' tales that he would later use in his novels. The pedimental sculptures of the Grecian temple–like facade portray Justice and other allegorical figures. City Hall, completed in 1929, now houses a number of government ministries. It was here that the British surrender took place in 1942, followed by the surrender of the Japanese in 1945.

Continuing north on St. Andrew's Road, which runs along the Padang, cross Coleman Street toward the green lawns that ⑮ surround the Anglican **St. Andrew's Cathedral.** The first church was built on this site in 1834; after being struck twice by lightning, it was demolished in 1852. Indian convicts were brought in to construct a new cathedral in the 12th-century English Gothic style. The structure, completed in 1862, with bells cast by the firm that made Big Ben's, resembles Netley Abbey in Hampshire, England. The cathedral's lofty interior is white and simple, with stained-glass windows coloring the sunlight as it enters. Around the walls are marble and brass memorial plaques, including one remembering the British who died in the 1915 Mutiny of Native Light Infantry. Within easy walking ⑯ distance is the huge **Raffles City** complex, easily recognized by the towers of the two Westin hotels.

From the cathedral, return to Coleman Street and turn right (away from the Padang). Cross Hill Street, and on the right-⑰ hand corner is the **Armenian Church** or, more correctly, the Church of St. Gregory the Illuminator, one of the most endearing buildings in Singapore. It was built in 1835, which makes it the oldest surviving church in the republic. A dozen wealthy Armenian families supplied the funds for the ubiquitous Coleman to design this church. It is, perhaps, his finest work.

Behind the church is **Fort Canning Rise.** Seven centuries ago this hill was home to the royal palaces of the Majapahit rulers, who no doubt chose it for the cool breezes and commanding view of the river. Raffles established government house (headquarters for the colonial governor) on the Rise. In 1859, a fort was constructed; its guns were fired to mark dawn, noon, and night for the colony. Little remains of these grand construc-⑱ tions, but **Fort Canning Park** offers a green and peaceful retreat from the city center. On the slope, beneath the ruins of ⑲ the fort, is an **old European cemetery.** Farther up the slope and ⑳ to the left is the sacred **tomb of Iskandar Shah.** The government once decided to have the grave opened to determine whether the ruler was actually buried here, but no one would dig it up.

㉑ Exit the park via Percival Road to reach the **National Museum and Art Gallery** (tel. 337–6077). Both the museum and the gallery have been closed down for repairs and renovations and are expected to reopen in late 1990. Housed in a grand colonial building topped by a giant silver dome, the museum originally opened as the Raffles Museum in 1887. Included in its collection are 20 dioramas depicting the republic's past; the Revere Bell, donated to the original St. Andrew's Church in 1843 by the daughter of American patriot Paul Revere; the 380-piece Haw Par Jade Collection, reputedly one of the largest of its kind in the world; ethnographic collections from Southeast Asia; and many historical documents. The Art Gallery displays contemporary works by local artists. Leaving the museum, walk east on Stamford Road and turn left onto Victoria Street. On the ㉒ right, you'll pass the **Convent of the Holy Infant Jesus,** one of Singapore's most charming Victorian buildings.

Turn right onto Bras Basah Road and walk toward the sea. On your left, opposite Singapore's tallest hotel and largest conven- ㉓ tion center, is the **Raffles Hotel.** The Raffles has had many ups and downs, especially during World War II, when it was first a center for British refugees, then quarters for Japanese officers, then a center for released Allied prisoners of war. After the war the hotel deteriorated. It survived mostly as a tourist site, trading on its heritage rather than its facilities. However, from now through mid-1991, a massive restoration and expansion project is under way. Until the reopening, the best you can hope for is a peek into the Palm Court garden. Across Nicoll ㉔ Highway is **Marina Square,** a minicity of its own, with its 200 shops and three smart atrium hotels. The whole area is built on reclaimed land.

To return to Collyer Quay and Clifford Pier, recross Nicoll Highway. In a park below Bras Basah Road you'll notice the four 70-m (230-ft) tapering white columns (known locally as ㉕ "The Four Chopsticks") of the **War Memorial,** which commemorates the thousands of civilians from the four main ethnic groups (Chinese, Malay, Indian, and European) who lost their lives during the Japanese occupation of Singapore. Another tribute to the war dead of all Allied nations is the **Kranji War Memorial,** a meticulously maintained cemetery in the north of the island, off Woodlands Road. This is a touching experience, a small but potent reminder of the greatness of the loss in war.

Farther south on Connaught Drive, across Stamford Road, is ㉖ an ornate **Victorian fountain,** sculpted with Greek-inspired figures wearing Empire dress. In 1882, the colonial government commissioned it as a memorial to Tan King Seng, a wealthy Chinese who helped provide Singapore with a fresh-water supply.

Time Out   Just behind the fountain is a delightful alfresco eating place. It is known as the **Satay Club,** but the open-air stalls offer other local dishes besides satay.

Continuing south, the imposing structure you'll see on the left ㉗ is the **Cenotaph War Memorial** to the dead of the two world wars. From here, you can cross over the grass to join **Queen Elizabeth Walk,** running alongside Marina Bay. It was opened in 1953 to mark the queen's coronation and remains a popular place to take the evening air.

㉘ A few yards farther on is the **Memorial to Major General Lim Bo Seng,** a well-loved freedom fighter of World War II who was tortured and died in a Japanese prison camp in 1944. At the end of Queen Elizabeth Walk is Anderson Bridge. On the other ㉙ side, in **Merlion Park,** stands a statue of Singapore's tourism symbol, the Merlion—half lion, half fish. In the evening, the statue—on a point of land looking out over the harbor—is floodlit, its eyes are lighted, and its mouth spews water. Once over the bridge, you are on Fullerton Road, which eventually becomes Collyer Quay.

Tour 2: Chinatown

In a country where 76% of the people are Chinese, it may seem strange to name a small urban area Chinatown. But Chinatown was born some 170 years ago, when the Chinese were a minority (if only for half a century) in the newly formed British settlement. In the belief that it would minimize racial tension, Raffles allotted sections of the settlement to different ethnic groups. The Chinese immigrants were given the area to the south of the Singapore River. Today, the river is still the northern boundary of old Chinatown, while Maxwell Road marks its southern perimeter and New Bridge Road its western. Before the 1933 land reclamation, the western perimeter was the sea. The reclaimed area between Telok Ayer Street and Collyer Quay/Shenton Way has become the business district, often referred to as Singapore's Wall Street.

Within the relatively small rectangle apportioned to the Chinese, immigrants from mainland China—many of them penniless and half starved—were crammed. Within three years of the formation of the Straits Settlement, 3,000 Chinese had moved in; this number increased tenfold over the next decade.

In the shophouses—two-story buildings with shops or small factories on the ground floor and living quarters upstairs—as many as 30 lodgers would live together in a single room. Life was transient, a fight for space and survival. What order existed was maintained not by the colonial powers but by Chinese guilds, clan associations, and secret societies, which fought for control of various lucrative aspects of community life.

Until recently, all of Chinatown was slated for the bulldozer, to be replaced by uniform concrete structures. However, the government finally realized not only the people's desire to maintain Chinese customs and strong family ties, but also the important role these play in modern society. Chinatown received a stay of execution, and an ambitious plan to restore a large area of shophouses is set for completion by mid-1990.

Numbers in the margin correspond with numbered points of interest on the Tour 2: Chinatown map.

The only way to appreciate Chinatown is to walk its streets, letting sights and smells guide your feet. The following excursion covers many of the highlights, but let your curiosity lead you down any street that takes your fancy.

We'll begin at Elgin Bridge, built to link Chinatown with the colonial administrative center. At the south end of the bridge, logically enough, South Bridge Road begins. Off to the right is
❶ Upper Circular Road, on the left-hand side of which is **Yeo Swee Huat,** at No. 13 (tel. 533–4288). Here, paper models of the necessities of life—horses, cars, boats, planes, even fake money—are made, to be purchased by relatives of the deceased (you can buy them, too) and ritually burned so that their essence passes through to the spirit world in flames and smoke.

Back on South Bridge Road, at the corner of Circular Road, is
❷ the **Sam Yew Shop** (21 South Bridge Rd., tel. 534–4638). Here

Tour 2: Chinatown

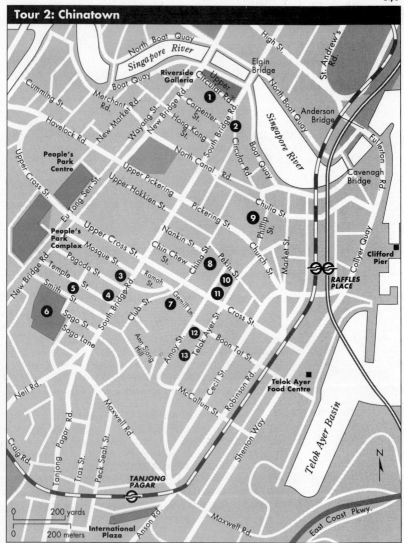

you can have your name—translated into Chinese characters—carved onto an ivory chop, or seal, for about S$60. Continuing

❸ down South Bridge Road, you'll pass the **Jamae Mosque**—built in the 1830s by Chulia Muslims from India's Coromandel

❹ Coast—before reaching **Sri Mariamman Temple,** the oldest Hindu temple in Singapore. Its pagodalike entrance is topped by one of the most ornate *gopurams* (pyramidal gateway towers) you are ever likely to see. Hundreds of brightly colored statues of deities and mythical animals line the tiers of this towering porch; glazed cement cows sit, seemingly in great contentment, atop the surrounding walls. Inside are some spectacular paintings that have been recently restored by Tamil craftsmen brought over from southern India.

At the junction of Trengganu and Temple streets, notice the old building on the corner. Reliable sources say this was a fa-

❺ mous **brothel** in its time. Opium dens and brothels played important roles in the lives of Chinese immigrants, who usually arrived alone, leaving their families behind, and worked long days, with little time for relaxation or pleasure.

You are now in the core of Chinatown, an area known as Kreta

❻ Ayer, dominated by **Chinatown Centre,** mobbed inside and out with jostling shoppers. At the open-air vegetable and fruit stands, women—toothless and wrinkled with age—sell their wares. Inside, on the first floor, hawker stalls sell a variety of cooked foods, but it is the basement floor that fascinates: Here you'll find a wet market (so called because water is continually sloshed over the floors), where an amazing array of meats, fowl, and fish are bought and sold.

Leaving the market, walk up **Sago Street** to South Bridge Road, then turn down Ann Siang Road. On the left, at No. 3, is a shop selling superb lion-head costumes and other masks. A left up Club Street takes you past old buildings that continue to house many clan associations.

A right off Club Street takes you to Gemmill Lane and several small shops where sculptures of deities are carved from sandalwood. Clients from all over Southeast Asia place orders for

❼ statues and temple panels at the **Say Tian Hong Buddha Shop,** at No. 6. Continue along Club Street and turn left onto Ramah Street, where, at No. 12, paper-thin pancakes are cooked on a griddle and sent to restaurants to be turned into spring rolls. On the other side of Cross Street, Club Street becomes China Street. Here, at another pancake shop, **Chop Chuan An,** you can watch spring rolls being made—and sample the finished products. To the left off China Street are Chin Chew, Nankin, and Hokkien streets; all have a number of well-preserved shophouses selling coffees, Chinese wines, birds' nests, herbal medicines, candy, and funeral paper.

❽ Back on China Street, opposite Nankin Street, is the **Jen Foh Medical Hall,** where salesmen are very helpful in suggesting cures for diseases or inadequacies you never knew you had. Where China Street ends, turn right onto Church Street, then

❾ take the first left onto Phillip Street. Here you'll find the **Wak Hai Cheng Bio Temple,** built between 1852 and 1855 by Teochew Chinese from Guangdong Province and dedicated to the goddess of the sea. The wonderfully ornate roof is covered with decorations—including miniature pagodas and human figures—depicting ancient Chinese villages and scenes from opera.

Retrace your steps to Telok Ayer Street. On the next block is ⑩ the Taoist **Fuk Tak Chi Temple,** built by Hakka and Cantonese immigrants. Show deference to the two sinister gods on the left as you enter or risk losing your spirit to them. In front of you are small statues representing some of the many Chinese deities. In the far right corner is one of Tua Pek Kong, to whom this temple is dedicated. Represented as a bearded sailor dressed in mourner's sackcloth, this deity is appealed to by those hoping for a prosperous and safe voyage.

Continue south on Telok Ayer; at Cross Street, notice the ⑪ **Hakka Clan Hall** (Ying He Hui Guan), on the right-hand corner. It is set in a courtyard and features intricate wood carvings on its gables. At No. 134 is **Meow Choon Foh Yit Ken,** a well-known store for traditional medicines.

⑫ Past the **Nagore Durghe Shrine,** an odd mix of minarets and Greek columns built by southern Indian Muslims between 1828 ⑬ and 1830, is the **Thian Hock Keng Temple** (Temple of Heavenly Happiness), completed in 1841 to replace a simple shrine built 20 years earlier. This Chinese temple is one of Singapore's oldest and largest, built on the spot where, prior to land reclamation, immigrants stepped ashore from their hazardous journey across the China Sea. In gratitude for their safe passage, the Hokkien people dedicated the temple to Ma Chu P'oh, the goddess of the sea.

Thian Hock Keng is richly decorated with gilded carvings, sculptures, tile roofs topped with dragons, and fine carved-stone pillars. Outside, on either side of the entrance, are two stone lions. The one on the left is female and holds a cup, symbolizing fertility; the other, a male, holds a ball, a symbol of wealth. Inside, a statue of a maternal Ma Chu P'oh, surrounded by masses of burning incense and candles, dominates the room. On either side of her are the deities of health and of wealth. The two tall figures are her sentinels: One can see for 1,000 miles, and the other can hear for 1,000 miles. The gluey black substance on their lips—placed there by devotees in days past—is opium to heighten their senses. While the main temple is Taoist, the temple at the back is Buddhist and dedicated to Kuan Yin, the goddess of mercy. Her many arms represent how she reaches out to all those who suffer on earth.

Tour 3: The Indian District

Indians have been part of Singapore's development from the beginning. While Singapore was administered by the East India Company, headquartered in Calcutta, Indian convicts were sent there to serve their time. Other Indians came freely to seek their fortunes as clerks, traders, teachers, and money-lenders.

The area Raffles allotted to the Indian immigrants was north of the British colonial district. The heart of this area—known today as Little India—is Serangoon Road. A good starting point for a tour is the junction of Serangoon and Sungei roads. As you walk along Serangoon, your senses will be sharpened by the fragrances of curry powders and perfumes, by tapes of high-pitched Indian music, by jewelry shops selling gold, and stands selling garlands of flowers. Other shops supply the colorful dyes used to mark the *tilak*—the dot seen on the forehead of Indian women.

In the first block on the left is **Zhu Jiao Centre,** one of the largest wet markets in the city. The array of fruits, vegetables, fish, herbs, and spices is staggering. Upstairs are shops selling brass goods, "antiques," porcelains, and textiles. On the right, just past Hastings Street, is **P. Govindasamy Pillai,** at No. 48/50, famous for Indian textiles, especially saris. Farther along, after Dunlop Street, at No. 82, is **Gourdatty Pillai,** with baskets filled with spices of every kind.

The streets to the right off Serangoon Road—Hastings Road, Campbell Lane, and Dunlop Street—are also filled with shops, many of them open-fronted, selling such utilitarian items as pots and pans, plus rice, spices, brown cakes of palm sugar, and every other type of Indian grocery item imaginable. Along Buffalo Road, to the left off Serangoon, are shops specializing in saris, flower garlands, and electronic equipment. Also along this short street are a number of moneylenders from the Chettiar caste—the only caste that continues to pursue in Singapore the role prescribed to them in India.

Continuing down Serangoon Road, you'll pass poster shops; the **Mi Ramassy Flour Mill** (at No. 92), where customers come for freshly ground flour; and shops selling silver charms and flower garlands. Down Cuff Road on the right, simple restaurants serve superb chicken, mutton, or fish curries, often on banana leaves with great mounds of boiled rice and an assortment of condiments.

A little farther down Serangoon Road on the left (opposite Veerasamy Road) you'll notice the elaborate gopuram—adorned with newly repainted sculptures—of the **Sri Veeramakaliamman Temple,** built in 1881 by indentured Bengali laborers working the lime pits nearby. It is dedicated to Kali the Courageous, a ferocious incarnation of Shiva's wife, Parvati the Beautiful. Inside is a jet-black statue of Kali, the fiercest of the Hindu deities, who demands sacrifices and is often depicted with a garland of skulls. More cheerful is the shrine to Ganesh, the elephant-headed god of wisdom and prosperity. Unlike Singapore's other temples, which are open all day, this one is open 8 AM–noon and 5:30–8:30 PM. At these times, you will see Hindus going in to receive blessings: The priest streaks devotees' foreheads with *vibhuti*, the white ash from burned cow dung.

Continue along Serangoon to Race Course Road and the Sakya Muni Buddha Gaya Temple. It is popularly known as the **Temple of 1,000 Lights** because, for a small donation, you can pull the switch that lights countless bulbs around a 15-m (50-ft) Buddha. The entire temple, as well as the Buddha statue, was built by the Thai monk Vutthisasala, who, until he died at the age of 94, was always in the temple, ready to explain Buddhist philosophy to anyone who wanted to listen. The monk also managed to procure relics for the temple: a mother-of-pearl-inlaid cast of the Buddha's footstep, and a piece of bark from the bodhi tree under which he received Enlightenment. Around the pedestal supporting the great Buddha statue is a series of scenes depicting the story of his search for Enlightenment; inside a hollow chamber at the back is a re-creation of the scene of the Buddha's last sermon.

Across the road is the charming **Leong San See Temple.** Its main altar is dedicated to Kuan Yin—also known as Bodhisattva Avalokitesvara—and framed by beautiful ornate carvings of flowers, a phoenix, and other birds. Backtrack on Race Course Road to Perumal Road; to the left is the **Sri Srinivasa Perumal Temple.** Dedicated to Vishnu the Preserver, the temple is easy to recognize by the 18-m (60-ft) high monumental gopuram, with tiers of intricate sculptures depicting Vishnu in the nine forms in which he has appeared on earth. From Sri Perumal, head back down Serangoon, exploring the side streets, or take a five-minute taxi ride to the Arab District.

Tour 4: The Arab District

Long before the Europeans arrived, Arab traders plied the coastlines of the Malay Peninsula and Indonesia, bringing with them the teachings of Islam. By the time Raffles came to Singapore in 1819, to be a Malay was also to be a Muslim. Traditionally, Malays' lives have centered on their religion and their villages, known as *kampongs.* These consisted of a number of wood houses, with steep roofs of corrugated iron or thatch, gathered around a communal center, where chickens and children would feed and play under the watchful eye of mothers and the village elders while the younger men tended the fields or took to the sea in fishing boats. The houses were usually built on stilts above marshes and reached by narrow planks serving as bridges. If the kampong was on dry land, flowers and fruit trees would surround the houses.

The area known as the Arab District, or Little Araby, while not a true kampong, remains a Malay enclave, held firmly together by strict observance of the tenets of Islam. At the heart of the community is the Sultan Mosque, or Masjid Sultan, originally built with a grant from the East India Company to the Sultan of Jahore. Around it are streets whose very names—Bussorah, Baghdad, Kandahar—evoke the fragrances of the Muslim world. This is a place to meander, taking time to browse through shops or enjoy Muslim food at a simple café. This tour begins at the foot of Arab Street, just across Beach Road from the Plaza Hotel.

The first shops on Arab Street are bursting with baskets of every description, either stacked on the floor or suspended from the ceiling. Farther along, shops selling fabrics—batiks, embroidered table linens, rich silks and velvets—dominate. However, don't go all the way up Arab Street yet. First turn right onto Baghdad Street (with more shops) and watch for the dramatic view of the Sultan Mosque when Bussorah Street opens up to your left. On Bussorah Street itself, on the right-hand side, are some interesting shops, including a Malay bridal shop, purveyors of batiks and Arab-designed cushion covers, and an importer of leather goods from Jogjakarta (Indonesia).

The first mosque on the site of the **Sultan Mosque** was built early in the 1820s with a S$3,000 grant from the East India Company. The current structure, built in 1928 by the same architects who designed the Victoria Memorial Hall, is a dramatic building with golden domes and minarets that glisten in the sunlight. The walls of the vast prayer hall are adorned with green and gold mosaic tiles on which passages from the Qur'an are written in decorative Arab script.

Two blocks east of the mosque, on Sultan Gate, is **Istana Kampong Glam,** the sultan's Malay-style palace. Rebuilt in the 1840s on a design by George Coleman, it is in a sad state of repair today. Next door, faring only slightly better, is another grand royal bungalow: the home of the sultan's first minister. Notice its gateposts surmounted by green eagles. Neither building is open to the public, but through the gates you can get a glimpse of the past.

Baghdad Street becomes Pahang Street at Sultan Gate, where several traditional Chinese stonemasons create statues curbside. At the junction with Jalan Sultan, turn right and, at Beach Road, left, to visit the endearing **Hajjah Fatimah Mosque.** The minaret is reputedly modeled on the spire of the original St. Andrew's Church in colonial Singapore, but it leans at a six-degree angle. No one knows whether this was intentional or accidental.

Return to Jalan Sultan and take a right. Past Minto Road is the **Sultan Plaza.** Inside, dozens of traders offer batiks and other fabrics in traditional Indonesian and Malay designs, and one store on the third floor (No. 26) sells handicrafts from the Philippines. Return to North Bridge Road and take a right back to Arab Street. North Bridge Road is full of fascinating stores selling costumes and headdresses for Muslim weddings, clothes for traditional Malay dances, prayer beads, scarfs, perfumes, and much more. Across Arab Street, Haji Lane, Shaik Madereah Lane, and Clyde Street offer a maze of small shops to explore. As you walk southeast along North Bridge Road you'll start seeing fewer signs in Arabic and fewer Malay names. Rochor Road is an unofficial boundary of the Arab District. The next right will bring you to **Bugis Street**—until recently, the epitome of Singapore's seedy but colorful nightlife.

Tourists (and Singaporeans, too, for that matter) used to delight in Bugis Street's red lights and bars, where transvestites would compete with the most attractive women for attention and favors. The government was *not* delighted, though, and so the area was razed to make way for a new MRT station. So strong was the outcry that Bugis Street is about to be reborn, albeit much tamed—sanitized, controlled, and programmed by a government-licensed entertainment corporation. Shophouses will be re-created on a site near the original street, and the emphasis will be on food and retail outfits.

Three blocks beyond where Bugis Street becomes Albert Street—past the **Fu Lu Shou** shopping complex (mostly for clothes) and the food-oriented **Albert Complex**—is Waterloo Street. Near the corner is the **Kuan Yin Temple,** one of the most popular Chinese temples in Singapore. The dusty, incense-filled interior, its altars heaped with hundreds of small statues of gods from the Chinese pantheon, transports the visitor into the world of Chinese mythology.

Tour 5: Orchard Road

If "downtown" is defined as where the action is, then Singapore's downtown is Orchard Road—an ultra-high-rent district that is very modern and very, very flashy, especially at night, when millions of lightbulbs, flashing from seemingly every building, assault the senses. Here are some of the city's most fashionable shops, hotels, restaurants, and nightclubs, plus a number of sights with which to break up a shopping trip.

Leaving the MRT station Dhoby Ghaut, with the **Plaza Singapura** shopping complex on your right, you'll see the enormous **Istana,** once the official residence of the colonial governor and now that of the president of the republic. It is open to the public only on National Day. On the first Sunday of each month, there's a changing-of-the-guard ceremony: The new guards leave Bideford Road at 5:30 PM and march along Orchard Road to the Istana, reaching the entrance gate punctually at 6.

On the other side of Orchard Road and a few steps on Clemenceau Avenue is the lovely old **Tan Yeok Nee House,** built around 1885 for a wealthy merchant from China. Whereas most homes built in Singapore at that time followed European styles, this town house was designed in a style popular in South China—notice the keyhole gables, terra-cotta tiles, and massive granite pillars. Since 1940 the Salvation Army has made the place its local headquarters. *207 Clemenceau Ave., tel. 734–3358. Admission free. Open weekdays 8:30–4:30, Sat. 9–noon, Sun. 8:30–6.*

Turn onto Tank Road and continue to the **Chettiar Temple,** which houses the image of Lord Subramaniam. The temple is a recent replacement (1984) of the original, built in the 19th century. The 21-m- (70-ft-) high gopuram, with its many colorful sculptures of godly manifestations, is astounding. The chandelier-lit interior is lavishly decorated; 48 painted-glass panels are inset in the ceiling and angled to reflect the sunrise and sunset. *Open daily 8–noon and 5:30–8:30.*

Return to Orchard Road and continue until you reach Cuppage Road, with a **market** (open every morning) known for imported and unusual fruit and a row of shops with a good selection of antiques.

Time Out For a quick break, try the **Cuppage Food Centre,** next to the Centrepoint shopping complex. Many of the stalls open out onto an attractive tree-lined walkway. The **Selera Restaurant** is famous for its Hainanese curry puffs.

Returning once more to Orchard Road, you'll pass the block-long **Centrepoint;** immediately after it is **Peranakan Place,** a celebration of Peranakan (also called Straits-born Chinese, or Baba) culture. This innovative blending of Chinese and Malay cultures emerged in the 19th century as Chinese born in the Straits Settlements adopted Malay fashions, cuisine, and architectural style, adapting them to their own satisfaction. At Peranakan Place, six old wooden shophouses, with fretted woodwork and painted in pastel colors, have been beautifully restored. Notice the typical Peranakan touches, like the distinctive use of decorative tiles and unusual fence doors.

Inside the buildings, ranged around a cobblestone forecourt, are shops selling Baba crafts; **Ba Chik's Foto Saloon,** where you can have a sepia-toned print of yourself, dressed in Peranakan clothing, taken; and two restaurants serving Nonya food, the distinctive cuisine of the Straits-born Chinese, both with outdoor tables. Costumed guides conduct tours through the **Show House Museum,** a re-creation of a turn-of-the-century Peranakan home. The unique mixture of Malay, Chinese, and European styles that characterizes Peranakan decor is represented by such furnishings as a Malay bed, a large Chinese altar, and an English sporting print. *180 Orchard Rd., tel. 732–6966. Admission free. Fee for Show House Museum tour. Open daily 10–6.*

Time Out In **Bibi's** charming colonial-style dining room one floor up, overlooking Peranakan Place, the S\$15 buffet luncheon is a good way to experience the marriage between Chinese and Malay cuisines. *Tel. 732–6966. Open daily noon–3 and 6:45–11. AE, DC, V.*

Pass the **Lucky Plaza** shopping center, packed with camera, electronic, and watch shops, to the corner of Orchard and Scotts roads. You are now at the heartbeat of downtown Singapore. Here, in the lobby of the **Dynasty Hotel,** you'll find a very special attraction: two facing walls of magnificently executed murals. These are, in fact, 24 gigantic panels of intricately carved teakwood, each 1.2 m (4 ft) wide and three stories high. Viewed as a whole, they present a vast panorama of 4,000 years of Chinese history and legend. The carving was done in China by 120 master carvers, mostly between 60 and 75 years old, on teak imported from the Burma-Thai border. (A book called *Tales of the Carved Panels* is available at the hotel desk.)

Retrace your steps to the intersection of Scotts and Orchard roads and continue up Orchard Road. Things quiet down a bit now. Walk on the right-hand side of the street past the **Liat Towers** complex (Hermès and Chanel are here), the **Far East Shopping Center,** the **Hilton** and its gallery of boutiques, and the **Ming Court Hotel.** At the Ming Court, veer left onto Tanglin Road, another main thoroughfare. Past the **Tudor Court Shopping Gallery** is the **Singapore Handicraft Centre,** with more than 40 shops showcasing the crafts of Asia, both contemporary and traditional. On Wednesday, Saturday, and Sunday nights (6–10) a *pasar malam* ("night bazaar") is held here. The mall and courtyard are jammed with stalls selling souvenirs and sundry wares.

Tour 5: Around the Island

Throughout the main island, there are numerous attractions to enjoy. Using the republic's excellent public transportation system, you can link several of these to make an East Coast tour, a West Coast tour, and a Center Island tour. Each can easily be accomplished in a morning or an afternoon. Alternatively, you can join one of the many organized tours that cover the attractions that interest you.

West Coast Near the satellite city of **Jurong,** Singapore's main industrial area, are a number of attractions that are covered in tours booked at the travel desk of any major hotel, or you can use the MRT or public buses to reach whichever attractions interest you.

Haw Par Villa (Tiger Balm Gardens), on the West Coast Highway, is an unusual landscaped garden with a bizarre series of displays, sculpted in cement and brightly painted, illustrating scenes from Chinese mythology, folk stories, and more. At press time, the gardens were closed and undergoing a series of renovations and expansions to create a huge theme park, scheduled for completion in 1990. *423 Pasir Panjang Rd., tel. 337-0134. Bus No. 143 from Orchard Rd. will get you here.*

Three popular west-coast attractions, relatively close to one another, are the Chinese Garden, the Japanese Garden, and the Jurong Bird Park. The easiest way to get to them is by air-conditioned express bus. The **Bird Park/Road Runner Service,** operated by Journey Express (tel. 339-7738), departs twice daily, in the morning and afternoon, from hotels along Orchard and Havelock roads. The round-trip fare is S$10 for adults, S$6 for children; there is also a shuttle service three times daily between the Bird Park and the Chinese Garden. Alternatively, you can take either the MRT (get off at Clementi Station) or the public bus (take the No. 10 or No. 30 from Clifford Pier or the No. 7 from Orchard Road to the Jurong Interchange; from the Interchange, you can walk to the gardens or take the No. 240, 242, or 406 bus). A taxi costs about S$12 to the Bird Park or the gardens from Orchard Road.

The 34.6-acre **Chinese Garden** (Yu Hwa Yuan) reconstructs an ornate Chinese Imperial garden, complete with temples, courtyards, bridges, and pagodas. It is beautifully landscaped, with lotus-filled lakes, placid streams overhung by groves of willows, and twin pagodas. *Off Yuan Ching Rd., Jurong, tel. 265-5889. Admission charge. (Combined ticket with Japanese Garden available.) Open Mon.-Sat. 9-7, Sun. 8:30-7.*

Adjacent to the Chinese Garden and connected with it by a walkway is the **Japanese Garden.** This delightful formal garden is one of the largest Japanese-style gardens outside Japan. Its classic simplicity, serenity, and harmonious arrangement of plants, stones, bridges, and trees induces tranquillity. *Off Yuan Ching Rd., Jurong, tel. 265-5889. Admission charge. Open Mon.-Sat. 9-7, Sun. 8:30-7.*

Across the water from the gardens is the **Singapore Science Centre,** dedicated to the space age and its technology. Subjects such as aviation, nuclear sciences, robotics, astronomy, and space technology are entertainingly explored through audiovisual aids and computers that you operate. The Omni-Theatre presents two programs: "Oasis in Space," which travels to the beginning of the universe, and "To Fly," which simulates the feel of travel in space. *Science Centre Rd., off Jurong Town Hall Rd., tel. 560-3316. Admission charge. Open Tues.-Sun. 10-6.*

The **Jurong Bird Park,** on 50 landscaped acres, boasts the world's largest walk-in aviary, complete with a 30-m (100-ft) man-made waterfall that cascades into a meandering stream. More than 3,600 birds from 365 species are here, including the colorful, the rare, and the noisy. If you get to the park early, try the breakfast buffet (from 9 to 11) at the Song Bird Terrace, where birds in bamboo cages tunefully trill as you help yourself to sausages, eggs, and toast. From there you can walk over to the Free Flight Show (held at 10:30), featuring eagles and hawks. In the afternoon, at 3:30, you might catch the Parrot Circus, complete with bike-riding bird-gymnasts. *Jurong Hill, Jalan Ahmad Ibrahim, tel. 265-0022. Admission charge. Open daily 9-6. Take bus No. 250, 251, or 253 from the Jurong Interchange.*

Next to the bird park is the **Jurong Crocodile Paradise.** Singaporeans seem to be fascinated with crocs, for at this five-acre park you'll find 2,500 more of them in various environments—in landscaped streams, at a feeding platform, in a breeding lake. You can feed the crocodiles, watch muscle-bound showmen (and a show*lady*) wrestle crocodiles, or buy crocodile-skin products at the shop. You can also watch the beasts through glass, in an underwater viewing gallery. *241 Jalan Ahmad Ibrahim, tel. 261–8866. Admission charge. Open daily 9–6.*

Into the Garden Isle Singapore is called the Garden Isle, and with good reason. Obsessed as it is with ferroconcrete, the government has also established nature reserves, gardens, and a zoo. This excursion from downtown Singapore takes you into the center of the island to enjoy some of its greenery. If you have only a little time to spare, do try to fit in the zoo, at least—it is exceptional.

The quickest way to reach the zoo is a 20-minute taxi ride (the fare is about S$11). Bus No. 171 *(Singapore Explorer)* from Orchard Boulevard or No. 137 from Upper Thomson Road will take you to the zoo in under 40 minutes for S$.80 any time of the day; other buses connect the nearby tourist sites. Alternatively, the air-conditioned **Zoo Express** bus (tel. 235–3111 or 777–3897) takes about 30 minutes, depending on which hotel you're collected from, and includes a short stopover at the Mandai Orchid Garden. The bus makes two runs a day, starting at 8:30 AM and at 1 PM. Cost (including round-trip and admission to the zoo and the Mandai gardens) is S$18 adults, S$11 children under 12. The **Zoo Road Runner Service** (tel. 339–7738) makes three runs a day, picking up at seven hotels. It also takes about 30 minutes and includes a stop at Mandai Orchid Garden. Cost (bus fare only): S$10 adults, S$6 children under 12.

Cliché though it may be, at the **Singapore Zoological Gardens,** humans visit animals as guests in their habitat. One gets the impression that animals come here for a vacation and not, as is often the case elsewhere, to serve a prison sentence. What makes the Singapore zoo different is that it is designed according to the open-moat concept, wherein a wet or dry moat separates the animals from the people. Try to arrive in time for the buffet breakfast. The food itself is not special, but the company is. At 9:30 AM, Ah Meng, a 24-year-old orangutan, comes by for her repast. Afterward, from glass windows beneath their watery grotto, you can watch the polar bears dive for their own fishy breakfast.

There are performances by snakes, monkeys, fur seals, elephants, free-flying storks, and other zoo inhabitants at various times throughout the day. In numerous miniparks reproducing different environments, giraffes, Celebese apes, bearded pigs, tigers, lions, and other of the zoo's 1,700 animals from among 160 species take life easy. Elephant rides are available for S$2 adults, S$1 children. For S$1.50, visitors can travel from one section of the zoo to another by train. *80 Mandai Lake Rd., tel. 269–3411. Admission charge. Open daily 8:30–6.*

The **Mandai Orchid Garden,** a half-mile down the road from the zoo (bus No. 171 links the two), is a commercial orchid farm. The hillside is covered with the exotic blooms, cultivated for domestic sale and export. There are many varieties to admire, some quite spectacular. *Mandai Lake Rd., tel. 269–1036. Admission charge. Open weekdays 9–5:30.*

For those who prefer their nature a little wilder than what the carefully manicured parks around the city can offer, the **Bukit Timah Nature Reserve** is the place to go. In these 148 acres around Singapore's highest hill, the tropical forest runs riot, giving a feel for how things were before anyone besides tigers roamed the island. Wandering along structured, well-marked paths, you may be startled by flying lemurs, civet cats, or long-tailed macaques. The view from the hilltop is superb. Wear good walking shoes—the trails are not smooth gravel but rocky, sometimes muddy, paths. *Km 12, Upper Bukit Timah Rd., no tel. Admission free. Open dawn to dusk. From the zoo or the Mandai Orchid Garden, take bus No. 171. The same bus departs from the Orchard and Scotts Rds. intersection.*

Back toward the city center are the **Botanic Gardens,** an ideal place to escape the bustle of downtown Singapore (and only a short bus ride away). The gardens were begun in Victorian times as a collection of tropical trees and plants. The beautifully maintained gardens are spread over some 74 acres, with a large lake, masses of shrubs and flowers, and magnificent examples of many tree species, including 30-m (98-ft) high fan palms. An orchid bed boasts specimens representing 250 varieties, some of them very rare. *Corner of Napier and Cluny Rds., tel. 474–1163. Admission free. Open weekdays 5 AM–11 PM, weekends 5 AM–midnight. Via bus No. 7, it's a 10-min ride to the Botanic Gardens from the top of Orchard Rd.*

The Islands

Sentosa In 1968, the government decided that Sentosa, the Isle of Tranquillity, would be transformed from the military area it was into the Disney-type resort playground it is, with museums, parks, golf courses, restaurants, and (soon) hotels. A tremendous amount of money has been poured into the island's development, and Singaporeans find Sentosa a very enjoyable place to spend some of their free time. Though Sentosa is certainly not a must-see in Singapore, there are two good reasons to go: the visual drama of getting there and the fascinating wax museum.

To reach Sentosa, take either the 1.8-km (1.1-mi) cable car (with gondolas holding four passengers each) or the ferry. Traveling out by cable car, the more dramatic method, heightens the anticipation; for variety, return by ferry.

The **cable car** picks up passengers from the Cable Car Towers, next to the World Trade Centre, and the Mt. Faber Cable Car Station. Since the trip from Cable Car Towers starts at the edge of the sea and is a bit shorter, it does not afford the panoramic views you get swinging down from Mt. Faber. At 113 m (377 ft), Mt. Faber is not particularly high, but it offers splendid views. There is no bus to the Mt. Faber station, and it's a long walk up the hill, so a taxi is the best way to get there. The Towers station *is* accessible by bus: from Orchard Road, take No. 10 or 143; from Collyer Quay, No. 10, 20, 30, 97, 125, or 146. *Off Kampong Bahru Rd., tel. 270–8855. Cost: S$6 round-trip, S$4.50 one way. Open Mon.–Sat. 10–7, Sun. and public holidays 9–7.*

Ferries ply between Jardine Steps at the World Trade Centre and Sentosa every 15 minutes from 7:30 AM, seven days a week; the crossing takes four minutes. The last ferry back from Sentosa departs at 11 PM Monday through Thursday. From Friday through Sunday and on public holidays, there are two extra return ferries, at 11:15 PM and midnight. Cost: S$2 one way.

Once on Sentosa, there is a **monorail** system—the first of its kind in Southeast Asia—whose six stations cover most of the major attractions (operates daily 9 AM–10 PM). Unlimited rides are included in the price of the admission ticket—you may get on and off at any of the stations at will. A free bus (daily 9–7) also provides transportation to most of the attractions. Bicycles are available for rent at kiosks throughout the island.

There are two main types of all-day (8:30 AM–10 PM) admission passes to the island, plus cheaper evening-only (5–10 PM) versions of the same. The **Day Charges Ticket** covers round-trip ferry, unlimited monorail and bus rides, swimming in the lagoon, and admission to the fountain shows and the Maritime Museum. Cost: day, S$3.50 adults, S$2 children under 12; night, S$3, S$2. The **Day Package Ticket** includes the above, plus admission to the Pioneers of Singapore/Surrender Chambers, the Coralarium, and Fort Siloso. Cost: day, S$7 adults, S$3.50 children under 12; night, S$5, S$3. Alternatively, you can pay for each individual attraction you visit. (S$1–S$2.50 each for adults).

A three-hour guided tour of Sentosa covers the major attractions, including the wax museum, the Maritime Museum, Fort Siloso, and the Coralarium. These tours depart daily at 10:30 AM. Tickets may be purchased at the Sentosa Cable Car Station ticket booth. You can certainly do as well on your own, however. A recording on the monorail points out sights as you pass, and audiovisual displays accompany many exhibits in the museums.

In front of the ferry terminal are the **Fountain Gardens;** several times each evening, visitors are invited to dance along with the illuminated sprays from the fountains to classical or pop music.

The **Butterfly Park and World Insectarium** has a collection of 2,500 live butterflies from 50 species, 4,000 mounted butterflies and insects, plus lots of insects that still creep, crawl, or fly. *Open weekdays 9:30–5:30, weekends, and holidays 9:30–7.*

Fort Siloso covers 10 acres of gun emplacements and tunnels created by the British as a fortress against invasion by the Japanese. Gun buffs will enjoy the range of artillery pieces in the fort. A photograph gallery documents the history of the war in the Pacific. *Open daily 9–7.*

The one Sentosa attraction that stands out from all the rest is the **Pioneers of Singapore/Surrender Chambers** wax museum. A series of galleries traces the development of Singapore and portrays the characters whose actions profoundly influenced the island's history. The second part of the museum is the Surrender Chambers, with wax tableaux depicting the surrender of the Allies to the Japanese in 1942 and the surrender of the Japanese in 1945. Photographs, documents, and audiovisuals highlight significant events in the Japanese occupation of Singapore and the various battles that led to the eventual defeat. *Open daily 9–9.*

The **Rare Stone Museum** is exactly what its name implies. Here you'll find some 4,000 rare and unique stones and other rocks that have been given interesting designs and shapes by nature. The collection includes a display of large rocks, such as 600,000-

year-old stalactites and stalagmites, and of fossils and dinosaur bones. *Open daily 9–7.*

The **Coralarium** has over 2,500 specimens of seashells and corals on display. In an air-conditioned artificial cave, unusual fish and live fluorescent coral can be viewed. Exhibits demonstrate how coral grows, how shells have evolved, and how typical coral reefs are structured. *Open daily 9–7.*

The **Maritime Museum** offers a small but interesting collection of ship models, pictures, and other items documenting Singapore's involvement with the sea in business and in war. *Admission free. Open daily 10–7.*

In addition to historical and scientific exhibitions, Sentosa offers a nature walk through secondary jungle, a night market with 40 stalls (open Fri.–Sun. 6–10 PM), campsites by the lagoon and tent rentals, and a wide range of recreational activities. Canoes, paddleboats, and bicycles are available for hire. There is swimming in the lagoon and at a small ocean beach, though the waters leave a lot to be desired. Golf is available at the Tanjong Course, and for anyone with balance, there is a roller-skating rink, said to be the largest in Southeast Asia. (For detailed information on Sentosa's recreational offerings, *see* Sports and Fitness, below.)

You may want to enjoy high tea or an early dinner at the **Rasa Sentosa Food Centre** (open 10 AM–10:30 PM), next to the ferry terminal. More than 40 stalls offer a variety of foods for alfresco dining amid groomed tropical surroundings.

Kusu   Kusu is approximately 30 minutes away by ferry from Jardine Steps (*see* Getting Around Singapore by Ferry, above), or you can take a day cruise on a junk or a luxury boat (*see* Guided Tours, above).

Also known as Turtle Island, Kusu is an ideal retreat (except on weekends) from the traffic and concrete of Singapore. There is a small coffee shop on the island, but you may want to bring a picnic lunch to enjoy in peace on the beach.

Next to the coffee shop is a small, open-fronted Chinese temple, **Tua Pek Kong,** built by Hoe Beng Watt in gratitude for the birth of his child. The temple is dedicated to Da Bo Gong, the god of prosperity, and the ever-popular Kuan Yin, goddess of mercy. This temple has become the site of an annual pilgrimage. From late October to early November, some 100,000 Taoists bring exotic foods, flowers, joss sticks, and candles, and pray for prosperity and healthy children. The Chinese believe in covering all bases, so while they are here, they will probably also visit the **Malay shrine** on top of the hill. To reach the shrine (called a *keramat*), you must climb 122 steps.

St. John's   St. John's is the most easily reached island for beach activities, and the one to which Singaporeans go for weekend picnics. The same ferries that go to Kusu go to St. John's. The trip takes an hour from Jardine Steps.

St. John's was first a leper colony, then a prison camp for convicts. Later it became a place to intern political enemies of the republic, and now it has become an island for picnicking and overnight camping. Without any temples or particular sights, it is quieter than Kusu.

Off the Beaten Track

A special Sunday-morning treat is to take breakfast with the birds at a **bird-singing café**. Bird fanciers bring their prize specimens, in intricately made bamboo cages, to coffee shops and hang the cages outside for training sessions: By listening to their feathered friends, the birds learn how to warble. One place to try is the coffee shop on the corner of Tiong Bahru and Seng Poh roads—get there around 9 AM on Sunday.

Pulau Sakeng is off the tourist track. Indeed, no public ferries cross to the island. You'll need to hire a bumboat from Jardine Steps for the 45-minute passage. The islanders have resisted change; the Malay fishing village on stilts is much as it was a century ago. About 150 families live in the kampong. Aside from a small, simple mosque to visit and local crafts to buy, there is little to do but enjoy the warmth and hospitality of the villagers. It is possible to go swimming off the shore, but there are no facilities. If you're changing on the beach, do remember to respect Malays' sense of propriety.

Shopping

Singapore is truly a shopping wonderland. What makes it so is the incredible range of goods brought in from all over the world to be sold in an equally incredible number of shops. Prices are competitive with places like Hong Kong, but the great savings of yesteryear no longer exist. Best buys are items indigenous to the region—leather, batiks, Oriental antiques, and silks. When shopping, look for the Singapore Tourist Promotion Board logo—a gold Merlion (a lion's head with a fish tail) on a red background. This signifies that the retailer is recommended by the STPB and the Singapore Retail Merchants Association.

Electrical Goods   Singapore's current is 220–240 volts at 50 cycles, similar to Australia's, Great Britain's, and Hong Kong's. Canada, Japan, and the United States use 110–120 volts at 60 cycles. When buying electrical equipment, verify that you can acquire special adapters, if required, and that these will not affect the equipment's performance.

Imitations   Street stalls or bargain shops have designer-label merchandise for ridiculously low prices; they are all fakes. Sport shirts with famous-name labels and logos filter in from Thailand and Hong Kong and are often of the same quality as the original product but at a third the price. Deeply discounted leather goods with such labels as Cartier, Etienne Aigner, and Gucci at these shops are most certainly frauds, and the quality may be inferior.

Street peddlers sell quartz watches, mainly from Taiwan, bearing the names of great Swiss or French watchmakers or European design houses for about S$30; they are fakes, but the timing mechanisms are just as good as those in watches that cost a hundred times more. Many Singaporeans consider the imitations the smarter buy.

Bargaining   Bargaining is widely practiced in Singapore; the type of store determines the potential "discount." Only department store prices are fixed—it's a good idea to visit one first to establish the base price of an item, then shop around. If you do not like to bargain, the department stores usually have the lowest initial ("first") price.

Shops in upscale complexes tend to give a 10%–15% discount on clothes. However, at a jewelry store, the discount can be as high as 50%. At less-upscale complexes, the discounts tend to be greater, especially if they view you as a tourist—that will boost their initial asking price.

How to Pay All department stores and most shops accept credit cards, and traveler's checks are readily accepted. Except at the department stores, paying with a credit card will mean that your "discounted price" will reflect the commission the retailer will have to pay the credit card company.

Guarantees Make sure you get international guarantees and warranty cards with your purchases. Check the serial number of each item against its card, and don't forget to mail the card in. Sometimes guarantees are limited to the country of purchase.

Complaints Complaints about either a serious disagreement with a shopkeeper or the purchase of a defective product should be lodged with the STPB (#01-19 Raffles City Tower, Singapore 0617, tel. 339–6622).

Shopping Districts

Throughout the city are complexes full of shopping areas and centers. Many stores will have branches carrying much the same merchandise in several of these areas.

Orchard Road The heart of Singapore's preeminent shopping district, Orchard Road is bordered on both sides with tree-shaded tiled sidewalks lined with modern shopping complexes and deluxe hotels that house exclusive boutiques. It is known for fashion and interior design shops with unusual Asian bric-a-brac.

Chinatown Once Singapore's liveliest and most colorful shopping area, Chinatown lost a great deal of its vitality when the street stalls were moved indoors (into the **Kreta Ayer Complex,** off Neil Road; the **Chinatown Complex,** off Trengganu Street; and the **People's Park Centre,** on Eu Tong Sen Street), but it is still fun to explore. South Bridge Road is the street of goldsmiths, specializing in 22K and even 24K gold ornaments in the characteristic orange color of Chinese gold. You *must* bargain here. On the same street, there are many art galleries, such as the **Seagull Gallery** (#62B, tel. 532–3491) and the **Wenian Art Gallery** (#95, tel. 535–4780), and seal carvers in the **Hong Lim Shopping Centre** and small shops will carve your name into your own personal chop.

Little India Serangoon Road is affectionately known as Little India. For shopping purposes, it begins at the **Zhu Jiao Centre,** on the corner of Serangoon and Buffalo roads. Some of the junk dealers and inexpensive-clothing stalls from a bazaar known as Thieves Market were relocated here when the market was cleared out.

All the handicrafts of India can be found here: intricately carved wood tables, shining brass trays and water ewers, handloomed table linens, fabric inlaid with tiny mirrors, brightly colored pictures of Hindu deities, and even garlands of jasmine for the gods. At dozens of shops here you can get the six meters of voile, cotton, Kashmiri silk, or richly embroidered Benares silk required to make a sari. For the variety, quality, and beauty of the silk, the prices are very low.

Arab Street The area really begins at Beach Road, opposite the Plaza Hotel. A group of basket and rattan shops first catches your eye. There are quite a few jewelers and shops selling loose gems and necklaces of garnet and amethyst beads. The main business is batiks and lace.

Holland Village Holland Village, 10 minutes from town by taxi, is the place to browse for unusual and inexpensive Asian items. Many shops specialize in Korean chests. Behind the main street is Lorong Mambong, a street of shophouses jammed with baskets, earthenware, porcelain, and all sorts of things from China and Thailand. The **Holland Village Shopping Centre** on Holland Avenue has quite a few shops, including **Lim's Arts and Crafts** (tel. 467–1300), selling inexpensive gifts and souvenirs; there always seems to be something out of the ordinary to pick up here.

Department Stores

Singapore has two homegrown chains. **Metro** stores are of two types: regular Metros offer a wide range of affordable fashions and household products; Metro Grands focus on upmarket fashion. Metro designs are up-to-the-minute, and the prices are unbelievably good by international standards. Look for Metros in Far East Plaza, The Paragon, and the Holiday Inn Building (25 Scotts Rd.); Metro Grands are in the Scotts Shopping Centre and in Lucky Plaza. **Klasse** department stores put the accent on budget buys but are best for Chinese imports. The most interesting Klasse store for tourists is at Lucky Plaza (tel. 235–0261).

Tang's (tel. 737–5500), also known as Tang's Superstore or C.K. Tang's, has just one branch, next to The Dynasty hotel on Orchard Road (#320). It looks upmarket but has some of the best buys in town. Its fashions are, at best, improving, but its accessories are excellent—especially the costume jewelry.

The **Chinese Emporium** (tel. 737–1411) in the International Building (360 Orchard Rd.) and the **Overseas Emporiums** in the People's Park Complex (tel. 535–0555) and the People's Park Centre (tel. 535–0967) offer Chinese silk fabric, silk blouses, brocade jackets, crafts, children's clothes, and china.

Singaporeans enjoy Japanese department stores, such as **Isetan**—in Wisma Atria (tel. 733–7777), the Apollo Hotel (Havelock Rd., tel. 733–1111), and Parkway Parade (Marine Parade Rd., tel. 345–5555); **Daimaru** (tel. 339–1111), in Liang Court, **Yaohan**, whose biggest store is in Plaza Singapura (tel. 337–4061), by far the most popular chain, especially for appliances and audio equipment; **Sogo** (tel. 339–1100) in Raffles City; and **Meitetsu** (tel. 732–0222) at the Delfi Orchard.

Printemps (tel. 733–9722), in the Hotel Meridien on Orchard Road, is good for lingerie and other women's fashions. **Galeries Lafayette** (tel. 732–9177) is at Liat Towers (541 Orchard Rd.). The English **Robinsons** (tel. 733–0888), in Centrepoint, is Singapore's oldest department store. It recently shed its fuddy-duddy image and rethought its pricing and is once again one of the best. **John Little** (tel. 727–2222), at the Specialists

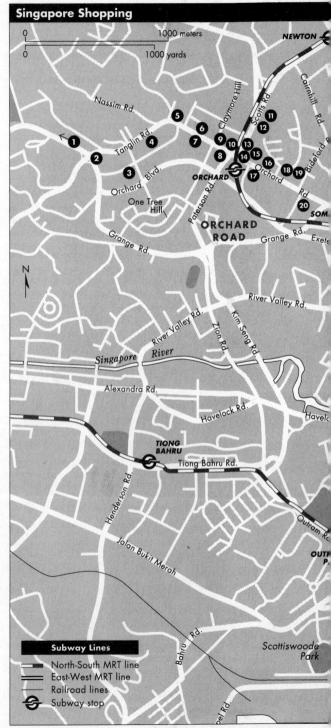

Singapore Shopping

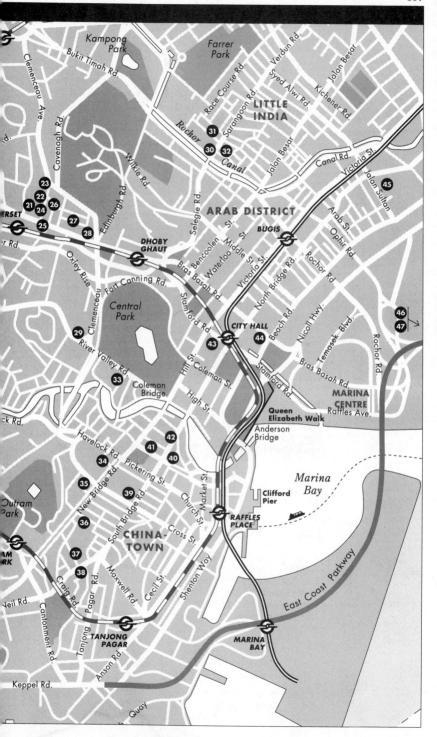

Centre, has a full range of offerings but is now targeting the young and trendy.

Hotel Shopping Arcades

The **Hilton Shopping Gallery,** in the Hilton (581 Orchard Rd.), is home to a number of top designer names—Giorgio Armani, Matsuda, Ferré, Valentino, Gucci, Davidoff, Vuitton, Dunhill —and a boutique with many other Italian and French fashion houses. The **Mandarin Shopping Arcade,** in the Mandarin Singapore (333 Orchard Rd.), has Courrèges, Givenchy, Ungaro, Versace, Hermès, A. Testoni, Bally, and Ferraud, plus two shops that offer a selection of haute couture names. The **Regent** (1 Cuscaden Rd., off Tanglin Rd.) has Hermès, Mikimoto, Pierre Balmain, Dunhill, and Patek Philippe. Other hotels with arcades include **The Dynasty** (320 Orchard Rd.), with a boutique for Porsche luggage and accessories, and the **Hyatt Regency** (10–12 Scotts Rd.), with a large shop for Lanvin.

Markets

Food Markets   Known as "wet markets" in Singapore because the floors are always being sluiced, food markets are always lively and are good places to absorb local color. The best for tourists is **Cuppage Centre** (on Cuppage Rd., off Orchard Rd.).

Street Markets   In the **Sungei Road area,** site of the once-notorious Thieves Market, a few street vendors creep back each weekend. The stalls sell mainly inexpensive shirts, T-shirts, children's clothes, and underwear, as well as odds and ends such as inexpensive watches, costume jewelry, and sunglasses. The **Kreta Ayer** complex in Chinatown may be modern, but it has all the atmosphere of a bazaar. Some of Chinatown's elderly junk peddlers refuse to leave the streets. In the afternoon, they line up along **Temple Street** and lay out a strange variety of goods—old bottles, stamps, bits of porcelain or brass, old postcards, etc.— on cloths in front of them. The bazaar at the **Singapore Handicraft Centre,** held from 6:30 to 10 PM on Wednesdays and from Friday through Sunday, is a good place to buy souvenirs at a good price.

Specialty Shops

Antiques   At the Tanglin Shopping Centre, try **Antiques of the Orient** (tel. 734–9351), specializing in maps; **Funan Selected Works of Art** (tel. 737–3442), with Buddhas and other religious items; and **Moongate** (tel. 737–6771), for porcelain. Off Orchard Road on Cuppage Road is a row of restored shophouses. Here, **Petnic's** (#41A, tel. 235–6564) specializes in antiques of the Straits Chinese; **Babazar** (31A–35A Cuppage Terr., tel. 235–7866) has jewelry, furniture, clothes, art, knickknacks, and antiques; and **Aizia Discoveries** (29B Cuppage Rd., tel. 734–8665) has yet more antiques. **Keng of Tong Mern Sern** (226 River Valley Rd., tel. 734–0761), near the Chettiar Temple, is a rabbit warren full of antiques. For primitive art and antique Indonesian batik and ikat (a woven fabric of tie-dyed yarns), there is **Tatiana** (tel. 235–3560) in the Tanglin Shopping Centre.

Art   Singapore has more than its share of fine artists. For a range of art, try **Art Forum** (tel. 737–3448) and **Raya Gallery** (tel. 732–0298), both in the Promenade; for local Singapore artists, **Sun**

Craft (tel. 737–1308), in the Tanglin Shopping Centre, and **Collectors Gallery** (tel. 339–8007), in Raffles City. There are also many galleries on South Bridge Road in Chinatown (*see* Chinatown, above).

Batik A traditional craft item of Singapore, Malaysia, and Indonesia, batik is now also important in contemporary fashion and interior design. **Blue Ginger** (tel. 737–5500) and **Design Batik** (tel. 235–5468), both in the Handicraft Centre, sell clothes and fabrics in modern designs. Traditional batik sarong lengths can be bought in the shops on **Arab Street** and in the **Textile Centre** on Jalan Sultan—try **Eng Leong Seng** (#01-37, tel. 294–4945). **Tang's** sells inexpensive batik products, including a good range of men's shirts.

Cameras Photographic equipment may not be the bargain it once was, but the range can be matched only in Hong Kong. All department stores carry cameras, and there are so many in Lucky Plaza that you can do all your comparison-shopping in one spot.

Cost Plus Electronics (#04-08/17 Scotts Shopping Centre, tel. 235–1557), something of a supermarket of cameras and electronics, has low listed prices, and no further discounts are given. For more-personalized service, try **Bobby O Store** (43 Stamford Rd., tel. 337–2191), near Raffles City.

Carpets Afghan, Pakistani, Persian, Turkish, and Chinese carpets—both antique and new—are very attractively priced in Singapore. In the Handicraft Centre, try **Chinese Carpets** (tel. 235–6548) or **Oriental Carpet Palace** (tel. 235–8259).

Curios Curio shops sell a fascinating variety of goods, mainly from China, including reverse-glass paintings, porcelain vases, cloisonné, wood carvings, jewelry, ivory carvings, embroidery, and idols. These shops—such as the International Building's **Asia Arts** (#01-02, tel. 737–3631), Orchard Towers' **Chen Yee Shen** (#01-12, tel. 737–1174), **Ivory Palace** (tel. 737–1169)—are great places for those who seek the unusual.

Fun Fashion In department stores and small boutiques all over the island—but especially on Orchard Road—locally made ladies' fashions and Japanese imports sell for a song. Three of the better-known boutiques are **Mondi** (#02-13 Scotts, tel. 235–1812; #03-36 Centrepoint, tel. 734–9672), **Man and His Woman** (#02-07 The Promenade, tel. 737–9492), and **Trend** (Centrepoint, tel. 235–9446; Plaza Singapura, tel. 337–1038).

High Fashion Singapore has its own designers: **Tan Yoong** has his shop in Lucky Plaza (tel. 734–3783), **Lam** has his in Liang Court (tel. 336–5974), and **Benny Ong** (who is based in London) sells through Tang's and China Silk House (*see* Silk, below). For European couture, check the arcades of the **Regent** hotel, the **Hilton International,** and the **Mandarin,** as well as the more fashionable shopping centers. Men's fashions are represented by such names as **Dunhill** (tel. 737–8174) in the Hilton; **Mario Valentino** in the Scotts Shopping Centre (tel. 235–0876); **Ralph Lauren** (tel. 732–0608) in the Promenade; and **Melwani** (tel. 339–6075) in the Metro department store at Marina Square.

Jewelry Singapore is a reliable place to buy jewelry, and there are so many jewelers that prices are competitive. Never accept the first price offered by any jeweler, no matter how posh the store. All jewelers give enormous discounts, usually 40% or more, but some only when pressed.

In Chinatown, particularly along South Bridge Road and in People's Park, there are dozens of Chinese jewelers selling 22K gold. Many of these, such as **Poh Heng** (27/28 N. Canal Rd., tel. 535–4933), are old family firms. On Orchard Road, the jewelry shops are often branches of Hong Kong firms or are local firms modeled along the same lines. They sell 18K set jewelry, often in Italian designs, as well as loose investment stones. **Larry's** (tel. 734–8763), with branches in Orchard Towers and Lucky Plaza, is one popular store. One of the many other small jewelers in Lucky Plaza is **The Hour Glass** (tel. 734–2420), which carries a large selection of designer watches.

Luggage and Accessories Luggage is a bargain in Singapore. Every complex boasts several stores carrying all the designer names in luggage and leather accessories. **Dunhill** (tel. 737–8174) is in the Hilton; **Etienne Aigner** is in Shaw Centre (tel. 737–6141), Scotts Shopping Centre (tel. 235–2742), and Delfi Orchard (tel. 732–9700); **Louis Vuitton** (tel. 737–5820) is in the Hilton; **Hermès** is at Liat Towers (541 Orchard Rd., tel. 734–1353) and at Daimaru in Liang Court, (tel. 339–1111); and **Charles Jourdan** (tel. 737–4988) is in the Promenade. The **Escada** boutique (tel. 734–7624) at Delfi Orchard has a range of accessories and custom-made luggage.

Pewter and Dinnerware Malaysia is the world's largest tin producer, and pewter is an important craft item in the region. **Selangor Pewter,** the largest pewter concern in Singapore, has a great product range on display at its main showrooms in the Thong Sia Building (30 Bideford Rd., tel. 235–6677), as well as at branch outlets in the Handicraft Centre (tel. 235–6633), Marina Square (tel. 339–3115), and Raffles City (tel. 339–3958).

Reptile-Skin Products Check the import restrictions on these goods. Singapore issues no export certificate for these or for ivory. The price of alligator, crocodile, and snake skins is lower here than anywhere else except Hong Kong. In the old shops around the Stamford Road-Armenian Street area, hard bargaining will yield dividends. The range is widest at big stores such as the showroom at the **Crocodilarium** (730 East Coast Pkwy., tel. 447–3722) and **Nan Hen** (Bright Chambers, 108 Middle Rd., tel. 338–3702).

Silk Indian silk, in sari lengths, is found in the dozens of sari shops in the Serangoon Road area at a fraction of what you would pay elsewhere. Try **Maharanee's** (#01-05 Buffalo Rd., tel. 294–9868) and **P. Govindasamy Pillai** (48/50 Serangoon Rd., tel. 337–2050). Chinese silk is found in all the emporiums. **China Silk House** (Tanglin Shopping Centre, tel. 235–5020, and Centrepoint, tel. 733–0555) has a wide range of fabrics in different weights and types, plus silk clothing. Thai silk comes in stunning colors by the meter or made up into gowns, blouses, and dresses. **Design Thai** (tel. 235–5439) in the Tanglin Shopping Centre is one of the largest shops.

Tailoring Tailors who offer 24-hour service rarely deliver, and their quality is pretty suspect. Allow four to five days for a good job. **Justmen** (tel. 737–4800) in the Tanglin Shopping Centre is one of a number of excellent men's tailors. For ladies, shops such as the Tanglin branch of **China Silk House** (tel. 235–5020) and the Specialists Centre's **M.B. Melwani** (tel. 737–5342) and **Bagatelle Shoppe** (tel. 737–7090) offer good tailoring.

Participant Sports and Fitness

Golf Some of the top Singapore hotels, including the Oriental, have special arrangements for guests at local golf clubs, or you can make your own arrangements. Ask the STPB for its brochure on golf clubs.

Jurong Country Club (Science Centre Rd., tel. 560–5655) has an 18-hole, par 71 course on 120 acres. **Keppel Club** (Bukit Chermin, tel. 273–5522) is the nearest 18-hole course to the city. **Seletar Country Club** (Seletar Airbase, tel. 481–2391, Tues.–Fri. only) is considered the best nine-hole course on the island. **Sembawang Country Club** (17 km Sembawang Rd., tel. 257–0642) is an 18-hole, par 70 course known as the commando course for its hilly terrain. There are also squash courts available. **Sentosa Golf Club** (tel. 472–2722) permits visitors to play on the 18-hole, par 71 Tanjong course on the southeastern tip of the island. **Singapore Island Country Club** (tel. 459–2222 or 466–2244) permits visitor use of its four 18-hole, par 71 courses—two at Upper Thomson Road and two (including the world-class Bukit course) on Sime Road—on weekdays.

Horseback Riding Arrangements may be made through the **Singapore Polo Club** (Thomson Rd., tel. 256–4530) or the **Saddle Club,** which is associated with the Singapore Turf Club (Bukit Timah Rd., tel. 469–3611, ext. 295).

Hotel Health Facilities Several of the hotels have health and fitness facilities. For addresses and telephone numbers, *see* Lodging, below.

Jogging Singapore has numerous parks, and a number of leading hotels offer jogging maps. Serious joggers can tackle the 10-km (6.2-mi) **East Coast Parkway track,** then cool off with a swim at the park's sandy beach. One of the most delightful places to run is the **Botanic Gardens** (off Holland Rd. and not far from Orchard Rd.), where you can jog on the paths or on the grass until 11 at night.

Squash and Racquetball Several hotels have their own squash courts (*see* Lodging, below), and there are numerous public squash and racquetball courts available, including **East Coast Recreation Centre** (East Coast Pkwy., tel. 449–0541), **Kallang Squash and Tennis Centre** (National Stadium, Kallang, tel. 348–1258), and **Singapore Squash Centre** (Fort Canning Rise, tel. 336–0155).

Swimming *See* Beaches and Water Parks, below.

Tennis Several public clubs welcome visitors, including **Alexandra Park** (Royal Rd. off York Rd., tel. 473–7236) and **Changi Courts** (Gosport Rd., tel. 545–2941). Also try the **Singapore Tennis Centre** (East Coast Pkwy., tel. 442–5966) and **Tanglin Tennis Courts** (Minden Rd., tel. 473–7236).

Waterskiing The center of activity for waterskiing is Ponggol, a village in northeastern Singapore. **Ponggol Boatel** (17th Ave., Ponggol, tel. 481–0031) charges S$60 an hour for a boat with ski equipment. Some of the local boats are for hire at considerably lower rates. Make sure the proper safety equipment is available.

Windsurfing **East Coast Sailing Centre** (1210 East Coast Pkwy., tel. 449–5118) has sailboard rentals and lessons. Windsurfing is also available on **Sentosa Island.**

Spectator Sports

In addition to the sports listed below, international matches of golf, tennis, cycling, formula motor racing, swimming, badminton, and squash are held on and off. Most events are detailed in the newspapers; information is also available from the **National Sports Council** (tel. 345–7111).

Cricket From March to September, games take place on the Padang grounds in front of the old **Cricket Club** (tel. 338–9271) every Saturday at 1:30 PM and every Sunday at 11 AM. Entrance to the club during matches is restricted to members, but you can watch the game from the sides of the playing field.

Horse Racing The **Singapore Turf Club** (Bukit Timah Rd., tel. 469–3611), about 10 km (6 mi) from the city center, is set in lush parkland, and its facilities are superb. Races are usually held on Saturday, beginning at about 2:15 PM. Gambling on the tote system (automatic gambling organized by track operators) is intense. For the S$15 admission price, you can watch the action either live or on a huge video screen.

You can get to the races easily by way of an organized tour. An air-conditioned coach picks you up from selected hotels and takes you to the club for a buffet lunch, followed by an afternoon of races and a guided tour of the paddock. Passports are required for the tour. *RMG Tours, tel. 337–3377; Singapore Sightseeing, tel. 737–8778. Cost (both): S$48.*

Polo The **Singapore Polo Club** (Thomson Rd., tel. 256–4530) is quite active, with both local and international matches. Spectators are welcome to watch Tuesday, Thursday, Saturday, and Sunday matches, played in the late afternoon.

Rugby Rugby is played on the Padang grounds in front of the Singapore **Cricket Club.** Kickoff is usually at 5:30 PM on Saturdays from September through March.

Soccer Soccer is the major sport of Singapore. Important matches take place in the **National Stadium** at Kallang (season: Sept.–Mar.).

Beaches and Water Parks

CN West Leisure Park. This huge complex boasts a flow pool, a baby pool with slide, a wave pool, and a 50-m (164-ft) water slide. Also here are amusement rides, such as minicars and a minijet merry-go-round. *9 Japanese Garden Rd., Jurong, tel. 261–4771. Admission charge. Open Tues.–Fri. noon–6, weekends and holidays 9:30–6.*

East Coast Park. Here you'll find an excellent beach and a lagoon where you can rent sailboards, canoes, and sailboats. The Aquatic Centre has four pools—including a wave pool—and a giant water slide called The Big Splash. *East Coast Pkwy., tel. 449–5118. Admission charge. Open Mon., Tues., Thurs., Fri. noon–6; weekends 9–6.*

Sentosa Island. Sentosa offers a range of recreational facilities, including a reasonable beach and a swimming lagoon, with changing and refreshment facilities, as well as rowboats, sailboards, and canoes for rent. You can camp here, play golf or tennis, or roller-skate.

Offshore Islands. The islands of Kusu and St. John's have reasonable small beaches and swimming facilities.

Desaru, Malaysia. The best beach area near Singapore is on peninsular Malaysia, 100 km (60 mi) east of Johore Bahru. Lots of resort-type activities on the water, as well as an 18-hole golf course, are available. You can charter a taxi from Johore Bahru for about M$50 (US$20). For overnight accommodations, Desaru has two hotels and several chalets (the Desaru View Hotel will collect you from Singapore). For more information, *see* Chapter 5.

Dining

by Violet Oon

Violet Oon, Singapore's leading culinary authority, is the publisher and editor of a monthly newspaper, The Food Paper, *and author of a cookbook on Nonya (Straits-born Chinese) foods. She is especially interested in chronicling and preserving the diverse food cultures of Singapore.*

Singapore offers the greatest feast in the East, if not in the world. Here you'll find excellent restaurants specializing in home-grown fare (known as Nonya, or Peranakan, cuisine) and in foods from Malaysia, Indonesia, Thailand, Vietnam, Korea, Japan, all parts of China, and north and south India, as well as from France, Germany, Italy, Britain, and the United States. At the hawker centers—semioutdoor markets with as many as 200 vendors selling wonderfully cooked, authentic foods—you can sample all these cuisines in the same meal!

With the Chinese making up about 76% of Singapore's population, their varied cuisines predominate. While Cantonese chefs are the most numerous, the earthy cooking of Teochew; spicy-hot Szechuan; refined Pekingese (known for its crackly crisp ducks); chickens poached with ginger, garlic, and onions from Hainan; soups and stews from Fukien; rustic foods from Hunan; and the provincial food of the Hakkas are all represented.

Hot and spicy food is found at restaurants owned by southern Indians, while their northern countrymen use aromatic spices from Kashmir to create less hot dishes, the most popular of which is tandoori chicken (marinated in yogurt and spices and cooked in a clay urn).

Malay cuisine is hot and rich, using turmeric root, lemongrass, coriander, prawn paste, chilies, and shallots. Nonya cooking is a mixture of Malay and Chinese, combining the finesse of the latter with the spiciness of the former.

Thai cuisine is also quite popular. The larger Thai restaurants here are actually seafood markets where you can pick your own swimming creature and tell the waitress how you want it cooked. In fact, seafood is among Singapore's greatest contributions to the gourmet world, and generally very inexpensive (though elegant and expensive seafood meals featuring delicacies like shark's fin, dried abalone, and lobster are served in some Chinese restaurants). The countryside area of Ponggol is famous for seafood, as is the **Seafood Centre** on the East Coast Parkway, with no less than eight restaurants in terracelike pavilions looking out toward the sea. Dishes marked "market price" on the menu are the premium items. Before ordering, be sure to find out exactly how much each dish will cost.

The many Continental restaurants have impeccable service and high-quality food. Perhaps the most important gastronomic gift from France is its famous visiting chefs, who have raised Singapore's standard of French cooking—classic or nouvelle—to great heights.

While some cultures consider atmosphere, decor, and service more important than food, in Singapore, a good meal means good food cooked with fresh ingredients. Gourmet cooking can be found as easily in small, unpretentious, open-front coffee shops as in the most elegant restaurants in the world, with service that's second to none. Most of the latter are located in hotels—Singaporeans love to make a grand entrance through a sparkling, deluxe hotel lobby.

At the other end of the scale are the hawker centers, agglomerations of individual vendor-chefs selling cooked foods in the open air. These vendors originally traveled from door to door selling their wares from portable stalls. Some years ago, Singapore decided to gather them in food centers for reasons of hygiene. (And these new centers *are* all perfectly clean—the health authorities are very strict.) Visitors and locals alike find these centers a culinary adventure. You can check out each stall—see the raw materials and watch the cooking methods—then choose whatever strikes your fancy from as many different stalls as you like. Find a seat at any of the tables (the government owns the centers and the seats; the hawkers rent only their stalls). Note the number of your table so you can tell the hawkers where to deliver your orders, then sit down and wait for the procession of food to arrive. Someone will come to your table to take your drink order. You pay at the end of the meal. Most dishes cost S$1 or slightly more; for S$3, you can get a meal that includes a drink and a slice of fresh fruit for dessert.

The most touristy center is **Newton Circus.** Many people find Newton *the* place to see life at night—it's raucous and noisy, and the mood is really festive. Go to Newton if you must for the experience, but avoid the seafood stalls: They are known to fleece tourists. Feast, instead, at stalls offering the traditional one-dish meals, such as fried Hokkien noodles, roast-duck rice, *rojak*, or Malay *satay* (*see* Glossary of Food Terms, below). These stalls have prices displayed prominently in the front. When you place your order, specify whether you want a S$2, S$3, or S$4 order.

Other hawker centers include **Cuppage Centre,** on Cuppage Road; **Empress Place,** behind the immigration office; **Telok Ayer Transit Food Centre,** on Shenton Way in the financial district; and **Bugis Square,** at Eminent Plaza (this one's open 7 AM–3 AM).

Another experience in Singaporean dining is to visit the **stir-fry stalls,** fondly called "wok-and-roll" by Americans. These stalls, most half restaurant and half parking lot, can be found in abundance on East Coast Road. They are characterized by open kitchens and a stream of waiters yelling and running about. As a rule of thumb, always follow the crowd to the busiest place.

The most popular dish at the stir-fry stalls is chili crab, with crusty bread to dip into a hot, rich, tasty sauce. Other favorites are deep-fried baby squid and steamed prawns or fish, accompanied by fried noodles. There is certainly no elegance here—just good, fresh food cooked according to tried-and-true recipes. Prices are very reasonable. Stalls open for business at 5 PM.

Dim sum—called *dian xin* ("small eats") in Singapore—is a particularly Cantonese style of eating, featuring a selection of bite-size steamed, baked, or deep-fried dumplings, buns, pastries, and pancakes, with a variety of savory or sweet flavorings. The selection, which may comprise as many as 50 separate offerings, may also include such dishes as soups, steamed pork ribs, and stuffed green peppers. Traditionally, dim sum are served three on a plate in bamboo steamer baskets on trolleys that are pushed around the restaurant. You simply wait for the trolleys to come around, then point to whichever item you would like. Dim sum is usually served for lunch from noon to 2:30 PM, though in some teahouses in Chinatown, it is served for breakfast from 5 to 9. An excellent place for dim sum in the financial district is the **Mayflower Restaurant** (6 Shenton Way, #04-02 DBS Bldg., tel. 220–3133), a huge room heavy with Chinese decor. **Tung Lok Shark's Fin Restaurant** (Liang Court Complex, 177 River Valley Rd., tel. 336–6022) has a vast dim sum selection. Also try **New Nam Thong Tea House** (*see* listing below).

High tea has become very popular in Singapore, and in many hotels, such as the **Goodwood Park Hotel** and the **Holiday Inn Park View,** is accompanied by light Viennese-style music. Though British-inspired, the Singapore high tea is usually served buffet style and includes dim sum, fried noodles, and other local favorites in addition to the regulation finger sandwiches, scones, and cakes. Teas are usually served between 3 and 6 PM.

Glossary of Food Terms The following are dishes and food names you will come across often at the hawker centers.

char kway teow—fried flat rice noodles mixed with soy sauce, chili paste, fish cakes, and bean sprouts and fried in lard.
Hokkien prawn mee—fresh wheat noodles in a prawn-and-pork broth served with freshly boiled prawns.
laksa—a one-dish meal of round rice noodles in coconut gravy spiced with lemongrass, chilies, turmeric, galangal, shrimp paste, and shallots. It is served with a garnish of steamed prawns, rice cakes, and bean sprouts.
mee rebus—a Malay version of Chinese wheat noodles with a spicy gravy. The dish is garnished with sliced eggs, pieces of fried bean curd, and bean sprouts.
rojak—a Malay word for "salad." Chinese rojak consists of cucumber, lettuce, pineapple, *bangkwang* (jicama), and deep-fried bean curd, tossed with a dressing made from salty shrimp paste, ground toasted peanuts, sugar, and rice vinegar. Indian rojak consists of deep-fried lentil and prawn patties, boiled potatoes, and deep-fried bean curd, all served with a spicy dip sweetened with mashed sweet potatoes.
roti prata—an Indian pancake made by tossing a piece of wheat-flour dough into the air until it is paper-thin and then folding it to form many layers. The dough is fried until crisp on a cast-iron griddle, then served with curry powder or sugar. An ideal breakfast dish.
satay—small strips of meat marinated in fresh spices and threaded onto short skewers. A Malay dish, satay is barbecued over charcoal and eaten with a spiced peanut sauce, sliced cucumbers, raw onions, and pressed rice cakes.

thosai—an Indian rice-flour pancake that is a popular breakfast dish, eaten with either curry powder or brown sugar.

The Nitty-Gritty
Dress

Except at the fancier hotel dining rooms, Singaporeans do not dress up to eat out. An open-neck shirt and a jacket represent the upper limit of formality. Generally, though, shorts, thongs, and track suits are not considered appropriate.

Hours

Most restaurants are open from noon to 2:30 or 3 for lunch and from 7 to 10:30 PM (last order) for dinner. Seafood restaurants are usually open only for dinner and supper, until around midnight or 1 AM. Some hotel coffee shops (and the Indian coffee shops along Changi Road) are open 24 hours a day; others close between 2 and 6 AM. At hawker centers, some stalls are open for breakfast and lunch while others are open for lunch and dinner. Late-night food centers like Eminent Plaza in Jalan Besar are in full swing until 3 AM.

Taxes and Charges

Hawker stalls and small restaurants do not impose a service charge. Most medium-size and larger restaurants, however, add 10% service charge as well as a 3% government tax to the bill. Most Chinese restaurants also automatically add to the bill a charge of S$2 per person for tea, peanuts, pickles, and rice.

Tipping

Do not tip in restaurants and hawker centers unless you really feel the service deserves an extra bit of recognition. (The 10% service charge is shared by a restaurant's staff.)

Alcohol

Liquor is very expensive in Singapore. A bottle of wine in a restaurant costs about S$36; a cocktail, S$6–S$8.

Highly recommended restaurants are indicated by a star ★.

Category	Cost*
Very Expensive	over S$50 (US$25)
Expensive	S$25–S$50 (US$13–US$25)
Moderate	S$10–S$25 (US$5–US$13)
Inexpensive	under S$10 (US$5)

per person, excluding tax, tip, and drinks

Chinese: Cantonese
Very Expensive–
Expensive
★

Li Bai. When it opened, the Li Bai set a new standard in Chinese restaurants. Its dining room evokes richness without overindulgence: deep maroon wall panels edged with black and backlighted, elaborate floral displays that change with the seasons, jade table settings, and ivory chopsticks. The service is very fine, as is the cooking, which is modern and innovative, yet deeply rooted in the Cantonese tradition. The chef's unusual creations include deep-fried diamonds of egg noodles in a rich stock with crabmeat and mustard greens; fried lobster in black bean paste; and double-boiled shark's fin with Chinese wine and *jinhua* ham. The restaurant is deliberately small, seating fewer than 100 people, to enhance the mood of exclusivity. *Sheraton Towers Hotel, 30 Scotts Rd., tel. 737–6888. Reservations advised. Dress: smart casual to elegant. AE, CB, DC, MC, V.*

Expensive–Moderate

Ruyi. This is Singapore's most beautiful Chinese restaurant. Such touches as Chinese screens and paintings, porcelain lamps, subdued lighting, and artistic presentation of food combine to make dining out at the Ruyi a memorable experience.

The cooking is purist. Try the minced pigeon on lettuce leaves or the beef-and-carrot rolls fried in delicate black-pepper sauce. Instead of Peking duck, try chicken cooked in a similar way; the skin is sliced and enclosed in paper-thin spinach-flavored pancakes with sweet plum sauce and spring onions. There's dim sum at lunch. *Hyatt Regency Hotel, 10-12 Scotts Rd., tel. 733–1188. Reservations advised. Dress: smart casual to elegant. AE, CB, DC, MC, V.*

Moderate **Majestic Restaurant.** The food at this restaurant, set in a cloistered part of Chinatown on a street of gentlemen's clubs, is considered among the best for traditional Cantonese cooking. Famous dishes include suckling pig barbecued over glowing charcoal and braised superior shark's fin with chicken (each dish costs about S$100 and feeds 10); fried-shark's-fin-and-crabmeat omelet (wrap a spoonful in a lettuce leaf, fold the leaf over, and eat); and roast Cantonese chicken. The decor is premodern Chinese with hints of red; the seating's comfortable; the service is fast but without finesse. *31-37 Bukit Pasoh Rd., tel. 223–5111. No reservations. Dress: casual. AE, DC, V.*

Inexpensive **New Nam Thong Tea House.** Absolutely inelegant but totally authentic is this teahouse in Chinatown. Breakfast here between 5 and 9:30 for a view of real Singapore life. Older folk, mainly men, congregate daily to meet and gossip with friends and read the Chinese papers. Situated above an open-front shophouse, the teahouse is not air-conditioned and can be muggy, but it serves hearty, giant-size dim sum—*char siew pow* (steamed barbecued pork buns), *siew mai* (prawn-and-minced-pork dumplings), and other assorted dishes. Wash it all down with piping-hot Chinese tea. They don't understand English here, so just point. *8-10A Smith St., tel. 223–2817. No reservations. Dress: casual. No credit cards.*

Chinese: Hunanese **Cherry Garden.** The Cherry Garden restaurant is a beautiful
Expensive setting for a meal. It is done in the Chinese courtyard style: A wood-roofed pavilion with walls of antique Chinese brick encloses a landscaped courtyard. Artworks are tastefully chosen and displayed. The service is impeccable, and the food is a welcome change from the usual Cantonese fare. An unusual dish is the steamed rice in woven bamboo baskets. Also try the minced-pigeon broth with dry scallops steamed in a bamboo tube, and the superior Yunnan honey-glazed ham served between thin slices of steamed bread. *Oriental Hotel, 6 Raffles Blvd., Marina Square, tel. 338–0066. Reservations advised. Dress: smart casual to elegant. AE, CB, DC, MC, V.*

Chinese: Pekingese **Pine Court.** Baked tench, marinated lamb, and fried dry scal-
Expensive lops are just a few of the dishes that distinguish the cooking of the Pine Court. The restaurant's Peking duck is famed for its crisp, melt-in-your-mouth skin and delicate pancake wrapping. The carved-wood wall panels create the ambience of a Chinese mansion; the service is fine and caring, by staff dressed in Chinese style. *Mandarin Hotel, 333 Orchard Rd., tel. 737–4411. Reservations advised. Dress: smart casual. AE, CB, DC, MC, V.*

Chinese: Szechuan **Dragon City.** Singaporeans consider Dragon City the best place
Expensive–Moderate for Szechuan food. Set in a courtyard and entered through a flamboyant red moongate door, the restaurant is a large room that looks Chinese but is not particularly appealing. The food is

Dining

Annalakshmi, **36**
Aziza's, **24**
Banana Leaf
Apollo, **27**
Bingtang Timur, **18**
Cherry Garden, **38**
Dragon City, **12**
Gordon Grill, **15**
Heday Kopi, **25**
Her Sea Palace, **6**
La Brasserie, **1**
Latour, **10**
Le Restaurant de
France, **28**
Li Bai, **14**
Long Beach Seafood
Restaurant, **40**
Majestic
Restaurant, **31**
Min Jiang, **16**
Nadaman, **11**
New Nam Thong Tea
House, **32**
Pine Court, **21**
Ristorante Italiano
Prego, **35**
Ruyi, **19**
Tandoor, **26**
UDMC Seafood
Centre, **41**

Lodging

Apollo Singapore, **30**
Boulevard Hotel, **4**
Cairnhill Hotel, **23**
Carlton Hotel, **34**
Crown Prince
Hotel, **22**
The Dynasty, **20**
Goodwood Park, **17**
Hilton International, **5**
Hotel Bencoolen, **33**
Ladyhill Hotel, **7**
Marco Polo, **2**
Mitre Hotel, **29**
The Oriental, **39**
Peninsula Hotel, **37**
The Regent, **3**
RELC International
House, **9**
Shangri-La, **8**
Sheraton Towers, **13**

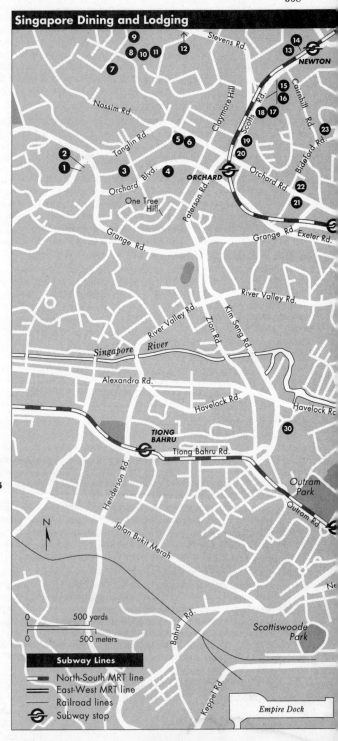

Singapore Dining and Lodging

Subway Lines

— North-South MRT line
= East-West MRT line
— Railroad lines
⊖ Subway stop

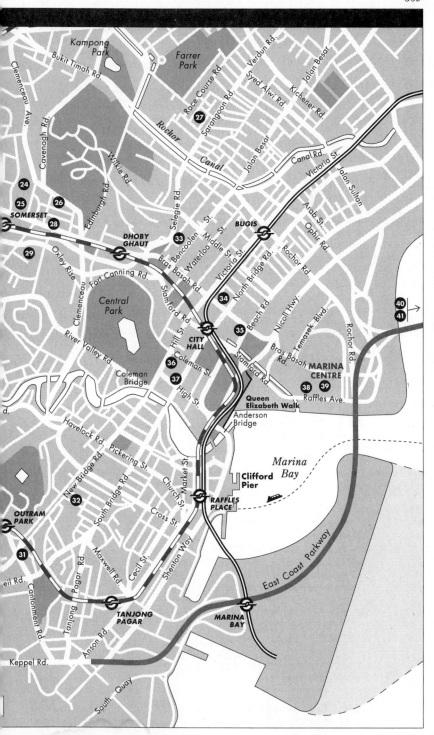

where all the artistry is. Choose from such Szechuan staples as *kung po* chicken and prawns, in which the meat is deep-fried with whole dried chili peppers and coated with a sweet-and-sour sauce; or try the delicious minced-pork soup in a whole melon, steamed red fish with soybean crumbs, or smoked Szechuan duck. *Novotel Orchid Inn, Plymouth Wing, 214 Dunearn Rd., tel. 254–7070. Reservations advised. Dress: smart casual. AE, CB, DC, MC, V.*

Moderate **Min Jiang.** Housed in a Chinese pavilion on the grounds of the Goodwood Park, Min Jiang is always packed, thanks to its delicious food, fast service, and reasonable prices. The decor is very Chinese in a mellow, resplendent style. The camphor-smoked duck, kung po chicken, and long beans fried with minced pork are favorites. *22 Scotts Rd., tel. 737–7411. Reservations advised. Dress: smart casual. AE, CB, DC, MC, V.*

Continental **Latour.** Come to this restaurant at the Shangri-La hotel for a
Very Expensive taste of the grand European style of dining. Floor-to-ceiling
★ windows provide a spectacular view of the palm-fringed swimming pool and the garden. Inside, an eclectic luxury reigns: salmon-pink walls, comfortable rattan chairs, batik paintings, and Austrian chandeliers, plus elegant crystal, china, and silver table settings. The food is French-based but with the lightness of nouvelle cuisine. Thinly sliced beef marinated in lemon pepper à la Cipriani, cream of smoked salmon soup, lobster medallions, and deboned rack of lamb with herbed morello sauce are some of the star dishes. The wine list is considered one of the best in town and includes a fine selection from France's Château Latour. *22 Orange Grove Rd., tel. 737–3644. Reservations required. Dress: smart casual to elegant; no jeans. AE, CB, DC, MC, V.*

Expensive **Gordon Grill.** I love the Gordon Grill for its hint of the heather and the grouse, the feel of the fireside. The Scottish country/hunting lodge look, with heavy draped curtains, is lightened with celadon and soft apple greens, light-wood chairs and accents, and glass panels etched with delicate drawings of Scottish lairds. Tradition is served up here very much as it always has been, including excellent roast beef, perfect steaks, and the best sherry trifle in town. You can go Scottish by ordering haggis with neeps and tatties and parcel of Scotch salmon. *Goodwood Park Hotel, 22 Scotts Rd., tel. 737–7411. Reservations advised. Dress: smart casual. AE, CB, DC, MC, V.*

French **Le Restaurant de France.** French master chef Louis Outhier is
Very Expensive– the consultant for the menus and recipes here and makes annu-
Expensive al appearances. The cooking is light, creamy, and full of surprises thanks to the way Outhier combines new ingredients he finds in Singapore's markets. Le Restaurant offers sheer elegance, from the opulent and romantic decor—pink-on-pink tones, chandeliers, fabric-covered chairs, huge displays of lilies, and gleaming crystal—to the superbly discreet French style of service. On the terrace, you may dine beside a fountain under a trellis entwined with vines. *Le Meridien Singapour, 100 Orchard Rd., tel. 733–8855. Reservations advised. Dress: smart casual to elegant. AE, CB, DC, MC, V. No lunch weekends.*

Expensive–Moderate **La Brasserie.** Often named as the favorite French restaurant in Singapore, this is an informal place, with *garçons* clad in traditional ankle-length aprons serving hearty traditional fare like French onion soup, *émincé de veau à la crème* (sliced veal with mushrooms in cream sauce), and fluffy lemon pancakes with vanilla ice cream. Here you'll dine on the spirit of Paris as well as the food: Red-checked tablecloths, antique wrought -iron lamps, exuberant French art, lace curtains, gleaming copper pans, and two very attractive bar counters bring this brasserie to life. *Marco Polo Hotel, Tanglin Rd., tel. 474–7141. Reservations advised. Dress: smart casual. AE, CB, DC, MC, V.*

Indian
Expensive
★

Tandoor. The food has a distinctly Kashmiri flavor at this luxurious restaurant, where Indian paintings, rust and terra-cotta colors, and Indian musicians at night create the ambience of the Moghul court. The clay oven, seen through glass panels across a lotus pond, dominates the room. After you place your order for tandoori chicken, lobster, fish, or shrimp—marinated in yogurt and spices, then roasted in the oven—sit back and watch the chef at work. The tender spice-marinated roast leg of lamb is a favorite of the regulars. Spiced masala tea at the end of the meal seems to wash down the richness of the meal perfectly. Service is exceptionally attentive. *Holiday Inn Park View, 11 Cavenagh Rd., tel. 733–8333. Reservations advised. Dress: smart casual. AE, CB, DC, MC, V.*

Moderate

Annalakshmi. At this Indian vegetarian restaurant run by a Hindu religious and cultural organization, the decor is lush, with carved-wood wall panels and chairs, Indian paintings, and fabric wall hangings studded with small mirrors. The paper-thin *dosai* pancakes are delicious in the special Sampoorna dinner, confined to only 30 servings per night and presented on silver. The vegetarian selection often includes cabbage curry, potato roast, *raita* (a condiment of cucumber and yogurt), *channa dhal* (a sort of lentil stew), *kurma* (a mild vegetable curry with ground spices like cumin, coriander, cinnamon, and cardamom, cooked in soured milk or cream), and *poori* (a puffy, ball-shaped bread). *Excelsior Hotel & Shopping Centre (#02-10), 5 Coleman St., tel. 339–9993. Reservations advised. Dress: smart casual. AE, DC, MC, V. Closed Thurs.*

Inexpensive
★

Banana Leaf Apollo. Walls tiled up to waist level, Formica-topped tables, a hodgepodge of colors—just general bad taste is what makes eating here such fun. It's so bad it's good. The food itself is fabulous, though you may end up crying yourself through the fiery, southern-Indian-style meals. Each person is given a large piece of banana leaf: Steaming-hot rice is spooned into the center; then two *papadam* (deep-fried lentil crackers) and two vegetables, with delicious spiced sauces, are arranged neatly around the rice. All this—and as much of it as you can eat—can be had for S$1.50–S$2. *56/58 Race Course Rd., tel. 298–5054. No reservations. Dress: very casual. No credit cards.*

Italian
Moderate

Ristorante Italiano Prego. I can't quite decide whether I like the rampantly red-and-green decor, but there's no doubt about the pastas: They're the best in town, all made on the spot by the Italian chef. Center stage at this long, narrow restaurant is the pizza-and-pasta kitchen, glassed in on three sides so you can see what's going on. The spaghetti *con vongole* (with clams in a cheese sauce) is a particular favorite, as are the seafood stew and scaloppine. The chef is very proud of his zabaglione. The service can be annoyingly slow. *Westin Stamford Hotel, 3rd floor, 2 Stamford Rd., tel. 338–8585, ext. 16310. Reservations required. Dress: smart casual. AE, CB, DC, MC, V.*

Japanese
Expensive
★

Nadaman. There's nothing quite as exciting as watching a teppanyaki chef perform his culinary calisthenics at this 23rd-floor restaurant, which boasts the Singapore skyline as a backdrop. Considered by many to be Singapore's finest Japanese restaurant, the Nadaman offers sushi, sashimi (the fresh lobster sashimi is excellent), teppanyaki, tempura, and kaiseki. Those on a budget should try one of the *bento* lunches—fixed-price meals (less than S$20) beautifully decorated in the Japanese manner and served in lacquer trays and boxes. The decor is distinctly Japanese, and the service is discreetly attentive. *Shangri-La Singapore, 24th floor, 22 Orange Grove Rd., tel. 737–3644. Reservations advised. Dress: smart casual. AE, DC, MC, V.*

Malay
Expensive

Aziza's. Hazizah Ali has brought elegant Malay cooking out of the home and into her intimate street-front restaurant on the charming Emerald Hill Road. It's the spicy cooking of the Malay Peninsula you get here—lots of lemongrass, galangal, shallots, pepper, coriander, cloves, and cinnamon. Try the beef *rendang* (stewed for hours in a mixture of spices and coconut milk), *gado gado* (a light salad with a spiced peanut sauce), or *bergedel* (Dutch-influenced potato cutlets). The oxtail soup is especially delicious. Ask for *nasi ambang* and you'll get festive rice with a sampling of dishes from the menu. *36 Emerald Hill Rd., tel. 235–1130. Reservations required for dinner. Dress: smart casual. AE, DC, MC, V.*

Moderate–Inexpensive

Bintang Timur. This is a very pleasant restaurant done up in green and light wood, with a good view from picture windows. Owner Aloyah Alkaff taught cooking before launching this restaurant, which serves Malay food with a touch of Indonesian and Arab influences. Try deep-fried satay *goreng*, the prawn satay, fish-head curry (cooked Malay-style, with lots of fresh spices and herbs, such as galangal and lemongrass), or *ikan pepes* (flaked fish mixed with a ground hot-spice paste, wrapped in banana leaves, then grilled over charcoal). *Far East Plaza (#02-08/13), ground floor, 14 Scotts Rd., tel. 235–4539. No reservations. Dress: casual. AE, DC, V.*

Nonya
Moderate–Inexpensive

Keday Kopi. This is the ground-floor restaurant in the preserve of Baba culture called Peranakan Place, a charming enclave with a palm-lined mall next door to the up-market Centrepoint shopping complex. The restaurant, with lots of carved-wood detail, is decorated to re-create the languid, easy Baba lifestyle at the turn of the century. The food itself is representative of the Nonya kitchen but is not the best example of it in town. A dish to savor here is the *buak keluak ayam* (a spicy, sour gravy made with chicken and a black Indonesian nut that has a creamy texture and the smokiness of French truffles). *Peranakan Place, 80 Orchard Rd., tel. 732–6966. No reservations. Dress: casual. AE, DC, V.*

Seafood
Expensive–Moderate

Long Beach Seafood Restaurant. The Long Beach is a 30-minute cab ride from town but is considered one of Singapore's finest seafood restaurants. The decor—pretty garish, with lots of plastic and clashing colors—is pure 1950s Singapore chic, complete with multicolored fairy lights strung outside. You eat either indoors (there's no air-conditioning) or out. If your tastebuds can withstand the hotness, try the pepper crabs—large Indonesian crabs chopped into pieces, then fried in a mixture of freshly ground black pepper, oyster sauce, and butter. Make up the rest of your meal with drunken prawns (live prawns mixed with cognac or Chinese wine, left for a few minutes to soak up the liquor, then lightly poached), barbecued fish, and stuffed deep-fried dough sticks called *you tiao*. *Bedok Rest House, 610 Bedok Rd., tel. 445–8833 or 344–7722. No reservations. Dress: casual. AE, DC, MC, V. Dinner only (5–12:15 weeknights, 5–1:15 weekends).*

Moderate **UDMC Seafood Centre.** You *must* visit this place at the East Coast Parkway, near the entrance to the lagoon. It gives you a true picture of the way Singaporeans eat out, as well as real value for the money (prices here are generally cheaper than in other seafood restaurants). Walk around the eight open-fronted restaurants before you decide where to eat. Chili crabs, steamed prawns, steamed fish, pepper crabs, fried noodles, and deep-fried squid are the specialties. *East Coast Pkwy. Tel.: Bedok Sea View, tel. 241–4173; Chin Wah Heng, tel. 444–7967; East Coast Park Live Seafood, tel. 448–2020; Golden Lagoon, tel. 448–1894; Jumbo, tel. 442–3435; Kheng Luck, tel. 444–5911; Red House, tel. 442–3112. No reservations. Dress: casual. AE, DC, MC, V. Dinner only (5–midnight).*

Thai **Her Sea Palace.** A runaway success of the late 1980s, Her Sea
Expensive–Moderate serves Thai food with a Teochew Chinese touch. Dishes to savor
★ are the thick soup of sliced fish maw (stomach lining) that has been dried and then deep-fried, mixed with lots of fresh crabmeat; pickled-olive rice; and Thai chili crabs, rich with coconut milk. The decor is pleasant, the service not possessed of much finesse; but the food is absolutely delicious. *Forum Galleria (#01-16), 583 Orchard Rd., tel. 732–5688. Reservations required. Dress: smart casual. DC, V.*

Lodging

With tourists and business travelers now flocking to Singapore in record numbers, hotels are recording 70% to 80% occupancy rates and are sometimes fully booked. However, except perhaps during the busiest periods—in August and at Christmas—you should be able to get reservations at the hotel of your choice. If you're willing to take the gamble and arrive without reservations, you are likely to find hotels willing to offer discounts. The Singapore Hotel Association maintains two reservations counters at Changi Airport and can set you up with a room—and often a discount if the hotels are having a slow period—upon your arrival. There is no fee for the booking.

Compared with other capital-city destinations, Singapore offers relatively low-cost lodgings.

The best of Singapore's hotels are equal to the best anywhere else in the world and certainly offer more value for the money than most. The staff go to great lengths to meet guests' needs. Guest rooms are spacious and fitted out with the latest amenities, from bedside computer control panels to marble-tiled bathrooms with telephone extensions and speakers for the television. Many hotels offer business and fitness centers loaded with the latest technology and equipment.

Perhaps because Singapore's top hotels set such high standards, less-expensive properties appear to work harder. Indeed, a major reason why Singapore makes such a convenient and comfortable base from which to explore Southeast Asia is the overall high quality of its lodgings. And, with more than 70 hotels and 24,000 guest rooms to choose from, there's certain to be a place just right for you. If all you're looking for is a bunk, there are dormitory-type guest houses on Bencoolen Street where you can sleep for no more than S$8 a night.

Your choice of hotel location may be influenced by your reason for visiting Singapore. Certainly the Orchard and Scotts roads area favors the shopper and evening reveler. Marina Square would be the logical choice for those attending conventions in the complex or who like the openness of space the area offers. For those doing business in the financial district, a hotel close to Shenton Way is ideal; likewise, hotels along the Singapore River are convenient for anyone making trips to the industrial city of Jurong. But location should not be overly emphasized. Singapore is a relatively compact city, and taxis and public transportation, especially the new subway, make travel between one area and another a matter of minutes. No hotel is more than a 30-minute cab ride from Changi Airport.

For a map pinpointing locations, *see* Dining, above.

Highly recommended hotels are indicated by a star ★.

Category	Cost*
Very Expensive	over S$200 (US$100)
Expensive	S$150–S$200 (US$75–US$100)
Moderate	S$100–S$150 (US$50–US$75)
Inexpensive	S$50–S$100 (US$25–US$50)
Budget	under S$50 (US$25)

All prices are for a standard double room, excluding 3% tax and a 10% service charge.

Very Expensive
★

Goodwood Park. Ideally located just off Scotts Road and within minutes of Orchard Road, the Goodwood Park has a tradition of hospitality that dates back to 1900, when it began life as a club for German expatriates. It may be overshadowed by the glitz of modern high-rise hotels, but for those who appreciate personal service and a refined atmosphere, plus all the creature comforts of a modern hotel, this one stands alone. Guests are remembered and greeted by name, high tea is accompanied by a string quartet, and guest rooms are furnished in the style of a country house. All the guest rooms have been recently renovated to offer the latest in amenities. Many look onto the garden and pool area, which was newly landscaped in 1989. For ultimate elegance, there is the Brunei Suite, possibly the most prestigious digs in Singapore, complete with oak-paneled study, formal dining room, sauna and steambath, and private elevator. *22 Scotts Rd., Singapore 0922, tel. 737–7411 or 800/421–0536. 235 rooms, including 64 suites. Facilities: 4 restaurants, 24-hr coffee shop, lounge for afternoon tea and light meals, 24-hr room service, beauty salon, business center, baby-sitting, tour desk, 3 outdoor pools, 5 function rooms. AE, DC, MC, V.*

The Oriental. Within this triangular Marina Square hotel, architect John Portman has created a 21-story atrium with interior balconies that are stepped inward as they ascend. Through the center of the atrium, glass elevators glide from floor to floor. The Oriental is smaller than many of the modern deluxe hotels in Singapore; this permits the staff to give personalized attention to each guest. Because of the hotel's pyramidal shape, guest rooms have one of three views. The south harbor view overlooks the harbor and the high rises of the City Centre beyond. The west harbor view looks out to sea, where hundreds of ships lay anchored. Garden-view rooms, overlooking a park, offer less-dramatic vistas but slightly more space. All the guest rooms are decorated in soft hues of peach and green; hand-woven carpets and paintings of old Singapore add to the feeling of understated elegance. The Italian-marble-tiled bathrooms offer separate tubs and showers. *6 Raffles Blvd., #01-200, Singapore 0103, tel. 338–0066 or 800/526–6566. 640 rooms. Facilities: 5 restaurants, 24-hr room service, outdoor pool, jogging track, tennis and squash courts, fitness center with sauna and massage, travel desk, arrangements for golf, business center, banquet and function rooms. AE, DC, MC, V.*

★ **Shangri-La.** This hotel has consistently ranked as one of the top three in Singapore since it opened in 1971. The most attractive rooms are in the newer Valley Wing, with its own entrance, check-in counter, concierge, and boardrooms. These guest rooms are exceptionally spacious, and the bathrooms are delightfully indulgent, with huge tubs, separate showers, and terry-cloth bathrobes. By 1990, the rooms in the main building and the Garden Wing will be upgraded to the standards, if not the size, of the Valley Wing rooms. The lobby lounge area is slightly dated and is visually dominated by a 10-foot mosaic mural of the zodiac, with a map of the world indicating the time in key cities. Set amid 15 acres of gardens in a residential area at the top of Orchard Road, the Shangri-La is a pleasant 10-minute walk from the shopping areas; taxis are always on call for those in a hurry. *22 Orange Grove Rd., Singapore 1025, tel. 737–3644 or 800/457–5050. 914 rooms (136 in the Valley Wing). Facilities: restaurants, 24-hr room service, tennis and squash courts, fitness center, indoor and outdoor pools, poolside bar, putting green, live evening entertainment (jazz and contemporary music), disco, 24-hr business center, meeting and banquet rooms. AE, DC, MC, V.*

Expensive **Boulevard Hotel.** Located at the top end of Orchard Road, the Boulevard is away from the main thoroughfare but within easy walking distance of the Singapore Handicraft Centre and the main Orchard Road area. It has two wings: the old wing, with renovated rooms; and the new 15-story Orchard Wing (opened in 1984), with a large, airy atrium lobby dominated by a floor-to-ceiling sculpture. The emphasis is on the traveling executive. Guest rooms include large work desks, minibars, IDD telephones, and pantries with coffee- and tea-making facilities. The 72 "executive suites" each have a lounge area. *200 Orchard Blvd., Singapore 1024, tel. 737–2911 or 800/421–0536. 528 rooms. Facilities: 3 restaurants (American, Japanese, Northern Indian), 24-hr coffee shop, 24-hr room service, fitness center, 2 outdoor pools, business center, hair-dresser, drugstore, disco, tour desk, shops. AE, DC, MC, V.*

★ **The Dynasty.** The 33-story, pagoda-inspired Dynasty is a striking landmark, dominating Singapore's "million-dollar corner"—the Orchard and Scotts roads intersection. It is the one hotel in Singapore that celebrates the island's Chinese heritage to the hilt. Depending on your taste, the three-story lobby in rich, deep red—the Chinese color for good fortune—is either opulent or garish. Notice especially the 153-bulb crystal chandelier and 24 remarkable carved-teak wall panels, each four feet wide and 40 feet high. Guest rooms, on the other hand, are decorated in cool colors and accented by lacquered paintings; minibars are discreetly camouflaged behind fine carvings. Indulge for a night in the splendid Imperial Suite, which will take you back to a China of long ago: The furnishings are museum-quality antiques, and the stage-set bathroom fulfills fantasies. A rooftop pool and garden, with trickling waters, weeping willows, and bamboo, give the feeling of an imperial Chinese courtyard. *320 Orchard Rd., Singapore 0923, tel. 734-9900 or UTELL International reservations 800/448-8355. 400 rooms, including 22 suites. Facilities: restaurants, 24-hr coffee shop, 24-hr room service, business center, fitness center, Twilight disco, outdoor pool with poolside bar, ballroom, function rooms. AE, DC, MC, V.*

Hilton International. Compared with some of the newer Singapore hotels, the Hilton is short on glitter and dazzle. Nevertheless, its renovated rooms have all the standard amenities of a modern deluxe property, and for what the hotel offers, the rates are highly competitive. The most prestigious lodgings are the Givenchy suites, each designed by Hubert de Givenchy and serviced by a personal valet. The Hilton has a fortunate location: a spacious, tree-lined pedestrian walkway out front leads to countless shops, cinemas, and restaurants, and the entertainment spots on Orchard and Scotts roads are minutes away. *581 Orchard Rd., Singapore 0923, tel. 737-2233 or 800/445-8667. 435 rooms. Facilities: 4 restaurants, 2 bars, 24-hr room service; rooftop outdoor pool; health club with sauna, steambath, whirlpool, and massage; shopping arcade; business center; large ballroom; 10 function rooms. AE, DC, MC, V.*

Marco Polo. Set on four acres in a high-rent residential district and only five minutes by taxi from Orchard Road, this hotel has undergone several changes since it opened in 1968. The most recent renovation (1989) gave the lobby and lounge areas a completely new look, creating a modern ambience that blends with the hotel's traditional European atmosphere. The guest rooms in the Continental Wing have been refurbished with Chippendale reproductions and marble-tiled bathrooms. These rooms have also been equipped with room safes, writing desks, and hand-held controls for television and lights. At night, a basement bar turns into a private-membership disco open to hotel guests. Perhaps because the British and Australian High Commissions are right across the road, guests are frequently from the Commonwealth. *Tanglin Rd., Singapore 1024, tel. 474-7141 or 800/223-5652. 603 rooms, including 30 suites. Facilities: 3 restaurants, lobby lounge and bar, disco, hair dryers, minibars, coffee- and tea-making facilities, 24-hr room service, landscaped outdoor pool, fitness center, business center, function rooms. AE, DC, MC, V.*

The Regent. In 1988, Regent International took over as managers of what was then the Pavilion Inter-Continental; at press time, plans for major renovations to bring the property up to Regent standards were being worked out. About a 10-minute walk from the Orchard and Scotts roads intersection, The Regent offers a quiet location that is close to the downtown action. Entering the sun-dappled atrium lobby, with greenery cascading from the balconies, is a soothing escape from the city heat, especially when the sound of violins from the Lower Bar fills the air. At the center is a bank of glassed-in elevators, which permit an overview of lounges and dining areas as you glide between floors. Guests rooms are comfortable and spacious, decorated in soft pastels and featuring an odd combination of bamboo and white-lacquer-and-brass furniture. All the rooms have writing desks and marble bathrooms; rooms on the terrace east and west sides have balconies overlooking green spaces. Service is characteristically Regent—which is to say first-rate. *1 Cuscaden Rd., Singapore 1024, tel. 733–8888 or 800/545–4000. 441 rooms, including 44 suites. Facilities: 4 restaurants; large outdoor pool; fitness center with sauna, steam room, hydro-pool, massage; business center; 24-hr room service; arcade with prestigious shops and pastry shop. AE, DC, MC, V.*

Sheraton Towers. Service at this hotel, which opened in 1985, is a key attraction. For example, guests are asked upon arrival if they'd like their suits pressed at no charge, and complimentary early morning coffee or tea is delivered to the rooms. Also complimentary are inhouse movies, breakfast, and evening cocktails. The pastel-decorated guest rooms have all the deluxe amenities, including a small sitting area with sofa and easy chairs. The hotel's dramatic visual is the cascading waterfall—the rocks are fiberglass—seen through a 30-foot glass panel from the Terrazza restaurant (especially welcoming for a superb high tea). *39 Scotts Rd., Singapore 0922, tel. 737–6888 or 800/325–3535. 406 rooms. Facilities: 3 restaurants, 24-hr coffee lounge, 24-hr room service, health center with sauna and massage, outdoor pool, poolside snack bar, business center, disco, ballroom, function rooms. AE, DC, MC, V.*

Moderate **Apollo Singapore.** Located to the south of the Singapore River and to the west of Chinatown and the business district, and without amenities like swimming pools and fitness centers, this semicircular 19-story hotel is more suited to business travelers than to tourists. At considerable expense, the facilities in this eight-year-old hotel were upgraded in 1988. Its main appeal is its clean, efficient, simply furnished but brightly colored rooms. *405 Havelock Rd., Singapore 0316, tel. 733–2081. 317 rooms. Facilities: 3 restaurants (Cantonese, Indonesian, Japanese), 24-hr coffee shop, disco, banquet rooms. AE, DC, MC, V.*

Carlton Hotel. Near Raffles City, between Orchard Road and the financial district of Shenton Way, this stark, pristine hotel—one of the newest (1988) in Singapore—has yet to develop a personality of its own. The lobby is an open forum echoing the footsteps of guests coming and going. However, everything is up-to-date and modern, and compared with other hotels in its class, this one's tariff is reasonable. Guest rooms have individually controlled air-conditioning, minibars, IDD telephones with bathroom extensions, and coffee- and tea-making facilities. The upper five stories are concierge floors, with express check-in and complimentary breakfast and evening cocktails. *76 Bras Basah Rd., Singapore 0718, tel. 338–8333 or UTELL*

International reservations 800/448–8355. 420 rooms, including 53 suites. Facilities: 2 restaurants (Cantonese and Continental), 24-hr coffee shop, wine bar, lounge bar, outdoor pool with poolside grill and bar, 24-hr room service, fitness center, business center, function rooms. AE, DC, MC, V.

Crown Prince Hotel. This Japanese-chain hotel, which opened in 1984, has a large, sparse lobby decorated with Italian marble and glass chandeliers. For drama, the elevators are glassed in and run along the outside of the building, which allows guests to check out the traffic congestion on Orchard Road. Guest rooms are neat, trim, and decorated in pastel colors; amenities include televisions with Teletext. The general ambience is one of efficiency rather than warmth. Many of the hotel's clients are Japanese. *270 Orchard Rd., Singapore 0923, tel. 732–1111 or 800/223–2094. 303 rooms, including 6 corner executive suites with steam baths. Facilities: 3 restaurants, outdoor pool, business center, 24-hr room service, 3 function rooms, banquet hall. AE, DC, MC, V.*

★ **Ladyhill Hotel.** Unlike most Singapore hotels, which cater to both business travelers and tourists, Ladyhill emphasizes home comforts and relaxation. Located in a residential area, a good 10-minute walk uphill from Orchard Road, the hotel consists of a main building and a series of cottages surrounding a pool. In the main building are the intimate Swiss-style restaurant Le Chalet, a cozy split-level bar with a Filipino band in the evenings, and some guest rooms. All the guest rooms are furnished in slightly dreary colors. The better ones are in the cottages. The "superior" rooms are larger—an extra bed may be added for the economy-minded guest traveling with children—and look out to the pool area. Usually in the evening there is a poolside barbecue. *1 Ladyhill Rd., Singapore 1025, tel. 737–2111 or 800/421–0536. 171 rooms. Facilities: coffee shop, outdoor pool, bar/cocktail lounge with live band, 2 small conference rooms. AE, V.*

Inexpensive **Cairnhill Hotel.** Once an apartment block, this hotel is a 10-minute walk from Orchard Road. While the building is not particularly attractive, its location on a hill does allow many of its guest rooms a good view of downtown Singapore. Also, for a smallish hotel, it offers a good range of amenities, from a small pool to an executive business center. Its Cairn Court restaurant serves Pekingese and Szechuan food, as well as regional fare. *19 Cairnhill Circle, Singapore 0922, tel. 734–6622. 220 rooms. Facilities: 24-hr coffee shop, business center, fitness center, pool with drink service, shopping arcade, small function room. AE, V.*

Peninsula Hotel. Near the Padang and between the fashionable areas of Orchard Road and Singapore's commercial district, this hotel offers the basic creature comforts. The fairly spacious guest rooms are clean—the best are on the newly refurbished 17th floor—though one may have to tolerate water stains in the bathtub. All rooms have televisions with Teletext, minibars, and self-coded safes. The lobby area is small, serving only as a place where guests register or gain access to the entertainment and dining rooms. *3 Coleman St., Singapore 0617, tel. 337–2200. 315 rooms, including 4 suites. Facilities: 24-hr coffee shop, cocktail lounge, nightclub with floor shows and hostesses, outdoor pool, fitness center with sauna and massage, 24-hr room service. AE, MC, V.*

★ **RELC International House.** This is less a hotel than an international conference center often used by Singapore's university for seminars. However, the upper floors of the building are guest rooms and offer one of the best bargains in Singapore. The centrally air-conditioned rooms are large and furnished with the basic comforts. The wide windows throw in welcome daylight, and though the bathrooms have rather sloppy plaster repair work, they are clean and functional. The building is in a residential neighborhood, up a hill beyond the Shangri-La Hotel; it's a stiff 10-minute walk to the Orchard and Scotts roads intersection. Because of its good value, it is often completely booked, so reservations are strongly advised. *30 Orange Grove Rd., Singapore 1024, tel. 737–9044. 128 rooms. Facilities: coffee shop, laundry facilities. No credit cards.*

Budget **Hotel Bencoolen.** On the commercial street that leads from Orchard Road to Little India, this hotel has recently been refurbished to add a fresher feel to its air-conditioned rooms, which include IDD phones. Usually, one can negotiate a discount on the room tariff, making the Bencoolen an especially good value. *47 Bencoolen St., Singapore 0718, tel. 336–0822. 69 rooms. Facilities: restaurant, rooftop garden. MC, V.*

Mitre Hotel. This small hotel is a relic. Overhead fans whirl in sparsely furnished bedrooms; downstairs, in the lounge/lobby bar, old-timers ruminate on how life used to be. If you are looking for shades of Sidney Greenstreet, staff who can manage Pidgin English at best, and a Conrad-esque atmosphere, the Mitre is for you. It does not have modern amenities, nor is it listed with the Singapore Tourist Promotion Office, so you will likely be the only Westerner in residence. *145 Killiney Rd., Singapore 0923, tel. 737–3811. 25 rooms with shared bath. Facilities: Count only on breakfast and drinks at the bar. No credit cards.*

The Arts and Nightlife

The Arts

Singapore Tourist Promotion Board (STPB) has listings of events scheduled for the current month. You can also find the schedules of major performances in the local English-language newspaper, the *Straits Times,* or in the free monthly *Arts Diary* brochure (available at most hotel reception desks).

Chinese, Indian, and Malay cultural events are limited to sporadic performances and to festivals, but some commercial shows drawing on Asian culture are given nightly for tourists. Indian music, drama, and dance performances are staged during some of the major festivals at the more important temples. Themes are from the ancient epics—tales of gods, demons, and heros.

The best of what there is in the area of serious international theater and classical concerts may be found at the **Victoria Theatre and Memorial Hall,** in two adjoining Victorian buildings. This is the home of the 85-member **Singapore Symphony Orchestra,** which was founded in 1979 and has built an excellent reputation for its wide repertoire, including popular classics as well as works by local and Asian composers. Also presented here from time to time are Chinese opera and Indian classical dance, as well as performances by Singapore's various theatrical and operatic societies. Several times a year, festivals featuring music and dance groups from throughout Southeast Asia are held in these auditoriums.

Concerts The **Singapore Symphony Orchestra** gives concerts on Friday and Saturday evenings twice a month at the Victoria Theatre (*see* above). Tickets may be reserved by telephone (tel. 338–1239, American Express or Visa accepted). Three times a year, the 70-member **Chinese Orchestra of the Singapore Broadcasting Corporation** performs Chinese classical music, also at the Victoria (tel. 338–1230 or 256–0401, ext. 2732).

Theater **Theatreworks** (tel. 280–0188) is a professional drama company focusing on contemporary works. **Act 3** (tel. 734–9090) concentrates on children's plays. **Stars** (tel. 468–9145) is a community theater that offers performances of family shows, such as American musicals and Christmas specials, as well as classic and modern dramas. **Hi! Theatre** (tel. 468–1945) is Singapore's theater of the deaf; its mask, mime, black-light, and sign-language performances appeal as much to the hearing as to the nonhearing.

Dance Performances are given throughout the year by the **Singapore Ballet Academy** (tel. 737–5772) and by the **Sylvia McCully** dance group (tel. 457–6995), who perform a combination of ballet and jazz.

Cultural Shows **"ASEAN Night"** at the Mandarin Hotel offers traditional songs and dances from the various countries of ASEAN. The shows are held at poolside, and dinner is available during performances. *333 Orchard Rd., tel. 737–4411. Tues.–Sun. Dinner starts at 7, the show at 7:45. Cost: dinner and show, S$40; show only, S$18.*

"Cultural Wedding Show" is a 45-minute re-creation of a Peranakan wedding ceremony. The presentation is part of a three-hour immersion in the culture of Straits-born Chinese that includes a tour of Peranakan Place's Show House Museum and dinner at Bibi's restaurant, serving Nonya food. *Peranakan Place, 180 Orchard Rd., tel. 732–6966. Weeknights 6:30 PM. Cost: S$36 adults, S$18 children.*

"Instant Asia" is a 45-minute revue of Chinese, Indian, and Malay dance. At the end of the show, members of the audience are invited onto the stage to participate. The show is cliché and commercial, but fun if you've never seen this kind of thing before. *Singa Inn Seafood Restaurant, 920 East Coast Pkwy., tel. 345–1111, Mon., Wed., Fri. at 7:30 PM. Free to diners.*

"Malam Singapura" is the Hyatt Regency's colorful 45-minute show of song and dance (mostly Malay) performed at poolside with or without dinner. *10–12 Scotts Rd., tel. 733–1188. Nightly. Dinner starts at 7, the show at 8. Cost: dinner and show, S$38; show only, S$18.*

Chinese Opera Chinese operas—called *wayangs*—are fascinating. Usually they are performed on temporary stages set up near temples, in market areas, or outside apartment complexes. Wayangs are staged all year, but are more frequently seen in August and September, during the Festival of the Hungry Ghosts. The wayangs, based on legends, are full of action. Gongs and drums beat, maidens weep, devils leap, and heros reap the praise of an enthusiastic audience. The characters are weirdly made up and gorgeously costumed.

Nightlife

Music clubs, offering everything from serious listening to jazz to the thumping and flashing of discos, are becoming more popular as Singaporeans take up the Western custom of dating. The increasingly popular *karaoke* ("empty orchestra") bars, where guests take microphones and sing along to the music track of a video, offer chronic bathroom singers the opportunity to go public.

Nightclubs with floor shows are also popular, and the feeling seems to be that the bigger the place is, the better—some accommodate as many as 500 guests. Often these clubs have hostesses (affectionately called public relations officers, or PRO's) available for company. Depending on the establishment, companionship is remunerated by either a flat hourly fee (the term used is "to book the hostess") or a gratuity given at the end of the evening.

At nightclubs or music bar/lounges, there is usually a cover charge or first-drink charge (cover plus one free drink) of about S$15 weeknights and S$25 weekends. At the nightclubs where there are floor shows and hostesses, the common practice is to buy a bottle of brandy, which may cost as much as S$300. You are advised to let your "hostess" drink from your bottle, rather than order her own.

Prostitution is not exactly legal, but certain areas, such as Geylang, do have red-light districts. The bars along Keppel Road are not recommended. Ladies have been known to slip sleeping draughts into men's drinks.

Dance and Theater Nightclubs The most popular nightclubs among Singaporeans are those with floor shows and hostesses. You are not under any obligation to select a hostess, however. The cost of going to these clubs is in the bottle of brandy you are expected to buy (if you don't mind losing face, you can forgo the brandy and order whatever you want from the bar). There are also "dinner theater" evenings held from time to time at the Hilton, Hyatt, and Shangri-La hotels. Dinner and a show at the **Shangri-La,** which often has some good comics, runs about S$85.

Golden Million. Here you can either dine or just listen to Hong Kong bands play a mixture of Mandarin, Cantonese, and Western music. The decor is rich and expansive, with lots of gold and red to give a feeling of extravagance. *Peninsula Hotel, 3 Coleman St., 5th floor, tel. 336–6993. Open nightly 8–2.*

Kasbah. The decor is Moroccan in this long-established, tiered nightclub where, on occasion, good artists from abroad entertain. Dancing is both fast and slow, and the music allows for conversation. The crowd, too, is more subdued and "properly" dressed. *Mandarin Hotel, Orchard Rd., tel. 737–4411. Open nightly 9–2.*

Marco Polo. A four-piece band plays popular dance music to which diners can take a turn on the floor between courses in the formal and elegant split-level Le Duc Continental restaurant in the Marco Polo Hotel. *Tanglin Rd., tel. 464–7141. Dinner for 2: approximately S$70. Open nightly 8–11.*

Neptune. This sumptuous two-story establishment, designed as an Oriental pavilion, is reputed to be the largest nightclub in

Southeast Asia. Cantonese food is served, and there is a gallery for nondiners. Local, Taiwanese, and Filipino singers entertain in English and Chinese; occasionally a European dance troupe is added to the lineup. *Overseas Union House, Collyer Quay, tel. 224-3922; for show information and reservations, tel. 737-4411. Open nightly 8-2.*

Tropicana. Australian and European belles demonstrate their legginess and live bands entertain at this popular spot. Cantonese cooking is served. The Tropicana is one of the old-timers in "tease dancing" and has become slightly sleazy; the second show is rather leggier than the first. *9 Scotts Rd., tel. 737-6433. Shows at 9 PM and 10:30 PM. Open nightly 8-2.*

Discos and Dance Clubs

Brannigans. This is currently the in place for Yuppies. Outside, lines of people wait to enter and be entertained by a variety of musical groups. *Hyatt Hotel, 10-12 Scotts Rd., tel. 733-1188. Open nightly 8-3.*

Caesars. The decor and the waitresses dressed in lissome togas give this disco an air of decadent splendor. DJ-spun music plus imported live bands make it a hot venue. *Orchard Towers front block (#02-36), 400 Orchard Rd., tel. 737-7665. Open Sun.-Thurs. 8-2, Fri. and Sat. 8-3.*

Celebrities. Having moved from Centrepoint to Orchard Towers, this establishment is now considered a sophisticated night spot. Dance music spun by a DJ is interspersed with live pop music; one of the key attractions is the all-girl band Heaven Knows. There is ample room to drink at the 150-foot-long bar. *Orchard Towers rear block (#B1-41), 400 Orchard Rd., tel. 734-5221. Open Sun.-Thurs. 8-2, Fri. and Sat. 8-3.*

Rumours. One of the largest discos in Singapore, this is a current favorite among the younger crowd. The two-level glass dance floor is designed to make you feel as though you are dancing in space; the play of mirrors adds to the distortion. *Forum Galleria (#03-08), 483 Orchard Rd., tel. 732-8181. Open Sun.-Thurs. 8-2, Fri. and Sat. 8-3.*

Top Ten. This old, converted cinema has a decor of cityscapes, as well as a four-tier bar, a dance floor, and a stage. Imported bands alternate with disco music. There is a popular "happy hour" in the lobby bar between 5 and 9 PM. *Orchard Towers (#04-35/36), 400 Orchard Rd., tel. 732-3077. Open nightly 9-3.*

Pubs and Beer Gardens

Dickens Tavern. At this mixture of a pub and a lounge, regulars listen to bands while being served by friendly waitresses (not hostesses). It's a good place to visit if you do not want to have a raucous and expensive evening. *Parkway Parade (#04-01), 80 Marina Parade Rd., tel. 440-0215. No cover. Open nightly 8-2.*

Jim's Pub. Try this cozy bar, owned and managed by pianist Jimmy Chan, for an evening of light music from a vocalist or instrumentalist. *Hotel Negara, 15 Claymore Dr., tel. 737-0811. Open nightly 7-1.*

Jazz

Saxophone. At this club, which offers both jazz and popular rock, the volume is loud and the space is compact, with standing room only. However, there is a terrace outside where you can sit and still hear the music. *23 Cuppage Terr., tel. 235-8385. Open nightly 6-1.*

Somerset Bar. The New Orleans-style jazz played here has attracted a loyal following over the past four years. With a larger space than the Saxophone, it offers room to sit and relax, making it more popular with the older crowd. *Westin Plaza, 4 Stamford Rd., 3rd floor, tel. 338–8585. Open nightly 5–2.*

Country-and-Western **Golden Peacock Lounge.** The star attraction is Matthew Tan, Singapore's own singing cowboy, who has a unique vintage country twang. *Shangri-La Hotel, 22 Orange Grove Rd., tel. 737–3644. Open nightly 8–2.*

Rock **Anywhere.** Crowds gather in this smoke-filled room to hear the local rock band Tania. *Tanglin Shopping Centre (#04-08), 19 Tanglin Rd., tel. 734–8233. Open Sun.–Thurs. 8–2, Fri. and Sat. 8–3.*

8 Taiwan

Introduction

Taiwan, also known as the Republic of China, is fast beginning to rival Hong Kong and Singapore for efficiency and comfort. First-rate hotels abound, trains are clean and run on time, service is cordial and swift. Signs of the country's economic development are everywhere. Walk around the capital, Taipei, and you'll see 7-Eleven stores and McDonald's on more than a few corners. You'll pass automated teller machines, slimming centers, and Alfa Romeo dealerships. At night, you may wonder if the Taiwanese didn't invent the neon sign.

Prosperity has come after a varied and somewhat bitter history. The island is believed to have been inhabited for at least 10,000 years, the earliest settlers most likely having been migrants from other Pacific islands. Today descendants of these aboriginal tribes live in villages on Lanyu Island and at Sun Moon Lake, where they stage performances of traditional dance for tourists. The aborigines first saw Europeans in the 1500s, when the Portuguese landed on Taiwan and named it Ihla Formosa ("beautiful island"). The Dutch drove out the Portuguese in 1624, only to lose the island two years later to the Spanish. The Dutch then reclaimed it in 1641.

Chinese from the neighboring mainland began migrating to Taiwan in large numbers only after Cheng Cheng-kung, better known as Koxinga, drove out the Dutch in 1661 and claimed the island for the fallen Ming dynasty. His grandson was forced to surrender to Ching dynasty troops two decades later, and the island eventually became a province of China. At the close of the Sino-Japanese War in 1895, Taiwan was ceded to the Japanese, and the island entered a bleak 50-year period of sometimes brutal colonial rule.

The history of Taiwan as the Republic of China began on the mainland long before the current government was set up on the island in 1949. After the collapse of the Ching dynasty in 1911, the republic was founded on the mainland in 1912 under the leadership of Sun Yat-sen. But civil war followed shortly, with Chiang Kai-shek's Nationalist Party eventually emerging as the dominant power. Chiang soon had his troubles. He had to face not only an incipient Communist movement but also Japanese invaders who landed in Manchuria in 1931. The Japanese then struck at Beijing, Shanghai, and Nanking in 1937. It wasn't until the Japanese surrender at the end of World War II that Chiang could give full attention to the Communist rebels. But Mao Tse-tung and his Red Chinese proved invincible. In 1949, Chiang and the Nationalists were forced to flee to Taiwan, where the Republic of China was relocated for what was to be a temporary period until the non-Communists reclaimed the mainland. The standoff continues to this day.

By the late 1950s, Taiwan began to recognize that living well is the best revenge, and economic prosperity could distinguish the island from the impoverished mainland. Gradually, foreign investors realized that Taiwan offered cheap, industrious labor for manufacturing. And the country's "economic miracle" took shape. Today, after several years of rapid development, Taiwan is regarded as one of Asia's Four Tigers, along with Hong Kong, Singapore, and Korea.

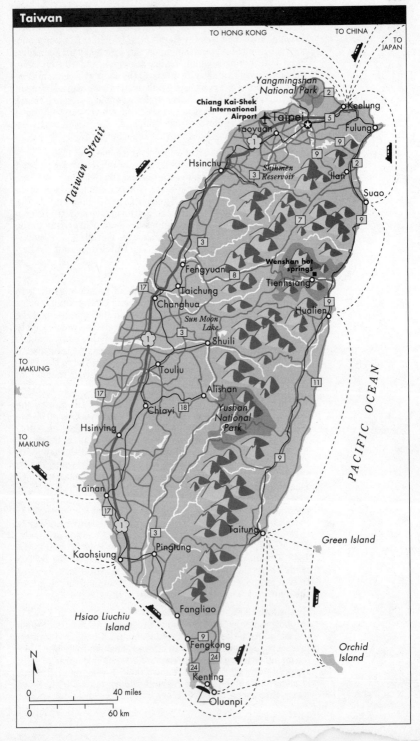

Taiwan

TO HONG KONG TO CHINA TO JAPAN

Yangmingshan National Park

Chiang Kai-Shek International Airport

Keelung

Taipei

Taoyuan Fulung

Taiwan Strait

Hsinchu *Shihmen Reservoir* Ilan

Suao

Fengyuan

Taichung

Changhua

Sun Moon Lake

Shuili

Touliu

Alishan

Chiayi

Yushan National Park

Hsinying

Wenshan hot springs

Tienhsiang

Hualien

TO MAKUNG

TO MAKUNG

PACIFIC OCEAN

Tainan

Kaohsiung Pingtung

Taitung *Green Island*

Hsiao Liuchiu Island

Fangliao

Fengkong

N

Kenting

Oluanpi

Orchid Island

0   40 miles
0   60 km

While economic success has made the island an easy place to spend time, its preoccupation with Western-style development also has some drawbacks. Don't come to Taiwan hoping to bask in an atmosphere of traditional Chinese culture. Although many families continue to observe ancient rituals in the home, street life shows little evidence of cultural continuity. Taiwan's 40 years as an exile society cut the island off from its cultural roots on the mainland. While its giant neighbor may be troubled and backward, Taiwan seems to have emerged as an economic powerhouse at some cost to its identity. The alienation of modern Taiwan from its Chinese past can be seen— symbolically perhaps—in the location of the National Palace Museum. This stunning institution, the world's finest storehouse of Chinese culture, is located in Taipei's northern suburbs—far from the heartbeat of the thriving capital.

Given Taiwan's commercial success, it's not surprising that 85% of its visitors are businesspeople. Many hotels offer a range of services catering to the business traveler, including secretaries, fax and telex machines, and special lounges for entertaining clients. The Taipei World Trade Center—a trade hub, not a tourist trap—is a sleek monument to the type of commerce that has driven Taiwan's development. The focus of the city's activity is gravitating toward this business complex, bringing with it a rejuvenation of Taipei's eastern district. A convention center and Hyatt Regency hotel are scheduled for completion at the WTC in early 1990.

Taipei is the hub of Taiwan and, since the island is so small— 402 km (250 mi) north to south and 89 km (55 mi) wide—the main jumping-off point for exploration. Most excursions from Taipei can be completed in a day, though overnight stays in some places may be more convenient. The island has many natural scenic attractions. Just north of Taipei, you can hike on Yangmingshan mountain. To the east, you can head for the beach at Fulung (though you'll have to travel to Taiwan's southern tip for the best beaches and spectacular ocean views). The island's central mountains offer the lush forests of Alishan. In the southwest, you can immerse yourself in Taiwan's history at Tainan, the oldest city on the island, with more than 200 temples.

Tourists and local honeymooners flock to Sun Moon Lake, a sparkling natural reservoir in central Taiwan that is popular with boaters and anglers. In the south, you can get caught up in the whir of Taiwan's second boomtown, Kaohsiung. This industrial hub is the country's largest port and the departure point for the Pescadores, a group of 64 islands off the west coast. The main island of Penghu has the archipelago's characteristic flat, windswept terrain, with dry brush and grasslands. There you'll find coral at bargain prices and excellent beaches.

Taipei itself provides sensory exhilaration—sometimes overload. Traffic is always a snarl, car horns blare, and music pounds from open-air shops. In the evening, people pour into the streets seeking bargains at the night markets, and the many excellent restaurants are crowded with diners. Taiwan is famous for its variety of Chinese cuisine, and it's the rare meal that doesn't please. After dinner, the perfect antidote to a frenzied day is relaxing over a cup of elaborately brewed tea in one of the city's many teahouses.

Especially since some airlines permit free stopovers from Japan, Hong Kong, and the Philippines, you may want to consider a diversion to Taiwan when planning your Asia itinerary.

Staying in Taiwan

Getting Around

Throughout this section, unless otherwise specified, all telephone numbers are for Taipei.

By Plane Taiwan is so small that any location is just a hop away by plane. One of the longest flights, between Taipei and the southern port city of Kaohsiung, is just 40 minutes. Be prepared for strict security inspections. Take your passport whenever you head for the airport. You'll be required to present it before boarding.

China Airlines (tel. 02/715–2626), the national carrier, and **Far Eastern Air Transport** (tel. 02/712–1555) offer jet service between Taipei and other major cities, including Kaohsiung, Hualien, Tainan, and Taitung. **Formosa Airlines** (tel. 02/507–4188) and **Taiwan Airline Co.** (tel. 02/537–3660) fly propeller planes on less-traveled routes. These carriers service Orchid and Green islands from Kaohsiung and Taitung.

By Train Taiwan has extensive rail service on two major lines along the west and east coasts. Seats on the air-conditioned trains must be reserved at least one day but not more than three days before departure. Hotels and travel agencies will make arrangements for you. Reservations can also be made at the **Taipei Central Railway Station** or by phoning 02/312–2255. You can get a 15% discount on round-trip tickets, but reservations for your return must be made once you arrive at your destination. The express trains are comfortable and clean, and some have dining cars. But since most trains provide only rice dishes served in cardboard boxes, it's a good idea on longer trips to carry your own food. Nonsmoking cars are available.

By Bus Express bus service along the North–South Highway, stretching for 370 km (230 mi) from Taipei to Kaohsiung, is faster and slightly cheaper than train travel. The whole route takes five hours. If you prefer a bus with a rest room, you'll pay a little more for the convenience. Reservations should be made up to two days in advance. Bus companies include **Chung Hsing Bus Co.** (tel. 02/771–2000), **Chuen Hwa Express Transit Co.** (tel. 02/597–5181), and **Three Star Touring Bus Co.** (tel. 02/731–1211).

By Boat If you're unrushed, ferries are a pleasant way to reach Orchid, Green, Hsiao Liuchiu, and the Pescadores islands. For service to Lanyu and Green islands from Taitung, contact the **Lanyu Shipping Agency** (tel. 098/322210). Boats to Hsiao Liuchiu from Kaohsiung are operated by **Jan An Boat Co.** (tel. 07/211–2123). **Taiwan Navigation Corp.** (tel. 07/311–3882) runs boats between Kaohsiung and the Pescadores. You can also ride from Keelung to Hualien on boats operated by **Taiwan Car Ferry Co.** (tel. 02/522–1215); the trip takes six hours. Passports are required for all boat trips.

By Car A private car is a good idea only if you travel outside Taipei. Inside the capital, it's best to rely on taxis and buses, since driving can be a harrowing experience. Roads are often horribly congested, and Taipei drivers tend to be rather madcap. On trips outside the capital, you'll spare yourself some anxiety by keeping the gas tank fairly full at all times; gas stations in remote areas may be hard to find. The speed limit downtown is 40 kph (25 mph); on the highways, 90 kph (56 mph). If you're involved in an accident or have a breakdown, phone the Foreign Affairs Police; their number in Taipei is 02/537–3852.

Rentals To rent a car, you need an international driver's license. Rentals range from NT\$1,300 to NT\$1,800 a day at **Hertz Rent-A-Car** (tel. 02/717–3673), **Avis** (tel. 02/500–6633), **Gordon's Rent-A-Car** (tel. 02/881–9545), and **China Rent-A-Car** (tel. 02/500–6088), among other Taipei companies.

Cars also can be rented with a driver who serves as your guide. Your hotel can usually make the arrangements. Prices start at about NT\$500 per hour, minimum three hours, or NT\$3,800 a day.

Road Conditions Taiwan's roads are generally good, though traffic on some of the scenic highways can get heavy. Most major locations are designated in English, but it's a good idea to watch the signposts for route numbers.

Telephones

Local Calls You'll find two types of public pay phones. The older ones permit only three-minute calls, then disconnect. If you want to resume your conversation, you have to drop another coin into the slot and dial again. The newer phones allow you to pump in money to keep the line alive, and a digital display lets you watch your money being consumed. If you want to keep talking, keep inserting coins. Local calls cost NT\$1 for three minutes. Domestic long-distance calls can be dialed from private or public pay phones. Public phones have a NT\$5 slot for long-distance calls. First insert a NT\$5 coin, then dial the area code and the number.

International Calls Overseas calls can be placed from private phones and at offices of the International Telecommunications Administration (ITA). The main Taipei ITA office (at 28 Hangchou South Rd., Section 1, tel. 02/344–3781) never closes. To place a call, dial 100 for an overseas operator. For specifics on discounts and direct dialing, call 02/321–2535.

Information To reach an English-speaking operator or to get directory assistance, dial 02/311–6796.

Mail

Taiwan's postal service puts those of most countries to shame. Postmen make their rounds every day of the year, usually delivering intra-island mail within two days.

Red mailboxes on the street are for international and domestic express letters; domestic surface mail goes in the green boxes. Post offices are open Monday–Saturday 8–5 and Sunday and holidays 8–noon. Taipei's Central Post Office (CPO), two blocks west of the Hilton Hotel at the North Gate intersection, packs parcels for a small fee.

Postal Rates Rates to the United States and Europe are NT\$16 for letters weighing 10 g (0.4 oz), NT\$12 for each additional 10 g. Postcards cost NT$11. The domestic rate for a regular letter is NT$2; express delivery within 24 hours costs NT$5. Mail to the United States and Europe takes six to seven days, but deliveries to other Asian countries are speedier.

Receiving Mail The CPO in Taipei holds letters for travelers and is a convenient place to pick up mail. Also in Taipei, **American Express** (214 Tunhwa North Rd., tel. 02/715–2400) holds mail for cardmembers and nonmembers alike.

Currency

The unit of currency is the New Taiwan dollar. Bills come in denominations of 50, 100, 500, and 1,000, and coins in units of NT$1, NT$5, and NT$10. At press time the exchange rate was NT$25.62 = US$1.

What It Will Cost

Prices have climbed considerably in recent years, because the New Taiwan dollar (NT$) has appreciated 45% since 1986. With the possible exception of hotel rates, Taipei prices now are comparable to those in Hong Kong and other major Asian cities.

Sample Prices Cup of coffee at a hotel, $3.30; can of soda from a 7-Eleven, 75¢; meal of diced chicken with cashew nuts, $9.35; 2-mile taxi ride, $2.15; double room, under $70 inexpensive, $70–$115 moderate, $115–$175 expensive, over $175 very expensive.

Language

Taiwan's national language is Mandarin Chinese, although more than half the population speaks the dialect of Fukien Province, from which many Taiwan residents trace their roots. The Hakka dialect is spoken among the small percentage of émigrés from China's Guangdong Province. Some older Taiwanese can speak Japanese because of the island's 50-year occupation by Japan. In general, taxi drivers are not likely to speak English; be sure to have your hotel write in Chinese characters the name of a destination you are trying to reach by taxi. At hotels there should be no problem at all.

Opening and Closing Times

Banks are open weekdays 9–3:30, Saturday 9–noon. **Government offices** are open weekdays 8:30–12:30 and 1:30–5:30, Saturday 8:30–12:30. **Department stores** open daily at 10:30 or 11 and close at 9:30. Most other **shops** open at 9 or 10 and close 12 hours later. **Museums** are open daily 9–5.

National Holidays

Founding of the Republic of China, Jan. 1; Youth Day, Mar. 29; tomb-sweeping day and death of Chiang Kai-shek, Apr. 5; birthday of Confucius, Sept. 28; Double Ten National Day, Oct. 10; Taiwan Retrocession Day, Oct. 25; birthday of Chiang Kai-shek, Oct. 31; birthday of Sun Yat-sen, Nov. 12; Constitution Day, Dec. 25.

Festivals and Seasonal Events

The following is a sampling of festivals. The dates vary from year to year because they're based on the lunar calendar; those below cover 1990. For additional information, contact the Taiwan Tourism Bureau (*see* Important Addresses and Numbers, below).

Jan. 1: Founding Day, celebrating the establishment of the Republic of China, is marked with parades, dragon dances, and fireworks.

Jan. 27: The **Lunar New Year** is the most important Chinese holiday. The country grinds to a halt in the days leading up to the celebration as families clean their houses and prepare for large feasts. You'll be awestruck by the nonstop firecracker explosions on New Year's Eve.

Feb. 10: The **Lantern Festival** marks the end of the New Year holiday season. The streets glow with a dazzling array of hanging lanterns.

Mar. 15: The **Birthday of Kuan Yin,** goddess of mercy, is celebrated with offerings of fruits and vegetables presented in colorful ceremonies at major temples throughout Taiwan.

Apr. 18: The **Birthday of Matsu,** goddess of the sea, is marked at many temples by sacrificial offerings of food and by the burning of incense and money.

May 28: The **Dragon Boat Festival** commemorates the death of Chu Yuan, a poet and statesman who drowned himself in 299 BC to protest government corruption. Colorful boat races are held in several cities.

June 5: The **Birthday of Cheng Huang,** Taipei's city god, is celebrated with parades of stilt walkers and dragon dancers at Cheng Huang Temple.

Oct. 3: The **Mid-Autumn Moon Festival** brings Chinese streaming into the streets to gaze skyward. It's believed that on this night, the 15th day of the eighth lunar month, the moon is at its brightest of the year. The festival has a traditional food: the moon cake, a round, sweet bean pastry.

Oct. 10: Double-Ten National Day commemorates the overthrow of the last Chinese dynasty, on the 10th day of the 10th month in 1911. A military parade takes place in the morning near the Presidential Building on Jenai Road.

Tipping

Tipping is not required; tax and a service charge totaling 15% are added to both hotel and restaurant bills. **Bellhops** are an exception; they get about NT$30 for carrying bags to your room.

Shopping

Taiwan's economic success has raised shopping to a national pastime. In Taipei, most stores open onto the street, and their shelves are packed. Although shopping mavens still insist that they must travel to Hong Kong or Singapore to satisfy their bargain-hunting urges, Taipei has quite a lot to offer, especially in handicrafts, jewelry, and furniture. Huge department stores, such as the Japanese-owned Sogo, offer a wide range of items from toys to cookware. Some smaller, elegant shops specialize in antique artifacts. Products worth looking for are bamboo crafts, rugs, marbleware, and cloisonné.

Outside Taipei, Hualien is famous for marble; the Pescadores are reputed to be one of only two places in the world that produce veinstone, used in elegant but inexpensive bracelets, rings, and necklaces; and Taiwan's pottery and ceramics center is just north of the capital, in Peitou.

Once quite prevalent, bargaining now seems less effective, though some shopkeepers will still yield to the persistent.

Sports and Beaches

Sports enthusiasts won't have trouble finding a place to exercise. The major hotels all have gyms, saunas, and swimming pools; some have jogging tracks. One way to combine physical activity with sightseeing is to head for the mountains just north of Taipei. The central mountains, including Alishan, also offer scenic hikes. Bowling is one of the most popular sports in Taipei, with many alleys around the city. Golfers can choose from 23 courses throughout Taiwan. Beach lovers won't have far to travel: Just 40 minutes north of Taipei is Fulung, a white-sand resort area, though the finest beaches are in the south at Kenting.

Dining

Eating is one of the greatest pleasures of a visit to Taiwan. An array of regional specialties is available, including Peking, Cantonese (and dim sum, also known as *yum cha*), Shanghainese, Hunanese, Szechuan, Taiwanese, and Mongolian. If you want a break from Chinese cuisine, you can choose from many other menus, including Japanese, Italian, Continental, Korean, and Indian.

Throughout this chapter, the following restaurant price categories will apply:

Category	Cost*
Very Expensive	over NT$700 (US$25)
Expensive	NT$500–NT$700 (US$18–US$25)
Moderate	NT$300–NT$500 (US$10–US$18)
Inexpensive	under NT$300 (US$10)

per person, excluding drinks, 10% service charge, and 5% value-added tax

Lodging

In Taipei, hotels range from the posh Lai Lai Sheraton to the functional YMCA. The higher-end places tend to cater to businesspeople, and many provide such a range of services that it's hardly necessary to step outside. Besides offering secretarial help, these hotels usually have several restaurants, a bar, a night spot, exercise facilities, and a shopping arcade.

Throughout this chapter, the following hotel price categories will apply:

Category	Cost*
Very Expensive	over NT$4,500 (US$175)
Expensive	NT$3,000–NT$4,500 (US$115–US$175)
Moderate	NT$1,800–NT$3,000 (US$70–US$115)
Inexpensive	under NT$1,800 (US$70)

All prices are for a standard double room, excluding 10% service charge and 5% value-added tax.

Taipei

Taipei, the heart of Taiwan, is known as the fastest-growing city in Asia. As the nation's capital, it is home to the island's finest monuments, such as the Chiang Kai-shek Memorial and the Sun Yat-sen Memorial. It is also the commercial center, with the recently completed Taipei World Trade Center signaling a shift in international business activity toward the eastern part of the city. Shoppers will want to stroll in the fashionable Dinghao district along Chunghsiao East Road, between Fuhsing Road and Tunhua Road, in eastern Taipei. The cuisine, ranging from every type of Chinese to Swiss and German, is first-rate.

Arriving and Departing by Plane

Airports and Airlines International flights arrive at Chiang Kai-shek International Airport, 40 km (25 mi) southwest of Taipei near Taoyuan. **China Airlines,** the national carrier, has flights from San Francisco, Los Angeles, New York, Honolulu, and Anchorage. The U.S. airlines serving Taipei are **Northwest Orient** and **United Airlines.** When leaving Taiwan, you'll have to pay an airport tax of NT$300. All domestic arrivals and departures use Sungshan Domestic Airport in northeast Taipei.

Between the Airport and Downtown Buses and taxis run regularly from both airports to the downtown hotels. Some hotels provide free shuttle service, but check in advance whether a representative will meet you. Travel time between Chiang Kai-shek International and downtown is about 45 minutes in off-peak hours; during rush hours, the ride can take up to 90 minutes. From Sungshan airport, you can get downtown in 10 minutes.

By Bus Buses leave every 15 minutes from Chiang Kai-shek International during the airport's operating hours, 6 AM to midnight, stopping at a cluster of downtown hotels. Fare is NT$72.

By Taxi Since the numerous drivers at Chiang Kai-shek International have to wait for fares, they're permitted to tack on 50% to the metered rate. The fare will run about NT$1,000 to downtown.

Getting Around

Taipei traffic is miserable, especially during the morning and evening rush hours, so plan on delays. Addresses can be confusing. Before setting out, ask your hotel to write the address of your destination in Chinese, including the section number, lane, and alley, if applicable. It's also a good idea to carry the name of your hotel in Chinese for your return trip.

By Bus Buses are cheap and efficient, though jammed in rush hours. The fare is NT$10 per zone aboard an air-conditioned bus, NT$8 without air-conditioning. For information, call 02/321–6511 or 02/351–4367.

By Taxi Taxis are numerous and fairly inexpensive. Be prepared for a wild ride: The drivers apparently try to outdo one another's daredevil stunts. If a driver is particularly reckless, ask him to pull over, pay the fare, and try another. In an effort to improve taxi travel, the government has begun rewarding drivers who have the fewest complaints and accidents to their credit—you can spot them by the letter N (for New Environment) above the TAXI sign on the car's roof—but these drivers account for only about one-fourth of the total in Taipei. The initial fare is NT$35, plus NT$5 for each additional half-kilometer. Tipping isn't required, but it's customary to let the driver keep any change.

Important Addresses and Numbers

Tourist Information The **Taiwan Tourism Bureau** provides maps and brochures on everything from Chinese food to calligraphy. The office is near the Sun Yat-sen Memorial (at 280 Chunghsiao East Rd., Section 4, 9th floor, tel. 02/721–8541). The bureau also operates **Travel Service Centers** at Chiang Kai-shek and Sungshan airports. A tourist information hotline (tel. 02/717–3737) takes calls daily 8–8.

Embassies The United States does not maintain diplomatic relations with Taiwan, but the **American Institute in Taiwan** (134 Hsinyi Rd., Section 3, La. 1, tel. 02/709–2000) serves as an unofficial representative office. The United Kingdom's unofficial office is the **Anglo-Taiwan Trade Committee** (36 Nanking East Rd., Section 2, tel. 02/521–4116). Canada's representative is the **Canadian Trade Office** in Taipei (205 Tunhua North Rd., tel. 02/713–7268).

Emergencies The **Foreign Affairs Police** speak English; dial 02/537–3852. For **Fire** and **ambulance,** call 119.

Doctors The **Adventist Hospital** (424 Pateh Rd., Section 2, tel. 02/771–8151), near the Municipal Stadium, has a staff of foreign-trained doctors who speak English.

English-Language Bookstores **Caves Books** (103 Chungshan North Rd., tel. 02/541–4754), the **Book Exchange** (669 Wenlin Rd., Shihlin, tel. 02/832–7434), **Lucky Bookstore** (128-1 Hoping East Rd., Section 1, tel. 02/392–7111), **Bookman Books Ltd.** (3 La. 62, Roosevelt Rd., Section 4, tel. 02/392–4715).

Travel Agencies Many Chinese agencies are listed in the phone book; the principal international office is **American Express** (4th floor, 214 Tunhwa North Rd., tel. 02/715–2400).

Guided Tours *Orientation* Two bus tours will show you the major monuments and Taipei by night. The daytime tours include the Chiang Kai-shek Memorial (*see* Exploring Taipei, below), the Martyrs Shrine (*see* Off the Beaten Track, below) and the National Palace Museum

(*see* The Arts and Nightlife, below). The night tours begin with
a Mongolian barbecue dinner, followed by a visit to the night
markets, Lungshan Temple, and the Chinese Opera. Companies operating these tours include **Grey Line** (tel. 02/551–5544),
Edison Travel Service (tel. 02/563–5313), **Pinho Travel Service**
(tel. 02/551–4136), and **Taiwan Coach Tours** (tel. 02/595–5321).
Your hotel can help make arrangements.

Highlights for First-time Visitors

Chiang Kai-shek Memorial (*see* Taipei Walking Tour)
Chinese opera performance (*see* The Arts)
Lungshan Temple (*see* Taipei Walking Tour)
National Palace Museum (*see* The Arts)
Snake Alley night market (*see* Nightlife)
Sun Yat-sen Memorial (*see* Taipei Walking Tour)
Taiwan Folk Art Museum (*see* Excursions from Taipei)
Yangmingshan National Park (*see* Excursions from Taipei)

Exploring Taipei

Taipei isn't very large, but the noisy battle among motorbikes,
cars, and buses on the crowded streets can be daunting. There
is order beneath the confusion, however. Chunghsiao Road,
running east and west, slices the city into its north and south
sections. Chungshan Road, running north and south, defines
Taipei's east and west sections. You'll find it convenient to get
around by bus and taxi. Exploring on foot is easy, too, since the
many underpasses let you cross busy streets without difficulty.

Taipei Walking Tour This tour takes you past the office buildings of Taiwan's central
government, stopping at the Chinese Handicraft Mart on your
way to the Chiang Kai-shek Memorial. From there, you can
walk to nearby Taipei New Park for a rest.

*Numbers in the margin correspond with numbered points of
interest on the Taipei map.*

❶ At the corner of Chungshan and Chunghsiao roads you'll see
the domed structure that houses the **Control Yuan,** the watch-
dog branch of government, which keeps an eye on state
accounts and public officials. You can't tour the building, but no
one will holler if you peek in the entry at the impressive cupola.
The building was constructed in 1915 as a headquarters by the
Japanese, who took control of Taiwan after the first Sino-
Japanese War.

❷❸ Walk south on Chungshan across Chingtao West Road. The
brick building on your left is the **Legislative Yuan,** Taiwan's
parliament. After crossing Chinan Road, you'll see the **Ministry of Education** on your left. Note the mixture of modern
architecture with the sloping Chinese eaves over the entrance.

❹ At Hsuchou Road, turn left and walk the short distance to the
Taiwan Handicraft Mart. This state-sponsored shop was created to promote Taiwanese handicrafts, so prices are
competitive. On the market's three floors you'll find ceramics,
jade carvings, marble vases, cloisonné, kites, jewelry, and furniture. *1 Hsuchou Rd., tel. 02/321–7233. Open daily 9–5:30.*

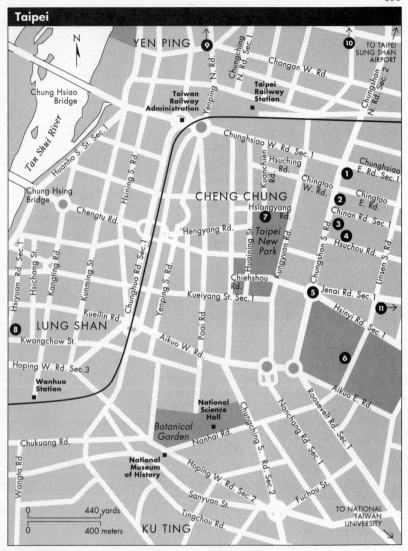

Taipei

Chiang Kai-shek
Memorial, **6**

Confucian Shrine, **9**

Control Yuan, **1**

East Gate, **5**

Legislative Yuan, **2**

Lungshan Temple, **8**

Martyrs Shrine, **10**

Ministry of
Education, **3**

Sun Yat-sen Memorial
Hall, **11**

Taiwan Handicraft
Mart, **4**

Taiwan Provincial
Museum, **7**

Return to Chungshan Road and continue south to the rotary at
⑤ Hsinyi Road. In the center sits the **East Gate,** one of five entrances in a 5.4-m- (18-ft-) high wall that surrounded the city in
the 19th century. All the gates were reconstructed in the style
of China's imperial palace; the North Gate was stripped of lacquer in 1979 to restore it to the original dark red brick and
yellow-gray stone.

Go around the rotary to Hsinyi and walk east beside the tall
⑥ white wall topped by blue tiles that encloses the **Chiang Kai-
shek Memorial.** Enter through the large gate. In the morning,
Chinese often do tai-chi exercises in the vast (62-acre) park,
and old men gather with their caged birds—an "outing" for the
beloved pets. As you approach the memorial hall, pause for a
moment at the bottom of the steep stairs and gaze upward for
the full, dizzying impact of the gargantuan structure. The
Ming-style archway at the entrance is 30 m (100 ft) high and
75 m (250 ft) wide. Inside, you are greeted by a statue of Chiang
Kai-shek, Taiwan's founder, flanked by two rigid uniformed
guards who are replaced each hour on the hour in a carefully
choreographed ceremony. The hall contains photographs and
personal effects of the president. In the park, you can stroll
along the paths to a lovely carp pond that catches the reflection
of the memorial hall. *Tel. 02/394–3171. Admission free. The
hall is open daily 9–5, the park daily 5 AM–midnight.*

Return to the rotary, go west on Chiehshou Road to Kungyuan
Road, and turn right. Follow Kungyuan to Hsiangyang Road
and turn left. At Hsiangyang and Kuanchien Road, enter Taipei New Park, with tree-sheltered paths and a pond with carp,
⑦ for which you can buy food. The **Taiwan Provincial Museum**
within the park has crafts of Taiwan's aborigines (believed to
have come from Polynesia and Malaya) and an art gallery. *2
Hsiangyang Rd., tel. 02/381–4700. Admission charge. Open
daily 9–5.*

Time Out   For a dim sum snack any time or a full Cantonese lunch, try
Rebar Restaurant, on the sixth floor of the Rebar Department
Store. From the east side of the park, walk east along
Hengyang Road to Yenping South Road. *110 Yenping South
Rd., tel. 02/381–8606. No reservations needed. Dress: casual.
No credit cards.*

Temple touring is a major attraction in the city. One of the larg-
⑧ est and most colorful Buddhist temples is the **Lungshan
Temple,** the first to be built in Wanhua, the oldest district in the
city. The magnificent stone sculpture, intricate wood carving,
gold-leafed idols, and ornate roof decorations of this 200-year-
old edifice fascinate visitors. It was built by settlers coming
from three districts in Fukien Province who wished to continue
their worship of Kuan Yin, the goddess of mercy, and Ma Tsu,
the goddess of the sea, as they had done at home. Although first
constructed in 1738, it has been rebuilt twice—once after a severe earthquake in 1816, and again after bomb damage during
World War II.

⑨ The **Confucian Shrine,** located in the northwest Taipei district
of Tatung, west of the **Taipei City Zoo** (*see* What to See and Do
with Children, below), is dedicated to the great Chinese philosopher and is similar in architectural design to a Buddhist
temple. The interior, however, is quite different: Instead of im-

ages and icons, the shrine's altar holds only a wood plaque carved with the Chinese ideographs "The most sacred, respected Master Confucius"—a reminder that Confucianism is a philosophy, not a religion.

⑩ A chief attraction of the **Martyrs Shrine,** just east of the Grand Hotel in north Taipei, is the changing-of-the-guard ceremony, performed hourly 9–5 each day. The shrine honoring Taiwan's fallen soldiers is a cavernous, mostly empty, Ming-style building that you can't enter. *139 Peian Rd., tel. 02/594–5041. Admission free. Open daily 9–5.*

⑪ The **Sun Yat-sen Memorial Hall,** in the heart of downtown, near the Tourism Bureau, is a peaceful memorial to Dr. Sun Yat-sen, the Father of the Republic. Inside is a 5.7-m (19-ft) bronze statue of the man, whose life is told in daily multimedia shows in English. *Section 4, Jenai Rd., tel. 02/702–2411. Admission free. Open daily 9–5.*

What to See and Do with Children

The new **Taipei City Zoo** covers 455 acres in the suburb of Mucha and is said to be Asia's largest. It features a Butterfly Aviary, a petting zoo, a sea lion aquarium, and areas featuring animals from different continents, in addition to a large collection of native animals. You can take a shuttle bus from area to area, or you can stroll leisurely around. *Buses available from World Trade Centre and other Taipei locations. Tel. 02/938–2300. Admission charge. Open daily 9–5.*

Shopping

Department Stores Three huge department stores are located within a few blocks along Chunghsiao East Road. At **Ming Yao** (200 Chunghsiao East Rd., Section 4, tel. 02/772–9728), an English-language directory at the elevator will guide you around the store's 11 floors. For those craving the tastes of home, there's a Pizza Hut and a Swensen's on the top floor. Across the street (at No. 201) is **Tonlin** (tel. 02/752–2222), with five floors. Look for the directory by the escalator. Taipei's biggest department store is **Sogo** (45 Chunghsiao East Rd., Section 4, tel. 02/771–3171), a massive structure with red marble columns. A guide to its 13 floors is by the front door.

Markets Vendors turn a parking lot along Chienkuo South Road into a **Flower Market** every Saturday and Sunday from 8 to 5. You'll see mostly tropical plants, including an array of orchids. Local growers also exhibit their latest hybrids. The market stretches for about 2 km (1.2 mi) between Hsinyi Road and Jenai Road.

Every weekend from 9 to 5 you can bargain for jade jewelry and carvings from vendors at the sidewalk **Jade Market,** along Hsinsheng South Road at Pateh Road. Prices are good, but don't expect to find genuine antiques here. Vendors may swear to the age of their products, but only the established antiques stores offer certificates of authenticity.

Specialty Stores
Antiques Antiques lovers won't want to miss the opulent relics for sale at **My Humble House.** The shop has the ambience of a museum, with such pieces as Qing Dynasty snuff bottles and *tien huang* chop stones. *260 Wenlin North Rd., tel. 02/831–9551. Open daily 10–6:30.*

Furniture Traditional Chinese furniture is available at the factory show-room of **Lu Furniture Mfg. Co.** in Peitou. The company produces high-quality rosewood pieces: coffee tables for NT$38,000 and screens for NT$62,000, as well as Japanese-style items. *64 Chungyang South Rd., Peitou, tel. 02/891-4111. Open daily 9– 5:30.*

Handicrafts **Taiwan Crafts Center,** a nonprofit outlet of the Taiwan Handi-craft Institute, has tasteful displays of handpainted umbrellas, bamboo carvings, five-piece rattan furniture sets, and more. *7th floor, Rebar Department Store, 110 Yenping South Rd., tel. 02/331-1507. Open Tues.–Sun. 10–6.*

The **Taiwan Handicraft Mart** has a broad range of souvenir crafts, including cloisonné and porcelain vases and such oddi-ties as pictures made entirely of butterfly wings. *1 Hsuchou Rd., tel. 02/321-7233. Open daily 9–5:30.*

One of the last wood-bucket makers in Taiwan carries on a fami-ly trade at the **Lin Tien Cooperage,** a tiny, cramped workshop north of the Chiang Kai-shek Memorial. Lin Chan Lin turns out two or three 14-inch buckets a day, which sell for NT$1,000 each. Besides the buckets, he carves bathing basins and toilet seats. *108 Chungshan North Rd., Section 1, tel. 02/541-1354. Open daily 9–5.*

Qipao You can have a traditional Chinese gown, known as a *qipao,* made at **Chien Long Fang** (118 Hunyang Rd., tel. 02/371-5751). Choose the design from photos or bring your own pattern or picture. The mainland-Chinese tailor can reproduce any de-sign—in polyester, silk, wool, or silk brocade—in about a week. Prices begin at NT$1,800. Traditional Chinese jackets for men are also available, from NT$3,000 to NT$10,000.

Tea Tea sellers abound in Taiwan. Best-known are the **Tien Ren** shops, with 45 outlets throughout the island and 14 in Taipei. You can choose among 15 types of tea and taste the varieties before making your decision. The shops also sell tea parapher-nalia, such as tiny pots and thimble cups, and you can pick up an English-language pamphlet explaining step-by-step the ritual of Chinese tea preparation. Ask your hotel for nearby loca-tions. The shops are open daily from 8:30 AM to 10:30 PM.

Sports and Fitness

Many of the better hotels have health clubs with pools, gyms, and saunas (*see* Lodging, below). For beaches in the area, *see* Paishawan, Chinshan, Pitou Chiao, and Fulung in the Excur-sions from Taipei that follow. Water sports are available in some of these areas.

Bowling **Chia Chia Bowling Center** (223 Sungjiang Rd. at Minsheng East Rd., tel. 02/503-7216), **Sun Bowling Center** (87 Wuchang St., Section 2, tel. 02/361-0679), **Yuan Shan Bowling Center** (6 Chungshan North Rd., Section 5, tel. 02/881-2277).

Golf Taiwan's oldest and best course, with 27 holes, is at the **Taiwan Golf and Country Club** in Tanshui, 20 km (12.4 mi) north of Tai-pei. For other courses, contact the Golf Association (tel. 02/ 711-3046).

Jogging Taipei streets and sidewalks are too congested for joggers, so your best bet is to run at the outdoor track at the **Taipei Munici-pal Sports Stadium** (Nanking East Rd. and Tunhua North Rd., tel. 02/771–1202, open daily) or in **Chiang Kai-shek Memorial Park.**

Tennis There are courts at the **Grand Hotel** (1 Chungshan North Rd., Section 4, tel. 02/596–5565), **Taipei Tennis Club** (4 Nanking East Rd., Section 4, tel. 02/771–6557), and the **Youth Park Tennis Club** (199 Shuiyuan Rd., tel. 02/303–2451).

Dining

by Bruce Shu

Bruce Shu is an American journalist based in Hong Kong. From 1986 to 1988, he was news editor for the China Post, *an English-language newspaper in Taipei.*

The traditional Chinese preoccupation with food is thriving in Taiwan, fed by a desire for novelty and the ability to pay for it. The result: a mushrooming of restaurants serving foreign cuisine and a renaissance in Chinese regional cooking.

A startling trend has developed: While their mainland Chinese counterparts preserve and refine regional traditions, Taiwan's restaurateurs are melding disparate styles on the same menu and even on the same plate. Taipei diners are no longer surprised, for instance, to find minced pork with chili peppers served in an establishment calling itself Shanghainese.

Meanwhile, some top Chinese restaurants are introducing more refined, Western-style service and plusher interiors, moving away from the noisy, bright, and bustling dining rooms that still characterize most eateries in Taiwan. Recent changes in trade policy allow the import of just about any fresh or frozen ingredient. High tariffs, however, keep menu prices at a level at least 50% higher than that for comparable dining in Europe or North America.

Most restaurants in Taiwan add a value-added tax and a service charge to the bill, and additional tipping is not necessary. Virtually all restaurants close for several days during the Chinese New Year festival; some also close during the Dragon Boat Festival and the Moon Festival. Highly recommended restaurants are indicated by a star ★.

Very Expensive **Sun Tung Lok Shark's Fin Restaurant.** Sun Tung Lok is among
Cantonese the upscale Chinese restaurants offering a somewhat incongruous Western style of service: A hostess in a *cheongsam* (traditional Chinese sheath dress with side slits) conducts diners to a small dining room with plush European fittings. The house specialty enjoys equal fame in Hong Kong and Taipei: chunks of shark's fin braised in a brown sauce thick from half a day's simmering. Lobster with vermicelli in casserole is flavored with a light but piquant curry sauce. The standard Chinese delicacies—abalone, swallow's nest, and drunken prawns—enjoy top treatment. *592 Tunhua South Rd., tel. 02/ 700–1818. Reservations advised. Jacket suggested. AE, DC, MC, V.*

Continental **Trader's Grill.** A restaurant with two identities, the Trader's
★ Grill is bright and airy by day and intimate and elegant by night. As the city lights up outside, the lights inside dim for candlelight dinners in a room with large, well-spaced tables and parquet floors. The kitchen may be Taipei's most disciplined. Chef Michel Sram offers the grill standards, as well as such specialties as beer-fed sirloin steak with Japanese vegetables and roasted duck breast in lime-and-honey sauce. *Hilton International Taipei, 38 Chunghsiao West Rd., Section 1, tel. 02/311–5151, ext. 2231/2178. Reservations advised. Jacket and tie required. AE, CB, DC, MC, V.*

French **Les Célébrités.** The emphasis here is on freshness, from the bright, flowered upholstery and powder-rose tablecloths to the meats and fish flown in weekly from Europe and the United States. Chef Jean-Louis Mermet contends that French food will never taste the same outside France, hence creations with the flair of pan-fried scallops with shark's fin sauce and flambéed tomato soup with vodka served with abalone. More classic fare is available, as are light dishes prepared without butter, eggs, or cream. *Hôtel Royal Taïpeï, 37-1 Chungshan North Rd., Section 2, tel. 02/542-3266, ext. 380. Reservations advised. Jacket and tie suggested. AE, DC, MC, V.*

Expensive **The Chinese Restaurant.** Delicate architecture imitating the
Hangchou pagodas and temples lining Hangchou's scenic West Lake
★ makes the basement of the Ritz hotel almost balmy, and the food is similarly light. The menu in English is woefully incomplete, so ask the server to introduce Hangchou dishes from the Chinese version. Shrimp sautéed with tea leaves and pork steamed in lotus leaf pay tribute to the produce of West Lake. Crispy rolled bean-curd sheets with minced chestnuts, shrimp, and pork are served with a pleasant sweet sauce. *155 Minchuan East Rd., tel. 02/597-1234, ext. 1240. Reservations advised. Jacket and tie suggested. AE, CB, DC, MC, V.*

Hunanese **Beautiful Garden.** Noise and bustle are part of the old-fashioned charm of Beautiful Garden. Grand red pillars and a mural depicting an ancient court scene serve as a backdrop for special family feasts and Taiwan-style business talks. Hunanese standard dishes include steamed onion-paste shrimp and clay pot spring chicken; for the more adventurous, there's pigeon served in a melon half. *230 Tunhua North Rd., tel. 02/715-3921. No reservations. Dress: casual. No credit cards.*

Japanese **Yoshisono.** Fifty years of Japanese occupation and continuing close business ties have done well by Japanese cuisine in Taiwan, and Yoshisono has emerged as the East Side favorite of businessmen and shoppers. Specialties include *kaibashira yaki*, scallops grilled in foil with bean sprouts and mushrooms, and *kani mushi*, whole crab in cream sauce. The kitchen wraps the first-floor dining room on two sides, and the bustling service staff have a tendency to shout at one another, so diners who require tranquility are advised to reserve a room or table on the second floor. *No. 9, La. 27, Jenai Rd., Section 4, tel. 02/781 -6607. Reservations advised for parties of 4 or more. Dress: casual. No credit cards.*

Seafood **Tainan Tan Tsu Mien.** Here is Taiwan's true story of the noodle vendor who made good. Thirty years later, the Snake Alley stall selling southern Taiwan-style minced-meat noodles is one of Taipei's best-loved seafood restaurants. There is no menu. The freshest-available offerings—local fish, crabs, abalone, snails, and gray salamanders (a Taiwanese delicacy), some still squirming—are displayed on ice outside. Selections are steamed, stir-fried, or grilled to order, and diners still get a small serving of noodles as a reminder of harder times. *31 Huahsi St., tel. 02/308-1123. Reservations accepted. Dress: casual. AE, DC, MC, V.*

Shanghainese **Tao Tao.** Shanghainese cooking—featuring light dishes prepared well—provides a refreshing change from the bloated banquets of traditional China and has become a sort of Taiwanese nouvelle cuisine. Crunchy baby beans poached with clams

Taipei Dining and Lodging

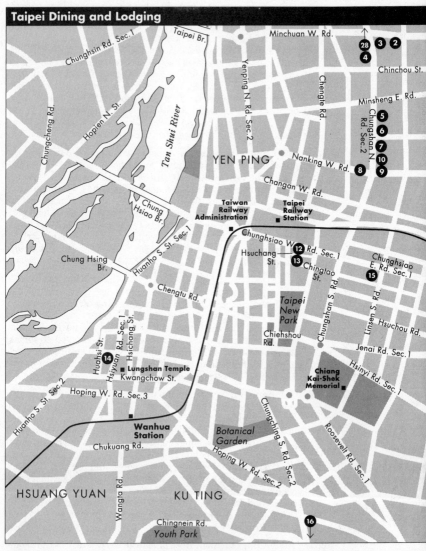

Dining
Beautiful Garden, **27**
Celestial, **8**
Chalet Swiss, **25**
Chinese Restaurant, **1**
Green Leaf, **9**
Heavenly Lotus, **24**
Hizen-ya, **10**
I'R, **22**
Les Célébrités, **7**

New World Soybean
Milk Magnate, **16**
Rong Shing, **11**
Royal Thai, **17**
Sun Tung Lok Shark's
Fin Restaurant, **19**
Tainan Tan Tsu
Mien, **14**
Tao Tao, **6**
Trader's Grill, **12**
Wistaria, **18**
Yoshisono, **21**

Lodging
Ambassador, **5**
Asiaworld Plaza, **26**
Fortune Dragon, **23**
Grand Hotel, **28**
Hilton
International, **12**

Hotel New Asia, **3**
Hotel Royal Taipei, **7**
Howard Plaza, **20**
Lai Lai Sheraton, **15**
Majestic, **2**
Ritz Taipei, **1**
Taipei Fortuna, **4**
YMCA International
Guest House, **13**

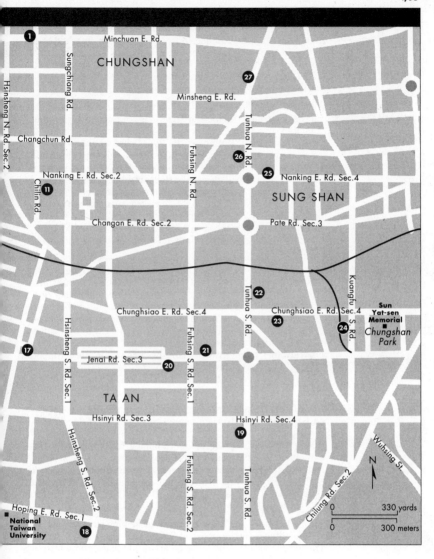

Minchuan E. Rd.

CHUNGSHAN

Sungchiang Rd.

Hsinsheng N. Rd. Sec. 2

Changchun Rd.

Chilin Rd.

Nanking E. Rd. Sec.2

Changan E. Rd. Sec.2

Fuhsing N. Rd.

Minsheng E. Rd.

Tunhua N. Rd.

Nanking E. Rd. Sec.4

SUNG SHAN

Pate Rd. Sec.3

Chunghsiao E. Rd. Sec.4

Tunhua S. Rd.

Chunghsiao E. Rd. Sec.4

Kuangfu S. Rd.

Sun Yat-sen Memorial ■

Chungshan Park

Fuhsing S. Rd. Sec.1

Jenai Rd. Sec.3

Hsinsheng S. Rd. Sec. 1

TA AN

Hsinyi Rd. Sec.3

Fuhsing S. Rd. Sec.2

Hsinyi Rd. Sec.4

Tunhua S. Rd.

Chilung Rd. Sec.2

Wuhsing St.

Hsinsheng S. Rd. Sec. 2

Hoping E. Rd. Sec.1

■ National Taiwan University

N

0   330 yards

0   300 meters

and tender morsels of stewed beef brisket come in easy-to-take portions. Save room for dessert: Shanghai's sweets are the best in China, and Tao Tao does a fine pan pie with smashed-date filling. A sleek turquoise interior and efficient, unobtrusive service bear the marks of Tao Tao's Japanese management. *57-1 Chungshan North Rd., Section 2, tel. 02/564-1277. Reservations advised for dinner. Jacket suggested. AE, DC.*

Swiss/German **Châlet Swiss.** The setting—across from the baseball stadium
★ on the edge of the financial district—is not exactly Alpine, but a melted, cheesy raclette will make any Swiss long for home. Proprietor Horst Trummer, the Swiss chef who came to Taiwan for two months and stayed for 22 years, is something of a legend in Taiwan food circles. At cozy tables under dark wood timbers, he offers dishes that are hearty but refined: roasted pig knuckle, steaks, and chateaubriand from chilled U.S. prime beef, and—if the right fowl are available—*gueggeli*, spring chicken roasted to perfection. The Châlet is a favorite for business lunches. *47 Nanking East Rd., Section 4, tel. 02/715-2051. Reservations advised. Dress: casual. AE, MC, V.*

Szechuan **Rong Shing.** Every second Chinese restaurant in Taipei seems to say it cooks Szechuan food, but none comes close to matching Rong Shing's 18-year history of steady, dependable service. The restaurant was recently redecorated, and gilded ebony pillars and chandeliers affirm its position as Taipei's grande dame of Szechuan cuisine. The *ma po tofu*, bean curd in hot sauce, is a perennial favorite, and shrimp with four sauces shows off Taiwan's home-grown giant prawns, which are dipped into boiling water and then sliced thin. *45 Chilin Rd., tel. 02/521-5341. Reservations accepted. Dress: casual. No credit cards.*

Thai **Royal Thai.** Despite several changes of management, the kitchen here continues to turn out a spicy, gentle cuisine that is consistently superior. Flowery, orchid-toned booths and natural light give the place an airy, homey feel, but while the surroundings are modest, the cooking is not. The seafood steamed in coconut cream and spices is much talked about. Pork sautéed with curry paste in coconut cream and frogs' legs with chili and basil also deserve notice. *49 Jenai Rd., Section 2, tel. 02/351-0960. Reservations accepted. Dress: casual. AE.*

Moderate **I'R.** Street-level garden windows—for looking out and looking
Continental in—put diners in the midst of Taipei's trendy East District. The local clientele is likely to be attired in black and white to match the marble-and-tile interior and espresso served in porcelain demitasses. Sorbets and ice creams made in I'R's own kitchens go into tantalizing summer cocktails with fresh fruit juices. Entrées such as spaghetti carbonara or Chinese noodles in beef stew come in minute portions, beautifully arranged, but are usually not well prepared. The people watching, however, is first class. The restaurant's name seems to be a mystery. *381 Tunhua South Rd., tel. 02/711-1089. No reservations. Dress: casual. No credit cards.*

Peking-style **Celestial.** For those who've become jaded about Cantonese dim sum, Celestial offers a heartier alternative at lunch: northern Chinese dumplings and breads, presented on carts in noisy, big-hearted southern Chinese style. The Peking duck is well respected; other specialties include a refreshing celery salad in pungent hot mustard sauce and an unusual baked bean curd with shrimp caviar. *2/F, 1 Nanking West Rd., tel. 02/563–2380, for reservations 02/563–2171. Reservations suggested. Dress: casual. No credit cards.*

Taiwanese **Green Leaf.** Simple food in simple surroundings makes this a standout among Taiwanese restaurants, most of which have unsuccessfully tried to elevate home cooking to haute cuisine. The noodles in soup and omelet with dried radish are tasty and down-to-earth. Green Leaf is usually packed until 2 AM with night owls enjoying traditional midnight snacks of rice porridge with sweet potato accompanied by small, savory dishes. An added attraction: The menu previews all dishes with photographs. *No. 1, La. 105, Chungshan North Rd., Section 1, tel. 02/551–7957. No reservations. Dress: casual. No credit cards.*

Vegetarian **Heavenly Lotus.** Buddhism and business combine for healthful eating at Heavenly Lotus, where the proprietors observe strict religious rules against alcohol and stimulants. Vegetables are cleaned by ultrasound to remove chemical residues and are prepared without MSG, alcohol, or eggs. Even mustard—a stimulant—is banned. The fare is no less than savory, though, as attested by the vegetarian chicken with dried chili peppers and steamed vegetarian codfish, both made from mushrooms. Smoking and alcoholic beverages are not permitted. *No. 1, La. 240, Kuangfu South Rd., tel. 02/731–2503. No reservations. Dress: casual. No credit cards. Main restaurant is in the northern suburb of Tienmu: 47 Tienmu East Rd., tel. 02/831–5928.*

Inexpensive **Hizen-ya.** Smoke blowing out a vent above the front door has
Japanese made Hizen-ya's sign an oily brown, and smoke will permeate
★ both you and the bare-timbered walls as you eat, but it's all for a good cause: arguably the best grilled eel with rice in Asia. Until recently, only Japanese expatriates knew about this tiny dive tucked away in an alley, but a knowledgeable young Taiwanese crowd now queues for lunch and dinner seven days a week. The sashimi is first-rate, selected at dawn each morning by chef/proprietor Wang Shih-wen himself. Be prepared to order by the Japanese names of dishes; English is not spoken—except "eel rice." *No. 18-1, La. 121, Chungshan North Rd., Section 1, tel. 02/561–7859. No reservations. Dress: casual. No credit cards.*

Northern Chinese **New World Soybean Milk Magnate.** This Taipei institution—open 24 hours a day—serves the staple breakfast fare of northern China and has become the unlikely nighttime haunt of Taiwan movie stars and other assorted glitterati. Metal stools and tables cozy up to fryers and an oven that can only be described as grimy, but the soy milk breakfasts that come out are undisputedly Taipei's best. Steaming bowls of soy milk—sweet or tangy—go with *shaobing youtiao* (sesame-covered bread enveloping crunchy fried dough sticks), *xiaolong bao* (juicy, steamed dumplings), *luobo danbing* (salty egg pancake with radish filling), and *subing* (flaky pastries filled with red beans, peanuts, or spring onion). *284 Yungho Rd., Section 2, Yungho, tel. 02/922–2334. No reservations. Dress: casual. No credit cards.*

Tea House **Wistaria.** Taipei's oldest tea house is an oasis for reflection and repose. Just down the street from National Taiwan University, Wistaria has become a gathering place for intellectuals, artists, and progressive political figures who linger on tatami mats around low tables. The island's celebrated oolong tea is complemented by flaky homemade pastries and fruit candies. The staff speaks English and gives primers on the appreciation of Chinese tea and on traditional tea-steeping techniques, which have recently come back into vogue. Light meals, usually of rice and simply cooked vegetables, are available; the menu changes weekly. *No. 1, La. 16, Hsinsheng South Rd., Section 3, tel. 02/363-9459. No reservations. Dress: casual. No credit cards.*

Lodging

Visitors will find a certain uniformity among Taipei's higher-priced hotels because of the country's massive push toward Westernization. If you prefer, however, to steep in Chinese ambience, the Grand Hotel, some distance from the city center, is a monument to Chinese architecture and design.

For a map pinpointing locations, *see* Dining, above. Highly recommended hotels are indicated by a star ★.

Very Expensive **Ambassador.** Stone lions flank the entrance in the wide, sprawling lobby of this 13-story high rise. Standard rooms are spare, but some deluxe suites are outfitted with carved-wood furniture in ornate, traditional style. All rooms of this 25-year-old hotel were fully renovated in 1986. *63 Chungshan North Rd., Section 2, tel. 02/551-1111. 500 rooms. Facilities: Western, Cantonese, and Szechuan restaurants, coffee shop, cocktail lounge, duty-free shop, business center, tour desk, outdoor pool. AE, DC, MC, V.*

Asiaworld Plaza. If shopping tops your list of preferred activities, this former Hyatt is for you: Your first sight in the lobby is not the reception desk but the recently expanded shopping arcade, and the giant Asiaworld Department Store is next door. Popular with tour groups, this enormous hotel retains the Hyatt ambience with its atrium coffee shop in a tropical setting. The guest rooms are modern, with rosewood furnishings. *100 Tunhwa North Rd., tel. 02/715-0077 or 800/228-3278. 1,057 rooms, including 260 suites. Facilities: 27 food and beverage outlets, business center, gym, sauna, outdoor pool, poolside snack bar, children's amusement center. AE, CB, DC, MC, V.*

Hilton International. Built in 1973, this Hilton near Taipei New Park underwent a major renovation in 1988–89. The redesigned lobby emphasizes pink granite and rosewood, with a complement of mirrored pillars. Three floors are devoted exclusively to business travelers, who can get complimentary buffet breakfast and cocktails in the executive lounge and access to a separate concierge. Executive rooms have such amenities as large desks and pants-pressing machines. All rooms are tastefully and soothingly decorated in a combination Western/Oriental style. Bathrooms are equipped with separate shower and tub and heated towel racks. *38 Chunghsiao West Rd., Section 1, tel. 02/311-5151. 413 rooms, including 51 suites. Facilities: Hunan, Western, and Italian restaurants, pub, coffee shop, gym, sauna, roof garden with sun deck and Jacuzzi, 2 nonsmoking floors, business center, shopping arcade. AE, CB, DC, MC, V.*

Hôtel Royal Taïpeï. The white wicker furniture, latticework, and floral carpeting and draperies in the lobby convey the southern French motif, which carries over to both the garden-style coffee shop and Les Célébrités restaurant, with its resident French chef. The rooms are cheerfully decorated in contemporary French style with tasteful wood shutters. An elegant and imposing touch is the chandelier that descends three stories into the sparkling white, marble-floored lobby. *37-1 Chungshan North Rd., Section 2, tel. 02/542-3266 or 800/645-5687. 203 rooms. Facilities: French, Japanese, and Cantonese restaurants, rooftop pool, gym, sauna, business center. AE, CB, DC, MC, V.*

★ **Howard Plaza.** Don't be put off by the bland exterior of this brick high rise in Taipei's emerging eastern business district. Inside, the airy atrium—with hanging plants, fountain pools, and a four-story cascade—and lobby with Chinese sculptures on pedestals create a successful blend of East and West. There are some rich details, such as the stained glass in the European restaurant, created by the Taiwanese owner's son. Handcarved rosewood furniture lends a sense of opulence to the modern guest rooms. *160 Jenai Rd., Section 3, tel. 02/700-2323. 606 rooms, including 47 suites. Facilities: Cantonese, Shanghainese, Taiwanese, Continental, and Japanese restaurants, coffee shop, 800-seat conference hall, outdoor pool, gym, sauna, business center, four-story shopping mall, art gallery. AE, DC, MC, V.*

Lai Lai Sheraton. Since it opened in 1981, this 18-story Sheraton has been considered the finest hotel in Taipei. It has a lot to offer, including first-rate service. Guest rooms are decorated in modern Chinese style. Despite some concessions to the local environment, such as banquet rooms decorated in Chinese imperial style, you will never forget you're at a Western-managed Sheraton. Popular with executive travelers, the extensively renovated hotel has a business center that receives the AP-Dow Jones newswire service. *12 Chunghsiao East Rd., Section 1, tel. 02/321-5511. 705 rooms. Facilities: 12 restaurants (Taiwanese, Shanghainese, Japanese, French, and Italian cuisine), rooftop gym, jogging track, outdoor pool, 2 squash courts, 3 bars, nightclub, 57 shops, clinic, nonsmoking floor, women's floor with special amenities, in-room safety deposit boxes, business center, shopping arcades. AE, DC, MC, V.*

The Ritz Taipei. Personalized service is the keynote at this business traveler's hotel; the management even maintains guest histories to anticipate return visitors' requests. Built in 1979, the Ritz underwent renovations in 1984 and 1989. The lobby and all suites are decorated in the art deco style, emphasizing black, gray, pink, and burgundy. Guest rooms are peach-colored, with marble-top furniture and silk wallpaper. *155 Minchuan East Rd., tel. 02/597-1234 or 800/223-6800. 204 rooms, including 100 suites. Facilities: French bistro-style coffee shop, French and Hunan restaurants, piano bar, business center, gym, Jacuzzi, sun deck, jogging track, room safes, baby-sitting service, library. AE, DC, MC, V.*

Expensive **Fortune Dragon.** A major renovation in 1988 didn't bring this high rise quite up to snuff, and the management continues to upgrade the lounge bar and coffee shop. The hotel's chief advantage is its location, in the fashionable Dinghao shopping district, near several major department stores. Rooms are basic but comfortable. *172 Chunghsiao East Rd., Section 4, tel. 02/772-2121. 312 rooms, including 92 suites. Facilities: Chinese and French restaurants, business center, handicapped* accommodations, in-room safes, baby-sitting. AE, DC, MC, V.

★ **Grand Hotel.** The name says it all. You approach along a sweeping tree-lined drive and enter through massive 20-foot-high Chinese-style doors. The vast, red-pillared lobby is reminiscent of an imperial palace. Designed with careful attention to traditional Chinese architecture, the hotel was built in two stages: The main building went up in 1973, dwarfing the original structure built in 1956. The rooms, decorated with heavy rosewood furniture, vary in size and quality. The more expensive ones have elaborately painted Chinese patios and views of Yuanshan Mountain. The hotel's major drawback is its location, on 20 acres in Taipei's northern outskirts. In addition, the service is not quite up to the standards of the modern first-rate hotels in the city center. If you don't stay here, however, make an effort to visit simply for a walk around the magnificent grounds. *1 Chungshan North Rd., Section 4, tel. 02/596–5565. 650 rooms. Facilities: Olympic-size outdoor pool, 3 tennis courts, bowling alley, billiards, Cantonese and Western restaurants, coffee shop, tea house, 500-seat banquet room, 1,200-seat convention hall, shopping arcade, baby-sitting. AE, CB, DC, MC, V.*

Majestic. A floor-to-ceiling Chinese painting sets the tone in the lobby of this high rise hotel on the busy corner of Min Chuan and Chung Shan roads. You can watch the street life from the ground-floor coffee shop's wide windows. Built in 1974, the hotel has a not-quite-contemporary mood. Guest rooms have almost modern rosewood furnishings. *2 Minchuan East Rd., tel. 02/581–1711. 405 rooms. Facilities: Cantonese and Western restaurants, disco. AE, DC, MC, V.*

Taipei Fortuna. You'll have to search for the Chinese accent at this high rise. The lobby, often crowded with tour groups, has the appearance of one of the better Holiday Inns. Guest rooms are modern and bright. The gym is pleasant, with a wall of windows. *122 Chungshan North Rd., Section 2, tel. 02/563–1111 or 800/223–9868. 300 rooms. Facilities: revolving 14th-floor Western restaurant, Cantonese restaurant, coffee shop, banquet rooms, gym, sauna, steambath, Jacuzzi, business center. AE, CB, DC, MC, V.*

Moderate **Hotel New Asia.** Built in 1969, this 120-room hotel is in need of a face-lift. You check in at a worn marble reception counter in a tiny lobby that has a coffee shop jammed into the rear. The small rooms are decorated with Western-motel-style paintings. However, the price and central location are right. *139 Chungshan North Rd., Section 2, tel. 02/511–7181. 120 rooms. Facilities: Chinese restaurant, bar. MC, V.*

Inexpensive **YMCA International Guest House.** For the budget traveler, this
★ YMCA provides a quiet, clean resting place. The rooms may remind you of a low-end motel—thin bedspreads and wobbly furniture—but they have private baths, all of which were renovated in 1987. Couples should be prepared to prove they're married if they intend to share a room. *19 Hsuchang St., tel. 02/311–3201. 86 rooms, including 4 suites. Facilities: Chinese restaurant. MC, V.*

The Arts and Nightlife

The English-language monthly magazine *Bang* and Taiwan's two English-language newspapers, *China Post* and *China*

News, provide details on local theater, dance, and film offerings.

The Arts The **National Palace Museum** is justifiably renowned as the
Museums world's finest treasure house of Chinese artifacts. A good many
of the pieces were looted by defeated Nationalists fleeing the
Chinese mainland in 1949. The museum's range is staggering:
porcelain, bronze, lacquerware, jade, enamel, calligraphy, and
paintings. The collection includes some 600,000 pieces, although only 15,000 items are on view at any one time. Most
astonishing is the immaculate condition of the relics, such as
the near-perfect 4,500-year-old earthenware bowls and cups.
Don't miss the Ching dynasty furniture exhibit on the second
floor. English-language tours are conducted daily. For a rest in
elegant surroundings, try the museum's Tea Room, where live
birds chirp in wood cages. The museum is in Waishuanghsi, a
suburb just north of Taipei. *Tel. 02/881-2021. Admission
charge. Open daily 9-5.*

The **Taipei Fine Arts Museum** houses modern Chinese and
Western art in a contemporary, concrete facility. Chinese
paintings include traditional landscapes and calligraphy, as
well as abstracts and oil portraits. Non-Chinese shows range
from works by Christo to posters by Japanese graphic artists.
181 Chungshan North Rd., Section 3, tel. 02/595-7656. Admission charge. Open Tues.-Sun. 10-6, (Sat. until 8).

Chinese Opera Although you won't be able to understand the dialogue (except
when plot synopses in English are provided), the costumes and
stylized movements are well worth seeing. Free performances
are given at the **Sun Yat-sen Memorial Hall** (505 Jenai Rd., Section 4, tel. 02/702-2411) Saturday at 2. The **Armed Forces
Cultural Activities Center** (69 Chunghwa Rd., tel. 02/331-5438)
also mounts productions.

Nightlife Perhaps because Taipei is so hectic by day, locals flock to serene
Tea Houses tea houses by night. The experience should not be missed. Besides tea, you may have a choice of coffee, juice, watermelon
seeds, or dried fruits. The atmosphere varies from traditional
Chinese or Japanese to rustic Western. Private rooms are usually available. In addition to the following, *see* Wistaria in
Dining, above.

Hsuan Ki is a small, Japanese-style tea house with bamboo
screens and tatami mats. *2nd floor, 50 Hengyang Rd., tel. 02/
331-6127. Open daily 10 AM-11 PM.*

Liyu Tea Center isn't as cozy as some places, but it has three
unusual private rooms: one in imperial style, with marble-inlay
tables and rosewood chairs; one in aboriginal style, with carved
wood chairs and a stone table; and a third in European style,
with a leather sofa. *64 Hengyang Rd., tel. 02/331-6636. Open
daily 10-10.*

The hardwood floors, modern portraits, and piped-in opera music give a trendy touch to the **Cafe Vernal**. *2nd floor, 110 Jenai
Rd., tel. 02/706-0401. Open daily 10-12:30.*

MTVs Named after the music-video television station in the United
States, these audiovisual centers now number about 800 in Taipei. For about NT$100, you can rent a videotaped movie and
watch it in a private room with a sofa and coffee table. The fee
includes a beverage. Most MTVs are clean, trendy places with
videotapes lining the walls; a few emphasize a theme. Walking

into **Hi Fi Rock** (2nd floor, 144 Nanking East Rd., Section 2, tel. 02/562–8903) is like boarding a sci-fi spaceship. The entry has chessboard carpeting and a black, circular sofa with moon-and-star upholstery. To get to a viewing room, you pass through a push-button glass door and walk along a metallic corridor lined with strings of tiny white lights.

Other MTVs: **Image** (2nd floor, 293 Chunghsiao East Rd., Section 4, tel. 02/751–4911), **Earthquake Hi-Fi Video Center** (2nd floor, 70 Nanchang Rd., Section 1, tel. 02/351–6973), and **Cash Box Video Center** (3rd floor, 62 Nanking East Rd., Section 2, tel. 02/571–9211).

Night Markets Lively between sundown and midnight, Taipei's night markets can be garish, loud, and sometimes repugnant. That's exactly why they draw crowds every night. By far the wildest is at **Snake Alley** near the Lungshan Temple off Kangting Road. You'll see Chinese weightlifters hawking health tonics and chefs killing turtles to make drinks with their fresh blood. Salesmen bark into electronic amplifiers, each trying to drown out the competition and stalls brim with videotapes, clothing, clocks, shoes, candy, and noodles. Taipei's other night markets appear tame in comparison with Snake Alley. One that attracts the collegiate crowd is in the lanes opposite Taiwan University, on the Roosevelt Road side of campus. Taipei's largest night market is in the northern suburb of Shihlin, near the Grand Hotel.

Excursions from Taipei

Taiwan's northern mountains and coast are tranquil retreats from the capital's frenzied pace. Less than an hour from Taipei, you can dig your feet into the sand or hike through lush mountain foliage. For the two expeditions below, we recommend renting a car or hiring a car with driver. Both trips can be accomplished easily in a day, though you may want to stay over at the beach in Fulung.

Peitou, the North Coast, and Yangmingshan National Park

Escorted Tours Companies that operate bus tours to Yangmingshan and the north coast include **Grey Line** (tel. 02/551–5544), **Edison Travel Service** (tel. 02/563–5313), **Pinho Travel Service Co.** (tel. 02/551–4136), and **Taiwan Coach Tours** (tel. 02/595–5321).

Getting Around *By Car* Chungshan North Road goes north out of Taipei and joins Route 2, known as the Northeast Coast Highway. Route 2 loops around the northern tip of the island.

Exploring *Numbers in the margin correspond with points of interest on the Excursions from Taipei map.*

❶ At the **Peitou hot springs,** 30 minutes from downtown Taipei on Route 2, steam seeps from the earth in a dreamlike mist, and crowds of Chinese squat on stone blocks set in the shallow water. If you have any doubt about the extreme temperature of the springs, just buy a goose or chicken egg at one of the nearby stands and place it in the water for five minutes. When you take it out, be careful not to touch the water. A sign in Chinese warns: "Watch out! The water is hot enough to boil an egg. Think what it can do to a person!"

Excursions from Taipei

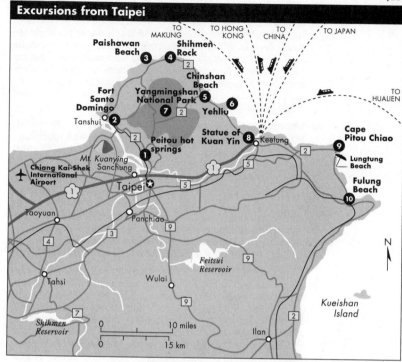

The **Taiwan Folk Art Museum,** also in Peitou, contains aboriginal and Chinese crafts in a beautiful Tang Dynasty–style building. You must remove your shoes to enter. Displays range from a carved wood canoe used by the Yami tribe to tiny embroidered shoes once worn by Chinese women with bound feet. Most of the descriptions are printed in English. *32 Yuya Rd., Peitou, tel. 02/891–2318. Admission charge. Open daily 9–8.*

② **Fort Santo Domingo,** in the quiet fishing village of **Tanshui,** also on Route 2, is a relic of Spain's brief control of north Taiwan (1624–42). Built in 1629, the fort has been restored and is empty now except for a few photo exhibits on Tanshui's early days as a bustling port. When Tanshui fell to the Dutch in 1642, the fort became known to locals by its current Chinese name, Hung Mao Ch'eng, or Fort of the Red-Haired Barbarians. The hilltop site provides some lovely views of Mt. Kuanying and the Taiwan Strait.

Far more interesting than the fort is the **former British consulate** next door, built in 1891. The two-story building, typical of colonial redbrick architecture, contains antique dining room and bedroom furniture that reflects the era. *Tel. 02/623–1001. Admission charge. Open Tues.–Sun. 9–5.*

③ North of Tanshui, the beach at **Paishawan** isn't the best Taiwan has to offer, but it draws summer crowds because it's close to Taipei. The white-sand beach has snack bars and changing rooms.

❹ Continuing north along Route 2, you come to **Shihmen Rock** at the tip of the island. The rock is distinctive for the giant hole in its center, bored by eons of wave action. Look for the **Eighteen Kings Temple** just beyond the rock on the opposite side of the road. This tiny temple, identified by women outside carrying bags of incense for sale, resembles a roadside market. Inside is a tomb for 17 people and a dog who were lost at sea here. Note the canine statues honoring the dog and the offerings of lighted cigarettes mounted on spikes in front of the altar.

❺ **Chinshan** beach, about 20 minutes from Shihmen, offers boating and waterskiing in addition to sunbathing and swimming. Its lovely park and wide beach make Chinshan one of the best seaside areas close to Taipei.

❻ Not long after Chinshan, you come to the bizarre rock formations at the fishing village of **Yehliu.** The mushroom-shape designs, produced by long exposure to the wind and sea, bear descriptive names such as Queen's Head and Candle Rock. The **Yehliu Ocean Park** offers performances by sea lions, dolphins, and more. *Tel. 032/921111. Admission charge. Shows weekdays 10:30, 1:30, 3:30; Sat. 10:30, 1, 2:30, 4; Sun. 9:30, 11, 1, 2:30, 4.*

❼ Returning to Chinshan, take Alternate Route 2 south into **Yangmingshan National Park.** The road climbs into lush mountains past stands selling mountain vegetables (believed to be sweeter than lowland varieties). Rocks spew steam from subterranean hot springs. Follow signs to the park headquarters, where you can park your car (for NT$30). Then wander along the tidy paths through the mountain vegetation. The spring cherry blossoms are particularly lovely. The murmur of running creek water adds to the soothing environment. The park is just a tiny part of the 28,000-acre national forest. Visitors with more time can hike deeper into the mountains to remote waterfalls and hot springs. Maps are available at the park headquarters. *Tel. 02/861–0187. Admission charge. Open daily 7:30–5.*

Keelung and Fulung

Getting Around
By Car Take Chungshan North Road north from Taipei, then Route 5 north. At Keelung take Route 2 toward Fulung.

Escorted Tours *See* listings for the above excursion.

Exploring **Keelung,** Taiwan's second-largest port after Kaohsiung, is a rainy but bustling city that you may want to just pass through on your way to Fulung beach. The city's chief tourist attraction
❽ is the giant **statue of Kuan Yin,** the goddess of mercy. You can't miss it: The 22-m- (74-ft-) high statue stands on a 4-m (14-ft) pedestal on a hillside of Chung Cheng Park. Climb the stairs inside the statue to reach a platform with a panoramic view. If you happen to be passing through at night, you may want to stop at the city's **night market** on Ai San Lu, near McDonald's. The market is renowned for its variety of Chinese food. In the daytime, shipping enthusiasts may enjoy watching what the city does best: loading container cargo onto huge vessels at dockside.

❾ Route 2 travels along the Pacific coast, offering some views of the rocky cliffs and bringing you to **Cape Pitou Chiao.** Rocks jut into the ocean, providing perches for fishermen and natural pools for swimming. A lifeguard is on duty during the summer. The area has showers and a snack bar. Hikers may want to trek along a stone path to the lighthouse. Three-plus km (2 mi) along the highway is a less-developed swimming spot at **Lungtung.**

⑩ The best beach in northern Taiwan is at **Fulung,** 57 km (35 mi) from Taipei. Enter at the Northeast Coast National Scenic Area Administration headquarters (228 Jenho Rd., Aoti, Kungliao, tel. 032/991118), which has an English-speaking staff. The wide, white-sand beach, stretching for 3 km (1.86 mi), is crowded on weekends. The area has one hotel, a campground, a restaurant, and showers.

Dining   **Hsin Kan.** You won't be knocked out by the decor—Formica tables and plastic plates—but the tanks holding a variety of fish and crabs should tip you off to the freshness of the fare. Specialties include steamed shrimp, sashimi, and excellent seaweed soup. *60 Hsinkan St., Aoti (just north of Fulung), tel. 032/901061. No reservations. Dress: casual. No credit cards. Moderate.*

Lodging   **Fulung Public Hostel.** Operated by the tourism bureau, this is a complex of 15 seaside, chalet-style buildings. The spare rooms have tile floors and rattan furniture. The restaurant, serving Chinese and Western food, is a high-ceilinged, wood-beam structure that resembles a camp dining hall. *40 Fulung St., Kungliao, tel. 032/991211. 71 rooms, suites with kitchens, campground with tent rentals. 40% Nov.–May discount weekdays, 20% weekends. 1-month advance booking in summer. No credit cards. Moderate.*

Island Excursions

Outside the bustling cities, Taiwan is an island of canyons, beaches, and mountains. The following excursions take you into the deep ravines of Taroko Gorge, onto the warm, white-sand beaches of Kenting, and into the frigid forests of Alishan Mountain.

Taroko Gorge

Getting Around   Flights depart for Hualien, jumping-off point for the gorge,
By Plane   from Taipei's Sungshan Domestic Airport. The flight takes 30 minutes (*see* Getting Around Taiwan by Plane in Staying in Taiwan, above).

By Car   Take Route 9 south out of Taipei to Hualien (total driving time: six hours). The 100-km (62-mi) stretch between Suao and Hualien is slow and a bit treacherous, but the sheer cliffs and mountain scenery are your reward.

By Train   Trains leave from Taipei's Central Railway Station and take 2½ to four hours.

By Bus   Buses depart from Taipei's East Bus Station, next to the Central Railway Station, and get to Hualien in under seven hours. Contact the **Taiwan Motor Transport Co.** (tel. 02/381–0731).

Escorted Tours   *See* Escorted Tours in Excursions from Taipei, above. From Hualien, **A-One Tours** (tel. 038/338121) operates rafting trips at a nearby river, as well as tours to the gorge.

Exploring Marble mania rages in Hualien, the largest city on the east coast. You'll walk on marble sidewalks, lean on marble walls, and shop for marble vases, bookends, and goblets. The airport even claims to have the world's only marble terminal. However, don't expect grand architectural designs. Marble simply happens to be a handy building material, excavated from the nearby gorge. The **Retired Servicemen's Engineering Agency** mines the stone and operates the factory that shapes and polishes it for sale at home and abroad. You can take a free tour of the factory (106 Huahsi Rd., near the airport, tel. 038/358361) and shop in its showroom.

Two temples also bear signs of the marble mania. The **Temple of Eastern Purity,** a short walk up the hill beside the Marshal Hotel, has marble columns and shrines. The more impressive **Temple of Motherly Love,** a 10-minute taxi ride from downtown, has been renovated with the local stone. As Taiwan's Taoist headquarters, it attracts hundreds of followers every year for the Lantern Festival celebration.

Hualien's chief attraction is its proximity to the spectacular **Taroko Gorge,** 27 km (17 mi) away. To reach the gorge, rent a car or Jeep, hire a car and driver, join a bus tour, or take the public bus. Consult your hotel for details.

Route 8, quite an engineering feat, snakes through cavelike tunnels along sheer cliffs. The 17-km (10½-mi) drive takes you over a marble bridge past several dizzying lookouts to Tienhsiang, at the top of the 19-m- (12-mi-) long gorge. For the full impact, you may want to get out and hike along the road, gazing up at the sharp canyon peaks and down at the steep drop below.

A short ride beyond the lodge are the **Wenshan hot springs.** Beyond the Wenshan road sign, just before a tunnel, you'll see a red stair railing leading down into the gorge. The 15-minute walk winds into the canyon and over a hanging bridge, to a small pool that's naturally heated to 104°F (40°C). Be prepared to share it with crowds in summer.

Dining **Lotus Pavilion.** Cantonese specialties are served in a large, elegant hotel banquet room, with polished-rosewood paneling. English menus are available. *Chinatrust Hotel, 2 Yunghsing Rd., Hualien, tel. 038/221171. No reservations. Dress: casual. AE, DC, MC, V. Very Expensive.*

Tang Nan. Every table has a built-in gas burner that heats the only dish served at this popular family restaurant: the traditional hot pot. The friendly staff delivers to your table plates of squid, shrimp, beef, vegetables, tofu, and noodles, and you drop it all into the broth boiling inside the hot pot. When the food is done to your liking, draw out the ingredients and eat. The setting is casual: bamboo-covered walls, noisy Taiwanese pop music, and fluorescent lights. *209 Linshen Rd., Hualien, tel. 038/360308. No reservations. Dress: casual. No credit cards. Open 11 AM–2 AM. Very Expensive.*

Lodging **Chinatrust Hotel.** This beachside hotel has a red-tile lobby with a wood-beam ceiling. Aboriginal designs adorn the bedspreads and curtains. *2 Yunghsing Rd., Hualien, tel. 038/221171. 237 rooms. Facilities: Cantonese restaurant, coffee shop, pool, bar. AE, DC, MC, V. Moderate.*

Marshall Hotel. The decor of this centrally located hotel's lobby is consistent with the Hualien theme: white marble floor, black marble reception desk, and mountain scene on a marble panel behind the desk. The rooms don't live up to the promise of the lobby—they smack of American roadside motel—but the full-moon windows are a nice touch. *36 Kungyuan Rd., Hualien, tel. 038/326123. 350 rooms. Facilities: restaurant, pool, sauna. AE, MC, V. Inexpensive.*

Tienhsiang Lodge. This peaceful lodge at the top of Taroko Gorge has a charming Chinese courtyard. Some rooms have rosewood furniture and mountain views. *18 Tienhsiang, Fuhsi, Hualien, tel. 038/691155. 48 rooms. Facilities: restaurant, bar, outdoor pool. No credit cards. Inexpensive.*

Kenting

The southern port of Kaohsiung, Taiwan's second-largest city, is a popular transit point for the beach at Kenting, 96 km (60 mi) away on a lovely coast highway. Bus, plane, and train service from Taipei to Kaohsiung is frequent.

Getting Around
By Car From Kaohsiung, drive south on Route 17, which joins Route 1 at Fangliao, then connects with Route 24 to Kenting. Car rentals are available at the airport.

By Bus Express-bus service departs from the main Kaohsiung bus station.

By Train Train service goes only as far as Fangliao. It's best to rely on bus or car transport to reach Kenting.

Escorted Tours For tours to Kenting from Taipei, *see* Escorted Tours in Island Excursions, above.

Exploring Traveling south from Kaohsiung, the highway rises above the shore at Fengkong and offers views of the rocky coastline and the broad, flat sea. The beaches at Kenting are easily the best in Taiwan, not only because of the long stretches of white sand in enclosed bays but also because of the year-round warm temperatures. This is a place for relaxing and exploring the bluffs.

You can walk a loop path through the **Kenting Forest Recreation Area** in about an hour and a half. It's a rather tame forest of bougainvillea and magnolias, but you'll also encounter such botanical oddities as the *Heritiera littoralis ait,* a tree whose roots rise from the earth like narrow wood planks. Unusual rock formations add a touch of the mysterious. The most interesting is the Fairy Cave, a dark, narrow passageway that snakes 146 m (160 yd) through coral rock. You can get ice cream or soft drinks at the Ocean Tower, then climb to the top for a 360° ocean view. *Tel. 08/886–1211. Open daily 8–5.*

From the recreation area, drive toward the tip of the peninsula, taking a moment to peer at **Sail Rock.** With only a tiny stretch of the imagination, you may recognize in the rock's natural shape the nose-and-cheek profile of Richard Nixon. At **Oluanpi,** you can visit the lighthouse and explore the bluffs for panoramic views of Bashi Channel and the Pacific Ocean. From there, hike down to a rocky white-sand beach tucked into the eastern side of the peninsula. Plant enthusiasts will enjoy strolling through the park at Oluanpi, where the ficus and formosa trees are identified in English. A leisurely walk along shaded paths will take you to ocean lookouts.

Dining **Orchid Garden.** This is an intimate, tasteful place with Oriental carved-wood paneling. Cantonese specialties include corn soup with shredded chicken and large, tender slices of beefsteak in a sweet sauce. *Caesar Park Hotel, tel. 08/889–5222. No reservations. Dress: casual. AE, DC, MC, V. Very Expensive.*

Hai Si Shen. This out-of-the-way place deviates from the plastic-plate, vinyl-chair syndrome common to smaller restaurants: You sit on colonial-style wood chairs and eat from real china. Seafood specialties include shrimp in ginger, squid, and clam soup. *26 Chungchen Rd., Section 1, Tung Kong, tel. 08/ 832–9809. No reservations. Dress: informal. No credit cards. Moderate.*

Lodging **Caesar Park Hotel.** The sunken bar, with potted palms dividing
★ the seating areas, will help put you in that get-away-from-it-all mood. It also doesn't hurt to know that one of Kenting's finest beaches is just across the road. The rooms, tastefully appointed with rattan furniture, all have decks overlooking the sea or the hills. *6 Kenting Rd., tel. 08/889–5222. 233 rooms. Facilities: Cantonese, Japanese, and Continental restaurants, disco, table tennis, billiards, nursery, gym, sauna, pool, tennis courts, children's playground, shopping arcade, barber shop, water sports. AE, DC, MC, V. Very Expensive.*

Kenting House. This motel-style inn has a main building near the forest recreation area and an annex at the beach. The vinyl armchairs and floral wallpaper in the rooms take you back to the 1950s. *451 Kenting Rd., tel. 08/886–1370. 72 rooms in the forest, 152 at the beach. Facilities: restaurant. No credit cards. Inexpensive.*

Kenting Youth Activity Center. This beach-area dormitory lodging caters to young people (minimum: three to a room). The single-story buildings with traditional tile roofs are clustered around a courtyard, like an early Chinese village. The rooms have whitewashed walls and bunk beds. *17 Kenting Rd., Hengchun, tel. 08/886–1221. 80 rooms. Facilities: restaurant. No credit cards. Inexpensive.*

Alishan

The departure point for Alishan is Chiayi, a city at the foot of the Alishan mountains. Cash traveler's checks there, because it may be difficult in the remote mountain area. Alishan is cold, even in summer, so bring warm clothing.

Getting Around From Taipei, take the North–South Highway to Chiayi, then
By Car Route 18 to Alishan.

By Bus Buses depart from the West Bus Terminal in Taipei for Chiayi, and from the Chiayi bus station six times daily for the two-hour ride to Alishan.

By Train Trains out of Taipei serve Chiayi; from there, a train trip at least one way to Alishan is a must. The train climbs for three hours through dense forest to about 2,250 m (7,500 ft) on a narrow-gauge line originally laid by the Japanese in 1915. You'll chug through 50 tunnels and cross 80 bridges. The train leaves three times a day from the Chiayi train station, next to the bus station (tel. 05/228095).

Escorted Tours *See* Escorted Tours in Excursions from Taipei, above.

Exploring A loop trail through the **Alishan National Forest** takes you past the major scenic points. You can join the trail outside Alishan House, the Train Hotel, or the Alishan Gou Hotel (*see* Lodging, below). It's an easy walk along dirt paths and steps built of train ties. The Taiwan red maple and red cypress trees are marked in English. A high point for both kids and adults is the narrow-gauge steam locomotive, built in 1881, that rests on the tracks beside the Train Hotel. A pleasing rest spot is the thatch pavilion in the middle of Elder Sisters Pond. Perhaps because of the forest's popularity with newlyweds, the authorities have given slightly humorous names to several of the tree formations. Two trees with interlocking trunks are called Forever United in Love, and another pair is identified as A Heavenly Couple. One of the oldest trees, a 4,100-year-old cypress, is also one of the tallest, at 48 m (157 ft), and aptly named Giant Tree. You may want to linger in the free **Alpine Museum** (tel. 05/227–7006; open Tues.–Sun. 9–noon and 2–5), which has English-language dioramas and exhibits explaining the forest's animal and insect life.

Alishan's chief attraction is the sunrise at **Chushan.** Your hotel will rouse you for a 6-km (3.7-mi) train ride in the dark, but don't expect a solitary experience with nature. This is a highly organized mass pilgrimage to platforms built on a mountainside looking east. Even vendors are out at this hour, hawking film and Chinese snacks such as prunes and bamboo shoots. When the sun peeks over the mountaintops, cameras click and the crowd comes alive. The site is then immediately deserted, as the early risers stream back onto the train for the return trip. Most visitors grab a hurried breakfast and catch the 9 AM train to **Monkey Rock.** You can escape the throngs there by venturing off onto some of the most pleasant and scenic trails at Alishan. Monkey Rock itself is an amusing sight: a towering formation that looks strikingly like the profile of a seated monkey.

Dining and **Alishan House.** This is an older mountain resort (built in 1967) **Lodging** among the pines. The lobby has dark wood paneling and a maroon-felt sofa. The rooms, which are unheated but supplied with heavy comforters, will give you the feeling that you're roughing it a bit. The restaurant has an elegance that far exceeds the rest of the hotel: glass-topped tables and china plates. The food, however, is standard, and the prices are moderate. *2 West Alishan, Shan Lin Village, Wu Feng, Hsiang Chiayi, tel. 05/267–9811. 60 rooms. Facilities: coffee shop, bar. No credit cards. Inexpensive.*
Alishan Train Hotel. This hotel is an actual train, and you sleep inside the bright red railway cars. It is operated by the Alishan House; inquire there when you arrive, and the Train Hotel will send a car for you. The setting—a cleared area in the forest—is quiet and restful. *2 West Alishan, tel. 05/267–9811. 18 rooms. No credit cards. Inexpensive.*

9 Thailand

Introduction

Thailand is unique among Southeast Asian nations in having developed its culture independently of western colonialism, and the Thais are innately proud of their history. The kingdom's Buddhism is the purest in the region. Its language is like no other but is enormously rich, with an extraordinary capacity for exact expression of the finest nuances of human relationships, a sign of the importance Thais place on dealing with one another peaceably and with dignity. Contrasts abound in the country, both geographically and socially. In a land the size of France, beach resorts run the gamut from sleazy Pattaya to dignified Hua Hin. Idyllic island hideaways of virgin beaches sheltered by palm groves and lapped by gentle waters contrast with the frenetic capital.

Bangkok is a sensory kaleidoscope in which temples and palaces of amazing beauty stand alongside ramshackle homes on the banks of evil-smelling *klongs* (canals); appetizing odors of exotic street food mix with the earthy pungency of open drainage systems; and graceful classical dancers perform on stages next door to bars where go-go girls gyrate in clinical nakedness. BMWs stall in traffic jams while *tuk-tuks* (three-wheel cabs) scoot between them; deluxe hotels share the same block with tin-roof stalls; and designer boutiques compete with street vendors hawking knockoff Pierre Cardin shirts.

Chiang Mai, Thailand's second largest city, is situated in the mountainous north of the country. It is older than Bangkok—in fact, older than the Thai Kingdom. Chiang Mai's cultural heritage reflects those of its neighbors, Burma and Laos, as much as it does Bangkok's. The surrounding hills are dotted with small villages of a people collectively known as the hill tribes, whose way of life has, until the last two decades, remained independent from Thailand's national development and the 20th century. To the northeast is the Golden Triangle, once notorious for opium trafficking and still famous for its mountainous scenery spreading over three countries—Thailand, Burma, and Laos.

The small, sleepy market towns of Sukhothai and Ayutthaya contain (restored) ruins that witness their mighty pasts as the capitals of the Thai kingdom.

Away from the towns are no fewer than 50 national parks. Phu Kradung in the northeast, for example, is 60 square miles of tableland covered with pine trees and tropical flora. Just to the south of Bangkok is the province of Kanchanaburi, filled with breathtakingly lush forests and cascades.

Forest cover, though, is declining in Thailand, down from 57% in 1961 to 32% today. The mighty elephant, who used to work the great teak forests, has joined the ranks of the unemployed. What work he picks up nowadays is performing for tourists a charade euphemistically called "Elephants at Work."

Just as tourism has given a new lease on life to the elephants, so has it created alternative opportunities for a population that is 70% agrarian. More than 4 million visitors flock to Thailand each year to seek a quick fix of the exotic at bargain prices. Their demands and willingness to pay top dollar for their pleasures have changed the Thai view of the foreigner. No longer a

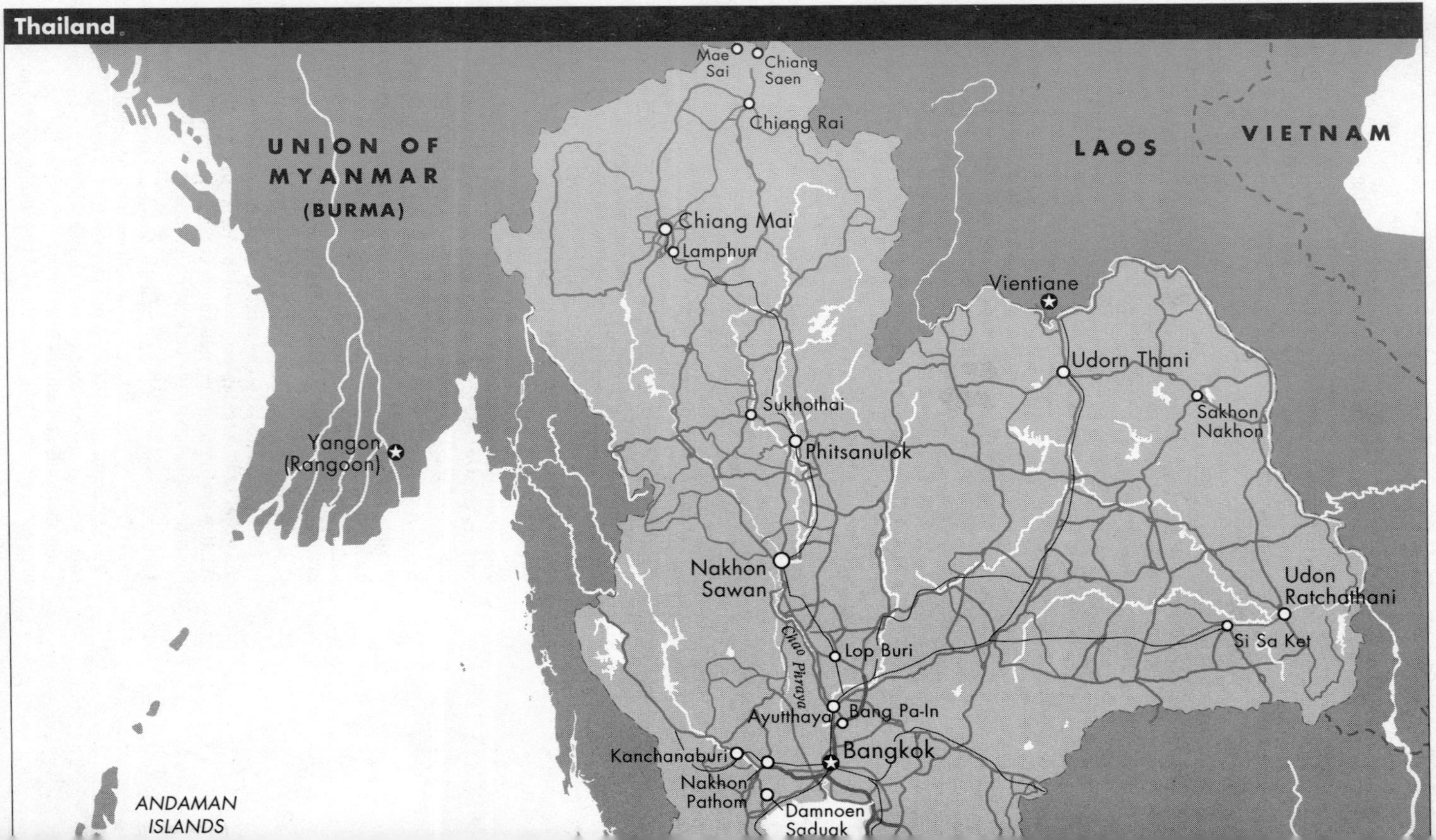

Thailand.

UNION OF
MYANMAR
(BURMA)

Yangon
(Rangoon)

ANDAMAN
ISLANDS

Mae
Sai

Chiang
Saen

Chiang Rai

Chiang Mai

Lamphun

LAOS

Vientiane

Udorn Thani

Sakhon
Nakhon

Udon
Ratchathani

Si Sa Ket

VIETNAM

Sukhothai

Phitsanulok

Nakhon
Sawan

Lop Buri

Bang Pa-In

Ayutthaya

Chao Phraya

Bangkok

Kanchanaburi

Nakhon
Pathom

Damnoen
Saduak

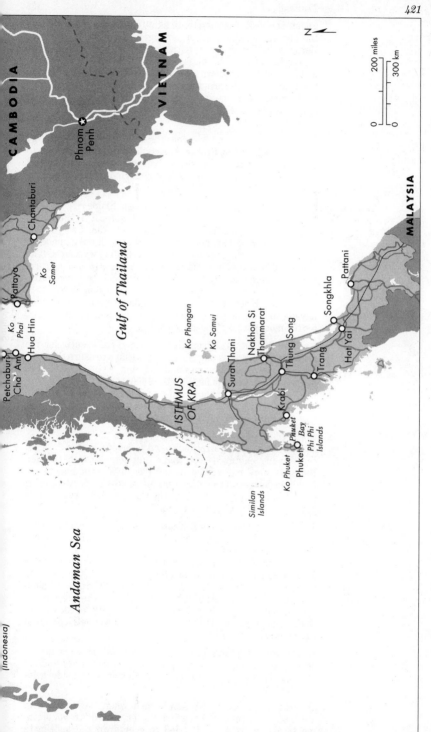

guest, the visitor is something akin to a one-armed bandit: If the Thai can jerk the tourist just right, he will hit the jackpot. Because the Thai does this with a smile, the foreigner keeps on coming back for more. This is not the Thai heritage. In the past, making money for its own sake was frowned upon. Important to the Thai was social harmony and the simple goal of enough "fish in the rivers and rice in the fields" for everybody—an idyllic state associated with the 13th-century founding of the kingdom.

Thailand's origins may even reach as far back as 5,600 years ago to the world's oldest Bronze Age civilization. From the 6th to the 13th centuries, known as the Dvaravati period, people from the southern Chinese province of Yunnan moved into the fertile basin of the Chao Phraya River.

The Sukhothai period began when two Siamese chieftains banded together, captured the Khmer outpost of Sukhothai and established the first Thai kingdom in 1238. Early in the Sukhothai period Thailand's first great king, Ramkhamhoeng, came to power. Not only was he an outstanding warrior, but he made two lasting and significant contributions to Thai culture. He revised and adapted the Khmer alphabet to the requirements of the Thai language, and he invited Ceylonese monks to purify the Khmer-corrupted Theravada (sometimes called Hinayana) Buddhism and establish the religion in a form that is, for the most part, still practiced today.

By 1350 Sukhothai's strength had waned sufficiently for the rising and dynamic young state of Ayutthaya to usurp the reins of power. For four centuries and 33 kings, Ayutthaya was the heart and brain of Thailand. In the 1650s, the city's population exceeded that of London and—according to many foreign travelers—with its golden spires, waterways, and roads, it was the most glorious capital not just in Asia, but in all the world.

In 1768 the Burmese attacked the city. After a 15-month siege, they finally captured Ayutthaya and plundered it. Golden Buddhas were melted down, the treasuries ransacked, and buildings burned. Thais who were unable to escape were killed or sent into slavery; by the time the Burmese left, Ayutthaya's population had dropped from 1 million to 10,000.

The Thais, under General Taksin, regrouped, established a capital on the Chao Phraya River at Thonburi (opposite present-day Bangkok), and set about successfully expelling the Burmese from Thailand. In 1782 Chao P'ya Chakri, a supporter of General Taksin, who had briefly been crowned king, became the first king of the current Chakri dynasty. (The present monarch, King Bhumipol Adulyadej, is the ninth in the line.) One of the first acts of P'ya Chakri, or Rama I (all kings of the Chakri dynasty are given the title Rama), was to move the Thai capital to Bangkok.

In the last 200 years, Thailand has had two prime concerns: staving off foreign encroachment on its sovereignty and restructuring its society to meet the demands of modern industrialism.

Western powers were first welcomed when they arrived in 1512, but the French (from whom the Thai word *farang*, meaning foreigner, is derived) tried to overthrow the legitimate government and install a puppet regime. The result was that the Thais not only threw out the French but also closed their doors to all outsiders until the middle of the 19th century. When the West again threatened Thailand's sovereignty, King Mongkut (Rama IV, 1851–1868), through a series of adroit treaties, kept the colonial forces at bay. His efforts were continued by King Chulalongkorn (Rama V, 1868–1910). Thai independence was eventually secured by the cession to the British of a little of what is now Malaysia and to the French of a little of what is now Kampuchea.

Thailand's other concern was adapting to modern social pressures. Under King Chulalongkorn, slavery was abolished, hospitals and schools were established, and some upper-class Thais received European educations so they could replace Western advisers. Under King Prajadhipok (Rama VII, reigned 1925–1935), the world's economic depression brought its share of discontent to Thailand. The pressure for sweeping reform ended in 1932 with the military demanding the establishment of a constitutional monarchy on lines similiar to that of Great Britain. Since then, quasimilitary governments and a strong bureaucracy have administered the country. Changes in government have as often been by coup as by election. As the new coalition of power holders customarily promises what the previous government promised when it came to power, the nation's policies have been remarkably consistent in fostering the expansion of the industrial economy.

Up to now, the Thais' strong belief in Buddhism (except in the south, where most of Thailand's 2 million Muslims live) has accounted for their tolerant attitude, which can be summed up by their expression *mai pen rai* ("never mind, it does not matter"). The Thais' respect and deference for the monarchy (it is an indictable offense to slander the monarchy) has fostered an acceptance of political authority, and a coup is treated with the attitude of mai pen rai. Whether the resilience of the Thai culture can withstand the pressures of the late 20th century is the current question.

Thailand's attraction rests with the people. Proud of their independence, the Thais believe in accommodation rather than confrontation. Thais believe there is, or at least should be, a way to resolve differences politely and amicably. Demands, displays of anger, and any behavior that upsets harmony are frowned upon. The Thais communicate by smiles, which have many meanings, some of which we are probably better off not knowing.

Staying in Thailand

Getting Around

By Plane The domestic airline is **Thai Airways,** which connects Bangkok with all major cities and tourist areas in Thailand with the exception of Ko Samui, where an airport is still being planned. Virtually all planes go through Bangkok. On popular tourist routes during peak holiday times, flights are often fully booked. Make sure you have reservations and make them well in advance of your travel date. Flights should be reconfirmed when you arrive in Thailand. Thai Airways has a good record for keeping to schedule. During the rainy season, you may expect delays due to the weather.

By Train The State Railway of Thailand has three lines, all of which terminate in Bangkok. The Northern Line connects Bangkok with Chiang Mai and passes through Ayutthaya and Phitsanulok; the Northeastern Line travels up to Udorn Thani near the Laotian border; and the Southern Line goes all the way south through Surat Thani—the stop for Ko Samui—to the Malaysian border and on to Kuala Lumpur and Singapore, a journey that takes 52 hours. (There is no train to Phuket, though you can go as far as Surat Thani and change onto a scheduled bus service.)

Most trains offer second- (air-conditioning and non-air-conditioning) or third-class tickets, but the overnight trains to the north (Chiang Mai) and to the south offer first-class sleeping cabins. Couchettes, with sheets and curtains for privacy, are available in second class. Do not leave valuables unguarded on these overnight trains as professional thieves have been known to board the train and take what they fancy.

Tickets may be bought at the railway stations. Travel agencies can also sell tickets for the overnight trains. Reservations are strongly advised for all long-distance trains. Train schedules in English are available from travel agents and from major railway stations.

Fares are reasonable. A second-class couchette, for example, for the 14-hour journey from Bangkok to Chiang Mai is B530, first class is B980.

By Bus Long-distance buses are cheaper and faster than trains, and there are buses into every corner of the country. A typical fare for the nine-hour trip between Chiang Mai and Bangkok is B230. The level of comfort depends on the bus company. Air-conditioned buses are superior, but the air-conditioning is always turned on full blast. The most comfortable long-distance buses are operated by private travel/tour companies. For the most part, these private buses serve only resort destinations. Travel agents have the bus schedules and can make reservations and issue tickets.

By Car Cars are available for rent in Bangkok and in major tourist destinations. An international driving license is required. Driving is on the left; speed limits are 60 kph (37 mph) in cities and 90 kph (56 mph) outside. It is advisable to hire a driver. The additional cost is small, and the peace of mind great. If a foreigner is involved in an automobile accident, he—not the Thai —is likely to be judged at fault.

In Chiang Mai, Ko Samui, Pattaya, and Phuket, hiring a jeep or motorcycle is a popular and convenient way to get around. Be aware that many rentals, especially those from small companies, are not covered by insurance, and you are liable for any damage to the vehicle, regardless of who is at fault. **Avis** (16/23 N. Sathorn Rd., Bangkok, tel. 02/233–0397) and **Hertz** (1620 Petchburi Rd., Bangkok, tel. 02/252–4903) rental companies are more expensive but tend to offer better insurance coverage.

Also be aware that motorcycles easily skid on gravel roads or on gravel patches on the pavement. In Ko Samui, a sign posts the year's count of foreigners who never made it home from their vacation!

The major roads in Thailand tend to be very congested and street signs are often in Thai only. But the limited number of roads and, with the exception of Bangkok, the straightforward layout of cities combine to make navigation relatively easy. Driving at night in rural areas, especially north and west of Chiang Mai and in the south beyond Surat Thani is not advised, as highway robberies have been reported.

By Taxi Taxis do not have meters; fares are negotiated. Taxis waiting at hotels are more expensive than those flagged down while cruising. Never enter the taxi until the price has been established. Most taxi drivers do not speak English, but all understand the finger count. One finger means B10, two is for B20 and so on. Ask at your hotel to find out what the appropriate fare from one point to another should be. Never pay more than what the hotel quotes, as they will have given you the high price. If in doubt, accept 65% to 75% of the cabbie's quote.

With any form of private travel, never change your initial agreement on destination and price unless you clearly communicate and establish a new "contract." Moreover, if you agree to the driver's offer to wait for you at your destination and be available for your onward or return journey, you will be charged for waiting time, and, unless you have fixed the price, the return fare can be double that of the outbound fare.

By Samlor Often called tuk-tuks for their spluttering sound, these three-wheel cabs are slightly less expensive than a taxi and, because of their maneuverability, the most rapid form of travel through congested traffic. All tuk-tuk operators drive as if your ride will be their last, but, in fact, they are remarkably safe. Tuk-tuks are not very comfortable, though, and are best used for shorter journeys.

By Songthaew Songthaews seat passengers on side bench seats and can serve as minibuses or as private taxis. If they travel as a minibus, they will follow a fixed route and the fare is set. If they are used as a taxi, then the fare must be negotiated.

By Bicycle Rickshaws For short trips bicycle rickshaws are a popular, inexpensive form of transport. They become expensive for long trips. Fares are negotiated. It is imperative to be very clear with these drivers about what price is agreed upon. They have a tendency to create a misunderstanding leading to a nasty scene at the end of the trip.

Telephones

Public telephones are available in most towns and villages and take B5 pieces. For a long-distance call in Thailand, dial the area code and then the number. To make overseas calls, you are advised to use either your hotel switchboard—Chiang Mai and Bangkok have direct dialing—or the overseas telephone facilities at the central post office and telecommunications building. You'll find one in all towns. In Bangkok the overseas telephone center, next to the general post office, is open 24 hours; up-country the facilities' hours may vary, but they usually open at 8 AM and some stay open until 10 PM. If you wish to receive assistance for an overseas call, dial 100/233–2771. For local telephone inquires, dial 100/183, but you will need to speak Thai. In Bangkok, you can dial 13 for an English-speaking operator.

Mail

Thailand's mail service is reliable and efficient. Major hotels provide basic postal services. Bangkok's central general post office on Charoen Krung (New Road) is open 8–6, weekends and public holidays 9–1. Up-country post offices close at 4:30 PM.

Airmail postcard rates to the United States are B7.50; B6.50 to the United Kingdom. The minimum rate for airmail letters is B12 to the United States and B10 to the United Kingdom. Allow about two weeks for your mail to get to its overseas destination. If you want to speed that process, major post offices offer overseas express mail (EMS) services, where the minimum rate (200 g or 8 oz) is B230.

You may have mail sent to you "poste restante." Usually, there is a B1 charge for each piece collected. Thais write their last name first, so be sure to have your last name written in capital letters and underlined.

Currency

The basic unit of currency is the baht. There are 100 satang to one baht. There are five different bills, each a different color: B10, brown; B20, green; B50, blue; B100, red; and B500, purple. Coins in use are 25 satang, 50 satang, B1, and B5. One-baht coins are smaller than B5 coins; both come in three different sizes—get the feel of them quickly.

The baht is considered a stable currency. All hotels will convert travelers' checks and major currencies into baht, though exchange rates are better at banks and authorized money changers. The rate tends to be better in Bangkok than up-country. Major international credit cards are accepted at most tourist shops and hotels.

What It Will Cost

The cost of visiting Thailand is very much up to you. It is possible to live and travel quite inexpensively if you do as Thais do—eat in local restaurants, use buses, and stay at non-air-conditioned hotels. Once you start enjoying a little luxury, prices jump drastically. For example, crossing Bangkok by bus is a 10¢ ride, but by taxi the fare may run to $10. Prices are typically higher in resort areas catering to foreign tourists, and Bangkok is more expensive than other Thai cities. Anything purchased in a luxury hotel is considerably more expensive than if purchased elsewhere. Imported items are heavily taxed.

At press time, B23.25 = US $1.

Sample Prices Continental breakfast at a hotel, $8; large bottle of beer at a hotel, $3; dinner at a good restaurant, $15; 1-mile taxi ride, $1.50; double room, $20–$40 inexpensive, $40–$80 moderate, $80–$120 expensive.

Language

Thai is the country's national language. As it uses the Khmer script and is spoken tonally, it is confusing to most foreigners. What may sound to a foreigner as "krai kai kai kai" will mean to a Thai, said with the appropriate pitch, "who sells chicken eggs?" However, it is easy to speak a few words, such as "sawahdee krap" (good day) and "khop khun krap" (thank you). With the exception of taxi drivers, Thais working with travelers in the resort and tourist areas in Bangkok generally speak sufficient English to permit basic communication.

Some words that may be useful to know as you visit places of interest in Thailand are:

Bot: The main chapel of a wat (*see* below), where ordinations occur and the chief image of the Lord Buddha is kept.
Chedi: A pagoda built in Thai style with a bell-shaped dome tapering to a pointed spire, often where holy relics are kept.
Farang: Foreigner.
Klong: Canal.
Ko (often written *Koh*): Island.
Nam: Water, often used to mean river.
Prang: A chedi built in the old Khmer style with an elliptical spire.
Soi: Small street, or lane, often assigned a number and described in conjunction with the abutting main street.
Stupa: Another word for chedi.
Viharn: The large hall in a wat where priests perform religious duties.
Wat: The complex of buildings of a Buddhist religious site (monastery), or temple.

Opening and Closing Times

Thai and foreign **banks** are open weekdays 8:30–3:30, except for public holidays. Most **commercial concerns** in Bangkok operate on a five-day week and are open 8–5. **Government offices** are generally open 8:30–4:30 with a noon–1 lunch break. Many **stores** are open daily 8–8.

National Holidays

The following are national holidays: New Year Day, January 1; Magha Puja, February, on the full moon of the third lunar month; Chakri Day, April 6; Songkran, mid-April; Coronation Day, May 5; Visakha Puja, May, on the full moon of the sixth lunar month; Queen's Birthday, August 12; King's Birthday, December 5. Government offices, banks, commercial concerns, and department stores are usually closed on these days, but smaller shops stay open.

Festivals and Seasonal Events

The festivals listed below are national and occur throughout the country unless otherwise noted. Many events follow the lunar calendar, so dates vary from year to year.

Dec. 31–Jan. 2: New Year celebrations are usually at their best around temples. In Bangkok, special ceremonies at Pramanae Ground include Thai dances.

Feb.: Magha Puja commemorates the day when 1,250 disciples spontaneously heard Lord Buddha preach the cardinal doctrine on the full moon of the third lunar month.

Feb.–Apr.: Kite-flying contests are held (in Bangkok, see them at the Pramanae Ground). Barbs attached to kite strings are used to destroy the other contestants' kites.

Apr. 6: Chakri Day. This day commemorates the enthronement of King Rama I, founder of the present dynasty, in 1782.

Mid-Apr.: Songkran. This marks the Thai New Year and is an occasion that is used for earning merit, setting caged birds and fish free, visiting family, dancing, and water-throwing where everyone splashes everyone else in good-natured merriment. The festival is at its best in Chiang Mai with parades, dancing in the streets, and a beauty contest.

May: Plowing Ceremony. At the Pramanae Ground in Bangkok, Thailand's king and queen take part in a traditional ritual that serves to open the rice-planting season.

May 5: Coronation Day: The king and queen take part in a procession to the Royal Chapel to preside over ceremonies commemorating the anniversary of their coronation.

May: Visakha Puja: On the full moon of the sixth lunar month the nation celebrates the holiest of Buddhist days—Lord Buddha's birth, enlightenment, and death. Monks lead the laity in candle-lit processions around their temples.

Aug. 12: Queen's Birthday. Queen Sirikit's birthday is celebrated with religious ceremonies at Chitralda Palace.

Nov.: Loi Krathong Festival. Held on the full moon of the 12th lunar month, this is the loveliest of Thai festivals. After sunset people throughout Thailand make their way to a body of water and launch small lotus-shaped banana-leaf floats bearing lighted candles. The aim is to honor the water spirits and wash away one's sins of the past year.

Nov.: Golden Mount Festival. Of all the fairs and festivals in Bangkok, this one at the Golden Mount is the most spectacular, with sideshows, food stalls, bazaars, and crowds celebrating.

Nov.: Elephant Roundup. Held at Surin in the northeast, this is a stirring display of 100 noble animals' skills as traditional beasts of war, as bulldozers, and even soccer players.

Dec. 5: King's Birthday. A trooping of the colors is performed in Bangkok by Thailand's elite Royal Guards.

Tipping

A **taxi driver** is not tipped unless hired as a private driver for an excursion. **Hotel porters** expect at least a B20 tip, and **hotel staff** who have given good personal service are usually tipped. A 10% tip is appreciated at a **restaurant** when no service charge has been added to the bill.

Shopping

Thailand offers some of the world's best shopping, and Bangkok and Chiang Mai are the best shopping cities. The critical factor in successful shopping is to know the product, especially if it is a precious stone or an antique. Another requirement for a successful buy is bargaining. It's a process that takes time, but it saves you money and wins respect from the vendor.

Thailand produces several specialties to tempt shoppers:

Bronzeware Uniquely handcrafted bronzeware can be bought in complete table services, coffee and creamer and bar sets, letter openers, bowls, tankards, trays, and candlesticks. Lately, the designs have become modern and classically simple. Traditional methods are still used, but a silicon coat is added to prevent tarnishing. Chiang Mai is a good source for this product.

Nielloware This special kind of silver with its inlaid design, which looks black when held against the light at an angle and white when looked at straight on, is also available with color inlays. Nielloware comes as cufflinks, lights, jewelry, ashtrays, creamer sets and a host of other articles. Bangkok or the southern province of Nakhon Si Thammarat are good places to buy it.

Thai Silk Through the efforts of Jim Thompson, Thai silk has become a much sought-after luxury fabric. The prices are fairly high, but they are much less than what you would pay at home. Be aware that the weights and quality do differ. Most yardage comes 40 inches wide and may be bought by the yard or as ready-made goods. Rivaling Thai silk is the handwoven cotton made in the Chiang Mai area.

Precious Stones Rubies and sapphires are most associated with Thailand. These can be bought loose or in jewelry. Unless you are a gemologist, you may wish to make your purchases from a Tourism Authority of Thailand–approved store. You should also get a guarantee and receipt written in English.

Dolls The more expensive dolls come dressed in Thai silk and represent classical Thai dancers or mythological characters.

Lacquerware Lacquerware, which is usually made into small tables or boxes, is lightweight and commonly comes in a gold-and-black color scheme. You'll find the better pieces are made in Chiang Mai.

Carved Wood Teakwood carvings, in the form of boxes, trays, or figures, are popular. Beware, there is a very convincing technique that makes carvings into instant antiques! You'll find wood carving all over Thailand, but Chiang Mai is its main center.

Thai Celadon The ancient art of making this type of pottery has been revived, and the ware can be found mostly around Chiang Mai, though some can be purchased in Bangkok. Also made in the Chiang Mai area is Sukhothai stoneware. Near Bangkok, the kilns produce a very fine blue and white porcelain.

Antiques The Thai government has very strict regulations on the export of antiques and religious art. Images of the Lord Buddha are not permitted to be exported. By law no antique may leave the country, and even reproductions not sold as antiques may need an export permit issued by the Fine Arts Department. A reputable dealer can obtain these permits in about one week.

Aside from traditional crafts, Thailand offers a host of other good buys, ranging from local handicrafts to ready-made clothes from designer to knockoffs. There are also knockoff watches with designer names. A "Rolex" can be purchased for $20, though the emblem may be a little crooked. Pirated cassettes are another phenomenally inexpensive item. However, be aware that it is illegal to import pirated goods into the United States. Beauty is a big business in Thailand, and walk-in beauty parlors are ubiquitous. For 40¢ to $2 you can have a manicure or pedicure; facials, permanents, and massages can be had at correspondingly low prices.

Prices are fixed in department stores. In fashion boutiques, there is no harm in asking for a small discount. In stores selling artifacts, price is open to negotiation, and in bazaars and street-side stalls, bargaining is essential.

Sports

Spectator Sports
Thai Boxing
Thai boxing, known locally as *muay Thai*, allows boxers to use their feet, knees, thighs, and elbows as well as their gloved fists to hit an opponent. Moreover, all parts of the opponent's body can be struck, and points are awarded for any blow. Thai boxing requires years of training, and prior to each bout, boxers indulge in ritual praying that involves complicated maneuvers designed to limber up the body.

Motorcycle Racing
With the opening of the Bira Pattaya Circuit, on Route 36 between Pattaya and Rayong, international motorcycle events are held regularly.

Takro
This sport involves passing a small rattan ball back and forth as long as possible before it falls to the ground. All parts of the body may be used. The more complicated the pass, the better it is judged. Other forms of takro require a hoop or net.

Kite-fighting
This sport dates back hundreds of years. Elaborate kites armed with barbs, designated *pakpao* (female) or *chula* (male), struggle for dominance, trying to ensnare or cut the opponent's line. A good place to watch this is at Bangkok's Pramanae Ground near the Royal Palace, particularly in March and April.

Horse Racing
Races are held at tracks in Bangkok *(see* Bangkok section, below).

Boat Racing
With so many rivers, Thailand has many kinds of boat racing. Teams from various towns or provinces vie for honors in colorful paddle-powered boats. Annual races are held in Bangkok, Pichit, Ayutthaya and Nan.

Participant Sports
Golf
Some 50 excellent golf courses are spread around the kingdom, though the majority are in the Bangkok region. Three of the best are Navatanee golf course, site of the 1975 World Cup tournament, the Rose Garden course, and the Krung Thep Kreta course.

Horseback Riding
Though some of the beach resorts may have horses, only Pattaya has a permanent stable, where horse treks into the countryside are available to the public.

Hiking and Trekking
Hiking is especially popular in the north, where groups go in search of hill-tribe villages and wildlife. The main center for northern treks is Chiang Mai. But with dozens of national parks around the country, you may hike in tropical jungles and isolated highlands alike. Contact the Tourism Authority of Thailand for information on bungalow-style accommodations in the national parks.

Water Sports
With its long coastline and warm waters, Thailand offers splendid opportunities for all sorts of water sports, including waterskiing, surfing, windsurfing, and parasailing. It is possible to rent power boats, water scooters, and sailboats. Scuba diving and snorkeling in the clear waters are also available, especially in Pattaya and Phuket, where rentals, instruction, and

trips to uninhabited islands may be arranged. Big-game fishing is a feature at Bang Saray, near Pattaya.

Beaches

The beaches of Thailand, both on the Gulf of Siam (the south and east coasts) and on the Andaman Sea (the southwest coast) are becoming increasingly popular with Europeans. Full-scale resort areas have been developed on both coasts—Pattaya, Hua Hin and Cha' Am on the Gulf, Phuket on the Andaman Sea. New resort areas are developing all the time. Ko Samui on the Gulf is becoming increasingly popular, as is Ko Phi Phi off Phuket. For those who like idyllic havens of beaches and no people, the area around Krabi facing the Andaman Sea is paradise, and Ko Samet on the Gulf (near Pattaya) has a number of small beaches and bungalows for rent. The waters around Bangkok are tropical, warm, and inviting, but do check on two factors before you plunge in: the undertow and the presence of stinging jelly fish. Sand tends to be golden in color and slightly coarse. Scuba diving and snorkeling are best off Ko Samui and among the Similan Islands off Phuket.

Dining

Thai cuisine is distinctive, often hot and spicy, and perfumed with herbs, especially lemon grass and coriander. It is influenced by the cooking styles of China, India, Java, Malaysia, and Portugal. Rice, boiled or fried, forms the basis for most Thai meals, though noodles can also play this role. Meats, poultry, and seafood are highly seasoned with herbs and chilis. Soups are also important in Thai cuisine and are usually spiced with lemon grass and chilis. All courses of a Thai meal are served at the same time.

Each region has its own specialties. The Northeast favors sticky rice served with barbecued chicken and shredded green papaya mixed with shrimp, lemon juice, fish sauce, garlic, and chilies. In the North, a local sausage, *naem*, is popular, while in the South there is an abundance of fresh seafood. Dessert is usually exotic fresh fruit or sweets made of rice flour, coconut milk, palm sugar, and sticky rice. Singha beer and Mekong whiskey (made from rice) are the usual beverages. Western food is available in most hotels and at many restaurants in resort areas.

For more on Thai food, *see* Dining in Bangkok, below.

Except in the Bangkok Dining section, the following dining price categories apply throughout this chapter:

Category	Cost*
Very Expensive	over B500 ($21.50)
Expensive	B250–B500 ($10.75–$21.50)
Moderate	B100–B250 ($4.30–$10.75)
Inexpensive	under B100 ($4.30)

per person, including service charge

Lodging

Every town of reasonable size offers accommodation. In the smaller towns the hotels may be fairly simple, but they will usually be clean and certainly inexpensive. In major cities or resort areas, there are hotels to fit all price categories. At the high end, the luxury hotels can compete with the best in the world. Service is generally superb—polite and efficient—and most of the staff usually speaks English. At the other end of the scale, the lodging is simple and basic with a room that has not much more than a bed. The least expensive places may have Asian toilets (squat type with no seat) and a fan rather than air-conditioning.

All except the budget hotels have restaurants and offer room service throughout most of the day and night. Most will also be happy to make local travel arrangements for you—for which they receive commissions. All hotels advise that you use their safe-deposit boxes.

During the peak tourist season, October–March, hotels are often fully booked and charge peak rates. At special times, such as December 30–January 2 and Chinese New Year, rates climb even higher. Weekday rates at some resorts are often lower, and during the off-season it is possible to negotiate a reduced rate. Breakfast is never included in the room tariff.

An 11% government tax is sometimes included in and sometimes added to hotel bills. In addition, deluxe hotels often add 10%–15% service charge.

Throughout this chapter the following lodging price categories apply:

Category	Cost*
Very Expensive	over B2,500 ($108)
Expensive	B1,500–B2,500 ($65–$108)
Moderate	B1,000–B1,500 ($43–$65)
Inexpensive	B500–B1,000 ($21.50–$43)
Budget	under B500 ($21.50)

per double room, including service and tax

Bangkok

A foreigner's reaction to Bangkok is often as confused as the city's geography. Bangkok has no downtown, and the streets, like the traffic, seem to veer off in every direction. The oldest quarter clusters around the eastern bank of the Chao Phraya River. The river winds between two cities, Thailand's current capital and Thonburi, where the Thais first established their capital after the fall of Ayutthaya in 1767.

Even Bangkok's name is disconcerting. Foreigners call the city Bangkok, but Thais refer to their capital as Krung Thep, the City of Angels. When Thailand's capital was Ayutthaya, to the north of present-day Bangkok, foreign vessels would reach there by the Chao Phraya. After the fall of Ayutthaya, King Rama I decided in 1782 to move his capital from Thonburi to a new site across the river. Foreigners looked at their navigational charts and understood the capital to be where the village of Bangkok was marked.

In the last 20 years, the face of Bangkok has changed. Before the Vietnam War, and before Bangkok became the R & R destination for American servicemen, the city had a population of 1.5 million. Then, the flaunting of U.S. dollars attracted the rural poor to the city. Within two decades, it grew to 6 million, 40 times the size of any other city in Thailand. Space to live and breathe is inadequate. Air pollution is the worst in the world. Traffic jams the streets from morning to evening, and no cure is in sight. Use the pedestrian crosswalks—the traffic will stop if you insist—or use the pedestrian flyovers.

Yet, while hurtling headlong into the world of modern commercialism and technology, Bangkok strangely gives a sense of history and timelessness, even though it is only 200 years old. This is perhaps because King Rama I was determined to build a city as beautiful as the old capital of Ayutthaya had been before the Burmese ransacked it. Bangkok requires an adjustment on our part. Let the gentle nature of the Thai and his respect for others win your heart, and let the serenity of the temples soothe your spirit.

Arriving and Departing by Plane

Airports and Airlines Bangkok's Don Muang Airport's new international terminal, adjacent to what is now the domestic terminal, has relieved passenger congestion and presents international passengers with modern efficiency on arrival. As you exit customs, you find an array of information desks where you can make arrangements for taxis into Bangkok and transport to other destinations; a reservation desk for Bangkok hotels (no fee); and a TAT (Tourist Authority of Thailand) desk that has a large selection of free brochures and maps. Both terminals have luggage-checking facilities (tel. 02/535–1250).

There is a tax of B150 for international departures and B20 for domestic departures.

Don Muang is 25 km (15 mi) from the city center. The road is often congested with traffic. Be prepared for a 90-minute journey by taxi, though there are times when it can take less than 40 minutes.

Thai International and **Thai Domestic Airlines,** the national airlines, have the most flights coming in and out of Don Muang. Thai International has direct flights from the west coast of the United States and from Toronto in Canada. The airline also has daily flights to Hong Kong, Singapore, Taiwan, and Japan, and direct flights from London.

United Airlines is the major U.S. carrier with service to Bangkok. There are direct flights from the West Coast, and connecting flights from the East Coast with one change of plane at San Francisco, Tokyo, or Hong Kong. A round-trip can be designed to include Tokyo and Hong Kong, which allows you to enjoyably break the 20-hour flight from the East Coast or the 17-hour flight from the West Coast. **Northwest** also has flights, and **Delta** plans daily service from Portland, Oregon, by the end of 1989. **Singapore Airlines** flies in from Singapore, and **British Airways** flies in from London. In total 35 airline companies have flights to and from Bangkok and more are seeking landing rights.

Also see Travel Agencies, below, concerning discounted airfares.

Between the Airport and Center City
By Taxi Obtain a taxi reservation at the counter (at either terminal) and a driver will lead you to the taxi. The fare for any Bangkok destination is B300 from the international terminal and B200 from the domestic. Taxis to the airport from downtown Bangkok are, with negotiation, approximately B130.

By Minibus Thai Airways has a minibus service between the airport and Bangkok's major hotels. They depart when the minibus is full. Cost: B100.

By Bus Bus No. 4 goes to Rama Garden Hotel, Indra Regent, Erawan, and Dusit Thani hotels, and down Silom Road. Bus No. 10 goes to Rama Garden Hotel, the Northern Bus Terminal, the Victory Monument, and the Southern Bus Terminal. Buses are airconditioned. Cost: B15.

By Train Trains into Bangkok's central railway station run approximately every 30 minutes from 5:30 AM to 9 PM. The fare is B5 for a local train, B13 for an express.

Arriving by Train and Bus

By Train **Hualamphong Railway Station,** (Rama IV Rd., tel. 02/223–7461) is the city's main station and serves most long-distance trains. There is also **Bangkok Noi** on the Thonburi side of the Chao Phraya River, used by local trains to Hua Hin and Kanchanaburi.

By Bus Bangkok has three main bus terminals. **Northern/Northeast Bus Terminal** (Phaholyothin Rd., tel. 02/279–4484 for airconditioned buses, tel. 02/279–6222 for non-air-conditioned buses) is for Chiang Mai and the north. **Southern Bus Terminal** (Charansanitwong Rd., tel. 02/411–4978 for air-conditioned buses, tel. 02/511–0511 for non-air-conditioned buses), on the Thonburi side of the river, is for Hua Hin, Ko Samui, Phuket and points south. **Eastern Bus Terminal** (Sukhumvit Rd., Soi 40, tel. 02/391–3310 for air-conditioned buses, tel. 02/392–2391 for non-air-conditioned buses) is for Pattaya and points southeast.

Getting Around

There is no subway, and road traffic is horrendous. Allow twice the normal travel time during rush hours, 7–10 AM and 4–7 PM.

By Bus Though buses can be very crowded, they are convenient and inexpensive for getting around. For a fare of only B2, B3 for the blue buses, and B5 for the less frequent air-conditioned buses, you can travel virtually anywhere in the city. Buses operate from 5 AM to around 11 PM. The routes are confusing, but usually someone at the bus stop will know the number of the bus you need to catch. It is even simpler if you pick up a route map. These are available at most bookstalls for B35. Be aware of purse snatchers on the buses.

By Taxi Taxis are not metered, and bargaining is essential before climbing into the taxi. As a rough guide to price, a taxi fare from the Hilton to the Grand Palace may run B60 ($2.34) and from the Hilton to the Oriental Hotel would be about B50 ($2.15).

By Samlor Tuk-tuks are slightly cheaper than taxis and best used for short trips in congested traffic.

By Boat Water taxis and express (ferry) boats ply the Chao Phraya River. For the express boats the fare is based on zones, but B5 will cover most trips that you are likely to take. You'll also have to pay a B1 jetty fee. The jetty adjacent to the Oriental Hotel is a useful stop. In about 10 minutes you can travel up the river, making half a dozen stops, to the Grand Palace, or farther up to the other side of Krungthon Bridge in about 15 minutes. It is often the quickest way to travel in a north–south direction.

Long-tailed (so called for the extra-long propeller shaft that extends behind the stern) boats may be hired for about B250 an hour.

Important Addresses and Numbers

Tourist Information The **Thailand Tourist Authority (TAT)**; Ratchadamnoen Rd., tel. 02/282–1143) tends to have more in the way of colorful brochures than hard information. The staff does try to be helpful, and you may want to drop in when you are near the Democracy Monument in the northern part of the city, but you can probably get all the brochures you want from the TAT branch at the airport.

Telephone information, English-speaking operator: tel. 13.

Immigration Division (Soi Suan Sathorn Tai Rd., tel. 02/286–9176) is the place to go for a visa extension. Visas are not required for many nationalities, but tourists are permitted to stay only 15 days in the country without an extension.

Embassies Most nations maintain diplomatic relations with Thailand and have embassies in Bangkok. Should you need to apply for a visa to another country, the consulate hours are usually 8–noon: **Australian Embassy** (37 Sathorn Tai Rd., tel. 02/287–2680); **British Embassy** (1031 Wireless Rd., tel. 02/253–0191); **United States Embassy** (95 Wireless Rd., tel. 02/252–5040).

Emergencies **Tourist Police** (509 Vorachak Rd., tel. 02/221–6209) is open daily 8 AM–midnight.

Police, tel. 195; **fire,** tel. 199; **ambulance,** tel. 02/246–0199.

Hospitals **Chulalongkorn Hospital** (Rama I Rd., tel. 02/252–8181).

English-Language Bookstores The English-language dailies, the *Bangkok Post* and *The Nation*, are available at newsstands.

Asia Books (221 Sukhumvit Rd., Soi 15, tel. 02/252–7277) has a wide selection, as does DK Books or, more properly, **Duang Kamol Bookshop** (244–6 Siam Sq., tel. 02/251–6335).

Pharmacies There is no shortage of pharmacies in Bangkok. Compared to the United States, fewer drugs require prescriptions, but should you need them, you must have a prescription written in Thai. Be aware that over-the-counter drugs are not necessarily of the same chemical composition as those in the United States.

Travel Agencies In virtually every major hotel a travel desk books tours in and around Bangkok. Smaller travel agencies sometimes do not live up to their promises, so for significant purchases and arrangements, you may want to select a larger and more established agency, such as **Diethelm** (544 Phoenchit Rd., tel. 02/252–4041) or **World Travel Service** (1053 New Charoen Krung Rd., tel. 02/233–5900).

Bangkok used to be the world's leading center for discounted airline tickets. The prices are not as competitive as they used to be, but agencies still offer some good prices, usually on lesser-known airlines. Be sure that you read the restrictions on the ticket carefully before you part with any money. You are safer buying open tickets rather than those naming a specific flight and time.

Guided Tours

Numerous tours cover Bangkok and its environs. Each tour operator offers some slight variation, but, in general, they cover the following itineraries.

Floating Market Tour. This half-day tour is a boat ride on the Chao Phraya and into the klongs, former site of a lively floating market with vendors selling vegetables, fruits, meats, and other fare from their sampans. Most of these vendors have long since disappeared, and the visual splendor has gone. Recommended, instead, is a tour to the floating market at Damnoen Saduak, south of Bangkok.

Grand Palace and Emerald Buddha Tour. Because you can easily reach the palace by taxi or public transport and hire a guide on the spot, you may want to visit these sights independently.

City and Temples Tour. In half a day you can visit some of Bangkok's most famous temples: Wat Po with the reclining Buddha; Wat Benjamabopit, famous for its marble structure; and Wat Traimitr, with the five-ton golden Buddha. This tour does not include the Grand Palace.

Thai Dinner and Classical Dance. This evening tour includes a buffet-style Thai dinner with a show of classical dancing. You can manage it just as well on your own.

Excursions **Damnoen Saduak Floating Market Tour.** With the wilting of Bangkok's floating market, Damnoen Saduak offers one of the most exotic and colorful sights of vendors selling produce from sampans. The tour leaves around 8 AM to cover the 100 km (62 mi) to Damnoen Saduak by 9:30, when the market is bustling. This tour may be combined with a visit to the Rose Garden, or Kanchanaburi, and the Bridge over the River Kwai (*see* below).

Rose Garden Tour. In the same direction as Damnoen Saduak is a complex that commercially replicates a Thai village. Amid flowers and gardens containing 20,000 rose bushes, there are traditional Thai houses and a stage where a "cultural show" of dance, Thai boxing, sword fighting, and a wedding ceremony are performed at 2:15 and 3:15. The park also contains hotels, restaurants, swimming pools and other playground activities. Though this afternoon tour is popular, the Rose Garden is a sterile tourist resort. Should you wish to go there independently, reserve through the *Rose Garden booking office, 264/4 Siam Sq.*, tel. *02/251–1935*.

Kanchanaburi and the Bridge over the River Kwai. Usually a full day is necessary to travel the 140 km (87 mi) to Kanchanaburi to visit the Allied war cemeteries, the infamous bridge over the river, and to tour the lush tropical countryside.

Ayutthaya and Bang Pa-In. This visit to Thailand's former glorious capital and the royal palace of Bang Pa-In takes a full day. Tours may travel the 75 km (46 mi) to Ayutthaya either both ways by coach, or in one direction by cruise boat and the other by coach. The most popular trip is aboard the *Oriental Queen*, managed by the Oriental Hotel. This tour may be booked through most travel agents or tour desks, or at the desk in the Oriental Hotel.

Highlights for First-time Visitors

Damnoen Saduak floating market (*see* Tour 3)

Ferry ride on the Chao Phraya River (*see* Tour 5)

Grand Palace and Wat Phra Keo (Temple of the Emerald Buddha) (*see* Tour 1)

Jim Thompson's House (*see* Tour 2)

National Museum (*see* Tour 2)

Wat Po (Temple of the Reclining Buddha) (*see* Tour 1)

Thai dance performance (*see* Tour 2)

Wat Traimitr (Temple of the Golden Buddha) (*see* Tour 1)

Orientation

Because confusion is part of Bangkok's fascination, learning your way around is a challenge. It may help to think of Bangkok as a triangle lying on its side with the base abutting the *S* curve of the Chao Phraya and the apex ending down Sukhumvit Road, somewhere around Soi 40 (*see* map).

Beginning at the apex of this conceptual triangle is Sukhumvit, once a residential neighborhood. In the last decade it has developed into a district of hotels, shops, nightclubs, and restaurants while retaining some of its warm, residential atmosphere. Westward, toward the Chao Phraya, you come to spacious foreign embassy compounds, offices of large corporations, and modern international hotels. Slightly farther west, stores, offices, and more hotels are more closely packed. Now you reach the older sections of Bangkok. On the southern flank is Silom Road, a shopping and financial district. Parallel to Silom Road is Suriwongse Road with more hotels, and between the two is the entertainment district of Patpong. Continue farther, and you reach two of the leading hotels on the riverbank: the Oriental and the Shangri-La.

Traveling down Rama I Road in the center of the triangle, pass the Siam Square shopping area and the National Stadium. Continue in the direction of the Hualamphong railway station. Between Hualamphong and the river is Chinatown, a maze of streets with restaurants, goldsmiths, and small warehouses and repair shops.

In the northern part of the triangle, moving westward, you pass through various markets before reaching Thai goverment buildings, the Victory Monument, Chitlada Palace, the Dusit Zoo, the National Assembly, the National Library, and, finally, the river. Slightly to the south of this route are the Democracy Monument, the Grand Palace, and the Temple of the Emerald Buddha.

Knowing your exact destination, its direction, and approximate distance are important in negotiating taxi fares and planning your itinerary. Crossing and recrossing the city is time-consuming—many hours can be spent in frustrating traffic jams.

Numbers in the margin correspond with points of interest on the Bangkok map.

Tour 1: The River Tour

❶ Start the tour with breakfast on the terrace of the **Oriental Hotel,** overlooking the Chao Phraya River. The hotel itself is a Bangkok institution. To the side of the Oriental's entrance, a small lane leads to the river and a landing stage for the river buses that ply it. Take the river bus upstream to the Grand Palace and Wat Phra Keo.

❷ The **Grand Palace** is Bangkok's major landmark. This is where Bangkok's founder, King Rama I, built his palace and walled city in 1782. Subsequent Chakri monarchs enlarged the walled city, though today the buildings are used only for state occasions and royal ceremonies. The compound—but not all of the buildings—is open to visitors.

The official residence of the king—he actually lives elsewhere, at Chitlada Palace in Bangkok—is the Chakri Maha Prasart palace. Occasionally its state function rooms are open to visitors, but most of the time only the exterior can be viewed. To the right of Chakri Maha Prasart is the Dusit Maha Prasart, a classic example of Thai royal palace architecture.

To the left of the palace is the Amarin Vinichai Hall, the original audience hall built by King Rama I and now used for the presentation of ambassadors' credentials. Note the glittering gold throne.

Visit this compound first, because none of these buildings excites such awe as the adjoining royal chapel, the most sacred temple in the kingdom, the **Temple of the Emerald Buddha** (Wat Phra Keo). No other wat in Thailand is so ornate and so embellished with murals, statues, and glittering gold. For many, it is overly decorated, and as your wat experience grows, you may decide that you prefer the simplicity of the lesser known wats, but you'll never quite get over the elaborate richness of Wat Phra Keo.

As you enter the compound, take note of a number of 6-m- (20-ft-) tall helmeted and tile-encrusted statues in traditional Thai battle attire standing guard and surveying the precincts. They set the scene—mystical, majestic, and awesome. Turn right as you enter and notice along the inner walls the lively murals (recently restored), depicting the whole *Ramayana* (*Ramakien* in Thai) epic.

The main chapel, with its gilded, glittering three-tiered roof, dazzles the senses. Royal griffins stand guard outside, and shining gold stupas in the court establish serenity with their perfect symmetry. Inside sits the Emerald Buddha.

Carved from one piece of jade, the ¾-m- (31-in-) high figure is one of the most venerated images of the Lord Buddha. No one knows its origin but, in 1464, history records it in Chiang Rai, in northeast Thailand. From there it traveled first to Chiang Mai, then to Lamphun, and finally back to Chiang Mai, where the Laotians stole it and took it home with them. Eventually, the Thais sent an army into Laos to secure it. The statue reached its final resting place when King Rama I built the chapel. The statue is high above the altar and visitors can see it only from afar.

Walk to the back of the royal chapel and you'll find a scale model of Angkor Wat. As Angkor Wat, in Kampuchea, is difficult to reach nowadays, this is a chance to sense the vastness of the old Khmer capital. *Admission charge. Open daily 8:30–11:30 and 1–3:30*

3 When you leave the Grand Palace, walk south to the oldest and largest temple in Bangkok, the **Temple of the Reclining Buddha** (Wat Po, or Wat Phya Jetuphon). Much is made of the size of this statue—the largest in the country, measuring 46 m (151 ft) in length. Especially noteworthy are his 3-m- (10-ft-) long feet, inlaid with mother-of-pearl designs depicting the 108 auspicious signs of the Lord Buddha.

Walk beyond the chapel containing the Reclining Buddha and enter Bangkok's oldest open university. A hundred years before Bangkok was established as the capital city, a monastery was founded to teach classical Thai medicine. The school still gives instruction in the natural methods of healing. Around the walls are marble plaques inscribed with formulas for herbal cures, and stone sculptures squat in various postures demonstrating techniques for relieving muscle pain.

Don't be perturbed by the sculpted figures that good-naturedly poke fun at farangs. Referred to as Chinese rock sculptures, they are gangling 3.6-m.- (12-ft-) high figures, the most evil of demons, which scare away all other evil spirits. With their top hats, they look farcically Western. In fact, they were modeled after the Europeans who plundered China during the Opium Wars.

These tall statues guard the entrance to the northeastern quarter of the monastery and a very pleasant three-tier temple. Inside are 394 seated Buddhas. Usually, a monk sits cross-legged at one side of the altar, making himself available to answer your questions (you will need to speak Thai or have a translator). On the walls bas relief plaques salvaged from Ayutthaya depict stories from the *Ramayana*. Around this temple area are four tall chedis, decorated with brightly colored procelain, each representing one of the first four kings of the Chakri (present) dynasty. *Admission charge. Open daily 7–5.*

Time Out The monks of Wat Po still practice ancient cures and have become famous for their massage technique. The massage lasts for one hour, growing more and more pleasurable as you adjust

Bangkok

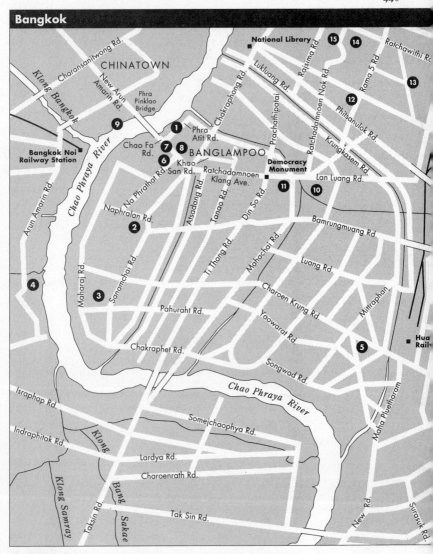

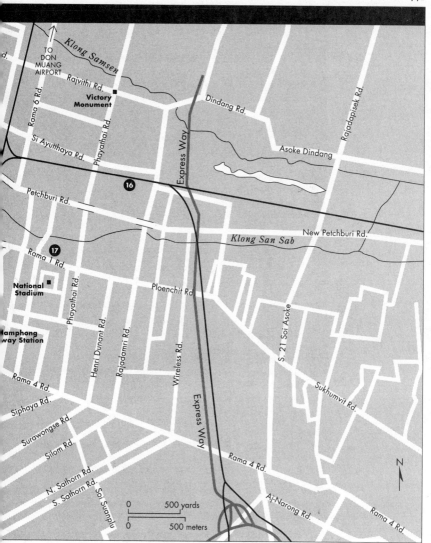

TO DON MUANG AIRPORT

Klong Samsen

Rajvithi Rd.

Rama 6 Rd.

Victory Monument

Phayathai Rd.

Dindang Rd.

Asoke Dindang

Rajadapisek Rd.

Si Ayutthaya Rd.

16

Petchburi Rd.

Express Way

New Petchburi Rd.

Klong San Sab

17

Rama 1 Rd.

National Stadium

Phayathai Rd.

Ploenchit Rd.

S. 21 Soi Asoke

lamphong way Station

Henri Dunant Rd.

Rajadamri Rd.

Wireless Rd.

Rama 4 Rd.

Siphaya Rd.

Surawongse Rd.

Silom Rd.

Express Way

Rama 4 Rd.

Sukhumvit Rd.

N. Sathorn Rd.

S. Sathorn Rd.

Soi Suanplu

Aj-Narong Rd.

Rama 4 Rd.

N

0   500 yards

0   500 meters

to the technique. Masseurs are available 7–5. Cost: B150. When you're ready for refreshment, there is a pleasant snack bar in the northeastern compound, where the fare includes delicious chilled coconut milk.

From Wat Po, if you walk halfway back to the Grand Palace and then cut down to the river past a small market, you'll reach the jetty for the ferry to cross over the Chao Phraya to **Wat Arun** on the western bank of the river.

Wat Arun means "Temple of the Dawn," and at sunrise, it is inspiring. It is still marvelous toward dusk, however, when the setting sun casts its amber tones. Within the square courtyard, the temple's architecture is symmetrical, containing five Khmer-style prangs (stupas). The central prang, towering 86 m (282 ft), is surrounded by its four attendant prangs in the corners. All of the prangs are covered in mosaics of broken Chinese porcelain. The surrounding grounds are a peaceful haven in which to relax and watch the sun go down. The more energetic climb the steep steps of the central prang for the view over the Chao Phraya River. *Admission charge. Open 8–5:30.*

Wat Arun has a small park around it, and, by the river, is a pleasant spot in which to linger. However, if time is short, cross back to the eastern shore and wander inland through Chinatown. You may want to take a tuk-tuk as far as Pahuraht Road.

With Bangkok's first tall buildings, **Chinatown** used to be the prosperous downtown neighborhood, but, as Bangkok has grown, new, taller office buildings have sprung up to the east, and Chinatown, losing some of its bustle and excitement, has become less the hub of activity. Red lanterns and Chinese signs still abound, and numerous Chinese restaurants line the streets. Pahuraht Road is full of textile shops, with nearly as many Indian dealers here as Chinese. Down Pahuraht Road, and a zigzag to the left, is Yaowarat Road, Chinatown's main thoroughfare, crowded with numerous gold and jewelry shops. Between Yaowarat and Charoen Krung roads is the so-called Thieves Market (Nakorn Kasem), an area of small streets with old wood houses, where you can buy all sorts of items ranging from hardware to porcelains. Bargains are hard to find nowadays; nevertheless, these small cluttered streets are fascinating to walk through and, who knows, a porcelain vase may take your fancy. Bargain hard!

South along Yaowarat Road is Charoen Krung (New Road). On the opposite corner is **Wat Traimitr** (Temple of the Golden Buddha). The main temple has little architectural merit, but off to the side, next to the money changing wagon, is a small chapel. Inside is the world's largest solid gold Buddha image, cast about nine centuries ago. Weighing 5½ tons and standing 3 m (10 ft) high, the statue gleams with such a richness and purity that even the most jaded are inspired by its strength and power. Sculpted in Sukhothai style, the statue is believed to have been brought first to Ayutthaya. When the Burmese were about to sack the city, the statue was covered in plaster. Two centuries later, the plaster still covering the image, it was regarded as just another Buddhist statue. Then, when it was being moved to a new temple in Bangkok, it slipped from the crane. Leaving the statue in the mud, the workmen called it a day. During the night, a temple monk dreamed that the statue was divinely inspired. First thing in the morning he went to see the Buddha image. Through a crack in the plaster, he saw the glint of yellow. Opening the plaster farther, he discovered that the statue was pure gold. *Admission charge. Open daily 8:30–5.*

Tour 2: Temples, Museums and Villas

Unless you can get an early start to visit some temples and beat the heat, the **National Museum** should be your first stop. Try to make it on a Tuesday, Wednesday, or Thursday, when free, guided, 90-minute tours in English start at 9:30 AM. Volunteers who specialize in different aspects of Thai art explain the complexities of Thai culture and give visitors a general orientation to the vast collection of treasures in the museum. The tours meet at the entrance to the main building, which was originally built in 1783 as a palace for surrogate kings (a position abolished in 1874). The two new wings were added in 1966.

This extensive museum has one of the world's best collections of Southeast Asian art in general, and Buddhist and Thai art in particular. As a result it offers the best opportunity to trace Thailand's long history, beginning with ceramic utensils and bronzeware from the Ban Chiang civilization, thought to have existed 5,000 to 6,000 years ago. Before entering the Kingdom of Thailand's 700-year history and most of the museum's exhibits, continue to the bronze sculptures dating to the 1,000-year-old Dvaravati and Khmer empires. The majority of the great masterpieces of art created during the Sukhothai and Ayutthaya periods, as well as those works from the northern provinces, have found their way into the Bangkok National Museum. *Admission charge. Open Tues.–Thurs. and weekends 9–noon and 1–4.*

❼ Next door is the **National Theatre,** where classical Thai dance and drama performances are held (*see* The Arts, below).

❽ Opposite is the **National Art Gallery,** with exhibits, both modern and traditional, by Thai artists. *Chao Fa Rd., tel. 02/281–2224. Admission charge. Open Tues.–Thurs. and weekends 9–noon and 1–4.*

❾ Walk or take a tuk-tuk across the Phra Pinklao Bridge to the dockyard, where the royal **ceremonial barges** are berthed. The ornately carved barges, crafted in the early part of this century, take the form of famous mythical creatures featured in the *Ramayana.* The most impressive is the red-and-gold royal flag barge, *Suphannahongse* (Golden Swan), used by the king on (very) special occasions. *Admission charge. Open Tues.–Thurs. and weekends 9–noon and 1–4.*

❿ Back across river is **Wat Sakret.** It's too far to walk, so take a tuk-tuk for B20. You'll first pass the tall and imposing Democracy monument, and, at the next main intersection, right across the street will be Wat Sakret.

Wat Sakret (the Temple of the Golden Mount) is a notable landmark of the old city and was, for a long time, the highest building around. King Rama III started the building of this mound and temple, which were completed by Rama V. To reach the gold-covered chedi, you must make an exhausting climb up 318 steps winding around the mound. Don't even attempt it on a hot day, but on a cool, clear day, the view over Bangkok from the top is worth the effort. Every November, the temple compound is the site of Bangkok's largest temple fair, with food stalls, stage shows, and merrymaking. *Admission charge. Open daily 8–5.*

⑪ Across from Wat Sakret is **Wat Rachanada,** built to resemble the mythical castle of the gods. According to legend, a wealthy and pious man built a fabulous castle, Loha Prasat, following the design laid down in Hindu mythology for the disciples of the Lord Buddha. Wat Rachanada, built in metal, is meant to duplicate that castle and is the only one of its kind remaining. In its precincts are stalls selling amulets that protect the wearer from misfortune—usually of the physical kind, though love amulets and charms are also sold. They tend to be rather expensive, but that's the price of good fortune. *Admission charge. Open daily 8–6.*

A short tuk-tuk ride away—no more than B20—is one of

⑫ Bangkok's most photographed temples, the **Marble Temple** (Wat Benjamabopit), built in 1899. Go north from Wat Rachanada, up Ratchadamnoen Nok Road and past the Tourist Authority of Thailand office, toward the equestrian statue of King Chulalongkorn. Just before the statue is Si Ayutthaya Road. Take a right, and Wat Benjamabopit will be on your right.

Wat Benjamabopit is more than a splendid temple. It is a place of learning that appeals to Buddhist monks with intellectual yearnings. It was here that Thailand's present king came to spend his days as a monk before his coronation. *Admission charge. Open daily 7–5.*

Leaving Wat Benjamabopit, you can take another short tuk-tuk ride to Vimarnmek Palace. Ask the driver to go there by

⑬ way of Rama V Road past **Chitlada Palace,** one of the king's residences. The palace will be on the right. On the left will be the

⑭ **Dusit Zoo,** a place to visit perhaps when you are exhausted by Bangkok's traffic and want to rest in a pleasant expanse of greenery.

⑮ **Vimarnmek Palace** is the largest teak structure in the world. This four-story palace was built by King Rama V, grandfather of the present king, as a suburban palace. Now, with the capital's growth, it's in the center of administrative Bangkok, right next door to the entrance of the National Assembly building.

The Vimarnmek Palace fits its name, "Castle in the Clouds." Its extraordinarily light and delicate appearance is enhanced by the adjacent reflecting pond. King Rama's fascination with Western architecture shows in the palace's Victorian style, but the building retains an unmistakable Thai delicacy. Most of the furniture was either purchased in the West or given as gifts by European monarchs. Some of the exhibits by late 19th-century craftsmen are exquisite—porcelain, handcrafted furniture, and crystal—and some have more novelty value, such as the first typewriter to have been brought to Thailand. *Admission charge. Open daily 9:30–4.*

⑯ By way of contrast with Vimarnmek Palace, visit the **Suan Pakkard Palace** next. You'll need a taxi or a tuk-tuk; it's a good B30 ride due east down Ayutthaya Road. Five traditional Thai houses, built high on teak columns, adorn the perfectly kept grounds, which include undulating lawns, shimmering lotus pools, and lush shrubbery. The center of attraction, the Lacquer Pavilion, is at the back of the garden. Inside it is gold-covered paneling with scenes from the life of Buddha. On display in the houses are porcelain, Khmer stone heads, old paintings, and statues of Buddha. The serene atmosphere of the houses and grounds makes Suan Pakkard one of the most relaxing places in which to absorb Thai culture. *Admission charge. Open Mon.–Sat. 9–4.*

17 Another compound of traditional Thai architecture and Southeast Asian furnishings—**Jim Thompson's House**—is fairly close by, no more than a B30 tuk-tuk ride. Go south on Phayathai Road and then west (right) on Rama I. Entrance to the compound of teak houses and grounds with lush tropical plants is down Soi Kasemsong, an unprepossessing alley off Rama I.

American Jim Thompson was once an architect in New York; he joined the OSS in World War II and went to Asia. After the war, he stayed in Thailand and took it upon himself to revitalize the silk industry, which had virtually become extinct. His project and product met with tremendous success. That, in itself, would have made Thompson into a legend, but, in 1967, he went to the Malaysian Cameron Highlands for a quiet holiday and was never heard from again.

Aside from reestablishing the Thai silk industry, Thompson also left us his house. Using parts of old up-country houses, some as old as 150 years, he constructed a compound of six Thai houses, three of which are exactly the same as their originals, including all the details of the interior layout. With true appreciation of Southeast Asian art, Thompson then set out to collect what are now priceless works of art to furnish his home. *Admission charge. Open Mon.–Sat. 9–5.*

Both of the tours above are long, full-day ventures. Each would be managed more comfortably in two days, allowing time to discover your own Bangkok. Moreover, these tours have left out at least 290 other Buddhist temples!

Tour 3: Damnoen Saduak and Nakhon Pathom

Do not bother visiting the floating market in Bangkok. It was a real market 20 years ago, when many vendors sold their wares and vegetables from boats. Since then, it has wilted down to one or two boats that, it has been suggested, are paid by the tour operators to paddle around. Instead, head for Damnoen Saduak, 100 km (62 mi) southwest of Bangkok in the province of Rajburi.

Damnoen Saduak is a morning's excursion from Bangkok. In this excursion, Nakhon Pathom and Kanchanaburi have been included to make a day's excursion—longer if you decide to cover extensively the natural beauty of Kanchanaburi province.

Getting There Most hotels can arrange for you to be collected, either by a regular tour coach or by private car/taxi. It is cheaper if you negotiate with a car firm outside your hotel. Speak to the concierge on the "quiet" and, nine times out of 10, he will have a good resource. A private car or taxi is far superior to a tour bus because you can reach the market by 9 AM, before the tours. Then, by the time the hordes of tourists arrive, you can be away to explore other places. If there are two of you and you have negotiated well with your driver, the cost will be no more than the tour bus. For a round-trip to Damnoen Saduak, the rate could be as low as B600. If you keep the car and combine Nakhon Pathom and Kanchanaburi to make a long day's excursion, the rate could be B1,000.

Public buses, both air-conditioned and non-air-conditioned, leave from the Southern Bus Terminal on Charan Sanitwong Road for Damnoen Saduak every 20 minutes from 6 AM onward. The fare on an air-conditioned bus is B50; B30 for a non-air-conditioned one. From the Damnoen Saduak bus station, walk for a mile on the passage on the right-hand side along the canal, or take a taxi boat at the pier to the nearby Floating Market.

Exploring
Damnoen Saduak

Once at Damnoen Saduak, hire a sampan for about B300—outrageous, but enough tourists pay the price so that you cannot get it down much lower. Then, for an hour or more, lazily travel the canal.

If you think Bangkok traffic is bad, witness true congestion and gridlock from a *ruilla pai* (sampan) in the middle of a mess of boats, each trying to shove its way along the klong. Farmers' wives dressed in baggy pants, long-tailed shirts, and straw hats sell produce from their sampans, paddling back and forth, or rather pushing and barging their way through the congestion. Other women are busy cooking tasty treats on little stoves and paddling to the rescue of any voracious appetite in another boat or on the shore. It's an authentic and colorful slice of Thai life.

For refreshment, a wharf alongside the klong has tables and chairs. Buy your drinks from the stall and your food from any one of the ruilla pai. At about 11 AM, you will be ready to leave Damnoen Saduak.

En route to Kanchanaburi (or even if you are returning to Bangkok) is the city of Nakhon Pathom, about 30 minutes from Damnoen Saduak.

Nakhon Pathom

Nakhon Pathom is reputed to be Thailand's oldest city. Its main attraction is **Phra Pathom Chedi,** the tallest Buddhist monument in the world. It was erected in the 6th century, but today one sees a larger chedi, built in 1860 to encase the ruins of the old. It stands at 127 m (417 ft), a few meters (or yards) higher than the Shwe Dagon Chedi of Burma. Established here about 1,000 years ago, Phra Pathom Chedi also marks the first center of Buddhist learning on the Thai peninsula. The terraces around the temple complex are full of fascinating statuary, including a Dvaravati-style Buddha seated in a chair, and the museum contains some Dvaravati (6th–11th century) sculpture. Occasionally classical Thai dances are performed in front of the temple, and during Loi Krathong festival, bazaars and a fair are set up in the adjacent park. *Museum open Wed.–Sun. 9–noon and 1–4.*

Sanam Chan Palace, built during the reign of King Rama VI, stands in a pleasant park. The palace is not open to the public but the park around it is a lovely place for relaxation between Damnoen Saduak and Bangkok.

Tour 4: Kanchanaburi

The movie *The Bridge over the River Kwai* from Pierre Boulle's novel gave the area of Kanchanaburi a certain fame—or, more accurately, the Japanese gave the area the dubious distinction of being the site of the Death Railway. Even without this publicity, Kanchanaburi province would attract tourists. Lush tropical vegetation and rivers with waterfalls and gorges make it one of the most beautiful national parks in Thailand.

Getting There You can visit Kanchanaburi on the same excursion as Damnoen Saduak or come straight from Bangkok.

By Train From Bangkok Noi Thonburi Station (tel. 02/411–3102) the train for Kanchanaburi leaves at 8 AM and 1:55 PM. The State Railway of Thailand also offers a special excursion train on Saturday, Sunday, and holidays that leaves Hualamphong Railway Terminal at 6:15 AM and returns at 7:30 PM. On the program are stops at Nakhon Pathom, the River Kwai Bridge, and Nam-Tok, from where minibuses are used to continue on to Khao Phang Waterfall. Tickets for this full-day, round-trip outing may be purchased at Bangkok Railway Station (tel. 02/223–7010), and advance booking is recommended. Cost: B75 for adults, B40 for children.

By Bus Air-conditioned and non-air-conditioned buses leave the Southern Transportation Bus Station, Charansanitwong Road, near Tha Phra intersection (tel. 02/411–0511 or 02/411–4978) every half hour. The journey takes about 2½ hours.

Tourist Information The TAT office (Saeng Chuto Rd., Kanchanaburi, tel. 034/511–200) has good maps and brochures and has a knowledgeable and helpful staff. If you wish to take a minibus tour, daily guide services are available from B.T. Travel (Saeng Chuto Rd., KB, tel. 034/511–967) next door to the TAT.

Exploring One may forgive, but one cannot forget the inhumanity that caused the death, between 1942 and 1945, of more than 16,000 Allied prisoners of war and 49,000 impressed Asian laborers. Forced by the Japanese under abysmal conditions to build a railway through the jungle from Thailand into Burma, one person died for every sleeper of the track.

A reconstruction of the now famous bridge (it was successfully bombed by the Allies toward the end of the war) stands just north of the small, sleepy town of **Kanchanaburi**. Nearby are two Allied war cemeteries with the remains of 8,732 POWs. To reach the bridge, go through town on Saeng Chuto Road, the main street. **Kanchanaburi War Cemetery** is on the left. In row upon row of neatly laid out graves rest 6,982 American, Australian, British, and Dutch prisoners of war. A commemorative service is held every April 25. After the cemetery, take the next road to the left and make a right at the *T* junction. Notice the Japanese War Memorial Shrine there. Be sure to read the plaque—it has an English translation. Just up the street from the memorial, the road opens out to a plaza—the bridge is on the left.

Upriver, on the road leading back to town, is the **JEATH War Museum** (JEATH stands for Japan, England, America, Australia, Thailand, and Holland). Founded by a monk from the adjoining temple, the museum consists of a reconstructed bamboo hut, the type used to house the POWs, and a collection of utensils, railway spikes, clothing, aerial photographs, newspaper clippings, and illustrations designed to show the atrocities inflicted on the POWs by the Japanese. *Admission charge. Open daily 8–5.*

Another Allied burial ground, the **Chong-Kai War Cemetery**, lies across the river. To get there, take the ferry from the pier below the park off Patana Road.

Kanchanaburi province is much more than the Death Railway. It is also spectacular countryside. The **Erawan Waterfall,** perhaps the most photographed waterfall in Thailand, is worth the trip. Located in the beautifully forested Khao Salop National Park, the falls are at their most enjoyable in early autumn. To reach the falls, located 65 km (40 mi) from Kanchanaburi on the Kanchanaburi-Srisawat Highway, either take a tour bus from Kanchanaburi or use the public bus.

Tour 5: Ayutthaya and Bang Pa-In

Toward the end of the 16th century, Europeans described Ayutthaya with its 1,700 temples and 4,000 golden images of Buddha as more beautiful than any capital in Europe. Certainly, the Ayutthaya period was also Thailand's most glorious.

Ayutthaya never recovered from the Burmese invasion in 1767. Today it is a small provincial town with partially restored ruins, where, with imagination, the visitor may re-create some of the magnificent architecture and fabulous statuary that were the glory of Ayutthaya.

Getting There Ayutthaya is 72 km (45 mi) north of Bangkok and may be visited either as an excursion from Bangkok or en route between Bangkok and Thailand's northern provinces. As midday can be very hot, it is best to get an early start in order to visit as many sights as possible before 1 PM. Then take a long lunch and, if you have time, continue sightseeing in the late afternoon and catch the sunset before you leave.

By Train Between 4:30 AM and late evening, trains depart frequently from Bangkok's Hualamphong station, arriving in Ayutthaya 80 minutes later. Halfway between the two cities (in time, not distance) is Don Muang Airport. Many travelers on their way south from Chiang Mai will stop at Ayutthaya and then continue by train only as far as the airport, from which they will fly on to their next destination instead of going all the way into Bangkok.

By Bus Buses leave Bangkok's Northern Terminal on Phaholyothin Road (tel. 02/271–0101) every 30 minutes between 6 AM and 7 PM.

By Boat The Oriental Hotel organizes a daily boat/bus excursion to Ayutthaya, with lunch served on the boat. Travelers may go upriver by boat and return by coach, or vice versa. Returning by boat with the current is about three hours faster. The tour guide hustles you past a few of the sights, but because of the length of the river trip, there is not enough time to see many of the attractions, including the museum. The trip is overpriced and the service leaves a lot to be desired. All travel agencies can make bookings. *Oriental Hotel, Oriental Lane, Charoen Krung Rd., tel. 02/236–0400. Cost: B740, including a buffet lunch. Departure: 8 AM.*

Getting Around For a three-hour tour of the sights, tuk-tuks can be hired within Ayutthaya for approximately B100, or get a four-wheel samlor for about B300. You may also want an English-speaking guide, and there are plenty available; they usually hang around the station.

Exploring Ayutthaya Ayutthaya is situated within a large loop of the Chao Phraya River, where it meets the Nam Pa Sak and Lopburi rivers. To completely encircle their capital by water, the Thais dug a canal along the northern perimeter, linking the Chao Phraya to the Lopburi. Although the new provincial town of Ayutthaya, including the railway station, is on the east bank of the Nam Pa Sak, most of Ayutthaya's ancient glory is on the island. An exception is Wat Yai Chai Mongkol, about a B20 tuk-tuk ride southeast of the railway station and south of Bangkok Road.

Wat Yai Chai Mongkol was built in 1357 by King U-Thong for meditation. After King Naresuan defeated the Burmese by killing the Burmese Crown Prince in single-handed combat on elephants in 1582, he enlarged the temple. The complex was totally restored in 1982 and, with the contemporary images of Buddha lining the courtyard and the neatly groomed grounds, looks a little as if it had been constructed for tourists. A souvenir shop, a beverage stand, and morning arrivals of tour buses from Bangkok add to the impression. *Admission charge. Open daily 8–5.*

The road continues to **Wat Phanan Choeng,** a small temple on the banks of the Lopburi just before it enters the Chao Phraya River. The temple predates the time when Ayutthaya became the Thai capital. In 1324 one of the U-Thong kings was to marry a daughter of the Chinese emperor. He had come to this spot on the river and, instead of entering the city with his fiancée, arranged an escort for her. Thinking she had been deserted, she was confused and, in despair, threw herself into the river and drowned. The king tried to atone for his thoughtlessness by building the temple. The story has great appeal to Thai Chinese; you'll see many a romantic pilgrimage here. *Admission charge. Open daily 8–6.*

Returning to the main road, go left, over the bridge, and cross onto the island. Continue on Rojana Road for about a mile to the **Chao Phraya National Museum.** It can be kept for later and visited only if you have time, as Ayutthaya's more important historical masterpieces are in Bangkok's National Museum. If you do visit the museum, try to find a guide who can highlight the evolution of Ayutthaya art over four centuries. *Admission charge. Open Wed.–Sun. 9–noon and 1–4.*

Just beyond the Chao Phraya National Museum, turn right onto Si Samphet Road. Pass the city hall on the left and continue for about half a mile to **Wat Phra Si Samphet,** on the left. It is easy to recognize by the huge parking lot. The shining white marble temple nearby not only looks modern but is. Built three decades ago (1956), **Viharn Phra Mongkol Bopitr** houses one of Thailand's largest bronze images of Buddha, one of the few that escaped the destruction wrought by the Burmese.

Wat Phra Si Samphet was the largest in Ayutthaya and the temple of the royal family. Built in the 14th century, it lost its 15-m- (50-ft-) high Buddha, Phra Si Samphet, to the Burmese, who melted it down for its gold in 1767—170 kg (374 lb) worth. The chedis, restored in 1956, survived to become the best examples of Ayutthaya architecture. Enshrining the ashes of Ayutthaya kings, they stand like eternal memories of a golden age. *Open daily 8–5.*

Before you leave this area, visit some of the stalls in the market behind those selling souvenirs to see a marvelously colorful array of vegetables, fruits, and foods. Then, after wandering around, stop at the café at the Viharn end of the market for refreshment—try the chilled coconut in its shell.

From the large coach park, Naresuan Road crosses Si Samphet Road and continues past a small lake to nearby **Wat Phra Mahathat** on the corner of Chee Kun Road.

Continue down Naresuan Road, now called Chao Phnom Road, to the Mae Nam Po Sak River. Here, go either left, up U-Thong Road to **Chandra Kasem Palace,** or right, down to the bridge to the mainland. The reconstructed 17th-century palace is used as Ayutthaya's second national museum. For instant energy, take a right on U-Thong Road. Just before and after the bridge over the Mae Nam Po Sak are two floating restaurants. If you have a train to catch try **Tevaraj,** a good Thai restaurant near the railway station, for a tasty freshwater lobster dish.

The numerous ruins in and around Ayutthaya give it a melancholy charm, especially at sunset, when the city's modern grime is no longer visible.

About 5 km (3 mi) to the north of Ayutthaya is the **Elephant Kraal,** the only intact royal kraal remaining in the country. A stockade built from massive teak logs, it was formerly used to pick prime elephants out of a wild herd to be trained for martial service.

The more popular attraction out of Ayutthaya is Bang Pa-In, 20 km (12 mi) to the south. Minibuses leave Chao Prom Market in Ayutthaya regularly starting from 6:30 AM. (Fare: B10.) The trip takes 50 minutes. Boats also make the 40-minute run back and forth on the river between Ayutthaya and Bang Pa-In. (Fare: B150.) From Bangkok, there is regular train service to Bang Pa-In railway station, from which a minibus runs to the palace. (Fare: B2.)

Exploring Bang Pa-In
On the bank of the Mae Nam Pa Suk, 70 km (43 mi) from Bangkok, **Bang Pa-In Summer Palace** is a popular attraction in Ayutthaya. King Prusat Thong (1630–55) originally built a palace here that was used by the Ayutthaya kings until the Burmese invasion. Neglected for 80 years, it was rebuilt during the reign of Rama IV (1851–68) and became the favored summer palace of King Chulalongkorn (Rama V, 1868–1910). It also has a sad tale. Delayed in Bangkok, the king had sent his wife on ahead by boat. The boat capsized and she drowned. She could easily have been saved, but the body of a royal personage was sacrosanct and could never be touched by a commoner, on pain of death. King Chulalongkorn could never forgive himself. In her memory, he built a touching pavilion. Be sure to read the inscription engraved in the memorial—it is in Thai, but an English translation is given.

You may want to take the cable car across the river to the unique wat south of the palace grounds. In his fascination with Western architecture, King Chulalongkorn had this Buddhist temple, **Wat Nivet Thamaprawat,** built in Gothic style. It looks as much like a Christian church as a wat, complete with belfry and stained-glass windows. *Admission charge to Bang Pa-In Palace. Open 8–3; closed Mon. and Fri.*

The palace is a popular weekend jaunt for Thais. A tour boat departs from Bangkok's Maharat Pier at 8:30 AM and travels up the Chao Phraya River to Bang Pa-In in time for lunch, returns downriver to the Bang Sai Folk Arts and Craft Centre, and then back to Bangkok by 5:30. The tour is operated by the Chao Phraya Express Boat Co. (2/58 Aroon-Amarin Rd., Maharat Pier, Bangkok, tel. 02/222–5330).

Bang Sai Folk Arts and Craft Centre is 24 km (15 mi) south of Bang Pa-In on the Chao Phraya River. The center was set up by the queen in 1976 to equip families with handicraft skills. The products are sold throughout Thailand at the Chirlada handicraft shops. The park is a pleasant place for a picnic, and very crowded on weekends with Thai families. It also has a small restaurant. The handicrafts on sale include fern vine basketry, wood carvings, dyed silks, and handmade dolls.

Tour 6: Nearby Beach Resorts

Pattaya, 147 km (91 mi; a three- to four-hour drive by hotel limousine, taxi, or public bus) southeast of Bangkok, is a booming beach resort for Thais and tourists alike. It offers more activities than any other Thai resort, from deep-sea fishing to windsurfing, to golf, to visiting an elephant kraal, and is often used as a base or as a way stop for trips farther south. The town has something tacky for everyone, but most obviously flaunted are the bars and nightclubs catering to the foreign male. Raw sewage flows into the bay, virtually guaranteeing a case of hepatitis for anyone foolish enough to swim in the once-clear waters.

The clear waters and sea life of the coral reefs around Pattaya's offshore islands are ideal for snorkeling and scuba diving, and the beaches are free of crowds. These islands may all be reached in approximately one hour by converted fishing trawlers. **Ko Larn** is the nearest and most popular. Farther offshore, and without facilities, so take along your own lunch, are **Ko Rin** and **Ko Phai.**

Beaches are the reason to go to **Ko Samet.** The other name for Ko Samet is Ko Kaeo Phitsadan (Sand Like Crushed Crystal) and, indeed, its fine sand is in much demand by glassmakers.

Farther away is the idyllic island of **Ko Samui,** which is rapidly developing as the new choice resort. To reach there you can either take a train (12 hours) or fly 40 minutes to Surat Thani and then take a short ferry ride to the island. Ko Samui has numerous beaches with guest houses and a few international resort hotels, of which the Imperial is the best. North of Ko Samui is a cluster of small islands, the sparkling Angthong Marine National Park.

Hua Hin and **Cha' Am** are more refined alternatives to the beach resort of Pattaya and considerably less crowded with package-tour vacationers. Located on the western shore of the Gulf of Siam about 100 km (60 mi) (a three-hour drive by hotel limousine, public bus, or train) from Bangkok, the area was especially popular in the 1920s when King Rama VI built his summer palace (Klai Kangwon) in Hua Hin. The small, sleepy town of Hua Hin has, aside from the beach and fishing pier, a number of shops, restaurants, and cafés to explore in the evening.

Off the Beaten Track

A relaxing way to see Bangkok is to hire a motorboat for an hour or two and explore the small canals (klongs). The cost is about B250, and a boat can seat four easily.

Alternatively, you can travel on the Chao Phraya river on the ferry boats. One good trip past waterside temples, Thai-style houses, the Royal Barge Museum, and Khoo Wiang Floating Market starts at the Chang Pier near the Grand Palace and travels along Klong Bang Khoo Wiang and Klong Bang Yai. Boats leave every 20 minutes between 6:15 AM and 8 PM and cost B10.

Stroll around the **Banglampoo** section of Bangkok, the area where the backpackers gravitate. The main thoroughfare, Ko-Sahn Road, is full of cafés, second-hand book stalls, and inexpensive shops. In the evening, the streets are full of stalls and food stands serving the needs of young Westerners on their grand around-the-world tour.

Visit the **Pratu Nam night market** at the junction of Phetchaburi and Rajprarop roads. Locals come here for noodles and other tasty dishes after an evening out at the cinema. The market is a good place to meet Thais and eat tasty, inexpensive Thai and Chinese food.

Shopping

Bangkok, with its range of goods produced in all regions of the country and offered at competitive prices, is a shopper's paradise.

Shopping Districts The main shopping areas are along Silom Road and at the Rama IV end of Suriwongse for jewelry, crafts and silk; along Sukhumvit Road for leather goods; along Yaowarat in Chinatown for gold; and along Silom Road, Oriental Lane, and Charoen Krung Road for antiques. The Oriental Plaza (across from the Oriental Hotel) and the River City Shopping Centre next to the Sheraton Orchid Hotel have shops with collector-quality goods ranging from antiques to fashion.

Street Markets Bangkok's largest is the **Weekend Market,** where virtually everything is offered for sale. When it was located near Wat Phra Keo, it had the excitement of a lively bazaar, but at its new quarters at Chaturhak Park it lacks an exotic character. While there is still a great deal of activity from Saturday morning until closing on Sunday evening, the market is more like an open-air department store, selling a range of goods, most of them mass-produced items for local consumption. If you are looking for inexpensive chinaware or a tough pair of boots, this market will suit your needs. *Open weekends 9–9.*

The other all-purpose market is **Pratunam Market** along Ratchaprarop Road. This is a beehive of activity on and off the sidewalk. It is best for deeply discounted clothing. *Open daily 9–8.*

Another lively market for goods that are cheap but inflated for the tourist is in **Patpong.** Along Silom Road stalls are set up in the afternoon and evening to sell tourists everything from "Rolex" watches to leather belts and knockoff designer shirts. **Thieves Market** in Chinatown, once a place for bargains in antiques, has become more utilitarian in its wares but is still fun to browse through. *Open daily 8–6.*

Department Stores Good quality merchandise may be found at **Robinson Department Store** (459 Rajavithi, tel. 02/246–1624), which has several locations including one at the top of Silom Road. For Japanese-inspired goods, **Sogo** (Amarin Plaza, Ploenchit Rd., tel. 02/256–9131) presents its wares in modern glitter. However, the locals shop at the **Central Department Store** (306 Silom Rd., tel. 02/233–6930; 1691 Phaholyothin Rd., tel. 02/513–1740; and 1027 Phoenchit Rd., tel. 02/251–9201). Prices are good and the selection is extensive.

Specialty Stores
Art and Antiques Suriwongse Road, Charoen Krung Road, and the Oriental Plaza (across from the Oriental Hotel) have many art and antiques shops. **Peng Seng** (942 Rama IV, tel. 02/234–1285), at the intersection with Suriwongse Road, is one of the most respected dealers in Bangkok. The price may be high, but the article is likely to be genuine. Thai antiques and old images of Buddha need a special export license.

Clothing and Fabrics Thai silk gained its world reputation only after World War II, when technical innovations were introduced to its silk-weaving industry. Two other Thai fabrics are worth noting. Mudmee (tie-dyed) silk is produced in the northeast of Thailand. Thai cotton is soft, durable, and easier on the wallet than silk.

The Jim Thompson Thai Silk Company (9 Suriwongse Rd., tel. 02/234–4900), begun by Jim Thompson, has become *the* place for silk by the yard and for ready-made clothes. There is no bargaining and the prices are high, but the staff is knowledgeable and helpful. **Choisy** (9/25 Suriwongse, 02/233–7794) is run by a Frenchwoman who offers Parisian-style ready-to-wear dresses in Thai silk. **Design Thai** (304 Silom Rd., tel. 02/235–1553) has a large selection of silk items in all price ranges—a good place for that gift you ought to take home. (It's not standard practice, but you can usually manage a 20% discount here.)

For factory-made clothing, the **Indra Garment Export Centre** is behind the Indra Regent Hotel on Ratchaprarop Road, where you can visit hundreds of shops selling discounted items, from shirts to dresses.

The custom-made suit in 48 hours is a Bangkok specialty, but the suit often hangs on the shoulders just as one would expect from a rush job. If you want a custom-made suit of an excellent cut, give the tailor more time. The best in Bangkok is **Marco Tailor** (430/33 Siam Sq., Soi 7, tel. 02/252–0689), where, for approximately B10,000 your suit will equal those made on Savile Row.

Jewelry While the government **Narayana-Phand** store (295/2 Rajapraroh, Payatai, tel. 02/245–3293) has a selection of handcrafted jewelry, **Polin** (860 Rama IV Rd., tel. 02/234–8176), close to the Montien Hotel, has jewelry of interesting design, and the **A.A. Company** (in the Siam Centre, tel. 02/251–7283), across from the Hotel Siam Intercontinental, will custom-make your jewelry.

Leather Leather is a good buy in Bangkok, with possibly the lowest prices in the world, especially for custom work. Crocodile leather is popular, but be sure to obtain a certificate that the skins came from a domestically raised reptile; otherwise U.S. Customs people may confiscate the goods. For shoes, try **River Booters** at the River City Shopping Centre (tel. 02/235–2966), next to the Sheraton Orchid Hotel.

Silverware, Nielloware, and Bronzeware
You may wish to wait until you travel to Chiang Mai for these goods. However, **Anan Bronze** (157/11 Petchburi Rd., tel. 02/215–7739) and **S. Samran** (302/8 Petchburi Rd., tel. 02/215–8849) have good selections at fair prices. Both will arrange for shipping purchases home.

Sports and Fitness

Golf Although weekend play requires advance booking, golf courses are usually available during the week. Two good ones are the **Krungthep Sports Golf Course** (522 Gp 10 Huamark, tel. 02/374–0491) or the **Rose Garden Golf Course** (4/8 Soi 3 Sukhumvit, tel. 02/253x400297).

Jogging Because of the heat and the humidity (which rarely falls below 60%), the crowds, and the air pollution, the best time to run is early in the morning. For a quick jog, the hotel's small running track may be the best bet. The **Siam Inter-Continental Hotel** has a 700-m (½-mi) jogging track in its parkland gardens. But **Lumphini Park,** whose pathways are paved, is 52 acres and about 1.25 km (2 mi) around. Many hotels are nearby. **Chatuchak Park,** twice as large, is north of the city, and also a popular place to run. A third park is **Sanam Luang,** in front of the Grand Palace. There is grass in the middle, but as in all city parks, follow Thai runners, and stay off the grass. Some people like to jog around Chitlada, the Thai royal residence. It is best not to run in the parks at night, but women can run alone safely during the day.

Spectator Sports

Horse Racing There are horse races every Sunday at the Royal Bangkok Sports Club (02/251–0181) or the Royal Turf club (02/280–0020), alternately. Each meeting has up to 12 races, and public betting is permitted.

Thai Boxing The two main stadiums are **Lompini** on Rama IV Road and **Ratchadammon** on Ratchadammon Nok Road, in Bangkok. Understanding the rules of this sport is close to impossible. All manner of punches seem to fly from feet as well as fists, and sometimes more than two boxers are in a ring at once.

Dining

by Robert Halliday

Robert Halliday has lived in Thailand for 20 years and writes about Thai food for many publications, most recently as food editor of the Bangkok Post.

Thais are passionate about food. Eating, like politics or boxing, is a perpetual subject for discussion, and everyone has very definite ideas on which restaurant is best at what. What's more, there is no such thing as a standard Thai recipe, so that even the commonest dish can surprise you in a creative new interpretation at some obscure little shop. In Thailand, seeking out the out-of-the-way food shop that prepares some specialty better than anyone else, then dragging friends off in groups to share the discovery, is a national pastime.

Some of Bangkok's best restaurants are in the big hotels, and many visitors will be content to look no further. But the gastronomically curious will be eager to get out and explore. Wonders await those prepared to try out small, informal eating places, but there are also dangers.

As a general rule, steer clear of open outdoor stands in markets and at roadsides. Most of these are safe, but you're far better off sticking to the clean, well-maintained food shops on major roads and in shopping centers. These rarely cause problems and will give you a chance to taste the most popular Thai dishes in authentic versions, and at very low prices.

Water is much less of a problem these days than in the past, but it's best to drink it bottled or boiled. Clear ice cubes with holes through them are safe, and most restaurants use them.

Among the myths that just won't die is the one about Thai food being unrelievedly hot and spicy. There are plenty of pungent dishes, of course, but most Thai recipes are not especially aggressive. Indeed, many Thais do not care for very spicy food and tend to avoid it. A normal Thai meal is composed of several dishes, including one hot and spicy one—a curry perhaps, or a hot stir-fried dish—which is balanced with a bland soup, a salad, and a vegetable dish or stuffed omelet.

Thai food is eaten with a fork and tablespoon, with the spoon held in the right hand and the bottom of the fork used like a plow to push food into the spoon. Chopsticks are used only for Chinese dishes, like noodle recipes. After you have finished eating, place your fork and spoon on the plate at the 5:25 position; otherwise the server will assume you would like another helping.

In compiling the following list, we have placed the emphasis on those restaurants that prepare Thai food authentically and deliciously but will not sabotage your vacation with anything your fresh-off-the-plane stomach can't handle. Also included is a smattering of the city's best Western-style dining rooms and others that feature non-Thai Asian cuisines. Another popular category of Thai eating place, the seafood restaurant, is represented by only an example or two, although many excellent ones exist.

A word should also be said about price categories. No restaurant in Bangkok is very expensive in the sense one understands the term in New York, London, or Paris. Even the priciest dining rooms in the city will rarely go above $75–$100 per person, unless one is *determined* to spend more. There are individual luxury dishes like the famous Chinese pot dish *phra kradode kamphaeng* ("Monk jumps over the wall"), a mixture of everything expensive—abalone, fancy mushrooms, large shrimp, lobster—that can run to $400 or more for a party of four or five. In the inexpensive places, a large and tasty meal can be had for as little as a dollar or two.

Because the English translations, when they are provided at all, can be bizarre, it is not a bad idea to be armed with a few food-related words in Thai when you take to the streets in search of an authentic meal. This short list will give you a head start.

jued ("jood," sounding like "good")—bland. A *kaeng jued* is a clear soup without chili, often with clear vermicelli noodles and wood-ear mushrooms added for texture.
kaeng (pronounced "gang")—curry, although the term covers

many thin, clear, souplike dishes very far from what most Westerners think of as curry.

kaeng khio waan ("gang khee-yo wahn")—a rich curry made with coconut cream and a complicated mixture of spices and other flavorings pounded into a paste, as well as eggplant and meat or fish (chicken, beef, shrimp, and a fish ball called *luuk cheen plaa krai* are the most common). The Thai name means "green, sweet curry," but it is very rarely sweet. "Green, hot curry" is more like it.

nam plaa ("nahm plah")—fish sauce used instead of salt in Thai cooking.

phad ("pot")—stir-fried.

phad bai kaphrao ("pot by ka-*prow*")—stir-fried with fresh basil, hot chili, garlic, and other seasonings.

phad phed ("pot pet")—popular dishes in which meat or fish is stir-fried with hot chili, sweet basil, onion, garlic, and other seasonings. They can be *very* phed, so watch it.

phed or **phet** ("pet")—spicy hot.

phrik ("prik")—any hot chili pepper. The notorious, nuclear-strength bird chilies are called *phrik kee noo*, and you can always find them on the table in a Thai restaurant, cut into pieces and steeping in *nam plaa* (*see* above). They should be approached with respect.

thawd ("taught")—deep-fried.

tom khaa ("tome khah")—a rich soup made with coconut cream, lime, hot chilies, *khah*, a root spice related to ginger, and chicken (or, less commonly, shrimp).

tom yam ("tome yom")—a semiclear hot-and-sour soup based on lime juice and small hot chilies, with lemongrass, mushrooms, and fresh coriander. Popular versions are made with shrimp, chicken, or fish.

yam ("yom")—a hot-and-sour saladlike dish, served cold and flavored with hot chilies, lime juice, and onions.

For Bangkok restaurants, the following price categories apply.

Category	Cost*
Very Expensive	over B1,000 (US$43)
Expensive	B500–B1,000 (US$21.50–$43)
Moderate	B100–B500 (US$4.30–$21.50)
Inexpensive	under B100 (US$4.30)

per person without tax, service, or drinks

Thai ★ **Spice Market.** Here is Thai home cooking as it was when domestic help was cheap. The decor also re-creates a once-familiar sight—the interior of a well-stocked spice shop, with sacks of garlic, dried chilies, and heavy earthenware fish sauce jars lined up as they were when the only way to get to Bangkok was by steamer. The authentic recipes are prepared full-strength; a chili logo on the menu indicates peppery dishes. The Thai curries are superb, and there is a comprehensive selection of old-fashioned Thai sweets. *Regent of Bangkok Hotel, 155 Rajadamri Rd., tel. 02/251–6127. Reservations suggested on weekends. Dress: casual. AE, DC, MC, V. Moderate.*

★ **Lemongrass.** Elegance and a certain adventurousness have made this restaurant a favorite with both Thais and resident Westerners. Embellished with Southeast Asian antiques, the dining rooms and the outdoor garden dining area all have plenty of atmosphere. Among regional specialties, two southern Thai favorites are the notoriously hot fish curry *kaeng tai plaa*, a good point of departure for those ready to explore, and the *kai yaang paak phanan*, a wonderfully seasoned barbecued chicken-type dish. Be sure to try a glass of *nam takrai*, the cold, sweet drink brewed from lemongrass. *5/1 Sukhumvit Soi 24, tel. 02/258–8637. Reservations suggested. Dress: casual. AE, DC, MC, V. Moderate.*

★ **Sanuknuk.** Named for one of the oldest surviving works of Thai literature, Sanuknuk was originally conceived as a drinking place for the city's intellectual community, particularly writers and artists. Its unique menu includes dishes that had been virtually forgotten until they were resurrected by the owner and his wife through interviews with old women in up-country areas. The eccentric, collagelike decor—which features original work by the artist owner and many others among the city's most prominent creative figures—is of near-museum quality. Sanuknuk's writer-artist crowd drinks a good deal and keeps things lively. Go with a Thai friend if you can, as the menu—a series of cards in a tape cassette box—is written only in Thai. Especially good are the many types of nam phrik and the soups like *tom khaa kai*, chicken with coconut cream, chili, and lime juice. *411/6 Sukhumvit Soi 55 (Soi Thong Law) at the mouth of Sub-soi 23 inside the soi, tel. 02/390–0166 or 392–2865. Reservations suggested on weekends. Dress: very casual. No credit cards. Dinner only. Closed 2nd and 3rd Sun. of each month. Moderate.*

Sala Rim Naam. Definitely a tourist restaurant, but with style to spare. This elegant *sala* (room), on the bank of the Chao Phraya River across from the Oriental Hotel, realizes many of the images that come to mind with the word *Siam*. Thais place great importance on the visual presentation of food, and here some dishes are indeed so beautifully prepared that eating them feels like vandalism. Try some of the hot-and-sour salads, particularly the shrimp version called *yam koong*. The excellently staged Thai dancing will be either a bonus or a distraction, depending on preferences. *Use free boat service from the Oriental Hotel, tel. 02/437–6211. Reservations required on weekends and Oct.–late Feb. Dress: casual. AE, DC, MC, V. Moderate.*

Ton Po. This is open-air riverside dining without tourist trappings. Ton Po (Thai for the Bo tree, of which there is a large, garlanded specimen at the entrance) takes the form of a wide, covered wooden veranda facing the Chao Phraya. To get the breeze that blows even in the hottest weather, try to wangle a riverside table. Many of its dishes are well-known, none more so than the *tom khlong plaa salid bai makhaam awn*, a delectable but very hot and sour soup made from a local dried fish, chili, lime juice, lemongrass, tender young tamarind leaves, mushrooms, and a full frontal assault of other herbal seasonings. Less potent but equally good are the *kai haw bai toei* (chicken meat wrapped in fragrant pandanus leaves and grilled) and *haw moke plaa* (a type of curried fish custard, thickened with coconut cream and steamed in banana leaves). *Phra Atit Rd., no phone. No reservations. Dress: casual. AE, DC, MC, V. Moderate.*

★ **Soi Polo Fried Chicken.** Although its beat-up plastic tables, traffic noise, and lack of air-conditioning make this place look

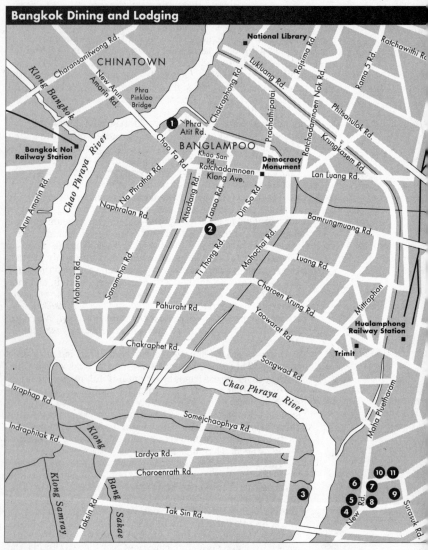

Bangkok Dining and Lodging

CHINATOWN

National Library

Charansanitwong Rd.
New Arun Amarin Rd.
Klong Bangkok
Chakraphong Rd.
Lukluang Rd.
Raisima Rd.
Ratchawithi Rd.
Phra Pinklao Bridge
Prachathipatai
Ratchadamnoen Nok Rd.
Phitsanulok Rd.
Rama 5 Rd.
Krungkasem Rd.

1 Phra Atit Rd.
BANGLAMPOO
Bangkok Noi Railway Station
Chao Fa Rd.
Khao San Rd. Ratchadamnoen Klang Ave.
Democracy Monument
Lan Luang Rd.

Na Phrahat Rd.
Atsadang Rd.
Tanao Rd.
Din So Rd.
Naphralan Rd.
2
Ti Thong Rd.
Mahachai Rd.
Bamrungmuang Rd.
Luang Rd.
Arun Amarin Rd.
Maharaj Rd.
Sanamchai Rd.
Charoen Krung Rd.
Mittraphan
Chao Phraya River
Pahurath Rd.
Yaowarat Rd.
Hualamphong Railway Station
Chakraphet Rd.
Songwad Rd.
Trimit

Israphap Rd.
Chao Phraya River
Somejchaophya Rd.
Maha Phuetharam

Indraphitak Rd.
Klong
Lardya Rd.
Charoenrath Rd.
10 **11**
6 **7**
3
5 **8** **9**
Klong Samray
Klong Bang Sakae
Tak Sin Rd.
4
New Rd.
Surasuk Rd.

Dining
Coca Noodles, **15**
Genji, **21**
Himali Cha Cha, **8**
Isaan Classic, **13**
Le Cristal, **20**
Le Dalat, **29**
Lemongrass, **32**
Le Normandie, **5**
Mandalay, **25**

Pan Pan, **22, 31**
Royal Kitchen, **18**
Sala Rim Naam, **3**
Sanuknuk, **34**
Saw Ying Thai, **2**
Soi Polo Fried Chicken, **27**
Spice Market, **20**
Thai Room, **17**
Thong Lee, **30**
Ton Po, **1**
Tumnak Thai, **35**

Lodging
Ambassador Hotel, **24**
Dusit Thani, **19**
Executive House, **11**
Hilton International, **21**
Imperial Hotel, **23**
Landmark Hotel, **26**
Mermaid's, **28**

Manohra Hotel, **10**
Montien, **16**
Narai Hotel, **12**
New Trocadero, **7**
Oriental Hotel, **5**
Shangri-La Hotel, **4**
Siam Inter-Continental, **14**
Silom Plaza Hotel, **9**
Swan Hotel, **6**
Tara Hotel, **33**

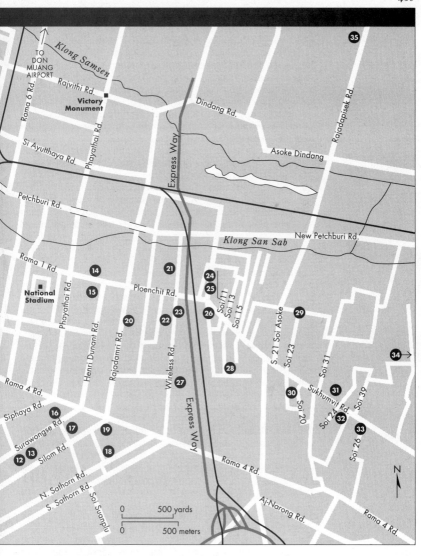

TO
DON
MUANG
AIRPORT

Klong Samsen

Rama 6 Rd.

Rajvithi Rd.

Phayathai Rd.

Victory
Monument

Si Ayutthaya Rd.

Dindang Rd.

Asoke Dindang

Rajadapisek Rd.

Express Way

Petchburi Rd.

Klong San Sab

New Petchburi Rd.

Rama 1 Rd.

National
Stadium

Phayathai Rd.

Henri Dunant Rd.

Rajadamri Rd.

Wireless Rd.

Ploenchit Rd.

Soi 11
Soi 13
Soi 15

S. 21 Soi Asoke

Soi 23

Soi 31

Sukhumvit Rd.

Soi 39

Rama 4 Rd.

Siphaya Rd.

Surawongse Rd.

Silom Rd.

N. Sathorn Rd.

S. Sathorn Rd.

Soi Suanplu

Express Way

Rama 4 Rd.

Aj-Narong Rd.

Rama 4 Rd.

Soi 20

Soi 24

Soi 26

N

0   500 yards

0   500 meters

14 15 20 21 22 23 24 25 26 27 28 29 30 31 32 33 34 35
12 13 16 17 18 19

like a sure thing for stomach trouble, it is one of the city's most popular lunch spots. The reason: its world-class fried chicken flavored with black pepper and plenty of golden-brown, crisp-fried garlic. The chicken should be sampled with sticky rice and perhaps a plate of the restaurant's excellent *som tam* (hot-and-sour raw papaya salad, a hydrogen bomb of a hot coleslaw from the northeast). Try to get there a bit before noon, or landing a table will be a problem. *Walk into Soi Polo from Wireless Rd. (the restaurant is the last in the group of shops on your left as you enter the soi), no phone. No reservations. Dress: very casual. No credit cards. No dinner. Inexpensive.*

Thong Lee. This small but attractive shophouse restaurant has an air-conditioned upstairs dining area. Although prices are very low, Thong Lee has a devoted upper middle-class clientele. The menu is not adventurous, but every dish has a distinct personality—evidence of the cook's artistry and imagination. Almost everyone orders the *muu phad kapi* (pork fried with shrimp paste); the *yam hed sod* (hot-and-sour mushroom salad) is memorable but very spicy. *Sukhumvit Soi 20, no phone. No reservations. Dress: casual. No credit cards. Inexpensive.*

Isaan Classic. Northeast Thailand's distinctive, Lao-style cuisine has been in vogue for several years now in Thailand. Many of the standard Isaan dishes are appealing to visitors who find chili-intensive food too much. Isaan Classic is a chain of restaurants featuring this cuisine in clean, if somewhat crowded and brightly lit, surroundings. The one to visit is on Silom Road, across from the Silom Plaza entertainment complex. Order the *kai yaang* (grilled chicken), *som tam* (raw papaya salad, one Isaan dish that *is* hot, so beware), and *laab neua* (a minced-beef dish with lime juice and seasonings). For some reason, the place is called "Isn't Classic" in English. *Silom Rd., no phone. No reservations. Dress: casual. AE, CB, DC, MC, V. Inexpensive.*

Tumnak Thai. The biggest restaurant in the world, according to the *Guinness Book of World Records*, Tumnak Thai seats 3,000 and is so extensive that the staff zips around on roller skates. The menu attempts to encompass the cuisine of the entire country and, not surprisingly, some dishes come off much better than others. Well worth trying are dishes based on rare freshwater fishes, which are now being farmed in Thailand. The bizarre *plaa buek*, a type of firm-fleshed, white, slightly sweet-flavored catfish that also makes the *Guinness Book* as the world's biggest freshwater fish, is featured in several dishes, including a tasty tom yam. Also worth trying is the sweet-fleshed *plaa yeesok* fish. *131 Rajadapisek Rd., tel. 02/276–1810. No reservations. Dress: casual. AE, DC, MC, V. Inexpensive.*

Saw Ying Thai. Unless you speak Thai or are accompanied by a Thai friend, it may not be worth your while to track down this place. Saw Ying Thai has been open for almost 60 years and has an extremely devoted clientele, many of whom have been regulars for decades. It is rare to find a tourist at Saw Ying Thai, and the circle of even long-term expatriate customers is small. The menu, written on placards on the wall, is in Thai only, and none of the staff speaks English. If you do go, be sure to order the *kai toon*, a chicken soup with bamboo sprouts; *plaa du thawd krawb phad phed*, crisp-fried catfish stir-fried with curry spices and herbs; and *khai jio neua puu*, an omelet full of crabmeat. For many years the decor consisted of long-out-of-date posters on the walls. Recently it has been spiffed up, but the charm remains the same. This restaurant would rate a star were it more accessible. *Cor. Bamrungmuang and Tanao Rds., no phone. No reservations. Dress: casual. No credit cards. Inexpensive.*

Non-Thai Asian

★ **Royal Kitchen.** Perhaps the most elegant of Bangkok's many Chinese restaurants, the Royal Kitchen consists of a number of small, atmospherically decorated dining rooms where everything, right down to the silver chopsticks on the tables, has been carefully considered. The menu is a reference resource for southern Chinese delicacies, including such offerings as *Mieng nok*, with finely minced, seasoned pigeon served on individual fragrant leaves. At lunchtime, dim sum is served, and it, too, is probably Bangkok's best, as beautiful to look at as it is subtle in taste. *N. Sathorn Rd., across from Alliance Française, tel. 02/ 234-3063. Reservations required. Jacket and tie suggested. AE, DC, MC, V. Expensive.*

Genji. Bangkok has many good Japanese restaurants, although a number of them give a chilly reception to those not of the city's insular Japanese community. Genji is a happy exception. Although culinary purists may wince to learn that it is located in a large international hotel, they would be wrong to stay away. The atmosphere is authentic and the food on a par with that of almost any of the *noli-me-tangere* ("don't touch me") joints, as the large Japanese clientele attests. There is an excellent sushi bar and several small, private rooms. Try some of the sushi, especially the succulent grilled eel. Set menus for lunch and dinner are well-conceived. *Hilton International, 2 Wireless Rd., tel. 02/253-0123. Reservations recommended. Dress: casual. AE, DC, MC, V. Expensive.*

★ **Mandalay.** One of only two Burmese restaurants in Thailand, Mandalay offers food that looks similar to Thai but tastes very different indeed. Many of the highly seasoned, saladlike dishes are real surprises. One marvel called *lo phet* (made from marinated young tea leaves, peanuts, sesame, garlic, toasted coconut, and several aromatic herbs) is a stunner, but remember the caffeine content of the tea leaves—too much will keep you awake. Also available are excellent, very thick beef and shrimp curries and an unusual pork curry called *hangle*. On the walls are Burmese antiques from the owner's famous shop, Elephant House, and taped Burmese popular music plays in the background. An unusual touch is a plate of Burmese cheroots and lumps of coconut sugar placed on the table after the meal. *77/5 Soi 11 Sukhumvit (behind the Ambassador Hotel), tel. 02/ 250-1220. Reservations recommended on weekends. Dress: casual. AE, DC, MC, V. Moderate.*

Le Dalat. Once a private home and now a very classy Vietnamese restaurant, Le Dalat consists of several intimate and cozily decorated dining rooms. Much Vietnamese cuisine is based on flavor juxtapositions striking to the Western palate, and here it's all served up with style. Try *naem neuang*, which requires you to take a garlicky grilled meatball and place it on a round of *mieng* (edible thin rice paper used as a wrapper), then pile on bits of garlic, ginger, hot chili, star apple, and mango, spoon on a viscous sweet-salty sauce, and wrap the whole thing up in a lettuce leaf before eating. The restaurant has become a favorite with Bangkok residents. *51 Sukhumvit Soi 23, opposite Indian*

Embassy, tel. 02/258–9298. Reservations suggested. Dress: casual. AE, DC, MC, V. Moderate.

Himali Cha Cha. Cha Cha, who prepares the food at this popular Indian restaurant, was once Nehru's cook. He serves up north Indian cuisine in a pleasantly informal setting with the usual decor. Far from usual, however, is the quality of the food, which has kept the place a favorite for a decade. The chicken tandoori is locally famous, and there are daily specials that Cha Cha himself will recommend and explain. Always good are the breads and the fruit-flavored *lassis* (yogurt drinks—the mango ones are especially successful). *1229/11 New Rd., tel. 02/235–1569. Reservations recommended for dinner. Dress: casual. AE, DC, MC, V. Moderate.*

Coca Noodles. This giant, raucous restaurant is as high-spirited as any in town. On evenings and weekends it is full of Chinese families eating a daunting variety of noodle dishes with noisy gusto. Both wheat- and rice-based pastas are available in abundance, and in combination with a cornucopia of meats, fish, shellfish, and crunchy Chinese vegetables. Try some of the green, wheat-based noodles called *mee yoke*, topped with a chicken thigh, red pork, or crabmeat. Also, on a gas ring built into the table, you can prepare yourself an intriguing Chinese variant of sukiyaki. *In Siam Square shopping center facing Henri Dunant Rd., tel. 02/251–6337 or 251–3538. Reservations suggested on weekends. Dress: casual. No credit cards. Inexpensive.*

Western Cuisine

★ **Le Normandie.** Perched atop the Oriental Hotel, this legendary Bangkok restaurant commands a panoramic view across the Chao Phraya River. Periodically, it persuades the most highly esteemed chefs in France to temporarily abandon their three-star restaurants and take over in Le Normandie's kitchen, where they prepare their specialties for a period of time. These artists usually import important ingredients from home, and at such times the restaurant's patrons enjoy what is literally the finest French food in the world. Even when no superstar chef is on the scene, the cuisine is unforgettable, with the menu often including rare dishes taught to Le Normandie's own master chef by the visiting chefs. *48 Oriental Ave., tel. 02/234–8690. Reservations required. Jacket and tie. AE, DC, MC, V. Very Expensive.*

★ **Le Cristal.** This is a strikingly designed, high-fashion French restaurant that resembles the interior of a Siamese palace. Appearing on the menu from time to time are such memorable dishes as fresh goose liver in raspberry vinegar (this can be specially prepared if requested a day or so in advance). Excellent endive salads and lobster dishes, one with a subtle goose liver sauce, are regularly featured on the menu. Le Cristal is currently being enlarged to encompass an outdoor terrace overlooking the imaginatively landscaped grounds of the Regent of Bangkok Hotel, where it is located. *155 Rajadamri Rd., tel. 02/251–6127. Reservations required. Jacket and tie. AE, DC, MC, V. Very Expensive.*

Pan Pan. Both branches of this Italian-food-and-ice-cream chain are among the most popular restaurants in Bangkok. They are pleasingly decorated with Italian kitchen items and spices. Tables are comfortable, and the relaxed feeling in both places invites long, intimate talks. The long list of pasta includes generous and delicious dishes: linguini with a sauce of salmon, cream, and vodka that is a taste of high-calorie heaven;

or "Chicken Godfather," with its cream-and-mushroom sauce, which is similarly disappointment-proof. But save room for the ice cream. It is of the thick, dense Italian type, and there is a fine durian-flavored one for those who dare. The branch on Sukhumvit Road offers a buffet-style antipasto and a large selection of extremely rich desserts. *6–6/1 Sukhumvit Rd., near Soi 33, tel. 02/258–9304 or 258–5071; or 45 Soi Lang Suan, off Ploenchit Rd., tel. 02/252–7104. Reservations suggested. Dress: casual. AE, DC, MC, V. Moderate–Inexpensive.*

Thai Room. A time capsule that has remained virtually unchanged since it opened during the Vietnam War, in 1966, the Thai Room was usually packed in the evening with GIs on R&R. Not a molecule of the decor has changed since then, and it is not unusual to see a veteran of that war quietly reminiscing. Around him, however, will be local residents and tourists in from the tawdry riot of Patpong. The Mexican food is a peculiar hybrid of Mexican and Thai cuisines, and the result is not unpleasing. Some of the Italian items, like the eggplant parmigiana, are very good by any standard, however, and the Thai food can be excellent. Local clients feel great affection for this one-of-a-kind restaurant. *30/37 Patpong 2 Rd. (between Silom and Suriwongse Rds.), tel. 02/233–7920. No reservations. Dress: casual. AE, DC, MC, V. Inexpensive.*

Lodging

The surge in tourism has taxed Bangkok's hotels to the limit, despite a construction boom that should extend through 1991. During the peak season, from November through March, securing hotel rooms can be very difficult without advance reservations. That is not to say you will be unable to find shelter, but perhaps not at the hotel you might have preferred, or even chosen. Because of the dearth of hotels, room prices have escalated in the last two years, but hoteliers have often not reinvested their profits in refurbishment. Aside from the top international hotels, in the expensive–moderate category, the carpets tend to have stains, plasterwork is patched, and, if your room faces the street, the only way to deaden the traffic noise is to hope the air conditioner works and that its clanking will drown out the street noise.

That said, Bangkok hotels are not expensive by European standards, and the deluxe hotels are superb. Indeed, the Oriental Hotel has been rated by some as the world's best hotel, and the Shangri-La surely is also in running for that position. Such hotels are about $200 for a double. An equivalent hotel in Paris would be close to $400.

There are many hotels in the $80–$100 range, and these, too, have every modern creature comfort imaginable, with fine service, excellent restaurants, health centers, and facilities for businesspeople. For $50 you can find respectable lodgings in a hotel with an efficient staff. Rooms in small hotels with limited facilities are available for around $10 and, if you are willing to share a bathroom, guest houses are numerous.

The four main hotel districts are next to the Chao Phraya and along Silom and Suriwongse roads; around Siam Square; in the foreign embassy neighborhood; and along Sukhumvit Road. Other areas, such as Ko-Sahn Road for inexpensive guest houses favored by backpackers, and across the river, where modern high-rise hotels are sprouting up, are not included in the following list. The latter are inconveniently located, and finding a room in Ko-Sahn, especially in the peak season, requires going from one guest house to another in search of a vacancy—which is best done around breakfast, as departing residents check out.

Very Expensive **Dusit Thani.** At the top end of Silom Road, this low-key 23-story hotel with distinctive, pyramid-style architecture is the flagship property of an expanding Thai hotel group. An extensive shopping arcade, a Chinese restaurant, and an elegant Thai restaurant are at street level. One floor up is the lobby, reception area, and a delightful sunken lounge, especially pleasant for enjoying afternoon tea while listening to piano music and looking out over a small courtyard garden. Rooms are stylishly furnished in pastels, and the higher floors have a panoramic view over Bangkok. The Dusit Thani is particularly noted for the spaciousness and concierge service of its Landmark suites. *Rama IV Rd., Bangkok 10500, tel. 02/233–1130, 800/223–5652, or in NY, 212/593–2988. 525 rooms, including 15 suites. Facilities: 7 restaurants, 24-hr coffee shop, disco, cocktail lounge, small outdoor pool, health center, business center, meeting and banquet rooms, shopping arcade. AE, DC, MC, V.*

Hilton International. This five-story hotel in the embassy district opened in 1983. Its most notable feature is the 8½ acres of landscaped gardens, which, aside from the large swimming pool and the poolside terrace restaurants, contain a wonderful retreat of greenery—mango, rose apple, broad-leaf breadfruit, durian, sapodilla, and mangosteen trees. Some rooms, decorated in soft pastels, have bougainvillea-draped balconies that overlook the garden. *2 Wireless Rd., Bangkok 10500, tel. 02/253–0123. 389 rooms and suites. Facilities: concierge floor, 4 restaurants, music bar, pool terrace bar, outdoor pool, fitness center, 2 tennis courts, squash courts, drugstore, French pastry shop, shopping arcade. AE, DC, MC, V.*

Imperial Hotel. With its lobby redesigned and renovated in 1989, this hotel is stylishly modern. On 6 acres in the embassy district, the hotel has an attractive lawn, lush gardens, and a large swimming pool. Guest rooms facing the garden are most preferred. The rooms are decorated with pale cream walls accented by bright, often red, bedspreads and draperies. *Wireless Rd., Bangkok 10500, tel. 02/254–0023. 400 rooms. Facilities: 4 restaurants (Chinese, Japanese, Thai, Western), tennis court, 2 squash courts, fitness center, sauna, putting green, shops. AE, DC, MC, V.*

Landmark Hotel. Calling itself Bangkok's first high-tech hotel, it has created an ambience suggestive of a grand European-style hotel by the generous use of teakwood in its reception areas. Guest rooms are unobtrusively elegant, geared to the international business traveler, and include a good working desk and a TV/video screen that can be tuned into information banks linked to the hotel's business center. *138 Sukhumvit Rd., Bangkok 10110, tel. 02/254–0404. 360 rooms and 55 suites. Facilities: 4 restaurants, 24-hr coffee shop, outdoor pool with snack bar, fitness center, 2 squash courts, sauna, shopping complex, business center, meeting rooms. AE, DC, MC, V.*

★ **Oriental Hotel.** Often cited as the best hotel in the world, the Oriental has set the standard toward which all other Bangkok hotels strive. Part of its fame stems from its past roster of famous guests, including Joseph Conrad, Somerset Maugham, and Noël Coward. Today's roster is no less impressive, though it now features heads of state and film personalities. The Oriental's location overlooking the Chao Phraya River has been unrivaled. The Garden Wing, with duplex rooms looking out on the gardens and the river, has been refurbished, and these rooms—along with the main building's luxury suites—are the hotel's best. The Oriental radiates elegance and provides superb service, though in recent years some of the crispness and panache have disappeared, perhaps because the staff is continually wooed away by other hotels. *48 Oriental Ave., Bangkok 10500, tel. 02/236–0400. 398 rooms. Facilities: 3 restaurants, outdoor pool, 2 tennis courts, jogging track, golf practice nets, 2 squash courts, health club, business center. AE, DC, MC, V.*

★ **Shangri-La Hotel.** For decades the Oriental could safely claim to be Bangkok's finest, but the Shangri-La is now challenging this position. Service is excellent (many top staff from the Oriental were enticed to the Shangri-La). The facilities are impeccable, and the open marble lobby, with crystal chandeliers, gives a feeling of spaciousness that is a relief from the congestion of Bangkok. The lobby lounge, enclosed by floor-to-ceiling windows, looks over the Chao Phraya River. The gardens, with a swimming pool alongside the river, are a peaceful oasis, interrupted only by the river boat traffic. The spacious guest rooms are decorated in pastels. The Club 21 rooms, on the executive floor, have outstanding views of the river, and their teak paneling adds warmth and intimacy. *89 Soi Wat Suan Phu, New Rd., Bangkok 10500, tel. 02/236–7777. 650 rooms and 47 suites. Facilities: 4 restaurants, 24-hr coffee shop, 2 bars, outdoor pool, 2 tennis courts, 2 squash courts, extensive fitness center, sauna, massage, business center. AE, DC, MC, V.*

Siam Inter-Continental. In the center of Bangkok on 26 landscaped acres, the Siam Inter-Continental has a soaring pagoda roof. The lobby, with its lofty space and indoor plantings and cascades, echoes the pagoda roof and the gardens. Its modern Thai-style architecture and feeling of space make this hotel stand out from all others in Bangkok. Each of the air-conditioned rooms is stylishly decorated with teak furniture and trim, upholstered wing chair and love seat, and a cool blue color scheme. Especially attractive are the teak-paneled bathrooms with radio, telephone extension, and built-in hair dryer. *967 Rama 1 Rd., Bangkok 10500, tel. 02/253–0355. 411 rooms and suites. Facilities: 4 restaurants, 2 bars, conference rooms, 24-hr room service, swimming pool, .8-km (½-mi) jogging track, putting green and driving range, outdoor gym with workout equipment. AE, DC, MC, V.*

Expensive **Ambassador Hotel.** This hotel, with three wings of guest rooms, a complex of restaurants, and a shopping center, is virtually a minicity, which perhaps explains the impersonal service and limited helpfulness from the staff. Milling convention delegates contribute to the impersonal atmosphere. Guest rooms are compact, decorated with standard pastel hotel furnishings. There is plenty to keep you busy at night: the Dickens Pub garden bar, the Flamingo Disco, and The Club for rock music. *171 Sukhumvit Rd., Soi 11–13, Bangkok 10110, tel. 02/254–0444. 1,050 rooms, including 24 suites. Facilities: 12 restaurants, 24-hr coffee shop, 24-hr room service, outdoor pool,* *poolside snack bar, health center with massage, 2 tennis courts, business center with secretaries, 60 function rooms. AE, DC, MC, V.*

Montien. Across the street from Patpong, this hotel has been remarkably well maintained over its two decades of serving visitors, especially those who want convenient access to the corporations along Silom Road. The concierge is particularly helpful. The guest rooms are reasonably spacious, though not decoratively inspired. *54 Surawongse Rd., Bangkok 10500, tel. 02/234-8060. 500 rooms. Facilities: 2 restaurants, 24-hr coffee shop, disco with live music, outdoor pool with pool bar, business center, banquet rooms. AE, DC, MC, V.*

Narai Hotel. Conveniently located on Silom Road near the business, shopping, and entertainment areas, this friendly, modern hotel offers comfortable, utilitarian rooms, many of which are decorated with warm, rose-colored furnishings. The most distinguishing feature of the hotel is Bangkok's only revolving restaurant. *222 Silom Rd., Bangkok 10500, tel. 02/233-3350. 500 rooms, including 10 suites. Facilities: 3 restaurants, 24-hr coffee shop, nightclub, outdoor pool, small fitness center. AE, DC, MC, V.*

Moderate **Manohra Hotel.** An expansive marble lobby characterizes the pristine efficiency of this hotel located between the river and Patpong. Rooms have pastel walls, rich patterned bedcovers, and dark green carpets. Notwithstanding Bangkok's polluted air, the hotel's roof garden is an attractive place to relax, and, for evening action, there is the Buccaneer Night Club. A word of caution: If the Manohra is fully booked, the staff may suggest its new sister hotel, the Ramada (no relation to the American-managed Ramada), opposite the general post office at 1169 New Road (tel. 02/234-897). Unless you are desperate, decline. The Ramada is overpriced and has small, poorly designed rooms. The Manohra, on the other hand, is attractive and well run, with a helpful, friendly staff. *412 Surawongse Rd., Bangkok 10500, tel. 02/234-5070. 230 rooms. Facilities: 2 restaurants, coffeehouse, nightclub, indoor pool, meeting rooms. AE, DC, MC, V.*

Silom Plaza Hotel. Opened in 1986 in the shopping area close to the Oriental, this hotel offers clean, well-maintained though compact rooms with modern decor in soft colors. The more expensive rooms have river views. The hotel caters to business travelers who want to be close to Silom Road. The staff is quick to be of service. The facilities are limited, but nearby is all the entertainment you could wish for. *320 Silom Rd., Bangkok 10500, tel. 02/236-0333. 209 rooms. Facilities: Chinese restaurant, coffee shop, 24-hr room service, indoor pool, poolside bar, gym, sauna, 4 function rooms. AE, DC, MC, V.*

Tara Hotel. Brand-new in 1989, the Tara is in the developing restaurant-and-nightlife section of Sukhumvit Road. Guests register in a check-in lounge, with tea or coffee served while the formalities are completed. The lobby is spacious, lined with teakwood carving. Guest rooms, which are on the small side, are decorated with pale pastels, and many overlook the eighth-floor outdoor swimming pool. *Sukumvit Soi 26, Bangkok 10110, tel. 02/259-0053. 200 rooms and 20 suites. Facilities: restaurant, 24-hr coffee shop, outdoor pool, poolside bar, banquet room. AE, DC, MC, V.*

Inexpensive **The Executive House.** Though it offers only limited services, this hotel has a friendly staff at the reception desk that will help with travel questions and a coffee shop that will deliver food to your room until midnight. The rooms are spacious for the price, the air-conditioning works, and, even if the decor is drab and a bit run down, the rooms on the upper floors have plenty of light. The 16th-floor rooms are the best. It is next to the Manohra Hotel, down a short driveway. *410/3–4 Surawongse Rd., Bangkok 10500, tel. 02/235–1206. 120 rooms. Facilities: coffee shop, small business center. AE, DC, MC, V.*

New Trocadero. This hotel, between Patpong and the Chao Phraya River, has been a Westerner's standby for six decades. Recently refurbished, it offers big double beds in smallish rooms and clean bathrooms. Service is friendly, with a helpful travel/tour desk in the lobby. *343 Surawongse Rd., Bangkok 10500, tel. 02/234–8920. 130 rooms. Facilities: 24-hr coffee shop, small outdoor pool. AE, DC, MC, V.*

Swan Hotel. Close to Bangkok's most expensive hotel, the Oriental, the Swan offers basic accommodation and friendly service. The air-conditioned rooms are functional, nothing more, and could benefit from a good spring cleaning. Ask for a quiet room in the back. *31 Soi Charoenkrung 36, New Rd., 10500, tel. 02/234–8594. 45 rooms. Facilities: coffee shop, small outdoor pool. No credit cards.*

Budget **Mermaid's.** Down a small, partly residential street off Sukhumvit Road near the Ambassador Hotel, this Scandinavian-owned hotel seems more like a guest house. The value is good, even if the staff's attitude is a little perfunctory at times. Rooms are clean and neat, and each of the more expensive ones has a private balcony. *39 Sukhumvit Soi 8, 10110, tel. 02/253–3410. 70 rooms with fan or air-conditioning, some with private bath. Facilities: restaurant, lounge with video, small outdoor pool, travel desk. AE, DC.*

The Arts and Nightlife

The English-language newspapers, the *Bangkok Post* and *The Nation*, have good information on current festivals, exhibitions, and nightlife. TAT's weekly *Where* also lists events.

The Arts Thai classical dance is the epitome of grace. Themes for the
Classical Thai dance drama are taken from the *Ramayana* (*Ramakien* in
Dance Thailand). A series of controlled gestures uses eye contact, ankle and neck movements, and hand and finger gestures to convey the stories' drama. The accompanying band consists of a woodwind instrument called the piphat, which sounds like an oboe, and percussion instruments.

Thai dance drama comes in two forms, the *khon* and the *lakhon*. In khon the dancers (originally all men) wear ferocious masks, and in the lakhon both male and female roles are played by women. In the old days of the courts of Siam, the dance drama would last for days. Now, seen mostly at dinner shows in hotels, only a few selected scenes are presented about how Rama (a reincarnation of Vishnu) battles with the demon king Ravana and how he frequently has to rescue the beautiful princess Sita.

Occasionally you may find a performance of *nang taloung*, a form of shadow puppet theater using silhouettes made from buffalo hide. These plays are similar to those found in Java and Bali, Indonesia.

Various restaurants, such as the **Baan Thai** (Soi 22, Sukhumvit Rd., tel. 258–5403) and the **Sala Rim Naam** (Oriental Hotel, 489 Charoen Nakom Rd., tel. 02/437–6211), offer a classical dance show with dinner. At the **National Theatre** (Na Phra That Rd., tel. 02/221–5861), performances are given most days at 10 AM and 3 PM.

Nightlife Most of Bangkok's nightlife is geared to the male tourist. Unfortunately, tourism has propagated its most lurid forms. Live sex shows, though officially banned, are still found in Patpong and other areas. Expect to be ripped off if you indulge.

Cabaret Most of the nightlife will be found on three infamous side streets that link Surawongse and Silom roads. Patpong I and II are packed with go-go bars with hostesses by the dozen. Patpong III caters to homosexuals. Patpong is quite safe, well patrolled by police, and, indeed, Patpong I has a night market where Thai families shop.

Bars Just beyond Soi Cowboy in the curving side streets (Soi 23 to Soi 31) off Sukhumvit are several small, pleasant bars, often with a small live band playing jazz or country music. **Rang Phah** (16 Sukhumvit 23 Soi, tel. 02/258–4321) is a restaurant with excellent Thai food, but you can sit in the garden outside the marvelous Thai house and drink, eat a little, and gaze at the stars. **September** (120/1 Sukhumvit 23, tel. 02/258–5785), another restaurant, is designed in a Victorian Thai style with a heavy teak bar. **Fred and Barts** (123/1 Sukhumvit, tel. 02/258–4541), a modern bar with stainless steel furnishings, has enthusiastic hostesses if you need companionship. Around the corner the friendly and cozy **Drunken Duck Pub** (59/4 Soi 31, Sukhumvit Road, tel. 02/258–4500) has a three-piece band playing popular jazz. A country and Western band plays at the nearby **Trail Dust** (43/2 Sukhumvit 31, tel. 02/258–4590), a large tavern with tables both in its patio garden and inside.

Friendly pubs and cafés, popular with yuppie Thais and expats, can be found along Sarasin Road (north of Lumphini Park). The three best are **Brown Sugar** (231/20 Soi Sarasin, tel. 02/250–0103), which has a clutter of small rooms humming with animated conversation; the **Old West Saloon** (231/17 Soi Sarasin, tel. 02/252–9510), which re-creates the atmosphere of America's Old West aided by a four-piece band; and the **Burgundy Pub** (231–18 Soi Sarasin, tel. 02/250–0090), good for conversation and relaxation.

Discos **Silom Plaza** (320/14 Silom Road, tel. 02/234–2657 and nearly opposite the Patpong District) is the hot new disco and pub center. Discos, such as the **Virgin,** and bars thumping out music from loud stereos line either side of the plaza both at ground level and one story up. In the center of the plaza are tables where you can also drink and eat while watching the comings and goings of young Thais swinging to the latest beat.

Dinner Cruises Strictly for tourists are the dinner cruises on the Chao Phraya River. Boats such as the *Wan Foh* (tel. 02/433–5453)—built to look like a traditional Thai house—start at the Mae-Nam Building near the Shangri-La Hotel. During the two-hour trip, a Western/Thai dinner is served. Your hotel staff will make reservations. The difference between one and another is marginal. Cost: B450 per person.

Cultural Shows   **Silom Village** (286 Silom Rd., tel. 02/234–4448) may perhaps be
rather touristy, but its appeal also reaches out to Thais. The
block-size complex, open 10 AM–10 PM, has shops, restaurants,
and performances of classical Thai dance. A couple of the restaurants feature chefs cooking tasty morsels in the open, and you
may select from them what takes your fancy or order off a menu.
The best cultural show is at the dinner restaurant **Ruan Thep**
(reservations, tel. 02/234–4581). Dinner starts at 7 and
showtime is at 8:30. Cost: dinner and show, B350; show only,
B200.

Chiang Mai

Introduction

Chiang Mai is the second most popular city to visit in Thailand.
Its rich culture stretches back 700 years. Under King Mengrai,
several small tribes banded together to form a new "nation"
called Anachak Lanna Thai, and made Chiang Rai (north of
Chiang Mai) their capital. In 1296 they moved the capital to the
fertile plains between Doi Suthep mountain and the Mae Ping
River and called it Napphaburi Sri Nakornphing Chiang Mai.

Lanna Thai eventually lost its independence to Ayutthaya and
later, Burma. Not until 1774—when General Tuksin (who
ruled as king before Rama I) drove the Burmese out—did the
region revert to Thailand. After that, the region developed independently of southern Thailand. Even the language is
different, marked by its relaxed tempo.

Only in the last 50 years have communications between Bangkok and Chiang Mai opened up. No longer a small, provincial
town, it has exploded beyond its moat and gates. Some of its in-
nocence has gone, but except for the hustling of *samlor*
(trishaw) cyclists and tuk-tuk drivers, Chiang Mai has few of
the big-city maladies that engulf Thailand's capital.

About 26 km (16 mi) south of Chiang Mai is Lamphun, a lovely
old village (founded in AD 600) known for its serenity and its silk
weaving. Farther south is Sukhothai, the first capital of the Thai
Kingdom, which produced great art, sculpture, and architecture
during the 13th century. The 70-sq-km (27-sq-mi) Sukhothai Historical Park evokes the magnificence of the old capital. Phitsanulok, an hour's ride to the west, is a busy market town whose
major landmark is Wat Phra Sri Mahathat, which houses the revered Phra Jinaraj bronze statue of Buddha.

Phitsanulok is on the railway line between Bangkok and Chiang
Mai, and frequent buses run between Phitsanulok and Sukhothai.
Both Phitsanulok and Sukhothai may be reached directly by bus
from either Chiang Mai or Bangkok.

Chiang Mai is also a base for exploring the north. Many travelers
take lodging for a month or longer and make excursions, returning to Chiang Mai to rest. The farther one goes from Chiang Mai,
the less commercial are the hill tribe villages. Chiang Rai is becoming a popular jumping-off point to the more frequented
villages and the Golden Triangle. The town itself is not very interesting, but the recently opened Dusit Hotel offers good
accommodations.

The most exciting way to reach Chiang Rai—180 km (112 mi) from Chiang Mai—is a five-hour boat trip from Tha Ton (five hours by bus from Chiang Mai) down the Kok River, but you can also make the trip over land. Chiang Rai province is 78% mountains and therein lies its beauty. Akha, Teo, Lisu, Lahu, Karen, and Meo hill tribe villages are scattered in the hills surrounding the town. Also near town are the 70-m (230-ft) Tart Mork Falls. Elephant treks and rafting trips can be arranged in town.

Chiang Saen, 60 km (37 mi) from Chiang Rai, was once a heavily fortified capital, and some fortifications and an old moat still remain. It is now a one-street village with temple ruins and a relaxed, timeless atmosphere undiluted by its guest houses and small hotels.

The Golden Triangle, 9 km (6 mi) north of Chiang Saen, is the place where the Mekong River, with Laos to the east, and the Mae Ruak River, dividing Thailand and Burma, meet.

Mae Sai is a village on the Burmese border where foreigners may walk on the bridge over the Mae Sai River and put one foot over the frontier.

Arriving and Departing by Plane

Thai Airways has seven or more flights daily between Chiang Mai and Bangkok. The flight takes about an hour and costs approximately B1,300. During the peak season, flights are heavily booked.

Arriving and Departing by Train and Bus

By Train The State Railway links Chiang Mai to Bangkok and points south. Trains depart from Bangkok's Hualamphong Railway Station and arrive at Chiang Mai Depot (Charoenmuang Rd., tel. 053/244–795). As the journey from Bangkok takes about 13 hours and there is little to see but paddy fields, the overnight sleeper (departs Bangkok 6 PM, arrives Chiang Mai 7:05 AM) is the best train to take. For the return trip, the train departs Chiang Mai at 5:25 PM and arrives in Bangkok at 6:25 AM. Not only is this train the cleanest of the State Railways, but the bunks in second class, in either the air-conditioned or the fan-cooled coaches, are comfortable. First class has only the advantage of two bunks per compartment for twice the price.

By Bus Numerous companies run buses both day and night between Bangkok and Chiang Mai. The buses are slightly faster than the trains (time is about 11 hours) and less expensive—approximately B240 for an air-conditioned bus. State-run buses leave from Bangkok's Northern Terminal (Phahonyothin Rd., Bangkok, tel. 02/279–4484).

Private tour coach operators have more luxurious buses and cost B30 to B60 more. Try Top North (tel. 02/252–2967) or Chan Tour (tel. 02/252–0349).

Getting Around

The city itself is compact and can be explored easily on foot or by bicycle, with the occasional use of public or other transport for temples, shops, and attractions out of the city center.

By Car A car, with a driver and guide, is the most convenient way to visit three of the five key temples located outside Chiang Mai as well as the Elephant Camp and hill tribe villages. For a morning's visit to the 6-km- (3.8-mi-) long craft factory/shopping area, the price for a car should not be more than B100, as the driver will be anticipating commissions from the stores you visit.

By Motorcycle Motorcycles are popular. Rental agencies are numerous, and most small hotels have their own agency. Shop around to get the best price and a bike in good condition.

By Samlor Most trips within Chiang Mai should cost less than B30.

By Songthaew These red minibuses follow a kind of fixed route but will go elsewhere at a passenger's request. Name your destination before you get in. The cost is B5.

By Bus The Arcade bus terminal serves Bangkok, Sukhothai, Phitsanulok, Udorn Thani, and Chiang Rai (and towns within the province of Chiang Rai). The other terminal, Chiang Phuak, serves Lamphun, Fang, Tha Ton, and destinations within Chiang Mai province.

Important Addresses and Numbers

Tourist Information TAT (135 Praisani Rd., tel. 053/235–334) has extensive information on everything in the region.

Emergencies **Police** and **ambulance** (tel. 191). **Tourist Police** (135 Praisani Rd., tel. 053/222–9777 or 053/232–508 for late-night emergencies).

Hospitals **Lanna Hospital** (103 Superhighway, tel. 053/211–037) has 24-hour service and up-to-date equipment.

English-Language Bookstores **D.K. Books** (234 Tapae Rd., opposite Wat Buparam, tel. 052/235–151) has one of the best selections of English-language books, including guidebooks. **Suriwongs Centre** (54/1–5 Sri Douchai Rd., tel. 053/252–052) also carries a range of English-language books, with a large selection of Thai/English dictionaries.

Guided Tours

Every other store seems to be a tour agency here, so you'd be wise to pick up a list of TAT-recognized agencies before choosing one. Also, each hotel has its own travel desk and association with a tour operator. **World Travel Service** (Rincome Hotel, Huay Kaeo Rd., tel. 053/221–1044) is reliable, but it is the guide who makes the tour great, so meet yours before you actually sign up. Prices vary quite a bit, so shop around, and carefully examine the offerings.

For plane, train, or bus tickets, one efficient and helpful agency is **ST&T Travel Center** (193/12 Sridonchai Rd., Amphur Muang, tel. 053/251–922), on the same street as the Chiang Plaza Hotel.

For trekking, unless you speak some Thai, know the local geography, understand the local customs, and are stricken with the romance of adventure, use the services of a certified guide. Dozens of tour operators, some extremely unreliable, set up shop on a Chiang Mai sidewalk and disappear after they have your money. Obtain a list of trekking tour agencies from TAT. **Top North** (Chiang Mai Hill Hotel, 18 Huay Kaeo Rd., tel. 053/221–254) and **Summit Tour and Trekking** (Thai Charoen Hotel, Tapas Rd., tel. 053/233–351) offer good tours at about B350 a day (more for elephant rides and river rafting). However, it is less the tour agency than the individual guide who determines the quality of the tour and the villages visited. Be sure yours knows several hill tribe languages as well as good English.

Because areas quickly become over-trekked and guides come and go, the only way to select a tour is to obtain the latest information by talking to travelers in Chiang Mai. What was good six months ago may not be good today. It is imperative, also, that you discuss with your proposed guide the villages and route before setting out. You usually can tell whether the guide is knowledgeable and respects the villagers. Finally, it can become very cold at night, so take something warm as well as hiking shoes that are sturdy. Otherwise, travel light.

Exploring Chiang Mai

Tour 1 : The Outer City

Numbers in the margin correspond with points of interest on the Chiang Mai map.

❶ **Wat Prathat Doi Suthep** is perched high up—1,080m (3,542 ft)—on Doi Suthep, a mountain that overlooks Chiang Mai. It is a 30-minute drive (16 km, or 10 mi) from Chiang Mai, then a cable car ride or a steep climb up 290 steps beside a marvelous balustrade in the form of *nagas* (mythical snakes that bring rain to irrigate the rice fields, then cause the waters to retreat so the crop may be harvested), with scales of inlaid brown and green tiles, to the chedi.

❷ Across from Wat Prathat is the **Phuping Palace,** the summer residence of the Thai Royal Family. Though the palace may not be visited, the gardens are open on Friday, Sunday and public holidays. The blooms are at their best in January.

❸ On Suthep Road is **Wat Suan Dok,** one of the largest of Chiang Mai's temples, said to have been built on the site where some of Lord Buddha's bones were found. Some of these relics are said to be housed in the chedi; the others went to Wat Prathat on Doi Suthep. At the back of the viharn is the bot housing Phra Chao Kao, a superb bronze Buddha made in 1504. In a graveyard alongside the wat, Chiang Mai nobility are buried in stupas.

❹ On the Superhighway between its intersection with Huay Kaew Road and Highway 107 is the **National Museum.** In this northern Thai-style building are numerous statues of the Lord Buddha as well as a huge footprint of Buddha's made from wood and inlaid with mother-of-pearl. The upper floor houses collections of archaeological items, including a bed with mosquito netting used by one of the early princes of Chiang Mai. *Admission charge. Open weekdays 8:30–noon and 1–4:30.*

❺ From the museum you can walk to **Wat Photharam Maha Viharn,** more commonly known as Wat Chedi Yot (Seven-Spired Pagoda). Built in 1455, it is a copy of the Mahabodhi temple in Bodh Gaya, India, where the Lord Buddha achieved enlightenment. The seven spires represent the seven weeks that Lord

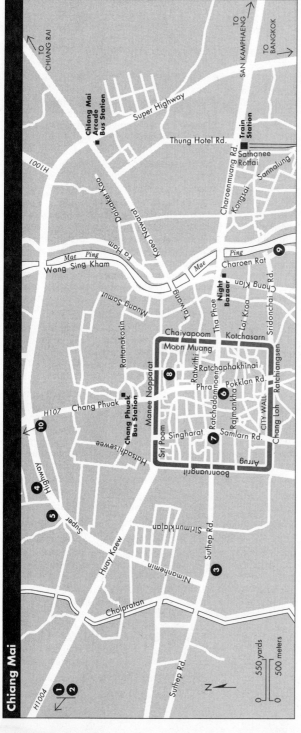

Chiang Mai

TO CHIANG RAI

TO SAN KAMPHAENG

TO BANGKOK

Chiang Mai Arcade Bus Station

Super Highway

Thung Hotel Rd.

Train Station

Sathanee Rottai

Sannaluang

Kongsai

Charoenmuang Rd.

H1001

Dois-ket-Kao

Kaeo Nawarat

Fa Ham

Mae Ping

Wang Sing Kham

Muang Samut

Mae Ping

Taiwang

Charoen Rat

Ping

Rattanakosin

Manee Nopparat

Chang Phuak

H107

Chang Phuak Bus Station

Chaiyapoom

Moon Muang

Ratchaphakhinai

Rawithi

Phra Pokklan Rd.

Ratchadamnoen

Rajmankha

Night Bazaar

Tha Phae

Lai Kroa

Kotchasarn

Sridonchai Rd.

Chang Klan

Ratchiangsen

Chang Loh Ratchiangsen

CITY WALL

Singharat

Samlarn Rd.

Sri Poom

Hatsadhisewee

Boonruangrit

Arrug

Suthep Rd.

Sirimunkajan

Nimahemin

Huay Kaew

Cholpratan

Suthep Rd.

H1004

N

0   550 yards
0   500 meters

Elephant Training
Centre, **10**
National Museum, **4**
Phuping Palace, **2**
Wat Chaimongkol, **9**
Wat Chedi Luang, **6**

Wat Chiang Man, **8**
Wat Photharam
Maha, **5**
Wat Phra Singh, **7**
Wat Prathat Doi
Suthep, **1**
Wat Suan Dok, **3**

Buddha spent in Bodh Gaya after attaining enlightenment. The sides of the chedi have marvelous bas-relief sculptures of celestial figures.

Tour 2: The Inner City

Three of the most important temples are within Chiang Mai's city walls, all in easy walking distance of one another. The first is **Wat Chedi Luang** on Phra Pokklan Road just before it crosses Rajmankha Road. In 1411 a vision commanded King Saen Muang Ma to build a chedi to a "height as high as a dove could fly." He died before it was finished, as did the next king, and, during the third succeeding king's reign, an earthquake knocked down 100 feet of the 282-foot-high chedi. It is now a superb ruin. Don't miss the naga balustrades flanking the entrance steps to the viharn—they are considered the finest of their kind.

Nearby at the junction of Ratchadamnoen and Singharat roads in the middle of town is Chiang Mai's principal monastery, **Wat Phra Singh**, with the Buddha image Phra Singh. The serene and benevolent facial expression of this statue has a radiance enhanced by the light filtering into the chapel. Be sure to note the temple's facades of splendidly carved wood, the elegant teak beams and posts, and the masonry. In a large teaching compound, student monks often have the time and desire to talk.

Wat Chiang Man, Chiang Mai's oldest (1296) monastery, typical of northern Thai architecture, has massive teak pillars inside the bot. Two important images of the Buddha sit in the small building to the right of the main viharn. Officially, they are on view only on Sunday, but sometimes the door is unlocked.

Each of Chiang Mai's multitude of temples has merit, but the one that counts is the one that inspires you. One that may, for example, is **Wat Chaimongkol,** along the Mae Ping River, near the Chiang Mai Plaza Hotel. It's small, with only 18 monks in residence, and foreigners rarely visit. Though the little chedi is supposed to contain holy relics, its beauty is the quietness and serenity of the grounds.

If you have not visited an "elephant camp" elsewhere in Thailand, visit the **Elephant Training Centre** about 20 km (12 mi) from Chiang Mai at **Mae Sa.** As commercial and touristy as it is, elephants are such magnificent beasts that the show cannot fail to please. Action begins at 9:30. The mahouts bring their beasts to the river for a thorough wash-down. The elephants frolic in the water, loving every moment of it. They then stage a dull demonstration of dragging 30-m-(100-ft) long teak logs into the "camp," where the strongest nudge the logs onto a pile. At the end of the show, some tourists choose to ride an elephant around the camp. Far better is riding the elephant on a 2½-hour trek through the jungle to the Mae Sa Valley waterfall (reserve ahead—price is B300), where your driver-guide will meet you with the car. In the valley, lunch at the Mae Sa Valley Resort (tel. 053/251–1662) with well-appointed thatched cottages among beautiful landscaped and flower-filled gardens. Ask the owner for the honey-cooked chicken with chili.

Shopping

Always negotiate prices. Even if the shop lists prices, there is room for negotiation. Most of the shops honor major credit cards. A further discount for cash is often possible. One excursion you will surely want to make is along the 16-km (10-mi) stretch of road from Chiang Mai to San Kamphaeng. On both sides, large emporiums sell crafts and goods for which the region has particular expertise—silverware, ceramics, cottons and silks, wood carvings, hill tribes crafts and artifacts, lacquerware, bronzeware, and hand-painted umbrellas. Most of these emporiums include a factory workshop where you can watch the goods being made, an experience worth the trip whether you buy anything or not. Any taxi driver will happily spend a couple of hours taking you around for about B50 to B100, depending on the level of your intent to make purchases. If you make purchases, he receives a commission.

Markets One of Thailand's fullest and most exciting markets is the Night Bazaar in the center of town. On the sidewalk on the main street and inside the covered building is a congestion of stalls selling anything from intricately woven Burmese rugs to designer-label shirts made in Thailand. The clothing can be very inexpensive, and, at times, good quality. The "Dior" and "Lacoste" shirts can be excellent at a third of the price of their cousins in the West. Some objets d'art are instant antiques. If you are careful and inspect the goods thoroughly, this is a shopper's heaven for crafts made in the rural villages throughout Burma, Laos, and northern Thailand.

Specialty Stores **Borisooki Antiques** (15/2 Chiang Mai–San Kamphaeng Rd., tel.
Antiques 053/351–777) has a reputation for expertise in Thai and Burmese antiques, though it is always recommended that you have some expertise yourself before you settle on a purchase. Borisooki also manufactures Ming Dynasty–style furniture.

Ceramics **Siam Celadon** (40 Moo 6, San Kamphaeng Rd., Km 10, tel. 053/ 331–526) has the largest collection of Thai Celadon. Celadon is a type of ceramicware modeled on the Sawankholoke pottery that was much in demand throughout Thailand hundreds of years ago. Its character comes from the mixtures of Chiang Mai and Lumpang clays. The deep, cracked, glazed finish is achieved with a wood-ash formula developed a thousand years ago. Celadon tends to be expensive, but prices are better here than in Bangkok.

Handicrafts **Prempracha's Collection** (224 Chiang Mai–San Kamphaeng Rd., tel. 053/331–540). In a single 2,000-sq-m (21,600-sq-ft) complex next to Bo Sang (the umbrella village) is displayed an array of products from ceramics, instant antiques, batik, and Thai silk, to wood carvings and bronze statues. Prices tend to be high here, though, and bargaining is discouraged.

Hilltribe and Handicraft Centre, Co, Ltd. (172 Moo 2, Bannong Khong, Chiang Mai-San Kamphaeng District, tel. 053/331–977). Handicrafts and fabrics from the six hill tribes (Meo, Yao, Lisu, Igo, Muser, and Karen) are on display. Goods range from dolls, dressed in multicolored traditional costumes, to elaborate half-moon necklaces and clothes made from natural hemp.

Pen's House (267/11 Chang Klarn Rd., Ampher Maung, tel. 053/ 252–917). To the side, somewhat artificially, are hill-tribe-style houses where craftsmen "perform" their craft. There are also musical instruments, including antique Karen elephant bells, which go for B30,000. Shoulder bags in traditional hill tribe designs make especially good gifts.

Lacquerware **Chiang Mai Laitong** (80/1 Moo 3, Chiang Mai–San Kamphaeng Rd., tel. 053/331–178). This shop offers a vast array of lacquerware, ranging from small boxes to tables, and is a good place to see what is available. The shop attendants explain the seven-step process, and visitors can watch the artists at work.

Leather **BU Leather** (Boonkrong Leather Chiang Mai, 919 Chiang Mai–San Kamphaeng Rd., tel. 053/242–753). The offering here is a variety of bags (including Vuitton) and shoes made from a range of skins, particularly cow and elephant.

Silk and Cotton **San Kamphaeng** (toward the end of the Golden Mile) has the best Thai silk at good prices. **Shinawatra** (on the Golden Mile) has the most stylish silk clothing and fabrics. For cotton, the best is south of Chiang Mai at **Passang,** near Lamphun.

Jolie Femme (8/3 Chiang Mai–San Kampaeng Rd., 500 m—545 yd—beyond the superhighway intersection, tel. 053/247–222) has Thai silk garments designed in the United Kingdom or will custom-make clothes in 24 hours. **Anongpoin** (208–19 Thepae, tel. 053/236–654) has a wide selection of fabrics and handicrafts from the hill tribes. It is especially good for colorful cloth shoulder bags.

Silverwork The silverwork along the Golden Mile is delicate, using close to 100% pure silver (look for the marks certifying percentage). The silversmiths here are known for their bowls with intricate hammered designs depicting stories from the life of the Buddha or scenes from *Ramayana*.

Hill tribe jewelry is chunky but attractive and can be bought at the villages (that of the Meos has the most variety) or at the **Thai Tribal Crafts** (208 Bamrung Rd., tel. 053/233–493, closed Sun.) a nonprofit store run by church groups.

Umbrellas A fascinating traditional craft still continues at **Baw Sang** (off the Golden Mile). Here villagers make paper umbrellas, beginning with soaking mulberry wood and ending by hand-painting with colorful designs.

SA Paper and Umbrella Handicraft Centre (999/16 Ban Nongkhong, Chiang Mai–San Kamphaeng Rd., tel. 053/331–973). At one of the largest manufacturers of hand-made paper, umbrellas, and fans, the selection is extensive—the hand-painted fans make an attractive gift.

Umbrella Making Centre (111/2 Basang, Chiang Mai, tel. 053/331–324). This manufacturer and retailer has some of the most colorful displays of hand-painted umbrellas and fans.

Wood Carvings Modern carvings of all sorts abound, most of which are suitable for the woodpile. An inexpensive but useful souvenir is a teak salad bowl. Some furniture stores on the Golden Mile have teak furniture carved in incredible detail with jungle and other scenes in deep relief. These *must* be seen. Some also have "antique" wood carvings of the Buddha, but religious carvings need an export certificate.

Dining

In all the top hotels, restaurants serve Continental and Thai cuisines. For Thai food, though, some of the best dining in Chiang Mai is in its restaurants.

Arun Rai. This is one of Chiang Mai's best restaurants for northern Thai cuisine. Don't expect great ambience at this open-air garden restaurant; the focus is on the food. Try *phak nam phrik* (fresh vegetables in pepper sauce), *tabong* (bamboo shoots boiled then fried in batter), *sai owa* (sausage filled with minced pork and herbs). The menu is available in English. The Arun Rai often has the delicacy *jing kung* (an insect much like a cricket) that you may want to try. *45 Kotchasarn Rd., tel. 053/ 236–947. No reservations. Dress: casual. No credit cards. Moderate.*

Baen Suan. This delightful restaurant is off the San Kamphaeng Road (the shopping/factory street) and a B40 tuk-tuk ride from downtown. The northern-style teak house sits in a peaceful garden, and the excellently prepared food is from the region. Try the hot Chiang Mai sausage (the recipe originally came from Burma), broccoli in oyster sauce, green curry with chicken, and a shrimp and vegetable soup. *51/3 San Kamphaeng Rd., tel. 053/242–116. Reservations suggested. Dress: casual. No credit cards. Moderate.*

Riverside. On the banks of the Mae Nam Ping, in a 100-year-old teak house, this restaurant serves primarily Western food given zest by the Thai chef. In the casual, conversation-laden atmosphere with lots of beer flowing, the food receives only partial attention. The choice tables are on the terrace over the river. Bands play light jazz or popular music after 7 PM. *9–11 Charoen Rat Rd., tel. 053/243–239. No reservations. Dress: casual. No credit cards. Moderate.*

Whole Earth. On the road leading to the Chiang Plaza Hotel, this long-established restaurant serves delicious vegetarian and health foods. On the second floor of an old, attractive Thai house, the dining room takes full advantage of any breezes. *88 Sridonchai Rd., tel. 053/232–463. No reservations. Dress: informal. No credit cards. Moderate.*

Lodging

With Chiang Mai on every tourist's itinerary, hotels of every persuasion flourish, with new construction making possible many new choices. Even in high season most hotels have a few rooms unoccupied. Hotels cluster in three main Chiang Mai districts. The commercial area, between the railway station and the city walls, offers modern accommodations, some with pools, convenient to markets and tours. Within the old city walls, the hotels, quieter and less numerous, are centrally located between markets and temple sites. The west side of town, near Doi Suthep, has attracted the posh hotels, which are quietest but also farthest from points of interest.

Expensive ★ **Chiang Mai Orchid Hotel.** The change of management in 1989 promises improvements in this leading hotel. The goal is to become the only four-star hotel in the northern capital. So far the new management has added new facilities and renovated the guest rooms. An additional 200 rooms will be completed by 1991. This is a grand hotel in the old style, with teak pillars in the lobby. Rooms are tastefully furnished and trimmed with wood. You can choose among the formal Continental restaurant, Le Pavillon, the new Japanese restaurant, or the informal Thai coffee shop, and find entertainment in the lobby bar or the cozy Opium Den. The suites include the Honeymoon Suite, which, we are told, is often used by the Crown Prince. The drawback is that the hotel is a 10-minute taxi ride from Chiang Mai center. *100–102 Huay Kaeo Rd., Chiang Mai 50000, tel. 053/222–099; Bangkok reservations, tel. 02/233–8261. 267 rooms, including 7 suites, with a proposed addition of 200 rooms. Facilities: 3 restaurants, 2 bars, disco, business center, Clark Hatch fitness center, sauna, outdoor pool with poolside bar, meeting room, beauty salon, drugstore, doctor on call 24 hours. AE, DC, MC, V.*

Dusit Inn. If you like to wander the streets and soak up the atmosphere, the Dusit Inn is well located. Step out of its front door, and you are in the heart of Chiang Mai, just a few minutes' walk from the Night Bazaar. Formerly the Chiang Mai Palace, it has undergone two years of refurbishing. The rooms, though comfortable enough, have utilitarian furniture and uninspired decor. There is a Thai/Western restaurant, a cocktail/tea lounge, and the Jasmine restaurant for some of the best Cantonese food in town. *112 Chang Khan Rd., Chiang Mai 50000, tel. 053/251–033; Bangkok reservations, tel. 02/233–1130. 200 rooms. Facilities: 2 restaurants, small outdoor pool with poolside service, airport shuttle service, meeting room. AE, DC, MC, V.*

Mae Ping Hotel. This high-rise hotel opened in 1988. Its advantage is the newness of the rooms, decorated in ever-popular pastels. An executive club floor offers escape from the tour groups massing in the remainder of the hotel. The service staff could use more training. Two restaurants serve Thai and Western food and Italian specialties, respectively. *153 Sridonchai Rd., Changklana Muang, Chiang Mai 5000, tel. 053/251–060; Bangkok reservations, tel. 02/391–4090. 400 rooms. Facilities: 2 restaurants, outdoor pool with poolside bar, garden terrace, meeting rooms. AE, DC.*

Moderate **Chiang Inn.** Around the corner from the Dusit Inn and close to the Night Market and the center of Chiang Mai, the Chiang Inn has offered well-kept guest rooms for the last 14 years. As the hotel is set back from the main street, the rooms are quiet (the higher the better). Appealingly decorated in light pastels with locally handwoven fabrics produced from home-grown cotton and dyed with purely natural herbs, the rooms are reasonably spacious. For dining, La Grillade serves Thai-influenced French cuisine in a formal atmosphere, or, more casual, the Ron Thong Coffee House serves Thai and Western dishes. The only problem is that the Chiang Inn is usually swamped with tour groups arriving and departing, and its facilities are geared to that kind of traffic. *100 Chang Khlan Rd., Chiang Mai 50000, tel. 053/235–655; Bangkok reservations, tel. 02/ 251–6883. 170 rooms, including 4 suites. Facilities: 2 restaurants, disco, outdoor pool with poolside service, meeting room, travel/tour desk. AE, DC, MC, V.*

Suriwongse Hotel. Located near the Night Bazaar, this hotel always smells of the last meal, despite ranking as one of Chiang Mai's five first-class hotels. It is popular with tour groups, especially French, as it is owned by the Novotel chain. The Suriwongse offers all tourist facilities, including a pickup point for the airport shuttle bus. The rooms, with standard first-class amenities, are clean but tend to be well worn. *110 Chang Khlan Rd., Chiang Mai 50000, tel. 053/236–733, Bangkok reservations, tel. 02/251–9883, U.S. reservations, tel. 800/221–4542. 170 rooms, including 4 suites. Facilities: restaurant, coffee shop, tour desk, airport shuttle bus stop. AE, DC, MC, V.*

Inexpensive   **Grand Apartments.** In the old city, this new building offers rooms by the day or by the month, making it a useful place for an extended stay at very reasonable rates (B4,000 per month). The rooms are efficient and clean, and guests have access to telex and fax machines. *Phra Pok Kico Rd., Chang Pluck Gate, 50000, tel. 053/217–291. 36 rooms. Facilities: café for breakfast and snacks. MC, V.*

★   **River View Lodge.** Facing the Mae Nam Ping and within an easy 10-minute walk of the Night Bazaar, the hotel is tastefully furnished with Thai furniture and rust-colored clay floor tiles. The more expensive rooms have private balconies overlooking the river. The small restaurant is better for breakfast than for dinner, and the veranda patio is good for relaxing with a beer or afternoon tea. The owner speaks nearly fluent English and will assist in planning your explorations. Some seasoned travelers to Chiang Mai say this is the best place to stay in the city. *25 Charoen Phrathet Soi 2, Chiang Mai 50000, tel. 053/251–109. 36 rooms. Facilities: restaurant. AE, DC, MC, V.*

Budget   **Galor Guest House.** On the Mae Ping riverfront, this guest
★   house has many advantages: its good location, within five minutes' walk of the Night Bazaar; friendly service from its staff; small but clean rooms with air-conditioning or fan; and a restaurant. It is also the best value in town. *7 Charcoplathat Rd., Chiang Mai 50000, tel. 053/232–885. Facilities: restaurant. No credit cards.*

Lai Thai. On the edge of the old city walls, and a 10-minute walk from the Night Bazaar, this friendly guest house offers rooms around a garden courtyard and a casual open-air restaurant that serves Thai, European, and Chinese food. The rooms are either air-conditioned or cooled by fan. Bare, polished floors and simple furniture give them a fresh, clean look. The rooms farthest back from the road have less traffic noise. *111/4–5 Kotchasarn Rd., Chiang Mai 50000, tel. 053/251–725. 80 rooms. Facilities: restaurant, laundry, tour/travel desk, motorbike rental. MC.*

The Arts and Entertainment

No first visit to Chiang Mai should be without a Khantoke dinner, which usually consists of sticky rice (molded into balls with your fingers for eating), delicious *kap moo* (spiced pork skin), a super spicy dip called *nam prink naw* with onions, cucumber, and chili, and *kang kai*—a chicken and vegetable curry. All this is to be washed down with Singha beer.

Often the Khantoke dinner includes performances of Thai and/ or hill tribe dancing. One such "dinner theater" is at the back of the **Diamond Hotel** (tel. 053/234–155), which offers a commercial repertory of Thai dancing in a small, comfortable restaurant-theater setting. The other place for a Khantoke dinner and dance is at the **Old Chiang Mai Cultural Centre** (tel. 053/235–097), a complex of buildings just out of Chiang Mai designed as a hill tribe village. Both places charge B200 per person. The show at the Cultural Centre is the more elaborate and is authentic in its dance.

For more mundane evening entertainment, aside from the "love palaces," of which Chiang Mai has its share, there are several pub restaurants. The **Riverside** *(see* Dining, above) is one of the most popular, especially for its location next to the Mae Ping and the small bands that drop in to perform throughout the evening. For a casual evening, with a jazz trio, you may want to stop off at the European-style **Rikker Pub** (84/5–6 Sridonchai Rd., no phone).

Phuket

Backpackers discovered the beauty of Phuket less than 20 years ago. The word got out about its long, white sandy beaches, cliff-sheltered coves, waterfalls, mountains, fishing and seafood, clear waters and excellent scuba diving, rainbow colors shimmering off the turquoise Andaman Sea, and fiery sunsets. Entrepreneurs were quick to see Phuket's potential. They built massive developments, at first clustering around Patong, and then spreading out to other tranquil bays and secluded havens. Most formerly idyllic deserted bays and secluded havens now have at least one hotel impinging on the beauty.

Phuket's popularity continues because, despite the tourist development and commercialism, the island is large enough (so far) to absorb the influx.

When to Go

Phuket has two seasons. During the monsoon season, from May until October, hotel prices are considerably lower. Though the rain may be intermittent during this time, the seas can make some of the beaches unsafe for swimming. The peak season is the dry period from November to April.

Important Addresses and Numbers

Tourist Information The **TAT office** (73–75 Phuket Rd., Phuket Town, tel. 076/212–213), located near the bus terminal, has information on all Phuket hotels as well as free maps. The TAT desk at the airport offers limited help.

Emergencies **Police** (tel. 076/212–046); **ambulance** (tel. 076/212–297). **Tourist police** (tel. 076/212–115) are the best officials to seek in an emergency. They are located next to the TAT office.

Arriving and Departing by Plane

Thai Airways has daily 70-minute flights from Bangkok and 30-minute flights from Hat Yai. **Thai International** has flights also from Penang (Malaysia) and from Singapore. A departure tax of B150 on international flights, and B20 on domestic flights is charged.

Between the Airport and the Beaches/ Center City Phuket's airport is at the northern end of the island. Phuket Town is 32 km (20 mi) to the south. Most of the hotels are on the west coast south of the airport. Many send their own limousine minivans to meet arriving planes. These are not free, just convenient. For Phuket Town, take a Thai Airways minibus—buy the B75 ticket at the transportation counter in the terminal. Sporadically, songthaews run between the airport and Phuket Town for B20.

Arriving and Departing by Train and Bus

By Train   The closest station is on the mainland at Surat Thani, where trains connect to Bangkok and Singapore. A bus/coach service links Phuket with Surat Thani. Traveling time between Phuket and Bangkok is five hours on the bus and nine hours on the overnight train(with sleeping bunks).

By Bus   Non-air-conditioned buses leave throughout the day from Bangkok Southern Bus Terminal. The one air-conditioned bus leaves in the evening. Tour companies also run coach service. These are slightly more comfortable, and often the price of a one-way fare includes a meal. **Songserm** (121/7 Soi Chapermla, Phyathai Rd., Bangkok 10400, tel. 02/252–9654) is one such company. The bus trip from Bangkok to Phuket takes 13 to 14 hours.

Getting Around

By Taxi   Fares are, to a large extent, fixed between different destinations. If you plan to use taxis frequently, obtain a fare listing from the TAT office, because drivers are not above charging more. A trip from Phuket Town to Patong Beach is B100 and to Promthep Cape is B120.

By Bus   Songthaews, the minibuses that seat six people, have no regular schedule, but all use Phuket Town as their terminal. Songthaews to the beaches leave from Rangong Road near the day market and Fountain Circle. They ply back and forth to most beaches, and a few make the trip to the airport. Should you want to travel from one beach to another along the western shore, you will likely have to go into Phuket Town first and change songthaew. Fares range from B10 to B40, depending on the length of the trip.

By Rental Car and Scooters   As Phuket has so many different types of beaches, your own transport offers the most convenience for exploring. Driving poses few hazards, except for the motor scooter—potholes and gravel can cause a spill, and some minor roads are not paved.

Many hotels have a car/jeep/scooter rental desk, but their prices are 25%–40% higher than those in Phuket Town. Try the Phuket Car Centre (Takuapa Rd., Phuket Town, tel. 076/212–671). Prices for jeeps start at B620 per day. Motor scooters range up from B150. The larger, 150 cc scooters are safer. Both **Avis** (tel. 076/311–358) and **Hertz** (tel. 076/311–162) have offices at the airport, as well as at some hotels.

Guided Tours

You may want to take advantage of a set tour to visit some of the attractions. These can be arranged through your hotel or by any travel agent and can be enjoyed privately or by joining a group.

Two reputable tour operators on the island are **New World Travel Service** (Hotel Phuket Merlin, tel. 076/212–866, ext. WTS)

and **Songserm** (64/2 Ressada Rd., Phuket Town 83000, tel. 076/
216–820), which, in addition to standard tour bookings, operates several cruise boats, air-conditioned buses to Bangkok,
and minibuses to Surat Thani, Hat Yai, Penang, and Singapore.

Orientation Tour   A half-day Phuket sightseeing tour includes Wat Chalong,
Rawai Beach, Phromtrep Cape, and Khao Rang.

Excursions   A full-day boat tour goes from Phuket to Phang Nga Bay on the
mainland with visits to other islands. Another full-day tour visits the Phi Phi Islands for swimming and caving. The full-day
Ko Hav (Coral Island) tour features snorkeling and swimming.
The nine islands of the Similan group offer some of the world's
clearest waters and most spectacular marine life. Full-day
cruises, costing B1,500, operated by Songserm (tel. 076/216–
820), are often available.

Special-Interest   A half-day tour features the Thai Cultural Village, for folk
Tours   dances, Thai boxing, and Thai martial arts (Krabea-Krabong).
The half-day Naga pearl tour visits cultured pearl farms on
Naga Noi Island.

Exploring Phuket

Orientation   Shaped like a teardrop pendant with many chips, Phuket is
linked to the mainland by a causeway. The airport is at the
northern end of the island. Phuket Town is in the southeast,
and the best beaches are on the west coast. Typically, tourists
go directly to their hotels on arrival and then make day trips to
various other beaches. Hence, the exploring section below is
less an itinerary than an overview of places to visit.

*Numbers in the margin correspond with points of interest on
the Phuket map.*

Tour 1: Phuket Town

①   About one-third of the island's population lives in **Phuket Town,**
the provincial capital, but very few tourists stay here. The
town bustles as the island's administrative and commercial center, though drab modern concrete buildings have replaced the
old Malay-Colonial-influenced architecture. A few hours of
browsing through the tourist shops are not wasted.

Most of the shops and cafés are along Phang-Nga Road and
Rasda Road. By bus, you arrive in Phuket on the eastern end of
Phang-Nga Road at the Phuket Bus Terminal.

Time Out   Sidewalk tables in front of the **Thavorn Hotel** on Rasda Road
provide a good place to do a little people-watching while sip-
ping a cold beer.

East of the Thavorn Hotel, Phuket Road forks right off Rasda
Road. On the left are the TAT office and the Tourist Police. In
the opposite direction (west) along Rasda Road, crossing the
traffic circle (Bangkok Circle), is Ranong Road. Here, on the
left, is the **local market,** Phuket Town's busiest and most colorful spectacle—a riot of vegetables, spices, meats, sellers and
buyers, and rich aromas. On the next block down Ranong Road
is the Songthaew Terminal for minibus service to Patong, Kata,
Kamala, Karon, Nai Yeng, and Surin beaches. Songthaews for
Rawai and Nai Marn beaches stop at Bangkok Circle. Diagonal-

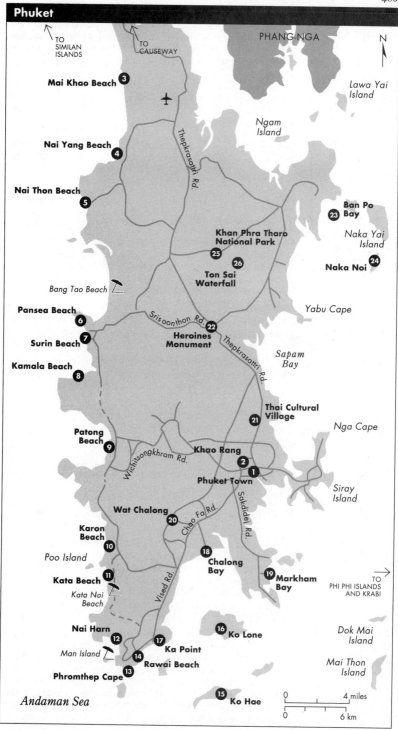

ly across town from Phuket's market is the Provincial Town Hall, whose claim to fame is that it was used as the French Embassy in the movie *The Killing Fields*. Perhaps the most relaxing way to see Phuket is from the top of **Khao Rang** (Rang Hill) in the northwest of the town. The elevation permits a view of both Phuket Town and the island's interior.

Time Out While enjoying the view from Khao Rang, try the **Tunka Café** (tel. 076/311–5000), which serves good Thai food for lunch and dinner.

But don't come to Phuket Island for its town. It is an island of beaches, sand cliffs, and hypnotic colors of the Andaman Sea. These are the places to explore.

Tour 2: The Beaches

Starting from the north and working down the west coast, the first beach is **Mai Khao Beach,** just 5 km (3 mi) from the airport. This beach is the island's largest, often ignored by Western tourists because at low tide it turns slightly muddy, and its steep drop-off makes it unpopular with swimmers. The absence of farangs attracts the Thais, who appreciate the peacefulness of the beach. Giant sea turtles like it, too. They come between November and February to lay their eggs.

Nai Yang is really a continuation of Mai Khao—making a 10-km (6-mi) stretch of sand. It curves like a half-moon, with casuarina trees lining the shore. It is also popular with Thais.

The next beach is **Nai Thon,** tucked in the center of a headland. Its rough waters keep swimmers away, and the village remains a peaceful fishing port. South of the headland, the shore curves in to form **Bang Tao Beach,** which, with the exception of the posh new Dusit Laguna Hotel, has been left undisturbed.

Next in line are **Pansea** and **Surin** beaches, with the island's most elegant resort, Amanpuri. Tucked in a small cove with a complete feeling of privacy, the hotel blends into the cliffside. Surin Beach, despite a long stretch of golden sand, is not good for swimming because of strong currents. On the headland south of Surin are several small intimate and romantic coves. Each requires a climb down a cliff. Surrounded by palms and rocks, the tiny beach is, with luck, your personal haven.

After the headland is **Kamala** Beach. It's only a small curving strip of sand with coconut palms and a few bungalows rented by Krathomtip Cottages. It is unfortunately rumored that the Sheraton Hotel Group has plans to build here. A small dirt road leads on from Kamala Beach to Patong—passable, but very tricky and not advised if it's your first time on a motor scooter. If you don't use this dirt road, drive inland to join the main road before turning west again for Patong.

Patong is Phuket's mini-Pattaya, complete with German restaurants, massage parlors, hustlers selling trinkets, or places like Tatum's, a combined coffeehouse, disco, and go-go dance floor. The abundance of hotels, ranging from deluxe to small cottages, attests to Patong's popularity among the charter groups flying into Phuket. Most tourists seek it out for at least one night's revelry, and the long, white sandy beach still justifiably attracts swimmers to its safe waters.

⑩ Beyond Patong is **Karon,** which is divided into two areas. Karon Noi is a small bay surrounded by verdant hills. It is truly beautiful, but virtually taken over by Le Meridien Hotel. Occasionally, cruise ships anchor offshore from this beach, doubling the crowds. Because of its good swimming and surfing, the other part of Karon, Karon Yai, is becoming increasingly popular, and several hotels and a minitown have sprung up to join the first of the luxury hotels.

⑪ **Kata** is the next beach south, 17 km (10.2 mi) due west of Phuket Town. The sunsets are as marvelous as ever, but the peace and quiet are fading fast. Club Meditérranée has moved in, but there are still stretches of sand with privacy, and the center of town has only a modest number of bars. Nearby is **Kata Noi** *(noi* means small) in the shelter of a forest-clad hill. A few inexpensive bungalows share the quiet beach with a resort that's popular with tour groups.

The road beyond Kata cuts inland across the hilly headland to
⑫ drop into yet another gloriously beautiful bay, **Nai Harn.** Protected by Man Island, the deep-water bay has been a popular anchorage for international yachtsmen. On the north side, a huge, white stucco, stepped building, the Phuket Island Yacht Club, rises from the beach in stark contrast to the verdant hillside. From the Yacht Club's terrace, the view of the sun, dropping into the Andaman Sea behind Man Island, is superb. The beach is good for sunning and swimming in the dry season, but beware of the steep drop-off.

From Nai Harn, the road swings around to climb up to
⑬ **Phromthep Cape.** Its panorama includes Nai Harn Bay, the island's coastline, and the far-off horizon of the Andaman Sea. At sunset, the view is supreme. This evening pilgrimage has become so popular that policemen organize parking, and a row of souvenir stands lines the parking lot. But, once away from this congestion, you can find space enough to enjoy the colors of the setting sun in contemplative solitude.

⑭ Down from Phromthep is **Rawai Beach.** The shallow, muddy beach is not so attractive, but the shoreline, with a small fishing village set in a coconut grove, has the charm you may have expected in all of Phuket.

⑮ Cruise boats leave Rawai for **Ko Hae** (Coral Island), 30 minutes
⑯ from shore. Slightly farther out is **Ko Lone.** Both are choice islands for snorkeling and sunbathing. Ko Hae has a couple of cafés and receives more visitors than Ko Lone. *Boat fare: B750.*

At the southern end of Rawai Beach is a small gypsy village. The inhabitants are descendants of the original tribes living on Phuket. Called Chao Nam (Water People) by the Thai, they tend to shy away from the modern world, preferring to stay among their own. They are superb swimmers, able to fish at 27-m (90-ft) depths in free dives. One of the three tribes of the Chao Nam is believed to have been the sea gypsies who pirated 17th-century trading ships entering the Burmese-Singapore waters. Though there are two other Chao Nam villages on Phuket, the one at Rawai Beach is the easiest to visit.

⑰ South of Rawai is **Ka Point,** where most of the promontory is owned by the huge Phuket Island Resort, virtually a small township, with several restaurants, two swimming pools, and a minibus to take guests from one facility to another. Along the

(18) southern coast is **Chalong Bay,** with several good inexpensive outdoor seafood restaurants—try Kanning II for delicious crabs and prawns. To the southeast of Chalong Bay is the pen-
(19) insula with **Markham Bay,** the place to catch the ferry boat to the Phi Phi Islands and Krabi.

Tour 3: Inland and Pearl Island

(20) Turning inland from Chalong Bay, rather than take the main road to Phuket Town, take the road at the traffic circle to **Wat Chalong.** Phuket has 20 Buddhist temples—all built since the 19th century—but Wat Chalong is the largest and most famous. It enshrines the gilt statues, wrapped in saffron robes, of two revered monks who helped quell an 1876 rebellion by Chinese immigrants.

(21) North of Phuket Town, toward the airport, is the **Thai Cultural Village.** In a 500-seat amphitheater it presents various aspects of southern Thai culture, including classical Thai dance, shadow puppets, exhibition Thai boxing, sword fighting, an "elephants-at-work" show, and more. *Admission charge. Show times: 10:15, 11, 4:45, 5:30.*

(22) Farther north on the airport road, you'll notice a statue of two women; they rallied the Thais in 1785 to ward off a siege by the Burmese, who had sacked Ayutthaya four years earlier. A
(23) right turn (east) at this crossroads of the **"Heroines Monument"** leads to **Ban Po Bay,** where you can take a 20-minute
(24) boat ride over to **Naka Noi,** the Pearl Island. A small restaurant offers refreshment after you tour the facilities. The tour demonstrates how pearls are formed by placing an irritant inside an oyster—the same method perfected by the Japanese.

(25) Turning inland from Ban Po, the road traverses **Khan Phra Tharo National Park,** the last remaining virgin forest on Phu-
(26) ket. You may want to stop at **Ton Sai waterfall,** a few minutes off the road. It's a popular picnic spot all year, but the falls are best during the rainy season.

After a few miles, the road joins the main island road, with the airport 10 km (6 mi) to the north, and Phuket Town 22 km (14 mi) to the south.

Excursions from Phuket

Ko Phi Phi, Krabi and Ao Phrang Bay, and Phang Nga can each be individual day trips from Phuket. Each deserves much longer to fully appreciate, but it is possible to link them together to make a circular minimum three-day tour starting from Phuket.

Ko Phi Phi **Phi Phi** is an idyllic island with secret silver sand coves and beaches and sheer limestone cliff walls dropping precipitously into the sea. Ten years ago, you could find a hammock hung between two coconut trees and spend the night for B10. Now, tourists come over from Phuket to escape the commercialism, only to bring commercialism to Phi Phi. Several comfortable air-conditioned hotels have been built as well as a range of more modest bungalow accommodations.

Getting There From Phuket, boats leave Markham Bay at approximately 8:30 and 2:30. The cost is B250 for the two-hour journey. **Songserm Travel Agency** (64/2 Rasada Rd., Phuket Town, tel. 076/216–

820), is the best company. There are also two boats a day from Krabi. Phi Phi is 48 km (30 mi) from Phuket Town and 42 km (26 mi) from Krabi.

Exploring Ko Phi Phi is comprised of two main islands, **Phi Phi Don** and Phi Phi Lae. Only the Don is inhabited. Shaped like a butterfly, the two hilly land portions are linked by a 300-m- (327-yd-) wide sandbar, 2 km (1.2 mi) long. Except for two moderately priced deluxe hotels, all accommodations and the main mall (no vehicles are on the island) with shops and restaurants are on this sandbar. On either side are bays, Ton Sai and Lohdalum. Boats come into Ton Sai.

The popular way to explore is by boat, either with others on a cruise boat or by hiring a long-tail boat that will seat up to six people.

The only nightlife consists of strolling the walkway along the sandbar, where numerous small restaurants serve the catch of the day, displayed on ice in big bins outside.

Krabi and Ao Phrang Bay On the mainland, 43 km (27 mi) east of Ko Phi Phi is **Krabi,** the provincial capital of the region. Once a favorite harbor for smugglers bringing in alcohol and tobacco from Malaysia, it has settled into being a fishing port and a gateway to the province's beaches, particularly **Ao Phrang Bay,** and offshore islands.

Getting There Two to four ferries make the two-hour run between Krabi and Phi Phi. Bookings can be made on Phi Phi Don. The fare is B150. To reach Ao Phrang Bay, take a songthaew for B20 or, if you are reserving Ao Phrang Bay accommodation in Krabi, you can probably arrange a free ride.

Exploring **Ao Phrang Bay,** less than 20 minutes by road from Krabi, is just being discovered by land speculators. Only one deluxe hotel, the Krabi Resort, intrudes itself with a new concrete eyesore that professes to have all the civilized modern amenities of Bangkok. Aside from this, there are only rustic bungalows, some more commodious than others. The beaches are of fine sand and sheltered by verdant jungles inland and islands offshore. Though Windsurfers are available for rent, the waters are often too calm for enthusiastic sailors.

Phang Nga Bay Halfway between Krabi and Phuket is **Phang Nga Bay,** made famous by the James Bond movie, *The Man with the Golden Gun*. Frequent bus service links Phang Nga town with Krabi or Phuket. Phang Nga town is 10 km (6.2 mi) from the bay, and other than for transport, there is no reason to go to it.

At the bay, hire a boat and tour the islands. The outcroppings of limestone, some rising 270 m (900 ft) straight up from the sea, are weird and wonderful. The key sights to visit are **Ko Panyi** with its Muslim fishing village built on stilts, **Ko Phing Kan** (now known as James Bond Island), **Ko Tapu,** which as its name implies looks like a spike driven into the sea, **Tham Kaeo** grotto, which will remind you of Capri, and **Tham Lot,** where a cave has evolved into an arch large enough to allow a cruise boat to pass through. To do it all, and to appreciate the sunsets—marvelous ones from **Ko Mak**—you really need two days. They will be unforgettable, as long as they don't fall in the monsoon season, when seas often become too rough for boats.

Dining

Restaurants abound on Phuket and serve all types of cuisine, including versions of Western cooking. Fresh seafood is the number-one specialty.

Isouw. Right on the main street of Krabi, this "floating" restaurant stands on stilts over the water. It is a wonderful place to sit, enjoy lunch, and watch the river traffic. The menu specializes in grilled fish with sweet and sour sauce, and the *mee krob* here has an abundance of fresh, sweet shrimp. *256/1 Uttarakit Rd., Krabi, tel. 075/611–956. No reservations. Dress: casual. No credit cards. Moderate.*

Kan Eang. Some of the best seafood in town is served at this beachside restaurant in Chalong Bay. The cooking is Thai, perhaps a little too softened to accommodate Western taste, but the fish is fresh and the spices Thai. Choose a mild evening to eat outdoors under the coconut palms and indulge in the crabs. *9/3 Chaofa Rd., Chalong Bay, Phuket, tel. 076/216–288. No reservations. Dress: casual. AE, V. Moderate.*

Lodging

Phuket has accommodations of every variety in virtually all of its main beach areas. You can choose from the most elegant resorts, such as Amanpuri, to modest, thatch-roof bungalows that are a fraction of the price. In all, approximately 100 hotels or cottages offer various levels of hospitality. Hotel tariffs fluctuate widely, depending on high and low season, weekend or weekday, and holiday periods, when they can more than double.

Very Expensive **Amanpuri.** For relaxation amid tasteful and elegant surroundings, there is no finer place in Thailand—nor is any place quite as expensive. The main building is completely open, with polished floors, modern bamboo furniture and pitched, thatch roofs. Individual pavilions, staggered up the hillside back from the beach, house guests. The architectural style is distinctly Thai, adapted with flair to accommodate modern creature comforts and maximize cooling breezes from the sea. Furnishings are handcrafted with local woods, and each suite has its private sun deck. A split-level bar perches on the hill affording a romantic view of the sun setting into the Andaman Sea. Meals are prepared by an enthusiastic French chef who takes full advantage of local fresh produce and the daily catch. The swimming pool is up from the beach, and the beach itself is secluded and private. Should you wish even more privacy, arrangements may be made for an overnight stay on one of the uninhabited islands. Guests are greeted and cared for individually by personally assigned staff. *Pansea Beach, Phuket 83110, tel. 076/311–394; Bangkok reservations, tel. 02/250–0746. 55 rooms. Facilities: 2 restaurants, bar, outdoor pool, 2 tennis courts, water sports, custom tours arranged, gift and drugstore. AE, V.*

★ **Phuket Yacht Club.** Set in an extremely picturesque westward-facing bay, this stepped, modern luxury hotel looks like an ambitious condominium complex. The architectural inappropriateness aside, its comfort, service, and amenities make the Phuket Yacht Club extremely pleasant. Whether you stay here or not, make a point of dining in the open-sided restaurant that overlooks the bay. Furnishings in the guest rooms are modern and stylish, but, like the exterior, lack any identification with the environment. *Nai Harn Beach, Phuket 83130, tel. 076/214–020; Bangkok reservations, 02/251–4707. 108 rooms, including 8 suites. Facilities: 2 restaurants, outdoor pool and poolside bar, 2 tennis courts, water sports arranged, and tour desk. AE, DC, MC, V.*

Expensive **Diamond Cliff Hotel.** North of town, away from the crowds, this is one of the smartest and architecturally most pleasing resorts in Patong. The beach across the road has mammoth rocks that create the feeling of several private beaches. The swimming pool is built on a ledge above the main part of the hotel, providing an unobstructed view of the coast and the Andaman Sea. Rooms are spacious, full of light, and decorated in pale colors to accentuate the open feel of the hotel. Dining is taken seriously, with the fresh seafood cooked in European or Thai style. Guests may dine indoors or on the restaurant's terrace looking out to sea. *61/9 Kalim Beach, Patong, Kathu District, Phuket 83121, tel. 076/321–501; Bangkok reservations, tel. 02/246–4515. 140 rooms. Facilities: restaurant, cocktail/tea lounge, outdoor pool, pool bar, water sports arranged, tour desk, and pharmacy. AE, MC, V.*

Dusit Laguna. This resort hotel is off by itself on the northwestern part of the island. The rooms, with picture windows opening onto private balconies, have modern pastel decor and commodious bathrooms. The hotel is popular with upmarket Thais seeking refuge from the more commercial areas of Patong. It offers barbecue dining on the terrace, and after dinner, dancing to the sounds of the latest discs. Business groups also come here to mix work and pleasure. *390 Srisoontorn Rd., Cherngtalay District, Amphur Talang, Phuket 83110, tel. 076/311–320; Bangkok reservations, tel. 02/236–0450. 240 rooms, including 7 suites. Facilities: 3 restaurants, outdoor pool, 2 tennis courts, water sports, putting green, tour desk, meeting rooms. AE, DC, MC, V.*

Moderate **Phuket Cabana.** This hotel's attraction is its location, in the middle of Patong, fronting 300 m (1,000 ft) of beach. Laid-back and casual describe guests as well as staff, but the basic resort amenities are here, with a good tour desk and a reputable dive shop to arrange outings. Modest rooms are in chalet-type bungalows furnished with rattan tables and chairs. The restaurant serves a hybrid Western-Thai cuisine. *94 Taveewong Rd., Patong Beach, Phuket 83121, tel. 076/321–138; Bangkok reservations, tel. 02/278–2239. 80 rooms. Facilities: restaurant, outdoor pool, airport bus, tour desk, dive shop. AE, MC, V.*

Budget **Friendship Bungalows.** In Kata, a four-minute walk from the
★ beach, two rows of single-story buildings house modest, sparsely furnished, but spotlessly clean rooms, each with its own bathroom (there is usually hot water). The owners are extremely hospitable and encourage guests to feel at home. The small restaurant/bar on a terrace offers good Thai food; Western food is also available. What you leave will probably be enjoyed by the two monkeys, who play throughout the day on the restaurant's wall. *6/5 Patak Rd., Kata Beach, Phuket 83130, no phone. 30 rooms. Facilities: restaurant. No credit cards.*

Phi Phi Island **P.P. International Resort.** The most expensive resort on the is-
★ land is on the north cape of Laemthong. Accommodations at
this isolated retreat range from standard double rooms to deluxe rooms in bungalows with sea views, more space, and
double the price. All rooms are air-conditioned, with small refrigerators, and color TV. The terraced restaurant (serving
Thai and European cuisine) does have splendid views of the
sea, and the fish is absolutely fresh. *Cape Laemthong, Phi Phi;
Bangkok reservations, tel. 02/250–0768; in Phuket, tel. 076/
214–297; in Ko Samui, tel. 077/421–228. 120 rooms. Facilities:
restaurant, water sports and island tours arranged. AE, V.
Expensive.*
Pee Pee Cabana and **Ton Sai Village.** Facing the sea amid coconut palms, these two adjacent hotels are owned by the same
management. Ton Sai Village, farthest from the ferry dock—
about a 10-minute walk—abuts cliffs. It is the quieter of the
two and has slightly larger rooms than Pee Pee Cabana. These
two hotels offer the best accommodation in the center of Phi
Phi. Both have either air-conditioned or fan-cooled rooms, and
their outdoor restaurants serve food similar to that found in the
village at twice the price. *Reservations: Pee Wee Marina Travel Co., 201/3–4 Uttararij Rd., Amphur Muang, Krabi
Province, tel. 075/612–196. No credit cards. Moderate.*
Krabi Pee Pee Resort. In the center of the isthmus on the opposite side of the pier, this collection of small bungalows in a
coconut grove—watch for falling coconuts—offers clean, simple, fan-cooled rooms with private Asian-style toilet and
shower. No guests seem to frequent the restaurant, but some
do hang around the bar, which faces the bay. This is the best
value on the island. *Lohdalum Bay, Phi Phi, Krabi Province;
Krabi reservations, tel. 075/611–484. 60 rooms. Facilities: restaurant, bar, dive shop. No credit cards. Inexpensive.*
Pee Pee Island Village. Near the P.P. International Resort, this
hotel offers more modest accommodation in small thatched
bungalows. It provides the same water sports and tours as its
neighbor, but the service is more casual and the atmosphere
more laid-back. Views from the hotel are less stunning but do
include panoramas of the sea and palm-clad hills. *Cape
Laemthing, Phi Phi; Bangkok reservations, tel. 02/277–0038;
in Phuket, tel. 076/215–014. 65 rooms. Facilities: restaurant,
water sports and island tours arranged. AE, V. Inexpensive.*

Vocabulary

To truly experience the culture of a foreign country, one must feast on its cuisine, learn the history of its monuments, and speak its native tongue. Southeast Asian languages, like its history, are as diverse as its people and customs.

To simplify communications, Fodor's has compiled a vocabulary chart of six languages you may encounter throughout your travels in the region. This easy-reference listing includes important words and significant phrases in English, Cantonese, Malay, Mandarin, Tagalog, and Thai. Use the phonetical chart to assist you in getting around, asking directions, and dining out.

English	Cantonese	Malay
Basics Yes/No	hai/mm'hai	ya/**tee´**-dak
Please	m'goy	**see**-la/**min**–ta
Thank you (very much).	doy-jeh/fehseng doh jeh	**tree**-ma **ka**-say (**ban**-yak)
You're welcome.	foon ying	**sa**-ma **sa**-ma
Excuse me.	dai'm jee	ma-fkan sa-ya
Hello	wa´	apa khabar or "hello"
Goodbye	joy geen	se-**la**-mat **jalan**/ se-**la**-mat **ting**-gal
Numbers One	yaht	sa-too
Two	eee	doo-a
Three	som	tee-ga
Four	say	em-pat
Five	m'	lee-ma
Six	look	e-nam
Seven	chut	tu-juh
Eight	baht	la-pan
Nine	gou	sem-bee-lan
Ten	sup	se-pu-luh
Days and Time Today	gäm-yät	**ha**-ree ee-nee
Tomorrow	ting-yat	**ay**-sok (also **bay**-sok)
Yesterday	chum-yät	kel-**mar**-in
Morning	joo-joh	**pa**-gee
Afternoon	ahn-joh	**pe**-tang
Night	man-hak	**ma**-lam
Monday	lye bye **yaht**	**ha**-ree **iss**-nin
Tuesday	lye bye **ee**	**ha**-ree se-**la**-sa
Wednesday	lye bye **som**	**ha**-ree **ra**-boo
Thursday	lye bye **say**	**ha**-ree **ka**-mees
Friday	lye bye m	**ha**-ree **ju**-ma-at
Saturday	lye bye **look**	**ha**-ree **sab**-too
Sunday	lye bye **yaht´**	**ha**-ree a-had (also **ha**-ree **ming**-gu)

Mandarin	Tagalog	Thai	English
shee/pu shee	oh-oh/hin-dee′	mai kha (F)/ mai khrap (M)	Yes/No
ching	pah-kee′	dai prōd	Please
sy-eh sy-eh nee	(mah-rah′-ming) sah-lah-maht	khob khun khrap	Thank you (very much).
boo sy-eh	wah-lahng′ ah-noo-mahn′	doo-ay kwam yin dee	You're welcome.
too-eh pu-shee	pah-oo′-manh-hin′ po	kaw-tōd	Excuse me.
way	kuh-moos-tah′/ heh-lo′	sa-wat dee khrap (M)/sa-wat dee kha (F)	Hello
tsay jen	pah-ah-lam nah po′	sa-wat dee khrap (M)/sa-wat dee kha (F)	Goodbye
ee	ee-sah′	nung	One
err	dah-lah-wah′	song	Two
san	taht-loh′	sam	Three
soo	ah′-paht	see	Four
woo	lee-mah	hah	Five
lee-oo	ah′-neem	hōk	Six
chee	pee-toh′	jet	Seven
bah	wah-lo′	paat	Eight
joo	see-yahm′	kaw	Nine
shur	sahm-poo′	sip	Ten
chin tien	nga-yohn′	wun nee	Today
ming tien	boo′-kahss	proong nee	Tomorrow
tso tien	kah-ha′-pon	moo-ah-wan-nee	Yesterday
shang wu	oo-mah′-gah	toan-chao	Morning
sha wu	hah′-pon	toan-klang-wun	Afternoon
wan shang	gah-beh′	toan-klang-koon	Night
lee-pa-ee	loo′-ness	wun-chan	Monday
lee-pa-ayr	mahr-tess′	wun-ung-khan	Tuesday
lee-pa-san	moo-yehr′-koh-less	wun-poot	Wednesday
lee-pa-soo	hoo-whe′-bess	wun-pru-roo-hud	Thursday
lee-pa-wu	bee-yehr′-ness	wun-sook	Friday
lee-pa-lee-oo	sah′-bah-doh	wun-sao	Saturday
lee-pa-tien	leeng-goh′	wun-ar-teet	Sunday

	English	Cantonese	Malay
Useful Phrases	Do you speak English?	nay gäng m' gäng ying män	ta-hoo-kah ber-ba-**ha**-sa **Ing**-gris?
	I don't speak . . .	ah m' woiy gäng gäng dōōng wah.	sa-ya **tee**-dak ber-**cha**-kap ba-**ha**-sa
	I don't understand.	äh m' sic	sa-ya **tee**-dak **fa**-ham
	I don't know.	äh m' jee	sa-ya **tee**-dak ta-hoo
	I am American/British.	ä hay may gäc yan/ying gäk yan	sa-ya o-rang Amerika/**Ing**-gris
	I am sick.	ä beng **jah**	**sa**-ya sa-kit
	Please call a doctor.	m goy nay gew yee sung	**see**-la ta-**lee**-pon **dok**-ter
	Have you any rooms?	nay yaw mohfäng	**bi**-lik a-da
	How much does it cost?	gay´ däh chien	**har**-ga-nya ber-a-pa
	Too expensive	gai´ gway	ter-**la**-loo **ma**-hal
	It's beautiful.	hoh leng	**chan**-tik
	Help!	bong jô	**to**-long
	Stop!	ting jee	ber-**hen**-ti
Getting Around	How do I get to . . .	deem yerng huy . . .	ba-gai-ma-ner boh-lee per-gee-ku . . .
	. . . the train station?	fäw che´ jäm	**stay**-shen **kray**-ta a-pee dee **ma**-na
	. . . the post office?	yaw jing gook	pe-**ja**-bat pos dee **ma**-na
	. . . the tourist office?	le hang se´	ja-bat-ban pe-**lan**-chong des **ma**-na
	. . . the hospital?	yee´ yuen	**roo**-mah sa-kit dee **ma**-na
	Does this bus go to . . . ?	ga ba se´ huy m huy . . .	a-da-kah bas ee-nee per-gee ke . . .

Mandarin	Tagalog	Thai	English
nee fweh sho yung yoo ma´	mah-roo-nohng hoh kay-yohng´ mahg-Ing-glehs?	khun pood pas-sa ung-grid dai-mai	Do you speak English?
wo pu fweh sho (thai kway yoo)	hin-dee´ a-koh mah-roo-nohng mahg-tah-gah´-lohg	chun mai pood (Thai)	I don't speak . . .
wo pu lee-oo chee-ay	hin-dee´ koh nah-ee-een-tin-dee´-hahn	chun mai kao chai	I don't understand.
wo pu tung	hin-dee´ koh ah-lahm	chun mai rue	I don't know.
wo sher may kwo jen/ing kwo jen	ah-ko ay Ah-meh-ree-kah-noh/Ing-glehs	chun pen (American/ung-grid)	I am American/British.
wo sheng ping ler	ah-ko ay may sah-kit	chun mai sa-bai	I am sick.
ching chow ee sung li	pah-kee-tah-wahg nang dook-tohr	dai-prod re-ak moa mai	Please call a doctor.
nee hay yoo fwang chien ma	may-roh-ohn kah-yong´mang-ah kuh-wahr-toh	khun-mee hong-mai	Have you any rooms?
to shaw chien	mahg-kah´-noh?	ra-ka tao rye	How much does it cost?
tao kwa la	mah-hal mah-shah-doh	pa-eng goo-pai	Too expensive
chen pee-ow lee-ang	mah-gahn-dah	soo-ay ma	It's beautiful.
choo-ming	sahk-loh-loh	choo-ay doo-ay	Help!
ting	hin-toh´	yoot	Stop!
wo tsen yang tao . . .	pah-pah-no pah-poon-tah sah . . .	chun ja pai . . . dai yang-rye	How do I get to . . .
. . . fwa chu chan	ee-stah-syon nahng tren	sa-tai-nee rod-fai	. . . the train station?
. . . yu choo	post oh-pis/tahn-gah-pahn nahng koh-reo	pai-sa-nee	. . . the post office?
. . . kuan kuang choo	oh-pee-see-nah nahng too-ris-moh	sam-nak-ngan tóng-tee-oh	the tourist office?
. . . ee-yuen	oh-spee-tal	rung-pa-ya-bal	. . . the hospital?
chu pu pa shur tao . . . ma	poo-moo-poon-tah bah ee-tohngboos sah . . .	rod-mai-nee pai-nai . . . chai mai	Does this bus go to . . . ?

English	Cantonese	Malay
Where is the W.C.?	say soh gahn herng been doh	**tan**-das **a**-da dee **ma**-na
Left	jäh	**kee**-ree
Right	yäw	**ka**-nan
Straight ahead	chiem mein	troos

Dining Out

English	Cantonese	Malay
Hot/not hot (spicy)	moh´ lät´	**pe**-das/**tee**-dak **pe**-das
Please bring me . . .	me goy ne ling lay	to long ba-wa un-tuk sa-ya . . .
Menu	chan pie	**me**-noo
Bill/check	dän	bill
Fork	chä´	**gar**-poo, or "fork"
Knife	bä´ doh	**pee**-sow
Spoon	chee gung	**soo**-doo
Napkin	jee gan	serviette (if paper) or too-ala (if cloth) or "napkin"
Bread	mean bou	**ro**-tee
Butter	ow yôw	men-tay ga or "butter"
Milk	nĭh	**soo**-soo
Pepper	woo jew fähn	**la**-da
Salt	yeem	**ga**-ram
Sugar	tông	**goo**-la
Water/bottled water	suy/jun suy	a-yer/a-yer **bo**-tol

Mandarin	Tagalog	Thai	English
chaw soo tsai na lee	sah-ahn ahng bahn-nioh	hong-nam yoo tee-nai	Where is the W.C.?
tso	kah-lee-wah´	sai	Left
yoo	kah-nahn	kuah	Right
ching sung chien tson	dee-reh-tsoh	trong-pai	Straight ahead
la/pu la	mah-hang-hang/ hoo-wahg mah-hang-hang	mai ped	Hot/not hot (spicy)
chin dee keh wo . . .	pah-kee-dah-la moh ah-ko nahng . . .	prod pah chun	Please bring me . . .
tsai tan	meh-noo´	rai-kran ar-han	Menu
chang tan	koo-when-tah/ tseh-keh	bill/check (bai-sed)	Bill/check
cha	tee-nee-dohr	som	Fork
tao	kuh-tsee-lee-yo	mead	Knife
tang-sher	kuh-tsa-rah	chen	Spoon
tsan-chin-chu	sir-bee-lee-yeah-tah	kra-dard ched park	Napkin
mien-paw	tee-nah-pie	kha-nom-pang	Bread
nyoo-yoo	mahn-teh-kíll-yah	no-ee	Butter
nyoo-nyai	gah´-tahss	nom	Milk
hoo-chao	pee-myen´-toh	pik-tai	Pepper
yen	ah-sin´	kloo-ah	Salt
tang	ah-soo´-kahl	nam-pan	Sugar
shoo-ay/ping shoe-ay	too-big/too-big sah boh´-teh	nam/nam koo-at	Water/bottled water

Index

Personal Itinerary

Departure *Date*

Time

Transportation

Arrival *Date*   *Time*

Departure *Date*   *Time*

Transportation

Accommodations

Arrival *Date*   *Time*

Departure *Date*   *Time*

Transportation

Accommodations

Arrival *Date*   *Time*

Departure *Date*   *Time*

Transportation

Accommodations

Personal Itinerary

Arrival *Date*   *Time*

Departure *Date*   *Time*

Transportation

Accommodations

Arrival *Date*   *Time*

Departure *Date*   *Time*

Transportation

Accommodations

Arrival *Date*   *Time*

Departure *Date*   *Time*

Transportation

Accommodations

Arrival *Date*   *Time*

Departure *Date*   *Time*

Transportation

Accommodations

Personal Itinerary

Arrival *Date*   *Time*

Departure *Date*   *Time*

Transportation

Accommodations

Arrival *Date*   *Time*

Departure *Date*   *Time*

Transportation

Accommodations

Arrival *Date*   *Time*

Departure *Date*   *Time*

Transportation

Accommodations

Arrival *Date*   *Time*

Departure *Date*   *Time*

Transportation

Accommodations

Personal Itinerary

Arrival *Date*   *Time*

Departure *Date*   *Time*

Transportation

Accommodations

Arrival *Date*   *Time*

Departure *Date*   *Time*

Transportation

Accommodations

Arrival *Date*   *Time*

Departure *Date*   *Time*

Transportation

Accommodations

Arrival *Date*   *Time*

Departure *Date*   *Time*

Transportation

Accommodations

Personal Itinerary

Arrival *Date*   *Time*

Departure *Date*   *Time*

Transportation

Accommodations

Arrival *Date*   *Time*

Departure *Date*   *Time*

Transportation

Accommodations

Arrival *Date*   *Time*

Departure *Date*   *Time*

Transportation

Accommodations

Arrival *Date*   *Time*

Departure *Date*   *Time*

Transportation

Accommodations

Addresses

Name	*Name*
Address	*Address*
Telephone	*Telephone*
Name	*Name*
Address	*Address*
Telephone	*Telephone*
Name	*Name*
Address	*Address*
Telephone	*Telephone*
Name	*Name*
Address	*Address*
Telephone	*Telephone*
Name	*Name*
Address	*Address*
Telephone	*Telephone*
Name	*Name*
Address	*Address*
Telephone	*Telephone*
Name	*Name*
Address	*Address*
Telephone	*Telephone*
Name	*Name*
Address	*Address*
Telephone	*Telephone*

Addresses

Name	*Name*
Address	*Address*
Telephone	*Telephone*
Name	*Name*
Address	*Address*
Telephone	*Telephone*
Name	*Name*
Address	*Address*
Telephone	*Telephone*
Name	*Name*
Address	*Address*
Telephone	*Telephone*
Name	*Name*
Address	*Address*
Telephone	*Telephone*
Name	*Name*
Address	*Address*
Telephone	*Telephone*
Name	*Name*
Address	*Address*
Telephone	*Telephone*
Name	*Name*
Address	*Address*
Telephone	*Telephone*

Fodor's Travel Guides

U.S. Guides

Alaska
Arizona
Atlantic City & the
  New Jersey Shore
Boston
California
Cape Cod
Carolinas & the
  Georgia Coast
The Chesapeake Region
Chicago
Colorado
Disney World & the
  Orlando Area

Florida
Hawaii
Las Vegas
Los Angeles, Orange
  County, Palm Springs
Maui
Miami,
  Fort Lauderdale,
  Palm Beach
Michigan, Wisconsin,
  Minnesota
New England
New Mexico
New Orleans

New Orleans (Pocket
  Guide)
New York City
New York City (Pocket
  Guide)
New York State
Pacific North Coast
Philadelphia
The Rockies
San Diego
San Francisco
San Francisco (Pocket
  Guide)
The South

Texas
USA
Virgin Islands
Virginia
Waikiki
Washington, DC

Foreign Guides

Acapulco
Amsterdam
Australia, New Zealand,
  The South Pacific
Austria
Bahamas
Bahamas (Pocket
  Guide)
Baja & the Pacific
  Coast Resorts
Barbados
Beijing, Guangzhou &
  Shanghai
Belgium &
  Luxembourg
Bermuda
Brazil
Britain (Great Travel
  Values)
Budget Europe
Canada
Canada (Great Travel
  Values)
Canada's Atlantic
  Provinces
Cancun, Cozumel,
  Yucatan Peninsula

Caribbean
Caribbean (Great
  Travel Values)
Central America
Eastern Europe
Egypt
Europe
Europe's Great
  Cities
France
France (Great Travel
  Values)
Germany
Germany (Great Travel
  Values)
Great Britain
Greece
The Himalayan
  Countries
Holland
Hong Kong
Hungary
India,
  including Nepal
Ireland
Israel
Italy

Italy (Great Travel
  Values)
Jamaica
Japan
Japan (Great Travel
  Values)
Kenya, Tanzania,
  the Seychelles
Korea
Lisbon
Loire Valley
London
London (Great
  Travel Values)
London (Pocket Guide)
Madrid & Barcelona
Mexico
Mexico City
Montreal &
  Quebec City
Munich
New Zealand
North Africa
Paris
Paris (Pocket Guide)
People's Republic of
  China

Portugal
Rio de Janeiro
The Riviera (Fun on)
Rome
Saint Martin &
  Sint Maarten
Scandinavia
Scandinavian Cities
Scotland
Singapore
South America
South Pacific
Southeast Asia
Soviet Union
Spain
Spain (Great Travel
  Values)
Sweden
Switzerland
Sydney
Tokyo
Toronto
Turkey
Vienna
Yugoslavia

Special-Interest Guides

Health & Fitness
  Vacations
Royalty Watching

Selected Hotels of
  Europe

Selected Resorts and
  Hotels of the U.S.
Shopping in Europe

Skiing in North America
Sunday in New York

Help us evaluate hotels and restaurants for the next edition of this guide, and we will send you a free issue of Fodor's newsletter, TravelSense.

Title of this guide:

1 Hotel ❏   Restaurant ❏   *(check one)*

Name

Number/Street

City/State/Country

Comments

2 Hotel ❏   Restaurant ❏   *(check one)*

Name

Number/Street

City/State/Country

Comments

3 Hotel ❏   Restaurant ❏   *(check one)*

Name

Number/Street

City/State/Country

Comments

General Comments

Please complete for a free copy of TravelSense

Name

Number/Street

City/State/Zip

Business Reply Mail

First Class   Permit Nº 7775   New York, NY

Postage will be paid by addressee

Fodor's Travel Publications

201 East 50th Street
New York, NY 10022